T0238645

Communications in Computer and Information Science 776

Commenced Publication in 2007
Founding and Former Series Editors:
Alfredo Cuzzocrea, Xiaoyong Du, Orhun Kara, Ting Liu, Dominik Ślęzak,
and Xiaokang Yang

More information about this series at http://www.springer.com/series/7899

J.K. Mandal · Paramartha Dutta
Somnath Mukhopadhyay (Eds.)

Computational Intelligence, Communications, and Business Analytics

First International Conference, CICBA 2017
Kolkata, India, March 24–25, 2017
Revised Selected Papers, Part II

Springer

Editors
J.K. Mandal
Department of Computer Science
  and Engineering
University of Kalyani
Kalyani, West Bengal
India

Somnath Mukhopadhyay
Department of Information Technology
Calcutta Business School
Kolkata
India

Paramartha Dutta
Department of Computer and System
  Sciences
Visva Bharati University
Bolpur Santiniketan, West Bengal
India

ISSN 1865-0929   ISSN 1865-0937   (electronic)
Communications in Computer and Information Science
ISBN 978-981-10-6429-6   ISBN 978-981-10-6430-2   (eBook)
DOI 10.1007/978-981-10-6430-2

Library of Congress Control Number: 2017953403

Printed on acid-free paper

This Springer imprint is published by Springer Nature
The registered company is Springer Nature Singapore Pte Ltd.
The registered company address is: 152 Beach Road, #21-01/04 Gateway East, Singapore 189721, Singapore

Foreword

Preparing a foreword for the proceedings of an international conference, in the form of an edited volume, cannot but be an intellectual pleasure which I can ill afford to desist myself from. Accordingly, I avail myself of an opportunity to write a few words for the foreword of the recently concluded First International Conference on Computational Intelligence, Business Analytics, and Communication (CICBA 2017). It was organized by Calcutta Business School in association with the Computer Society of India, on March 24–25, 2017 at the Calcutta Business School campus. The conference was technically sponsored by IEEE Kolkata Chapter, IEEE Young Professionals Kolkata, as well as the IEEE Computational Intelligence Society, Kolkata Chapter. The proceedings of the conference have been published by Springer Nature, in their CCIS series.

With the presence of Prof. Dr. Sankar Pal, former director, of the Indian Statistical Institute, Padmashri; Prof. Dr. Edward Tsang, University of Essex, UK; and Dr. P.N. Suganthan, Nanyang Technological University, Singapore as Keynote speakers, as well as luminaries from leading industries and research/academic institutes as invited speakers, the event could attain the true international standard that it had the intention to achieve. With Prof. Dr. L.M. Patnaik, Indian Institute of Science, Bangalore gracing the occasion as the chief guest, it was further praiseworthy to have had representatives from the Indian Institute of Management Kolkata, the Indian Statistical Institute Kolkata, the Defence Research and Development Organization, the Government of India, IBM, Wipro, Capgemini, Tata Consultancy Service, Accenture, Rediff.com, and LinkedIn for invited speeches and panel discussions.

As per my information, there were 276 papers submitted from across the globe including countries like Australia, the UK, Singapore, Bangladesh, Portugal, Saudi Arabia, Taiwan, Nepal, Thailand, Russia, and the USA – out of which 90 papers were accepted and presented. There were 8 technical tracks at the conference, each chaired by experts in the respective domains, as well as 18 technical sessions, where the authors presented their respective research work in front of the session chairs from academia and industry. The three best papers were awarded by Springer Nature with prizes worth € 250, € 200, and € 150 respectively. Some more awards were also offered by Calcutta Business School, the host, and IEEE Young Professionals Kolkata.

From my experience in general and by virtue of being present in person for some hours during the event, I strongly believe that it was undoubtedly commendable on the part of the organizers of the conference to have made it a grand success, especially this being the first one in the series. I am sure that subsequent events of this conference series will definitely be able to prove its standing as a successful series within the research community in the years ahead.

Last but not the least, I want to avail myself of this opportunity to express my heartfelt thanks to the chairs of the Program Committee of CICBA 2017, along with all my good wishes for the upcoming CICBA series of conferences.

With best wishes

July 2017   Sushmita Mitra

Preface

Calcutta Business School, in collaboration with the Computer Society of India, organized the First International Conference on Computational Intelligence, Communication, and Business Analytics (CICBA 2017), during 24–25 March 2017 at the Calcutta Business School campus. This is the first activity of the Computer Society of India in the eastern region with Springer Nature as the publication partner. This mega event covered all aspects of computational intelligence, communications, and business analytics, where by the scope was not only limited to various engineering disciplines, such as computer science, electronics, and electrical, mechanical, or biomedical engineering, but also included work from allied communities like general science, educational research, and management science, etc.

The volume constitutes a collection of high-quality peer-reviewed research papers received from all over the world. CICBA 2017 attracted a good number of submissions from the different areas spanning eight tracks in various cutting-edge technologies of specialized focus, which were organized and chaired by eminent professors. The eight special sessions focused on computational intelligence, data science and advanced data analytics, signal processing and communications, microelectronics, sensors, intelligent networks, computational forensics (privacy and security), computational intelligence in bio-computing, computational intelligence in mobile & quantum computing, and intelligent data mining & data warehousing. After a rigorous peer-review process, with the help of our Program Committee members and external experts as reviewers (from inland as well as abroad), top-quality papers could be identified for presentation and publication. The review process was extremely stringent with a minimum of three reviews for each submission and occasionally up to six reviews duly supplemented by checks on similarity and overlaps as well. Submitted papers geographically encompass countries like Australia, the UK, Singapore, Bangladesh, Portugal, Saudi Arabia, Taiwan, Nepal, Thailand, Russia, and the USA. Out of the pool of papers submitted, only 30% have been included in these final proceedings.

The Organizing Committee of CICBA 2017 consisted of international academic and industrial luminaries, and the Program Committee comprised around 200 technical experts. These proceedings are published in one volume of Springer's Communications in Computer and Information Science (CCIS) series. We, in the capacity of the volume editors, convey our sincere gratitude to Springer for providing the opportunity to publish the proceedings of CICBA 2017.

Representatives from the Indian Institute of Management Kolkata, the Indian Statistical Institute Kolkata, the Indian Institute of Science Bangalore, the Defence Research Development Organization, the Government of India, IBM, Wipro, Capgemini, TCS, Accenture, Rediff.com, and LinkedIn participated in the panel discussions, keynote addresses, and invited talks. The conference included many distinguished keynote addresses by eminent speakers such as Prof. Dr. Sankar Pal, Indian Statistical Institute, Dr. P.N. Suganthan, Nanyang Technological University, Singapore,

Prof. Dr. L.M. Patnaik, Indian Institute of Science Bangalore, and Prof. Dr. Edward Tsang, University of Essex, UK. Speakers for panel discussions included luminaries from academia and industry, such as Dr. Gautam Mahapatra, RCI Labs, Defence Research Development Organization, Hyderabad; Mr. Lawrence Mohanraj, IBM India Pvt. Ltd., Chennai; Mr. Somnath Chatterjee, Capgemini, Kolkata; Mr. Ajit Balakrishnan, Rediff.com; Dr. Arindam Pal, Data and Decision Sciences Group, TCS Innovation Labs Kolkata, India; Mr. Rajeev Ranjan Kumar, Virtual Desk, Wipro Tech. Hyderabad, etc. Invited talks were delivered by Ms. Suvira Srivastav, Springer Nature and Prof. Dr. Sushmita Mitra, Machine Intelligence Unit, Indian Statistical Institute, Kolkata.

The editors would like to express their sincere gratitude to Prof. Dr. Kalyanmoy Deb, Michigan State University, for taking the time to inaugurate the Call for Papers of CICBA 2017. They also thank the International Advisory Committee and the Chief Guest of CICBA 2017, Prof. Dr. L.M. Patnaik, for providing valuable guidance and inspiration to overcome various difficulties in the process of organizing the conference. We moreover want to avail ourselves of this opportunity to extend our heartfelt thanks to the Honorary Chair of this conference, Prof. Dr. Anirban Basu, Computer Society of India, for his active involvement from the very beginning till the end of the conference, without whose support this conference could never have assumed such a successful shape. Sincerest thanks are due to Prof. Dr. P.K. Roy, APIIT, India, for his valuable suggestions regarding enhancing the editorial review process. The editors also thank the Best Paper Award Committee of CICBA 2017 for taking the trouble to select the best papers from a pool so many formidable acceptances. The conference was sponsored by Calcutta Business School and IEEE Young Professionals.

Special words of appreciation are due to the Calcutta Business School, for coming forward to host the conference, which incidentally was the first in the series. It was indeed heartening to note the enthusiasm of all faculty, staff, and students of Calcutta Business School to organize the conference in a professional manner. Involvement of faculty coordinators and student volunteers are particularly praiseworthy in this regard. The editors also thank technical partners and sponsors for providing all the support and financial assistance.

It is needless to mention the role of the contributors. But for their active support and participation, the question of organizing a conference is bound to fall through. The editors take this opportunity to thank the authors of all the papers submitted as a result of their hard work, more so because all of them considered the conference as a viable platform to ventilate some of their latest findings, not to speak of their adherence to the deadlines and patience with the lengthy review process. The quality of a refereed volume primarily depends on the expertise and dedication of the reviewers who volunteer their efforts with a smiling face. The editors are further indebted to the Program Committee members and external reviewers, who not only produced excellent reviews but also did these in short timeframes, in spite of their very busy schedules. It is because of their quality work that it has been possible to maintain the high academic standard of the proceedings.

A conference is only complete when it has managed to attract a high level of participation. A conference with good papers accepted and devoid of any participants is perhaps the worst form of curse that may be imagined. The editors therefore thank the participants for attending the conference.

Last but not the least, the editors would offer cognizance to all the volunteers for their tireless efforts in meeting the deadlines and arranging every minute detail meticulously to ensure that the conference achieved its goals, academic or otherwise.

J.K. Mandal
Paramartha Dutta
Somnath Mukhopadhyay

Organization

Steering Committee

Chief Patron
S.K. Birla   Calcutta Business School, India

Patron
Shekhar Chaudhuri   Calcutta Business School, India

Honorary Chair
Anirban Basu   Computer Society of India, India

Chief Guest
L.M. Patnaik   Indian Institute of Science Bangalore, India

General Chairs
Sankar K. Pal   Indian Statistical Institute Kolkata, India
Ponnuthurai Nagaratnam   Nanyang Technological University, Singapore
  Suganthan
Edward Tsang   University of Essex, UK

Program Chairs
J.K. Mandal   University of Kalyani, India
Paramartha Dutta   Visva Bharati University, India
Somnath Mukhopadhyay   Calcutta Business School, India

Convener
Somnath Mukhopadhyay   Calcutta Business School, India

Co-conveners
Indranil Ghosh   Calcutta Business School, India
Sanjib Biswas   Calcutta Business School, India

Organizing Chair
Tamal Datta Chaudhuri   Calcutta Business School, India

Finance Chair
T.K. Basu   Calcutta Business School, India

Organizing Committee

J.K. Mandal	University of Kalyani, India
Somnath Mukhopadhyay	Calcutta Business School, India
Sanjana Mondal	Calcutta Business School, India
Siddhartha Sen Gupta	Calcutta Business School, India
Sanjay Mohapatra	Computer Society of India, India
M.K. Sanyal	University of Kalyani, India
Paramartha Dutta	Visva Bharati University, India
Sanjib Biswas	Calcutta Business School, India
Indranil Ghosh	Calcutta Business School, India
Pinaki Ranjan Bhattacharyya	Calcutta Business School, India
Suman K. Dawn	Calcutta Business School, India
Arindam Sarkar	University of Kalyani, India
Madhumita Sengupta	Indian Institute of Information, India Technology Kalyani, India
Phalguni Mukherjee	Computer Society of India Kolkata Chapter, India
Rajdeep Chakraborty	Netaji Subhash Eng. College, India
Subimal Kundu	Computer Society of India Kolkata Chapter, India
Sudipta Ghosal	Future Institute of Engineering & Technology, India
K.L. Hasan	Aliah University, India
Radha Krishna Bar	Computer Society of India, Kolkata Chapter, India
Sanjeev Mitra	Calcutta Business School, India
Subir Lahiri	Computer Society of India Kolkata Chapter, India
Rituparna	Datta Calcutta Business School, India
Utpal Nandi	Vidyasagar University, India
Somdatta Chakroborty	Govt of Eng & Ceramic Technology, Kolkata, India
Tanmoy Kanti Halder	Prasannadeb Women's College, India
Sujoy Chatterjee	University of Kalyani, India
Ranjan Kumar Barman	National Institute of Cholera and Enteric Diseases (ICMR) Kolkata, India
Mili Ghosh	Visva Bharati University, India

Editorial Board

J.K. Mandal	University of Kalyani, India
Paramartha Dutta	Visva Bharati University, India
Somnath Mukhopadhyay	Calcutta Business School, India

Advisory Board

Kalyanmoy Deb	Michigan State University, USA
Aynur Unal	Stanford University, USA
Valentina E. Balas	Aurel Vlaicu University of Arad, Romania
Y. Narahari	Indian Institute of Science Bangalore, India

Prith Banerjee	Schneider Electric, USA
Hyeona Lim	Mississippi State University, USA
Rajkumar Buyya	University of Melbourne, Australia
Shikharesh Majumdar	Carleton University, Canada
Amiya Nayak	Ottawa University, Canada
Sajal Das	University Texas at Arlington, USA
Santosh Mohanty	TCS Mumbai, India
Zbigniew Michalewicz	University of Adelaide, Australia
Arun Baran Samaddar	National Institute of Technology, Sikkim, India
Subhansu Bandyopadhyay	Calcutta University, India
Somnath Mukhopadhay	Texas University, USA
A. Kaykobad	Bangladesh University of Engineering & Technology, Bangladesh
Bidyut Baran Chaudhuri	Indian Statistical Institute Kolkata, India
Girijasankar Mallik	University of Western Sydney, Australia
Atal Chowdhury	Jadavpur University, India
Ujjwal Maulik	Jadavpur University, India
A. Damodaram	Jawaharlal Nehru Technological University, India
Atulya Nagar	Liverpool Hope University, UK
B.K. Panigrahi	Indian Institute of Technology Delhi, India
Bani K. Sinha	Calcutta Business School, India
Barin Kumar De	Tripura University, India
Basabi Chakraborty	Iwate Prefectural University, Japan
Mrinal Kanti Naskar	Jadavpur University, India
Nandini Mukhopadhyay	Jadavpur University, India
K.V. Arya	Indian Institute of Information Technology & Management Gwalior, India
Millie Pant	Indian Institute of Technology Roorkee, India
Rahul Kala	Indian Institute of Information Technology Allahabad, India
Subarna Shakya	Tribhuvan University, Nepal
Pronab Sen	International Growth Centre, India Central, India
Siddhartha Bhattacharjee	RCC Institute of Information Technology, India

Publication Committee Chairs

Durgesh Misra	Computer Society of India, India
D.P. Sinha	Computer Society of India, India

Best Paper Award Committee

Dipti Prasad Mukherjee	Indian Statistical Institute, Kolkata, India
Pradosh K. Roy	Asia Pacific Institute of Information Technology, India
Vipin Tyagi	Jaypee University of Engineering and Technology, India

Website and IT Committee

Radha Krishna Bar   Computer Society of India, Kolkata Chapter, India
Sunil Ray   Calcutta Business School, India

Technical Sponsors

IEEE Computational Intelligence Society Kolkata, India
IEEE Young Professionals Kolkata, India
IEEE Kolkata Chapter, India
Computer Society of India Kolkata Chapter, India

Associate Partner

Computer Society of India Division V (E&R), India

Knowledge Partner

Computer Society of India Division IV (Communications), India

Financial Sponsor

Union Bank of India, Kolkata, India

Technical Program Committee

Arindam Pal	TCS Innovation Lab., India
Anindita Roy	B P Poddar Institute of Management & Technology, India
A.C. Mondal	University of Burdwan, India
A. Chattopadhyay	Siliguri Institute of Technology, India
A.M. Sudhakara	University of Mysore, India
Abhishek Bhattacharya	Institute of Engineering & Management, India
Ambar Dutta	Computer Society of India Kolkata Chapter, India
Amiya Kumar Rath	Veer Surendra Sai University of Technology, India
Amlan Chakrabarti	Calcutta University, India
Andrew M. Lynn	Jawaharlal Nehru Technological University, India
Angshuman Bhttacharyya	National Institute of Technology Durgapur, India
Angsuman Sarkar	Kalyani Government Engineering College, India
Anirban Guha	Jadavpur University, India
Anupam Baliyan	Bharati Vidyapeeth's Institute of Computer Applications & Management, India
Anuradha Banerjee	Kalyani Government Engineering College, India
Arnab K. Laha	Indian Institute of Management Ahmedabad, India
Arpita Chakraborty	Techno India Salt Lake, India

Arun K. Pujari	University of Hyderabad, India
Arundhati Bagchi Misra	Saginaw Valley State University, USA
Asad A.M. Al-Salih	University of Bagdad, Iraq
Ashok Kumar Rai	Gujarat University, India
Asif Ekbal	Indian Institute of Technology Patna, India
Asok Kumar	MCKV Institute of Engineering, India
Atanu Kundu	Heritage Institute of Technology, India
Ayan Datta	IACS, Kolkata, India
B.B. Pal	University of Kalyani, India
Balakrushna Tripathy	Vellore Institute of Technology, India
Banshidhar Majhi	National Institute of Technology Rourkela, India
Bhaba R. Sarker	Louisiana State University, USA
Bhabani P. Sinha	Indian Statistical Institute Kolkata, India
Bhagvati Chakravarthy	University of Hyderabad, India
Bhaskar Sardar	Jadavpur University, India
Bibhas Chandra Dhara	Jadavpur University, India
Biplab K. Sikdar	Indian Institute of Engineering Science and Technology Shibpur, India
Brojo Kishore Mishra	C.V. Raman College of Engineering, India
Buddhadeb Manna	University of Calcutta, India
C.K. Chanda	Indian Institute of Engineering Science & Technology, India
C. Srinivas	Kakatiya Institute of Technology & Science, India
Carlos A. Bana e Costa	Universidade de Lisboa, Portugal
Chandan Bhar	Indian School of Mines, India
Chandreyee Chowdhury	Jadavpur University, India
Chilukuri K. Mohan	Syracuse University, USA
Chintan Mandal	Jadavpur University, India
D.D. Sinha	Calcutta University, India
Dakshina Ranjan Kisku	National Institute of Technology Durgapur, India
Debashis De	Maulana Abul Kalam Azad University of Technology, India
Debasish Nandi	National Institute of Technology Durgapur, India
Debdatta Kandar	North East Hill University, India
Debesh Das	Jadavpur University, India
Debidas Ghosh	National Institute of Technology Durgapur, India
Debotosh Bhattacharjee	Jadavpur University, India
Deepak Khemani	Indian Institute of Technology Madras, India
Deepak Kumar	Amity University, India
Dhananjay Bhattacharyya,	Saha Institute of Nuclear Physics, Kolkata, India
Dhananjay Kumar Singh	Global ICT Standardization Forum for India (GISFI), India
Diganta Goswami	Indian Institute of Technology Guwahati, India
Dilip Kumar Pratihar	Indian Institute of Technology Kharagpur, India
Dipanwita Roychowdhury	Indian Institute of Technology Kharagpur, India

Dulal Acharjee	Purushottam Institute of Engineering & Technology, India
Durgesh Kumar Mishra	Computer Society of India, India
Esteban Alfaro Cortés	University of Castilla-La Mancha, Spain
Ganapati Panda	Indian Institute of Technology Bhubaneswar, India
Goutam Sarker	National Institute of Technology Durgapur, India
Goutam Sanyal	National Institute of Technology Durgapur, India
Govinda K.	Vellore Institute of Technology, India
Gunamani Jena	Roland Institute of Technology, India
H.S. Lalliel	University of Derby, UK
Hirak Maity	College of Engineering and Management Kolaghat, India
Indrajit Bhattacharjee	Kalyani Govt. Engineering College, India
Indrajit Saha	National Institute of Technical Teachers' Training & Research Kolkata, India
J.V.R. Murthy	Jawaharlal Nehru Technological University Kakinada, India
Jimson Mathew	University of Bristol, UK
Jyoti Prakash Singh	National Institute of Technology Patna, India
K. Kannan	Nagaland University, India
K. Srujan Raju	CMR Group of Institutions, India
K. Suresh Basu	Jawaharlal Nehru Technological University, India
Kameswari Chebrolu	Indian Institute of Technology Bombay, India
Kandarpa Kumar Sarma	Gauhati University, India
Kartick Chandra Mandal	Jadavpur University, India
Kausik Dasgupta	Kalyani Govt. Engineering College, India
Koushik Majumder	Maulana Abul Kalam Azad University of Technology, India
Kui Yu	University of South Australia, Australia
Kunal Das	Narula Institute of Technology, India
Lothar Thiele	Swiss Federal Institute of Technology Zurich, Switzerland
M. Ali Akber Dewan	Athabasca University, Canada
M.S. Prasad Babu	Andhra University, India
M. Sandirigama	University of Peradenia, Sri Lanka
Malay Bhattacharyya	Indian Institute of Engineering Science and Technology, India
Malay Pakhira	Kalyani Govt. Engineering. College, India
Manas Kumar Bera	Haldia Institute of Technology, India
Manas Ranjan Senapati	Centurion University of Technology & Management, India
Manish Kumar Kakhani	Mody University, India
Massimo Pollifroni	University of Turin, Italy
Md. Iftekhar Hussain	North East Hill University, India
Mohammad Ubadullah Bokhari	Aligarh Muslim University, India

Mohd Nazri Ismail	Universiti Pertahanan Nasional Malaysia, Malaysia
N.V. Ramana Rao	Jawaharlal Nehru Technological University, India
Nabendu Chaki	Calcutta University, India
Nibaran Das	Jadavpur University, Kolkata, India
Nilanjan Dey	Techno India College of Technology, India
P. Premchand	Osmania University Hyderabad, India
P.S. Neelakanta	Florida Atlantic University, USA
Parag Kulkarni	iknowlation Research Labs Pvt. Ltd., India
Parama Bhaumik	Jadavpur University, India
Partha Pratim Sahu	Tezpur University, India
Pawan Kumar Jha	Purbanchal University, Nepal
Pawan Lingras	St. Mary's University, Canada
Pradosh K. Roy	Asia Pacific Institute of Information Technology, India
Pramod Kumar Meher	Nanyang Technological University, Singapore
Pranab K. Dan	Indian Institute of Technology Kharagpur, India
Prasanta K. Jana	Indian School of Mines Dhanbad, India
Prashant R. Nair	Computer Society of India, India
Pratyay Kuila	National Institute of Technology Sikkim, India
Priya Ranjan Sinha Mahapatra	University of Kalyani, India
R.K. Jana	Indian Institute of Social Welfare and Business Management, India
R.N. Lahiri	Batanagar Institute of Engineering Management & Science, India
R. Sankararama Krishnan	Indian Institute of Technology Kanpur, India
Rajeeb Dey	National Institute of Technology Silchar, India
Ram Sarkar	Jadavpur University, India
Rameshwar Dubey	South University of Science & Technology of China, China
Ranjan Kumar Gupta	West Bengal State University, India
Ray Zhong	University of Auckland, New Zealand
Rober Hans	Tshwane University of Technology, South Africa
S.V.K. Bharathi	Symbiosis International University, India
S.D. Dewasurendra	University of Peradenia, Sri Lanka
S.G. Deshmukh	Indian Institute of Technology, Mumbai, India
S.K. Behera	National Institute of Technology Rourkela, India
S.P. Bhattacharyya	Texas A & M University, USA
Saikat Chakrabarti	CSIR-IICB, Kolkata, India
Samar Sen Sarma	University of Calcutta, India
Samiran Chattopadhyay	Jadavpur University, India
Sandip Rakshit	Kaziranga University, India
Sanjib K. Panda	Berkeley Education Alliance for Research in Singapore Limited, Singapore
Sankar Chakraborty	Jadavpur University, India
Sankar Duraikannan	Asia Pacific University of Technology & Innovation, Malaysia

Santi P. Maity	Indian Institute of Engineering Science and Technology Shibpur, India
Sarbani Roy	Jadavpur University, India
Satish Narayana Srirama	University of Tartu, Estonia
Saurabh Dutta	Dr. B.C. Roy Engineering College Durgapur, India
Seba Maity	College of Engineering and Management Kolaghat, India
Shangping Ren	Illinois Institute of Technology Chicago, USA
Soma Barman	University of Calcutta, India
Soumya Pandit	University of Calcutta, India
Sripati Mukhopadhyay	Burdwan University, India
Sruti Gan Chaudhuri	Jadavpur University, India
Subhadip Basu	Jadavpur University, India
Subho Chaudhuri	BIT Mesra Kolkata, India
Subhranil Som	Amity University Noida, India
Subir Sarkar	Jadavpur University, India
Subrata Banerjee	National Institute of Technology Durgapur, India
Sudhakar Sahoo	Institute of Mathematics & Applications, India
Sudhakar Tripathi	National Institute of Technology Patna, India
Sudip Kumar Adhikari	Cooch Behar Government Engineering College, India
Sudip Kumar Das	Calcutta University, India
Sudip Kundu	Calcutta University, India
Sudipta Roy	Assam University, India
Sukumar Nandi	Indian Institute of Technology Guwahati, India
Sumit Kundu	National Institute of Technology Durgapur, India
Sunirmal Khatua	Calcutta University, India
Supratim Sengupta	Indian Institute of Engineering Science and Technology Shibpur, India
Sushmita Mitra	Indian Statistical Institute Kolkata, India
Suvamoy Changder	National Institute of Technology Durgapur, India
Swagatam Das	Indian Statistical Institute Kolkata, India
Swapan Kumar Mandal	Kalyani Government Engineering College, India
Syed Samsul Alam	Aliah University, India
T.K. Kaul	Sikkim University, India
Tamaghna Acharya	Indian Institute of Engineering Science and Technology, India
Tandra Pal	National Institute of Technology Durgapur, India
Tanushyam Chattopadhyay	Innovation Lab, TCS Kolkata India
Tapan K. Ghosh	West Bengal University of Animal & Fishery Sciences, India
Tushar Kanti Bera	Yonsei University, South Korea
U. Dinesh Kumar	Indian Institute of Management Bangalore, India
Utpal Biswas	University of Kalyani, India
V. Prithiviraj	Pondicherry Engineering College, India
Vikrant Bhateja	Shri Ram Swaroop Memorial Group of Professional Colleges, India

Vladimir A. Oleshchuk   University of Agder, Norway
Yoshihiro Kilho Shin   University of Hyogo, Japan
Zaigham Mahmood   University of Derby, UK
Muheet Ahmed Butt   University of Kashmir, India
Arijit Chowdhury   TCS Innovation Lab., India
Hemanta Dey   Techno India College of Technology, India
Samir Malakar   MCKV Institute of Engineering, Howrah, India
Snehasis Banerjee   TCS Innovation Lab., India

Contents – Part II

Intelligent Data Mining and Data Warehousing

Computational Intelligence

Contents – Part I

Signal Processing and Communications

Microelectronics, Sensors, Intelligent Networks

Computational Forensics (Privacy and Security)

Computational Intelligence in Bio-computing

Protein Function Prediction from Protein Interaction Network Using Bottom-up L2L Apriori Algorithm

Abhimanyu Prasad[1], Sovan Saha[1(✉)], Piyali Chatterjee[2], Subhadip Basu[3], and Mita Nasipuri[3]

[1] Department of Computer Science and Engineering, Dr. Sudhir Chandra Sur Degree Engineering College, Dumdum, Kolkata 700 074, India
prasad.abhi150@gmail.com, sovansaha12@gmail.com
[2] Department of Computer Science and Engineering, Netaji Subhash Engineering College, Garia, Kolkata 700152, India
chatterjee_piyali@yahoo.com
[3] Department of Computer Science and Engineering, Jadavpur University, Kolkata 700032, India
subhadip@cse.jdvu.ac.in, mitanasipuri@yahoo.com

Abstract. Detection of unannotated protein functions in a protein interaction network generates a lot of beneficial information in the field of drug discovery of various kinds of diseases. Though most of the various computational methods have succeeded in predicting functions of huge amount of unknown proteins at recent times but the main problem is the simultaneous increase of false positives in most of the predicted results. In this work, a bottom-up predictor of existing Apriori algorithm has been implemented for protein function prediction by exploiting two most important neighborhood properties: closeness centrality and edge clustering coefficient of protein interaction network. The method is also unique in the fact that the functions of the leaf nodes in the interaction network have been back propagated and thus labeled up to the root node (target protein) using a bottom-up level to level approach. An overall precision, recall and F-score of 0.86, 0.65 and 0.74 respectively have been obtained in this work which are found to be better than most of the current state-of-the-art.

Keywords: PPI (Protein-Protein Interaction) · Apriori algorithm · PIN (Protein Interaction Network) · L2L (Level to Level) approach · Closeness centrality · Edge clustering coefficient

1 Introduction

Computational methods for protein function prediction have succeeded to draw the limelight in comparison to the biological/experimental methods since they comprehensively reduce time, effort and cost. Though most of the recent methodologies outperform the previous ones still the fact cannot be denied that they provide the foundation without which the advancement in this area of research is not possible. Function prediction from PPI (Protein-Protein Interaction Network) is one of the most important fields in protein function prediction which is considered in this work. In a PIN, each node represents a protein while the corresponding edge between two nodes/proteins represents its

© Springer Nature Singapore Pte Ltd. 2017
J.K. Mandal et al. (Eds.): CICBA 2017, Part II, CCIS 776, pp. 3–16, 2017.
DOI: 10.1007/978-981-10-6430-2_1

interaction. It is believed that proteins in the neighborhood of unannotated protein (target protein) will also perform similarly as that of unannotated one. But all the functions of all neighborhood proteins cannot be assigned to the unknown since it is not logically justified that the target protein will perform all the functions. Moreover, it will enhance the percentage of false positives. In reality it has been observed in various researches that the unknown protein only performs only few of the functions performed by the proteins in its neighborhood. So selection of a protein with specific functionality among a large number of neighborhood proteins is proved to be a very crucial as well as a challenging task indeed. But before proceeding into further details of this work, some of the previous works have been discussed in the upcoming section to have a clear concept about the types of work in this PIN and other areas of protein function prediction.

The pioneering attempt start with the simplest neighbourhood-counting method [1, 2]. The concept of functional similarity of two proteins has been introduced in the work of Chen et al. [3] where both level-1 and level-2 proteins of interaction network has been considered. While Vazquez et al. [4] highlights the concept of maximum connectivity of the unannotated protein through his simulated annealing optimizing method. Exploration and embedding other features of a protein in a PIN opens another way of function prediction. This has been observed in the work of Karaoz et al. [5] where gene ontology has been taken into consideration along with the gene expression data and PIN. Other important approaches like markov random field [6], flow based approach [7], probabilistic methods [8], binomial model based loopy belief propagation [9], UVCLUSTER based on bi-clustering [10] and network based statistical algorithm [11] also leave their marks in PIN based protein function prediction. Clustering of proteins is another essential aspect which has been highlighted in the works of Pruzli et al. [12] and King et al. [13]. Xiong et al. [14] combines PPI information and protein sequence information to increase the performance of the predictor. They add implicit edges to the network with explicit or existing edges and employ a collective classification algorithm to predict the function. While in some of the previous works [15–17], physicochemical properties and neighborhood properties collectively determine the functional group. Piovesan et al. [18] propose an unique approach of combining PPI information, sequence information and domain information for the protein function prediction. Zhao et al. [19] predicts protein function using a ranking methodology on a dynamic weighted interactome network enriched with PPI network, time course gene expression data, protein's domain information and protein complex information. Other exclusive works in this field are Wu et al. [20], Sandhan et al. [21], Huang et al. [22], Saha et al. [23, 24] and Zhao et al. [25].

All these studies have revealed the fact that there are still a lot of scopes for improvements in this field of improving accuracy level in the field of protein function prediction which motivates us not only to work in this field and to discover new methodologies which will reduce the rate of false positives as well as increases the precision, recall and F-score values. Our entire work can be described in two phases: In the first phase, closeness centrality of all the nodes in the PIN has been calculated. Then unannotated proteins or the target set is selected based on three thresholds (High, medium and low) estimated on closeness centrality of all nodes. In the second phase, PPI network is formed for each target protein, considering its level-1 and level-2 proteins. Then Apriori algorithm is used from bottom to top in a PIN using L2L approach (first it predicts the function of level-2 proteins and then level-1 proteins) and predicts functions of unannotated protein from the functions of leaf nodes which are only considered to be annotated in the respective PIN. Moreover since Apriori algorithm is used for prediction so all the possible combination of functions of leaf nodes has been taken into consideration which reduces the chances of missing any annotation while predicting protein function. In the upcoming section, we will discuss about the dataset, related terminologies, our proposed methodology and its associated results.

2   Dataset

Munich Information Center for Protein Sequences database (ftp://ftpmips.helmholtz-muenchen.de/fungi/Saccharomycetes/CYGD/PPI/) [15–17] has been used in this work. The overall network of yeast is shown in Fig. 1.

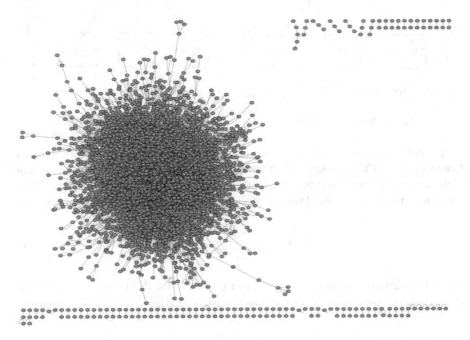

Fig. 1. PIN of yeast

3   Related Terminologies

The important component of proposed methodology of bottom-up L2L approach is Protein interaction network [15] which is represented by graph [15] where proteins are vertices and interactions are edges. Terminologies like Sub-graph [15], Edge Clustering Coefficient [16, 26], level-1 neighbors [15], level-2 neighbors [15] have their usual meaning. Proposed work uses Apriori Algorithm to predict the functional group of target protein by bottom-up approach. Initially it predicts the functional group of level-1 neighbors from the level-2 neighbors. Then using similar manner, the functional group of level-1 neighbors are again back propagated up to the target protein. The entire scenario has been shown in Fig. 2.

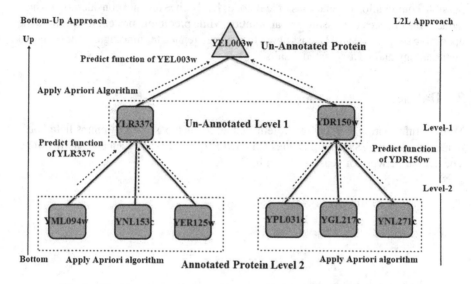

Fig. 2. Working of Bottom-Up L2L approach on target protein YEL003w

In order to select set of target proteins, a graph-theoretical measure Closeness Centrality Score (CCS) is taken. *CCS* of a node [27–29] is defined as a measure of the sum of the length of the shortest paths between the node and all other nodes in the graph. Thus the more central a node is, the closer it is to all other nodes. Mathematically, it is defined as

$$CCS(i) = \frac{|N_u| - 1}{\sum_j d_{ij}} \tag{1}$$

where i is the target protein, j is any another protein in the PPI network G_p, d_{ij} is the shortest distance between these two nodes and $|N_u|$ is the total number of node i's neighbour.

4   Methodology

The top level view of the proposed method has been shown in Fig. 2. Basically it can be subdivided into three phases. The phase-1 is basically for selecting unannotated proteins (target set) at three levels of thresholds based on the calculated closeness centrality of all nodes in the network which is executed in the algorithm *Select_Target*. Next, *Edge_Prune* eliminates less significant edges from the neighborhood graph of target proteins chosen by *Select_Target*. Thus filtered neighborhood graph of target protein is processed by *FunApriori*. The entire step by step approach of bottom-up L2L approach has been given below.

Algorithm: *Select_Target*

(Selection of target proteins whose functional groups
to be predicted)

Input: Protein Interaction Network represented by
          directed graph with edges labeled with function
          al groups

Output: Three sets of target proteins at three levels of
          threshold: P_U^{high}, P_U^{medium}, P_U^{low}

Begin

  $P_U = \emptyset;$

  for each protein i in G_P (PIN)

      Find closeness centrality Score $CCS(i)$ using
      equation 1.

  Sort them on their decreasing CCS values.

  Set the three threshold values (high, medium
  and low) based on range of CCS at random.

  for each protein i in G_P

      if $CCS(i) \geq threshold$ then

          $P_U = \{i\} \cup P_U ;$ // P_U^{high}, P_U^{meduim} and P_U^{low} at
          three thresholds

End.

Algorithm: Edge_Prune

(Pruning of less important interactions in the neighborhood graph of target proteins)

Input: P_U (set of Target Proteins) and G_P (PIN)

Output: G_{P_i}' (pruned neighborhood graph of target protein)

Begin

  //forming neighborhood graph G_{P_i}' for each target pro
  tein i upto $level-2$

  for each target protein i in P_U

      $N_U^1(i) = level-1$ **neighbors of protein** i

      for each target protein j **in** $N_U^1(i)$

          $N_U^2(i) = \{ level-1$ **neighbors of protein** $j\};$

  $G_{P_i}' = \{i\} \cup N_U^1(i) \cup N_U^2(i);$ // $G_{P_i}' = \{V_{P_i}', E_{P_i}'\}$ denotes the neighborhood graph of protein i

  for each edge l in G_{P_i}'

      calculate $ECC(l)$ // Edge Clustering Coefficient
      eliminate edge l if $ECC(l)$ falls under desired
      threshold
      $E_{P_i}' = E_{P_i}' - \{l\};$

  return $G_{P_i}';$

End.

Procedure: FunApriori (G'_{P_i}, minSupport)

// G'_{P_i} (neighborhood graph of target protein), minSupport is the Minimum Support or the threshold value

Begin

      $N_U^j(i)$=level-j neighbors of protein i; // j =1,2 for *level − 1* or *level − 2*

      L_1= Functional group of $N_U^j(i)$;

      for (k=2; $L_{K-1}! = \emptyset$; k + +)

            C_K = **candidates generated from** L_{K-1}

      //that is cartesian product of $L_{K-1} \times L_{K-1}$ and eliminating any k-1 size item set that is not frequent

      for each functional group of $N_U^j(i)$

            increment the count of all candidates in C_K that are contained in $N_U^j(i)$

      L_K = candidate in C_K with min support

End.

return $\cup_K L_K$;

Proposed Methodology

Input: G_P (PIN)

Output: Function prediction of target proteins

Begin

      //call Select_Target to select target proteins

      $P_U = Select\_Target(G_P)$; //$P_U^{high}, P_U^{medium}, P_U^{low}$

      //Call Edge_Prune to eliminate useless edges from neighborhood graph of target proteins

      $G'_P = Edge\_Prune(P_U, G_P)$;

      //Apply apriori algorithm to level-2 neighbors of target protein i

      $\cup_K L_K = FunApriori(G'_{P_i}$, minSupport);

      Propagate $\cup_K L_K$ back up to its parent node

      // Apply apriori algorithm to level-1 neighbors of target protein i

      $U_{K'}L_{K'} = FunApriori(G'_{P_i}$, minSupport);

      Propagate $U_{K'}L_{K'}$ back up to its parent node protein i

End.

It should be noted here that Edge Clustering coefficient [16] has been calculated in Phase-2 for each edge of the neighborhood graph of target protein. ECC for edge determines how much a protein is connected to densely connected proteins. Or, in other words, edges or interaction having low edge clustering coefficient values than the calculated threshold value should be pruned before ultimate prediction so that the prediction might not get hampered by the non-essential proteins.

4.1   Illustration of Methodology with Sample PIN

In Fig. 3 YEL003w is the protein of the target set whose function is to be predicted by our proposed methodology. Its corresponding level-1 neighbors are YLR337c and YDR150w. While it's Level-2 neighbors are YML094w, YNL153c, YER125w, YPL031c, YGL217c and YNL271c. In this work, functional groups of level-1 are not taken rather are assigned from their children or level-2 neighbors. So at first Apriori algorithm is applied on the

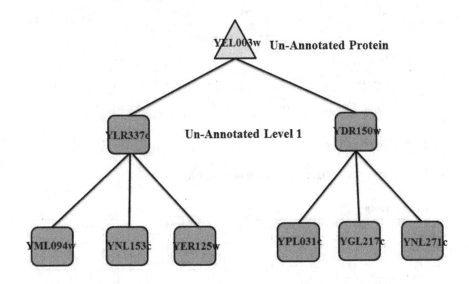

Fig. 3. Sample PIN of unannotated protein YEL003w

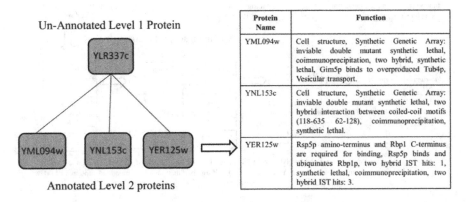

Fig. 4. Sub-network of YLR337c

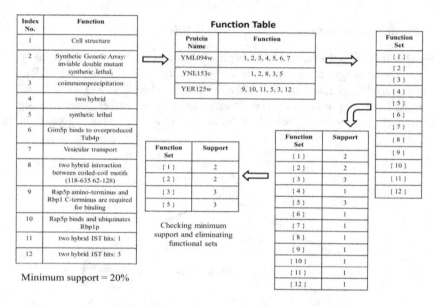

Index No.	Function
1	Cell structure
2	Synthetic Genetic Array: inviable double mutant synthetic lethal,
3	coimmunoprecipitation
4	two hybrid
5	synthetic lethal
6	Gim5p binds to overproduced Tub4p
7	Vesicular transport
8	two hybrid interaction between coiled-coil motifs (118-635 62-128)
9	Rsp5p amino-terminus and Rbp1 C-terminus are required for binding
10	Rsp5p binds and ubiquinates Rbp1p
11	two hybrid IST hits: 1
12	two hybrid IST hits: 3

Minimum support = 20%

Function Table

Protein Name	Function
YML094w	1, 2, 3, 4, 5, 6, 7
YNL153c	1, 2, 8, 3, 5
YER125w	9, 10, 11, 5, 3, 12

Function Set
{1}
{2}
{3}
{4}
{5}
{6}
{7}
{8}
{9}
{10}
{11}
{12}

Function Set	Support
{1}	2
{2}	2
{3}	3
{4}	1
{5}	3
{6}	1
{7}	1
{8}	1
{9}	1
{10}	1
{11}	1
{12}	1

Function Set	Support
{1}	2
{2}	2
{3}	3
{5}	3

Checking minimum support and eliminating functional sets

Fig. 5. Execution of apriori algorithm

Function Table

Protein Name	Function
YML094w	1, 2, 3, 4, 5, 6, 7
YNL153c	1, 2, 8, 3, 5
YER125w	9, 10, 11, 5, 3, 4, 12

Function Set	Support
{1}	2
{2}	2
{3}	3
{5}	3

Function Set
{1, 2}
{1, 3}
{1, 5}
{2, 3}
{2, 5}
{3, 5}

Function Set	Support
{1, 2}	2
{1, 3}	2
{1, 5}	2
{2, 3}	2
{2, 5}	2
{3, 5}	3

Selected Proteins are YML094w and YNL153c as it contains the maximum no. of functions matched out of the selected functions, Now all the interaction functions will be assigned to the respective un- annotated level 1 protein which is YLR337c

Checking minimum support and eliminating functional sets

Minimum support = 20%

Function Set	Support
{1, 2, 3, 5}	2

Function Set
{1, 2, 3, 5}

Checking minimum support and eliminating functional sets

Function Set	Support
{1, 2, 3}	2
{1, 2, 5}	2
{1, 3, 5}	2
{2, 3, 5}	2

Function Set
{1, 2, 3}
{1, 2, 5}
{1, 3, 5}
{2, 3, 5}

Similarly the remaining un-annotated level 1 protein functions of YDR150w is derived and using the same Apriori algorithm on recently annotated proteins i.e. YLR337c and YDR150w the functions of un-annotated protein YEL003w predicted.

Fig. 6. Illustration of working of proposed methodology with an example

neighborhood graph of YLR337c as shown in Figs. 4, 5 and 6. Similar process has been carried out for the network of YDR150w to predict its function. Then finally when functions of YLR337c and YDR150w are known, Apriori algorithm is applied on the functions of these two proteins to predict the function of target protein YEL003w as shown in Fig. 2.

5   Results and Discussion

The use of graph-theoretic measures like Closeness centrality for selection of target proteins and Edge-Clustering Coefficient for pruning less significant interactions from the neighborhood graph is the novelty of this work. Furthermore, discovering associations among functional groups along with proteins and thereby back propagating functional groups from distant to direct neighbors and from direct neighbors to target protein, application of *Apriori* algorithm is significant. In selection of target proteins using CCS three levels of thresholds are used where different set of targets are obtained and different performance scores are observed and shown as follows in Table 1, Figs. 7 and 8.

Table 1. Variation of number of unannotated proteins w.r.t the threshold values of closeness centrality

Threshold type	Threshold value	No. of target proteins
High	0.005533576	624
Medium	0.005518575	2301
Low	0.004879241	4357

**Closeness Centrality Threshold
Vs
No. of Target Proteins**

■ High Threshold (0.005533576)

■ Medium Threshold(0.005518575)

■ Low Threshold(0.004879241)

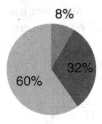

Fig. 7. Variation of target set with varied closeness centrality threshold

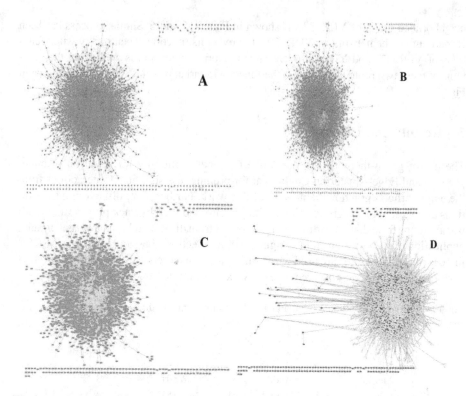

Fig. 8. A: Overall PPI network, B: PPI network of annotated and target proteins at high threshold, C: PPI network of annotated and target proteins at medium threshold, D: PPI network of annotated and target proteins at low threshold (Yellow colored triangle shape denotes target proteins while the rest round green rectangle shape represents annotated proteins) (Color figure online)

It is seen that at high threshold 8% of target set has been selected. But this should be borne in mind that proteins involving in this 8% have extremely high closeness centrality. While slight relaxation of threshold in medium and low threshold though incorporates 32% and 60% of target proteins but most of them have low closeness centrality score which will definitely hamper the prediction result as shown in the upcoming section.

The performance evaluation of our algorithm has been estimated using Precision (P), Recall (R) and F-Score (F) as performance metric given below:

$$P = \frac{TP}{TP + FP} \tag{2}$$

$$R = \frac{TP}{TP + FN} \tag{3}$$

$$F = \frac{2 \times (P \times R)}{(P + R)} \tag{4}$$

Where TP represents True Positives, FP represents False Positives and FN represents False Negatives. The overall precision, recall and F-score obtained in our work is shown in Table 2.

Table 2. Performance measures of proposed methodology

Levels of threshold	No. of target proteins	Precision	Recall	F-Score
High	624	0.8621	0.6592	0.7471
Medium	2301	0.5184	0.5993	0.5560
Low	4357	0.4245	0.5552	0.4811

It is observed from the Table 2 and Fig. 9 that the precision, recall and F-score obtained in high threshold is better in comparison to the other two since it incorporates only high closeness centrality proteins unlike others as discussed in earlier section which enhances the chances of incorporating more essential proteins of maximum connectivity in the target set. So it can be deduced that selection of target set proteins is equally important as that of protein function methodologies.

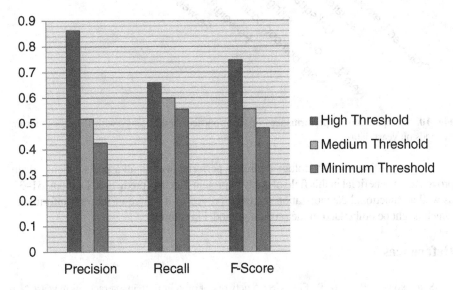

Fig. 9. Bar graph showing precision, recall and F-score measures achieved by the proposed methodology at three levels of thresholds

Figure 10 also includes other existing methodologies [16, 30] for unannotated protein function prediction like NRC,FS-weight #1 (#1 represents only level-1 proteins), FS-weight#1&#2 (#1 and #2 represents level-1 and level-2 proteins), Neighborhood counting#1(#1 represents only level-1 proteins), Neighborhood counting#1&#2 (#1 and #2 represents level-1 and level-2 proteins),Chi square#1(#1 represents only level-1 proteins) and Chi square#1&#2 (#1 and #2 represents level-1 and level-2 proteins).

These are the well-known and standard methods which have been considered in our work for comparison of our method's performance. It is clearly observed that the proposed methodology performs better compared to existing predictors. Use of Apriori algorithm empowered with Closeness Centrality and Edge Clustering Coefficient makes this methodology efficient compared to existing methods.

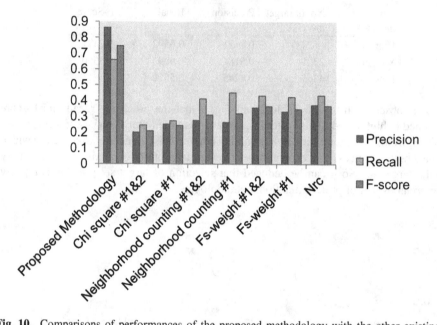

Fig. 10. Comparisons of performances of the proposed methodology with the other existing methods on yeast dataset

So, this prediction methodology definitely performs well in all aspects which is really proved to be beneficial in this field of study of protein function prediction. Domain [31–33] as well as functional categorization might be proved as a source of relevant information which might be embedded in the prediction model in future.

References

1. Schwikowski, B., Uetz, P., Fields, S.: A network of protein-protein interactions in yeast. Nat. Biotechnol. **18**, 1257–1261 (2000)
2. Hishigaki, H., Nakai, K., Ono, T., Tanigami, A., Takagi, T.: Assessment of prediction accuracy of protein function from protein–protein interaction data. Yeast. **18**, 523–531 (2001)
3. Chen, J., Hsu, W., Lee, M.L., Ng, S.-K.: Labeling network motifs in protein interactomes for protein function prediction. In: IEEE 23rd International Conference on Data Engineering, pp. 546–555. IEEE (2007)
4. Vazquez, A., Flammini, A., Maritan, A., Vespignani, A.: Global protein function prediction from protein-protein interaction networks. Nat. Biotechnol. **21**, 697–700 (2003)

5. Karaoz, U., Murali, T.M., Letovsky, S., Zheng, Y., Ding, C., Cantor, C.R., Kasif, S.: Whole-genome annotation by using evidence integration in functional-linkage networks. Proc. Natl. Acad. Sci. U. S. A. **101**, 2888–2893 (2004)
6. Deng, M., Mehta, S., Sun, F., Chen, T.: Inferring domain–domain interactions from protein–protein interactions. Genome Res., 1540–1548 (2002)
7. Nabieva, E., Jim, K., Agarwal, A., Chazelle, B., Singh, M.: Whole-proteome prediction of protein function via graph-theoretic analysis of interaction maps. Bioinformatics **21**(Suppl 1), i302–310 (2005)
8. Wu, D.D.: An efficient approach to detect a protein community from a seed. In: IEEE Symposium on Computational Intelligence in Bioinformatics and Computational Biology, pp. 1–7. IEEE (2005)
9. Letovsky, S., Kasif, S.: Predicting protein function from protein/protein interaction data: a probabilistic approach. Bioinformatics **19**, i197–i204 (2003)
10. Arnau, V., Mars, S., Marín, I.: Iterative cluster analysis of protein interaction data. Bioinformatics **21**, 364–378 (2005)
11. Samanta, M.P., Liang, S.: Predicting protein functions from redundancies in large-scale protein interaction networks. Proc. Natl. Acad. Sci. U. S. A. **100**, 12579–12583 (2003)
12. King, A.D., Przulj, N., Jurisica, I.: Protein complex prediction via cost-based clustering. Bioinformatics **20**, 3013–3020 (2004)
13. Asthana, S., King, O.D., Gibbons, F.D., Roth, F.P.: Predicting protein complex membership using probabilistic network reliability. Genome Res. **14**, 1170–1175 (2004)
14. Xiong, W., Liu, H., Guan, J., Zhou, S.: Protein function prediction by collective classification with explicit and implicit edges in protein-protein interaction networks. BMC Bioinf. **14**(Suppl 1), S4 (2013)
15. Saha, S., Chatterjee, P., Basu, S., Kundu, M., Nasipuri, M.: Improving prediction of protein function from protein interaction network using intelligent neighborhood approach. In: International Conference on Communications, Devices and Intelligent Systems (CODIS), pp. 584–587. IEEE (2012)
16. Saha, S., Chatterjee, P., Basu, S., Kundu, M., Nasipuri, M.: FunPred-1: protein function prediction from a protein interaction network using neighborhood analysis. Cell. Mol. Biol. Lett. **19**, 675–691 (2014)
17. Saha, S., Chatterjee, P.: Protein function prediction from protein interaction network using physico-chemical properties of amino acids. Int. J. Pharm. Biol. Sci. **4**, 55–65 (2014)
18. Piovesan, D., Giollo, M., Leonardi, E., Ferrari, C., Tosatto, S.C.E.: INGA: protein function prediction combining interaction networks, domain assignments and sequence similarity. Nucleic Acids Res. **43**, W134–140 (2015)
19. Zhao, B., Wang, J., Member, S., Li, M., Li, X., Li, Y.: A new method for predicting protein functions from dynamic weighted interactome networks. IEEE Trans. Nanobiosci. **15**, 131–139 (2016)
20. Wu, Q., Ye, Y., Ng, M.K., Ho, S.-S., Shi, R.: Collective prediction of protein functions from protein-protein interaction networks. BMC Bioinf. **15**(Suppl 2), S9 (2014)
21. Sandhan, T., Yoo, Y., Choi, J.Y., Kim, S.: Graph pyramids for protein function prediction. BMC Med. Genomics **8**, S12 (2015)
22. Huang, L., Liao, L., Wu, C.H.: Inference of protein-protein interaction networks from multiple heterogeneous data. EURASIP J. Bioinforma. Syst. Biol. **2016**, 8 (2016)

23. Saha, S., Chatterjee, P., Basu, S., Nasipuri, M.: Gene ontology based function prediction of human protein using protein sequence and neighborhood property of PPI network. In: Satapathy, S.C., Bhateja, V., Udgata, Siba K., Pattnaik, P.K. (eds.) Proceedings of the 5th International Conference on Frontiers in Intelligent Computing: Theory and Applications. AISC, vol. 516, pp. 109–118. Springer, Singapore (2017). doi:10.1007/978-981-10-3156-4_11

24. Saha, S., Chatterjee, P., Basu, S., Nasipuri, M.: Functional group prediction of un-annotated protein by exploiting its neighborhood analysis in saccharomyces cerevisiae protein interaction network. In: Chaki, R., Saeed, K., Cortesi, A., Chaki, N. (eds.) Advanced Computing and Systems for Security. AISC, vol. 568, pp. 165–177. Springer, Singapore (2017). doi:10.1007/978-981-10-3391-9_11

25. Zhao, B., Hu, S., Li, X., Zhang, F., Tian, Q., Ni, W.: An efficient method for protein function annotation based on multilayer protein networks. Hum. Genomics. 10, 1–15 (2016)

26. Peng, W., Wang, J., Wang, W., Liu, Q., Wu, F.-X., Pan, Y.: Iteration method for predicting essential proteins based on orthology and protein-protein interaction networks. BMC Syst. Biol. 6, 87 (2012)

27. Freeman, L.C.: A set of measures of centrality based on betweenness. Sociometry 40, 35–41 (1977)

28. Freeman, L.C.: Centrality in social networks conceptual clarification. Soc. Networks. 1, 215–239 (1978)

29. Opsahl, T., Agneessens, F., Skvoretz, J.: Article Node centrality in weighted networks Generalizing degree and shortest paths. Soc. Networks (2010)

30. Moosavi, S., Rahgozar, M., Rahimi, A.: Protein function prediction using neighbor relativity in protein-protein interaction network. Comput. Biol. Chem. 43, 11–16 (2013)

31. Chatterjee, P., Basu, S., Kundu, M., Nasipuri, M., Plewczynski, D.: PPI_SVM: prediction of protein-protein interactions using machine learning, domain-domain affinities and frequency tables. Cell. Mol. Biol. Lett. 16, 264–278 (2011)

32. Chatterjee, P., Basu, S., Kundu, M., Nasipuri, M., Plewczynski, D.: PSP_MCSVM: brainstorming consensus prediction of protein secondary structures using two-stage multiclass support vector machines. J. Mol. Model. 17, 2191–2201 (2011)

33. Chatterjee, P., Basu, S., Zubek, J., Kundu, M., Nasipuri, M., Plewczynski, D.: PDP-RF: Protein Domain Boundary Prediction Using Random Forest Classifier. In: Kryszkiewicz, M., Bandyopadhyay, S., Rybinski, H., Pal, Sankar K. (eds.) PReMI 2015. LNCS, vol. 9124, pp. 441–450. Springer, Cham (2015). doi:10.1007/978-3-319-19941-2_42

QSAR Model for Mast Cell Stabilizing Activity of Indolecarboxamidotetrazole Compounds on Human Basophils

Anamika Basu[1(✉)], Anasua Sarkar[2], and Piyali Basak[3]

[1] Gurudas College, Kolkata, India
basuanamikaami@gmail.com
[2] Department of Computer Science and Engineering, Jadavpur University, Kolkata, India
anasua.sarkar@cse.jdvu.ac.in
[3] School of Bioscience and Engineering, Jadavpur University, Kolkata, India
piyali_basak@yahoo.com

Abstract. Indolecarboxamidotetrazole compounds are well known as potential anti allergic agents due to their mast cell stabilizing activity on human basophils. A quantitative structure activity relationship (QSAR) model has been generated using Multiple Linear regression (MLR) for the prediction of inhibition efficiency of indolecarboxamidotetrazole derivatives. Twenty-one compounds with their activities expressed as % inhibition (PI) are collected. Descriptors are generated using Chemistry Development Kit. Three models are built and the models are evaluated using multiple correlation coefficient (R) and residual standard deviation (s). Considering the quality and accuracy of the predicted models, model 1 is the best, because it predicts biological activity which is almost closed to that of experimental value. This model is externally validated. This built model can be used to calculate inhibition efficiency of natural mast cell stabilizers containing caroxamidotetrazoles as antiallergic chemical in future.

Keywords: QSAR model · Multiple Linear Regression · Carboxamidotetrazole · Natural mast cell stabilizer

1 Introduction

Ethnopharmacology is the study of traditionally used drugs. Some approved drugs are identified by using ethanopharmacological data e.g. sodium salt of chromoglicic acid as mast cell stabilizer [1]. Mast cells are master players during type I hypersensitivity reaction in response to allergens. So, it acts as target site for the treatment of allergy. Mast cells are master players during type I hypersensitivity reaction in response to allergens. So, it acts as target site for the treatment of allergy [2]. These sensitized mast cells after exposure to allergen initiate different signaling pathways inside themselves. Finally, different mediators like histamine are released from mast cells after degranulation and acting on surrounding cells produce symptoms of allergy. Mast cell stabilizers are natural, semi-synthetic and synthetic compounds, which can prevent release of mediators from mast cells. But their mechanisms of actions remain unknown till now.

© Springer Nature Singapore Pte Ltd. 2017
J.K. Mandal et al. (Eds.): CICBA 2017, Part II, CCIS 776, pp. 17–29, 2017.
DOI: 10.1007/978-981-10-6430-2_2

Disodium cromoglycate, a chromone complex, is first discovered as orally active antiallergic drugs for mast cell stabilizer. This most commonly prescribed antiallergic drug, acts by inhibiting the release of mediators (histamine, leukotrienes) from mast cell as a prophylactic drug [3, 4]. It probably interferes with the antigen-mediated calcium ion influx into mast cells, as it acts on Calcium-activated potassium channel subunit alpha-1 [5, 6, 7]. But this drug has other targets for binding in human like Protein S100-P [8]. It plays an important role in cellular calcium signaling, which may cause adverse effect on our body.

Mastocytosis is the adverse reaction, which is reported during administration of Cromolyn Sodium as shown in different drug databases like DrugbindingDB etc. So, the designs of new oral and natural mast cell stabilizers are urgently needed, which are cheaper and with longer half-life period.

Several natural constituents, which are obtained from different herbs, like Holy Basil (*Ocimum Tenuiflorum*) [9], Chamomile (*Matricaria Recutita*) [10], flavonoids in peppermint [11], rhizome of Ginger [12], polyphenols of apple [13], are identified as mast cell stabilizers. Different types of chemical compounds are also analyzed in earlier research works as natural mast cell stabilizers like Flavonoids [14], Coumarins [15], phenols [16], terpenoids [17], tetrazoles [18] and amino acids [19].

Unangst et al. [18] in 1989, describe the inhibition of histamine release from human basophils by a group of Indolecarboxamidotetrazole compounds. They synthesize 31 derivatives. The percent inhibition (PI) of basophil histamine release for 31 derivatives along with two well-known inhibitors e.g. nedocromil (CHEMBL 746) and Cromolyn sodium (CHEMBL 74) is calculated at screening concentration of 10 µm. Among them, 16 compounds, which have PI values less than 50, are selected as training set for our QSAR study. For this study, log (PI/100-PI) is used as biological activity.

Quantitative structure–activity relationship (QSAR) analysis is used to identify mast cell stabilizing activity of different types of compounds [20, 21, 22]. This work is important because experimental methods are costly and time consuming. In this QSAR study of Indolecarboxamidotetrazole compounds, some parameters of selected chemical properties are correlated with biological activity by using mathematical equations. Quantitative parameters for physicochemical or biological or toxicological properties of a molecule, derived by the computational or experimental methods, are known as descriptors. Depending on the types of algorithms and dimensions of descriptors, QSAR analysis can be classified into 2D-QSAR, 3D-QSAR and so on. Among them, 2D-QSAR analysis is a less time consuming energy calculation, because its descriptors are simple and two dimensional. This type of analysis can be operated with direct mathematical algorithms [23].

In various models developed using MLR technique, the statistical parameters e.g. cross validated coefficient (CV) defines the goodness of prediction, whereas the non-cross validated conventional correlation coefficient (r^2) defines the goodness of fit of the QSAR model [24].

As stated earlier, Unangst et al., in 1989 [18], synthesize and analyze antiallergic potential of a series of novel indolecarboxamidotetrazoles compounds. These series of thirty-one compounds are derivatives of the following compound, where different substitutions are incorporated in R1, R2 and R3 positions. Bioactivity data for 21 inhibitors of IgE receptor α subunit for human basophils are collected [18] and subjected to descriptor determination [25]. First of all, various topological, electronic, geometrical and constitutional descriptors are calculated and among them five are finally selected by systemic search method [26]. Finally, a linear regression model is hypothesized using selected descriptors, which will be quite useful for finding structurally optimum inhibitor for mast cell stabilization (Fig. 1).

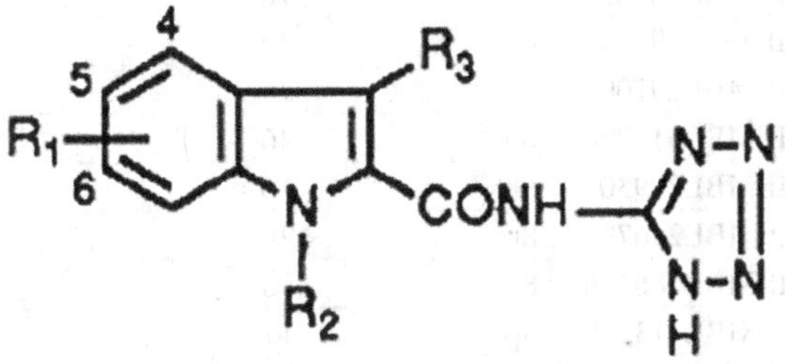

Fig. 1. Chemical structure of Indolecarboxamidotetrazole.

Carboxyamidotriazole binds to and inhibits non-voltage-operated calcium channels, blocking both Ca2 + influx into cells and Ca2 + release from intracellular stores, resulting in the disruption of calcium channel-mediated signal transduction.

2   Material and Method

There are several steps in QSAR model development. First a dataset of similar chemical compounds with same biological activity have been identified. Then different types of descriptors are calculated and using systemic search most suitable descriptors have been identified. With the help of these selected descriptors QSAR models are constructed.

2.1   Data

A data set of the compounds, which consists of twenty-one Indolecarboxamidotetrazole substituted compounds as inhibitors for histamine release for IgE Fc receptor, alpha-subunit from allergic donors, are obtained from the ChEMBL database and literature [27]. According to Unangst et al. [18] chemicals are marked as compound key e.g. 8 1, 3 g, 13 m etc. The chemical IDs and standard inhibition (PI) values and log (PI/100-PI) values are presented in Table 1. Among them first sixteen compounds form training set and last five compounds consist of test set for QSAR study.

Table 1. Compound id and standard inhibition and their logarithmic values for twenty one inhibitors

Compound no.	Title	Compound key	Percent inhibition (PI)	log(PI/100-PI)
1	CHEMBL27676	8 1	13	−0.8256
2	CHEMBL29967	8u	24	−0.5006
3	CHEMBL26520	8 m	30	−0.3680
4	CHEMBL281257	8z	18	−0.6585
5	CHEMBL29519	8y	7	−1.1233
6	CHEMBL29700	15	25	−0.4771
7	CHEMBL417298	8d	46	−0.0696
8	CHEMBL29930	8n	16	−0.7201
9	CHEMBL29679	8r	26	−0.4542
10	CHEMBL286486	8j	20	−0.6020
11	CHEMBL413319	8p	17	−0.6868
12	CHEMBL29720	8aa	40	−0.1760
13	CHEMBL29249	8b	46	−0.0696
14	CHEMBL284894	8f	43	−0.1224
15	CHEMBL30074	8o	7	−1.1234
16	CHEMBL29683	8q	18	−0.6585
17	CHEMBL71182	3 g	30	−0.3680
18	CHEMBL305750	3q	37	−0.2311
19	CHEMBL302045	13v	31.3	−0.3414
20	CHEMBL176486	13 m	27.5	−0.4210
21	CHEMBL417298	13X	46	−0.0696

2.2 Descriptor Generation and Calculation

In this study, SMILES structures, as they are obtained from ChEMBL [27], of all sixteen molecules are used as inputs to calculate 44 different types of molecular descriptors. These descriptors are categorized as topological, electronic, constitutional, and geometric classes for QSAR analysis. For our 2D QSAR study, we choose all 123 descriptors from Chemistry Development Kit (CDK v 1.03), an open source Java library for Chemoinformatics and Bioinformatics [25]. A total of 1,968 descriptors (123 descriptors for 16 compounds) are generated after the calculation using CDK for our experiment (Fig. 2).

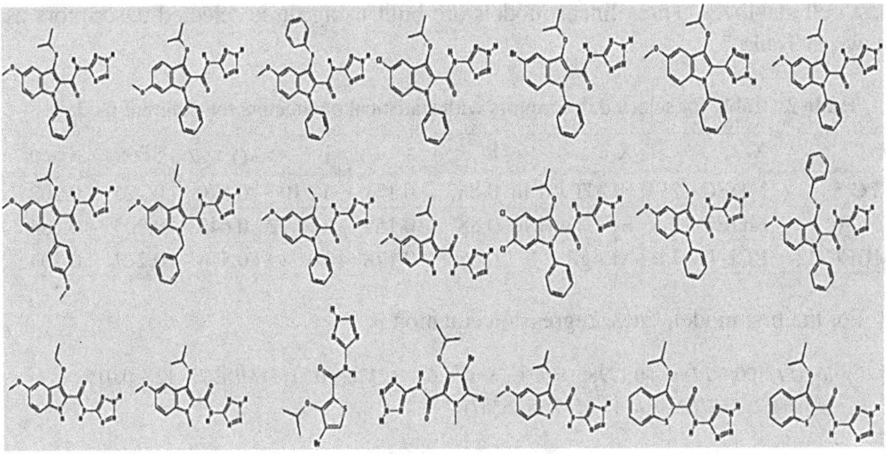

Fig. 2. Chemical structures of twenty-one inhibitors.

2.3 Descriptor Selection

Variable selection method in BuildQSAR software [28] is carried out by using the systematic search method, where controlling parameters are set, as described next. Considering log (PI/100-PI) as chosen biological activity and a correlation coefficient factor R is >0.84, cross validation of results is done by using least-one-out method. The number of descriptors per model is set to be 1 as the ratio of (number of compounds) to (number of descriptors) should be >= 5. Here the total twenty-one compounds are randomly divided into training and validation sets containing first sixteen molecules in training set and last five compounds in validation set.

From the summary table of CDK descriptor (wiki.qspr.thesaurus.eu) the above-mentioned descriptors are discussed here. SPC-6 is a type of Chi Path Cluster descriptor belongs to the class of topological descriptor. This type of descriptor reflects the molecular connectivity of a compound without its geometry information. This descriptor evaluates the value of the Kier & Hall Chi path cluster indices of order 6. The second descriptor MDEC-12 represents molecular distance edge descriptors for C as another topological descriptor. Similarly, another topological descriptor is BCUTw-1 h. This is an Eigen value based descriptor noted for its utility in chemical diversity. SPC-5 is the value of the Kier & Hall Chi path cluster indices of order 5. XLogP is a constitutional descriptor which predicts of logP based on the atom-type method.

2.4 Model Development

Three models are generated using one descriptor in each model by Multiple Linear Regression method in BuildQSAR software [28]. The QSAR Model is represented as QSAR equation, with the correlation coefficients calculated for each descriptor used in the regression model. By plotting the experimental activity (Yexp) vs predicted activity (Ypred), built models are evaluated for their predictive powers to determine activity as mast cell stabilizer. Three linear models are built using three selected descriptors as shown in Table 2.

Table 2. Table for selected descriptors with statistical parameters for different models.

X-1	X-2	X-3	R	s	F	Q^2	SPress	SDep
SPC-5	MDEC-12	BCUTw-1 h	0.867	0.171	12.104	0.570	0.225	0.202
SPC-6	MDEC-12	BCUTw-1 h	0.887	0.159	14.692	0.643	0.205	0.184
MDEC-12	BCUTw-1 h	XLogP	0.855	0.178	10.910	0.564	0.227	0.203

For the first model, linear regression equation is

$$log\,(PI/100 - PI) = +0.1798(\pm0.0689)\,SPC - 6 - 0.2126(\pm0.1115)\,MDEC - 12 - 0.0152$$
$$(\pm\,0.0062)\,BCUTw - 1h - 1.5559\,(\pm0.6567)$$

$$\left(n = 16; R = 0.887; s = 0.159; F = 14.692; p = 0.0003; Q^2 = 0.643; SPress = 0.205; SDEP = 0.184\right)$$

This equation is obtained by analyzing the three topological descriptors e.g. Chi Path Cluster descriptor, molecular distance edge descriptor and Eigen value based descriptor. Here n is number of molecules under analysis, R is the correlation coefficient, $r^2(R)$ is the squared correlation coefficient, s is the standard deviation and F is the F statistical value. The cross validated squared correlation coefficient, Q^2 is 0.643 and standard deviation of sum of square of difference between predicted and observed values, SPress is 0.205.

The second QSAR equation is

$$log(PI/100 - PI) = +0.3223\,(\pm0.1372)\,SPC - 5 - 0.2040\,(\pm0.1193)\,MDEC - 12 - 0.0135$$
$$(\pm0.0064)\,BCUTw - 1h - 1.9672\,(\pm0.8760)$$

$$\left(n = 16; R = 0.867; s = 0.171; F = 12.104; p = 0.0006; Q^2 = 0.570; SPress = 0.225; SDEP = 0.202\right)$$

This equation is obtained by analyzing the three topological descriptors. The cross validated squared correlation coefficient, Q^2 is 0.570 and SPress is 0.225.

The third model can be generated by using two topological and one constitutional descriptor. Here the values of Q^2 and SPress are 0.564 and 0.227 respectively.

$$log(PI/100 - PI) = -0.1717\,(\pm0.1189)\,MDEC - 12 - 0.0161\,(\pm0.0072)\,BCUTw - 1h$$
$$+ 0.1774\,(\pm0.0800)\,XLogP - 0.6188\,(\pm0.4605)$$

$$\left(n = 16; R = 0.855; s = 0.178; F = 10.910; p = 0.0010; Q2 = 0.564; SPress = 0.227; SDEP = 0.203\right)$$

3   Evaluating the Model

As stated earlier in various models developed using Multiple Linear Regression technique, the cross validated coefficient (CV) defines the goodness of prediction for developed models, whereas the non-cross validated conventional correlation coefficient (r^2) defines the goodness of fit of the QSAR model [24].

3.1 On the Basis of Goodness of Fit

Among the above three models, model 1 has produced high statistical quality *equation* ($n = 16$; $R = 0.887$; r^2 (R) = 0.7860; R^2-Adj. = 0.7325; $s = 0.159$; $F = 14.692$; $p = 0.0003$; $Q^2 = 0.643$; $SPress = 0.205$; $SDEP = 0.184$). It is seen that both models 2 and 3 have R values of 0.867 and 0.855 respectively, which are lower compared to the first model. Model 1 contents the lowest standard deviation value ($s = 0.159$) when compared to the other two models. The value of F, the calculated value of the F-ratio test, is 14.692, which is also highest among others F values for all models (Table 3). So, on the basis of R^2, s and F values, model 1 can be considered as the best one among the three models.

Table 3. MLR output for regression coefficient.

Model No.	R	R^2	s	F	Q^2	Sdep	SPress
1	0.887	0.7860	0.159	14.692	0.643	0.205	0.184
2	0.867	0.7516	0.171	12.104	0.570	0.225	0.202
3	0.855	0.7317	0.178	10.910	0.564	0.227	0.203

3.2 On the Basis of Predictive Power

According to the predictive powers of models, the models can be ranked (from the best to the worst) (considering the values of Q^2 in descending order), as 1, 2 and 3. When minimum value of SDEP is considered, the model 1 is the best model again on the basis of predictive power (Tables 4 and 5).

Table 4. Calculated and observed activity for model 1

Sl No.	Compound	log(PI/100-PI)	SPC-6	MDEC-12	BCUTw-1 h
1	CHEMBL27676	−0.826	11.711	4.429	31.972
2	CHEMBL29967	−0.501	11.664	3.725	15.997
3	CHEMBL26520	−0.368	12.012	2.022	31.972
4	CHEMBL281257	−0.659	11.732	2.278	34.969
5	CHEMBL29519	−1.123	11.732	2.278	78.918
6	CHEMBL29700	−0.477	11.008	3.585	15.996
7	CHEMBL417298	−0.696	11.711	3.585	15.997
8	CHEMBL29679	−0.454	10.375	3.166	15.997
9	CHEMBL286486	−0.602	11.173	3.293	31.972
10	CHEMBL29930	−0.720	12.213	4.632	15.998
11	CHEMBL413319	−0.689	7.803	1.842	15.997
12	CHEMBL29720	−0.176	12.739	1.992	34.970
13	CHEMBL29249	−0.070	11.173	2.648	15.997
14	CHEMBL284894	−0.122	11.788	1.924	15.997
15	CHEMBL30074	−1.123	7.268	2.054	15.997
16	CHEMBL29683	−0.659	9.683	2.645	15.997

Table 5. Residual table for model 1

No.	Compounds	Y(obs)	Y(calc)	Y(res)	StDev.Res
1	CHEMBL27676	−0.826	−0.880	0.054	0.340
2	CHEMBL29967	−0.501	−0.495	−0.006	−0.036
3	CHEMBL26520	−0.368	−0.314	−0.054	−0.340
4	CHEMBL281257	−0.659	−0.464	−0.194	−1.222
5	CHEMBL29519	−1.123	−1.134	0.011	0.069
6	CHEMBL29700	−0.477	−0.583	0.106	0.666
7	CHEMBL417298	−0.696	−0.457	−0.240	−1.506
8	CHEMBL29679	−0.454	−0.608	0.154	0.965
9	CHEMBL286486	−0.602	−0.735	0.133	0.835
10	CHEMBL29930	−0.720	−0.589	−0.131	−0.823
11	CHEMBL413319	−0.689	−0.789	0.100	0.628
12	CHEMBL29720	−0.176	−0.222	0.046	0.291
13	CHEMBL29249	−0.070	−0.354	0.284	1.788
14	CHEMBL284894	−0.122	−0.090	−0.033	−0.206
15	CHEMBL30074	−1.123	−0.930	−0.193	−1.216
16	CHEMBL29683	−0.659	−0.621	−0.037	−0.234

4   Graphical Analysis

The graphical analysis has been performed and the graph is shown in following Figs. 3, 4, 5 and 6. The graph has been plotted between the predicted and observed log (PI/100-PI)

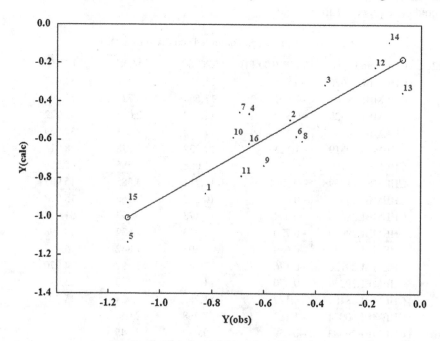

Fig. 3. Predicted activity vs. observed activity.

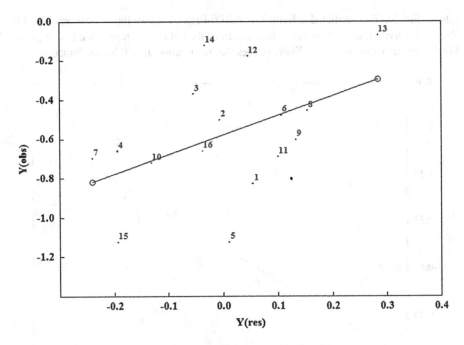

Fig. 4. Observed activity vs. residual activity.

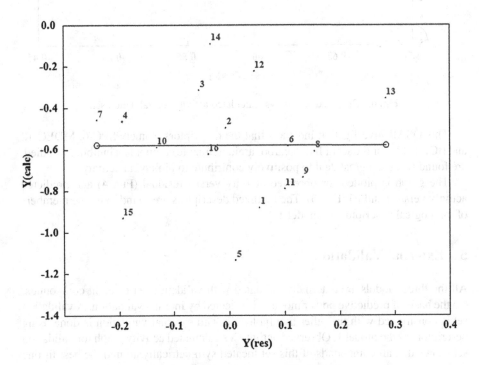

Fig. 5. Calculated activity vs. residual activity.

values (Fig. 3). The predicted activity log(PI/100-PI)pred shows linear relationship with observed activity log(PI/100-PI)obs, because fit of the data to the regression line is good. The higher the value for r^2, less likely proves that the relationship is due to chance.

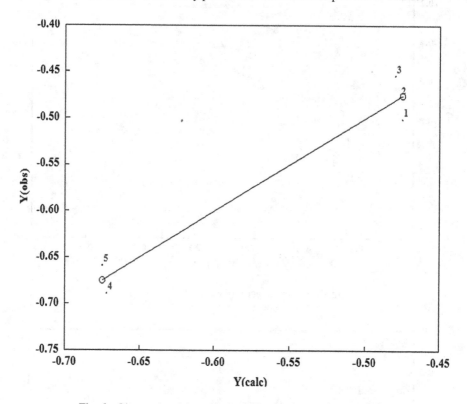

Fig. 6. Observed activity vs. calculated activity for validation set.

This QSAR investigation indicates that the descriptors, namely SPC-6, MDEC-12 and BCUT-1 h, for the set of Indolecarboxamidotetrazole compounds inhibitors studied, are found to have a great deal to positively contribute to biological activity.

The graph is plotted for observed activity versus residual (Fig. 4) and predicted activity versus residual (Fig. 5). The finalized descriptors are found to be the members of topological descriptors in model 1.

5   External Validation

All the three models are externally validated with validation set of eight compounds. On the basis of predictive power model 1 is selected by internal validation. A validation set is constructed with the other five molecules and external validation is done using descriptors of the model 1. Observed activity Vs calculated activity graph for validation set shows that all compounds of this set located symmetrically around the best fit line

(Fig. 6). Thus model 1 are externally validated with five compounds with the values 0.980 and 0.9606 for the correlation coefficient R and the squared correlation coefficient r^2(R) respectively.

$$log\,(PI/100 - PI) = -0.3700\,(\pm 2.0994)\,SPC - 6 + 0.8626\,(\pm 4.2198)\,MDEC - 12$$
$$+\,123.0171\,(\pm 1003.2860)\,BCUTw - 1h - 1967.2691\,(\pm 16043.2591)$$

$(n = 5; R = 0.980; s = 0.043; F = 8.120; p = 0.2512; Q^2 = Not\,Pred.; SPress = Not\,Pred.; SDEP = Not\,Pred.)$

6 Conclusion

Innumerable QSAR models have been built in last 50 years drug designing of antimycobacterial agents [30], antituberculosis agents [31], acetylcholinesterase inhibitors [31] and estrogen receptor agonist and antagonists [32]. Mast cell stabilizers can act as inhibitors on human basophil cells and thus they are potent anti allergic drugs.In earlier work, Unangst et al. in 1989 concludes that N –phenyl analogue of indolecarboxamidotetrazole inhibits histamine release from human leukocytes after stimulating with anti-IgE antibody (18), compared to the substitution N-H and N-methyl compounds. These compounds are marked as compound no. 7, 11 and 16 in our dataset respectively and their calculated activity using QSAR model correlates with their observed activity. In this QSAR model developed by using multiple linear regression (MLR) analysis, the cross-validated values of maximum Q^2 and minimum SDEP correlates with the goodness of prediction, whereas the non-cross-validated conventional correlation coefficient (R^2) defines the goodness of fit of the model. Based on the most predictable QSAR model 1, it can be inferred that inhibitory activity will be decreased with the following substituent, namely halogen substitution in 5th position at R1 of indole ring, OEt, OCH(Me)$_2$ substitutions in R3 of indole ring. The model is also valid for other five carboxamidotetrazole derivatives of furan, thiophene, naphthalene and benzothiophene derivatives. So, it can be concluded that irrespective of nature of substituents the basic structure of this twenty one compounds are responsible for their action as mast cell stabilizer.

We hope that the derived models and effect of substituents can be used in searching more potential mast cell stabilizers from the natural resources prior to experimental evaluation for our future work.

References

1. Atanasov, A.G., Waltenberger, B., Pferschy-Wenzig, E.-M., Linder, T., Wawrosch, C., Uhrin, P., Temml, V., Wang, L., Schwaiger, S., Heiss, E.H., Rollinger, J.M., Schuster, D., Breuss, J.M., Bochkov, V., Mihovilovic, M.D., Kopp, B., Bauer, R., Dirsch, V.M., Stuppner, H.: Discovery and resupply of pharmacologically active plant-derived natural products: a review. Biotechnol. Adv. 33(8), 1582–1614 (2015). http://doi.org/10.1016/j.biotechadv.2015.08.001
2. Finn, D.F., Walsh, J.J.: Twenty first century mast cell stabilizers. Br. J. Pharmacol. 170(1), 23–37 (2013)

3. Margit, N., Fedina, L., Balazs, R., Barta, B., nee Gyarmati, G.T., Marczis, J., Szasz, A.: Antiasthmatic aerosol preparation of sodium cromoglycate. U.S. Patent US5753208, issued June 1965

4. Heinke, S., Szucs, G., Norris, A., Droogmans, G., Nilius, B.: Inhibition of volume-activated chloride currents in endothelial cells by chromones. Br. J. Pharmacol. 115(8), 1393–1398 (1995)

5. Overington, J.P., Al-Lazikani, B., Hopkins, A.L.: How many drug targets are there? Nat. Rev. Drug Discov. 5(12), 993–996 (2006)

6. Imming, P., Sinning, C., Meyer, A.: Drugs, their targets and the nature and number of drug targets. Nat. Rev. Drug Discov. 5(10), 821–834 (2006)

7. Brogden, R.N., Speight, T.M., Avery, G.S.: Sodium cromoglycate (cromolyn sodium): a review of its mode of action, pharmacology, therapeutic efficacy and use. Drugs 7(3–4), 164–282 (1974)

8. Arumugam, T., Ramachandran, V., Logsdon, C.D.: Effect of cromolyn on S100P interactions with RAGE and pancreatic cancer growth and invasion in mouse models. J. Natl Cancer Inst. 98(24), 1806–1818 (2006)

9. Sridevi, G., Gopkumar, P., Ashok, S., Shastry, C.: Pharmacological basis for antianaphylactic, antihistaminic and mast cell stabilization activity of ocimum sanctum. Internet J. Pharmacol. 7(1) (2008)

10. Chandrashekhar, V.M., et al.: Anti-allergic activity of German chamomile (Matricaria recutita L.) in mast cell mediated allergy model. J. Ethnopharmacol. 137(1), 336–340 (2011)

11. Inoue, T., et al.: Antiallergic effect of flavonoid glycosides obtained from Mentha piperita L. Biol. Pharm. Bull. 25(2), 256–259 (2002)

12. Chen, B.-H., et al.: Antiallergic potential on RBL-2H3 cells of some phenolic constituents of Zingiber Officinale (Ginger). J. Nat. Prod. 72(5), 950–953 (2009)

13. Kanda, T., et al.: Inhibitory effects of apple polyphenol on induced histamine release from RBL-2H3 cells and rat mast cells. Biosci. Biotechnol. Biochem. 62(7), 1284–1289 (1998)

14. Kimata, M., Shichijo, M., Miura, T., Serizawa, I., Inagaki, N., Nagai, H.: Effects of luteolin, quercetin and baicalein on immunoglobulin E-mediated mediator release from human cultured mast cells. Clin. Exp. Allergy 30, 501–508 (2000)

15. Ninomiya, M., Itoh, T., Ishikawa, S., Saiki, M., Narumiya, K., Yasuda, M., et al.: Phenolic constituents isolated from Fragaria ananassa Duch. inhibit antigen-stimulated degranulation through direct inhibition of spleen tyrosine kinase activation. Bioorg. Med. Chem. 18, 5932–5937 (2010)

16. El-Agamy, D.S.: Anti-allergic effects of nilotinib on mast cell-mediated anaphylaxis like reactions. Eur. J. Pharmacol. 680, 115–121 (2012)

17. Itoh, T., Oyama, M., Takimoto, N., Kato, C., Nozawa, Y., Akao, Y., et al.: Inhibitory effects of sesquiterpene lactones isolated from Eupatorium chinense L. on IgE-mediated degranulation in rat basophilic leukemia RBL-2H3 cells and passive cutaneous anaphylaxis reaction in mice. Bioorg. Med. Chem. 17, 3189–3197 (2009)

18. Unangst, P.C., Connor, D.T., Stabler, S.R., Weikert, R.J., Carethers, M.E., Kennedy, J.A., Thueson, D.O., Chestnut, J.C., Adolphson, R.L., Conroy, M.C.: Novel indolecarboxamidotetrazoles as potential antiallergy agents. J. Med. Chem. 32(6), 1360–1366 (1989)

19. Connor, D.T., Cetenko, W.A., Mullican, M.D., Sorenson, R.J., Unangst, P.C., Weikert, R.J., Adolphson, R.L., Kennedy, J.A., Thueson, D.O.: Novel benzothiophene-, benzofuran-, and naphthalene Hocarboxamidotetrazoles as potential antiallergy agents. J. Med. Chem. 35(5), 958–965 (1992)

20. Kim, N.H., Jeong, H.J., Kim, H.M.: Theonine is a candidate amino acid for pharmacological stabilization of mast cells. Amino Acids **42**, 1609–1618 (2011)
21. Raj, N., Jain, S.K.: 2D QSAR study of substituted 2-Phenyl-Benzimidazole derivatives as potent anti allergic agents. Int. J. PharmTech Res. **4**(4), 1350–1360 (2012)
22. Zhou, Y.X., Xu, L., Wu, Y.P., Liu, B.L.: A QSAR study of the antiallergic activities of substituted benzamides and their structures. Chemometr. Intell. Lab. Syst. **45**(1), 95–100 (1999)
23. Ford, R.E., Knowles, P., Lunt, E., Marshall, S.M., Penrose, A.J., Ramsden, C.A., Summers, A.J.H., Walker, J.L., Wright, D.E.: Synthesis and quantitative structure-activity relationships of antiallergic 2-hydroxy-N-(1H-tetrazol-5-yl) benzamides and N-(2-hydroxyphenyl)-1H-tetrazole-5-carboxamides. J. Med. Chem. **29**(4), 538–549 (1986)
24. Roy, K., Narayan Das, R.: A review on principles, theory and practices of 2D-QSAR. Curr. Drug Metab. **15**(4), 346–379 (2014)
25. Golbraikh, A., Tropsha, A.: Predictive QSAR modeling diversity sampling of experimental data set and test set selection. J. Comput. Aided Mol. Des. **5**, 231–243 (2002)
26. Guha, R., Van Drie, J.H.: Structure-activity landscape index: identifying and quantifying activity cliffs. J. Chem. Inf. Model. **48**(3), 646–658 (2008)
27. Gonzalez, M.P., Teran, C., Saiz-Urra, L., Teijeira, M.: Variable selection methods in QSAR: an overview. Curr. Top. Med. Chem. **8**(18), 1606–1627 (2008)
28. Bento, A.P., Gaulton, A., Hersey, A., Bellis, L.J., Chambers, J., Davies, M., Kruger, F.A., Light, Y., Mak, L., McGlinchey, S., Nowotka, M., Papadatos, G., Santos, R., Overington, J.P.: The ChEMBL bioactivity database: an update. Nucleic Acids Res. **42**, 1083–1090 (2014)
29. De Oliveira, D.B., Gaudio, A.C.: BuildQSAR: a new computer program for QSAR analysis. Quant. Struct.-Activ. Relat. **19**(6), 599–601 (2001)
30. Stavrakov, G., Valcheva, V., Philipova, I., Doytchinova, I.: Design of novel camphane-based derivatives with antimycobacterial activity. J. Mol. Graph. Model. **51**, 7–12 (2014)
31. Arvind, A., et al.: Uridine monophosphate kinase as potential target for tuberculosis: From target to lead identification. Interdisc. Sci. Comput. Life Sci. **5**(4), 296 (2013)
32. Lee, S., Barron, M.G.: A mechanism-based 3D-QSAR approach for classification and prediction of acetylcholinesterase inhibitory potency of organophosphate and carbamate analogs. J. Comput. Aided Mol. Des. **30**(4), 347–363 (2016)
33. Lee, S., Barron, M.G.: Structure-based understanding of binding affinity and mode of estrogen receptor α agonists and antagonists. PLoS ONE **12**(1), e0169607 (2017)

Integrated Classifier:
A Tool for Microarray Analysis

Shib Sankar Bhowmick[1,4(✉)], Indrajit Saha[2], Luis Rato[3],
and Debotosh Bhattacharjee[4]

[1] Department of Electronics and Communication Engineering,
Heritage Institute of Technology, Kolkata, India
shibsankar.ece@gmail.com
[2] Department of Computer Science and Engineering,
National Institute of Technical Teachers' Training and Research, Kolkata, India
[3] Department of Informatics, University of Evora, Evora, Portugal
[4] Department of Computer Science and Engineering,
Jadavpur University, Kolkata, India

Abstract. Microarray technology has been developed and applied in
different biological context, especially for the purpose of monitoring the
expression levels of thousands of genes simultaneously. In this regard,
analysis of such data requires sophisticated computational tools. Hence,
we confined ourselves to propose a tool for the analysis of microarray
data. For this purpose, a feature selection scheme is integrated with the
classical supervised classifiers like Support Vector Machine, K-Nearest
Neighbor, Decision Tree and Naive Bayes, separately to improve the
classification performance, named as Integrated Classifiers. Here feature
selection scheme generates bootstrap samples that are used to create
diverse and informative features using Principal Component Analysis.
Thereafter, such features are multiplied with the original data in order
create training and testing data for the classifiers. Final classification
results are obtained on test data by computing posterior probability.
The performance of the proposed integrated classifiers with respect to
their conventional classifiers is demonstrated on 12 microarray datasets.
The results show that the integrated classifiers boost the performance
up to 25.90% for a dataset, while the average performance gain is 9.74%,
over the conventional classifiers. The superiority of the results has also
been established through statistical significance test.

Keywords: Feature selection · Microarray · Principle component analysis · Supervised classifiers · Statistical significance test

1 Introduction

Microarray technology facilitates the researchers to simultaneously measure the
expression levels of thousands of genes [1]. Generally, the technology works on

S.S. Bhowmick and I. Saha—Contributed equally.

glass slide, where the DNA molecules are fixed at specific location in an orderly manner [2]. Different technologies are used to fix these DNA molecules. Moreover, the fixed DNA molecules may correspond to the short stretch of an oligonucleotides, representing a gene. Microarray technology helps in understanding and analyzing large number of gene expressions in an efficient manner as well as it assists in exploring the genetic causes of anomalies occurring in a human body. All these analysis using microarray technology creating huge amount of data, analytical precision of which is influenced by a number of variables. Therefore, it is extremely important to reduce these huge data in to an informative one so that the best genes can be distinguished. Such set of genes is differentially expressed in normal and disease samples. To identify these differentially expressed genes, machine learning technology can be used.

Over the last decades, several methods for the integration of classifiers have been developed [3]. One such example of classifier integration is found in [4]. In this approach, evolutionary strategy is used with the integration of Multi-Layer Perception [5] to design a hybrid system for performing classification task. Recently, sequential integration of the classifiers is also proposed, where weights are assigned to the training samples. Based on the weights, samples are then propagated to the subsequent classifier as training data. Adaptive Boosting [6] is an example of such type of integrated classifier. In other approaches, different feature subsets are assigned to each single classifier and latter integration is performed on their results, e.g., mixture of experts [7] and ensemble averaging [8]. Moreover, classifiers are subjected to integrate by various forms of combination along with feature selection while implementing the intelligent decision making process. In this paper, we confined ourselves to this specific domain, referring to the classification problem where it is hard to find a single classifier that can be used for all pattern recognition tasks, since each has its own domain of competence. The above facts motivated us to propose a new technique for constructing Integrated Classifier (IC) that can use aggregated bootstrap samples after Principal Component Analysis (PCA). We expect the IC to exploit the strengths of the base classifier along with feature selection for microarray data to produce the high quality classification results which will overcome the performance of base classifier.

Unlike the other methods, in this study, PCA is used to compute additional features for training the classifier by increasing the diversity in the training set. To train the classifiers, the training dataset is split into different number of rotational non-overlapping subsets. Subsequently, PCA is used for each subset and all the principal components are retained to create diverse and informative features that preserve the variability information of the original training data. Thereafter, such informative features are multiplied with the original data to create the training and testing data for the classifiers. Finally, the posterior probability is computed to get the classification results while testing. In this study, we have used Support Vector Machine (SVM) [9], K-Nearest Neighbor (K-NN) [10], Decision Tree (DT) [11] and Naive Bayes (NB) [12] as an underlying base classifier to integrate with the above feature selection scheme and named

as individually, iSVM, iK-NN, iDT and iNB, all together Integrated classifiers
(ICs). The performance of the proposed method is demonstrated in comparison
with its Conventional Classifiers (CCs) on 12 microarray datasets [13–15] to see
the effectiveness in the classification task. The superiority of proposed ICs are
established quantitatively, and visually. Moreover, statistical significance test,
called Friedman test [16], is conducted to judge the efficacy of the results produced by ICs.

2 Integrated Classifiers

In order to describe the Integrated Classifiers (ICs) some notations are used, such
as a training set consisting of N labelled instances $\mathcal{L} = \{(x_i, y_i)\}_{i=1}^{N}$ in which each
instance (x_i, y_i) is described by m input attributes and an output attribute, i.e.,
$x \in \mathbb{R}^m$ and $y \in \mathbb{R}$, where y takes a value from the label space $\{c_1, c_2, \ldots, c_z\}$. In
a classification task, the goal is to use the information only from $\mathcal{L}$ to construct
a classifier which performs well on unseen data. Let X be an $N \times m$ matrix
consisting of the values of m input attributes for each training instance and Y
be an N dimensional column vector containing the output attributes of each
training instance in $\mathcal{L}$, which means that $\mathcal{L}$ can be expressed as concatenating
X and Y horizontally, i.e., $\mathcal{L} = [XY]$. Let denote $\mathcal{S} = \{X_1, X_2, \ldots, X_m\}^T$, the
attribute set comprised of m input attributes. Note that the parameter F which
specifies the number of subsets for the given attribute set $\mathcal{S}$ that should be split
off. In order to construct the training set for the classifier IC, the following steps
are necessary:

Step1: Randomly split $\mathcal{S}$ into F number of subsets. The lower and upper bounds
of feature subsets are chosen as $F_{min} = 2$ and $F_{max} = \frac{m}{2}$, respectively such
that $F_{min} \leqslant F \leqslant F_{max}$, i.e., the minimum number of subsets is 2 with atleast
2 features in each subset.
Step2: Repeat the following steps F times for each subset, i.e., $f = 1, 2, \ldots, F$.
  (a) A new submatrix X_f is constructed which corresponds to the data matrix
      X.
  (b) From this new submatrix, a bootstrap sample X_f' is considered where
      the sample size is generally smaller than X_f.
  (c) X_f' is then used for PCA and the coefficients of all computed principal
      components are stored in a new matrix D_f.
Step3: Arrange each D_f into a block diagonal sparse matrix R whose fth diagonal element is D_f, and then rearrange the columns of R so that the order
of them correspond to the original attributes in $\mathcal{S}$. During this rearrangement, columns with all zero values are removed from the sparse matrix. The
rearranged rotation matrix is denoted by R^a and the training set for classifier
IC is $[XR^a, Y]$.

The reason behind to do this rearrangement is that the feature set is split
randomly and the order of the attribute or feature subsets is not the same

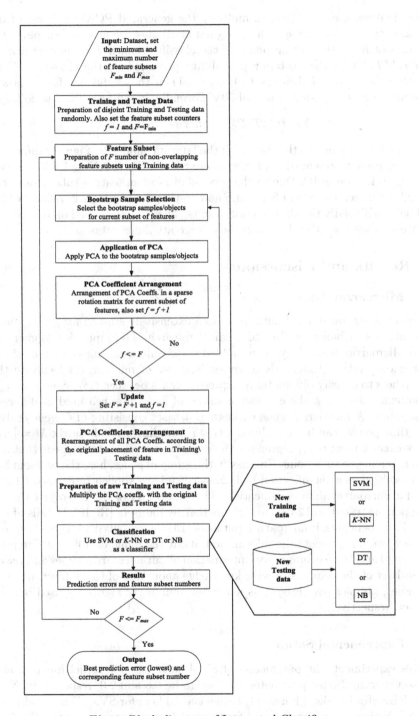

Fig. 1. Block diagram of Integrated Classifiers

as original feature set. Thus, to multiply the generated PCA coefficients from the subsets with its corresponding original attributes, we need to rearrange the columns of R. In the testing phase of the classification, if T is the test sample and $IC_i(TR^a)$ be the posterior probability produced by the classifier IC on the hypothesis that T belongs to class c_i. Then the confidence for a class is determined by the posterior probability. Formally, it can be defined as follows.

$$\psi_i(T) = IC_i(TR^a), \quad where \quad i = 1, 2, \ldots, z \tag{1}$$

Here T is assigned to the class with the largest confidence. Figure 1 shows the block diagram representation of ICs, where SVM, NB, K-NN and DT are used separately instate of IC. Due to the process of random feature subdivision, the classifier will get new sets of training and testing data in each iteration, which will help to diversify the classification results. The ICs are applied on microarray datasets to see how it performs on these large attribute datasets.

3   Results and Discussion

3.1   Microarray Data

In recent years, microarray data have been extensively studied for gene expression analysis in biological and biomedical research. The rapid development of DNA Microarray technology have enabled the simultaneous measurement of the expression levels of thousands of genes. The use of microarrays facilitate the researchers to classify differentially expressed genes between two or more groups of patients. Generally, the expression values of genes are measured at different time points. A microarray gene expression dataset consisting of G genes taken at T time points, can be thought as a $G \times T$ two-dimensional matrix $M = [g_{ij}]$, where each element of g_{ij} represents the expression level of the ith gene that has been taken at jth time point. To classify the group of genes, here the problem has been modeled as a classification task. Hence, we have applied Integrated Classifiers for microarray data classification. The superiority of the ICs over CCs has been demonstrated on 12 benchmark microarray datasets [13–15]. Details of the considered benchmark microarray datasets [13–15] are given in Table 1, where the first column presents the information about the name of different datasets, the second and third columns give information about microarray types and tissue types. Rest of the columns provide knowledge about size of the dataset, number of classes, samples per class, class name and number of attributes used in each dataset, respectively.

3.2   Experimental Setup

In this experiment, the parameters of SVM such as γ for kernel function and the soft margin C (cost parameter), are set to be 0.5 and 2.0, respectively. Note that, RBF (Radial Basis Function) kernel is used here for SVM. The K value for the K-NN classifier is chosen as 13 for the satisfactory operation of the classifier and for the case of DT, C4.5 classifier is used.

Table 1. Summery of the microarray datasets

Dataset	Array type	Tissue	Size	Number of classes	Samples per class	Classes	Total number of input attributes
Armstrong-2002-v2	Affymetrix	Blood	72	3	24, 20, 28	ALL, MLL, AML	2194
Bhattacharjee-2001	Affymetrix	Lung	203	5	139, 17, 6, 21, 20	AD, NL, SCLC, SQ, COID	1543
Chowdary-2006	Affymetrix	Breast, Colon	104	2	62, 42	B, C	182
Laiho-2007	Affymetrix	Colon	37	2	8, 29	Serrated CRC, Conventional CRC	2202
Liang-2005	Double Channel	Brain	37	3	28, 6, 3	GBM, ODG, Normal	1411
Nutt-2003-v1	Affymetrix	Brain	50	4	14, 7, 14, 15	CG, CO, NG, NO	1377
Pomeroy-2002-v2	Affymetrix	Brain	42	5	10, 10, 10, 4, 8	MD, Mglio, Rhab, Ncer, PNET	7129
Ramaswamy-2001	Affymetrix	Multi-tissue	190	14	11, 10, 11, 11, 22, 10, 11, 10, 30, 11, 11, 11, 11, 20	BR, PR, LU, CR, LY, ML, BL, UT, LE, RE, PA, OV, ME, CNS,	1369
Risinger-2003	Double Channel	Endometrium	42	4	13, 3, 19, 7	PS, CC, E, N	1771
Su-2001	Affymetrix	Multi-tissue	174	10	26, 8, 26, 23, 12, 11, 7, 27, 6, 28	PR, BL, BR, CO, GA, KI, LI, OV, PA, LU	1571
West-2001	Affymetrix	Breast	49	2	25, 24	ER+, ER−	1198
Yeoh-2002-v2	Affymetrix	Bone Marrow	248	2	43, 205	T-ALL, B-ALL	2526

3.3   Results

The performance of ICs is compared with the CCs like SVM, K-NN, C4.5 or DT and NB. As there is no separate training and testing data for the aforementioned datasets, hence, each of these datasets is randomly divided into 70% training and 30% testing datasets to compute the prediction error of each classifier. Tables 2 and 3 report the average results of prediction error produced by different integrated and conventional classifiers for microarray datasets, respectively. Figures 2(a–h) show the results for eight such best performing microarray datasets. In general, the results in Tables 2, 3 and Fig. 2 show that the average prediction error values corresponding to the ICs are better than the CCs. On the other hand, Tables 4 and 5 report the average values of Kappa-Index (KI) [17], Minkowski Score (MS) [18] and Adjusted Rand Index (ARI) [19] of different ICs and CCs for microarray datasets over 20 runs. The KI, MS and ARI values are also found better for ICs. Moreover, it is observed that the results of iSVM and SVM are superior in their corresponding groups, whereas the iSVM performs better than the SVM. Figures 3(a–h) show the boxplots indicating the

Table 2. Average values of prediction error (in %) and its standard deviation (σ) of different integrated classifiers for microarray datasets

Dataset	Mean & σ of integrated classifier							
	iSVM		iK -NN		iDT		iNB	
Armstrong-2002-v2	00.53	±0.16	01.91	±0.75	22.02	±3.95	06.17	±1.81
Bhattacharjee-2001	01.78	±1.18	03.45	±2.00	11.40	±1.21	12.35	±1.03
Chowdary-2006	01.03	±1.42	13.24	±1.84	02.79	±1.08	04.56	±2.06
Laiho-2007	01.67	±1.87	02.71	±2.54	06.25	±2.49	22.29	±3.39
Liang-2005	02.80	±1.90	09.40	±6.01	18.80	±2.93	25.80	±4.16
Nutt-2003-v1	07.42	±3.74	14.55	±7.83	24.70	±4.11	24.70	±5.35
Pomeroy-2002-v2	04.63	±2.90	08.33	±2.57	28.52	±3.96	25.00	±4.79
Ramaswamy-2001	30.00	±2.57	30.08	±3.35	29.88	±2.84	26.17	±2.77
Risinger-2003	08.15	±5.29	15.19	±9.04	20.00	±3.31	22.59	±4.94
Su-2001	05.31	±2.90	05.22	±3.00	29.96	±1.52	23.81	±1.60
West-2001	05.00	±2.59	04.38	±2.13	13.75	±3.11	14.06	±3.71
Yeoh-2002-v2	04.63	±2.12	19.16	±4.22	28.52	±5.12	25.00	±4.64

Table 3. Average values of prediction error (in %) and its standard deviation (σ) of different conventional classifiers for microarray datasets

Dataset	Mean & σ of conventional classifier							
	SVM		K-NN		DT		NB	
Armstrong-2002-v2	02.02	±1.12	02.45	±1.10	21.91	±1.62	12.13	±1.86
Bhattacharjee-2001	02.61	±1.88	04.17	±2.38	10.49	±1.36	11.74	±1.11
Chowdary-2006	02.28	±1.95	09.49	±2.65	14.12	±1.99	05.74	±1.49
Laiho-2007	07.29	±4.68	03.13	±1.66	08.33	±1.39	21.88	±2.29
Liang-2005	07.80	±2.94	10.40	±4.32	18.00	±4.58	26.80	±5.86
Nutt-2003-v1	14.70	±5.34	15.61	±4.51	25.91	±5.41	33.79	±5.23
Pomeroy-2002-v2	13.33	±4.89	07.96	±1.83	30.56	±5.56	32.78	±3.24
Ramaswamy-2001	28.99	±2.86	27.62	±5.71	31.29	±4.73	33.71	±3.03
Risinger-2003	12.78	±4.78	18.15	±4.27	19.44	±3.07	38.52	±5.87
Su-2001	05.75	±3.35	05.80	±1.32	31.48	±1.48	27.24	±3.61
West-2001	05.94	±2.46	11.25	±4.74	19.38	±2.46	18.44	±6.60
Yeoh-2002-v2	07.48	±3.35	17.73	±5.18	23.11	±2.28	31.55	±4.17

changes of prediction errors with incremental feature subset numbers for the "Armstrong-2002-v2", "Bhattacharjee-2001", "Chowdary-2006", "Laiho-2007", "Liang-2005", "Nutt-2003-v1", "Pomeroy-2002-v2" and "Su-2001" datasets, respectively. The performance of iSVM, iK-NN, iDT and iNB for each dataset is shown in four sub figures. The best feature subset number F for each dataset,

Table 4. Average values of KI, MS and ARI over 20 runs of different integrated classifiers for microarray datasets

Dataset	Integrated classifier											
	i SVM			iK -NN			i DT			i NB		
	KI	MS	ARI	KI	MS	ARI	KI	MS	ARI	KI	MS	ARI
Armstrong-2002-v2	0.84	0.21	0.82	0.81	0.31	0.80	0.69	0.39	0.68	0.79	0.35	0.79
Bhattacharjee-2001	0.81	0.32	0.82	0.82	0.30	0.84	0.75	0.38	0.72	0.77	0.32	0.76
Chowdary-2006	0.89	0.24	0.80	0.76	0.39	0.74	0.78	0.35	0.85	0.89	0.31	0.88
Laiho-2007	0.78	0.36	0.76	0.79	0.37	0.79	0.76	0.42	0.74	0.67	0.35	0.72
Liang-2005	0.70	0.39	0.77	0.80	0.36	0.77	0.82	0.35	0.89	0.77	0.37	0.81
Nutt-2003-v1	0.72	0.32	0.76	0.79	0.39	0.81	0.76	0.31	0.74	0.73	0.44	0.77
Pomeroy-2002-v2	0.88	0.29	0.84	0.87	0.26	0.85	0.73	0.46	0.76	0.70	0.48	0.74
Ramaswamy-2001	0.64	0.40	0.69	0.67	0.47	0.71	0.70	0.40	0.73	0.70	0.35	0.76
Risinger-2003	0.72	0.29	0.76	0.73	0.31	0.78	0.74	0.41	0.82	0.71	0.46	0.73
Su-2001	0.77	0.26	0.75	0.73	0.40	0.70	0.73	0.44	0.79	0.69	0.55	0.71
West-2001	0.78	0.31	0.78	0.75	0.36	0.76	0.75	0.39	0.74	0.72	0.31	0.75
Yeoh-2002-v2	0.80	0.32	0.85	0.79	0.42	0.71	0.76	0.45	0.75	0.79	0.45	0.71

Table 5. Average values of KI, MS and ARI over 20 runs of different conventional classifiers for microarray datasets

Dataset	Conventional classifier											
	SVM			K -NN			DT			NB		
	KI	MS	ARI	KI	MS	ARI	KI	MS	ARI	KI	MS	ARI
Armstrong-2002-v2	0.89	0.25	0.87	0.86	0.24	0.86	0.77	0.30	0.75	0.79	0.39	0.81
Bhattacharjee-2001	0.86	0.36	0.88	0.79	0.39	0.79	0.74	0.31	0.80	0.73	0.31	0.80
Chowdary-2006	0.87	0.28	0.90	0.81	0.38	0.83	0.76	0.37	0.76	0.88	0.26	0.85
Laiho-2007	0.78	0.42	0.71	0.82	0.38	0.80	0.73	0.31	0.78	0.72	0.40	0.75
Liang-2005	0.75	0.39	0.70	0.74	0.40	0.73	0.73	0.43	0.77	0.75	0.43	0.78
Nutt-2003-v1	0.71	0.37	0.75	0.73	0.39	0.75	0.67	0.43	0.63	0.63	0.41	0.64
Pomeroy-2002-v2	0.72	0.34	0.76	0.81	0.37	0.83	0.76	0.43	0.71	0.77	0.43	0.72
Ramaswamy-2001	0.76	0.33	0.70	0.76	0.45	0.79	0.68	0.41	0.71	0.65	0.46	0.65
Risinger-2003	0.81	0.30	0.81	0.81	0.32	0.77	0.76	0.39	0.72	0.73	0.43	0.68
Su-2001	0.85	0.31	0.81	0.89	0.33	0.88	0.74	0.46	0.78	0.72	0.45	0.78
West-2001	0.87	0.31	0.81	0.72	0.37	0.79	0.78	0.45	0.79	0.76	0.41	0.75
Yeoh-2002-v2	0.86	0.36	0.81	0.78	0.42	0.75	0.78	0.40	0.71	0.70	0.45	0.71

which are found from these figures, is reported in Table 6. In that table, best feature subset number, corresponding gain value and name of the classifier are also mentioned. The gain is computed according to the Eq. 2:

Table 6. Best "F" and gain (in %) values of different integrated classifiers for microarray datasets

Dataset	F	$\mathcal{G}$ (%)	Name of the classifier
Armstrong-2002-v2	650	06.78	iNB
Bhattacharjee-2001	322	00.86	iSVM
Chowdary-2006	12	13.18	iDT
Laiho-2007	662	06.07	iSVM
Liang-2005	122	05.42	iSVM
Nutt-2003-v1	308	13.73	iNB
Pomeroy-2002-v2	104	11.57	iNB
Ramaswamy-2001	122	11.37	iNB
Risinger-2003	602	25.90	iNB
Su-2001	587	04.73	iNB
West-2001	524	07.75	iK-NN
Yeoh-2002-v2	1042	09.57	iNB
Summery		**Avg. $\mathcal{G}$: 09.74 (%)**	**iSVM:3 times, iK-NN:1 times, iDT:1 times, iNB:7 times**

Table 7. The Friedman ranks of all classifiers for microarray datasets

Dataset	Integrated classifier				Conventional classifier			
	i**SVM**	iK -NN	i DT	i NB	SVM	K -NN	DT	NB
Armstrong-2002-v2	1	3	8	7	4	5	2	6
Bhattacharjee-2001	1	3	6	5	2	4	8	7
Chowdary-2006	1	7	3	8	2	6	4	5
Laiho-2007	1	2	4	6	5	3	8	7
Liang-2005	1	3	6	5	2	4	7	8
Nutt-2003-v1	1	2	5	6	3	4	7	8
Pomeroy-2002-v2	1	3	5	6	4	2	7	8
Ramaswamy-2001	4	5	3	6	2	1	7	8
Risinger-2003	1	3	6	5	2	4	8	7
Su-2001	2	1	7	8	3	4	5	6
West-2001	2	1	5	8	3	4	6	7
Yeoh-2002-v2	1	4	6	5	2	3	8	7
Average rank	**1.417**	**3.083**	**5.333**	**6.250**	**2.833**	**3.667**	**6.417**	**7.000**

$$\mathcal{G} = (\frac{PA\,of\,IC - PA\,of\,CC}{PA\,of\,CC}) \times 100 \qquad (2)$$

Here predicted error is used to compute the Prediction Accuracy (PA) for gain computation. From Table 6, it can be seen that the best produced gain is

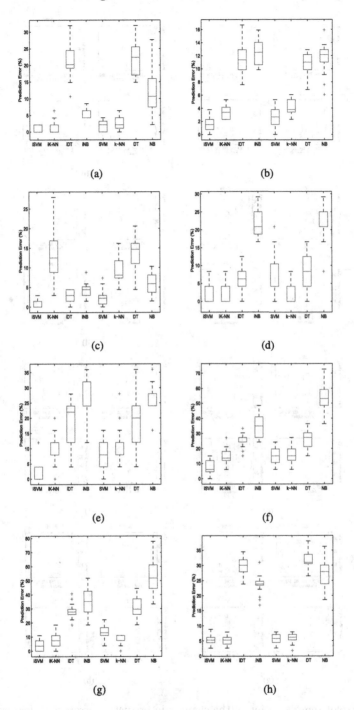

Fig. 2. Boxplot representation of prediction errors of different classification algorithms on (a) Armstrong-2002-v2 (b) Bhattacharjee-2001 (c) Chowdary-2006 (d) Laiho-2007 (e) Liang-2005 (f) Nutt-2003-v1 (g) Pomeroy-2002-v2 and (h) Su-2001 datasets

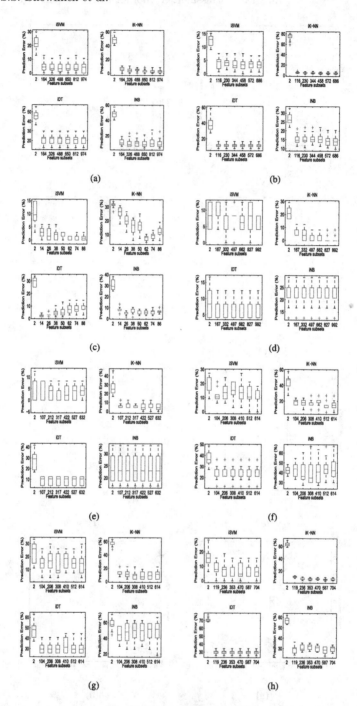

Fig. 3. Boxplot representation of the changes in prediction errors with feature subset numbers of different integrated classification algorithms on (a) Armstrong-2002-v2 (b) Bhattacharjee-2001 (c) Chowdary-2006 (d) Laiho-2007 (e) Liang-2005 (f) Nutt-2003-v1 (g) Pomeroy-2002-v2 and (h) Su-2001 datasets

25.90% for "Risinger-2003" dataset and the average of the best gain is 9.74%. It gives a better understanding about the superiority of the ICs over CCs. Moreover, the best gain produced by iSVM, iK-NN, iDT and iNB are 3, 1, 1 and 7 times respectively, which also reveal the same fact for ICs. Therefore, it indicates the superior performance of ICs for proper classification of microarray data.

Statistical test like Friedman test has been conducted for the used classifiers and the rank of these classifiers are reported in Table 7. The rank is determined based on the average prediction error values produced by the ICs and CCs. From Friedman test, the average rank of the classifiers, iSVM, iK-NN, iDT and iNB, is computed as 1.417, 3.083, 5.333 and 6.250. Based on average rank, the *chi-square* value: 60.861 and p value: 0.13×10^{-4} at $\alpha = 0.05$ significance level is obtained. This is also a strong evidence to reject the null hypothesis. Therefore, the results produced by the ICs are statistically significant.

4   Conclusion

Microarray expression analysis generates millions of data related to the biological interpretation of genes and their functions. However, sophisticated computational methods are required in order to successfully analyze these microarray data. In this regard, the developed method shows promising results. The present study can be viewed as a comparative analysis of integrated and conventional classifiers where 12 microarray datasets are used. The integrated classifier is developed based on feature selection scheme. In feature selection scheme, bootstrap samples are used to create diverse and informative set features using principal component analysis. Thereafter, such features are multiplied with the original data to construct the training and testing data for the Support Vector Machine, K-Nearest Neighbor, Decision Tree and Naive Bayes classifiers separately. Finally, the posterior probability is computed for each classifier to get the classification result. For microarray datasets, the values of prediction errors, Kappa-Index, Minkowski Score, Adjusted Rand Index as well as the statistical significant test, indicate the superior performance of integrated classifiers. Moreover, the gain produced by integrated classifiers over conventional classifiers has also verified the goodness of this integration. Therefore, judging all the results, it can be concluded that the proposed integrated classifiers are quantitatively, visually and statistically superior to their conventional counterparts for microarray data analysis.

The application of the proposed method could be beneficial for binding activity prediction of protein-peptide [20, 21]. Additionally, the developed method can also be used for miRNA marker [22–24] and gene selection [25].

References

1. DeRisi, J.L., Iyer, V.R., Brown, P.O.: Exploring the metabolic and genetic control of gene expression on a genomic scale. Science **278**(5338), 680–686 (1997)
2. Stears, R.L., Martinsky, T., Schena, M., et al.: Trends in microarray analysis. Nat. Med. **9**(1), 140–145 (2003)
3. Valentini, G., Masulli, F.: Ensembles of learning machines. In: Marinaro, M., Tagliaferri, R. (eds.) WIRN 2002. LNCS, vol. 2486, pp. 3–20. Springer, Heidelberg (2002). doi:10.1007/3-540-45808-5_1
4. Mitra, S., Mitra, P., Pal, S.K.: Evolutionary modular design of rough knowledge-based network using fuzzy attributes. Neurocomputing **36**, 45–66 (2001)
5. Khotanzad, A., Chung, C.: Application of multi-layer perceptron neural networks to vision problems. Neural Comput. Appl. **7**(3), 249–259 (1998)
6. Freund, Y., Schapire, R.E.: A desicion-theoretic generalization of on-line learning and an application to boosting. In: Vitányi, P. (ed.) EuroCOLT 1995. LNCS, vol. 904, pp. 23–37. Springer, Heidelberg (1995). doi:10.1007/3-540-59119-2_166
7. Jordan, M.I., Jacobs, R.A.: Hierarchical mixture of experts and the EM algorithm. Neural Comput. **6**, 181–214 (1994)
8. Hashem, S.: Optimal linear combination of neural networks. Neural Comput. **10**, 519–614 (1997)
9. Boser, B.E., Guyon, I.M., N.Vapnik, V.: A training algorithm for optimal margin classifiers. In: Proceedings of the Fifth Annual Workshop on Computational Learning Theory, pp. 144–152 (1992)
10. Sun, S.: Ensembles of feature subspaces for object detection. In: Yu, W., He, H., Zhang, N. (eds.) ISNN 2009. LNCS, vol. 5552, pp. 996–1004. Springer, Heidelberg (2009). doi:10.1007/978-3-642-01510-6_113
11. Quinlan, J.R.: C4.5: Programs for Machine Learning. Morgan Kaufmann Publishers, San Francisco (1993)
12. Duda, R.O., Hart, P.E.: Pattern Classification and Scene Analysis. Wiley, New York (1973)
13. Armstrong, S.A., Staunton, J.E., Silverman, L.B., Pieters, R., den Boer, M.L., Minden, M.D., Sallan, S.E., Lander, E.S., Golub, T.R., Korsmeyer, S.J.: MLL translocations specify a distinct gene expression profile that distinguishes a unique leukemia. Nat. Genet. **30**(1), 41–47 (2002)
14. Bhattacharjee, A., Richards, W.G., Staunton, J., Li, C., Monti, S., Vasa, P., Ladd, C., Beheshti, J., Bueno, R., Gillette, M., Loda, M., Weber, G., Mark, E.J., Lander, E.S., Wong, W., Johnson, B.E., Golub, T.R., Sugarbaker, D.J., Meyerson, M.: Classification of human lung carcinomas by mrna expression profiling reveals distinct adenocarcinoma subclasses. Proc. Natl Acad. Sci. **98**(24), 13790–13795 (2001)
15. Chowdary, D., Lathrop, J., Skelton, J., Curtin, K., Briggs, T., Zhang, Y., Yu, J., Wang, Y., Mazumder, A.: Prognostic gene expression signatures can be measured in tissues collected in rnalater preservative. J. Mol. Diagn. **8**(1), 31–39 (2006)
16. Friedman, M.: A comparison of alternative tests of significance for the problem of m rankings. Ann. Math. Stat. **11**, 86–92 (1940)
17. Cohen, J.A.: Coefficient of agreement for nominal scales. Educ. Psychol. Meas. **20**(1), 37–46 (1960)
18. Jardine, N., Sibson, R.: Mathematical Taxonomy. Wiley, New Jersey (1971)
19. Yeung, K.Y., Ruzzo, W.L.: An empirical study on principal component analysis for clustering gene expression data. Bioinformatics **17**, 763–774 (2001)

20. Saha, I., Rak, B., Bhowmick, S.S., Maulik, U., Bhattacharjee, D., Koch, U., Lazniewski, M., Plewczynski, D.: Binding activity prediction of cyclin-dependent inhibitors. J. Chem. Inf. Model. **55**(7), 1469–1482 (2015)
21. Mazzocco, G., Bhowmick, S.S., Saha, I., Maulik, U., Bhattacharjee, D., Plewczynski, D.: MaER: a new ensemble based multiclass classifier for binding activity prediction of HLA Class II proteins. In: Kryszkiewicz, M., Bandyopadhyay, S., Rybinski, H., Pal, S.K. (eds.) PReMI 2015. LNCS, vol. 9124, pp. 462–471. Springer, Cham (2015). doi:10.1007/978-3-319-19941-2_44
22. Bhowmick, S.S., Saha, I., Maulik, U., Bhattacharjee, D.: Identification of miRNA signature using next-generation sequencing data of prostate cancer. In: Proceedings of the 3rd International Conference on Recent Advances in Information Technology, pp. 528–533 (2016)
23. Lancucki, A., Saha, I., Bhowmick, S.S., Maulik, U., Lipinski, P.: A new evolutionary microRNA marker selection using next-generation sequencing data. In: 2016 IEEE Congress on Evolutionary Computation (CEC), pp. 2752–2759 (2016)
24. Saha, I., Bhowmick, S.S., Geraci, F., Pellegrini, M., Bhattacharjee, D., Maulik, U., Plewczynski, D.: Analysis of next-generation sequencing data of mirna for the prediction of breast cancer. In: Panigrahi, B.K., Suganthan, P.N., Das, S., Satapathy, S.C. (eds.) SEMCCO 2015. LNCS, vol. 9873, pp. 116–127. Springer, Cham (2016). doi:10.1007/978-3-319-48959-9_11
25. Bhowmick, S.S., Saha, I., Maulik, U., Bhattacharjee, D.: Biomarker identification using next generation sequencing data of RNA. In: 2016 International Conference on Advances in Computing, Communications and Informatics (ICACCI), pp. 299–303 (2016)

Study and Analysis of a Fast Moving Cursor Control in a Multithreaded Way in Brain Computer Interface

Debashis Das Chakladar$^{(\boxtimes)}$ and Sanjay Chakraborty

Computer Science and Engineering Department, Institute of Engineering and
Management, Kolkata, India
devs24u2008@gmail.com, sanjay.chakraborty@iemcal.com

Abstract. Now a days, 'Brain Computer Interface' is one of the fastest
growing technologies in which researchers are trying to communicate
between human brain and external devices effectively. Generally, brain
signal can be captured by EEG technique and the scalp voltage is measured in timely manner. The signal is then transferred to the external
devices for modification and finally, the scalp voltage level is transferred
into cursor movement (in multithreaded way). Then it will try to reach
the desired target inside the computer. In this paper, we propose an efficient technique to reach the cursor to the desired target with single brain
signal. This paper also shows that the time and space complexity of this
approach is quite less compared to the other existing approaches. If the
cursor can reach to the desired target quickly then human can respond
very quickly and the application would be more helpful for disabled or
paralysed people. For sake of simplicity, the proposed method is also carried out on 5 different amplitude levels of the same signal over different
time periods (within 1 ns) in this paper.

Keywords: Electroencephalography (EEG) · Cursor control · Multi-
threading · Brain computer interface (BCI) · Brain machine interface

1 Introduction

Electroencephalograph (EEG) was first introduced by Berger in 1929 by externally attaching several electrodes on the human skull [9]. These signals are connected with human brain and extract information about physiological functions
indirectly. We can peform several possible applications using such signals with
the help of various embedded technologies. Recent studies show that people can
learn to control the amplitude of electroencephalographic activity (EEG) over
sensorimotor cortex and use that control to move a cursor from the center of a
computer screen to a desired target [5]. Brain Computer Interface (BCI) system
has three main components: Signal acquisition, Signal processing and application
interface. Most of the previous works have been done based on signal processing
and useful feature extraction from those processed signals. Some works have also
done based on efficient communication technique between brain signal (analog)

© Springer Nature Singapore Pte Ltd. 2017
J.K. Mandal et al. (Eds.): CICBA 2017, Part II, CCIS 776, pp. 44–56, 2017.
DOI: 10.1007/978-981-10-6430-2_4

and computer (digital), so that device commands can easily interpret the brain signal and return feedback from application interface. Figure 1 shows the basic design of a BCI system. Generally, BCI system takes brain activity and classify them into a computer understandable signal using feature based extraction techniques. Different sort of brain activity patterns are captured in the form of EEG signals and converted to device commands by the BCI system. Such classification was undertaken by various methods and performed by machine learning algorithms [3,7]. BCI can be classified into synchronous BCI and asynchronous BCI. Synchrounous BCI has a plain design, whereas asynchronous BCI offering a natural mode of interaction, and without waiting for external cues [11].

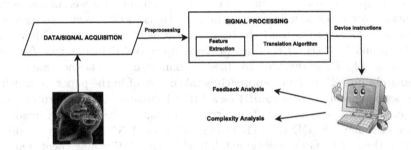

Fig. 1. Basic design of a BCI system

Several works have been done in this field. But no such work has been done yet that is based on an efficient methodology to move the cursor in multithreaded way to reach the desired target quickly. There is no need to fetch brain signal repeatedly through EEG, as this will cause extra overhead. If the signal processing (fetching, amplifying, extracting features etc.) has done repeatedly then the overhead associated with each components of BCI will be increased proportionately which will cause low efficiency. So in this paper, we proposed a technique which will fetch one brain signal at a time and capture the various levels of amplitudes of the signal over a specific time range. This paper is organized as following. Some prior works on brain Computer Interfacing through EEG based technologies are analyzed and discussed in Sect. 2. Section 2 also describes how this BCI technologies can be extensively used for communication and computer control. Section 3 describes the proposed algorithm for an efficient way of fast moving cursor. Section 4 discusses the effectiveness of this proposed technique on a demo user input signal. Section 5 shows the applications of the proposed technique on (1) Gamma waves-upto 31 Hz (2) Beta waves-(12–30) Hz (3) Alpha waves-(7.5–12) Hz (4) Theta waves-(3.5–7.5) Hz (5) Delta waves-(0.5–3.5) Hz. Section 6 throws some light on the time, space and computational complexity analysis of our proposed approach. Sections 7 gives a detail comparison of the proposed approach with other well-known approaches with respect to its advantages and disadvantages. Finally, Sect. 8 gives the conclusion and future work of this paper.

2   Literature Review

A number of techniques have been developed to assist various ways of communication between human and computer devices. In this section, we are dealing with some of the famous BCI techniques for communication problems. In the review papers [1,9,10], how the various time frequency methods (Fourier transform, autoregressive models, wavelets, and Kalman filter and spatio temporal techniques such as Laplacian filter and common spatial patterns) and feature classifications techniques (linear discriminant analysis, support vector machines, artificial neural networks, and Bayesian classifiers) [15] are used for signal processing task in BCI system. A study at the Wadsworth Center [4] shown that physically disabled people can control to move a cursor on a computer screen in one or two dimensions using the amplitude of μ or β rhythms in electroencephalographic (EEG) activity recorded from the scalp over sensorimotor cortex. They used 8–12 Hz μ and 13–28 Hz β rhythms in the scalp recorded EEG signal for communication [12]. These rhythms are directly connected with the movement areas of human brains. The similar approach is taken care of in the paper [5] which is called sensorimotor rhythm (SMR) based BCI technique. One important study is to analyze the performance of linear discriminant analysis (LDA), quadratic discriminant analysis (QDA) and K-nearest neighbor (KNN) algorithms in differentiating the raw EEG data obtained, into their associative movement, namely, left-right movement. It also includes the feature vector strategy to improve the performance accuracy [2]. A very interesting application of machine learning and pattern recognition algorithms on neural data classification in BCI is introduced in paper [6]. These algorithms take huge amount of neural data and classify them from non-informative brain signals. In this way, it will be able to decode the brain-states.

3   Proposed Methodology

The main approach of this paper is to find a suitable algorithm to move the cursor control towards desired target on the computer screen efficiently and effectively. The proposed technique is described in Algorithm 1 (Find Target). This algorithm follows the Greedy techinque as every time it takes the optimal amplitude from the queue to reach the target. The proposed algorithm first receives three user inputs, cursor and target location and five different amplitudes (based on the Brain signal). Then it stores that five different amplitudes of the brain signal into the queue in descending order. After that, it will check the difference between cursor and target values. Initially, it extracts the maximum amplitude from the queue and if the initial distance is large then the cursor location has been added with that maximum amplitude. Now, again based on the new cursor location check the difference (parallely) and reset the cursor and set the flag after modification of cursor location. Finally, call the same function recursively with the new cursor and target location and if the difference between them is zero, then stop the process as the cursor has reached to the target.

Algorithm 1. Find-Target Algorithm

1: **procedure** FINDTARGET(XCUR,XTAR)
2:      $xtar \leftarrow Targetlocation(x\text{-}axis)$
3:      $xcur \leftarrow Cursorlocation(x\text{-}axis)$
4:      $diff \leftarrow xtar\text{-}xcur$
5:      Queue Q (MaxPriority queue based on array ,which holds 5 different amplitude levels of EEG signal)
6:      **if** $(diff = 0)$ **then**
7:          *Write(Success!!Cursor has reached to the target)*
8:      **else**
9:          **while** $((Q! = NULL)or(diff >= amp[0]))$ **do**
10:              $xmax \leftarrow ExtractMax(Q)$
11:              **if** $(diff <= xmax)$ **then**
12:                  **for** $(i = 0$ to $n)$ **do**
13:                      **if** $(diff <= amp[i])$ **then**
14:                          $xmax \leftarrow amp[i]$
15:                      **end if**
16:                  **end for**
17:              **end if**
18:              $xcurnew \leftarrow xcur\text{+}xmax$
19:              $diffnew \leftarrow xtar\text{-}xcurnew$
20:              $diff \leftarrow diffnew$
21:              **if** $((diffnew = 0)or(flag = 1))$ **then**
22:                  *Write(Success after some attempts)*
23:              **else**
24:                  **if** $flag = 0$ **then**
25:                      **for** $(i = 0$ to $n)$ **do**
26:                          **if** $(diffnew = amp[i])$ **then**
27:                              $xcurnew \leftarrow xcur\text{+}amp[i]$
28:                              $flag \leftarrow 1$
29:                              **break**
30:                          **end if**
31:                      **end for**
32:                  **end if**
33:                  **if** $flag = 0$ **then**
34:                      **for** $(i = 0$ to $n)$ **do**
35:                          **if** $(diffnew < amp[i])$ **then**
36:                              $xmin \leftarrow amp[n\text{-}1]$
37:                              $xdiff \leftarrow xmin\text{-}diffnew$
38:                              $xcurnew \leftarrow xcur\text{+}xdiff$
39:                              $flag \leftarrow 1$
40:                              **break**
41:                          **end if**
42:                      **end for**
43:                  **end if**

Algorithm 2. Find-Target Algorithm- Part 2

```
44:             if flag = 0 then
45:                 for (i = 0 to n) do
46:                     if (amp[i + 1] < diff < amp[i]) then
47:                         smallest ← i
48:                         xmin ← diffnew-amp[i]
49:                         xmin1 ← diffnew-amp[i+1]
50:                         if (xmin < xmin1) then
51:                             shiftcur ← xcurnew+amp[i]
52:                             xcurnew ← shiftcur-xmin
53:                             flag ← 1
54:                             break
55:                         else
56:                             return
57:                         end if
58:                     end if
59:                 end for
60:             end if
61:         end if
62:     end while
63: end if
64: Findtarget(xcurnew,xtar)
65: end procedure
```

4   Illustrative Example

The amplitude of specific frequency will translated into cursor movement. Cursor always moves towards the Xaxis,
so here we derive the algorithm based on horizontal displacement of cursor towards the target

Step1 (UserInput): Set the target in computer
Step2 (UserInput): Initially set the cursor's location in any position based on EEG signal

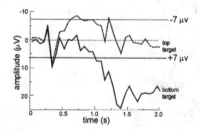

Fig. 2. Cursor movement towards the target after periodic interval [8]

Step3: Calculate difference between the cursor and target

Step4: Use MaxpriorityQueue which will contain the amplitudes (in descending order) of brain signal within very short time interval range (here for the sake of simplicity we have taken five different amplitudes)

The queue (Q) holds the following amplitudes **(5, 4, 3, 2, 1)** in microvolt

Step5:

Case 1:

(1) Target location (x-axis): tar = 20 and Cursor location (x-axis): cur = 10
(2) difference: (tar − cur) = 10
(3) Extract Maximum amplitude from Queue: MaxAmp = 5
(4) Now check the difference with maximum amplitude: (difference > MaxAmp)
(5) Reset Cursor location: (cur = cur + MaxAmp) = 10 + 5 = 15
(6) Check the new difference: (difference = tar − cur) = 20 − 15 = 5
(7) Check the new difference with all the amplitudes in the queue (using parallel for loop) and check whether any of the amplitude value is equal to the difference
(8) Reset Cursor location: (cur = cur + Maxamp) = 15 + 5 = 20
(9) Check the new cursor and target location: tar = 20 and cur = 20, so the difference=0–>**Success (cursor has reached to the target)**

Case 2:

(1) Target location (x-axis): tar = 10 and Cursor location (x-axis): cur = 1.2
(2) difference: (tar-cur) = 8.8
(3) Extract Maximum amplitude from Queue: MaxAmp = 5
(4) Now check the difference with maximum amplitude: (difference > MaxAmp)
(5) Reset Cursorlocation: (cur = cur + MaxAmp) = 1.2 + 5 = 6.2
(6) Check the new difference: (difference = tar − cur) = 10 − 6.2 = 3.8
(7) Check the new difference in the amplitudes of queue (using parallel for loop): the required difference is between the two amplitudes values (i:e ampval [2] = 2 and ampval [3] = 3) now check the distance between two amplitudes with difference diff: (difference-amp[3]) = (3.8 − 3) = .8 and diff1: (difference-amp [2]) = (3.8 − 4) = −.2, so we pick amplitude value 4, as the difference is closer to the amplitude value 4 (having minimum difference as negetive sign for crossing the target by shifting the value of .2)
(8) Reset Cursorlocation: cur = cur + ampval[4] = 6.2 + 4 = 10.2
(9) Reduce the extra shifted value from cursor:
(cursorlocation = cur-diff1) = cur = 10.2 − .2 = 10
(10) Check the new cursor and target location: tar = 10 and cur = 10, so the difference =0–>**Success (cursor has reached to the target)**

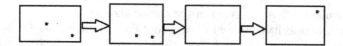

Fig. 3. Block Diagram of Cursor movement: (1) Initial position of Cursor (center at the screen) and Target (bottom right corner) (2)Cursor moves towards the fixed target (3) Cursor hits (cursor reach to the target) the fixed Target (4) Next Target (top right corner) has been set

Case 3:

(1) Target location (x-axis): tar = 20 and Cursor location (x-axis): cur = 16
(2) difference: (tar − cur) = 4
(3) Extract Maximum amplitude from Queue: MaxAmp = 5
(4) Check the nearest amplitude from the queue with difference: (difference < MaxAmp)
(5) Check the nearest amplitude from queue with difference: here ampvalue[2] = 4 which is matched with difference, so pick that nearest amplitude value
(6) Reset Cursor location: cur + ampvalue[2] = 16 + 4 = 20
(7) Check the new cursor and target location: tar = 20 and cur = 20, so the difference = 0–>**Success(cursor has reached to the target)**

Case 4: New amplitude values (5,4,3,2.5,2) in microvolt, so the queue (Q) also holds the new amplitude values

(1) Target location (x-axis): tar = 10 and Cursor location (x-axis): cur = 4
(2) difference: (tar-cur) = 6
(3) Extract Maximum amplitude from Queue: MaxAmp = 5
(4) Now check the difference with maximum amplitude: (difference > MaxAmp)
(5) Reset Cursor location: (cur = cur + MaxAmp) = 4 + 5 = 9
(6) Check the new difference: (difference = tar-cur) = 10 − 9 = 1
(7) Check the new difference in the amplitudes of queue (using parallel for loop): all the amplitudes are greater than the difference as the lowest amplitude (minamp = 2) which is greater than difference
(8) Take new difference between minimum amplitude and difference: newdifference = (minamp-difference): 2 − 1 = 1
(9) Reset Cursorlocation: (cur = cur + newdifference) = 9 + 1 = 10
(10) Check the new cursor and target location: tar = 10 and cur = 10, so the difference = 0–> **Success (cursor has reached to the target)**

5   Result and Analysis

The experimental analysis of the proposed algorithm has done on the following computing platform.

Application Environment: DEV C++ (version-4.9.9.2)

Hardware Environment: Operating System- Windows7 (64 bit), Processor-Intel Core (TM)i3, RAM-4 GB, Clock-2.26 GHZ

Performance Analysis: Execution time of the algorithm

Case 1: 8.79 s
Case 2: 8.85 s
Case 3: 8.89 s
Case 4: 8.63 s

EEG has classified the brain signals into five waves [13]

(1) Gamma waves-upto 31 Hz
(2) Beta waves-(12–30) Hz
(3) Alpha waves-(7.5–12) Hz
(4) Theta waves-(3.5–7.5) Hz
(5) Delta waves-(0.5–3.5) Hz

The above frequency range has been converted into amplitude levels for horizontal movement of the cursor. Target and cursor locations had been set initially. The cursor movement towards the target has been controlled by the above brain signals. We show here some brain signals(amplitude vs time) of different amplitude ranges and plot the cursor movement towards the target for that signal within the fixed time intervals.

Signal 1:

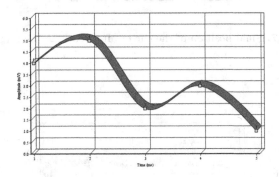

Fig. 4. Brian signal (Delta and Theta wave) with amplitude levels (in mV): 1, 2, 3, 4, 5

Result:

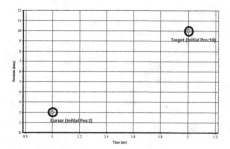 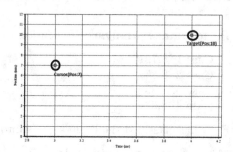

Fig. 5. Initial position of the target (20) and the Cursor (10)

Fig. 6. Cursor movement towards the fixed target

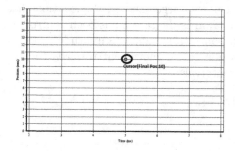

Fig. 7. Final position of the cursor after reaching the target

Signal 2:

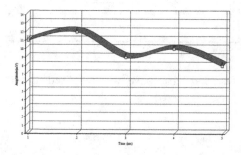

Fig. 8. Brian signal (Alpha wave) with amplitude levels (in mV): 8, 9, 10, 11, 12

Result:

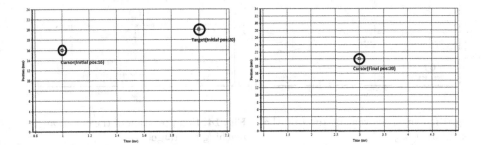

Fig. 9. Initial position of the target (20) and the cursor (16)

Fig. 10. Final position of the cursor after reaching the target

Signal 3:

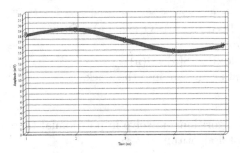

Fig. 11. Brain signal (Beta wave) with amplitude levels (in mV): 15, 16, 17, 18, 19

Result:

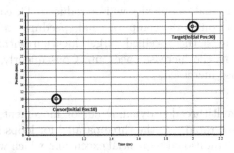

Fig. 12. Initial position of the target (30) and the cursor (10)

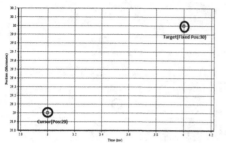 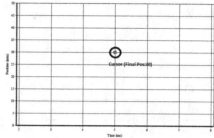

Fig. 13. Cursor movement towards the fixed target

Fig. 14. Final position of the cursor after reaching the target

6   Time-Space Tradeoff and Computational Complexity

Extractmax(from MaxPriorityQueue):–>O(logn)
Parallel for loop:' –>O(n) ,as all for loops will execute concurrently in different threads,

---

Total Time Complexity: T(n)=O(logn+n)->O(n)
Linear Time Complexity
Total Space complexity: S(n)=O(n)
Maximum 'n' elements can store into the stack.

   Class of P: the algorithm can solve in polynomial time as it is linear time (n) to execute the total algorithm.

7   Advantages and Disadvantages

This algorithm is based on multithreaded application. All the for loops will execute in parallel, (keyword: **"parallel for"** use for concurrent execution dynamically) so the computational complexity will be reduced. Threads are lightweight and very fast in execution so the computational speedup can be also increased. The cursor will reach to the specified target location within a very limited amount of time due to the increase speed up. Consequently, the speed of the human response is also increased.
So the main benefits are

Benefit 1: It is a multithreaded dynamic cursor movement, so the processor efficiency has increased rapidly as the three parallel for loops has executed concurrently rather than traditional sequential execution, which will increased computational speedup.
   Time complexity of the algorithm is linear in the input size.

Benefit 2: Previous algorithms(LDA, QDA and KNN) had been suffering from trial prediction and wavelet coefficient factor [2] but in this algorithm as the cursor can reach to the target very quickly in the first trial then immediately cursor will be ready for the next trial, so it is not dependent on the trial prediction

Benefit 3: For goal or target oriented cursor movement, there needs to be some complex output device for translating the target objective [1] but in this algorithm we have tried to implement the logic in a simple manner so that runtime complexity will be minimum.

Benefit 4: The KNN algorithm is unsuitable for huge distance as the approximation of nearest neighbour is not always successful for large distance, but in this algorithm Cursor can reach the target easily if they are located in a huge distance gap.

Disadvantage: Thread complexity will be merely increased. If one thread is blocked, then we need to add a new thread for executing the parallel task.

8 Conclusion and Future Scope

BCI consumes a bright future for a broad range of applications. Coupled with current technological advances and BCI are growing faster in a different field of applications. BCI, as a technology, has achieved a wide range of applications from control of robotic arms to multi-dimensional cursor manipulation. This paper is based on fast movement of the cursor (using multithreaded way) of the brain signal to the desired target in computer. If the cursor can reach the target very quickly, human response will be quick and interaction between human computer can also be done effectively. The algorithm will run in polynomial time so the computational complexity is also up to the mark. A brief comparison analysis shown that the proposed approach has a list of benefits over some well-known existing approaches.

Cursor movement in BCI has enhanced scope in various applications like wheelchair controller, Robot controller etc. [14]. If the movement of a cursor can handle quickly then human thinking capability can be improved effieciently in near future.

References

1. Ortiz-Rosario, A., Adeli, H.: Brain-computer interfaces technologies: from signal to action. Rev. Neurosci. **24**(3), 537–552 (2013). De Gruyter
2. Bhattacharyya, S., Khasnobish, A., Chatterjee, S., Konar, A., Tibarewala, D.N.: Performance analysis of LDA, QDA and KNN algorithms in left-right limb movement classification from EEG data. In: International Conference on Systems in Medicine and Biology, pp. 126–131. IEEE, IIT Kharagpur, India (2010)
3. Ramadan, R.A., Refat, S., Elshahed, M.A., Ali, R.A.: Basics of brain computer interface. In: Hassanien, A.E., Azar, A.T. (eds.) Brain-Computer Interfaces. ISRL, vol. 74, pp. 31–50. Springer, Cham (2015). doi:10.1007/978-3-319-10978-7_2
4. Wolpaw, J.R., McFarland, D.J., Vaughan, T.M.: Brain-computer interface research at the Wadsworth center. IEEE Trans. Rehabil. Eng. **8**(2), 222–226 (2012)

5. Yuan, H., He, B.: Brain-computer interfaces using sensorimotor rhythms: current state and future perspectives. IEEE Trans. Biomed. Eng. **61**(5), 1425–1435 (2014)

6. Lemm, S., Blankertz, B., Dickhaus, T., Muller, K.-R.: Introduction to machine learning for brain imaging. NeuroImage **56**, 387–399 (2011). Elsevier

7. Alamdari, N., Haider, A., Arefin, R., Verma, A.K., Tavakolian, K., Fazel-Rezai, R.: A review of methods and applications of brain computer interface systems. In: IEEE International Conference on Electro Information Technology (EIT) (2016)

8. Wolpawa, J.R., Birbaumerc, N., McFarlanda, D.J., Pfurtschellere, G., Vaughan, T.M.: Brain-computer interfaces for communication and control. Clin. Neurophys. **113**, 767–791 (2002). Elsevier

9. Suleiman, A.B.R., Fatehi, T.A.H.: Features extraction techniques of EEG signal for BCI applications. http://www.limu.edu.ly/pub/papers/f2465.pdf

10. Birbaumer, N., Cohen, L.G.: Brain computer interfaces: communication and restoration of movement in paralysis. J. Physiol. **579**(3), 621–636 (2007)

11. Allison, B.Z., Wolpaw, E.W., Wolpaw, J.R.: Brain-computer interface systems: progress and prospects. Expert Rev. Med. Devices **4**(4), 463–474 (2013)

12. Wolpaw, J.R., McFarland, D.J., Neat, G.W., Forneris, C.A.: An EEG-based brain-computer interface for cursor control. Electroencephalogr. Clin. Neurophysiol. **78**, 252–259 (1991). Elsevier

13. Larsen, E.A.: Classification of EEG signals in a brain-computer interface system, Ph.D. thesis. Norwegian University of Science and Technology, June 2011

14. SarangShastrakar, M., Bawane, N.G.: BCI based systems to control cursor movement using various techniques: survey report. Int. J. Eng. Sci. **6**, 3434 (2016). S. B. Jain Institute of Technology, Management and Research, Nagpur, Maharashtra, India

15. Classification of 2-Dimensional Cursor Movement Imagery EEG Signals by ÃÜnder Aydemir Department of Electrical and Electronics Engineering, Karadeniz Technical University. IEEE (2016)

A New Approach for Clustering Gene Expression Data

Girish Chandra[✉] and Sudhakar Tripathi

Department of Computer Science and Engineering, National Institute of Technology Patna,
Bihar, India
gcchandra440@gmail.com, stripathi.cse@nitp.ac.in

Abstract. Most of the clustering algorithms are sensitive to noise. Many of them cluster all the genes of the dataset. However, it may be possible that only a small part of genes of the gene expression dataset is involved in the biological processes for a particular set of experiment conditions or sample. To identify these genes clusters, we propose a method which identifies the co-expressed genes having chances of co-regulation in presence of non-functional genes and high level of noise. The proposed method clusters those genes that are within distance threshold t with respect to a specific gene in each experiment conditions and works on column wise distance calculation approach. To validate the proposed method an experimental analysis has been done with a real gene expression data and the experimental results show the significance of proposed method over existing one.

Keywords: Clustering · Gene expression data · Data mining

1 Introduction

DNA microarray technology is used to measure the expression level of thousands of genes simultaneously. Analysis of these data is helpful in study of functions of genes. In absence of any prior information regarding the gene expression data, clustering plays an important role in analysis of such data. Clustering is a process of grouping objects having a set of similar properties.

The gene expression data generated during DNA microarray experiment under different experiment conditions is arranged in a matrix $GE = \{E_{ij} \mid 1 \leq i \leq n; 1 \leq j \leq m\}$, where n is the number of rows and m is the number of columns. Each row of the matrix represents a gene. Similarly, each column of the matrix represents an experiment condition. An element, E_{ij}, of the matrix, a numerical value, is the expression level of the gene i in the experiment condition j.

Many clustering algorithms, such as the hierarchical agglomerative clustering algorithm [1], k-means algorithm [2], SOM [3], CLICK [4], fuzzy c-means algorithm [5] and SiMM-TS [6], have been efficiently employed for effective clustering of gene expression data. Most of them consider the assumption that all of the genes belong to a particular cluster. However, it has been observed that only a smaller number of genes participate in a biological process under a set of experiment condition [7]. Certain genes may not participate in any biological function. It is important to identify gene clusters with background of high level of noise and non-functional genes. The expression levels

© Springer Nature Singapore Pte Ltd. 2017
J.K. Mandal et al. (Eds.): CICBA 2017, Part II, CCIS 776, pp. 57–64, 2017.
DOI: 10.1007/978-981-10-6430-2_5

of the genes, which are not involved in any biological function, differ from the expression levels of rest of the genes of dataset. Their behavior is similar to that of the outliers corresponding to all of the co-expressed genes clusters.

In this paper, we propose a method which selectively identifies the clusters of genes that are co-expressed. The core concept is to identify genes that exist within a distance threshold t of a specific gene in each of the experiment conditions. Then, we apply the method on a gene expression dataset. Further, we utilize three clustering validation indices to evaluate the effectiveness of the method used. The method is compared with hierarchal algorithm, k-means algorithm and SOM.

In the Sect. 2, the proposed method is described in detail. In the Sect. 3, the proposed method implementation and their evaluation are given. The conclusion part of the paper is given in Sect. 4.

2 Proposed Method

A gene expression data set typically contains expression levels of the genes participating in cellular processes, some irrelevant genes which do not involve in any biological function and noise that is produced due to complex procedure of microarray experiment [14]. In other words, the data set contains a set of clusters of co-expressed genes, non-functional genes with expression levels differing from the expression levels of the remaining genes and some noise. To identify these clusters, we propose a method in which a column wise distance calculation approach is used. Those genes formed a cluster that are within the distance threshold t with respect to a specific gene in each experiment conditions. A gene not having any other gene within distance t in each experiment condition can be marked as noise. The detailed procedure of the proposed method is as follows.

Let us consider a gene expression data set $GE = \{E_{ij} \mid 1 \leq i \leq n; 1 \leq j \leq m\}$ having a set of n genes $G = \{g_1, g_2, \ldots, g_n\}$ and their expression levels measured under a set of m experiment condition $E = \{e_1, e_2, \ldots, e_m\}$.

To understand the proposed method, we define an unclustered gene set U consisting of all unclustered genes. Initially $U = \{g_1, g_2, \ldots, g_n\}$ i.e. all genes are unclustered. A marked gene set M is used for column wise distance calculations.

A gene g_i is randomly selected from U. Rest of the unclusterd genes are put in the marked gene set M. Let distance d, for an experiment condition e_j, between genes g_i and a marked gene g_k, is the difference of expression level E_{ij} of g_i with expression level E_{kj} of g_k.

$$d = \left| E_{ij} - E_{kj} \right|$$

The d is calculated for each marked gene $g_k \in M$. The gene g_k is removed from M if d is greater than a threshold t. This process is repeated for each experiment condition $\{e_1, e_2, \ldots, e_m\}$ one by one. It is evident that with each succession of experiment condition, the marked gene set reduces. After comparison of all the marked genes with g_i under the experiment conditions, if no marked gene is found in M then the gene g_i is marked as noise, otherwise all the marked genes are labelled as a cluster. Then, these clustered genes are removed from the unclustered gene set U. The aforementioned steps are repeated with rest of the unclustered genes of U until all of the genes are not clustered.

The algorithm can be summarized as follows:

The algorithm can be summarized as follows:
```
c=1        //cluster
for each unclustered gene g_i∈U
        M=U-{g_i}
        for each experiment e_j
                if |E_ij − E_kj | > t        //for all g_k ∈M
                        M=M-{g_k}
                end if
        end for
        if  M is NULL
                mark g_i as noise
        else
                mark genes of M as cluster c
        end if
        c=c+1
        update U
end for
```

3   Implementation and Analysis

In this section, detail analysis of the result obtained by applying the proposed method on yeast cell cycle data is presented. Three cluster validation indices have been used for evaluation of the proposed method. The result obtained by proposed method is compared with three clustering algorithms.

3.1   Data Set

The yeast cell cycle data consists of expression levels of 6220 genes measured over 17 time points, taken at an interval of 10 min and covers nearly two full cell cycles. Only 416 genes show significant changes during the course of experiment [8, 9]. The expression levels are normalized to have mean = 0 and variance = 1 [15]. The data set we are using is a subset of the yeast cell cycle data containing 384 genes and has been previously used in [10]. The data is available at http://faculty.washington.edu/kayee/cluster.

3.2   Cluster Validation Index

For evaluation of clusters, three cluster validation indices Dunn Index [11], Davies-Bouldin (DB) Index [12] and Connectivity [13] are used.

The Dunn Index is the ratio of the smallest distance between two clusters to the largest distance within a cluster. It is defined as

$$Dunn = \min_{1 \le i \le n, 1 \le j \le n, i \ne j} \left(\frac{d(i,j)}{\max_{1 \le k \le n} d'(k)} \right)$$

where n is the number of cluster, $d(i,j)$ is the distance between centers of cluster i and j and $d'(k)$ is the largest distance between two objects of cluster k. The range of Dunn Index is 0 to ∞ and it should be maximized.

The Davies-Bouldin Index (DB) is defined as

$$DB = \frac{1}{n} \sum_{i=1; i \ne j} max \left(\frac{\sigma_i + \sigma_j}{d(c_i, c_j)} \right)$$

where n is the number of cluster, σ_i is the average distances of all object with center c_i of cluster i and, $d(c_i, c_j)$ is the distance between centers c_i and c_j of cluster i and j respectively. The DB Index should be minimized.

Connectivity is defined as

$$conn = \sum_{i=1}^{n} \sum_{j=1}^{k} x_{ij}$$

where n is the number of objects that participate in clustering, x_{ij} is 0, if object i and jth nearest neighbor of i belong to the same cluster otherwise $1/j$, and k is taken as the parameter for the nearest neighbor consideration. The range of connectivity is 0 to ∞ and it should be minimized.

3.3   Implementation Platform

The proposed method is implemented on R. For validation of clustering algorithm and their result, two R packages, clValid [13] and clv [16], are used.

3.4   Results

The proposed method is applied on yeast cell cycle data with different values of threshold t. No cluster has been found for t less than 0.4 and greater than 4.3. The values of Dunn, DB and Connectivity indices, as shown in Table 1, indicate that highly coexpressed gene clusters are obtained when threshold t is small. It is also evident from the values of Dunn Index, DB Index and connectivity at threshold t = 0.4 that though the best cluster has been obtained, however, a very small number of genes have been identified in obtained clusters which is not desirable. So we can also consider some more clusters, having significant number of genes, obtained with moderate values of these indices. As we increase threshold t, more number of genes assigns to the clusters and compactness of the clusters decreases.

Table 1. Result of proposed method on yeast cell cycle data

Threshold t	Number of clusters	Total genes identifies in clusters	Dunn Index	DB Index	Connectivity
0.4	8	16	0.784855	0.534706	21.2
0.5	18	41	0.457198	0.831953	50.21667
0.6	29	79	0.315428	1.099389	106.75
0.7	32	108	0.274293	1.213592	130.1167
0.8	52	178	0.161777	1.310934	222.2333
0.9	67	233	0.159863	1.318261	311.5333
1	61	267	0.152332	1.555046	381.4333
1.1	63	307	0.127547	1.575846	424.3333
1.2	54	319	0.135242	1.660292	396.2
1.3	55	344	0.159944	1.795899	409.9833
1.4	45	354	0.147664	1.788297	384.0833
1.5	40	365	0.112127	1.91393	414.1
1.6	31	367	0.112127	2.08875	398.8167
1.7	27	371	0.132266	2.025547	350.0667
1.8	22	373	0.116361	2.095597	331.5
1.9	24	379	0.111185	2.130306	341.9
2	18	378	0.114503	2.129832	294.7167
2.1	12	379	0.106698	2.348927	248.8667
2.2	11	380	0.097003	2.337651	240.5333
2.3	11	380	0.097003	2.55091	253.5833
2.4	9	382	0.14735	2.398617	222.6833
2.5	8	382	0.149549	1.65122	190.5
2.6	7	383	0.149892	1.691213	190.7
2.7	6	382	0.147924	1.722208	202.95
2.8	7	383	0.091332	1.855697	240.7667
2.9	5	383	0.13633	2.016989	231.6333
3	5	383	0.111402	2.258458	235.5333
3.1	5	384	0.111402	2.06011	233.8
3.2	5	384	0.097045	2.580419	278.45
3.3	4	383	0.090158	2.178656	202.0333
3.4	4	384	0.093367	2.204393	184.3667
3.5	4	384	0.131954	2.156926	149.75
3.6	4	384	0.120302	2.05699	133.85
3.7	3	383	0.120302	2.02868	103.8333
3.8	3	384	0.112204	1.874462	74.95
3.9	2	383	0.112204	1.98153	52.05
4	2	383	0.113622	1.777664	31.08333
4.1	2	383	0.113622	1.978261	24.78333
4.2	2	384	0.387906	2.065439	6.266667
4.3	2	384	0.387906	2.065439	6.266667

Table 2. Dunn and connectivity indices for k-means, hierarchial and SOM algorithms

No. of clusters	hierarchical		k-means		SOM	
	Connectivity	Dunn	Connectivity	Dunn	Connectivity	Dunn
2	18.7833	0.2356	48.9333	0.1671	41.15	0.1754
3	26.0167	0.2362	35.85	0.1988	40.9833	0.1273
4	37.3	0.2362	41.9667	0.2103	41.9667	0.2103
5	50.4667	0.2546	48.2667	0.191	71.2333	0.2117
6	51.2	0.2546	65.5667	0.1843	105.2833	0.1741
7	51.8667	0.2546	74.3167	0.2252	114.15	0.1132
8	58.3	0.2321	103.3167	0.1971	126.5333	0.1625
9	60.5833	0.2321	85.4333	0.2431	128.55	0.1478
10	62.8667	0.2321	135.0167	0.1813	156.4167	0.1478
11	65.15	0.2321	137.75	0.1534	180.6833	0.1402
12	67.85	0.2321	149.4667	0.1534	180.1833	0.1414
13	83.9	0.255	164.7333	0.1534	200.25	0.1386
14	86.1833	0.255	187.65	0.103	204.5167	0.1007
15	87.9667	0.255	193.3667	0.103	210.1833	0.0882
16	90.2833	0.255	199.3333	0.1097	211.2333	0.162
17	98.2333	0.255	206.2333	0.1502	224.1667	0.1177
18	102.7667	0.2662	230.5	0.1375	235.8833	0.1405
19	103.2667	0.2662	222.6167	0.1551	234.05	0.1619
20	106.5333	0.2662	229.55	0.1147	257.5167	0.0916
21	107.0333	0.2662	239.5667	0.1086	236.5333	0.1672
22	109.1167	0.2662	243.3	0.1471	253.4333	0.106
23	114.1333	0.2674	239.3833	0.1157	271.7833	0.1612
24	116.45	0.2674	263.7833	0.1098	278.7667	0.1586
25	120.35	0.2674	247.5	0.157	281.0333	0.1336
26	130.9333	0.2674	257.5333	0.1179	305.1667	0.1299
27	133.2833	0.2674	260.2167	0.1179	303.95	0.1405
28	134.3667	0.2674	244.75	0.1853	306.3833	0.106
29	134.8667	0.2674	259.4333	0.1178	319.4	0.1743
30	139.35	0.277	271.9	0.1178	314.45	0.1488
31	141.1833	0.277	276.8	0.1179	302.7167	0.1702
32	147.7	0.277	285.4167	0.1179	309.6833	0.1626
33	149.3167	0.277	285.5333	0.1179	319.8	0.1714
34	152.1833	0.277	290.7333	0.1269	325.9333	0.1499
35	157.75	0.277	291.5833	0.1269	330.9333	0.1499
36	163.35	0.277	281.2833	0.1995	352.0167	0.1382
37	169	0.277	280.25	0.1189	341.7833	0.1403
38	170.7	0.277	282.9	0.1189	346.55	0.1442
39	170.95	0.277	286.8167	0.1189	353.95	0.1627
40	174.7667	0.277	290.8167	0.1189	345.1	0.1392
41	176.7167	0.277	289.6167	0.1189	350.85	0.178
42	182.3167	0.277	301.2	0.2295	361.9833	0.1663
43	185.9	0.277	305.9667	0.2295	373.75	0.1539
44	188.9667	0.277	308.05	0.2344	378.9	0.1435
45	192.7333	0.277	313.25	0.2365	392	0.1124
46	194.0167	0.277	322.2333	0.2295	377.4333	0.1566
47	196.4167	0.277	323.4	0.2295	380.2	0.1502
48	199.2833	0.277	327.0333	0.2365	378.85	0.171
49	200.1167	0.277	319.1167	0.2129	386.8667	0.1392
50	210.3667	0.263	326.9667	0.1355	388.95	0.1725

The Dunn and connectivity indices are also calculated for k-means, hierarchal and SOM algorithms as shown in Table 2. It is evident from Tables 1 and 2 that the Dunn index is greater for threshold t at 0.4, 0.5, 0.6, 4.2 and 4.3 when compared to the maximum values of Dunn index of SOM, k-means and hierarchal algorithms. This shows that the proposed method is performing well in comparison to k-means, SOM and hierarchal algorithms.

4   Conclusion

In this paper, a method is proposed for the identification of gene clusters in the presence of inactive genes and high levels of noise. The method works on column wise distance calculation approach. This works well in conducting the identification of highly co-expressed genes clusters. In this paper, the proposed method is compared with k-means, hierarchal and SOM algorithms. For evaluation and comparison three clustering validation indices, Dunn index, connectivity and DB index, are used.

References

1. Eisen, M.B., Spellman, P.T., Brown, P.O., Botstein, D.: Cluster analysis and display of genome-wide expression patterns. Proc. Nat. Acad. Sci. USA **95**(25), 14863–14868 (1998)
2. Tavazoie, S., Hughes, J.D., Campbell, M.J., Cho, R.J., Church, G.M.: Systematic determination of genetic network architecture. Nat. Genet. **22**(3), 281–285 (1999)
3. Tamayo, P., Slonim, D., Mesirov, J., Zhu, Q., Kitareewan, S., Dmitrovsky, E., Lander, E.S., Golub, T.R.: Interpreting patterns of gene expression with self-organizing maps: Methods and application to hematopoietic differentiation. Proc. Nat. Acad. Sci. USA **96**(6), 2907–2912 (1999)
4. Sharan, R., Shamir, R., CLICK: A clustering algorithm with applications to gene expression analysis. In Proceeding of Intelligent Systems for Molecular Biology (ISMB), pp. 307–316 (2000)
5. Dembele, D., Kastner, P.: Fuzzy c-means method for clustering microarray data. Bioinformatics **19**(8), 973–980 (2003)
6. Bandyopadhyay, S., Mukhopadhyay, A., Maulik, U.: An improved algorithm for clustering gene expression data. Bioinformatics **23**(21), 2859–2865 (2007)
7. Jiang, D., Tang, C., Zhang, A.: Cluster analysis for gene expression data: A survey. IEEE Trans. Knowl. Data Eng. **16**(11), 1370–1386 (2004)
8. Yee, Y.K., Haynor, D.R., Ruzzo, W.L.: Validating clustering for gene expression data. Bioinformatics **17**(4), 309–318 (2001)
9. Cho, Raymond: J.: A genome-wide transcriptional analysis of the mitotic cell cycle. Mol. Cell **2**(1), 65–73 (1998)
10. Ma, P.C.H., Chan, K.C.C.: A novel approach for discovering overlapping clusters in gene expression data. IEEE Trans. Biomed. Eng. **56**(7), 1803–1809 (2009)
11. Dunn, J.C.: Well-separated clusters and optimal fuzzy partitions. J. Cybern. **4**(1), 95–104 (1974)
12. Bolshakova, N., Azuaje, F.: Cluster validation techniques for genome expression data. Sig. Process. **83**(4), 825–833 (2003)

13. Brock, G., Pihur, V., Datta, S., Datta, S.: clValid, an R package for cluster validation. J. Stat. Softw. (Brock et al., March 2008) (2011)
14. Kerr, G., Ruskin, H.J., Crane, M., Doolan, P.: Techniques for clustering gene expression data. Comput. Biol. Med. **38**(3), 283–293 (2008)
15. Tamayo, P., Slonim, D., Mesirov, J., Zhu, Q., Kitareewan, S., Dmitrovsky, E., Lander, E.S., Golub, T.R.: Interpreting patterns of gene expression with self-organizing maps: methods and application to hematopoietic differentiation. Proc. Natl. Acad. Sci. **96**(6), 2907–2912 (1999)
16. Nieweglowski, L., Maintainer Nieweglowski, L.: Package 'clv' (2015)

Prediction of Diabetes Type-II
Using a Two-Class Neural Network

Somnath Rakshit[1], Suvojit Manna[1], Sanket Biswas[1], Riyanka Kundu[1],
Priti Gupta[1], Sayantan Maitra[2], and Subhas Barman[1(✉)]

[1] Jalpaiguri Government Engineering College, Jalpaiguri, West Bengal, India
somnath@cse.jgec.ac.in, davsuvo@gmail.com, sanketbiswas1995@gmail.com,
riyankakundu@gmail.com, pritigupta220596@gmail.com,
subhas.barman@gmail.com
[2] Institute of Pharmacy, Jalpaiguri, West Bengal, India
maitra_sayantan@yahoo.co.in

Abstract. Diabetes is one of the most frightful diseases that is creating
a terror in peoples mind all over the globe and all of them are putting
tremendous efforts to search for various methods to prevent this disease
at the budding stage by predicting the symptoms of diabetes. In this
paper, our main aim is to predict the onset of diabetes amongst women
aged at least 21 years using Two-class Neural Network and tabulate and
compare our results with others results. This approach has been tested
with the Pima Indians Diabetes Data Set downloaded from the UCI
Machine Learning data repository. The performance of our predictive
model has been measured and compared in terms of accuracy and recall.
Endocrinologists, dietitians, ophthalmologists and podiatrists can use
this model to predict how likely a patient is to suffer from diabetes.

Keywords: Diabetes mellitus · Machine learning · Pima Indians
diabetes data set · Two-class neural network

1 Introduction

To diagnose a disease, a number of tests are essential. And medical history data
plays a significant part of the testing procedure. Thus arises the need for a
powerful tool for analysing and extracting usable information for this complex
data [1]. Healthcare industries can benefit immensely from data mining applications [2,3]. This can improve patient compliance by maintaining high quality in
patient care and can help all concerned parties in limiting costs and enhancing
profits. This study focusses its attention on prediction of diabetes mellitus and
provides a detailed performance analysis of the same. Now, it is very important to develop predictive models using the risk factors for the development of
diabetes. Many studies have suggested traditional methods (statistical) as predictors [4,5]. The data mining process for diagnosis of diabetes can be divided
into five steps, though the underlying principles and techniques used for data

© Springer Nature Singapore Pte Ltd. 2017
J.K. Mandal et al. (Eds.): CICBA 2017, Part II, CCIS 776, pp. 65–71, 2017.
DOI: 10.1007/978-981-10-6430-2_6

mining diabetic databases may differ for different projects in different countries [1]. Data mining entails extraction of information from a data set and transformation into a comprehensible structure for further use. Statistical approaches like clustering, classification, regression, hypothesis testing and computer science applications like soft computing, machine learning and data visualizations largely contribute to solve different categories of data mining problems. Data Mining has been extensively used in diverse areas of science and engineering in recent times, ranging from bioinformatics to the fields of medicine and education.

Artificial neural network (ANN) is vastly used for diabetes prediction. Olaniyi and Adnan [6] used multilayer feed-forward neural network and trained with back-propagation algorithm to classify patients. Those were tested positive, assigned as binary 1 and those were tested negative as binary 0. They achieved a recognition rate of 82% by considering Pima Indians Diabetes Data Set. Similarly, Pradhan and Sahu propose an Artificial Neural Network (ANN) based classification for diabetes prediction [7]. In this paper, the ANN based classification model as one of the powerful methods in intelligent field was applied for classifying diabetic patients into two classes. Genetic algorithm (GA) is also used for feature selection for better accuracy. This model is trained with Back-propagation (BP) algorithm and GA (Genetic Algorithm) and 73.45% classification accuracy has been reported. On the other side, Smith et al. [8] proposed neural net-work ADAP algorithm to build associative models and obtained 76% accuracy of classification rate.

In this study, the features which carry more weight towards the outset of diabetes has been considered for training the neural network. The Pima Indians Diabetes dataset has been used to classify the positive and negative cases. The model is then scored and evaluated on the basis of accuracy and recall rate. The rest of the paper is organized as follows: Sect. 2 describes the proposed methodology. Section 3 deals with experimental results and analysis and finally, the paper is concluded in Sect. 4.

2   Proposed Methodology

Classification of data is a two phase process in which first step is the training phase. In this phase, the classifier algorithm builds a set of classification rules with the training set of tuples. The second phase is the test phase where the model is tested with well known cases to measure its accuracy. The performance of the model is then analyzed with the testing set of tuples [9]. A machine learning algorithm in general operates on a model and is iterated multiple times while manipulating the algorithm hyper-parameters to increase the accuracy of the classifier [2]. A model of neural network is given in Fig. 1.

2.1   Preprocessing of Data

The Pima Diabetes dataset has some biologically impossible data like there are 35 cases where diastolic blood pressure is 0, 231 cases where tricep skinfold

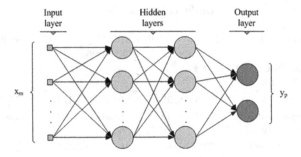

Fig. 1. General structure of totally connected Neural Network

value is zero, 11 cases where BMI is 0. These data points were assumed to have missing values and thus were removed. Shanker (1996) used all the cases from the datasets in his analysis [10]. Similarly, Kayaer et al. (2003) used all 768 cases which were normalized for better results [11]. Temurtas et al. (2009) used the first 576 cases as training data and the remaining 192 cases as testing data [12]. Preprocessing of data, such as cleaning the missing values is essential so that our model can correctly analyze the data [13]. A statistical analysis of the data as well as the feature scaling is given in Table 1. Scaling of all feature values were done to get the standardized feature values and to weight all features equally in their representation.

The main objective was to get all the data on same scale; if the scales for different features differ wildly, this can have a secondary effect on their ability to learn (depending on what methods are being used to do so). Having standardized feature values can implicitly weight all features equally in their representation.

2.2   Analyzing the Features

Features in machine learning are individual measurable properties of something to be interested in. In our given dataset, each row represents a female, and each column represents a feature of that female. For creating our predictive model, a good set of features were found. After a thorough study, it was inferred that some features performed better in predicting targets while some had a strong correlation with other features and hence they were removed.

2.3   Constructing the Model

After the data was prepared, a predictive model was constructed that consists of training and testing. The data was used to train the model, and then, the model was tested to see how closely it was able to predict the result. Training and testing the model was done by splitting the data into separate training and testing datasets. 80% of the data was used to train the model, and the remaining 20% was held back for testing.

Table 1. Data analysis

Feature ID	Feature name	Mean	Median	Standard deviation	Min/Max	Scaling process
F1	Number of pregnancies	3.301	2	3.2114	0/17	$\frac{F1}{10}$
F2	Age (years)	30.8648	27	10.2008	21/81	$\frac{F2}{100}$
F3	Triceps skinfold thickness (mm)	29.1454	29	10.5164	7/63	Ignored
F4	Diastolic blood pressure (mm Hg)	70.6633	70	12.4961	24/110	$\frac{F4}{80}$
F5	Body mass index (weight in kg/(height in m)^2)	33.0862	33.2	7.0277	18.2/67.1	$\frac{(F5-18)}{(25-18)}$
F6	Diabetes pedigree function	0.523	0.4495	0.3455	0.085/2.42	Unchanged
F7	Plasma glucose concentration a 2 h in an oral glucose tolerance test	122.6276	119	30.8608	56/198	$\frac{(F7-50)}{(120-50)}$
F8	2-Hour serum insulin (mu U/ml)	156.0561	125.5	118.8417	14/846	$\frac{(F8-14)}{(250-10)}$

3 Experimental Result and Analysis

In the following approach, the experiment was carried out to observe the accuracy, recall and precision with respect to prediction of Diabetes Type II.

3.1 Dataset

The following approach was used on Pima Indians Diabetes Dataset to measure the accuracy of prediction of Diabetes Type II. This database is publicly available [13] and the National Institute of Diabetes and Digestive and Kidney Diseases is the owner of the dataset. In this database, all patients are females of at least 21 years old of Pima Indian heritage. The dataset contains values for eight relevant vital attributes.

3.2 Experimental Setup

The Two Class Neural Network model was chosen to solve this problem. The model was configured using the following specifications:

1. Hidden layer specification:
   - The neural network consists of n hidden layers ($0 \leq n \leq 3$) each completely connected to its preceding layer, the first hidden layer is connected to input layer.
   - The output layer is fully connected to nth hidden layer, for $n > 0$, else it is connected to input layer.
   - The number of node in the input layer is determined by the number of features used.
   - Each hidden layer contains 100 nodes each.
   - The output layer contains 2 nodes, one each for positive and negative.
2. The global learning rate of 0.01 was found to be appropriate to train our model.
3. The model was trained over 1000 iteration.
4. The initial learning weights diameter was assigned as: 0.1
5. The momentum was kept 0 for optimum performance.
6. The trained model was then evaluated.

In the study, 392 cases of the data set were considered, out of which 314 was used for training the neural network model and 78 was used for testing the model. There were 262 negative cases (i.e., 67%) and 131 positive cases (i.e. 33%).

3.3   Experimental Result

In our implementation, we used R, SQL and Python within Microsoft Azure Machine Learning Studio and the results were compared with the existing approaches. The criterion taken for the comparison of classifiers were accuracy, precision and recall. In simple terms, high accuracy means that most of the measurements of a quantity were close to the true value. High precision means that an algorithm returned substantially more relevant results than irrelevant ones, while high recall means that an algorithm returned most of the relevant results [14].

The classification of data in this study was based on the usage of confusion matrix (given in Table 2) and were grouped into true positive (TP), true negative (TN), false positive (FP) and false negative (FN). The recall rate, precision and accuracy of the model were measured by varying the number of hidden layers of nodes and the results were plotted in Fig. 2.

$$Accuracy = \frac{(TP + TN)}{(TP + FP + TN + FN)} \tag{1}$$

$$Precision = \frac{TP}{(TP + FP)} \tag{2}$$

$$Recall = \frac{TP}{(TP + FN)} \tag{3}$$

Table 2. Confusion matrix

Actual vs Predicted	Positive	Negative
Positive	TP	TN
Negative	FP	FN

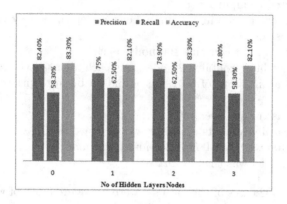

Fig. 2. Experimental results

3.4   Comparison of Performance

The results were compared with existing works and the comparison has been displayed in Table 3. In all cases, Pima Indians Diabetes Data Set was used for evaluations.

Table 3. Comparison of performance

Approaches	Models	Accuracy
Olaniyi and Adnan [6]	Multilayer feed-forward neural network	82%
Pradhan and Sahu [7]	ANN, GA, BP	73.45%
Our approach	Two-class neural network	83.3%

4   Conclusion

In summary, the two class neural network model is being used for predicting Diabetes Mellitus Type II using seven important attributes. Here the studies conclude that our model has achieved the highest accuracy of 83.3% for the given data. This model can be utilized to classify people at high risk of developing diabetes and provide timely medical intervention for women, aged 21 years and above. In this way, premature mortality and health risks can be diminished by implementing such predictive models. This paper presents an approach that can be used for hybrid model construction of community health services. This classification algorithm can be implemented for the prediction of other dominant diseases and classification with their suitable datasets. An another scope is to check whether by applying new algorithms, any improvement can be made over existing techniques.

References

1. Kandhasamy, J.P., Balamurali, S.: Performance analysis of classifier models to predict diabetes mellitus. Procedia Comput. Sci. **47**, 45–51 (2015)
2. Gaber, M.M., Zaslavsky, A., Krishnaswamy, S.: Mining data streams: a review. ACM Sigmod Rec. **34**(2), 18–26 (2005)
3. Palaniappan, S., Awang, R.: Intelligent heart disease prediction system using data mining techniques. In: 2008 IEEE/ACS International Conference on Computer Systems and Applications, AICCSA 2008, pp. 108–115. IEEE (2008)
4. Jia, Z., Zhou, Y., Liu, X., Wang, Y., Zhao, X., Wang, Y., Liang, W., Shouling, W.: Comparison of different anthropometric measures as predictors of diabetes incidence in a Chinese population. Diabetes Res. Clin. Pract. **92**(2), 265–271 (2011)
5. Tapak, L., Mahjub, H., Hamidi, O., Poorolajal, J.: Real-data comparison of data mining methods in prediction of diabetes in Iran. Healthc. Inf. Res. **19**(3), 177–185 (2013)
6. Olaniyi, E.O., Adnan, K.: Onset diabetes diagnosis using artificial neural network. Int. J. Sci. Eng. Res. **5**(10) (2014)
7. Pradhan, M., Sahu, R.K.: Predict the onset of diabetes disease using artificial neural network (ANN). Int. J. Comput. Sci. Emerg. Technol. **2**(2), 303–311 (2011)
8. Jack W Smith, JE Everhart, WC Dickson, WC Knowler, and RS Johannes. Using the adap learning algorithm to forecast the onset of diabetes mellitus. In Proceedings of the Annual Symposium on Computer Application in Medical Care, p. 261. American Medical Informatics Association, 1988
9. Jordan, M.I., Mitchell, T.M.: Machine learning: trends, perspectives, and prospects. Science **349**(6245), 255–260 (2015)
10. Shanker, M.S.: Using neural networks to predict the onset of diabetes mellitus. J. Chem. Inf. Comput. Sci. **36**(1), 35–41 (1996)
11. Kayaer, K.: Medical diagnosis on pima Indian diabetes using general regression neural networks
12. Temurtas, H., Yumusak, N., Temurtas, F.: A comparative study on diabetes disease diagnosis using neural networks. Expert Syst. Appl. **36**(4), 8610–8615 (2009)
13. UCI Machine Learning Repository pima Indian diabetes data set. https://archive.ics.uci.edu/ml/datasets/Pima+Indians+Diabetes
14. Powers, D.M.: Evaluation: from precision, recall and f-measure to ROC, informedness, markedness and correlation (2011)

Computational Intelligence in Mobile and Quantum Computing

Design of Two-Bit Gray Code Counter Using Two-Dimensional Two-Dot One-Electron QCA

Kakali Datta[1]([✉]), Debarka Mukhopadhyay[2], and Paramartha Dutta[1]

[1] Department of Computer and System Sciences, Visva-Bharati University, Santiniketan 731235, West Bengal, India
kakali.datta@visva-bharati.ac.in, paramartha.dutta@gmail.com
[2] Department of Computer Science, Amity School of Engineering and Technology, Amity University, Kolkata 700156, West Bengal, India
debarka.mukopadhyay@gmail.com

Abstract. Quantum-Dot Cellular Automata (QCA) is a well accepted for the next generation computer technology as it is capable of overcoming certain technical limitations of existing CMOS technology. We have designed the Gray code counter using two-dot one-electron QCA. As the Set-Reset flipflop is the building block of the Gray code counter, we also designed the Set-Reset flipflop. Computing the potential energies we have substantiated and analyzed the proposed design and calculated the energy and power related parameters. We have also compared our work with the four-dot two-electron QCA architecture and found that the proposed designs are superior to the existing ones in terms of space utilization, energy and power dissipation.

Keywords: Gray code counter · QCA · Coulomb's repulsion · Majority voter

1 Introduction

QCA technology of Lent and Tougaw [1] is now very popular in the nano technology domain as it requires extremely small space, consumes very low power and eliminates the disadvantage of the off-state leakage current. Thus the technology is very promising among the emerging technologies concerning future computers.

A four-dot two-electron quantum cell is square in shape with four charged wells or "dots" at the corners. Two electrons quantum-mechanically tunnel between neighboring dots within a cell. Coulomb's repulsion forces the electrons to take the corner positions. The concept is well addressed in [2–4]. Here, we are going to use two-dimensional two-dot one-electron QCA cells.

Gray code is a code assigned a set of integers, so that two adjacent code words differ by a single symbol thus having Hamming distance of 1 between them. Originally spurious output from electromechanical switches was prevented by the reflected binary code or the Gray code. Of late Gray codes also facilitates error correction in television systems, digital terrestrial, some cable TV and other

© Springer Nature Singapore Pte Ltd. 2017
J.K. Mandal et al. (Eds.): CICBA 2017, Part II, CCIS 776, pp. 75–84, 2017.
DOI: 10.1007/978-981-10-6430-2_7

digital communications. Gray code is used in genetic algorithms, in labeling the axes of Karnaugh maps, etc.

In Sect. 2, we reviewed of two-dimensional two-dot one-electron QCA. In Sect. 3, we discussed the design of SR flipflop. In Sect. 4, we discussed the design of 2-bit Gray code counter. Then we have verified the outputs of both the circuits using potential energy calculations in Sect. 5. The proposed architecture has been analyzed in Sect. 6 and lastly in Sect. 7, we have calculated energy and power requirements for our design. We have compared our work with that in [5] in Sect. 8 and finally we have concluded.

2   2-D Two-Dot One-Electron QCA

The two-dot one-electron QCA has rectangular cells, with two dots at the two ends. Through the tunnel between the two quantum dots, a free electron may move (Fig. 1). Binary information is represented by the position of electron within a cell that passes from one cell to another obeying Coulomb's principle.

    (a)   (b)   (c)   (d)

Fig. 1. Polarities of two-dot one-electron QCA cells

2.1   Clocking

Clocking is used for synchronization in CMOS technology. In QCA, the direction of signal flow is determined by clocking. Moreover, energy is supplied to input signals that are weak enabling it to propagate from the input cell to the output cell [2,4]. There are four clocking phases. Initially, the potential energy of the electron is least [6], so it is unable to move the adjacent quantum dots and the polarity is definite. In switch phase, the potential energy rises and attains its maximum at the end of this phase. In hold phase, this potential energy is maintained and the electron is delocalized. In release phase, the potential energy decreases and then a definite polarity is reached by the cell. Finally, in relax phase, it obtained the least potential energy and is at a definite polarity. All QCA architecture contains at most four clock zones and each clock zone consists of four phases. The phase difference between two consecutive clock zones is $\dfrac{\pi}{2}$ [2] (Fig. 2).

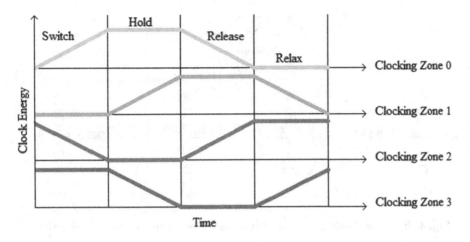

Fig. 2. The QCA clocking

2.2 Basic Building Blocks

A sequence of cells with same orientation makes up a binary wire (Fig. 3a); a differently oriented cell in between two cells of a binary wire gives an inverted output (Fig. 3b); the inverted outputs may also be obtained at two out of four turning at corners (Fig. 3c); if the same input is required to drive two systems then fan-out gate (Fig. 3d) may be used; the planar crossing wires (Fig. 3e) must have a zone difference of two.

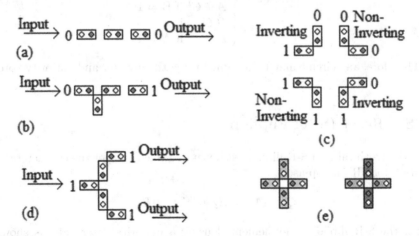

Fig. 3. The basic building blocks (a) binary wire (b) inverter (c) inverter at turnings (d) fan-out (e) planar wire crossing

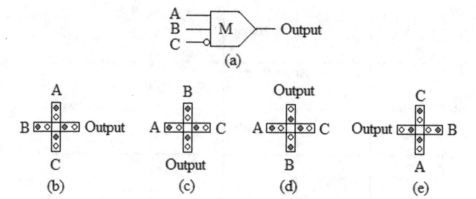

Fig. 4. Inputs and outputs of majority voter gates depending on their directions

The schematic diagrams and implementations of the majority voter gates having inputs A, B and C are shown in Fig. 4. The output function for Fig. 4(b)–(d) is given by

$$\text{Output} = AB + (A + B).C' \tag{1}$$

Thus, fixing the values of A, B and C, we get,

$$\text{Output} = \begin{cases} A.B & \text{if } C = 1 \\ A + B & \text{if } C = 0 \\ A.C' & \text{if } B = 0 \\ A + C' & \text{if } B = 1 \\ B.C' & \text{if } A = 0 \\ B + C' & \text{if } A = 1 \end{cases} \tag{2}$$

Therefore, any circuit may be designed using the inverter and majority voter gate.

3   Set-Reset (S-R) Flipflop

From the truth table of S-R flipflop is shown in Table 1, we get the characteristic equation for SR flipflop as:

$$Q(t + 1) = SQ + (S + Q)R' \tag{3}$$

So, the S-R flipflop is implemented using a majority voter gate as shown Fig. 5. Two alternative schematic diagrams and their respective implementations of SR flipflop is shown in Fig. 5(a)–(b).

Table 1. Truth table for S-R Flipflop

R	S	Q_{t+1}
0	0	Q_t
0	1	1
1	0	0
1	1	Q_t

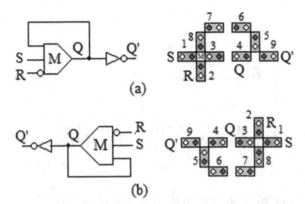

(a)

(b)

Fig. 5. S-R flipflop (a) schematic diagram and implementation (b) alternative schematic diagram and implementation

4   Gray Code Counter

Frank Gray coded a binary numeral system, the reflected binary code (RBC) or Gray code such that the successive values differed in one bit only.

The two-bit Gray code is shown in Table 2. By the "cyclic" property of a Gray code, decimal number rolls over to another decimal number with only one change of switch. This cycle is depicted in Fig. 6. The logic diagram of the Gray code counter is shown in Fig. 7. The same is implemented in Fig. 8.

Table 2. Truth table for Gray code

Decimal	Binary	Gray code	Gray as decimal
0	00	00	0
1	01	01	1
2	10	11	3
3	11	10	2

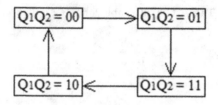

Fig. 6. Transition diagram of a 2-bit Gray code counter

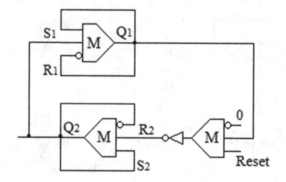

Fig. 7. Logic diagram of a Gray code counter

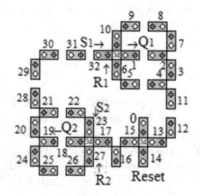

Fig. 8. Implementation of a Gray code counter

5   Determination of Output

Till date no simulator simulating two-dot one-electron QCA is available. To verify the circuit, we calculate the potential energy based on Coulomb's principle [4].

The potential energy, U between two point charges q_1 and q_2, at distance of r units is

$$U = \frac{Kq_1q_2}{r} = \frac{9 \times 10^9 \times (1.6)^2 \times 10^{-38}}{r} \tag{4}$$

$$U_T = \sum_{t=1}^{n} U_t \tag{5}$$

where K is the Boltzman constant and U_T is the sum of potential energies due to all neighboring electrons. As the electrons attains a position where potential energy is least. We calculate the potential energies of the possible electron positions and select the position with least potential energy. Thus we establish the outputs.

The outputs of the S-R flipflops shown in Fig. 5(a) and (b) have been established in Tables 3 and 4, respectively. As we have established the outputs of the S-R flipflop. We have used it as the basic building blocks for the Gray code counter shown in Fig. 8. The output states of the Gray code counter are established in Table 5.

Table 3. Output state of S-R flipflop as shown in Fig. 5(a)

Cell	Position of electron	Total potential energy	Remarks
1	-	-	Input cell S
2	-	-	Input cell R
8	-	-	Input cell Q_i
3	a	14.102×10^{-20} J	Output Q_{i+1}. Electron latches at
	b	1.368×10^{-20} J	the position b as energy is lesser
4	-	-	The same polarity of cell 3
5–7	-	-	The inverse polarity of cell 4
8	-	-	The inverse polarity of cell 7
9	-	-	The inverse polarity of cell 4

6   Analysis

Stable and maximum area utilization are the major criteria for QCA architectures [7]. If all input signals to the majority voter gates are of same strength and the outputs are obtained simultaneously then the architecture is stable. The architectures in Figs. 5 and 8 satisfy the above conditions, we may conclude that these designs are stable.

Let p nm $\times q$ nm be the dimension of a two-dot one-electron QCA cell. As Fig. 5 requires 9 cells, the covered area is $9\,pq$ nm^2. The covered area by the design is $(4p + 3q) \times 2(p + q)$ nm^2. Hence area utilization has the ratio $9\,pq$: $(4p + 3q) \times 2(p + q)$ is convincing. Also the number of clock zones required is 4.

Table 4. Output state of S-R flipflop as shown in Fig. 5(b)

Cell	Position of electron	Total potential energy	Remarks
1	-	-	Input cell S
2	-	-	Input cell R
8	-	-	Input cell Q_i
3	a	1.368×10^{-20} J	Output Q_{i+1}. Electron latches at
	b	14.102×10^{-20} J	position a as energy is lesser
4	-	-	The same polarity of cell 3
5–7	-	-	The inverse polarity of cell 4
8	-	-	The inverse polarity of cell 7
9	-	-	The inverse polarity of cell 4

Table 5. Output state of Gray code counter

Cell	Position of electron	Total potential energy	Remarks
1	a	14.102×10^{-20} J	Input cell Q_i and output
	b	1.368×10^{-20} J	Q_{i+1} Electron latches at position b
2–3	-	-	Same polarity as cell 1
4–6	-	-	The inverse polarity of cell 3
7–9	-	-	The inverse polarity of cell 2
10	-	-	The inverse polarity of cell 9
11–12	-	-	The inverse polarity of cell 3
3	-	-	The inverse polarity of cell 12
14	-	-	Input cell Reset
15	a	0.294×10^{-20} J	Output Q_{i+1}
	b	6.9056×10^{-20} J	Electron latches at position a
16–17	-	-	The inverse polarity of cell 15
18	a	-1.368×10^{-20} J	Output Q_{i+1}
	b	-14.102×10^{-20} J	Electron latches at position b
19–20	-	-	Same polarity as cell 18
21–23	-	-	The inverse polarity of cell 20
24–26	-	-	Attains the inverse polarity of cell 19
27	-	-	Attains the inverse polarity of cell 26
28–29	-	-	Attains the inverse polarity of cell 20
30–32	-	-	Attains the inverse polarity of cell 29

As Fig. 8 requires 33 cells, the covered area effectively is $33\,pq$ nm^2. The covered area by the design is $(5p + 6q) \times (5p + 6q)$ nm^2. Thus the ratio of area utilization is $33\,pq : (5p + 6q)^2$ is also convincing. Here the number of clock zones required is 8.

7   Energy and Power Requirements

For architectures of S-R flipflop and Gray code counter, the energy and power related parameters from [8] are in Table 6. Here, we have assumed $n = 10$ and $n_2 = 3$.

Table 6. Parameter calculated for the proposed two-dot one-electron QCA S-R flipflop and Gray code counter

Parameters [8]	Value for S-R flipflop	Value for Gray code counter
$E_m = E_{clock}$	3.21187×10^{-19} J	1.17769×10^{-18} J
E_{diss}	3.17975×10^{-19} J	1.16591×10^{-18} J
ν_1	8.81741×10^{14} Hz	3.23305×10^{15} Hz
ν_2	9.59256×10^{14} Hz	3.51727×10^{15} Hz
$(\nu_2 - \nu_1)$	7.75157×10^{13} Hz	2.84224×10^{14} Hz
$\tau_1 = \dfrac{1}{\nu_1}$	5.6706×10^{-16} s	1.54653×10^{-16} s
$\tau_2 = \dfrac{1}{\nu_2}$	5.21237×10^{-16} s	1.42156×10^{-16} s
τ	1.0883×10^{-15} s	2.96808×10^{-16} s
t_p	1.51617×10^{-14} s	1.43702×10^{-14} s

8   Comparative Study

In [5] we find the designs of S-R flipflop and Gray code counter using four-dot two-electron QCA. There are certain advantages of two-dot one -electron QCA over four-dot two-electron QCA. First and foremost is that the number of electrons two-dot one-electron QCA architecture with N cells is N but in case of four-dot two-electron QCA it is $2N$. In four-dot two-electron QCA, there are four ambiguous configurations out of the $^4C_2$ possible configurations [9], only two are valid configurations. But in two-dot one-electron QCA ambiguous situation does not arise. The wiring complexity is reduced in case of two-dot one-electron QCA. In Table 7 we see a comparative study of the designs in [5] with those in this article. From [9], we get $p = 13$ nm and $q = 5$ nm.

Table 7. Comparative study of S-R flipflop and Gray code counter

Parameters	S-R flipflop		Gray code counter	
	In [5]	In this article	in [5]	In this article
Number of cells	66	9	87	33
Area covered	$85140\,\text{nm}^2$	$2412\,\text{nm}^2$	$113844\,\text{nm}^2$	$9025\,\text{nm}^2$
Energy required	High (as there are 132 electrons)	Low (as there are 9 electrons)	High (as there are 174 electrons)	Low (as there are 33 electrons)

9 Conclusion

We have seen how to design a two-bit Gray code counter from two S-R flipflops. We have also analyzed the proposed design and calculated the energy required and the power dissipation for the same. This design may be extended to form three- or higher bit higher Gray code counters.

References

1. Lent, C., Tougaw, P.: A device architecture for computing with quantum dots. Proc. IEEE **85**, 541–557 (1997)
2. Mukhopadhyay, D., Dinda, S., Dutta, P.: Designing and implementation of quantum cellular automata 2:1 multiplexer circuit. Int. J. Comput. Appl. **25**(1), 21–24 (2011)
3. Mukhopadhyay, D., Dutta, P.: Quantum cellular automata based novel unit 2:1 multiplexer. Int. J. Comput. Appl. **3**, 22–25 (2012)
4. Mukhopadhyay, D., Dutta, P.: Quantum cellular automata based novel unit reversible multiplexer. Adv. Sci. Lett. **5**, 163–168 (2012)
5. Huang, J., Momenzadeh, M., Lombardi, F.: Analysis of missing and additional cell defects in sequential quantum-dot cellular automata. Integr. VLSI J. **40**, 503–515 (2007)
6. Blum, K.: Density Matrix Theory and Applications. Springer Series on Atomic, Optical and Plasma Physics. Springer, Heidelberg (2012)
7. Ghosh, M., Mukhopadhyay, D., Dutta, P.: A 2 Dot 1 electron quantum cellular automata based parallel memory. In: Mandal, J.K., Satapathy, S.C., Sanyal, M.K., Sarkar, P.P., Mukhopadhyay, A. (eds.) Information Systems Design and Intelligent Applications. AISC, vol. 339, pp. 627–636. Springer, New Delhi (2015). doi:10.1007/978-81-322-2250-7_63
8. Mukhopadhyay, D., Dutta, P.: A study on energy optimized 4 dot 2 electron two dimensional quantum dot cellular automata logical reversible flipops. Microelectron. J. **46**, 519–530 (2015). Elsevier
9. Iv, L.R.H., Lee, S.C.: Design and Simulation of 2-d 2-dot quantum-dot cellular automata logic. IEEE Trans. Nanotechnol. **10**(5), 996–1003 (2011)

A Study on Structural Benefits of Square Cells over Rectangular Cells in Case of 2Dot 1Electron QCA Cells

Mili Ghosh[1]([✉]), Debarka Mukhopadhyay[2], and Paramartha Dutta[1]

[1] Department of Computer and System Sciences, Visva Bharati University,
Santiniketan 731235, India
ghosh.mili90@gmail.com, paramartha.dutta@gmail.com
[2] Department of Computer Science, Amity School of Engineering and Technology,
Amity University, Kolkata 700156, India
debarka.mukhopadhyay@gmail.com

Abstract. Quantum-dot Cellular Automata i.e. QCA is emerged as a product of immense study made by researchers to find out an efficient replacement of CMOS technology in nanoscale. Nanoscale alternatives arise due to the fact that CMOS is near to face serious challenges due to the scaling limitation of this technology. The nanoscale implementation of CMOS also suffers from high power dissipation. In this present article, a study has been carried out over the structural advantages of square shaped 2Dot 1Electron QCA cells over the rectangular shaped cell. As an case study, a design strategy of a half subtractor as well as a full subtractor has been proposed using 2Dot 1Electron QCA and an analysis has been carried out with respect to the cell structure. The design of the half subtractor consists of only 25 many number of 2Dot 1Electron QCA cells. On the other hand, the full subtractor design contains 40 many number of cells. Using this design approach, we have achieved upto 67% and 65% of efficiency with respect to the cell count over the existing half and full subtractor implementation using 4-dot 2 electron QCA respectively. No such study has been carried out in this domain till date.

Keywords: 2Dot 1Electron QCA · Square shape cell · Subtractor · MV Gate · Clock signal energy · Stability · Robustness

1 Introduction

Predictions through studies [1] has been made towards the limitations of the ruling CMOS technology in nano-scale applications. The challenges get to be increased day by day due to the recent advancements of nanotechnology such as the necessity of high device density with low energy dissipation. These sort of requirements brought up severe challenges to the CMOS technology. Thus research community felt an urge for alternate technology which can surpass the limitations of CMOS technology and can cope up with the first pace development of the nano-scale technology. QCA came out to be the most befitting

© Springer Nature Singapore Pte Ltd. 2017
J.K. Mandal et al. (Eds.): CICBA 2017, Part II, CCIS 776, pp. 85–96, 2017.
DOI: 10.1007/978-981-10-6430-2_8

alternative to the CMOS technology in nanoscale. It simplifies the complexity of interconnection of CMOS. QCA also solves the energy and other limiting issues of CMOS in nanoscale. 2Dot 1Electron QCA is an emerging cellular variant of QCA. There are specific advantages compared to its 4Dot 2Electron variant [5]. The inter cell communication is achieved using the cell to cell interaction according to the Coulomb's principle. QCA also solves the energy and other limiting issues of CMOS in nanoscale. 2Dot 1Electron QCA is an emerging cellular variant of QCA. It possesses some proven benefits over the existing and well studied variant i.e. 4Dot 2Electron cellular QCA as mentioned in [5]. The inter cell communication is achieved using the cell to cell interaction according to the Coulomb's principle. In this present article, a study has been made to check the impact of cell structure on different design parameters of 2Dot 1Electron QCA structures. For this purpose analytical study has been carried out on subtractors. In the present scope we offer yet unexplored designs of half subtractor and full subtractor using 2Dot 1Electron QCA. The proposed designs are also analyzed with respect to some well established energy parameters to understand the energy efficiency of the proposed designs in a better way. Later the stability and the robustness of the presented designs are also discussed. Remaining part of this article is arranged in the following manner. Section 2 presents a brief study of the previous reportings in the domain of subtractors. We elaborate the operational details of 2Dot 1Electron QCA in section in Sect. 3. Whereas in Subsect. 3.1 the QCA clocking mechanism is discussed in detail. Section 4, explains the basics of subtractor. Our proposed work is then illustrated in Sect. 5. The output state is then evaluated in Sect. 6. The analysis of the proposed designs are then carried out in the Sect. 8. The conclusion is then made in the Sect. 10.

2   Literature Survey

The field of subtractor design has been well exploited in the purview of 4Dot 2Electron cellular variant QCA such as [8,10]. The field is yet to be explored using 2Dot 1Electron QCA. In [10], design of half subtractor as well as full subtractor was reported. The half subtractor consists of four majority voter gates and two inverters. The half subtractor implementation required 77 numbers of 4Dot 2Electron QCA cells. The half subtractor has 3 clock zone delays. The full subtractor design in [10] requires three majority voter(mv) gates and two inverters. The full subtractor had been implemented using 178 number of 4Dot 2Electron QCA cells. The full subtracor has 8 clock zone delays. The 1-bit full subtractor design in [8] requires four mv gates and three inverters. This full adder circuit consists of 4 clock zone delays. There are some more reportings as done in [2,3]. In [3] a new design methodology of XOR gate was proposed which is further used to develop half and full subtractor. The half subtractor design in [3] consists of 55 number of cells and has 3 clock zone delays whereas the full subtractor design consists of 136 number of cells and 7 clock zone delays. In [2] a reversible feynman gate was designed using 4Dot 2Electron QCA. The feynman gate was then used to develop a half subtractor. The half subtractor in [2] consists of 114 number of cells and has 3 clock zone delays.

3   Rudimentaries of 2Dot 1Electron QCA

Like any other variant of QCA, 2Dot 1Electron QCA is based on the concept of quantum dots and electrons. The structural unit of any QCA architecture. In a 2Dot 1Electron QCA rectangular cell, a single electron on being energized, may move from one dot to the other [5,7,9]. Thus the cells have two different alignments, horizontal and vertical. In QCA cells the binary data is depicted with the help of electron position within the quantum dots. So, 2Dot 1Electron QCA has different polarity representations for different alignments as shown in the Fig. 1. As presented in [9], 2Dot 1Electron QCA works on a few building blocks such as planar crossing of wires, binary wire, majority voter gate, inverter which are shown in Figs. 1g, c, f, d respectively.

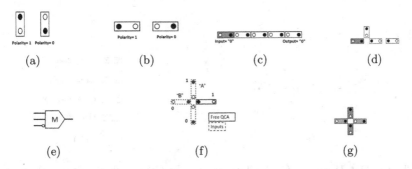

Fig. 1. Binary Encoding in 2Dot 1Electron QCA when (a) cells placed vertically and (b) cells placed horizontally and (c) 2Dot 1Electron QCA binary-wire and (d) Inversion by placing oppositely aligned cell and (e) MV Gate schematic diagram and (f) QCA cell Implementation and (g) Planar crossing of wires

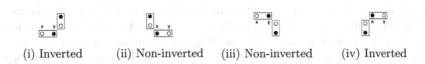

(i) Inverted   (ii) Non-inverted   (iii) Non-inverted   (iv) Inverted

Fig. 2. Data inversion by turning cells in proper direction

3.1   Clocking Mechanism

Clocking mechanisms for 2Dot 1Electron and for 4Dot 2Electron QCA are similar and quite different from CMOS clocking primarily used for synchronization. QCA clocking is used as an controller of the entire QCA architecture as it provides energy to weak input signals and helps to determine the data flow direction

[12]. QCA clocking incorporates four clock zones and each of which comprises of four clock phases: **switch, hold, release and relax**. With the initialization of the **switch** phase, the electrons starts to energize. Till the very end of the **switch** phase electron attains its maximum energy. The cell will lose its polarity at this stage. Maximum potential energy of the electron is retained during **hold** phase. With the beginning of the **release** phase the electron starts to lose its energy and the electrons starts to localize at the other quantum dot. Eventually the electron attains its polarity at the end of **release** phase followed by the begining of subsequent **relax** phase. Actual computation is done at this point. At the relax phase, the cell maintains its polarity. Each clock zone comprises of the aforesaid four clock phases. Each of these four clock zones are $\frac{\pi}{2}$ out of phase with its previous one as shown in the Fig. 3a. The color scheme we have used to represent different clock zones through out this paper is shown in the Fig. 3b.

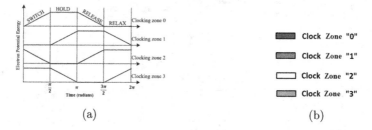

(a)   (b)

Fig. 3. (a) 2Dot 1Electron QCA Clocking and (b) Color code of various clock zones (Color figure online)

4   Subtractor

Subtractor serves the purpose of subtraction operation. Subtractor is a combinational architecture. Subtractor take two binary bits as inputs and provides two outputs which are difference and borrow. Like adder there are two kinds of subtractors, half subtractor and full subtractor. Half subtractor can perform subtraction of two bits at a time. The logic diagram of the half subtractor is shown in the Fig. 4a. The schematic diagram of the half adder using QCA majority voter logic as suggested in [10] is shown in the Fig. 4b. The logic functions of the half subtractor for the outputs difference and borrow is shown in Eqs. 1 and 2. The 2Dot 1Electron QCA implementation of the half subtractor in Fig. 6.

$$\text{Difference} = A \oplus B \tag{1}$$
$$\text{Borrow} = AB' \tag{2}$$

Similarly the full subtractor can be constructed. The schematic diagram of the full adder using QCA majority voter logic as suggested in [10] is shown in the Fig. 5. Figure 7 indicates the 2Dot 1Electron QCA implementation of the half subtractor.

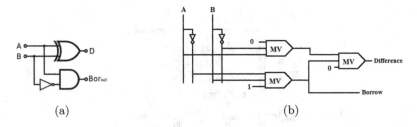

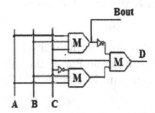

(a)   (b)

Fig. 4. (a) Logic diagram of half subtractor and (b) Schematic diagram of Half subtractor

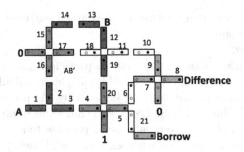

Fig. 5. Schematic diagram of full subtractor

5   Proposed Work

As we can see in the schematic diagram shown in Fig. 4b, the half subtractor consists of 3 majority voter gates and two inverters. The three majority voter gates built a Ex-OR gate as suggested in [6]. The Borrow output is obtained from the majority voter gate which produces $A'B$ as output. The half subtractor has been implemented using 4Dot 2Electron QCA in [10]. As stated in [5], 2Dot 1Electron QCA is advantageous over the 4Dot 2Electron QCA. In this article we have implemented the half subtractor using 2Dot 1Electron QCA as presented in the Fig. 6. The half subtractor component consists of 25 many 2Dot 1Electron QCA. The entire circuit has a delay of 4 clock zones as shown in the Fig. 6.

Fig. 6. Design of half subtractor

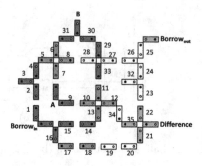

Fig. 7. Design of full subtractor

The full subtractor has also been implemented using 2Dot 1Electron QCA as shown in the Fig. 7. As shown in the Fig. 7, the full subtractor consists of 40 many 2Dot 1Electron QCA cells and it also has a delay of 4 clock zones.

6   Determination of Output States

There is no reported availability of any simulation software for 2Dot 1Electron QCA as yet. So, we have to justify the correctness of our proposed circuits using some well established principle. In the present purview, we are going to justify our proposed work using Coulomb's principle. The mathematical formulations based on coulomb's principle are shown in Eqs. 3 and 5. The potential energy calculations between two point charges are evaluated using the equations suggested in [5,11].

$$U = Kq_1q_2/r \tag{3}$$

$$Kq_1q_2 = 9 \times 10^9 \times (1.6)^2 \times 10^{-38} \tag{4}$$

$$U_T = \sum_{t=1}^{n} U_t \tag{5}$$

where
U : Potential energy persisting between two charged particles.
K : Boltzman's constant.
q_1, q_2 : Point charges.
r : Euclidean separation between the charged particles.
U_T: Potential energy due to the effect of all its neighbors calculated using Eq. 5. Quantum dots maintain positive charge induced by the presence of negatively charged electrons in 2Dot 1Electron QCA. Electron tends to align at the farthest position from another electron and as close as possible to a quantum dot. Electrons try to achieve a dot-position with least potential energy. Thus we have to calculate the potential energy of an electron at each possible position (for 2Dot 1Electron QCA cell only two possible positions) and the position which gives the minimum potential energy electron will attain that position. The size of a 2Dot 1Electron QCA cell is 13 nm × 5 nm and the distance between two likely oriented adjacent cells is 5 nm [9]. During the potential energy calculations we

mark the left quantum dot as x and the right quantum dot as y in horizontally aligned 2Dot 1Electron QCA cell. Similarly for vertical cells the upper quantum dots are marked as x and the lower quantum dot is marked as y. For clear understanding of potential energy calculations we have marked the cells with numbers as we can see the numbered half subtractor layout in Fig. 6 and the numbered full subtractor layout in Fig. 7. The potential energy calculations regarding the half subtractor is shown in Fig. 6 is presented in Table 1 and the potential energy calculations regarding the full subtractor shown in Fig. 7 is presented in Table 2.

Table 1. Output state of half subtractor

Cell	Electron position	Total potential energy	Comments
2	-	-	Achieves the inverted polarity of input cell A due to cell placement shown in Fig. 2(i)
3	-	-	Achieves the inverted polarity of cell A
16	-	-	Achieves the polarity of cell 2
17	x	$3.33 \times 10^{-20} J$	Electron will latch at dot-position y due to less energy
17	y	$0.54 \times 10^{-20} J$	
4	-	-	Achieves the polarity of cell 3
12, 13	-	-	Achieves the input polarity B
14, 19, 20	-	-	Achieves the input polarity B
5	x	$3.33 \times 10^{-20} J$	Electron will latch at dot-position y due to less energy
5	y	$0.54 \times 10^{-20} J$	
15	-	-	Achieves the inverted polarity of cell 14 due to cell placement shown in Fig. 2(iv)
18, 11, 10	-	-	Achieves the polarity of cell 17
9	-	-	Achieves the polarity of cell 10 due to cell placement shown in Fig. 2(iii)
6	-	-	Achieves the inverted polarity of cell 5 due to cell placement shown in Fig. 2(i)
21	-	-	Achieves the polarity of cell 5 due to cell placement shown in Fig. 2(iii)
7	-	-	Achieves the inverted polarity of cell 6 due to cell placement shown in Fig. 2(iv)
8	x	$3.33 \times 10^{-20} J$	Electron will latch at dot-position y due to less energy
8	y	$0.54 \times 10^{-20} J$	

Table 2. Output state of full subtractor

Cell	Electron position	Total potential energy	Comments
1, 2	-	-	Achieves the polarity of cell input $Borrow_{in}$ due to cell placement shown in Fig. 2(ii)
3	-	-	Achieves the polarity of cell 2 due to cell placement shown in Fig. 2(iii)
4	-	-	Achieves the inverted polarity of cell 3 due to cell placement shown in Fig. 2(i)
5	-	-	Achieves the inverted polarity of cell 4 due to cell placement shown in Fig. 2(iv)
31	-	-	Achieves the inverted polarity of cell B due to cell placement shown in Fig. 2(i)
6	-	-	Achieves the inverted polarity of cell 31 due to cell placement shown in Fig. 2(iv)
7	-	-	Achieves the inverted polarity of cell A due to cell placement shown in Fig. 2(iv)
9, 10	-	-	Achieves the polarity of cell A due to cell placement shown in Fig. 2(ii)
8	x	$6.75 \times 10^{-20} J$	Electron will latch at dot-position y due to less energy
8	y	$0.3 \times 10^{-20} J$	
28, 27, 26	-	-	Achieves the inverse polarity of cell 8
30	-	-	Achieves the polarity of cell 3 according to corner placement shown in Fig. 2(ii)
29, 33, 11	-	-	Achieves the polarity of cell 30 due to cell placement shown in Fig. 2(iii)
16	-	-	Achieves the polarity of cell $Borrow_{in}$ due to cell placement shown in Fig. 2(iii)
15, 14	-	-	Achieves the inverted polarity of cell 16 due to cell placement shown in Fig. 2(iv)
13	-	-	Achieves the inverted polarity of cell 14 due to cell placement shown in Fig. 2(i)
12	x	$6.75 \times 10^{-20} J$	Electron will latch at dot-position y due to less energy
12	y	$0.3 \times 10^{-20} J$	
34	-	-	Achieves the polarity 12 due to cell placement shown in Fig. 2(iii)
35	-	-	Achieves the polarity 34 due to cell placement shown in Fig. 2(ii)
25	-	-	Achieves the inverted polarity 26 due to cell placement shown in Fig. 2(i)

(*continued*)

Table 2. (*continued*)

Cell	Electron position	Total potential energy	Comments
Borrow$_{out}$	-	-	Achieves the inverted polarity 25 due to cell placement shown in Fig. 2(iv)
24	-	-	Achieves the polarity 26 due to cell placement shown in Fig. 2(iii)
32	-	-	Achieves the inverted polarity 24 due to cell placement shown in Fig. 2(i)
23, 22	-	-	Achieves the polarity 32 due to cell placement shown in Fig. 2(iii)
17, 18	-	-	Achieves the polarity 16 due to cell placement shown in Fig. 2(ii)
19, 20	-	-	Achieves the polarity 18
21	-	-	Achieves the inverse polarity 20 due to cell placement shown in Fig. 2(i)
Difference	x	$-13.41 \times 10^{-20} J$	Electron will latch at dot-position x due to less energy
Difference	y	$-1.38 \times 10^{-20} J$	

7   Compactness Analysis with Respect to Cell Shape

In this present article we have carried out a comparative study with respect to cell shape. We considered two probable cell shapes i.e. rectangular cell and square cell. We have shown the computations in Table 3 where the rectangular cell size is taken as 13 nm × 5 nm [5].

Table 3. Compactness of different designs due to different cell shapes

Designs	Rectangular cell	Square cell
Binary wire(With 4 cells)	59.77%	57.14%
Inverter	60.93%	50%
Inverter at turns	40.12%	50%
Fan-out	33.82%	33.33%
Majority voter gate	27.05%	44.44%
Half subtractor	20.48%	25.25%
Full subtractor	19.89%	25.64%

8   Analysis of the Proposed Designs

The article presents the designs of half subtractor and full subtractor using 2Dot 1Electron QCA. In this section we are going to analyze our proposed designs using different energy parameters, stability issues and robustness to justify the novelty of the designs. Instead of these analysis, 2Dot 1Electron QCA is beneficiary over the 4Dot 2Electron QCA from structural aspects [5]. Thus the proposed designs are better than those reported in the purview of 4Dot 2Electron QCA.

8.1   Energy Analysis

The energy related parameters which are going to be used to analyze the proposed designs are presented in [4]. These parameters are developed to analyze 4Dot 2Electron QCA but are applicable to any structural variant of QCA. The parameters we are going to use are namely E_{clock}, the minimum clock signal energy to be supplied to the QCA architecture; E_{diss} the dissipated energy from the architecture; v_1, the frequency of incident energy; v_2, the frequency of energy dissipation; τ_1, required time move from quantum level n to quantum level n_1; τ_2, required time to dissipate energy into the environment; τ, the switching time; t_p, propagation time through the architecture and $v_2 - v_1$ is the differential frequency. One vital parameter to judge the acceptability of any QCA architecture as suggested in [4] is EI (Efficiency Index) which is calculated using Eq. 6.

$$EI = 1 - \frac{E_{diss}}{E_{ev} + E_{clock}} \tag{6}$$

where E_{ev} is the input signal energy. EI calculates the ratio of dissipated energy over the applied energy to the architecture. This instead judge the energy efficiency of any QCA architecture. The energy parameters have been evaluated for the proposed designs and are shown in Table 4. For all the energy related calculations we have taken the electron quantum number i.e. n to be 11 and the intermediate electron quantum number i.e. n_1 to be 2 as the difference between quantum number and intermediate quantum number must be an odd number.

The energy requirement in case of the half and full subtractor implementation using 4Dot 2Electron QCA is higher than the proposed subtractors using 2Dot 1Electron QCA. The number of cells required has been reduced to a great extent in case of the proposed 2Dot 1Electron QCA implementations. Thus energy required to drive the proposed circuits in 2Dot 1Electron is much lesser than the existing ones in 4Dot 2Electron QCA.

9   Comparison with 4Dot 2Electron QCA Counter Part

In this section, we will compare the existing 4Dot 2Electron QCA subtractors with the proposed 2Dot 1Electron QCA subtractors. The comparison has been made with respect to number of cells in the architecture and the number of clock zones required to propagate the signal from input end to the output end (Table 5).

Table 4. Different Energy parameters of Subtractor

Parameters	Half subtractor	Full subtractor
$E_{clock} = \dfrac{n^2 \pi^2 \hbar^2 N}{ma^2}$	$8.919844244 \times 10^{-19}$	$1.427175079 \times 10^{-18}$
$E_{diss} = \dfrac{\pi^2 \hbar^2}{ma^2}(n^2 - 1)N$	$8.830645802 \times 10^{-19}$	$1.412903328 \times 10^{-18}$
$v_1 = \dfrac{\pi \hbar}{ma^2}(n^2 - n_1^2)N$	$1.245290748 \times 10^{15}$	$1.992465197 \times 10^{15}$
$v_2 = \dfrac{\pi \hbar}{ma^2}(n^2 - 1)N$	$1.291802664 \times 10^{15}$	$2.066884262 \times 10^{15}$
$v_2 - v_1 = \dfrac{\pi \hbar}{ma^2}(n_1^2 - 1)N$	4.6511916×10^{13}	$7.441906532 \times 10^{13}$
$\tau_1 = \dfrac{1}{v_1}$	$2.537365138 \times 10^{-16}$	$4.059784221 \times 10^{-16}$
$\tau_2 = \dfrac{1}{v_2}$	$2.6166578 \times 10^{-16}$	$4.18665248 \times 10^{-16}$
$\tau = \tau_1 + \tau_2$	$5.154022938 \times 10^{-16}$	$8.232630902 \times 10^{-16}$
$t_p = \tau + (k - 1)\tau_2 N$	$2.014033579 \times 10^{-14}$	$5.106309285 \times 10^{-14}$

Table 5. Comparison of existing Subtractor design in 4 Dot QCA with the proposed design in 2Dot 1Electron QCA

Parameters	Existing designs in [10]		Proposed designs	
	Half subtractor	Full subtractor	Half subtractor	Full subtractor
Number of cells	77	114	25	40
Delay (Clock Zones used)	4	4	4	4

10   Conclusion and Future Scope

In this article, design methodology of half subtractor along with full subtractor using 2Dot 1Electron QCA. The reported designs are justified using potential energy calculations to judge the correctness of the designs. Finally the designs are analyzed to estimate their energy efficiency. Then the stability and robustness aspects of the proposed designs are discussed to analyze their acceptability.

References

1. International Technology Roadmap for Semiconductor (ITRS). http://www.itrs.net
2. Akter, R., Jahan, N., Shanta, M.M.R., Barua, A.: A novel design of half subtractor using reversible feynman gate in quantum dot cellular automata. Am. J. Eng. Res. **3**, 87–92 (2014)
3. Akter, R., Jahan, N., Shanta, M.M.R., Barua, A.: Novel subtractor design based on quantum dot cellular automata (QCA) nanotechnology. Int. J. Nanosci. Nanotechnol. **11**(4), 257–262 (2015)
4. Dutta, P., Mukhopadhyay, D.: A study on energy optimized 4 Dot 2 Electron two dimensional quantum dot cellular automata logical reversible flip-flops. Microelectron. J. **46**, 519–530 (2015). Elsevier

5. Ghosh, M., Mukhopadhyay, D., Dutta, P.: A 2 Dot 1 Electron quantum cellular automata based parallel memory. In: Mandal, J.K., Satapathy, S.C., Sanyal, M.K., Sarkar, P.P., Mukhopadhyay, A. (eds.) Information Systems Design and Intelligent Applications. AISC, vol. 339, pp. 627–636. Springer, New Delhi (2015). doi:10.1007/978-81-322-2250-7_63

6. Ghosh, M., Mukhopadhyay, D., Dutta, P.: Design and analysis of two dot one electron qca ex-or gate in logically reversible gate design. In: 2015 IEEE International Conference on International Symposium on Advanced Computing and Communication (ISAAC), September 2015

7. Ghosh, M., Mukhopadhyay, D., Dutta, P.: A novel parallel memory design using 2 dot 1 electron qca. In: 2015 IEEE 2nd International Conference on Recent Trends in Information Systems (ReTIS), pp. 485–490, July 2015

8. Hayati, M., Rezaei, A.: Design of novel efficient adder and subtractor for quantum-dot cellular automata. Int. J. Circ. Theory Appl. 43, 1446–1454 (2014)

9. Hook IV, L.R., Lee, S.C.: Design and simulation of 2-d 2-dot quantum-dot cellular automata logic. IEEE Trans. Nanotechnol. 10(5), 996–1003 (2011)

10. Iakshmi, S., Athisha, G., Karthikeyan, M., Ganesh, C.: Design of subtractor using nanotechnology based qca. In: 2010 IEEE International Conference on Communication Control and Computing Technologies (ICCCCT), pp. 384–388, October 2010

11. Mukhopadhyay, D., Dutta, P.: Qca based novel unit reversible multiplexer. Adv. Sci. Lett. 16(1), 163–168 (2012)

12. Mukhopadhyay, D., Dutta, P.: Quantum cellular automata based novel unit 2: 1 multiplexer. Int. J. Comput. Appl. 43(2), 22–25 (2012)

A Flower Pollination Algorithm Based Task Scheduling in Cloud Computing

Indrajeet Gupta[✉], Amar Kaswan, and Prasanta K. Jana

Department of Computer Science and Engineering,
Indian Institute of Technology (ISM), Dhanbad, India
indrajeet7830@gmail.com, amarkaswan@gmail.com, prasantajana@yahoo.com
http://www.iitism.ac.in

Abstract. Flower pollination algorithm (FPA) is a nature inspired fascinating meta-heuristic technique, which is applicable to many real life optimization problems. Mapping of tasks on the virtual machines in cloud computing environment is a well known NP-complete problem. This paper propose a novel FPA-based algorithm to schedule the tasks on the virtual machines to minimize makespan and maximize cloud resource utilization. The proposed scheme uses an efficient pollen representation scheme and a novel multi-objective fitness function. We simulate the proposed scheme on one synthetic and two benchmark datasets of diverse configuration. The performance of the proposed scheme is compared with three other meta-heuristic based approaches, namely particle swarm optimization (PSO), genetic algorithm (GA) and gravitational search algorithm (GSA). The superiority of the proposed algorithm over other algorithms is exhibited by the simulation results.

Keywords: Flower pollination algorithm · Cloud computing · Task scheduling · Cloud utilization · Makespan

1 Introduction

Scheduling of tasks in cloud computing is a well studied problem which is NP-complete in nature. Therefore, several heuristics and meta-heuristics approaches have been proposed to address this problem that deal with independent or dependent tasks. This article describes the scheduling of independent tasks on the virtual resources and present a novel algorithm which is based on an efficient meta-heuristics approach, called flower pollination algorithm (FPA) [1]. It is noteworthy that there exist m^n possible schedules for n tasks to be mapped on m VMs. Therefore, the computational complexity to generate an optimal task-VM mapping by a brute force approach would be exponential. This also consumes huge space. Thus, a nature-inspired approach such as flower pollination algorithm (FPA) [1] can be very effective to generate a near optimal solution for the aforesaid task scheduling problem in cloud environment. Note that the FPA can produce better solution than other meta-heuristic approaches such as GA, PSO and has the highest convergence rate among them [1].

© Springer Nature Singapore Pte Ltd. 2017
J.K. Mandal et al. (Eds.): CICBA 2017, Part II, CCIS 776, pp. 97–107, 2017.
DOI: 10.1007/978-981-10-6430-2_9

The key goal of the proposed scheme is to map the tasks of a given application on the active virtual machines such that the overall application processing time namely makespan(M) is minimized and the average cloud resource utilization ($Avg.U_c$) is maximized. The proposed scheme is presented with the employed pollen representation scheme. A novel multi-objective fitness function is also derived by considering the aforesaid objectives which contradict each other. We perform rigorous experiments to compute the results of the proposed scheme using one synthetic dataset and two benchmark datasets instances. The performance results are compared with three other meta-heuristic based scheme i.e., PSO, GA and GSA. The simulated results demonstrate its superiority in terms of makespan and average cloud utilization.

Many researches have been carried out in recent years to address the task scheduling problem in [2–12,16,19,20]. Panda et al. [8] have proposed both online and off-line task scheduling algorithm to schedule the independent tasks for cloud environment. The proposed algorithms of task scheduling are shown to perform better than the cloud list scheduling (CLS) [17], Round Robin (RR) and Min-Min task scheduling algorithms [18]. In [16], the authors have used the linear programming to solve the problem of preemptive task scheduling in cloud computing. In [7], a two phase genetic algorithm with multi-parent crossover is suggested to minimize both makespan and energy consumption. However, they have not considered average cloud utilization. In [6], an improved genetic algorithm (IGA) is proposed, in which the virtual machines are selected on the basis of dividend policy. The performance of their algorithm is shown to outperform [7]. In [4], the authors have developed a PSO based algorithm for static task scheduling problem in a homogeneous cloud environment which supersedes the GA based approach. A multi-objective differential evolution (MODE) scheme is proposed in [2], as a solution to the task scheduling problem. In [5], the authors have addressed the problem of task scheduling in a grid environment and proposed a PSO based scheme to generate the task-VM mapping. The proposed algorithm is shown to produce the best solution for the task scheduling problem. Our proposed algorithm in this paper, is a novel approach in the sense that we are the first researchers to exploit the features of the meta-heuristic FPA to develop an efficient task scheduling algorithm for cloud computing. Further, there is novelty in the pollen representation and derivation of an efficient fitness function based on the two important objectives for task scheduling.

The remainder of the paper is systematized as follows. Section 2 describes the models and terminologies used in the proposed algorithm. The proposed algorithm is explained in Sect. 3. The simulation results are displayed in Sect. 4 followed by the conclusion in Sect. 5.

2   Preliminaries

2.1   Cloud and Task Model

Let us consider a cloud user's request which is expressed in the form of an application A consisting of a set of n tasks such that $A=\{T_1, T_2, \cdots, T_n\}$. The user submits his application to a cloud service provider (CSP) for the needful operations (i.e., computing, communication and storage). The CSP provides all the requested services to the users by negotiating a service level agreement (SLA).

Table 1. Notations used

Notations	Descriptions
n	Number of tasks in a application A
m	Number of active VMs
I_i	Size of the task T_i in million instructions
M_VM_i	Makespan of the ith virtual machine
PS_i	Processing speed of the ith virtual machine
$max(A)$	Return the maximum value form a set A
$Switch\_prob$	Switching probability of FPA

Consider an IaaS cloud model similar to the Amazon EC2, where m heterogeneous virtual machines (VMs) are deployed on a cloud. Each VM has different computing capability. Therefore, all VMs are able to execute the tasks of the given application. The key components of the assumed cloud model are as follows.

1. **Cloud user:** This is the end user of cloud resources. The cloud users initiate the various cloud service requests to execute their applications. These requests are submitted to the cloud scheduler via cloud service provider (CSP).
2. **Cloud scheduler:** Cloud scheduler is the recipient of the cloud users' service requests. The core responsibility of the cloud scheduler is to maintain status of all VMs and assign the tasks over the virtual machines so that the user's requirement is fulfilled.
3. **Cloud service provider (CSP):** The cloud service provider acts as an intermediary between the cloud users and the cloud scheduler. The CSP contains the resource pool of the active VMs. The user's application is executed on the active VMs as per the decided task scheduling algorithm.

2.2 Notations and Terminologies

Now, we define various terminologies used to derive the fitness function and analyze the simulation results as follows. The notations are shown in the Table 1 with their description.

1. **Processing speed** (PS): This is the processing speed of each VM say, VM_j which is measured in million instructions per second (MIPS) and denoted by PS_j.

2. **Execution time of a task** (ET_{ij}): Consider an application consisting of n tasks $\{T_1, T_2, T_3, \cdots, T_n\}$, where the size (I_i) of every task T_i is measured in million instructions (MIs). Therefore, the execution time of task T_i on virtual machine VM_j can be mathematically expressed as follows.

$$ET_{ij} = \frac{I_j}{PS_j} \tag{1}$$

3. **Makespan** (M): Let M_VM_i denote the makespan of the ith virtual machine, where $1 \leq i \leq m$. Then, we can mathematically express the overall makespan as follows.

$$M = max\{M\_VM_i \mid 1 \leq i \leq m\} \tag{2}$$

4. **Average makespan** $(Avg.M\_VM)$: It is the mean of the makespan of all the VMs. In other words,

$$Avg.M\_VM = \frac{\sum_{j=1}^{m} M\_VM_j}{m} \tag{3}$$

5. **Standard deviation of VM's makespan** $(Sd.M\_VM)$: It is the standard deviation of virtual machines' makespan. Hence,

$$Sd.M\_VM = \sqrt{\frac{\sum_{i=1}^{m}(Avg.M\_VM - M\_VM_i)^2}{m}} \tag{4}$$

6. **Average cloud utilization** $(Avg.U_c)$: It is the ratio of the average makespan $(Avg.M\_VM)$ and the overall makespan (M). Therefore,

$$Avg.U_c = \frac{Avg.M\_VM}{M} \tag{5}$$

2.3   Problem Definition

We address the following problem in this paper. Given an application with a set of n independent tasks, $A = \{T_1, T_2, T_3, \cdots, T_n\}$ and given a set of m virtual machines $C = \{VM_1, VM_2, VM_3, \cdots, VM_m\}$, the problem is to determine the task-VM mapping with the following objectives:

- Objective 1: The overall makespan (M) is minimized.
- Objective 2: The average cloud utilization $(Avg.U_c)$ is maximized.

3   Proposed Work

In this section, we present a FPA-based scheme to address the problem defined in Sect. 2.3. We first show the pollen representation scheme used in the proposed algorithm. We then design an efficient multi-objective fitness function to incorporate in the proposed algorithm.

3.1 Pollen Representation

Each pollen (P) is represented by an n-dimensional vector, where each element (say $p_{ij} \mid 1 \leq i, j \leq n$) has a random value in the range $(0, 1)$ i.e., $0 < p_{ij} < 1$. The employed mapping function is given by Eq. 6.

$$T\_VM_{ij} = floor(p_{ij} \times m) + 1 \mid 1 \leq i \leq p\_size \text{ and } 1 \leq j \leq n \qquad (6)$$

where, m denotes the total number of VMs, p_size denotes population size and n denotes the total number of tasks. This pollen representation is analogous to [15]. It is noteworthy that each pollen is able to produce entire solution for the task scheduling problem. To demonstrate this, we consider a hypothetical could-resource model where $n = 8$ and $m = 3$. The process of task-VM mapping is exhibited by considering a sample pollen as shown in Fig. 1.

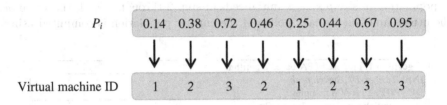

Fig. 1. Retrieval of task-VM mapping from a pollen

In Fig. 1, we can observe that the first task is mapped on virtual machine 1 since the value of p_{i1} is 0.14 and therefore, $floor(0.14 \times 3) + 1 = 1$. Remaining tasks are also mapped on the VMs following similar procedure. For instances, the tasks T_2 and T_3 are mapped onto VM_2 and VM_3 respectively using same formula given in Eq. 6.

3.2 Fitness Function

We consider two contradictory objectives to derive an efficient multi-objective fitness function for problem of independent task scheduling in cloud computing. The first objective is to minimize the makespan. The makespan can be minimized, if the standard deviation of makespan of all the VMs is minimized i.e., lower the value of $Sd.M\_VM$, lower will be the makespan. Therefore,

$$\text{Objective 1: Minimize } Sd.M\_VM \qquad (7)$$

Our second objective is to maximize the average cloud utilization. Therefore,

$$\text{Objective 2: Maximize} = Avg.U_c \qquad (8)$$

We combine both above-mentioned objectives into a single-objective for minimization problem by employing the weighted sum approach where the value of the first objective is multiplied with a weight value C_1 and reciprocal of the second objective is multiplied by C_2. Thus,

$$\text{Objective: Minimize}(C_1 \times Avg.M\_VM + \frac{C_2}{Avg.U_C}) \qquad (9)$$

We choose this is as the single objective fitness function in our proposed algorithm. In other words,

$$Fit = C_1 \times Avg.M\_VM + \frac{C_2}{Avg.U_C} \qquad (10)$$

3.3 FPA-based Task Scheduling Algorithm

The pseudo code of the proposed FPA-based algorithm is given in Fig. 2. In step 1, population of size p_size is initialized. In step 2 through step 4, the value of the fitness function for each pollen of the current population is computed using

---

Algorithm 1: Proposed FPA-based algorithm

INPUT: n, m, ET, $Switch.prob$

OUTPUT: Task-VM mapping

1. Initialize pollen P_k, $1 \le k \le P.size$
2. **for** $k = 1$ to m **do**
3. Fit_k = Compute the value of fitness function of jth pollen using Eq. 10
4. **end for**
5. Initialize $Best.fit = Init\_max$
6. Initialize $Best.pol = \emptyset$
7. **for** k = 1 to m **do**
8.   if $Best.fit > Fit_k$ **then**
9. $Best.fit = P_k$
10.   **end if**
11. **end for**
12. **for** $k = 1$ to m do
13.   **for** $k = 1$ to m **do**
14. $temp = rand(0, 1)$
15.   **if** $temp > Switch.prob$ **then**
16.   Draw a n – dimensional step L following a Levy distribution
17.   Apply global pollination using $P_{k+1} = P_k + L(Best.fit - P_k)$
18.   **else**
19.   Draw ε following a Uniform distribution
20.   Arbitrarily opt i and j among available solutions
21.   Apply local pollination using $P_k + 1 = P_k + \varepsilon(Pi - Pj)$
22.   **end if**
23.   Compute novel pollen
24.   **if** novel pollen is superior than current pollen **then** update the current pollen
25.   Identify new $Best.pol$
26.   **end if**
27.   **end for**
28. **end for**

Fig. 2. Proposed FPA-based task scheduling algorithm

Eq. 10. In step 5 and step 6, the fitness value of the best pollen is initialized to maximum value of the integer and the best pollen is initialized as an empty set respectively. In step 7 through step 11, the best pollen from the initial population is identified and stored as *Best_pol*. In step 12 through step 27, at each iteration for every pollen, a random number between 0 and 1 is generated and if the generated value is greater than the *Switch_prob* than the global pollination is applied to the pollen using Levy distribution, otherwise the local pollination is applied using uniform distribution [1].

The proposed algorithm FPA is tested through extensive simulations which were carried out on an Intel Core 2 Duo processor, 2.20 GHz CPU with 4 GB RAM running on Microsoft Windows 7 platform by using MATLAB R2012a version 7.14.0.739. We evaluate the performance for the simulation results on one synthetic dataset of 6 instances and two benchmark datasets of 12 instances. For the comparison purpose, we also simulate GA, GSA and PSO by employing the same solution representation and the fitness function. In simulation, the switching probability and the size of population (*p_size*) is considered as 0.5 and 100 respectively.

3.4 Datasets

In simulation, we considered two benchmark datasets as given in [13] with 512 and 1024 tasks respectively. The benchmark datasets comprises of 12 diverse dataset instances. These instances are described by u_x_yyzz, where u implies uniform distribution to generate the dataset, x refers for the consistency i.e., inconsistent (i), semi-consistent (s) or consistent(c) and yyzz refers the heterogeneity of task-VM i.e., hihi, hilo, lohi, lolo respectively [13,14]. Moreover, we created one synthetic dataset using the uniform distribution. This synthetic dataset also consists of 6 different instances, where size of each instance is $n \times m$, for n tasks and m VMs.

3.5 Experimental Results

We consider makespan (M) and average cloud utilization (please refer Sect. 2.2) as the performance metrics to show the dominance of the proposed algorithm over other simulated schemes. The comparison of cloud makespan for the dataset instances of size 512×16 size and 1024×32 are shown in Figs. 3 and 4 respectively by the bar graph. We also plot the average cloud resource utilization for both the benchmark datasets as shown in Figs. 5 and 6 respectively. Similarly, for synthetic dataset, we also calculated the makespan and average cloud resource utilization as shown by Fig. 7. It can be observed that the proposed FPA-based scheme has the minimum makespan and maximum average cloud utilization for all the dataset instances in comparison with GA, GSA and the PSO based approaches.

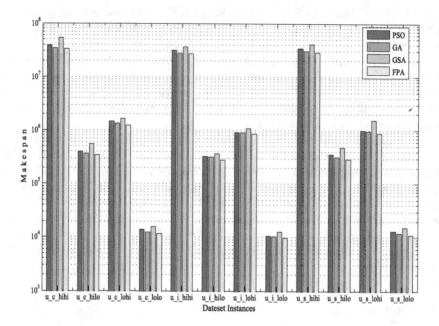

Fig. 3. Comparison of cloud makespan for 512×16 size dataset instances

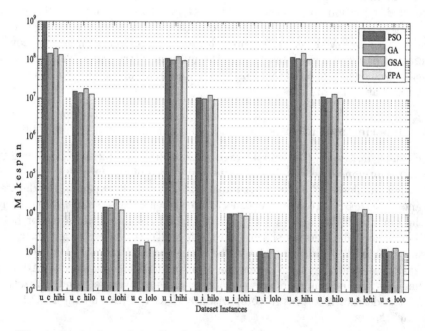

Fig. 4. Comparison of cloud makespan for 1024×32 size dataset instances

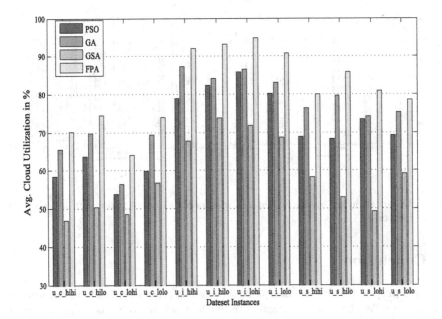

Fig. 5. Comparison of avg. cloud utilization for 512×16 size dataset instances

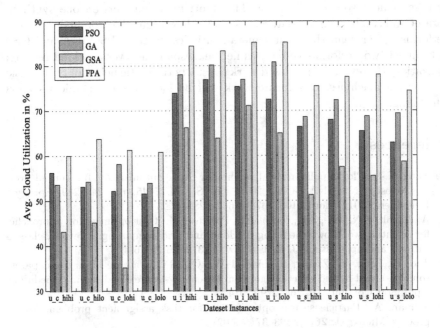

Fig. 6. Comparison of avg. cloud utilization for 1024×32 size dataset instances

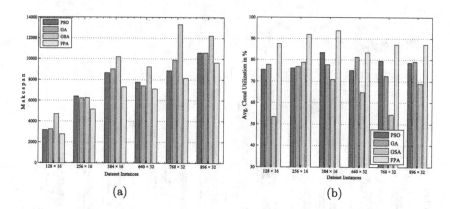

Fig. 7. Comparison for synthetic dataset instances (a) cloud makespan and (b) avg. cloud utilization

4   Conclusion

We have proposed a FPA-based task scheduling scheme in a cloud computing environment. We have demonstrated an efficient scheme of pollen representation and the process to retrieve the task-VM mapping from a given pollen. We have also shown the derivation of a single objective fitness function by combining two conflicting objectives, i.e., minimization of makespan and maximization of average cloud resource utilization. Through simulation runs on one synthetic dataset and two benchmark datasets, we have shown that the proposed technique performs better than the similar meta-heuristics, namely, PSO, GA and GSA in terms of two performance metrics i.e., makespan and average cloud resource utilization. However, the proposed work considers the static behavior of the tasks and virtual machines. Our future work will be focused on dynamic workflow scheduling.

References

1. Yang, X.-S.: Flower pollination algorithm for global optimization. In: Durand-Lose, J., Jonoska, N. (eds.) UCNC 2012. LNCS, vol. 7445, pp. 240–249. Springer, Heidelberg (2012). doi:10.1007/978-3-642-32894-7_27
2. Alkhanak, E.N., Lee, S.P., Rezaei, R., Parizi, R.M.: Cost optimization approaches for scientific workflow scheduling in cloud and grid computing: a review, classifications, and open issues. J. Syst. Softw. **113**, 1–26 (2016)
3. Tao, F., Feng, Y., Zhang, L., Liao, T.W.: CLPS-GA: a case library and pareto solution-based hybrid genetic algorithm for energy-aware cloud service scheduling. Appl. Soft Comput. **19**, 264–279 (2014)
4. Salman, A.: Particle swarm optimization for task assignment problem. Microprocess. Microsyst. **26**(8), 363–371 (2002)
5. Zhang, L., Chen, Y., Sun, R., Jing, S., Yang, B.: A task scheduling algorithm based on PSO for grid computing. Int. J. Comput. Intell. Res. **4**, 37–43 (2008)

6. Zhong, H., Tao, K., Zhang, X.: An approach to optimized resource scheduling algorithm for open-source cloud systems. In: ChinaGrid Conference (ChinaGrid), pp. 124–129. IEEE (2010)
7. Talukder, A., Kirley, M., Buyya, R.: Multi-objective differential evolution for scheduling workflow applications on global grids. Concurr. Comput. Pract. Exp. 21(13), 1742–1756 (2009)
8. Panda, S.K., Jana, P.K.: Efficient task scheduling algorithms for heterogeneous multi-cloud environment. J. Supercomput. 71(4), 1505–1533 (2015)
9. Panda, S.K., Jana, P.K.: Uncertainty-based QoS min min algorithm for heterogeneous multi-cloud environment. Arab. J. Sci. Eng. 41(8), 3003–3025 (2016)
10. Gupta, I., Kumar, M.S., Jana, P.K.: Compute-intensive workflow scheduling in multi-cloud environment. In: International Conference on Advances in Computing, Communications and Informatics (ICACCI), pp. 315–321 (2016)
11. Durillo, J.J., Prodan, R., Barbosa, J.G.: Pareto tradeoff scheduling of workflows on federated commercial clouds. Simul. Model. Pract. Theor. 58, 95–111 (2015)
12. Ding, Y., Qin, X., Liu, L., Wang, T.: Efficient scheduling of virtual machines in cloud with deadline constraint. Future Gener. Comput. Syst. 50, 62–74 (2015)
13. https://code.google.com/p/hcspchc/source/browse/trunk/AE/ProblemInstances/ HCSP. Accessed 26 July 2016
14. Xhafa, F., Carretero, J., Barolli, L., Durresi, A.: Immediate mode scheduling in grid systems. Int. J. Web Grid Serv. 3(2), 219–236 (2007)
15. Kuila, P., Jana, P.K.: Energy efficient clustering and routing algorithms for wireless sensor networks: particle swarm optimization approach. Eng. Appl. Artif. Intell. 33, 127–140 (2014)
16. Lawler, E.L., Jacques, L.: On preemptive scheduling of unrelated parallel processors by linear programming. J. ACM (JACM) 25(4), 612–619 (1978)
17. Li, J., Qiu, M., Ming, Z., Quan, G., Qin, X., Gu, Z.: Online optimization for scheduling preemptable tasks on IaaS cloud system. J. Parallel Distrib. Comput. 72, 666–677 (2012). Elsevier
18. Panda, S.K., Agrawal, P., Khilar, P.M., Mohapatra, D.P.: Skewness-based min-min max-min heuristic for grid task scheduling. In: 4th International Conference on Advanced Computing and Communication Technologies, pp. 282–289. IEEE (2014)
19. Panda, S.K., Jana, P.K.: SLA-based task scheduling algorithms for heterogeneous multi-cloud environment. J. Supercomput. 73, 1–33 (2017)
20. Panda, S.K., Jana, P.K.: Normalization-based task scheduling algorithms for heterogeneous multi-cloud environment. Inf. Syst. Front, 1–27 (2016)

An Efficient Design of Left Shifter in Quantum Cellular Automata

Biplab Das[1], Debashis De[1,2(✉)], Jadav Chandra Das[1], and Sagar Sarkar[1]

[1] Department of Computer Science and Engineering, Maulana Abul Kalam Azad University
of Technology, Kolkata, 700064, West Bengal, India
biplab.das52@gmail.com, dr.debashis.de@gmail.com,
jadav2u@gmail.com, sagar.djvu@gmail.com
[2] School of Physics, University of Western Australia, 35 Stirling Highway,
Crawley, Perth, WA 6009, Australia

Abstract. Quantum-dot Cellular Automata (QCA) is one of the rapidly growing nano-electronic computing technology. QCA is based on electron presents in quantum dots. QCA technology have features on high density, low power and smallest design compare to the other technologies. This paper proposed the basic paradigm of an efficient design of a 4-bit binary Logical Left Shifter circuit for single shift as well as multiple shifts. Due to inherent nature, QCA has been utilized in this paper to achieve low power faster circuit for proposed design. These shifter circuits are useful in floating point processing systems, particularly very useful for mantissa multiplication technique. All the designs are implemented with QCADesigner tool. The accuracy is verified comparing theoretical values and corresponding simulation results.

Keywords: QCA · Clock zone · Majority gate · Inverter · Shifter · Multiple shifter

1 Introduction

CMOS Technology is approaching its scaling end very fast. The important challenges that CMOS technology is facing can be divided in three categories as Physical challenges, Material challenges, and Power-thermal challenges [1]. So in order to enhance the performance of a system new technological approach should be taken into account. QCA is one of the rapidly growing nano-technology [1]. QCA cell is a collection of quantum dot cells arranged in an array format [3]. These cells are inter-connected with each other through the electron passing system from one cell to an-other cell. To accomplish the computation in QCA arrays, columbic interaction in cells is sufficient so wires are not required [2]. Recent research work have shown that this technology can achieve very high density computing elements, extremely low power dissipation, ultra-fast computing [4]. The main objective of our paper is to show a detailed design, QCA layout and simulation result of a Logical Left Shifter, Logical Left Shifter for Multiple Shifts with minimum complexity and cell count. The QCA circuits have been designed by the help of QCA designer tool [5].

© Springer Nature Singapore Pte Ltd. 2017
J.K. Mandal et al. (Eds.): CICBA 2017, Part II, CCIS 776, pp. 108–120, 2017.
DOI: 10.1007/978-981-10-6430-2_10

2   Motivation and Contribution

These shifter circuits are used in floating point processing systems. These circuits are particularly very useful for mantissa multiplication technique [20, 21]. Using the proposed design, we can enhance the overall performance of the floating point processing systems, by speeding up the process i.e. by decreasing the calculation time. QCA requires less power consumption and less clock delay having high device density. Thus QCA technology has been utilized in this paper to achieve low power faster circuit for proposed design [22]. The contributions of the paper are as follows.

- The design of a logical left shifter circuit to shift single bit.
- The design of left shifter circuit for shifting multiple bits.
- Single layer wire crossing has been used to provide easiest implementation of the designs.

3   QCA Overview

The basic building block of a QCA circuit, i.e., QCA cell, QCA wire, majority gate and inverter are explored in this section. Besides, clock cycles are introduced in QCA to guide the data propagation in the circuit.

3.1   QCA Cell

The fundamental element in this technology is QCA cell [7]. Each QCA cell consists of four quantum-dots in four corner of a square box cell as shown in Fig. 1. Among four quantum dots, two are filled with electrons which drive away from each other because of columbic interaction in between the quantum dots [8]. Due to electrostatic force of interaction, electrons take diagonally opposite holes in the cell [4–6]. As a result there are two polarizations of a QCA cell which are denoted as P = + 1(as binary '1') and P = −1(as binary '0'). Polarization, P = +1 is encoded as logical '1' and P = −1 is encoded as logical' 0' [9].

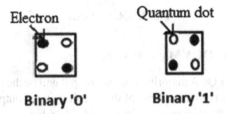

Fig. 1. QCA cell of polarization'−1' and polarization '1'

3.2 Representation of QCA Wire

QCA wire is an array representation of QCA cells, due to the columbic interaction between cells, the binary signal propagates from input to output [6]. The signal propagation in a 90° wire and 45° wire are shown in Fig. 2.

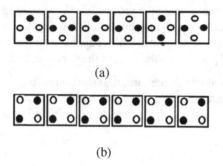

(a)

(b)

Fig. 2. QCA wire (a) 45° QCA wire (b) 90°QCA wire

3.3 Representation of QCA Inverter

By arranging QCA cell as shown in the Fig. 3. We can implement an Inverter. An inverter is basically a NOT Gate [11]. Logically it can be expressed as, A = A' [5–8].

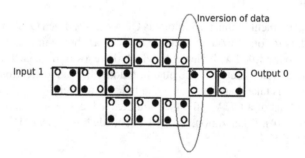

Fig. 3. QCA inverter

3.4 Representation of QCA Majority Gate

In QCA majority gate or QCA majority voter the output will be the majority of the inputs [13–25]. If binary '1' is the major input of the circuit then the output will be binary '1' and if major inputs are '0' then output will be '0' [10]. In Fig. 4 P,Q,R are inputs. Let's say, P = 0, Q = 0 and R = 1, So in this case the major inputs are '0' so the output will be '0'. We can easily construct 'AND' gate and 'OR' gate using majority gate or majority voter [11].

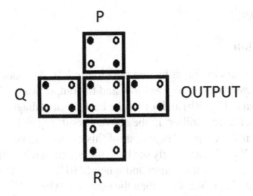

Fig. 4. QCA majority gate

3.5 Clock Zone

To guide the data flow in QCA circuits four clock signals are used [9]. Each clock signal is shifted in phase by 45° as shown in the Fig. 2. When clock signal is high, it opens the electron tunnel junctions in QCA cells which allows the electron in a QCA cell to travel between potential wells. A clock zone cycle through four phases are phase1, phase2, phase3 and phase4, the phase also called Switch, Hold, Release and Relax [11–13]. During the phase1 the inter-dot barriers are lifted so that the electrons within the cell can be altered by the case of electrons in their input cell [26]. In the hold phase the inter-dot barriers are kept high so that the cell can stay at their present state [9–11]. In phase3 and phase4 state the barriers are kept very low so that the cell remain unpolarized [17–19] (Fig. 5).

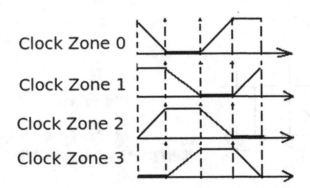

Fig. 5. Different clock zones

4 Proposed Work

4.1 Logical Left Shift

A logical left shifter shifts the input by one position to left. An example of left shift is shown below where we take <1100> as input and the output we get is <1000>.

The circuits shown in Fig. 6(b) and (c) are the basic logical diagram and QCA layout for a single output logical left shifter. In the above circuit, Fig. 6(b), 'X0' and 'X1' are two inputs and OUT is the output. The output of this circuit can be logically expressed as, OUT = S'.X0 + S.X1. We can clearly see from the equation when Shift is set 'S' = '0' then the input X0 is passed to the output and when SHIFT is set '1' then the input X1 is passed to the output., i.e. when S = 0 then the output will be 'OUT' = 'X0' and when 'S' = '1' then 'OUT' = 'X1'. 'Y1' is the output of the QCA layout. Figure 7 represents a four-bit Logical Left shifter where the input is <'X3','X2','X1','X0'> and output will

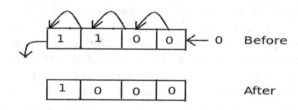

(a)

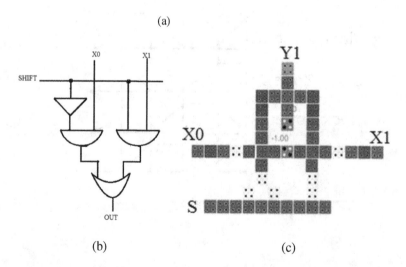

(b)   (c)

Fig. 6. (a) Left shift operation (b) Circuit diagram and (c) QCA layout for the basic element of logical Left shift

be <'Y3','Y2','Y1','Y0'> and 'S' is the controller of the circuit. The value of 'S' can be either '0' or '1'. So when S = 1, the circuit shifts input bits one position to its left.

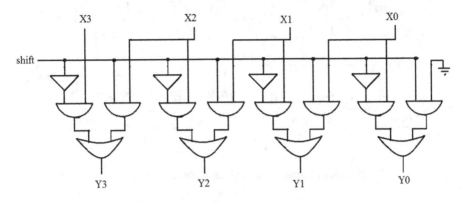

Fig. 7. Circuit diagram for logical left shift

Here, we have proposed a QCA design of 4-bit 'Logical left Shifter' with the objective of minimum area, minimum number of cells and less complexity. The circuit diagram and QCA layout of the ' Logical Left Shifter' circuit are shown in Figs. 7 and 8.

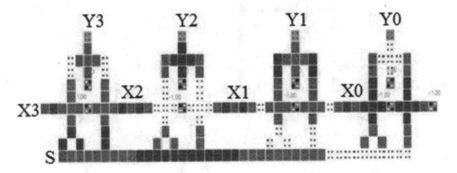

Fig. 8. QCA layout for logical left shift

4.2 Logical Left Shifter for Multiple Shifts

In case of 'Logical Left Shifter for Multiple Shifts' the shifting of input is controlled by two shifting signals. The input can be shifted from ' 0 to 3' places. Figure 9 shows the block diagram for 'Logical Left Shifter for Multiple Shifts'. In this diagram we have taken <'X3',' X2',' X1',' X0'> as input and <'Y3', 'Y2', 'Y1', 'Y0'> is the corresponding outputs. S0 and S1 are two shifting signals. The QCA layout for a Logical Left Shifter for Multiple Shifts is show in Fig. 10.

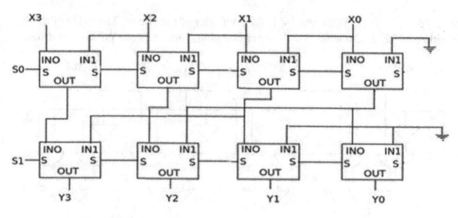

Fig. 9. Block diagram for logical left shifter for multiple shifts

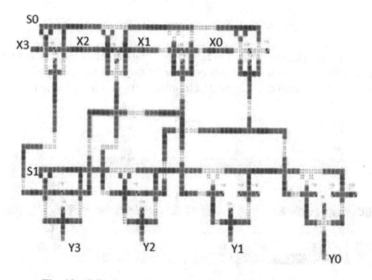

Fig. 10. QCA layout for logical left shifter for multiple shifts

This circuit basically acts more like a barrel shifter. As there are two shifting bits S1 and S0, there can be four possible combinations. The rules are as follows: (Table 1)

Table 1. The rules of case study

Case	Signals		Action	Top unit	Bottom unit
I	S1 = 0	S0 = 0	No shift	Shift 0	Shift 0
II	S1 = 0	S0 = 1	Shift Left by one place	Shift 1	Shift 0
III	S1 = 1	S0 = 0	Shift Left two places	Shift 0	Shift 2
IV	S1 = 1	S0 = 1	Shift Left three places	Shift 1	Shift 2

5 Result Analysis

Figure 11 shows the simulation result for a logical left shifter. Let's say we have taken input as <'1', '1', '1', '1'> i.e. 'X3' = '1', 'X2' = '1','X1' = '1' and 'X0' = '1'. As you can see from the Fig. 11 when S is '1' the input shift by 1 position to the left, thus the LSB bit becomes '0'. So the value of output bits <'Y3', 'Y2', 'Y1', 'Y0'> becomes <'1', '1', '1', '0'> .

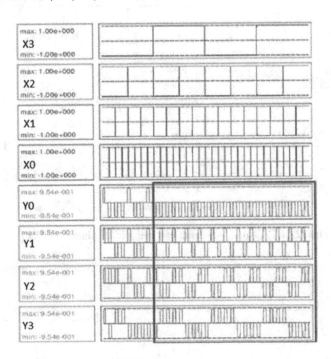

Fig. 11. QCA simulation for logical left shifter

Figure 12 shows the output of a multiple left shifter for case 1 i.e. when S1 = '0' and S0 = '0'. As mentioned earlier in this case no shifting occurs,so the input and the output will be the same, which means if the input bits are <'X3', 'X2', 'X1', 'X0'> and the output bits are <'Y3', 'Y2', 'Y1', 'Y0'> then, 'Y3' = 'X3', 'Y2' = 'X2', 'Y1' = 'X1' and 'Y0' = 'X0'. Figure 13 shows the output of a multiple left shifter for case 2 i.e. when 'S1' = '0' and 'S0' = '1'. In this case, the input bit shifts one position to its left. So if the input bits are <'X3', 'X2', 'X1', 'X0'> and the output bits are <'Y3',' Y2', ' Y1',' Y0'> then, 'Y3' = 'X2', 'Y2' = 'X1', 'Y1' = 'X0' and 'Y0' = '0'.

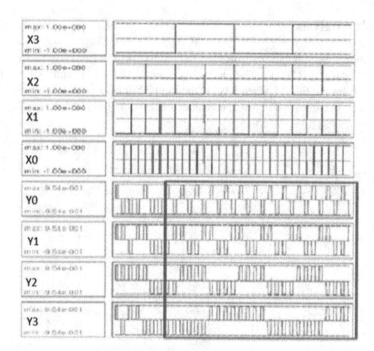

Fig. 12. QCA simulation result of a multiple left shifter for case1

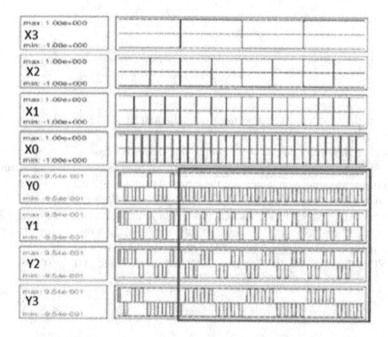

Fig. 13. QCA simulation result of a multiple left shifter for case 2

Figure 14 shows QCA simulation result of a multiple Left shifter for 'Case 3' i.e. when 'S1' = '1' and 'S0' = '0'. As mentioned earlier it will cause the input bits to shift two positions to its left, So if the input bits are < 'X3', 'X2', 'X1', 'X0' > and the output bits are <'Y3', 'Y2', 'Y1', 'Y0'> then, 'Y3' = 'X1', 'Y2' = 'X0', 'Y1' = '0' and 'Y0' = '0'. Now for 'Case 4' we have to select 'S1' = '1' and 'S0' = '1' which will cause the input bits to shift three position to its left, So if the input bits are <'X3', 'X2', 'X1', 'X0'> and the output bits are <'Y3', 'Y2', 'Y1', 'Y0'> then, 'Y3' = 'X0', 'Y2' = '0', 'Y1' = '0' and 'Y0' = '0'. The QCA simulation for the output of Case 4 is shown in Fig. 15.

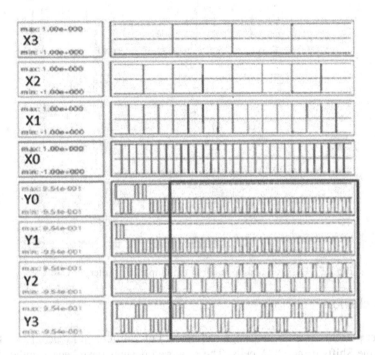

Fig. 14. QCA simulation result of a multiple left shifter for case3

To design a Left Shifter and a Left Shifter for multiple shift, we have used less number of cell and less area. We have used 158 cells for Left Shifter and 586 cells for Left Shifter for multiple shift. In this design the values of clock cycles values are 2 and 5.75 respectively [14–16] (Table 2).

Table 2. Complexity analysis

Component	No. of cell	Area(nm^2)	ClockZones
Left shifter	158	0.20	2
Multiple left shifter	586	129	5.75

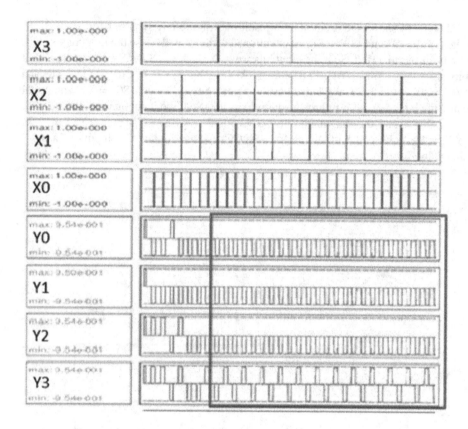

Fig. 15. QCA simulation result of a multiple left shifter for Case4

6   Conclusion

This paper presents an efficient design of Logical Left Shifter and Logical Left Shifter for Multiple Shifts using QCA cells. The proposed designs have been simulated and verified by QCA Designer. The proposed design consumes very low power and will be very useful to implement different complex circuits. However there is still scope to improve the design which has been proposed in this paper and could be taken for further studies to achieve greater density.

Acknowledgement. Authors are grateful to TEQIP-II, WB for providing financial assistance to completed the paper.

References

1. Lent, C.S., Tougaw, P.D., Porod, W., Bernstein, G.H.: Quantum cellular automata. Nanotechnology **4**(1), 49 (1993)

2. Lakshmi, S.K., Athisha, G.: Efficient design of logical structures and functions using nanotechnology based quantum dot cellular automata design. Int. J. Comput. Appl. **3**, 5 (2010)

3. Lakshmi, S.K., Athishi, G., Karthikeyan, M., Ganesh, C.: Design of subtractor using nanotechnology based QCA. In: Communication Control and Computing Technologies, pp. 384–388 (2010)

4. Orlov, A.O., Amlani, I., Toth, G., Lent, C.S., Bernstein, G.H., Snider, G.L.: Experimental demonstration of a binary wire for quantum-dot cellular automata. Appl. Phys. Lett. **74**(19), 2875–2877 (1999)

5. Niemier, M.T., Kogge, P.M.: Logic in wire: using quantum dots to implement a microprocessor. Electron. Circ. Syst. **3**, 1211–1215 (1999)

6. Das, J.C., De, D.: Novel low power reversible binary incrementer design using quantum-dot cellular automata. Microprocess. Microsyst. **42**, 10–23 (2016)

7. Agrawal, P., Sinha, S.R.P., Wairya, S.U.B.O.D.H.: Quantum dot cellular automata based parity generator and detector: a review. Int. J. Electron. Commun. Eng. **5**, 3 (2016)

8. Navi, K., Sayedsalehi, S., Farazkish, R., Azghadi, M.R.: Five-input majority gate, a new device for quantum-dot cellular automata. J. Comput. Theoret. Nanosci. **7**(8), 1546–1553 (2010)

9. Tougaw, P.D., Lent, C.S.: Logical devices implemented using quantum cellular automata. J. Appl. Phys. **75**(3), 1818–1825 (1994)

10. Vetteth, A., Walus, K., Dimitrov, V.S., Jullien, G.A.: Quantum-dot cellular automata carry-look-ahead adder and barrel shifter. In: IEEE Emerging Telecommunications Technologies Conference, pp. 2–4 (2002)

11. Zhang, R., Walus, K., Wang, W., Jullien, G.A.: A method of majority logic reduction for quantum cellular automata. IEEE Trans. Nanotechnol. **3**(4), 443–450 (2004)

12. Porod, W.: Quantum-dot devices and quantum-dot cellular automata. Int. J. Bifurcat. Chaos **7**(10), 2199–2218 (1997)

13. Walus, K., Dysart, T.J., Jullien, G.A., Budiman, R.A.: QCADesigner: a rapid design and simulation tool for quantum-dot cellular automata. IEEE Trans. Nanotechnol. **3**(1), 26–31 (2004)

14. Khan, A., Chakrabarty, R.: Novel design of high polarized inverter using minimum number of rotated cells and related kink energy calculation in quantum dot cellular automata. Int. J. Soft Comput. Eng. (IJSCE) **3**(1), 165–169 (2013)

15. De, D., Purkayastha, T., Chattopadhyay, T.: Design of QCA based programmable logic array using decoder. Microelectron. J. **55**, 92–107 (2016)

16. Das, J.C., Purkayastha, T., De, D.: Reversible nanorouter using QCA for nanocommunication. Nanomat. Energy **5**(1), 28–42 (2016)

17. Cho, H., Swartzlander Jr., E.E.: Adder and multiplier design in quantum-dot cellular automata. IEEE Trans. Comput. **58**(6), 721–727 (2009)

18. Das, J.C., De, D.: Operational efficiency of novel SISO shift register under thermal randomness in quantum-dot cellular automata design. Microsyst. Technol. **23**(9), 4155–4168 (2016). https://doi.org/10.1007/s00542-016-3085-y

19. Modi, S., Tomar, A.S.: Logic gate implementations for quantum dot cellular automata. In: Computational Intelligence and Communication Networks (CICN), pp. 565–567 (2010)

20. Imre, A., Csaba, G., Ji, L., Orlov, A., Bernstein, G.H., Porod, W.: Majority logic gate for magnetic quantum-dot cellular automata. Science **311**(5758), 205–208 (2006)

21. Hast, H., Khorbotly, S., Tougaw, D.: A signal distribution network for sequential quantum-dot cellular automata systems. IEEE Trans. Nanotechnol. **14**(4), 648–656 (2015)

22. Rasala, E.J., Young, C.J.: Data general corporation. Floating point data processing system. U.S. Patent No. 4,208,722 (1980)

23. Amdahl, G., Clements, M., Topham, L.: Right and left shifter and method in a data processing system, U.S. Patent No. 3,790,960 (1974)
24. Das, J.C., De, D.: Optimized multiplexer design and simulation using quantum dot-cellular automata. Indian J. Pure Appl. Phys. (IJPAP) **54**(12), 802–811 (2016)
25. Das, J.C., De, D.: Reversible binary to grey and grey to binary code converter using QCA. IETE J. Res. **61**(3), 223–229 (2015)
26. Das, J.C., De, D.: Quantum dot-cellular automata based reversible low power parity generator and parity checker design for nanocommunication. Front. Inf. Technol. Electron. Eng. **17**(3), 224–236 (2016)

Nano-Router Design for Nano-Communication in Single Layer Quantum Cellular Automata

Biplab Das[1], Jadav Chandra Das[1], Debashis De[1,2(✉)], and Avijit Kumar Paul[1]

[1] Department of Computer Science and Engineering, Maulana Abul Kalam Azad University
of Technology, Kolkata 700064, West Bengal, India
biplab.das52@gmail.com, jadav2u@gmail.com,
dr.debashis.de@gmail.com, kumaravijitece@gmail.com
[2] School of Physics, University of Western Australia, 35 Stirling Highway,
Crawley, Perth, WA 6009, Australia

Abstract. Quantum dot Cellular Automata(QCA) is a new electronics paradigm
for information technology and communication. It has been recognized as one of
the revolutionary nano-scale computing devices. In this work, we have selected
few basic gates using QCA to develop a 4: 4 router. The main function of this
design is to transfer information from four input ports through a DEMUX and
receive this information at the four different receiver port. The information that
has been provided is being routed via crossbar in the present study. We use a
parallel to serial converter to receive the information at the receiver port. This
router has been implemented with less clock delay and less QCA, which results
into an efficient router comparing to any other router. This Nano-router can be
used for distributed computing. The QCA Designer Software is used for designing
and simulating the circuits.

Keywords: QCA · Clock cycle · Majority voter · DEMUX · Router · Parallel to
serial converter · Nano-communication

1 Introduction

QCA automata technology is an alternative means to CMOS technology. QCA technology facilitates in the development of nanostructures from standard semi conductive
materials [1–10]. QCA is a promising nano technological platform. The majoty logic
gates is used to develop QCA circuits. Quantum-dot based QCA is a promising technology for implement nano-scale design. Quantum wells are modeled of this technology
[3]. QCA technology has a very efficient and novel design approach. In nanotechnology,
power loss is becoming a challenging issue for the designers [2, 3]. As the device sizes
are scaled down to sub-micron level power consumption has been found to increase.
Thus the need for a device which is of very small size as well as dissipates less power
is growing [7–9]. QCA is a likely substitutes, which take care of size, power and speed.
QCA is transistor less technology having very high density, ultra fast clocking speed
and negligible utilization of power. In QCA information system, transfers as well as
various computations are implemented with the help of mutual exchange between electrons [3]. QCA based nano communication is a growing field of research at present.

© Springer Nature Singapore Pte Ltd. 2017
J.K. Mandal et al. (Eds.): CICBA 2017, Part II, CCIS 776, pp. 121–133, 2017.
DOI: 10.1007/978-981-10-6430-2_11

2   Related Work

In this paper we have represented the architecture and implementation of a router with higher efficiency. In our references, various router design has been shown, reversible nano router [2], multi layer nano router [3]. A nano communication device has been designed using QCA to achieve efficiency in terms of cell count and less clock delay [1]. Some improvement has been done in the thermal behavior of QCA system in terms of their resistance to stray charge and fabrication imperfections by using nearest neighbour interactions in the QCA wire [11]. We have introduced a synthesis technique to implement symmetric boolean functions using QCA Logic [6–13]. For designing the QCA circuit, a rapid and accurate design tool has been used to simulate the circuit [12]. A DEMUX has been design with more efficiency in terms of clock delay. In the design of the DEMUX single layer wire, crossing has been used to achieve this efficiency [4]. Design of single layer technique based on difference of cell state has been done to get more accurate outcomes from the router at receiver port [5]. Nano communication for router has been used to achieve the goal [2]. The router design has been done based on the related work.

3   Motivation and Contribution

QCA based nanotechnology has been used to build an efficient router as it requires less power consumption and less clock delay. This is the first time a router is going to be implemented by using single layer wire crossing in QCA technology. We have designed a DEMUX using single layer wire crossing to implement the router using single layer wire crossing. This router provide the basic concept of routing, where incoming links are used to take input via different input port and sends them to different output port via parallel to serial converter. We have used QCA designer to implement the router.

4   Background and Materials

The main function of a router have already been discussed. In this section, we will discuss how different circuit has been implemented using QCA that helps to implement router. Firstly, we have provided QCA basics [9, 11–14]. After that we have provided details of all the related QCA circuit that has already been done. After this section, we have discussed proposed work and then we have shown our conclusion.

4.1   QCA Preliminaries

QCA circuit is based on the concept of free electrons within two different band-gap materials at a particular temperature [7–9]. The positions in a cell where electrons get confined are known as dot. A QCA cell contains four dots, where two additional electrons are added in four dots, whose positions will be fixed at the two diagonals due to columbic interaction [18]. So, based on the position of the electrons, we get two distinct polarizations viz. +1 and −1, which are represented as binary 1 and 0 respectively. Polarizations of a typical QCA cell are being shown in Fig. 1 [11, 12].

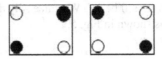

Fig. 1. Polarization cell '1' and '0'

Two and more QCA cell has been represented as an array and one array structure of QCA cell could be called as a QCA wire. Two types of QCA cell are available in QCA technology, which are 90^0 QCA cell wire and 45^0 QCA cell wire [10]. A 90^0 QCA cell array or wire has been shown in Fig. 2.

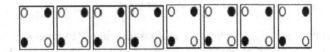

Fig. 2. QCA wire

QCA crossover is one of the main important part of the QCA technology. Two types of layer are available in the QCA technology, single layer crossover and multi layer crossover, which are shown in Fig. 3 [5].

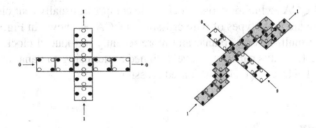

Fig. 3. QCA crossover

QCA inverter or NOT gate alter the input data '0' to '1' or '1' to '0' as output data. In QCA inverter, electrons are reversed in an output cell. A QCA inverter has shown in Fig. 4.

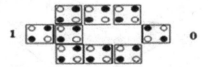

Fig. 4. QCA inverter

Majority gate or voter is required for design of any types of QCA design [2, 12, 15–18]. Majority voter has been displayed in the result of majority input. In majority voter, there are three inputs and one output. If major input are '1' then output will be '1' and if major input are '0' then output will be '0'. We can easily design the 'AND' gate and 'OR' gate. A majority gate has shown in Fig. 5.

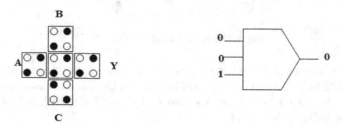

Fig. 5. Majority voter

The barrier between adjacent dots can be adjusted using QCA clocking. A QCA cell adjusts between two different polarizations i.e. −1 and +1. The electron between the adjoining dots in a cell when inter dot barrier is low [1, 2]. There are four different clock zones as well as four clock phases in QCA clocking, which are respectively switch, hold, release and relax. Due to increase in the tunneling energy between quantum dots, it shows a high value in the switch phase, which signifies a clock 0 situation. The tunneling energy between quantum dots seems to be low at room temperature, enabling it to be in a hold phase. These different clock zones has been shown in Fig. 6.

In a typical QCA technology, one clock cycle comprises usually four clock phases. Moreover, there are three types of wire crossing in QCA, as shown in Fig. 7 [17]. The three layers are multi-layer, coplanar and more recently introduced clock-zone based crossings [21–24]. In this paper, we have designed router using coplanar crossing both by using rotated cells and clock-zone based crossing.

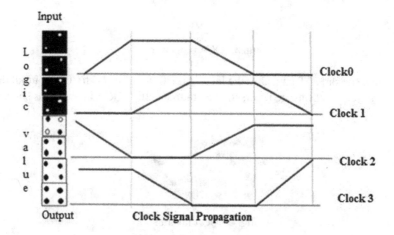

Fig. 6. QCA clock phase

Clock Zones

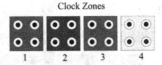

1   2   3   4

Fig. 7. QCA clocking zones

5 Proposed Work

There are designed 4:4 router in coplanar technique of QCA. The designed consists of four DEMUX, four parallel to serial converter. Switch fabric is a interconnection between DEMUX output and input of parallel to serial converter [3]. All components of the router design are shown in Table 1.

Table 1. Component for this design

DEMUX	Serial to parallel converter	Switch fabric
1:4	4:1	4:4

5.1 Design of 1:4 DEMUX

The DEMUX is commonly known as data distributor in communication systems. A DEMUX is a combinational which takes a single input through a single input line and used to select one output line to send the input data. This selection of the output line among many output lines depend on the select information. Here, we have used it to provide input to the router. To build this 4:4 router, we have used 1:4 DEMUX. The block diagram of a 1:4 DEMUX and the corresponding QCA implementation of a DEMUX has been shown in Figs. 8 and 9 respectively.

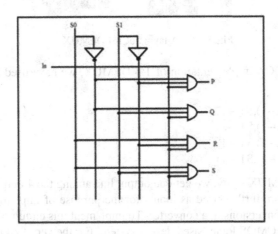

Fig. 8. Block diagram of 1:4 DEMUX

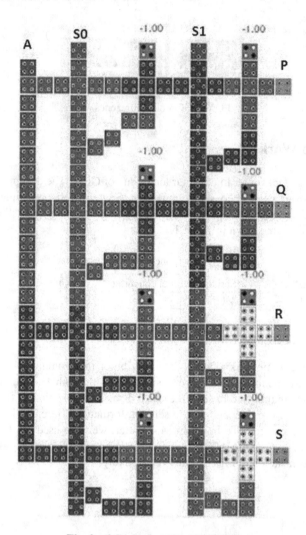

Fig. 9. QCA layout of 1:4 DEMUX

In the above QCA implementation of 1:4 DEMUX, we have used 8 M (Majority Voter).

$$O1 = M(M(S0,I,-1),S1,-1)$$
$$O1 = M(M(S0,I,-1),S1,-1)$$
$$O1 = M(M(S0,I,-1),S1,-1)$$
$$O1 = M(M(S0,I,-1),S1,-1)$$

From each DEMUX study, we get one output line among the 4 output lines. These four output lines are further used as inputs for the purpose of implementing various parallel to serial conversions in a converter. To implement this circuit of DEMUX, we have followed the CMOS logic based design system. For the very first time, DEMUX has been proposed with the help of QCA technology featuring single layer implementation.

5.2 Design of Parallel-to-Serial-Converter

Parallel to Serial Converter is used to hold the output signal coming from the incoming links and make delay at the output port. To design this router, we have used 4 parallel to serial converter. The QCA implementation of parallel to serial converter is shown in Fig. 10 [20]. The converter exhibits efficient performance employing QCA based technology.

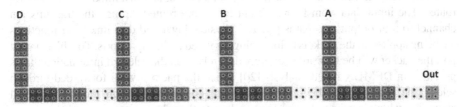

Fig. 10. QCA layout of parallel to serial converter

5.3 Design of 4:4 Router

A router is a major element in the world of Internet. It is employed in the transfer of data or packets between incoming and outgoing links. The minimum requirements for a basic router design should be that the speed of the access rate of memories sould at least match the speed of the line rate [20]. This makes it difficult for the router design to operate with fast lines, which makes packets to be transported flexibly to the Internet. QCA is an effective nano-scale technology, where the building blocks are of minute size, consume very less power and bear a clock rate within the terahertz range [3]. In this paper, an efficient router architecture based on QCA is proposed and also implemented

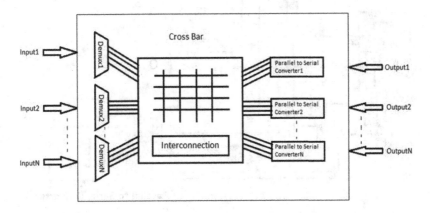

Fig. 11. Basic router block diagram

to bridge a gap between conventional router, communication domain and emerging QCA technology. The basic router block diagram has been shown in Fig. 11.

5.4　4:4 Router Architecture

A 4:4 router architecture overview has been provided in this section. A router has mainly two parts data plane and control plane. The incoming packets are routed by control plane while the data packets are forwarded with the help of data plane [3]. To build this router, we have used the basic concept of DEMUX, single layer crossbar and parallel to serial converter. This given architecture says that how does a router implement and works.

Here, we demonstrate the manner in which a packet is transmitted through the 4:4 router. The input data from four different inputs are routed through the transmission channel to four output data paths [3]. The physical layer and data link layer functions are being applied to the packets before being provided to the input ports. To which output port the packet will be forwarded entirely depends upon the selected information that is provided in DEMUX based analysis [20]. Once the packets were forwarded through select line mode, soon the information were converted through parallel to serial converter, which is used to forward the packets to the selected output port [3].

The QCA simulation of router has been shown in Fig. 12, which shows that if we provide data like 1100 to the input port then we get that data at the output port P where s0s1 is 00.

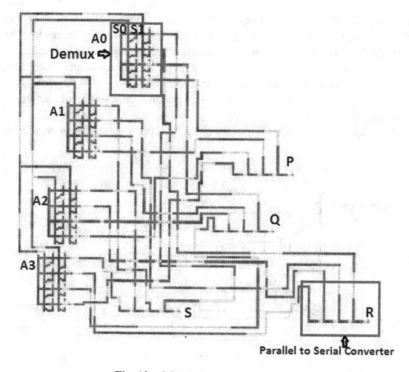

Fig. 12. QCA layout of the 4:4 router

Complexity analysis of all the component of the router design are shown in Table 2. There are given total cell count, latency and area of the design of DEMUX, parallel to serial converter and router.

Table 2. Complexity of the component

Component	Cell	Clock cycle	Area(nm²)
DEMUX	188	1	0.18
Parallel to serial converter	45	4	0.07
Router	3551	15	9.86

6   Simulation Result

Here whatever we provide in the input of the parallel to serial converter, we get that at the output of the parallel to serial converter with some delay that causes incoming information of the router to wait at the output port of the receiver. There we provide simulation results of DEMUX and 4:4 router respectively.

DEMUX simulation result is given in Fig. 13, where s0 and s1 are select line, binary '00','01','10' and '11' would be value of the select lines. This select lines are decided which data packets used for the communication.

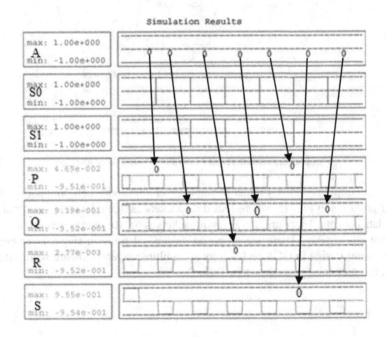

Fig. 13. QCA simulation result of DEMUX

Parallel to serial converter convert the parallel input to serial output. Simulation result of parallel to serial converter is shown in Fig. 14, where parallel input '0010' are shown serial output '0010'.

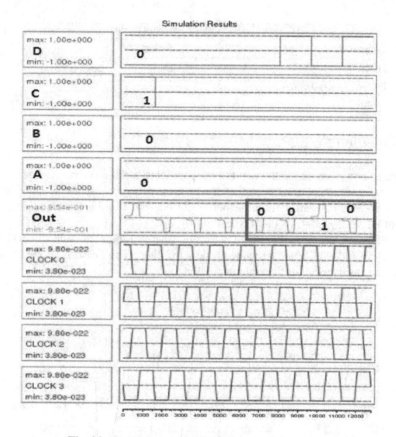

Fig. 14. Simulation result of parallel to serial converter

There are implemented 4:4 router in single layer with rotate cell. Simulation result of router is shown in Fig. 15, where four data packets as input data and so output will be four data packets. There are 'A' as input packets is '0110' output packets is '0110' with some clock delay. There are proposed design 4:4 route in single layer but the previous router design in QCA technology are multiple layer. Compare with different router in this technology are shown in Table 3.

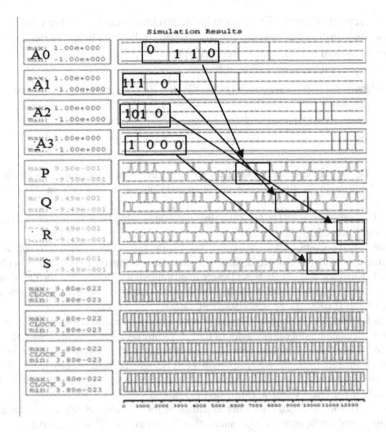

Fig. 15. Simulation result of router

Table 3. Comparison table for different router

Design	Cell count	Clock cycle	Area(nm^2)	Layers
[2]	4026	48	13.81	3
[12]	3057	24	7.91	3
Proposed design	3551	15	9.86	1

7   Conclusion and Future Work

In this paper, we have worked out with a 4:4 router that has the ability to transfer data from four different input link to four different output link. This transmission of data from different incoming link to different outgoing link depends on DEMUX, crossbar and the parallel to serial converter. This design is single layer design, which is more acceptable in QCA technology and its cell count and area much less than any other router design in this technology. This router is used to provide efficient output results in terms of less energy and less clock delay, which uses less number of QCA cells that facilitates to achieve an accurate outcome. The study helps in designing effective power system based on low power consumption and energy dissipation finding applications ranging from fault tolerant system to high speed circuit design.

Acknowledgement. Authors are grateful to TEQIP-II, WBUT for providing financial assistance to complete this paper.

References

1. Das, S., De, D.: Nanocommunication using QCA: a data path selector cum router for efficient channel utilization. In: Radar, Communication and Computing (ICRCC), pp. 43–47. IEEE (2012)
2. Das, J.C., Purkayastha, T., De, D.: Reversible nanorouter using QCA for nanocommncation. Nanomat. Energy **5**(1), 28–42 (2016)
3. Sardinha, L.H., Costa, A.M., Neto, O.P.V., Vieira, L.F., Vieira, M.A.: Nanorouter: a quantum-dot cellular automata design. IEEE J. Sel. Areas Commun. **31**(12), 825–834 (2013)
4. Iqbal, J., Khanday, F.A., Shah, N.A.: Design of quantum-dot cellular automata (QCA) based modular 2 n – 1–2n MUX-DEMUX. In: Multimedia, Signal Processing and Communication Technologies (IMPACT), pp. 189–193. IEEE (2013)
5. Shin, S.H., Jeon, J.C., Yoo, K.Y.: Design of wire-crossing technique based on difference of cell state in quantum-dot cellular automata. Int. J. Control Autom. **7**(4), 153–164 (2014)
6. Deb, A., Das, D.K.: A regular network of symmetric functions in quantum-dot cellular automata. In: 18th International Symposium VLSI Design and Test, pp. 1–6. IEEE (2014)
7. Cho, H., Swartzlander Jr., E.E.: Adder and multiplier design in quantum-dot cellular automata. IEEE Trans. Comput. **58**(6), 721–727 (2009)
8. Modi, S., Tomar, S.A.: Logic gate implementations for quantum dot cellular automata. In: Computational Intelligence and Communication Networks (CICN). IEEE (2010)
9. Imre, A., Csaba, G., Ji, L., Orlov, A., Bernstein, G.H., Porod, W.: Majority logic gate for magnetic quantum-dot cellular automata. Science **311**(5758), 205–208 (2006)
10. Lent, C.S., Tougaw, P.D., Porod, W., Bernstein, G.H.: Quantum cellular automata. Nanotechnology **4**(1), 49 (1993)
11. Hast, H., Khorbotly, S., Tougaw, D.: A signal distribution network for sequential quantum-dot cellular automata systems. IEEE Trans. Nanotechnol. **14**(4), 648–656 (2015)
12. Walus, K., Dysart, T.J., Jullien, G.A., Budiman, R.A.: QCADesigner: a rapid design and simulation tool for quantum-dot cellular automata. IEEE Trans. Nanotechnol. **3**(1), 26–31 (2004)
13. Amlani, I., Orlov, A.O., Snider, G.L., Lent, C.S., Bernstein, G.H.: Demonstration of a six-dot quantum cellular automata system. Appl. Phys. Lett. **72**(17), 2179–2181 (1998)
14. Frost, S.E., Rodrigues, A.F., Janiszewski, A.W., Rausch, R.T., Kogge, P.M.: Memory in motion: a study of storage structures in QCA. In: First Workshop on Non-Silicon Computing, vol. 2 (2002)
15. Narasimha, M.J.: The Batcher-banyan self-routing network: universality and simplification. IEEE Trans. Commun. **36**(10), 1175–1178 (1988)
16. Das, J.C., De, D.: Shannon's expansion theorem-based multiplexer synthesis using QCA. Nanomat. Energy **5**(1), 53–60 (2016)
17. Iyer, S., McKeown, N.W.: Analysis of the parallel packet switch architecture. IEEE/ACM Trans. Netw. (TON) **11**(2), 314–324 (2003)

18. Abedi, D., Jaberipur, G., Sangsefidi, M.: Coplanar full adder in quantum-dot cellular automata via clock-zone-based crossover. IEEE Trans. Nanotechnol. **14**(3), 497–504 (2015)
19. Cowburn, R.P., Welland, M.E.: Room temperature magnetic quantum cellular automata. Science **287**(5457), 1466–1468 (2000)
20. Kamaraj, A., Marichamy, P., Abinaya, M.: Design of reversible logic based area efficient multilayer architecture router in QCA. Int. J. Appl. Eng. Res. **10**(1), 140–144 (2015)
21. Das, J.C., De, D.: Quantum dot-cellular automata based reversible low power parity generator and parity checker design for nanocommunication. Front. Inf. Technol. Electron. Eng. **17**(3), 224–236 (2016)
22. Das, J.C., De, D.: Reversible comparator design using quantum dot-cellular automata. IETE J. Res. **62**(3), 323–330 (2016)
23. Das, J.C., De, D.: Operational efficiency of novel SISO shift register under thermal randomness in quantum-dot cellular automata design. In: Microsystem Technologies, pp. 1–14 (2016)
24. Das, J.C., De, D.: Optimized design of reversible gates in quantum dot-cellular automata: a review. Rev. Theoret. Sci. **4**(3), 279–286 (2016)

Intelligent Data Mining and Data Warehousing

Graph Based Clinical Decision Support System Using Ontological Framework

Nilanjana Lodh, Jaya Sil, and Indrani Bhattacharya(✉)

Indian Institute of Engineering Science and Technology, Shibpur, India
nilanjanalodh@gmail.com, jayaiiests@gmail.com,
indrani.84@hotmail.com

Abstract. Scarcity of doctors in rural areas of developing countries is a major problem and has serious impact in health sector of villages. Health kiosks driven by the health assistants in different remote places are the backbone of rural healthcare services. However, due to limited knowledge and experience of the health assistants, diagnosis is often ambiguous. Therefore, there is an increasing demand to develop a knowledge based decision-making system to treat the rural patients at primary level. In this paper, a graph based clinical decision support system (CDSS) has been proposed to facilitate the health assistants for provisional disease diagnosis of the patients. The graph-based knowledge base is developed by integrating the medical knowledge represented of different ontologies. We apply the modified depth first search algorithm and topological sort algorithm for achieving minimum cost in graph traversal for differential diagnosis of the diseases. Diagnosis may be performed in two modes – online and offline, in the presence of the patient and using patient records respectively.

Keywords: CDSS · Graph search · Differential diagnosis · Rural healthcare · Ontology

1 Introduction

Diagnosis of diseases is an extremely complex process, requiring expert knowledge and excellent reasoning skill. However, such expertise is not always available, especially in rural India where acute shortage of doctors is a very common scenario. In order to deal with the problem, development of an expert system to simulate the knowledge of human experts for assessing the health records and provide advice would be immensely valuable. Clinical decision support system (CDSS) aims at solving these problems, which incorporate domain knowledge and reasoning power of doctors for provisional diagnosis of diseases of the rural patients. The outcome is validated by the physicians for cross checking to avoid missing important pointers.

The CDSSs may be classified into two types: knowledge based and nonknowledge based [1]. Most of the knowledge based CDSSs try to simulate the decisions based on a predefined set of rules obtained in consultation with the physicians. However, the systems are usually difficult to update and maintain when the system encounters with new knowledge. Non–knowledge based CDSSs use statistical data, probabilistic techniques and machine learning methods to diagnosing the diseases. Nevertheless,

© Springer Nature Singapore Pte Ltd. 2017
J.K. Mandal et al. (Eds.): CICBA 2017, Part II, CCIS 776, pp. 137–152, 2017.
DOI: 10.1007/978-981-10-6430-2_12

such systems fail to handle rare diseases for which sufficient training data is not available.

One of the first attempts of developing a CDSS is acute abdominal pain help (AAP help) based on the naïve-Bayes' approach [2]. Symptoms of the patients suffering from abdominal pain and related diseases are obtained from the field (like hospitals) and later used to find the probability of a particular disease based on a given set of symptoms. Though the system performs well for a small set of diseases like abdominal pain, it has two shortcomings. Firstly, it is not flexible or easy to extend when the range of symptoms and diseases become diverse. Secondly, in case of rare diseases, insufficient data creates problem for reliable implementation of the system.

INTERNIST-I, was an expert system designed in the early 1970s which aimed to model the way clinicians diagnose diseases. INTERNIST used a tree-like database, which linked symptoms with potential diseases. The patient's observations were used to deduce the probable diseases with this tree-like knowledge base. However, this method required a lot of human-effort and thus was not very scalable. Nevertheless, the knowledge base created for this system proved to be very useful for developing CDSS (s) in the future.

MYCIN (1976) is a static rule-based CDSSwhich represented medical knowledge as a set of IF-THEN rules, with each rule having a probability factor the diagnoses [5]. One more rule based system is Arden Syntax (1989), where medical knowledge was represented as a set of production rules expressed in markup language. These rules relate input conditions to a set of diagnoses or actions. However, this form of representation was found to be inadequate for multistep diagnosis.

The Guideline Interchange Format (GLIF) (1998) is based on an object-oriented logical model of concepts and creates a flow-chart like structure for diagnosis steps. There are classes for all types of diagnosis entities [7].

The development of a CDSS for provisional diagnosis of diseases would require a huge pool of data about different diseases and symptoms in order to prepare the knowledge base. In addition, the knowledge representation method should be such that it not only describes the diseases and symptoms in a standardized manner, but also expresses the relations between them which is easy to interpret. Ontologies at the core of representing the knowledge would meet the challenges well. The advantages of ontologies are manifold [8], as they make it very easy to share medical knowledge and re-use reuse existing ones. Many such medical ontologies are already freely available in the public domain, which would lessen the human-effort required for the knowledge base creation phase. However, employing ontologies is not sufficient for performing differential diagnosis, since it comprises of disjoint knowledge like disease and symptom ontologies. Individual ontologies express hierarchical relationship within the same entity type, but fail to show the relationship between different entities. For example, disease ontologies show the relationship among different diseases and their characteristics but don't represent how different diseases and symptoms are related to each other.

In this paper, a graph based clinical decision support system (CDSS) by utilizing the framework of the ontology has been proposed. However, the disease and symptom ontologies obtained from public medical ontologies are disjoint and inadequate for performing differential diagnosis. For differential diagnosis, we require knowledge about individual diseases and symptoms as well as how they are related to each other. The disease and symptom ontologies have been merged to form disease-diagnosis graph (DDG) using domain knowledge from physicians. Each pair of related disease and symptom is linked with an edge where the edge weight indicates the strength of inter node relation. A modified depth first search algorithm has been proposed to search the most probable disease while applied on the weighted DDG. The proposed system can be used in two modes, namely online and offline. In online mode, the system interacts with the end user, prompting for input and accordingly traverses the DDG for diagnosing the disease. In the off-line mode, the end user is not available for answering the queries, and the diagnosis is performed on the basis of medical records of the patient, stored earlier. In the offline mode topological sort algorithm has been applied to the keywords of the medical record according to their 'depth' or location in the DDG.

Organization of the paper is as follows: Sect. 2 describes the detailed methodology to develop the proposed CDSS. The results for two cases are presented in Sect. 3 and conclusions are arrived at in Sect. 4.

2 Methodology

Figure 1 shows the basic components of the proposed graph based CDSS consisting of three main components:

1. The knowledge base of diseases and symptoms
2. Inference Engine
3. User Interface

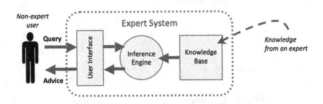

Fig. 1. Components of the proposed CDSS

2.1 Knowledge Base

The knowledge base of the proposed CDSS may be built using domain knowledge collected from the physicians or by using public medical ontologies. The disease and symptom ontologies are merged with the help of a priori data collected from the physicians relating different diseases and symptoms to create the proposed DDG.

Ontology based Framework

The raw medical data is first 'modeled' in ontological framework with respect to the diseases, patients and symptoms. While developing the ontology one need not build the entire knowledge base from scratch because different ontology based medical databases are available in the public domain such as (LOINC), ICD-9 CM [9], (SNOMED-CT) [10], MeSH [11] and UMLS [12]. For instance, SNOMED (systematic nomenclature of medicine) CT [13] uses an ontology based hierarchical model to systematically document all the concepts such as diseases and symptoms related with the medical domain. A description is attached with each concept of the SNOMED ontology. Some concepts may be referred to using many synonymous terms – these synonymous codes are also stored in a table [14].

Here, raw medical data comprises of different symptoms, diseases, symptom-disease relations and patient hierarchy details are obtained from the experts (physicians). Instead of creating the ontology from scratch by using data from the physicians, one may take help of the existing disease and symptom ontologies, available in the public domain such as DOID [15], SNOMED and DSO [16]. The method of importing public domain ontology is more scalable in the long run as it minimizes extra human effort. Figure 2 shows a small part of ontological hierarchy modeled in Protégé.

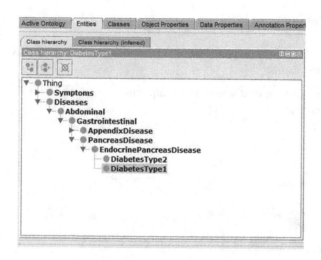

Fig. 2. Ontology hierarchy using Protégé

The ontological knowledge base is transformed into a class hierarchy using an object oriented programming language. Each concept of the medical ontology represents a class in the class hierarchy. For instance, the top-level concept 'Disease' in the patient ontology transforms to a 'Disease' class in the class hierarchy. For each of the sub-concepts of 'Disease', analogous child classes are created. This process is repeated recursively for each of the three ontology namely, patient, disease and symptom. Open source frameworks such as Protégé automates this process, and directly convert the ontology represented in XML/OWL format into Java code [17]. The proposed approach makes the process very scalable as human effort for knowledge base creation is minimized.

2.2   Disease Diagnosis Graph

The proposed disease diagnosis graph (DDG) has been constructed by considering the objects of the class hierarchy as the vertices/nodes of the graph. Each vertex of the graph is an object of one of the classes in the class hierarchy. We define a common interface, which underlines the common behavior of each vertex in the graph. All classes in the hierarchy implement this interface, as they all share the basic similarities in their properties and operations. However, different classes may have different implementation of the same method/behavior. For instance, one of the behaviors defined in the <Node> interface is the action performed on reaching to that node. Say, a 'Patient' type node may prompt for queries from the user, whereas a 'Disease' type node may display the disease detail.

The proposed DDG is a directed, weighted graph. Edge weight (EW) between two nodes, say node1 and node2 represents inter-node-relation as defined in Eq. (1). Equation (1) has been devised in such a way that higher the EW, the more closely node1 and node2 are related. The factors which determine EW are defined below:

1. Input from the physicians about the interrelations
2. Statistical data sampled for a large number of patients
3. Medical data of the current patient, i.e. the patient being diagnosed

Out of these three, the first two factors don't depend on the patient. The third factor may vary from patient to patient. Thus the edge weights, i.e. the internodes relations are different for different patients based on the particular patient's attributes. For instance, in case of the symptom of abdominal pain, the EW between 'abdominal pain' and 'acute appendicitis' would be greater for a 14-year-old patient than a 40-year-old patient, as appendicitis is more common in children in that age group.

$$EW(node1 \rightarrow node2) = \frac{w_p.P(node2|node1) * \sum_{k=1}^{n} W_k.Condition_k}{\sqrt{\sum_{k=1}^{n} W_k^2}} \qquad (1)$$

The terms used in Eq. (1) are defined below:

P(node2|node1) is a statistical term based on past medical data of a large number of patients. Although the probability distribution function is same for every patient, the value of P(node2|node1) for each patient x also depends on the attributes of the patients.

$$P_x(node2|node1) = f(attributes\ of\ patient\ x)$$

The probability distribution function f() is obtained a-priori by approximating a curve to the statistical data at the time of diagnosis; i.e., the relation between the probability and patient parameters(such as age, height, weight) is discovered with the help of the statistical data calculated At the time of diagnosis, the patient-specific attributes such as weight and height are substituted in the function to get the probability. In absence of statistical data, the posterior probability is set to a standard value say, 1/2 to avoid the effect of biasing. This is explained in further detail via an example in the following subsection.

$Condition_k$ is the textual data determining the state of the patients defined by the physicians and represented as a Boolean expression.Evaluation of the Boolean expression is used to establish the connection between two nodes, say node1 and node2 during diagnosis based on the patient details. For example, let node1 represent abdominal pain and node2 be a symptom node representing missed menstrual period. Based on the patient's information collected at node1 the following Boolean expression has been evaluated for finding the connection between node1 and node2.

$$\text{Sex} = \text{Female} \ \ \text{AND} \ \ \text{pain\_location} = \text{left}$$

Thus, only female patients are prompted for symptoms related to menstruation, while it evaluates to zero for male patients and edge weight is set to 0.

$W_1, W_2, \ldots W_n$ are the weights for n number of conditions. Intuitively, condition 'weights' represent the importance of each condition in the diagnosis. When explicit input is not available from the physician for the condition weights, they are set to a default value (say '1').

w_p is based on patient statistical data and may be interpreted as the weight assigned to the statistical term or the general biasing of the relation between node1 and node2. w_p is determined according to the data collected from physicians /domain experts.

Therefore, Eq. (1) allows us to incorporate both statistical features/conditions, and also permits us to choose the relative importance of each term with the help of the weight terms.

The disease diagnosis graph is first created using Algorithm1(explained below), and then the edge weights are assigned in accordance with Eq. (1).

The algorithm is explained with the help of an example in the following section.

Algorithm 1. Disease-diagnosis graph creation algorithm

Input: Disease Ontology, DO
Symptom Ontology, SO
Diagnoses, DGO
Output: Disease-diagnosis Graph G(V,E)
CreateGraph (DO,SO, DGO)
1. $V \leftarrow \Phi$ //Set of nodes
2. $E \leftarrow \Phi$ //Set of edges
3. For each diagnoses $d \in$ DGO
4. $V \leftarrow V \cup \{d\}$ //Add the node to V
5. For each $s \in$ SO
6. $V \leftarrow V \cup \{s\}$// Add the node to V
7.   For each $d \in$ DGO associated with $s \in$ S
8. $E \leftarrow E \cup \{(d,s)\}$// Add the edge to E
9. For each $d \in$ DO
10. $V \leftarrow V \cup \{d\}$// Add the node to V
11.   For each $s \in$ SO associated with $d \in$ DO
12. $E \leftarrow E \cup \{(d,s)\}$//Add the edge to E
// Calculation of weight of the edges
13. For each edge $e=(node1, node2) \in$ E
14. Define probability function $P(node2|node1)$ based on statistical data
15. Define conditions $C_1, C_2, ..., C_n$ for edge e
16. Set parameters w_p and $W_1, W_{2,...}, W_n$ in equation (1)
17. For each node $v \in$ V
18. Implement node specific behavior using<Node> interface.
19. Return G(V,E)

DDG Creation: Example

Each concept in the ontologies has a corresponding vertex in the DDG. Each vertex of the DDG implements the <Node> interface.

Let us consider the most top-level concept 'Patient of abdominal pain' in the patient ontology. It has a corresponding vertex in the DDG which is an object of the class 'PatientOfAbdominalPain' and implements the <Node> interface. This vertex serves as the root node of our example DDG (Fig. 3).

PatientOfAbdominalPain

Fig. 3. Creation of root node

The <Node> interface behavior of the class 'PatientOfAbdominalPain' acquires patient's primary information such as sex, age, pain location, pain duration and onset.

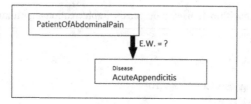

Fig. 4. Addition of second node in the DDG

Information has been acquired depending on which mode of querying is being used, online or offline. Next, consider the disease 'Acute Appendicitis' associated with the root node (Fig. 4).

EW between the vertices 'AcuteAppendicitis' and 'PatientOfAbdominalPain' is defined below using Eq. (1) with the help of statistical data collected and the following conditions provided by the physician.

C_1 = Age < 14
C_2 = (Onset Type == Suden Onset)
C_3 = (PainLocation = Central or Lower Abdomen)

$P(Acute\ Appendicitis|Patient\ Of\ abdomonial\ pain)$ is defined by finding the best-fit curve for the available statistical data by polynomial regression method [18]. The available data set is represented as a frequency distribution function of the attributes such as patient age, body weight, etc. An example of best fitted curve of a particular disease for age attribute is shown in Fig. 5.

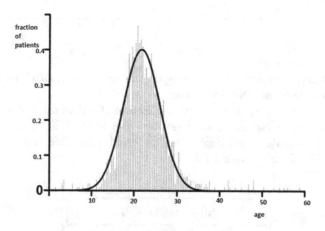

Fig. 5. Curve fitting to frequency distribution

Similar curves may be fit to data collected about other patient attributes such as height, weight, B.M.I, etc.The edge weight for every edge in the DDG is similarly calculated using Eq. (1). The depth first search (DFS) algorithm has been modified to visit the neighbors of a node in decreasing order based on their inter-node-relation with the current node. From a particular node, the strongly related edge is visited first, reducing the average path-count while interpreting diagnosis of a disease.

2.3 Query Classification

The DDG accepts patient data as query in two modes and classifies it into a set of probable diseases based on analysis of the DDG. In online, data is acquired by prompting a set of questions to the patients based on the initial query. Data is acquired in offline mode by consulting previous medical records of the patient. The modified depth first search (MDFS) algorithm has been applied on the DDG for differential diagnosis of the disease.

Modified Depth First Search (MDFS)
The MDFS algorithm has been devised which traverses neighbours based on the out-degree of a node in decreasing order based on the EW values. The neighbouring node with largest EW has been traversed first. Upon visiting any node, it executes two primary functions: carries out the <Node> specific behaviour defined for that node during graph creation and then calculates the EW for all the outgoing edges associated with it using Eq. (1). The MDFS algorithm ensures that the path with the highest edge weights in the DDG has been traversed first.

Online Mode
The MDFS algorithm is applied on the disease-diagnosis graph, starting from the parent diagnosis node. At each diagnosis node, the system prompts for input from the user. This online data determines which of the path next to follow and continues until a leaf node is reached. The query is classified as the disease represented by the leaf node.

Offline Mode
First, the fixed formatted medical record of a patient is processed to extract the basic patient information and the keywords corresponding to the symptoms experienced by the patient. Keywords are sorted according to their position (topologically) in the DDG to ensure that the keywords are handled in correct order. The MDFS algorithm can be used for offline query mode as well by assigning a topological 'level' to each of the query keyword appearing in the DDG as EW, sorted in topological order [19]. The query keywords are hashed and their hash-values and topological levels are stored in a look-up table so that the keywords extracted from the medical records can be sorted according to the topological levels stored in the hash table [20]. The MDFS algorithm has been applied on the DDG using level-wise sorted set of information. Both online and offline modes are described in Algorithm 2.

Algorithm 2. Disease- diagnosis algorithm (using previously constructed DDG)

Input: Disease-diagnosis graph G(V,E)
Query Q
Patient Record PR
MODE (offline or online)
Output: Diagnosed disease of the query
OnlineQuery (Q)
1. MDFS (G, Q, patient_head_node) // Modified Depth First Search
OfflineQuery (PR)
1. Q ← TopologicalSort (PR)
2. MDFS (G, Q)
Procedure 1:MDFS(G,Q,v)
1. Path_count←0
2. Path_count← Path_count + 1
3. If v is an enabled <Node>
4. Carry out <Node>specific behaviour on the basis of   Query Q
5. For each outgoing edge $e=(v,u)$
6.   Calculate edge-weight(e) using equation(1)
7. If MODE is 'offline'
8 Q ← extractNextQuery(Q)
9. Sort G.adjacentEdges(v) in increasing order of their edge
weights EW
10. For each edge e from v to w inG.adjacentEdges(v)
11.   If vertex w is not labeled as discovered
12.   MDFS(G,Q,w)
13. Return Depth First path and Path_count

Procedure 2: TopologicalSort (PR)
1.L←Φ // Set of sorted elements
2.S← Set of all nodes with no incoming edges
3. For each s∈ S
4.   Remove s from S
5.   Add s to tail of L
6.   For each m with edge e
7.   Remove e from G(V,E)
8.   If m has no other incoming edge
9.   S← m
10. Return L

As evident from the MDFS algorithm that the path count is a measure of the number of nodes in the graph that are traversed before reaching to the correct diagnosis. The MDFS algorithm ensures that the most likely disease/symptom association with the current node has been checked first, which leads to a minimum average path count.

Consider diseases D_1 and D_2 which are associated with the root node and their apriori probabilities as a function of age is shown in Fig. 6.

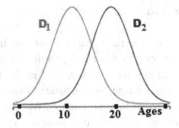

Fig. 6. The probability-density functions of two diseases as a function of age.

Let the conditions associated with the disease D_1 be C_1 and that with the disease D_2 be C_2. The conditions for these diseases are described in Fig. 7:

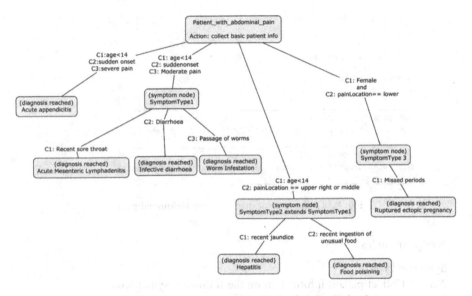

Fig. 7. Part of disease-diagnosis graph of abdominal pain

C_1 = PainLocation = Central abdomen
C_2:Sex = FemaleANDPainLocation = Lowerabdomen

Considering the weights of the conditions are unity, the edge weights for a particular patient is determined using Eq. (1), based on the data of that patient. Therefore, for a female patient with age 20, and pain in the lower abdomen, EW_2 is much higher than EW_1 indicating that disease D_2 is more probable for the patient. Consequently, the node D_2 is checked first, leading to a quicker query classification.

3 Results and Discussion

Patients' data are collected from the rural health kiosks in India. The kiosks provide primary level health care services to the rural people where dearth of doctors is a serious problem. Our proposed approach is deployed in the kiosk to assist the health workers for provisional diagnosis based on the patient's query and medical reports.

For experimentation, knowledge base is prepared with the help of domain experts. Domain knowledge has been mapped into ontological model, which is the basis of disease-diagnosis graph. The class hierarchy is obtained using object oriented programming language, like Java. It is also auto-generated from the ontology using open source ontology editor Protégé. From the class hierarchy the disease-diagnosis graph has been constructed, part of which for abdominal pain is shown in Fig. 7

Few of the important nodes of the DDG of Fig. 8 are described below:

```
([Patient@13c6d5a , Type1@103f2e5 , Type2@16761 , Type3@1bf7285 , Type
Name : nil
Sex :female
Pain Location :lower
Severity :severe
How did it start ?sudden
Age :12

nil is a Type 2 patient
Type 2  details : <14, F, Sudden, Severe, pain in central/Lower body

CONFIRMED Acute Appendicitis
Suggested diagnosis : Consult Doctor, Refer child to hospital
```

Fig. 8. Online patient diagnosis for abdominal pain

Symptom nodes:

SymptomType1:
Action: Collect patient information on the following symptoms-
Recent sore throat, diarrhea, passage of worms, vomiting
SymptomType2: (subclass of SymptomType1)
Action: Collect patient information on the following symptoms-
Loss of weight, recent jaundice, recent ingestion of unusual food
SymptomType3:
Action: Collect patient information on the following symptoms –
Missed periods, Date of Last menstrual period

We have applied our method on several cases. The results of a sample diagnosis in both modes are shown in the following case studies.

3.1 Case Study: Abdominal Pain (Online Mode)

A patient with severe lower abdominal pain is asked more questions for diagnosing the disease in online mode. The diagnosis is given in Fig. 8 with path count 4.

3.2 Case Study: Abdominal Pain (Offline Mode)

Patient record is obtained from rural health kiosk in the form as given in Fig. 9. The record contains basic statistics of health and symptoms along with demographic data of the patient. The patient record is analyzed and topologically sorted to arrange the extracted information in correct order. Finally, the patient has been diagnosed in offline mode as described in Fig. 10 with path count 8.

Barhra Rural Health Kiosk Prescription

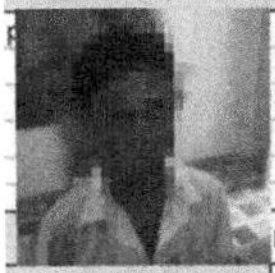

Reg. No.	10412	Status	New	Date:	100315	
Name	Prabir Maji			S/D/W of	Late Raicharan Maji	
Occup.	Electrician	Phone	9749400734	Address	Barhra	
Age	45	Gender	M	Height	161	cm
BMI		BP	95/85	Weight	41.4	kg
Pulse	79	spO2		Temp		C

Mother diabetic.

Medical History (H/O): 20 years ago Jaundice. Operation hydrocel, appendix.

Did patient bring any previous Diagnosis/Prescription: NA

C/O	On Examination
Upper Abdomen pain	
Duration : 24 hours for 2- 3 months	Rt Hyoychondrium and epigastric area - tender. No palpable mass

Fig. 9. Sample Patient record

```
([Patient@1454493 , Type1@1df513e , Type2@b5c51c , Type
MODE : OFFLINE
EXTRACTED INFORMATION :

Name : Prabir Maji
Sex : Male
Pain Location : upper right
Severity :Unknown
Duration : 24 hours >2 months
How did it start ?Unknown
Age :45

Fever : Yes
Suggested diagnosis : unknown

Passage of worms : no

Vomiting : Yes
Possible Diagnosis : Gastritis
Possible Diagnosis : Hepatitis
Diarrhoea : No
Diagnosis complete
```

Fig. 10. Diagnosis from patients' record in offline mode

3.3   Case Study: Diarrhea (Online Mode)

We consider another case of diarrhea, given in Fig. 11 where patient is diagnosed as diarrhea patient by prompting query form the system. The path count of the following diagnosis is 6.

Similarly, from the patient's past history and reports diarrhea patients are diagnosed using offline mode of proposed system.

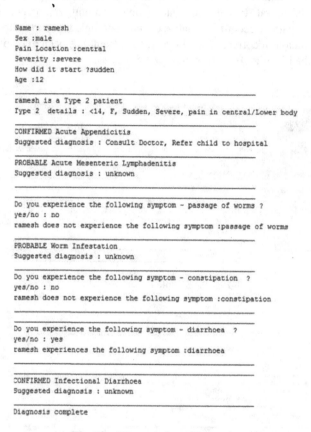

```
Name : ramesh
Sex :male
Pain Location :central
Severity :severe
How did it start ?sudden
Age :12

ramesh is a Type 2 patient
Type 2  details : <14, F, Sudden, Severe, pain in central/Lower body

CONFIRMED Acute Appendicitis
Suggested diagnosis : Consult Doctor, Refer child to hospital

PROBABLE Acute Mesenteric Lymphadenitis
Suggested diagnosis : unknown

Do you experience the following symptom - passage of worms ?
yes/no : no
ramesh does not experience the following symptom :passage of worms

PROBABLE Worm Infestation
Suggested diagnosis : unknown

Do you experience the following symptom - constipation  ?
yes/no : no
ramesh does not experience the following symptom :constipation

Do you experience the following symptom - diarrhoea  ?
yes/no : yes
ramesh experiences the following symptom :diarrhoea

CONFIRMED Infectional Diarrhoea
Suggested diagnosis : unknown

Diagnosis complete
```

Fig. 11. Diagnosis in online mode

4   Conclusion

In this paper, we propose a disease-diagnosis graph on the basis of existing medical ontologies in the public domain, would have great impact on the healthcare system in rural India. The presence of open source tools such as Protégé automates a significant portion of this process and minimizes human effort greatly, making the method scalable and interpretable. Thus, although the proposed approach has presently been studied with respect to abdominal pain related diseases and diarrhea, it represents a prototype for general framework and may be extended to any medical domain.

The proposed edge weight function allows us to incorporate both statistical and predefined conditional terms specified by the physicians, while giving us the flexibility of assigning variable weights to the different factors. Interaction with the patient is not always possible and the diagnosis depends on the past medical records of the patient. Our graph based approach enables us to apply simple graph algorithms such as topological sort and modified depth first search algorithm to solve this problem and so computationally inexpensive.

Acknowledgement. This work is supported by Information Technology Research Academy (ITRA), Govt. of India, under ITRA-Mobile Grant (ITRA/15(59)/Mobile/Remote Health/01).

References

1. Abbasi, M., Kashiyarndi, S.: Clinical decision support systems: a discussion on different methodologies used in health care. Marlaedalen University Sweden (2006)
2. Jadhav, V., Sattikar, A.: Review of application of expert systems in the medicine. National Conference on Innovations in IT and Management (2014)
3. Internist-I: https://en.wikipedia.org/wiki/Internist-I. Accessed 19 Jan 2016
4. Wolfram, D.: An appraisal of INTERNIST-I. Artif. Intell. Med. 7(2), 93–116 (1995)
5. Introduction to Expert Systems: MYCIN: 2016. http://psy.haifa.ac.il/~ep/Lecture%20Files/AI/Secure/Download/Introduction%20to%20expert%20systems%20-%20MYCIN.pdf. Accessed 19 Jan 2016
6. Samwald, M., et al.: The Arden Syntax standard for clinical decision support: experiences and directions. J. Biomed. Inf. 45(4), 711–718 (2012)
7. Ohno-Machado, L., et al.: The guideline interchange format: a model for representing guidelines. J. Am. Med. Inform. Assoc. 5(4), 357–372 (1998)
8. Anbarasi, M., et al.: Ontology based medical diagnosis decision support system. Int. J. Eng. Res. Technol. 2(4) (2013)
9. ICD - ICD-9-CM - International Classification of Diseases, Ninth Revision, Clinical Modification (2016). http://www.cdc.gov/nchs/icd/icd9cm.htm. Accessed 19 Aug 2016
10. Spackman, K., et al.: SNOMED RT: a reference terminology for health care. AMIA 1997 Annual Symposium (1997)
11. Lowe, H.: Understanding and using the medical subject headings (MeSH) vocabulary to perform literature searches. JAMA: J. Am. Med. Assoc. 271(14), 1103–1108 (1994)
12. Bodenreider, O.: The unified medical language system (UMLS): integrating biomedical terminology. Nucleic Acids Res. 32(90001), 267–270 (2004)
13. SNOMED CT: https://en.wikipedia.org/wiki/SNOMED_CT. Accessed 20 Oct 2016
14. Ciolko, E., et al.: Intelligent clinical decision support systems based on SNOMED CT. In: 32nd Annual International Conference of the IEEE EMBS Buenos Aires, Argentina, 31 August – 4 September (2010)
15. Human Disease Ontology | NCBO BioPortal (2016). https://bioportal.bioontology.org/ontologies/DOID. Accessed 20 Aug 2016
16. Mohammed, O., et al.: Building a diseases symptoms ontology for medical diagnosis: an integrative approach. In: The First International Conference on Future Generation Communication Technologies (2012)
17. ProtegeOWL API Programmers Guide - Protege Wiki (2016). http://protegewiki.stanford.edu/wiki/ProtegeOWL_API_Programmers_Guide. Accessed 20 Aug 2016

18. Dam, J.S., Dalgaard, T., Fabricius, P.E., Andersson-Engels, S.: Multiple polynomial regression method for determination of biomedical optical properties from integrating sphere measurements. Appl. Optics **39**(7), 1202–1209 (2000)
19. Pearce, D.J., Kelly, P.H.: A dynamic topological sort algorithm for directed acyclic graphs. J. Exp. Algorithmics (JEA) **11**, 1–7 (2007)
20. Rokach, L., Maimon, O., Averbuch, M.: Information retrieval system for medical narrative reports. In: Christiansen, H., Hacid, M.S., Andreasen, T., Larsen, H.L. (eds.) FQAS 2004. LNCS, vol. 3055, pp. 217–228. Springer, Berlin, Heidelberg (2004)

Use of Possibility Measures for Ranking of Interval Valued Intuitionistic Fuzzy Numbers in Solving Multicriteria Decision Making Problems

Samir Kumar[1] and Animesh Biswas[2(✉)]

[1] Department of Mathematics,
Acharya Jagadish Chandra Bose College, Kolkata 700020, India
kumarsamir2007@gmail.com
[2] Department of Mathematics, University of Kalyani,
Kalyani 741235, India
abiswaskln@rediffmail.com

Abstract. In this paper, three possibility degree measures for comparing interval valued intuitionistic fuzzy numbers have been defined as extensions of existing possibility degree formulas in interval numbers and their equivalence are established and some basic properties are also proved. A simple mechanism proposed for solving MCDM problems by directly employing the possibility degree matrix generated from the proposed possibility degree measures. The introduced approach presents possibility degree as supplementary information to the ranking of alternatives in interval-valued intuitionistic fuzzy decision making. The validity and effectiveness of the developed methods are demonstrated through the comparative analysis and discussion of the three illustrative examples.

Keywords: Intuitionistic fuzzy sets · Interval numbers · Interval-valued intuitionistic fuzzy numbers · Possibility degree · Multi criteria decision making

1 Introduction

As a generalization of fuzzy set theory [17], Atanassov [1] developed intuitionistic fuzzy sets (IFSs) for capturing the vagueness and incompleteness in the real situations in more effective and reliable manner. Atanassov and Gargov [2] further generalized IFSs for effective modelling of uncertainties inherent in the real-world problems and presented the concepts of interval-valued intuitionistic fuzzy sets (IVIFSs). Ranking of alternatives being at the core of every multicriteria decision making (MCDM) problem, the idea of ranking of interval numbers, IFSs, IVIFSs, etc. [3–5, 7, 11] was developed. Wang et al. [5] advanced a simple and pragmatic preference degree for ranking of interval numbers without using the midpoints of interval numbers. Tao et al. [11] presented the idea of intuitionistic fuzzy possibility degree as a tool for ordering of interval-valued fuzzy numbers and applied it to fuzzy multi-attribute decision making problems.

© Springer Nature Singapore Pte Ltd. 2017
J.K. Mandal et al. (Eds.): CICBA 2017, Part II, CCIS 776, pp. 153–167, 2017.
DOI: 10.1007/978-981-10-6430-2_13

Wei et al. [6] utilized the possibility degree measure [5] for comparing interval numbers to define order on intuitionistic fuzzy numbers (IFNs) by converting an IFN into an interval with consideration of membership degree as lower bound and fuzzy complement of non-membership degree as upper bound.

Xu [9] extended the concepts of accuracy function and score function for an IFN to the IVIF number (IVIFN) by defining them as the sum and difference of the midpoints of membership and non-membership interval degrees, respectively. Skalna et al. [15] overviewed the existing approaches for ordering of fuzzy numbers by dividing them into two groups - the first group being probabilistic, centroid point or radius of gyration approaches while the second group methods assign a crisp value to each fuzzy number like defuzzification, Yager ranking index or weighted average approaches. The degree of possibility approach assigns a crisp value as preference estimate for comparing two fuzzy numbers or IVIFNs.

Very few works are found towards extension of the concept of possibility degree measures to IVIFNs. Zhang et al. [10] proposed two possibility degree measures for comparing IVIFNs. The first possibility degree measure was proposed in the form of newly defined accuracy function while the second possibility degree measure was defined using existing possibility degree measure for interval numbers. Both the methods face the drawback of assigning parameter in an arbitrary way as decided by the decision makers. Dammak et al. [16] made a short study of the existing possibility degree measures for comparing the IVIFNs and applied them to solve numerous MCDM problems.

Wan and Dong [4] compared two intervals considering them as random variables following uniform distribution. In that approach the possibility of occurrence of the fuzzy event of comparing two intervals was explained from the probabilistic perspective. The possibility degree of comparing two IVIFNs are performed by taking the average value of the possibility degrees of the comparison of corresponding membership and non-membership intervals of the IVIFNs in reverse order.

So far, all the possibility measures defined for comparing IVIFNs were either functions of a parameter or average of the possibility measures for intervals. In this paper, the three possibility degree measures are defined for comparing IVIFNs which are independent of parameters as well as possibility measures for interval numbers satisfying the transitivity property. It is to be noted that the possibility degree measures furnish supplementary information regarding the degree of intensity for comparing the two IVIFNs.

2 Preliminaries

The notion of IVIFSs, the aggregation operators and the possibility degree measures for comparing two interval numbers are reviewed in brief in this section.

Definition 2.1 [2]. An IVIFS, A, defined on a universe of discourse $X(\neq \emptyset)$, is considered as a set of the form $A = \{\langle x, \mu_A(x), v_A(x) : x \in X\rangle\}$, where $\mu_A : X \rightarrow S[0,1], v_A : X \rightarrow S[0,1]$ with $0 \leq sup\mu_A(x) + sup v_A(x) \leq 1$, for each $x \in X$. The set $S[0,1]$ denotes the collection of all closed subintervals of $[0, 1]$.

The functional values $\mu_A(x)$ and $\nu_A(x)$ of the element $x(\in X)$ denote the interval degree of membership and non-membership to the set A, respectively. For brevity, let $\mu_A^l(x), \mu_A^u(x)$ and $\nu_A^l(x), \nu_A^u(x)$ be, respectively, the lower and upper end points of $\mu_A(x)$ and $\nu_A(x)$, for each $x \in X$. Thus, the IVIFS A takes the form

$A = \{\langle x, [\mu_A^l(x), \mu_A^u(x)], [\nu_A^l(x), \nu_A^u(x)]\rangle : x \in X\}$ with $0 \le \mu_A^u(x) + \nu_A^u(x) \le 1$, $\mu_A^l(x) \ge 0, \nu_A^l(x) \ge 0$

For IVIFS A in X, an associated function $\pi_A : X \to S[0, 1]$ defined by

$$\pi_A(x) = 1 - \mu_A(x) - \nu_A(x) = [\pi_A^l(x), \pi_A^u(x)]$$
$$= [1 - \mu_A^u(x) - \nu_A^u(x), 1 - \mu_A^l(x) - \nu_A^l(x)]$$

For each $x \in X$, the functional value $\pi_A(x)$ represents the interval-valued hesitancy degree (the unknown degree) of x in A.

Definition 2.2 [2]. Let IVIFS(X) denote the family of all IVIFSs in X and $A, B \in IVIFS(X)$. Then,

$A \subset B$ iff $\mu_A^l(x) \le \mu_B^l(x), \mu_A^u(x) \le \mu_B^u(x)$ and $\nu_A^l(x) \ge \nu_B^l(x), \nu_A^u(x) \ge \nu_B^u(x), \forall x \in X$

Definition 2.3 [9]. Assume that $A = \{\langle x, \mu_A(x), \nu_A(x)\rangle : x \in X\}$ be an IVIFS. Then, the associated ordered pair $\langle \mu_A(x), \nu_A(x)\rangle$, for each $x \in X$, is said to be an IVIFN.

For computational convenience, let us denote an IVIFN α_j as $\langle\left[a_j^-, a_j^+\right],$ $\left[b_j^-, b_j^+\right]\rangle$. The basic operations for combining the two IVIFNs are underlined below:

Definition 2.4 [9]. Let $\alpha_j = \langle\left[a_j^-, a_j^+\right], \left[b_j^-, b_j^+\right]\rangle (j = 1, 2)$ be two IVIFNs and $\lambda > 0$. Then,

1. $\alpha_1 + \alpha_2 = \langle\left[a_1^- + a_2^- - a_1^- a_2^-, a_1^+ + a_2^+ - a_1^+ a_2^+\right], [b_1^- b_2^-, b_1^+ b_2^+]\rangle$
2. $\alpha_1 \alpha_2 = \langle\left[a_1^- a_2^-, a_1^+ a_2^+\right], [b_1^- + b_2^- - b_1^- b_2^-, b_1^+ + b_2^+ - b_1^+ b_2^+]\rangle$
3. $\lambda \alpha_1 = \langle\left[1 - (1 - a_1^-)^\lambda, 1 - (1 - a_1^+)^\lambda\right], \left[(b_1^-)^\lambda, (b_1^+)^\lambda\right]\rangle$
4. $(\alpha_1)^\lambda = \langle\left[(a_1^-)^\lambda, (a_1^+)^\lambda\right], \left[1 - (1 - b_1^-)^\lambda, 1 - (1 - b_1^+)^\lambda\right]\rangle$

IVIF weighted geometric aggregation operator relating to IVIFNs proposed by Xu [9] as follows:

Definition 2.5 [9]. Let $\left\{\alpha_j = \langle\left[a_j^-, a_j^+\right], \left[b_j^-, b_j^+\right]\rangle \mid j = 1, 2, \ldots, n\right\}$ be a family of IVIFNs. Then, the IVIF weighted geometric aggregation operator is defined by $G_w(\alpha_1, \alpha_2, \ldots, \alpha_n) = \langle\left[\prod_{j=1}^n \left(a_j^-\right)^{w_j}, \prod_{j=1}^n \left(a_j^+\right)^{w_j}\right], \left[1 - \prod_{j=1}^n \left(1 - b_j^-\right)^{w_j}, 1 - \prod_{j=1}^n \left(1 - b_j^+\right)^{w_j}\right]\rangle$ where $w = (w_1, w_2, \ldots, w_n)^T$, with $w_j > 0$ and $\sum_{j=1}^n w_j = 1$, is the weight vector of $\alpha_j (j = 1, 2, \ldots, n)$.

The definitions of novel accuracy function [13] and general accuracy function [14] are given below.

Definition 2.6 [13]. Assume that $\alpha = \langle [a^-, a^+], [b^-, b^+] \rangle$ is an IVIFN. The novel accuracy function M is defined by $M(\alpha) = a^- + a^+ - 1 + \frac{b^- + b^+}{2}$.

Definition 2.7 [14]. Assume that $\alpha = \langle [a^-, a^+], [b^-, b^+] \rangle$ is an IVIFN. The general novel accuracy function LG is defined by $LG(\alpha) = \frac{a^- + a^+ + \delta(2 - a^- - a^+ - b^- - b^+)}{2}$, where δ is a parameter with $\delta \in [0, 1]$ which depends on the individual's preference for optimism.

The existing concepts of possibility degree measures used for comparing two interval numbers are revisited here.

Let $a_i = [a_i^-, a_i^+] (i = 1, 2)$ be two interval numbers and $L(a_i) = a_i^+ - a_i^-$ be the interval length of a_i. The degree of possibility for the order $a_1 \geq a_2$ implying "a_1 is not smaller than a_2" may be defined in one of the following ways:

Definition 2.8 [3]. Assume that $a_i = [a_i^-, a_i^+] (i = 1, 2)$ are two interval numbers with $0 \leq a_i^- \leq a_i^+ \leq 1$ and $L(a_i)$ be the interval length of a_i. Then, the possibility degree of $a_1 \geq a_2$, denoted by $p(a_1 \geq a_2)$, is defined by

$$p(a_1 \geq a_2) = min \left\{ max \left\{ \frac{a_1^+ - a_2^-}{L(a_1) + L(a_2)}, 0 \right\}, 1 \right\}$$

Definition 2.9 [5]. Assume that $a_i = [a_i^-, a_i^+] (i = 1, 2)$ are two interval numbers with $0 \leq a_i^- \leq a_i^+ \leq 1$ and $L(a_i)$ be the interval length of a_i. Then, the possibility degree of $a_1 \geq a_2$, denoted by $p(a_1 \geq a_2)$, is defined by

$$p(a_1 \geq a_2) = \frac{max\{0, a_1^+ - a_2^-\} - max\{0, a_1^- - a_2^+\}}{L(a_1) + L(a_2)}$$

Definition 2.10 [7]. Assume that $a_i = [a_i^-, a_i^+] (i = 1, 2)$ are two interval numbers with $0 \leq a_i^- \leq a_i^+ \leq 1$ and $L(a_i)$ be the interval length of a_i. Then, the possibility degree of $a_1 \geq a_2$, denoted by $p(a_1 \geq a_2)$, is defined by

$$p(a_1 \geq a_2) = max \left\{ 1 - max \left\{ \frac{a_2^+ - a_1^-}{L(a_1) + L(a_2))}, 0 \right\}, 0 \right\}$$

3   Possibility Degree Measures for IVIFNs

The limitations [4, 10] underlined in the possibility degree formulations for the comparison of IVIFNs need effective remedy by introducing a suitable extension of the existing concept of possibility degree measures for interval numbers. Motivated by the concepts in [3, 5, 7], the following definition as an extension of Definition 2.8 relating to possibility degree measure for two interval numbers [3] to IVIFNs is proposed as follows:

Definition 3.1. Let $\alpha_i = \langle [a_i^-, a_i^+], [b_i^-, b_i^+] \rangle = \langle a_i, b_i \rangle (i = 1, 2)$ be two IVIFNs and $L(a_i) = a_i^+ - a_i^-$, $L(b_i) = b_i^+ - b_i^-$ be the lengths of intervals a_i and b_i, respectively. Then, the possibility degree of $\alpha_1 \geq \alpha_2$, denoted by $p(\alpha_1 \geq \alpha_2)$, is defined by

$$p(\alpha_1 \geq \alpha_2) = min\left\{ max\left\{ \frac{a_1^+ - a_2^- + b_2^+ - b_1^-}{L(a_1) + L(a_2) + L(b_1) + L(b_2)}, 0 \right\}, 1 \right\} \tag{1}$$

Definition 3.2. Let α_1 and α_2 be two IVIFNs. If $p(\alpha_1 \geq \alpha_2) \gtreqqless p(\alpha_2 \geq \alpha_1)$ then α_1 is called superior or inferior to α_2 to the extent of degree $p(\alpha_1 \geq \alpha_2)$, denoted by $\alpha_1 \overset{p(\alpha_1 \geq \alpha_2)}{\succ} \alpha_2$ or $\alpha_1 \overset{p(\alpha_1 \geq \alpha_2)}{\prec} \alpha_2$. Further, if $p(\alpha_1 \geq \alpha_2) = p(\alpha_2 \geq \alpha_1) = 0.5$ then α_1 is said to be indifferent to α_2, denoted by $\alpha_1 \sim \alpha_2$.

Remark 3.1. For two IVIFNs α_1 and α_2, $p(\alpha_1 \geq \alpha_2) \gtreqqless p(\alpha_2 \geq \alpha_1) \Rightarrow$ $p(\alpha_1 \geq \alpha_2) \gtreqqless 1 - p(\alpha_1 \geq \alpha_2) \Rightarrow p(\alpha_1 \geq \alpha_2) \gtreqqless 0.5$.

Thus, $p(\alpha_1 \geq \alpha_2) \gtreqqless p(\alpha_2 \geq \alpha_1)$ and $p(\alpha_1 \geq \alpha_2) \gtreqqless 0.5$ are equivalent.

The possibility degree matrix obtained by pairwise comparison of IVIFNs $\alpha_i = \langle [a_i^-, a_i^+], [b_i^-, b_i^+] \rangle = \langle a_i, b_i \rangle (i = 1, 2, \ldots, n)$ takes the following form

$$P = \left(p(\alpha_i \geq \alpha_j) \right)_{n \times n} = \left(p_{ij} \right)_{n \times n}$$

This is an additive reciprocal fuzzy matrix representing fuzzy preference relation and the optimal degree ξ_i for an IVIFN $\alpha_i(i = 1, 2, \ldots, n)$ may be obtained by the optimal degree formula proposed by Xu and Da [8] which is given as

$$\xi_i = \frac{1}{n(n-1)} \left(\sum_{k=1}^{n} p_{ik} + \frac{n}{2} - 1 \right), \quad \text{for} \quad i = 1, 2, \ldots, n \tag{2}$$

The ranking of IVIFNs is based on the descending order of their optimal degrees. To describe Theorem 3.1, the Lemmas required are as follows:

Lemma 1: For two real numbers x and y, $min\{x, y\} = 1 - max\{1 - x, 1 - y\}$

Proof: *Case 1:* Let $x \leq y$. Then, $1 - y \leq 1 - x$

$$min\{x, y\} = x = 1 - (1 - x) = 1 - max\{1 - x, 1 - y\}$$

Case 2: Let $y < x$. Then, $1 - x < 1 - y$

$$min\{x, y\} = y = 1 - (1 - y) = 1 - max\{1 - x, 1 - y\}$$

Lemma 2: For two real numbers x and y, $max\{x,y\} = 1 - min\{1 - x, 1 - y\}$

Proof: As above.

Lemma 3: For any real number x, $max\{min\{x,1\},0\} = min\{max\{x,0\},1\}$

Proof:

Case 1: Let $x \leq 0$. So, $max\{min\{x,1\},0\} = 0 = min\{0,1\} = min\{max\{x,0\},1\}$
Case 2: Let $0 < x \leq 1$. $max\{min\{x,1\},0\} = x = min\{x,1\} = min\{max\{x,0\},1\}$
Case 3: Let $x > 1$. $max\{min\{x,1\},0\} = 1 = min\{x,1\} = min\{max\{x,0\},1\}$.

Theorem 3.1. Let $\alpha_i = \langle [a_i^-, a_i^+], [b_i^-, b_i^+] \rangle = \langle a_i, b_i \rangle (i = 1,2,3)$ be three IVIFNs and $L(a_i)$ and $L(b_i)$ be the lengths of intervals a_i and b_i. Then, the following properties hold:

   (i) $0 \leq p(\alpha_1 \geq \alpha_2) \leq 1$ (Boundedness)
  (ii) $p(\alpha_1 \geq \alpha_2) = 1$ iff $a_2^+ + b_1^+ \leq a_1^- + b_2^-$
 (iii) $p(\alpha_1 \geq \alpha_2) = 0$ iff $a_1^+ + b_2^+ \leq a_2^- + b_1^-$
 (iv) $p(\alpha_1 \geq \alpha_1) = 0.5$
  (v) $p(\alpha_1 \geq \alpha_2) + p(\alpha_2 \geq \alpha_1) = 1$
 (vi) $p(\alpha_1 \geq \alpha_2) \geq 0.5$ iff $a_1^+ + a_1^- + b_2^+ + b_2^- \geq a_2^+ + a_2^- + b_1^+ + b_1^-$
(vii) If $p(\alpha_1 \geq \alpha_2) \geq 0.5$ and $p(\alpha_2 \geq \alpha_3) \geq 0.5$ then $p(\alpha_1 \geq \alpha_3) \geq 0.5$
      (Weak transitivity property)

Proof: It is evident that

$$L(a_1) + L(a_2) + L(b_1) + L(b_2)$$
$$= (a_1^+ - a_1^-) + (a_2^+ - a_2^-) + (b_1^+ - b_1^-) + (b_2^+ - b_2^-) \tag{3}$$

(i) The inequality directly follows from the Eq. (1).

(ii) $p(\alpha_1 \geq \alpha_2) = 1 \Leftrightarrow \dfrac{a_1^+ - a_2^- + b_2^+ - b_1^-}{L(a_1) + L(a_2) + L(b_1) + L(b_2)} \geq 1$ (By Definition 3.1)

     $\Leftrightarrow a_1^+ - a_2^- + b_2^+ - b_1^- \geq L(a_1) + L(a_2) + L(b_1) + L(b_2)$

     $\Leftrightarrow a_2^+ + b_1^+ \leq a_1^- + b_2^-$ (By Eq. (3))

(iii) $p(\alpha_1 \geq \alpha_2) = 0 \Leftrightarrow \dfrac{a_1^+ - a_2^- + b_2^+ - b_1^-}{L(a_1) + L(a_2) + L(b_1) + L(b_2)} \leq 0$ (By Definition 3.1)

     $\Leftrightarrow a_1^+ - a_2^- + b_2^+ - b_1^- \leq 0$

     $\Leftrightarrow a_1^+ + b_2^+ \leq a_2^- + b_1^-$

(iv) $p(\alpha_1 \geq \alpha_1) = \dfrac{(a_1^+ - a_1^-) + (b_1^+ - b_1^-)}{L(a_1) + L(a_1) + L(b_1) + L(b_1)} = \dfrac{L(a_1) + L(b_1)}{2(L(a_1) + L(b_1))} = 0.5.$

(v) $\quad p(\alpha_1 \geq \alpha_2) = min\left\{ max\left\{ \dfrac{a_1^+ - a_2^- + b_2^+ - b_1^-}{L(a_1) + L(a_2) + L(b_1) + L(b_2)}, 0 \right\}, 1 \right\}$

$\qquad = min\left\{ max\left\{ 1 - \dfrac{a_2^+ - a_1^- + b_1^+ - b_2^-}{L(a_1) + L(a_2) + L(b_1) + L(b_2)}, 0 \right\}, \ 1 \right\}$ (By Eq. (3))

$\qquad = min\left\{ 1 - min\left\{ \dfrac{a_2^+ - a_1^- + b_1^+ - b_2^-}{L(a_1) + L(a_2) + L(b_1) + L(b_2)}, 1 \right\} \ 1 \right\}$ (Lemma 2)

$\qquad = 1 - max\left\{ min\left\{ \dfrac{a_2^+ - a_1^- + b_1^+ - b_2^-}{L(a_1) + L(a_2) + L(b_1) + L(b_2)}, 1 \right\}, \ 0 \right\}$ (Lemma 1)

$\qquad = 1 - min\left\{ max\left\{ \dfrac{a_2^+ - a_1^- + b_1^+ - b_2^-}{L(a_1) + L(a_2) + L(b_1) + L(b_2)}, 0 \right\}, \ 1 \right\}$ (Lemma 3)

$\qquad = 1 - p(\alpha_2 \geq \alpha_1)$

Hence, $p(\alpha_1 \geq \alpha_2) + p(\alpha_2 \geq \alpha_1) = 1$

(vi) Let $p(\alpha_1 \geq \alpha_2) \geq 0.5$

$$p(\alpha_1 \geq \alpha_2) \geq 0.5 \Leftrightarrow \frac{a_1^+ - a_2^- + b_2^+ - b_1^-}{L(a_1) + L(a_2) + L(b_1) + L(b_2)} \geq 0.5 \quad \text{(By Definition 3.1)}$$

$$\Leftrightarrow 2\left(a_1^+ - a_2^- + b_2^+ - b_1^- \right) \geq L(a_1) + L(a_2) + L(b_1) + L(b_2)$$

$$\Leftrightarrow a_1^+ + a_1^- + b_2^+ + b_2^- \geq a_2^+ + a_2^- + b_1^+ + b_1^- \quad \text{(By Eq. (3))}$$

(vii) Let $p(\alpha_1 \geq \alpha_2) \geq 0.5$ and $p(\alpha_2 \geq \alpha_3) \geq 0.5$

By property (vi),

$$p(\alpha_1 \geq \alpha_2) \geq 0.5 \Rightarrow a_1^+ + a_1^- + b_2^+ + b_2^- \geq a_2^+ + a_2^- + b_1^+ + b_1^- \qquad (4)$$

$$\text{and } p(\alpha_2 \geq \alpha_3) \geq 0.5 \Rightarrow a_2^+ + a_2^- + b_3^+ + b_3^- \geq a_3^+ + a_3^- + b_2^+ + b_2^- \qquad (5)$$

From inequalities (4) and (5), $a_1^+ + a_1^- + b_3^+ + b_3^- \geq a_3^+ + a_3^- + b_1^+ + b_1^-$

$$\Rightarrow p(\alpha_1 \geq \alpha_3) \geq 0.5 \qquad \text{(By property (vi))}$$

Hence, the weak transitivity property is established.

In view of Definition 3.1, the simple extensions of Definitions 2.9 and 2.10 relating to possibility degree measure for two interval numbers [5, 7] to IVIFNs are proposed as follows:

Definition 3.3. Let $\alpha_i = \left\langle [a_i^-, a_i^+], [b_i^-, b_i^+] \right\rangle = \langle a_i, b_i \rangle (i = 1, 2)$ be two IVIFNs and $L(a_i) = a_i^+ - a_i^-$, $L(b_i) = b_i^+ - b_i^-$ be the lengths of intervals a_i and b_i. Then, the possibility degree of $\alpha_1 \geq \alpha_2$, denoted by $p(\alpha_1 \geq \alpha_2)$, is defined by

$$p(\alpha_1 \geq \alpha_2) = max\left\{ 1 - max\left\{ \frac{a_2^+ - a_1^- + b_1^+ - b_2^-}{L(a_1) + L(a_2) + L(b_1) + L(b_2)}, 0 \right\}, 0 \right\} \qquad (6)$$

Definition 3.4. Let $\alpha_i = \langle [a_i^-, a_i^+], [b_i^-, b_i^+] \rangle = \langle a_i, b_i \rangle (i = 1, 2)$ be two IVIFNs and $L(a_i) = a_i^+ - a_i^-$, $L(b_i) = b_i^+ - b_i^-$ be the lengths of intervals a_i and b_i. Then, the possibility degree of $\alpha_1 \geq \alpha_2$, denoted by $p(\alpha_1 \geq \alpha_2)$, is defined by

$$p(\alpha_1 \geq \alpha_2) = \frac{max\{0, a_1^+ - a_2^- + b_2^+ - b_1^-\} - max\{0, a_1^- - a_2^+ + b_2^- - b_1^+\}}{L(a_1) + L(a_2) + L(b_1) + L(b_2)} \quad (7)$$

Theorem 3.2. Let $\alpha_i = \langle [a_i^-, a_i^+], [b_i^-, b_i^+] \rangle = \langle a_i, b_i \rangle (i = 1, 2)$ be two IVIFNs and $L(a_i) = a_i^+ - a_i^-$, $L(b_i) = b_i^+ - b_i^-$ be the lengths of intervals a_i and b_i. Then, Eqs. (1), (6) and (7) are equivalent.

Proof: By Eq. (1),

$$p(\alpha_1 \geq \alpha_2) = min\left\{ max\left\{ \frac{a_1^+ - a_2^- + b_2^+ - b_1^-}{L(a_1) + L(a_2) + L(b_1) + L(b_2)}, \quad 0 \right\}, \quad 1 \right\}$$

$$= max\left\{ min\left\{ \frac{a_1^+ - a_2^- + b_2^+ - b_1^-}{L(a_1) + L(a_2) + L(b_1) + L(b_2)}, \quad 1 \right\}, \quad 0 \right\} \qquad \text{(Lemma 3)}$$

$$= max\left\{ 1 - max\left\{ 1 - \frac{a_1^+ - a_2^- + b_2^+ - b_1^-}{L(a_1) + L(a_2) + L(b_1) + L(b_2)}, \quad 0 \right\}, \quad 0 \right\} \qquad \text{(Lemma 1)}$$

$$= max\left\{ 1 - max\left\{ \frac{a_2^+ - a_1^- + b_1^+ - b_2^-}{L(a_1) + L(a_2) + L(b_1) + L(b_2)}, 0 \right\}, \quad 0 \right\}$$

Thus, Eq. (1) implies Eq. (6) and vice-versa.
Now, the following cases are considered:

Case 1: $a_1^+ - a_2^- < 0, b_2^+ - b_1^- < 0, a_1^+ - a_2^- + b_2^+ - b_1^- < 0$

$$p(\alpha_1 \geq \alpha_2) = \frac{max\{0, a_1^+ - a_2^- + b_2^+ - b_1^-\} - max\{0, a_1^- - a_2^+ + b_2^- - b_1^+\}}{L(a_1) + L(a_2) + L(b_1) + L(b_2)}$$

$$= min\left\{ max\left\{ \frac{a_1^+ - a_2^- + b_2^+ - b_1^-}{L(a_1) + L(a_2) + L(b_1) + L(b_2)}, 0 \right\}, \quad 1 \right\}$$

Case 2: $a_1^- - a_2^+ > 0, b_2^- - b_1^+ > 0, a_1^- - a_2^+ + b_2^- - b_1^+ > 0$

$$p(\alpha_1 \geq \alpha_2) = \frac{max\{0, a_1^+ - a_2^- + b_2^+ - b_1^-\} - max\{0, a_1^- - a_2^+ + b_2^- - b_1^+\}}{L(a_1) + L(a_2) + L(b_1) + L(b_2)}$$

$$= min\left\{ max\left\{ \frac{a_1^+ - a_2^- + b_2^+ - b_1^-}{L(a_1) + L(a_2) + L(b_1) + L(b_2)}, \quad 0 \right\}, \quad 1 \right\}$$

Case 3: $a_1^- - a_2^+ < 0 < a_1^+ - a_2^-, b_2^- - b_1^+ < 0 < b_2^+ - b_1^-$ and $a_1^- - a_2^+ + b_2^- - b_1^+ < 0 < a_1^+ - a_2^- + b_2^+ - b_1^-$

$$p(\alpha_1 \geq \alpha_2) = \frac{max\{0, a_1^+ - a_2^- + b_2^+ - b_1^-\} - max\{0, a_1^- - a_2^+ + b_2^- - b_1^+\}}{L(a_1) + L(a_2) + L(b_1) + L(b_2)}$$

$$= \frac{a_1^+ - a_2^- + b_2^+ - b_1^-}{L(a_1) + L(a_2) + L(b_1) + L(b_2)} = min\left\{ max\left\{ \frac{a_1^+ - a_2^- + b_2^+ - b_1^-}{L(a_1) + L(a_2) + L(b_1) + L(b_2)}, \quad 0 \right\}, \quad 1 \right\}$$

It can be found that there may arise nineteen cases from all possible combinations of admissible signs of elements of intervals $a_1 - a_2$, $b_2 - b_1$ and $a_1 - a_2 + b_2 - b_1$. However, it is clear that irrespective of signs of elements of intervals $a_1 - a_2$ and $b_2 - b_1$, the nature of interval $a_1 - a_2 + b_2 - b_1$ can be represented by one of the three variants of the Fig. 1. Thus, the effect of remaining sixteen cases reduces them to exactly one of the three cases as described above. Hence, it can be found that

$$p(\alpha_1 \geq \alpha_2) = \frac{max\{0, a_1^+ - a_2^- + b_2^+ - b_1^-\} - max\{0, a_1^- - a_2^+ + b_2^- - b_1^+\}}{L(a_1) + L(a_2) + L(b_1) + L(b_2)}$$

$$= min\left\{ max\left\{ \frac{a_1^+ - a_2^- + b_2^+ - b_1^-}{L(a_1) + L(a_2) + L(b_1) + L(b_2)}, \ 0 \right\}, \ 1 \right\}$$

Therefore, Eq. (1) implies Eq. (7) and vice-versa.
Hence, Eqs. (1), (6) and (7) are equivalent and the theorem is established.

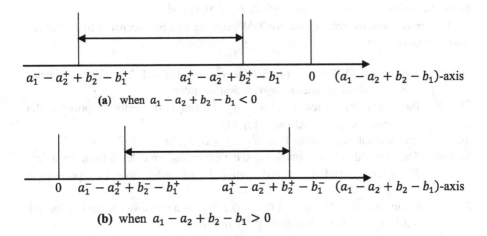

(a) when $a_1 - a_2 + b_2 - b_1 < 0$

(b) when $a_1 - a_2 + b_2 - b_1 > 0$

(c) when $a_1 - a_2 + b_2 - b_1$ admits either sign

Fig. 1. Representations of variations of sum of the differences between membership interval weights as well as non-membership interval weights in reverse order of two IVIFNs

4 MCDM Method Based on Possibility Degree Measures of IVIFNs

Let $A = \{A_1, A_2, \ldots, A_m\}$ and $C = \{C_1, C_2, \ldots, C_n\}$ be the sets of alternatives and criteria, respectively, in a multicriteria IVIF decision making problem generating IVIF decision matrix

$$D = (d_{ij})_{m \times n} = \left(\left\langle \left[\mu^l_{ij}, \mu^u_{ij} \right], \left[v^l_{ij}, v^u_{ij} \right] \right\rangle \right)_{m \times n}$$

$$= \begin{array}{c} \\ A_1 \\ A_2 \\ \vdots \\ A_m \end{array} \begin{pmatrix} \overset{C_1}{\left\langle \left[\mu^l_{11}, \mu^u_{11} \right], \left[v^l_{11}, v^u_{11} \right] \right\rangle} & \overset{C_2}{\left\langle \left[\mu^l_{12}, \mu^u_{12} \right], \left[v^l_{12}, v^u_{12} \right] \right\rangle} & \cdots & \overset{C_n}{\left\langle \left[\mu^l_{1n}, \mu^u_{1n} \right], \left[v^l_{1n}, v^u_{1n} \right] \right\rangle} \\ \left\langle \left[\mu^l_{21}, \mu^u_{21} \right], \left[v^l_{21}, v^u_{21} \right] \right\rangle & \left\langle \left[\mu^l_{22}, \mu^u_{22} \right], \left[v^l_{22}, v^u_{22} \right] \right\rangle & \cdots & \left\langle \left[\mu^l_{2n}, \mu^u_{2n} \right], \left[v^l_{2n}, v^u_{2n} \right] \right\rangle \\ \vdots & \vdots & \cdots & \vdots \\ \left\langle \left[\mu^l_{m1}, \mu^u_{m1} \right], \left[v^l_{m1}, v^u_{m1} \right] \right\rangle & \left\langle \left[\mu^l_{m2}, \mu^u_{m2} \right], \left[v^l_{m2}, v^u_{m2} \right] \right\rangle & \cdots & \left\langle \left[\mu^l_{mn}, \mu^u_{mn} \right], \left[v^l_{mn}, v^u_{mn} \right] \right\rangle \end{pmatrix}$$

Now, assume that the decision maker evaluates criteria assigning the weights given by the vector $\omega = (\omega_1, \omega_2, \ldots, \omega_n)$, where $\omega_j \in [0, 1]$ and $\sum_{j=1}^{n} \omega_j = 1$.

The procedures for solving the MCDM problem can be encapsulated in the following important steps:

Step 1:   Aggregated IVIF score of each alternative $A_i (i = 1, 2, \ldots m)$ is estimated using weighted geometric aggregation operator.

Step 2:   Possibility degree matrix $P = (p_{ij})_{m \times m}$ from IVIF vector of priorities for alternatives is generated using Eq. (1).

Step 3:   The alternative A_k ranks first, if $p_{kj} \geq max_i \, p_{ij}$, for $j = 1, 2, \ldots n$

Step 4:   The row and column containing the element p_{kk} are deleted from the matrix $P = (p_{ij})_{m \times m}$ and a reduced matrix P_1 of order $(m-1) \times (m-1)$ is obtained.

Step 5:   Go to Step 3 and Step 4 in that order getting alternatives ranked at second, third, etc., till the exhaustion of alternatives.

Step 6:   Two alternatives A_i and A_j are called indifferent or equivalent, denoted by $A_i \sim A_j$, if $p_{ik} = p_{jk}$, $k = 1, 2, \ldots n$.

Further, if optimal degrees or performance scores of alternatives are required for ranking and for being used as an intermediate step in a complex decision making procedure then step 2 should be followed by Step 7 and Step 8 in that order.

Step 7:   Optimal degrees ξ_i for alternatives $A_i (i = 1, 2, \ldots m)$ are computed using Eq. (2).

Step 8:   The decreasing order of the optimal degrees ξ_i generates the ranking of alternatives $A_i (i = 1, 2, \ldots m)$

5 Numerical Illustrations

In this section, the proposed definition of the possibility degree of IVIFNs and intu-itionistic fuzzy MCDM method are illustrated through the three illustrative examples.

5.1 Illustrative Example 1

Consider the four IVIFNs $\alpha_1 = \langle[0.3,0.5],[0.1,0.3]\rangle, \alpha_2 = \langle[0.3,0.45],[0.1,0.35]\rangle$, $\alpha_3 = \langle[0.3,0.4],[0.1,0.4]\rangle$, $\alpha_4 = \langle[0.3,0.4],[0.1,0.5]\rangle$.

Using Definition 2.2, it is obvious that $\alpha_1 > \alpha_2 > \alpha_3 > \alpha_4$.

The possibility degree matrix obtained by pairwise comparison of these IVIFNs using Eq. (1) is given by

$$
P = (p_{ij})_{4\times4} =
\begin{array}{c}
\\ \alpha_1 \\ \alpha_2 \\ \alpha_3 \\ \alpha_4
\end{array}
\begin{array}{cccc}
\alpha_1 & \alpha_2 & \alpha_3 & \alpha_4 \\
\left(\begin{array}{cccc}
0.5 & 0.56 & 0.62 & 0.67 \\
0.44 & 0.5 & 0.56 & 0.61 \\
0.38 & 0.44 & 0.5 & 0.56 \\
0.33 & 0.39 & 0.44 & 0.5
\end{array}\right)
\end{array}
$$

Following the ranking process discussed in Sect. 4, it is found that $\alpha_1 > \alpha_2 > \alpha_3 > \alpha_4$ which is consistent with the previous ranking.

Now, using Definition 2.6, the novel accuracy degrees (NADs) [13] for the IVIFNs are estimated as $M(\alpha_1) = 0$, $M(\alpha_2) = -0.025$, $M(\alpha_3) = -0.05$, $M(\alpha_4) = 0$. The ranking of alternatives thus becomes $\alpha_1 \sim \alpha_4 > \alpha_2 > \alpha_3$ which is untenable reflecting the shortcomings of the NAD developed by Ye [13].

The general accuracy functional values [14] of the IVIFNs are $LG(\alpha_1) = 0.4 + 0.4\delta$, $LG(\alpha_2) = 0.375 + 0.4\delta$, $LG(\alpha_3) = 0.35 + 0.4\delta$, $LG(\alpha_4) = 0.35 + 0.35\delta$ with $\delta \in [0,1]$ yielding ranking $\alpha_1 > \alpha_2 > \alpha_3 > \alpha_4$.

Remark 5.1. In the preceding example, it is observed that the possibility degree ranking of IVIFNs is consistent with the Definition 2.2 and GNAD based ranking [14], but inconsistent with the ranking by NAD [13]. Here, the NAD ranking counters the basic Definition 2.2 and hence amply outlines its shortcomings over other methods of ranking of IVIFNs. Furthermore, the possibility degree ranking provides additional information of degree by which one IVIFN is greater than another one as shown in Table 1. Thus, the validity and effectiveness of the proposed approach is strongly demonstrated.

5.2 Illustrative Example 2

The example considered by Nayagam and Sivaraman [14] illustrates the introduced approach. Consider following four IVIFNs

$\alpha_1 = \langle[0.2297,0.4266],[0.3674,0.4898]\rangle$,
$\alpha_2 = \langle[0.5102,0.7000],[0.1614,0.2616]\rangle, \alpha_3 = \langle[0.4181,0.6000],[0.2260,0.3618]\rangle$,
$\alpha_4 = \langle[0.4799,0.6411],[0.1000,0.2263]\rangle$.

Using general accuracy degree [14] two different rankings are found as:
$\alpha_2 > \alpha_4 > \alpha_3 > \alpha_1$, for $\delta \in [0, 0.484)$ and $\alpha_4 > \alpha_2 > \alpha_3 > \alpha_1$, for $\delta \in [0.484, 1]$.

Now, the possibility degree matrix obtained by pairwise comparison of these IVIFNs using Eq. (1) is given by

$$
P = \left(p_{ij}\right)_{4 \times 4} = \begin{array}{c} \\ \alpha_1 \\ \alpha_2 \\ \alpha_3 \\ \alpha_4 \end{array} \begin{pmatrix} \overset{\alpha_1}{0.5} & \overset{\alpha_2}{0} & \overset{\alpha_3}{0.0046} & \overset{\alpha_4}{0} \\ 1 & 0.5 & 0.7936 & 0.4935 \\ 0.9954 & 0.2064 & 0.5 & 0.1989 \\ 1 & 0.5065 & 0.8011 & 0.5 \end{pmatrix}
$$

Using the proposed ranking procedure, it is found that $\alpha_4 > \alpha_2 > \alpha_3 > \alpha_1$ which is identical with the ranking based on the general accuracy functional degree [14] with preference towards individual's optimism.

Now, using Definition 2.6, the NADs [13] are estimated as $M(\alpha_1) = 0.0849$, $M(\alpha_2) = 0.4217$, $M(\alpha_3) = 0.312$, $M(\alpha_4) = 0.2841$. The ranking of IVIFNs thus follows $\alpha_2 > \alpha_3 > \alpha_4 > \alpha_1$ which is different from possibility based ordering. The dissimilar rankings of IVIFNs could be attributed to the deficiency of NAD underlined in the previous example.

Remark 5.2. In the above example, the ranking of IVIFNs under proposed possibility degree method is identical with the ranking based on the GNAD [14] with preference towards individual's optimism while different with the individual's pessimism. However, the possibility degree ranking is incompatible with that of NAD [13]. Definition 2.2 ranks $\alpha_2 > \alpha_3 > \alpha_1$ and $\alpha_4 > \alpha_3 > \alpha_1$ but it cannot be applied to ranking of IVIFNs α_2 and α_4. The unique ranking of the proposed possibility degree approach with additional information of degree of comparison as given in Table 1 makes it more suitable over others.

5.3   Illustrative Example 3

This example, related to an intuitionistic fuzzy multiattribute decision making problem as described by Li [12], fairly illustrates the application of the proposed possibility degree measures in the context of MCDM problems and also demonstrates its effectiveness over other ranking methods. The problem is described below:

An investment company has planned to invest in four companies A_1 (Car), A_2 (Food), A_3 (Computer), and A_4 (Arms). These alternatives are to be evaluated under the three attributes C_1 (risk analysis), C_2 (growth analysis), and C_3 (environmental impact analysis). Due to inherent uncertainties involved in the decision analysis, the responses from an expert are expressed in terms of IVIFNs. The IVIF decision matrix is given as

$D = \left(\beta_{ij}\right)_{m \times n}$

$$
= \begin{array}{c}
A_1 \\
A_2 \\
A_3 \\
A_4
\end{array}
\begin{pmatrix}
\langle [0.4, 0.5], [0.3, 0.4] \rangle & \langle [0.4, 0.6], [0.2, 0.4] \rangle & \langle [0.1, 0.3], [0.5, 0.6] \rangle \\
\langle [0.6, 0.7], [0.2, 0.3] \rangle & \langle [0.6, 0.7], [0.2, 0.3] \rangle & \langle [0.4, 0.7], [0.1, 0.2] \rangle \\
\langle [0.3, 0.6], [0.3, 0.4] \rangle & \langle [0.5, 0.6], [0.3, 0.4] \rangle & \langle [0.5, 0.6], [0.1, 0.3] \rangle \\
\langle [0.7, 0.8], [0.1, 0.2] \rangle & \langle [0.6, 0.7], [0.1, 0.3] \rangle & \langle [0.3, 0.4], [0.1, 0.2] \rangle
\end{pmatrix}
$$

with column headers C_1, C_2, C_3.

Here $\beta_{ij} = \left\langle \left[a_{ij}^-, a_{ij}^+ \right], \left[b_{ij}^-, b_{ij}^+ \right] \right\rangle (i = 1, 2, 3, 4; j = 1, 2, 3)$.

The weight vector of the attributes C_1, C_2 and C_3 with IVIFNs as elements is
$W = (w_1, w_2, w_3)^T = (\langle [0.1, 0.4], [0.2, 0.55] \rangle, \langle [0.2, 0.5], [0.15, 0.45] \rangle, \langle [0.25, 0.6],$
$[0.15, 0.38] \rangle)^T$ The possibility degree matrix obtained by pairwise comparison of attributes using Eq. (1) is given by

$$
P(W) = \left(p\left(w_i \geq w_j\right)\right)_{3 \times 3} = \begin{array}{c} w_1 \\ w_2 \\ w_3 \end{array}
\begin{pmatrix}
0.5 & 0.36 & 0.27 \\
0.64 & 0.5 & 0.41 \\
0.73 & 0.59 & 0.5
\end{pmatrix}
$$

with column headers w_1, w_2, w_3.

Using Eq. (2), the crisp weight vector of optimal degrees for attributes becomes

$$
\omega = (\omega_1, \omega_2, \omega_3)^T = (0.27, 0.34, 0.39)^T.
$$

By Definition 2.5, the IVIF weighted geometric aggregation operator is given by

$$
\beta_i = \left\langle \left[\prod_{j=1}^{3} \left(a_{ij}^-\right)^{\omega_j}, \prod_{j=1}^{3} \left(a_{ij}^+\right)^{\omega_j} \right], \left[1 - \prod_{j=1}^{3} \left(1 - b_{ij}^-\right)^{\omega_j}, 1 - \prod_{j=1}^{3} \left(1 - b_{ij}^+\right)^{\omega_j} \right] \right\rangle,
$$

for $i = 1, 2, 3, 4$

Now, the weighted geometric aggregated values are given by
$\beta_1 = \langle [0.23, 0.44], [0.36, 0.49] \rangle, \beta_2 = \langle [0.51, 0.70], [0.16, 0.26] \rangle,$
$\beta_3 = \langle [0.44, 0.60], [0.23, 0.36] \rangle, \beta_4 = \langle [0.48, 0.58], [0.10, 0.24] \rangle.$

The possibility degree matrix obtained by pairwise comparison of these IVIFNs using Eq. (1) is given by

$$
P = (p_{ij})_{4 \times 4} = \begin{array}{c} \beta_1 \\ \beta_2 \\ \beta_3 \\ \beta_4 \end{array}
\begin{pmatrix}
0.5 & 0 & 0 & 0 \\
1 & 0.5 & 0.793 & 0.566 \\
1 & 0.207 & 0.5 & 0.245 \\
1 & 0.434 & 0.755 & 0.5
\end{pmatrix}
$$

with column headers β_1, β_2, β_3, β_4.

Utilizing the ranking procedure of Sect. 4, the IVIFNs are ranked as $\beta_2 > \beta_4 > \beta_3 > \beta_1$. Hence, the ranking of alternatives becomes $A_2 \succ A_4 \succ A_3 \succ A_1$ which is identical with that of Li [12]. It is to be mentioned here that the computational complexities are reduced through the proposed model and the acceptability of the method would be more convenient in solving different MCDM contexts relating to IVIFNs.

By Definition 2.6, the NADs [13] are given as $M(\beta_1) = 0.095, M(\beta_2) = 0.42, M(\beta_3) = 0.335, M(\beta_4) = 0.23$ yielding ranking $\beta_2 > \beta_3 > \beta_4 > \beta_1$ and hence the ranking of alternatives is $A_2 \succ A_3 \succ A_4 \succ A_1$.

By Definition 2.7, GNADs [14] are estimated as $LG(\beta_1) = 0.335 + 0.24\delta$, $LG(\beta_2) = 0.605 + 0.185\delta, LG(\beta_3) = 0.52 + 0.185\delta, LG(\beta_4) = 0.53 + 0.3\delta, \delta \in [0,1]$ giving two different rankings $\beta_2 > \beta_4 > \beta_3 > \beta_1$, for $\delta \in [0, 0.652)$ and $\beta_4 > \beta_2 > \beta_3 > \beta_1$ for $\delta \in [0.652, 1]$ relative to individual's pessimism and optimism

Table 1. Comparison of the proposed approach with other approaches

	Ranking of IVIFNs/Alternatives			
	Li [12]	NAD [13]	GNAD [14]	Proposed approach
Illustrative Example 1	–	$\alpha_1 \sim \alpha_4 > \alpha_2 > \alpha_3$	$\alpha_1 > \alpha_2 > \alpha_3 > \alpha_4$	$\alpha_1 >^{0.56} \alpha_2 >^{0.56} \alpha_3 >^{0.56} \alpha_4$
Illustrative Example 2	–	$\alpha_2 > \alpha_3 > \alpha_4 > \alpha_1$	$\alpha_2 > \alpha_4 > \alpha_3 > \alpha_1,$ for $\delta \in [0, 0.484)$ $\alpha_4 > \alpha_2 > \alpha_3 > \alpha_1,$ for $\delta \in [0.484, 1]$	$\alpha_4 >^{0.5065} \alpha_2 >^{0.7936} \alpha_3 >^{0.9454} \alpha_1$
Illustrative Example 3	$A_2 \succ A_4 \succ A_3 \succ A_1$	$A_2 \succ A_3 \succ A_4 \succ A_1$	$A_2 \succ A_4 \succ A_3 \succ A_1,$ for $\delta \in [0, 0.652)$ $A_4 \succ A_2 \succ A_3 \succ A_1,$ for $\delta \in [0.652, 1]$	$A_2 \succ^{0.566} A_4 \succ^{0.755} A_3 \succ^1 A_1$

respectively. Thus, the respective ranking of alternatives are $A_2 \succ A_4 \succ A_3 \succ A_1$ and $A_4 \succ A_2 \succ A_3 \succ A_1$.

Remark 5.3. In the illustrative example 3, the possibility ranking of alternatives using weighted geometric aggregation operator is consistent with the Li's method [12] and the procedure based on GNAD [14] with preference towards individual's pessimism while different with the individual's optimism and NAD [13] method. Definition 2.2 ranks $A_2 \succ A_3 \succ A_1$ but neither ranks A_3 and A_4 nor ranks A_2 and A_4. Hence, the proposed method is consistent enough with [2, 12] and also with the pessimistic part of [14]. A summary of comparisons is presented in the Table 1.

6 Concluding Remarks

In this study, three possibility degree measures for comparing IVIFNs are defined as simple extensions of existing possibility measures for interval numbers [3, 5, 7]. The equivalence of the proposed possibility degree measures are established just like their counterparts in interval numbers and related properties are proved. A simple mechanism for solving MCDM problems is proposed by directly employing the possibility degree matrix generated from the proposed possibility measures. The validity and effectiveness of the developed models are demonstrated through the comparative analysis and discussion of three illustrative examples. The proposed method has greater computational simplicity in solving MCDM problems and also provides the degree of possibility as supplementary information to the ranking of alternatives.

References

1. Atanassov, K.T.: Intuitionistic fuzzy sets. Fuzzy Sets Syst. **20**(1), 87–96 (1986)
2. Atanassov, K.T., Gargov, G.: Interval-valued intuitionistic fuzzy sets. Fuzzy Sets Syst. **31**(3), 343–349 (1989)
3. Facchinetti, G., Ricci, R.G., Muzzioli, S.: Note on ranking fuzzy triangular numbers. Int. J. Intell. Syst. **13**, 613–622 (1998)
4. Wan, S., Dong, J.: A possibility degree method for interval-valued intuitionistic fuzzy multi-attribute group decision making. J. Comput. Syst. Sci. **80**, 237–256 (2014)
5. Wang, Y.M., Yang, J.B., Xu, D.L.: A preference aggregation method through the estimation of utility intervals. Comput. Oper. Res. **32**, 2027–2049 (2005)
6. Wei, C.P., Tang, X.: Possibility degree method for ranking intuitionistic fuzzy numbers. In: IEEE/WIC/ACM International Conference on Web Intelligence and Intelligent Agent Technology, pp. 142–145 (2010)
7. Xu, Z.S., Da, Q.L.: The uncertain OWA Operator. Int. J. Intell. Syst. **17**, 569–575 (2002)
8. Xu, Z.S., Da, Q.L.: A possibility based method for priorities of interval judgment matrices. Chin. J. Manag. Sci. **11**, 63–65 (2003)
9. Xu, Z.S.: Methods for aggregating interval-valued intuitionistic fuzzy information and their application to decision making. Control Decis. **22**(2), 215–219 (2007)
10. Zhang, X., Yue, G., Teng, Z.: Possibility degree of interval-valued intuitionistic fuzzy numbers and its application. In: Proceedings of the International Symposium on Information Processing (ISIP 2009), Huangshan, China, pp. 33–36 (2009)
11. Tao, Z., Liu, X., Chen, H., Zhou, L.: Ranking interval-valued fuzzy numbers with intuitionistic fuzzy possibility degree and its application to fuzzy multi-attribute decision making. Int. J. Fuzzy Syst. **19**(3), 1–13 (2016)
12. Li, D.F.: Linear programming method for MADM with interval-valued intuitionistic fuzzy sets. Expert Syst. Appl. **37**, 5939–5945 (2010)
13. Ye, J.: Multicriteria fuzzy decision-making method based on a novel accuracy function under interval-valued intuitionistic fuzzy environment. Expert Syst. Appl. **36**, 6899–6902 (2009)
14. Nayagam, V.L.G., Sivaraman, G.: Ranking of interval-valued intuitionistic fuzzy sets. Appl. Soft Comput. **11**, 3368–3372 (2011)
15. Skalna, I., Rebiasz, B., Gawel, B., Basiura, B., Duda, J., Opila, J., Pelech-Pilichowski, T.: Ordering of fuzzy numbers. In: Advances in fuzzy decision making: Theory and Practice. Studies in Soft Computing, vol. 333, pp. 27–48 (2015)
16. Dammak, F., Baccour, L., Alimi, A.M.: An exhaustive study of possibility measures of interval-valued intuitionistic fuzzy sets and application to multicriteria decision making. Adv. Fuzzy Syst. **2016**, 1–10 (2016)
17. Zadeh, L.A.: Fuzzy sets. Inf. Control **8**, 338–353 (1965)

Music Classification Based on Genre and Mood

Ayush Shakya, Bijay Gurung, Mahendra Singh Thapa, Mehang Rai,
and Basanta Joshi[✉]

Institute of Engineering, Pulchowk, Lalitpur, Nepal
qwerty.ayush5@gmail.com, bjgurung10@gmail.com,
mahendrasinghthapa27@gmail.com, mehang.rai007@gmail.com,
basanta@ioe.edu.np

Abstract. The advent of internet and the growing number of digital media has increased the necessity of Music Information Retrieval systems within which Music Classification is a prominent task. Here, we present methods to perform genre based classification over five different genre and mood based classification using a mood model that maps mood onto a two-dimensional space along axes of arousal and valence. Support vector machine and a feed-forward artificial neural network are applied to achieve an overall accuracy of 88% for genre based classification and 73% and 67% accuracy for the arousal and valence axes respectively in mood based classification.

Keywords: Music classification · Genre · Mood · Artificial neural network · Support vector machine

1 Introduction

With the advent of the internet, the number of songs being created as well as the number available to the average person has grown a lot. Simply put, it's overwhelming. Sifting through the deluge of songs manually isn't practical or appealing. It needs to be automated.

Automatic classification of music is a growing field with the primary goal of making it easier for people to find songs they like and for vendors to present those songs to their listeners. It can also lay the foundation for figuring out ways to represent similarity between two musical pieces and in the making of a good recommendation system.

Given the perplexing nature of music, its classification requires specialized representations, abstraction and processing techniques for effective analysis, evaluation and classification that are fundamentally different from those used for other mediums and tasks.

2 Literature Review

2.1 History of MIR and Music Classification

The field of Music Information Retrieval (MIR) can be traced back to the 60s with reference to the works done by Kassler in [1]. Even Automatic Transcrip-

© Springer Nature Singapore Pte Ltd. 2017
J.K. Mandal et al. (Eds.): CICBA 2017, Part II, CCIS 776, pp. 168–183, 2017.
DOI: 10.1007/978-981-10-6430-2_14

tion of Music was attempted as early as the 70s [2]. However, there were two limiting factors that prevented progress in the field at the time. Firstly, the high computational requirements of the problem domain was simply not available. And secondly, other related fields of study such as Digital Signal Processing, Speech Processing, and Machine Learning were also not advanced enough. So, the field stalled for the next few decades.

In the 1990s, the field regained prominence as computational resources improved greatly and the rise of the internet resulted in massive online music collection. So, there was both an opportunity and demand for MIR systems. The organization of the first International Symposium on Music Information Retrieval (ISMIR 1) in 2000 highlights this resurgence of interest in the field. 280 people from 25 different countries participated in ISMIR Conference Malaga 2015.

As for the methodologies used, MIR in the 90s was influenced by the field of Text Information Retrieval (IR), techniques for searching and retrieving text documents based on user queries. So, most of the algorithms were developed based on symbolic representations such as MIDI files [3]. One such method is described in [4].

However, recognizing approximate units of meaning in MIR, like it is done in a lot of text-IR methods was difficult [5].

Instead, statistical non-transcriptive approaches for non-speech audio signals started being adopted in the second half of the 90s [3]. This was probably influenced by progress of such methods in other fields of speech processing. For example, in [6], the authors reported 98% accuracy in distinguishing music from speech in commercial radio broadcasts. This was based on the statistics of the energy contour and the zero-crossing rate.

In [7], the authors introduced similar statistical methods for retrieval and classification of isolated sounds. Similarly, in [8], an algorithm for music-speech classification based on spectral feature was introduced. It was trained using supervised learning.

And so, starting in the 2000s, instead of methods attempting note-level transcriptions, researchers focused on direct extraction of information of audio signals using Signal Processing and Machine Learning techniques.

Currently, three basic strategies are being applied in MIR: [9]

- Based on Conceptual Metadata - Suited for low-specificity queries.
- Using High-level Descriptions - Suited for mid-specificity queries. item Using Low-level Signal-based Properties - Used for all specificity.

But still most of the MIR techniques being employed at present use low-level signal features instead of high-level descriptors [10]. Thus, there exists a semantic gap between human perception of music and how MIR systems work.

2.2 Audio Processing

Particularly speaking, music signal processing may appear to be the junior relation of the large and mature field of speech signal processing, not least because many techniques and representations originally developed for speech have been applied to music, often with good results. However, music signals have certain characteristics that are different from spoken language and other signals [11].

2.3 Genre Based Classification

In [12], Scaringella et al. discuss how and why musical genres are a poorly defined concept making the task of automatic classification non-trivial. Still, although the boundaries between genre are fuzzy and there are no well-defined definitions, it is still one of the widely used method of classification of music. If we look at human capability in genre classification, Perrot et al. [13] found that people classified songs–in a ten-way classification setup–with an accuracy of 70% after listening to 3 s excerpts.

The features used for genre based classification have been heavily influenced by the related field of speech recognition. For instance, Mel-frequency Cepstral Coefficients (MFCC), a set of perceptually motivated features that is widely used in music classification, was first used in speech recognition.

The seminal paper on musical genre classification by Tzanetakis et al. [14] presented three feature sets for representing timbral texture, rhythmic content and pitch content. With the proposed feature set, they achieved a classification accuracy of 61% for ten musical genre.

Timbral features are usually calculated for every short-time frame of sound based on the Short Time Fourier Transform (STFT). So, these are low-level features. Typical examples are Spectral Centroid, Spectral Rolloff, Spectral Flux, Energy, Zero Crossings, and the afore-mentioned Mel-Frequency Cepstral Coefficients (MFCCs). Among these, MFCC is the most widely preferred feature [15,16]. Logan [17] investigated the applicability of MFCCs to music modeling and found it to be "at least not harmful".

Rhythmic features capture the recurring pattern of tension and release in music while pitch is the perceived fundamental frequency of the sound. These are usually termed as mid-level features.

Apart from these, many non-standard features have been proposed in the literature.

Li et al. [18] proposed a new set of features based on Daubechies Wavelet Coefficient Histograms (DWCH), and also presented a comparative study with the features included in the MARSYAS framework. They showed that it significantly increased the classifier accuracy.

Anglade, Amélie, et al. [19] propose the use of Harmony as a high-level descriptor of music.

Music classification has been attempted through a variety of methods. Some of the popular ones are SVM, K Nearest Neighbours and variants of Neural Networks. The results are also widely different. In [20], 61% accuracy has been achieved using a Multilayer Perceptron based approach. While in [21], the authors have achieved 71% accuracy through the use of an additional rejection and verification stage. Haggblade et al. [22], compared simpler and more naive approaches (k-NN and k-Means) with more sophisticated neural networks and SVMs. They found that the latter gave better results.

However, lots of unique methods – either completely novel or a variation of a standard method – have been put into use too. In [23], the authors propose a method that uses Chord labeling (ones and zeros) in conjunction with a k-window subsequence matching algorithm used to find subsequence in music sequence and a Decision tree for the actual genre classification.

It is also noted that high-level and contextual concepts can be as important as low-level content descriptors [19].

2.4 Mood Based Classification

As mood is a very human thing, Mood Based Classification, also known as Mood Emotion Recognition (MER), requires knowledge of both technical aspects as well as the human emotional system.

Generally, emotions are conceptualized in two ways:

Categorical Conceptualization. This approach to MER categorizes emotions into distinct classes. It requires a set of base emotions (happiness, anger, sadness, etc.) from which other secondary emotion classes can be derived [24]. However, this approach runs into the problem that the whole spectrum of human emotions cannot be captured by a small number of classes.

Dimensional Conceptualization. It defines Musical Values as numerical values over a number of emotion dimensions. So, the focus is on distinguishing emotions based on their position on a predefined space. Most of these conceptualizations map to three axes of emotions: valence (pleasantness), arousal (activation) and potency (dominance). By placing emotions on a continuum instead of trying to label them as discrete, this approach can encompass a wide variety of general emotions.

Thayer [25] proposed a similar two-dimensional approach that adopts the theory that mood is entailed from two factors: -Stress (happy/anxious) -Energy (calm/energetic). This divides music mood into four clusters: Contentment, Depression, Exuberance and Anxious/Frantic (Fig. 1).

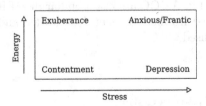

Fig. 1. Thayer's two-dimensional model of mood

Although, the two-dimensional approach has been criticized as deficient (leading to a proposal of the third dimension of potency), it seems to offer the right balance between sufficient "verbosity" and low complexity [26].

So, we use a similar simplified two-dimensional model based on *arousal* and *valence* (Fig. 2):

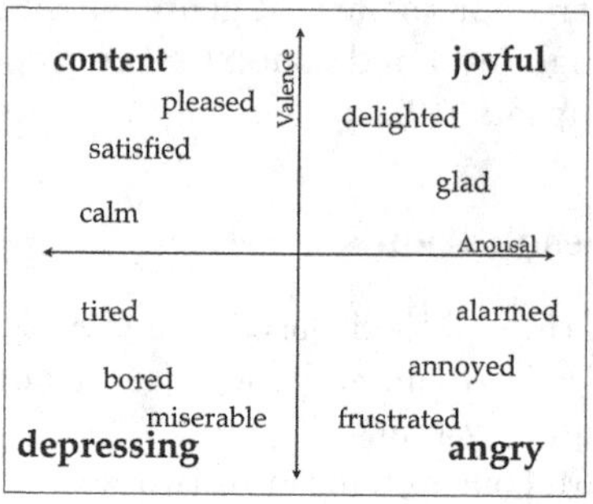

Fig. 2. Two-dimensional model of mood based on Arousal and Valence

2.5   Features in MER

Some of the commonly used features in MER are:

- Energy: Energy related features such as audio power, loudness, specific loudness sensation coefficients (SONE), are correlated to the perception of arousal. Lu et al. [27] used it to classify arousal.
- Melody: These include features such as Pitch (perceived fundamental frequency), chromogram centroid, etc.
- Timbre: As with the AMGC problem, MFCC is widely used in MER too. Apart from MFCC, octave-based spectral contrast as well as DWCH (Daubechies wavelets coefficient histogram) are also proposed in literature.

So, we see that the features used in MER are almost the same as those in AMGC. However, Fu et al. note in their extensive survey on Audio-based Music Classification [28] that although their effectiveness is debatable, mid-level features such as Rhythm seem to be more popular in MER.

The algorithms used in AMGC are also popular in MER. So, support vector machines, Gaussian mixture models, neural networks, and k-nearest neighbor are the ones regularly used.

3   Methodology

3.1   Audio Signal Pre-processing

The pre-processing in music classification systems is used in order to increase the efficiency of subsequent feature extraction and classification stages and therefore to improve the over-all system performance. Commonly pre-processing includes framing and windowing of the input signal. At the end of pre-processing, the smoothed frame are forwarded to the feature extraction stage.

Framing. Framing is the process of dividing the whole audio sample into frames. Although an audio signal changes continuously, the assumption that on short time scales it remains statistically stationary can be made. So, we frame the signal into 20–40 ms frames. A shorter frame gives too few samples while in a longer one, the signal varies too much.

Windowing. Windowing is necessary because whenever we do a finite Fourier transform, it is implicitly being applied to an infinite repeating signal. So, for instance if the start and end of a finite sample doesn't match then that will look just like a discontinuity in the signal, and show up a lots of high-frequency noise in the Fourier Transform, which is harmful. If the sample happens to be a perfect sinusoid but with an integer number of periods then it doesn't fit exactly into the finite sample and the FT will show appreciable energy in all sorts of places nowhere near the real frequency.

3.2 Feature Integration

As the features are temporal, the feature integration is also temporal. We used the mean and variance of the features for temporal feature integration although they capture neither the temporal dynamics nor dependencies among the individual feature dimensions. As seen below, the mean and standard deviation of MFCCs for a classical and a hiphop songs are sufficiently distinguishable. So, this representation of the features can be used to separate classes of music (Fig. 3).

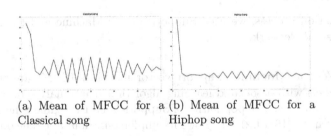

(a) Mean of MFCC for a Classical song

(b) Mean of MFCC for a Hiphop song

Fig. 3. Comparison of means for Classical and Hiphop songs

3.3 Dataset

The publicly available GTZAN dataset introduced in [14] has become one of the standard datasets for Music Genre Classification used by researchers across the world. We too used this dataset. The dataset contains 100 representative

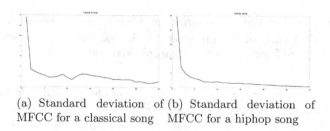

(a) Standard deviation of (b) Standard deviation of
MFCC for a classical song   MFCC for a hiphop song

Fig. 4. Comparison of standard deviations for Classical and Hiphop songs

excerpts from ten different genre. They were taken from radio, compact disk, and MP3 compressed audio files. All the files are stored as 22 050 Hz, 16-bit, mono audio files. The Genres dataset has the following classes: classical, country, disco, hiphop, jazz, rock, blues, reggae, pop, metal (Fig. 4).

For mood based classification, in 2013, Soleymani et al. [29] created a 1000 songs dataset for emotional analysis of music which uses the Valence-Arousal axes for representing emotional values for songs. The songs, in the dataset, each 45 s long, were collected from FMA. They used Amazon Mechanical Turk as a crowd sourcing platform for collecting more than 20,000 annotations on the 1,000 songs.

Furthermore, their analysis on the annotations revealed a higher agreement in arousal ratings compared to the valence ratings. We have used a filtered version (with some redundancies removed) of that dataset resulting in a final set of 744 songs. We further labeled them as high/low arousal and high/low valence songs based on the numerical values in the dataset. To achieve equal number of songs in each class, we finally used 600 songs of those 744 songs.

3.4   Classifier

For classification process, we used Support Vector Machine and Feed-Forward Artificial Neural Network.

Support Vector Machine. Support vector machines (SVM) are supervised learning models with associated learning algorithms that analyze data used for classification analysis. The popularity of Support Vector machine is huge as a lot of research papers [16,19,21,22] shows its implementation. For the construction of multi-class SVM, we use one vs one SVM classifier. This leads to $\frac{N(N-1)}{2}$ classifiers.

Genre Based Classification: In genre based classification linear kernel is used with the soft margin method.

Mood Based Classification: In mood based classification gaussian kernel and laplacian, the kernel is used which are the non linear type.

Feed-Forward Neural Network. A Feed-Forward Neural Network is a type of Neural Network architecture where the connections are "fed forward". Research papers [16,19–22] shows the implementation of artificial neural network in the field of music classification. For training, Backpropagation algorithm is used which calculates the error at a layer and propagates it back to the earlier layers.

Genre Based Classification: In genre based classification we used Cross-entropy error function for output as probabilities and softmax activation function.

Mood Based Classification: In mood based classification we used Least mean squares error function and logistic sigmoid activation function.

4   Results and Discussion

4.1   Effect of Frame Size

As seen in the figure, frame size of 11.5 ms and 23 ms performed considerably better than the bigger frame sizes. We chose the 23 ms (1024 samples) frame size because the smaller 512 sample frame size would lead to higher number of frames and hence necessitate more computation (Fig. 5).

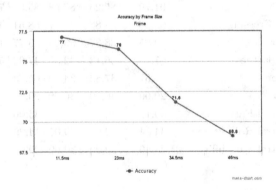

Fig. 5. Effect of frame size

4.2   Effect of Frame Overlap

We explored four different overlapping schemes: 0%, 25%, 50% and 75% overlap. In each of the cases, we received almost the same accuracy (75.4% on No-overlap, 75.8% on Quarter overlap, 76% on half-overlap, and 75.2% on three-quarters overlap). And so, as it seemed to indicate that the overlapping didn't have any bearing on our results, we chose the less computationally intensive option of using no overlap at all.

4.3 Comparison of Features

Genre Based Classification. MFCC was found to be the best feature for genre classification (in fact, it was found to do well in mood classification too) (Table 1).

Table 1. Genre classification using ANN and SVM

Algorithm	Feature	Classical	Hiphop	Jazz	Pop	Rock	Overall
ANN	Spectral Centroid	47.54	11.92	11.61	51.25	18.89	28.40
	MFCC	92.45	83.42	91.57	82.98	74.44	84.20
	Zero Crossing	63.29	48.31	39.83	52.65	52.00	51.20
	Pitch	37.83	15.00	34.80	61.73	1.67	28.00
	Compactness	81.53	81.75	57.67	28.39	45.55	58.60
	Timbre	6.25	20.00	30.00	20.00	28.46	20.60
	RMS	85.52	34.99	19.85	47.89	70.46	51.20
	Spectral Flux	87.94	26.71	19.77	43.63	57.45	46.40
	Spectral Roll off point	84.10	54.11	22.14	43.74	13.18	41.60
	Spectral Variability	83.10	32.98	25.98	51.24	71.76	52.40
SVM	Spectral Centroid	58.95	1.11	69.09	7.50	0.00	26.40
	MFCC	91.79	85.25	87.98	85.62	77.61	85.80
	Zero Crossing	63.20	48.86	41.47	58.51	44.31	50.00
	Pitch	59.95	38.37	36.04	35.77	13.64	36.20
	Compactness	67.18	66.13	42.30	47.93	53.60	55.60
	Timbre	1.67	37.83	34.80	61.73	15.00	28.00
	RMS	20.00	40.00	30.00	20.00	0.00	21.60
	Spectral Flux	59.17	10	20.91	33.06	0.00	27.20
	Spectral Roll off point	34.34	52.60	29.07	14.29	0.00	24.40
	Spectral Variability	28.46	20.00	30.00	20.00	6.25	20.60

Mood Based Classification. Results favor MFCC here too (Tables 2 and 3).

4.4 Effect of MFCCs on the Result

The results indicate that once we use more than 10 MFCC Coefficients, the accuracy plateaus and doesn't increase at all. So, using around 15 coefficients is found to be good enough for the problem domain (Fig. 6).

4.5 Effect of Number of Hidden Nodes

We used only one hidden layer as it should be enough for our problem domain. As seen in the figure, for any number of hidden numbers after six or so, we get

Table 2. Mood classification(Arousal) using ANN and SVM

Feature	ANN			SVM		
	Low arousal	High arousal	Overall	Low arousal	High arousal	Overall
Spectral Centroid	70.07	26.20	50.34	50.00	50.00	44.14
MFCC	69.32	75.09	71.38	73.22	71.77	72.41
Zero Crossing	70.70	64.03	67.24	74.00	67.07	70.69
Pitch	44.27	64.62	54.83	59.00	55.01	56.55
Compactness	59.73	51.71	57.24	47.22	78.45	62.76
Timbre	58.96	61.10	58.28	62.58	53.87	56.55
RMS	70.76	67.28	68.97	50.00	50.00	42.76
Spectral Flux	76.58	58.87	67.93	40.00	60.00	45.86
Spectral Roll off point	50.79	47.67	50.34	70.00	30.00	41.38
Spectral Variability	73.28	62.51	67.24	50.00	50.00	40.00

Table 3. Mood classification(Valence) using ANN and SVM

Feature	ANN			SVM		
	Low valence	High valence	Overall	Low valence	High valence	Overall
Spectral Centroid	37.69	60.63	51.38	40.00	60.00	44.83
MFCC	60.04	65.45	63.79	45.37	72.06	58.62
Zero Crossing	62.74	57.80	59.66	70.34	52.46	60.34
Pitch	66.29	35.46	50.69	53.56	52.53	49.66
Compactness	50.67	58.79	52.76	57.25	62.40	58.97
Timbre	61.75	57.69	56.90	60.50	61.19	60.34
RMS	63.85	44.87	53.79	50.00	50.00	44.83
Spectral Flux	70.19	47.50	59.31	60.00	40.00	40.34
Spectral Roll off point	57.56	44.94	48.28	60.00	40.00	41.72
Spectral Variability	63.99	45.13	51.03	50.00	50.00	41.83

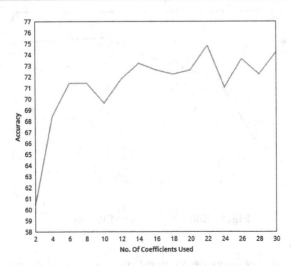

Fig. 6. Effect of number of MFCCs on result

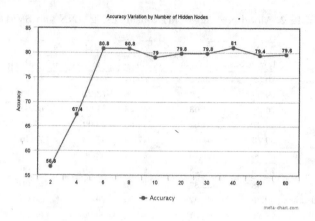

Fig. 7. Effect of number of hidden nodes

almost the same accuracy. As a rule of thumb, it is usually recommended that the number of nodes be around the mean of the number of inputs and outputs, so we chose 30 as our final number of hidden nodes (Fig. 7).

The number of nodes had minimal effect in regard to mood classification.

4.6 Effect of Number of Iterations

As seen in the figure, for genre classification, the number of iterations has an effect on the accuracy up to a certain point (around 20 iterations) (Fig. 8).

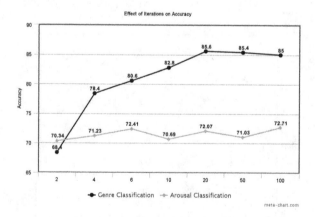

Fig. 8. Effect of number of iterations

As for Arousal, the increase in iterations had no effect on the accuracy (Fig. 9).

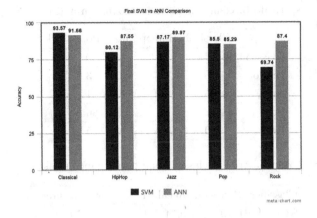

Fig. 9. Final SVM and ANN comparison based on genre

4.7   Final Results

Genre Classification. For our final model we used ANN with these feature: MFCC, Spectral Centroid, Zero Crossing, Compactness and RMS (Fig. 10 and Tables 4, 5 and 6).

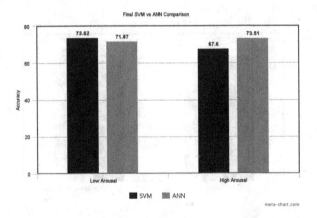

Fig. 10. Final SVM and ANN comparison based on arousal

Table 4. Genre classification performance measure

Classifier	Precision	Recall	F-Measure	Accuracy
SVM	0.87	0.94	0.89	83.00
ANN	0.94	0.92	0.92	88.80

Table 5. Genre classification confusion matrix

	Classical	Hiphop	Jazz	Pop	Rock
Classical	93	1	4	0	2
Hiphop	0	88	0	3	9
Jazz	5	0	90	1	4
Pop	2	7	0	86	5
Rock	0	4	4	5	87

Table 6. Arousal classification performance measure

Classifier	Precision	Recall	F-Measure	Accuracy
SVM	0.70	0.74	0.72	70.69
ANN	0.75	0.72	0.72	73.10

Mood Classification. For our final model we used ANN with these feature: Spectral centroid, MFCC, Zero Crossing, Compactness, Rhythm, Spectral Flux, RMS and Spectral Variability (Fig. 11 and Tables 7, 8 and 9).

For our final model we used ANN with these feature: Spectral centroid, MFCC, Zero Crossing, Compactness, Rhythm, Spectral Flux, RMS and Spectral Variability.

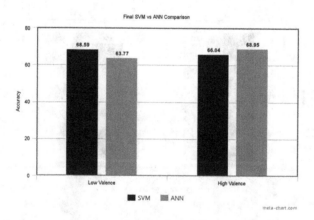

Fig. 11. Final SVM and ANN comparision based on valence

Table 7. Arousal classification confusion matrix

	Low arousal	High arousal
Low arousal	105	40
High arousal	38	107

Table 8. Valence performance measure

Classifier	Precision	Recall	F-Measure	Accuracy
SVM	0.68	0.69	0.68	67.59
ANN	0.68	0.64	0.65	67.24

Table 9. Valence confusion matrix

	Low valence	High valence
Low valence	95	52
High valence	43	100

5   Conclusion

Any type of classification of music is difficult simply because the classifications themselves don't have a clear definition. Still, we can work with fuzzy boundaries between these classes to get good enough results with Music Classification Systems.

In this paper, we studied many such components and approaches such as: types and combinations of features for proper representation of songs, feature integration approaches, classifier types, and their parameters, etc.

All these studies were done in order to tackle two related but distinct problems:

- In Automatic Music Genre Classification (AMGC), good performances were achieved with both of the classifiers employed: the final SVM model got 83% accuracy while the ANN model got 88% accuracy for five genres. These results are comparable with the state-of-the-art results, especially involving the same dataset.
- In Music Mood Classification however, the good results couldn't be replicated. The result along both axes of the music mood model used (arousal and valence) were underwhelming. Around 73% accuracy was achieved using ANN for the binary low/high arousal classification. SVM did even worse with around 70% accuracy. For low/high valence classification, both of the classifiers settled on 67% accuracy.

5.1   Limitations and Future Work

Distance Measure for Songs. One way to achieve song clustering or even classification is to develop distance measures to figure out the "distance" or difference between any two given songs. So, we tried to do the same. However, our initial attempts at using a simple Euclidean Distance measure were unsuccessful and later attempts using Gaussian Mixture Models proved to be too computationally intensive to be useful.

Future work could focus on figuring out appropriate distance measures for specific types of music being compared.

Feature Learning. Filtering and pre-processing might result in better high-level features. Or perhaps unsupervised feature learning methods as done in [30] might yield even better features. These approaches weren't explored in this paper.

Deep Learning. Future work could involve application of deep learning techniques in the problem domain.

Multi-tagging. A song can belong to multiple genre. So it is sure to consist of features characterizing multiple genre. Future work can be done to resolve this ambiguity.

References

1. Kassler, M.: Toward musical information retrieval. Perspect. New Music **4**, 59–67 (1966)
2. Andel, J.: On the segmentation and analysis of continuous musical sound by digital computer. Dissertation, Stanford University (1975)
3. Tzanetakis, G., Cook, P.: Manipulation, analysis and retrieval systems for audio signals. Princeton University, Princeton, NJ, USA (2002)
4. Alghoniemy, M., Tewfik, A.H.: Rhythm and periodicity detection in polyphonic music. In: 1999 IEEE 3rd Workshop on Multimedia Signal Processing. IEEE (1999)
5. Byrd, D., Crawford, T.: Problems of music information retrieval in the real world. Inf. Process. Manag. **38**(2), 249–272 (2002)
6. Saunders, J.: Real-time discrimination of broadcast speech/music. In: ICASSP, vol. 96 (1996)
7. Wold, E., et al.: Content-based classification, search, and retrieval of audio. IEEE Multimed. **3**(3), 27–36 (1996)
8. Scheirer, E., Slaney, M.: Construction and evaluation of a robust multifeature speech/music discriminator. In: IEEE International Conference on Acoustics, Speech, and Signal Processing, ICASSP-97, vol. 2. IEEE (1997)
9. Casey, M.A., et al.: Content-based music information retrieval: current directions and future challenges. Proc. IEEE **96**(4), 668–696 (2008)
10. Kaminskas, M., Ricci, F.: Contextual music information retrieval and recommendation: state of the art and challenges. Comput. Sci. Rev. **6**(2), 89–119 (2012)
11. Muller, M., et al.: Signal processing for music analysis. IEEE J. Sel. Top. Sig. Process. **5**(6), 1088–1110 (2011)
12. Scaringella, N., Zoia, G., Mlynek, D.: Automatic genre classification of music content: a survey. IEEE Sig. Process. Mag. **23**(2), 133–141 (2006)
13. Perrot, D., Gjerdigen, R.: Scanning the dial: an exploration of factors in the identification of musical style. In: Proceedings of the 1999 Society for Music Perception and Cognition (1999)
14. Tzanetakis, G., Cook, P.: Musical genre classification based on audio signals. IEEE Trans. Speech Audio Process. **10**(5), 293–302 (2002)
15. Lippens, S., Martens, J.-P., De Mulder, T.: A comparison of human and automatic musical genre classification. In: IEEE International Conference on Acoustics, Speech, and Signal Processing, Proceedings. (ICASSP 2004), vol. 4. IEEE (2004)

16. Kour, G., Mehan, N.: Music genre classification using MFCC, SVM and BPNN. Int. J. Comput. Appl. **112**, 12–14 (2015). ISSN 0975-8887
17. Logan, B.: Mel frequency cepstral coefficients for music modeling. In: ISMIR (2000)
18. Li, T., Ogihara, M., Li, Q.: A comparative study on content-based music genre classification. In: Proceedings of the 26th Annual International ACM SIGIR Conference on Research anD Development In Informaion Retrieval. ACM (2003)
19. Anglade, A., et al.: Improving music genre classification using automatically induced harmony rules. J. New Music Res. **39**(4), 349–361 (2010)
20. Neumayer, R.: Musical genre classification (2004)
21. Koerich, A.L.: Improving the reliability of music genre classification using rejection and verification. In: ISMIR (2013)
22. Haggblade, M., Hong, Y., Kao, K.: Music genere classification. Stanford University, Department of Computer Science (2011)
23. Nasridinov, A., Park, Y.-H.: A study on music genre recognition and classification techniques. Int. J. Multimed. Ubiquitous Eng. **9**(4), 31–42 (2014)
24. Ekman, P.: Are there basic emotions? Psychol. Rev. **99**, 550 (1992)
25. Thayer, R.E.: The Biopsychology of Mood and Arousal. Oxford University Press, New York (1990)
26. Juslin, P.N., Sloboda, J.A.: Music and Emotion: Theory and Research. Oxford University Press, Oxford (2001)
27. Lu, L., Liu, D., Zhang, H.-J.: Automatic mood detection and tracking of music audio signals. IEEE Trans. Audio Speech Lang. Process. **14**(1), 5–18 (2006)
28. Fu, Z., et al.: A survey of audio-based music classification and annotation. IEEE Trans. Multimed. **13**(2), 303–319 (2011)
29. Soleymani, M., et al.: 1000 songs for emotional analysis of music. In: Proceedings of the 2nd ACM International Workshop on Crowdsourcing for Multimedia. ACM (2013)
30. Lee, H., et al.: Unsupervised feature learning for audio classification using convolutional deep belief networks. In: Advances in Neural Information Processing Systems (2009)

Shape-based Fruit Recognition and Classification

Susovan Jana[✉] and Ranjan Parekh

School of Education Technology, Jadavpur University, Kolkata, India
jana.susovan2@gmail.com, rparekh@school.jdvu.ac.in

Abstract. Classification of fruits is traditionally done using manual resources due to which the time and economic involvements increase adversely with number of fruit types and items per class. In recent times computer based automated techniques have been used to alleviate this problem to a certain extent. These techniques utilize image analysis and pattern recognition methodologies to automatically classify fruits based on their visual features like color, texture, and shape. However, challenges of such techniques include the fact that fruit appearances differ due to natural environments, geographical locations, stages of growth, size, orientations and imaging equipments. In this paper, a shape based fruit recognition approach has been proposed which is independent of many of these factors. It involves a pre-processing step to normalize a fruit image with respect to variations in translation, rotation, scaling and utilizes features which do not change due to varying distances, growth stages and surface appearances of fruits. The proposed method has been applied to 210 images of 7 fruit classes. The overall recognition accuracy ranges from 88–95%.

Keywords: Fruit classification · Geometrical transformation · Morphological operation · Convex polygon · Naïve bayes classifier

1 Introduction

Agriculture and cultivation of fruits and vegetables are major revenue earners in many countries of the world. These, however, need expert resources and knowledge for planting, harvesting, sorting & packing [2]. In recent times, auto-harvesting robots are being used to reduce the manual effort to a large extent as well as the time involvement. Image analysis and pattern recognition techniques are used to identify fruits and vegetables using their visual characteristics. However, variation in viewpoints, distance, and illumination pose are the major challenges for an imaging system for reliable recognition. Additionally handling inter-class similarities and intra-class differences are required for robust classification systems. This research work studies recognition and classification of fruits for auto harvesting and attempts to address some of these challenges.

Extant literature consists of a number of automated fruit recognition approaches based on visual features like color [1, 3–8, 10–12], texture [5–12], shape [2–6, 8, 10, 11], and size [3, 10, 11]. But, these include a number of deficiencies and shortcomings. Shape-based approaches have translation, rotation, and scaling dependency, the surface features (color and texture) may be affected by surface defects, fruit size changes over different growth stages and so on. To overcome these challenges a shape-based

© Springer Nature Singapore Pte Ltd. 2017
J.K. Mandal et al. (Eds.): CICBA 2017, Part II, CCIS 776, pp. 184–196, 2017.
DOI: 10.1007/978-981-10-6430-2_15

recognition and classification method has been proposed, which is independent of translation, rotation, uniform scaling, surface features, and growth stage of fruit.

The rest of this paper is organized as follows. Section 2 surveys the related previous works. Section 3 contains the explanation of the proposed approach. Experimentation and corresponding results are reported in Sect. 4 followed by the analysis of results in Sect. 5. Finally, Sect. 6 concludes the work with future scopes.

2   Previous Work

There are a number of works related to fruit recognition and classification based on visual features captured from images. A color histogram based fruit recognition method has been proposed to recognize multiclass fruits [1]. In RGB color space, histogram of each color channel has been quantized to 16 bins. In total, it generates 48 features, but using chi-square method best 25 features have been selected. Experimentation results show that system performs well with k-NN classifier for 32 subclasses of fruit. A classification system has been developed to classify 3 sub-types of Mango fruit [2] with object contour model, region based descriptor, boundary based descriptor, and Bayes classifier. A new method for fruit recognition has been proposed combining color (Mean of RGB Color Values), shape (Roundness), and size (Area, Perimeter) features [3] to improve classification accuracy. The system archives up to 90% accuracy with Nearest Neighbor Classifier. Apple, strawberry, and orange classification process have been proposed using shape, color, Scale Invariant Feature Transform (SIFT) and Random Forest classifier [4]. The system has not been tested with the fruit type; whose color and shape both are nearly similar. Another fruit classification approach, based on combined texture (Hausdorff dimension), color (Mean of Hue values), and shape (Roundness) features using Neural Network Classifier, has been proposed [5]. The proposed approach has been experimented on 150 images of 6 fruit class. An automatic classification system has been proposed [6] for five classes of fruit. The authors combined color (Mean, Variance), shape (Area, Perimeter, and Eccentricity) and texture (Statistical features from GLCM) features and achieved best classification result with SVM classifier. A multiclass fruit detection method has been proposed using a fusion of Global Color Histogram, HOG, LBP and Gabor LBP features for multiple color channel of multiple color space [7]. Experimentation has been done with 5 classes of fruit. Due to the larger dimension of the feature vector, the detection speed is not acceptable in comparison to real-time image recognition. Based on a combination of color (HSV histogram), texture (LBP), shape (Roundness) features [8] and Back Propagation Neural Network classifier an automatic fruit type recognition method has been proposed. The method is not stable with different camera angle and lighting. Some researcher from GLA University proposed a texture feature and SVM based fruit and vegetable classification method [9]. A single histogram feature has been considered with the combination of sum and difference intensity of neighboring pixel for 3 color channels. This achieved a good accuracy but, intensity depends on various conditions like illumination. In paper [10], authors combined color (Mean of RGB Values), shape (Roundness), size (Area, Perimeter) and texture (Entropy) features, to achieve a most improved accuracy of fruit recognition.

The proposed method archives 95% overall accuracy for classification of 5 fruit class with k-NN classifier. The auto-identification method of sub-type of a Date fruit has been proposed to reduce manual effort of sorting in the Middle East [11]. The authors have experimented with 7 sub-types of Date. In total, color, shape, size and texture related fifteen features are used for recognition purpose. Neural Network Classifier shows satisfactory result than other classifiers. Each type of feature has its own limitations. Most of the authors considered combined approach of color, texture shape and size features to overcome those limitations. In this paper, a complete shape based approach has been proposed to overcome some limitations.

3   Proposed Approach

Challenges of an automated fruit recognition system include handling variations of visual features due to translation, rotation, and scaling of captured images, as well as changes pertaining to different growth stages of the fruit. A shape-based approach has been proposed here to deal with these challenges. Figure 1 depicts the flow diagram of the proposed method.

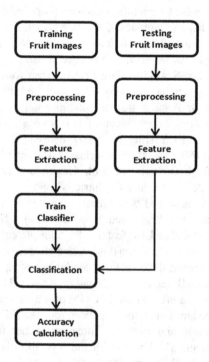

Fig. 1. Process flow diagram of complete proposed system

3.1   Pre-processing

An RGB color image of a fruit, Fig, 2(a), is converted to a grayscale image using the Eq. (1).

$$GrayImage = 0.2989 \times R + 0.5870 \times G + 0.1140 \times B \tag{1}$$

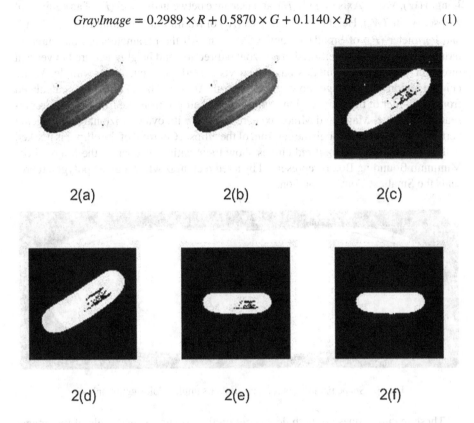

2(a)   2(b)   2(c)

2(d)   2(e)   2(f)

Fig. 2. (a) RGB Color Image (b) Grayscale Image (c) Binary Image (d) Background noises removed (e) Rotated Image (f) Inner holes filled (Color figure online)

The grayscale image, Fig. 2(b), is subsequently binarized using an appropriate threshold [13], Fig. 2(c). Background noise is removed using a threshold based on the actual number of pixels in the region, Fig. 2(d). The angle of orientation of the major axis of the fruit with respect to the horizontal is computed from the image and it is then rotated by this angle to align the major axis along with the horizontal, Fig. 2(e). This step is necessary to normalize the object of interest against arbitrary orientation factors which might affect the shape features, discussed in the next section. Any hole inside the fruit region which might have resulted from the binarization operation, is filled up by the morphological flood-fill operation, Fig. 2(f).

3.2 Feature Extraction

To classify the shape following shape based features are computed from the pre-processed image. These are Area (A), and Perimeter (P) of the fruit region, Major Axis Length (W), Minor Axis Length (H), and Distance between the Foci (F) of an equivalent ellipse, Width (W_b), Height (H_b), and Area (A_b) of Minimum Bounding Box, Area (A_c), and Perimeter (P_c) of Smallest Convex Polygon. All the parameters are measured in terms of pixels. Width measured in horizontal direction and height measured in vertical direction. In Fig. 3 parameters have been visualized for a cucumber sample. White colored region in this image shows the actual fruit Area, and fruit Perimeter is calculated from the border of the white region. Approximated ellipse from the fruit region is represented with blue. Major and Minor axis are marked with cyan horizontal and magenta vertical lines passing through the centroid of the ellipse. Centroid of the ellipse is marked with a red cross. Two small red circles show the position of Foci on the Major Axis. Minimum Bounding Box is represented by a red rectangle while a green polygon represents the Smallest Convex Polygon.

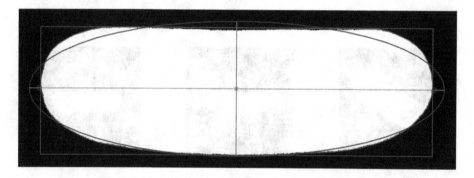

Fig. 3. Shape parameters for a cucumber sample (Color figure online)

These feature values are both dependent on the orientation and scale of the image. The variation due to orientation is normalized by the pre-processing step, as discussed in the previous section. To make the features independent of scaling factors, eight extended descriptors are derived from the basic shape descriptors as shown below.

$$sf_1 = F/W \tag{2}$$

$$sf_2 = H/W \tag{3}$$

$$sf_3 = 1 - (H_b/W_b) \tag{4}$$

$$sf_4 = P/(H + W) \tag{5}$$

$$sf_5 = A/P^2 \tag{6}$$

$$sf_6 = A/A_b \tag{7}$$

$$sf_7 = A/A_c \qquad (8)$$

$$sf_8 = P_c/P \qquad (9)$$

It is to be noted that all extended features are ratios which make them invariant to uniform scaling. Final feature vector (SF) contains those 8 extended shape descriptors.

$$SF = \{sf_1, sf_2, sf_3, sf_4, sf_5, sf_6, sf_7, sf_8\} \qquad (10)$$

3.3 Classification

A fruit class i contains a set of n number images. Each class is specified by its feature values T_i obtained at the time of training process. A test image S is said to belong from a specific class if the matching probability of its feature value is maximum for a specific training class. As such there is no standard mathematical model which can be used to classify from sample observed data.

Naïve Bayes classifier is one of the superior classification models which work on the basis of Bayes theorem of independent assumptions between predictors using Eq. (11). It assumes that the effect of the value of a predictor (X) on a given class (c) is not dependent on the values of other predictors.

$$P(c|x) = P(x|c).P(c)/P(x) \qquad (11)$$

In Eq. (11), $P(c|x)$ is the posterior probability, $P(x|c)$ is the likelihood, $P(c)$ is the class prior probability, and $P(x)$ is the predictor prior probability. This classifier is well known for sophisticated classification and handling large dataset.

Back Propagation Neural Network is an effective classifier known for its non-linear solution ability. It consists of multiple layers of neurons which can be varied according to the complexity of the problem and is thus also known as Multi-Layered Perception (MLP). During the learning process, the difference between actual output and desired output is calculated and back-propagated to the previous layer(s). To scale the accuracy, the connection weights are adjusted using a transfer function.

K-Nearest Neighbor (k-NN) is a simple and efficient classification algorithm which assigns the class of sample data based on a distance metric and the number of training samples within a specified distance in feature space. There are few types of distance metric e.g. Euclidean, cityblock, hamming etc. Here k is the number of nearest neighbor for the prediction. Larger k value gives smoother boundary but decreases efficiency.

4 Experiments and Results

To test the effectiveness of the proposed system, experimentations are performed on 210 digital images belonging to 7 fruit classes viz. Apple, Banana, Cucumber, Lemon, Mango, Strawberry, and Tomato. Most of the images are captured using a smartphone camera and some are downloaded from websites [14]. Each class contains 30 images.

Half of the images are used for training and rest for testing. Samples of the training and testing dataset are shown in Figs. 4 and 5 respectively.

Fig. 4. Training samples: (a) Apple (b) Banana (c) Cucumber (d) Lemon (e) Mango (f) Strawberry (g) Tomato

Fig. 5. Testing samples: (a) Apple (b) Banana (c) Cucumber (d) Lemon (e) Mango (f) Strawberry (g) Tomato

To introduce a large amount of variation the fruit images has been captured by varying camera to fruit distance, fruit orientation, and fruit size. Figure 6 represents the variations of some of the most discriminative shape features on 15 samples for each of the 7 fruit class training images. The horizontal axis represents the index of training image and the vertical axis represents corresponding feature value for each fruit class normalized within the range 0 to 1. Each fruit type is marked with a different color as given in the legend.

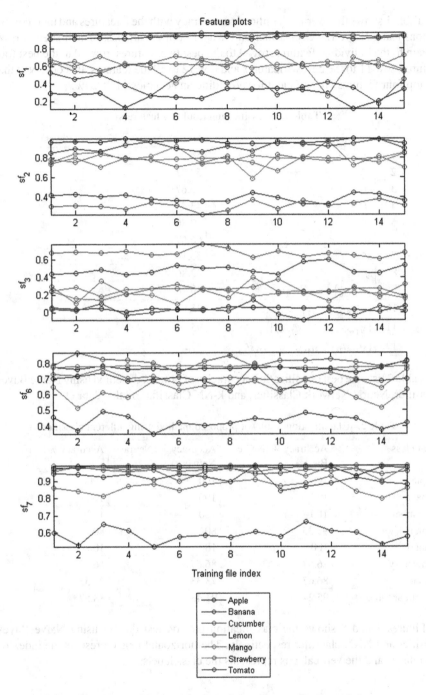

Fig. 6. Variation of features on the training dataset using legend shown

Table 1 shows the overall classification accuracy with the 8 features and their combinations using Naïve Bayes classifier on the dataset of 7 fruit class. The first eight rows pertain to the individual features, row 9 to the best two features, row 10 to the best four features, row 11 to the best six features and row 12 to all the features. It is observed that the top four features are sufficient for providing an accuracy of 95.24%.

Table 1. Classification results of feature(s)

	Feature(s)	Overall Accuracy % (Naïve Bayes)
1	sf_1	54.29
2	sf_2	53.33
3	sf_3	66.67
4	sf_4	43.81
5	sf_5	42.86
6	sf_6	66.67
7	sf_7	56.19
8	sf_8	42.86
9	$\{sf_3, sf_6\}$	90.48
10	$\{sf_1, sf_3, sf_6, sf_7\}$	95.24
11	$\{sf_1, sf_2, sf_3, sf_6, sf_7, sf_8\}$	95.24
12	$\{sf_1, sf_2, sf_3, sf_4, sf_5, sf_6, sf_7, sf_8\}$	95.24

Table 2 lists the best classification accuracies of proposed method using Naïve Bayes Classifier, Neural Network Classifier, and k-NN Classifier on this dataset.

Table 2. Classification results of proposed method using different classifier

Fruit class	Accuracy % (Naïve Bayes)	Accuracy % (Neural Network)	Accuracy % (k-NN)
Apple	100	100	100
Banana	100	100	100
Cucumber	100	100	100
Lemon	93.33	80	80
Mango	100	100	100
Strawberry	86.67	86.67	66.67
Tomato	86.67	73.33	73.33
Overall accuracy	95.24	91.43	88.57

Figures 7 and 8 shows the classification plot on test dataset using Naïve Bayes classifier and KNN classifier respectively. The horizontal axis represents the index of test images and the vertical axis represents the class labels.

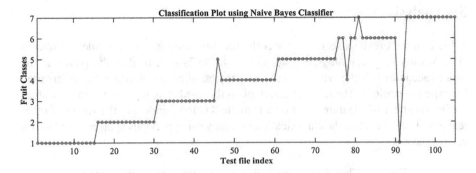

Fig. 7. Classification plot using Naïve Bayes Classifier

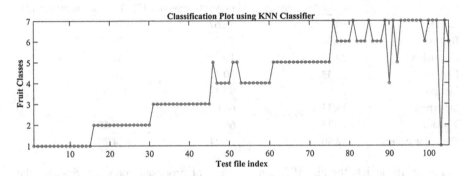

Fig. 8. Classification plot using KNN Classifier

Figure 9 shows the classification plot on test dataset using Neural Network Classifier. The horizontal axis represents the test file index and the vertical axis represents the classification output of corresponding class as mentioned in the legend.

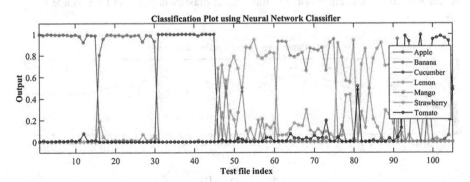

Fig. 9. Classification plot using neural network classifier

5   Analysis

Table 2 in the previous section depicts that the proposed method provides an overall classification accuracy ranging from 88.57% to 95.24%. It is also observed that the overall accuracy is better with the Naïve Bayes Classifier than the other classifiers used for experimentations. The reason behind this is that the Naïve Bayes Classifier assumes prediction effect of a feature value on a fruit class is independent of the values of other features. Table 3 depicts the classification accuracy using previous approaches [1–3] on current dataset.

Table 3. Classification results of previous approaches on this dataset

Fruit class	Accuracy % of previous approach [1]	Accuracy % of previous approach [2]	Accuracy % of previous approach [3]
Apple	100	66.67	100
Banana	66.67	73.33	26.67
Cucumber	93.33	100	6.67
Lemon	73.33	60	20
Mango	100	93.33	33.33
Strawberry	73.33	66.67	6.67
Tomato	73.33	66.67	46.67
Overall accuracy	82.86	75.24	34.29

Figure 10 depicts the classification accuracy of proposed approach vis-à-vis the previous approaches [1–3] for all the 7 classes of fruit. Performance is not satisfactory with the color-based approach in [1] for the fruit pair Banana- Lemon and Strawberry-Tomato because the color of the two fruit member of each pair is nearly similar to each other. The shape-based features used by in approach [2] are effective for classification of small number of classes and where there is a large amount of shape variation among the classes. In the current work, the number of classes is large and the shape-based

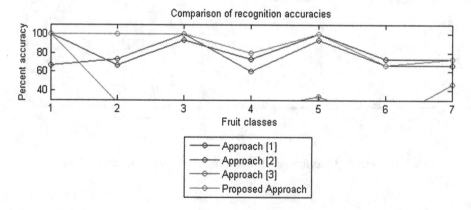

Fig. 10. Comparison of recognition accuracies with different approaches

descriptors, used by the authors [2], are closely similar for the classes like lemon, straw-berry, and tomato. Approach [3] is a mixed approach of color, shape, and size based features. The shape and size based descriptors, used by the authors, enormously diverges due to geometric transformation as well as different growth stages of a fruit. To establish the robustness of the proposed method this work introduces sufficient amount variation of shape, size and surface color for a particular class. This is the reason behind the very poor classification performance of previous approach [3]. Figure 11 Shows how the overall classification accuracy has been improved than the previous works.

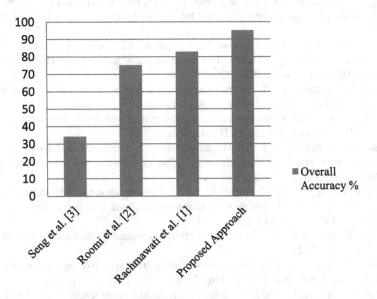

Fig. 11. Improvement of overall accuracy

6 Conclusions and Future Scopes

This work proposes a shape-based fruit class recognition and classification using a number of classifiers. It achieves 95.24% overall classification accuracy over seven classes of fruits varying in shape, color, size and orientation. The major contributions of this paper involves proposing schemes which are: (1) invariant to translation, rotation, and uniform scaling, (2) not dependent on surface based features (3) invariant to the different growth stage of fruit.

Fruit Recognition and classification is a very demanding research topic for the automation in the agricultural field. Recognition of fruit class in the 3D environment can be researched in future.

References

1. Rachmawati, E., Khodra, M.L., Supriana, I.: Histogram based color pattern identification of multiclass fruit using feature selection. In: 5th International Conference on Electrical Engineering and Informatics (ICEEI), pp. 43–48. IEEE (2015)
2. Roomi, S.M.M., Priya, R.J., Bhumesh, S., Monisha, P.: Classification of mangoes by object features and contour modeling. In: International Conference on Machine Vision and Image Processing (MVIP), pp. 165–168. IEEE (2012)
3. Seng, W.C., Mirisaee, S.H.: A new method for fruits recognition system. In: International Conference on Electrical Engineering and Informatics (ICEEI), vol. 1, pp. 130–134. IEEE (2009)
4. Zawbaa, H.M., Hazman, M., Abbass, M., Hassanien, A.E.: Automatic fruit classification using random forest algorithm. In: 14th International Conference on Hybrid Intelligent Systems (HIS), pp. 164–168. IEEE (2014)
5. Naskar, S., Bhattacharya, T.: A fruit recognition technique using multiple features and artificial neural network. Int. J. Comput. Appl. **116**(20), 23–28 (2015)
6. Al-falluji, R.A.A.: Color, shape and texture based fruit recognition system. Int. J. Adv. Res. Comput. Eng. Technol. **5**(7), 2108–2112 (2016)
7. Kuang, H.L., Chan, L.L.H., Yan, H.: Multi-class fruit detection based on multiple color channels. In: International Conference on Wavelet Analysis and Pattern Recognition (ICWAPR), pp. 1–7. IEEE (2015)
8. Wang, X., Huang, W., Jin, C., Hu, M., Ren, F.: Fruit recognition based on multi-feature and multi-decision. In: 3rd International Conference on Cloud Computing and Intelligence Systems (CCIS), pp. 113–117. IEEE (2014)
9. Dubey, S.R., Jalal, A.S.: Robust approach for fruit and vegetable classification. Procedia Eng. **38**, 3449–3453 (2012)
10. Ninawe, P., Pandey, S.: A completion on fruit recognition system using k-nearest neighbors algorithm. Int. J. Adv. Res. Comput. Eng. Technol. **3**(7), 2352–2356 (2014)
11. Haidar, A., Dong, H., Mavridis, N.: Image-based date fruit classification. In: 4th International Congress on Ultra Modern Telecommunications and Control Systems and Workshops (ICUMT), pp. 357–363. IEEE (2012)
12. Jana, S., Parekh, R.: Intra-class recognition of fruits using color and texture features with neural classifiers. Int. J. Comput. Appl. **148**(11), 1–6 (2016)
13. Otsu, N.: A threshold selection method from gray-level histograms. IEEE Trans. Syst. Man Cybern. **9**(1), 62–66 (1979). IEEE
14. Computers and Optics in Food Inspection. http://www.cofilab.com/portfolio. Accessed 15 Dec 2016

An Efficient Fragmented Plant Leaf Classification Using Color Edge Directivity Descriptor

Jyotismita Chaki[1(✉)], Ranjan Parekh[1], and Samar Bhattacharya[2]

[1] School of Education Technology, Jadavpur University, Kolkata, India
cjyotismita@yahoo.com, rparekh@school.jdvu.ac.in
[2] Department of Electrical Engineering, Jadavpur University, Kolkata, India
samar_bhattacharya@ee.jdvu.ac.in

Abstract. Plant species identification is one of the most important research branches of botanical science. The current work proposes an efficient methodology for recognition of plant species from whole as well as fragmented digital leaf images. The situation becomes challenging when only a partial portion of the leaf can be obtained. Since leaves are fragile and prone to be fragmentation due to various environmental and biological factors, the paper studies how recognition of fragmented leaves can be effectively done. In this study the combination of texture and color based method (Color Edge Directivity Descriptor) is used to extract the feature and Euclidean distance is used as the classifier for the classification of the fragmented as well as whole leaf images.

Keywords: Fragmented leaf · CEDD · Plant species · Whole leaf

1 Introduction

Plants are the most important species in the Earth's ecology as they provide us breathable oxygen, medicine, food and so on. For the ecological protection and automatic plant recognition system, plant recognition based on leaf images is very important and necessary. Currently the visual features that have been successfully used for plant identification and recognition include shape, color and texture. Different data modeling techniques used include Fourier descriptors [2], curvelets [10, 16], local binary descriptors (LBD) [3, 4], histogram of oriented gradients (HoG) [8], leaf margin [11], fractal dimensions [9, 12], pattern counting [15]. A variety of classifiers and comparison metrics have been used viz. artificial neural network [1], support vector machines [5, 7], multiscale distance matrix [6], random forest based sub classifier [10].

1.1 Contribution of the Paper

In this paper both the whole and partial leaf images recognition is done i.e. where parts of leaf area might be missing. Recognizing the fact that leaves are fragile and prone to various types of deformations due to environmental and biological factors, we consider cases where only about some portion of the leaf area might be intact. Sometimes the entire leaf blade is consumed by various insects. In this case only the tougher midvein

© Springer Nature Singapore Pte Ltd. 2017
J.K. Mandal et al. (Eds.): CICBA 2017, Part II, CCIS 776, pp. 197–211, 2017.
DOI: 10.1007/978-981-10-6430-2_16

remains. Sometimes distinct portions of the leaf is missing i.e. distinct notches cut from the leaf margin or may be circular holes cut from the margin of the leaf or some small randomly scattered holes in the leaf. Sun and high temperature, flooding, heavy rain, frost, snow and even high winds can damage the plant leaves. Such a leaf is referred to as "fragmented". Figure 1 shows a sample of fragmented leaf.

Fig. 1. Sample of fragmented leaf

Fragmented leaves would not contain adequate shape information for reliable classification, due to which their texture patterns are analyzed. It needs to be mentioned here that all the previous works surveyed by us, pertains to recognition of whole leaf images and we have not come across any other work aimed specifically to recognize partial leaf portions.

1.2 Paper Organization

The organization of the paper is as follows: Sect. 2 outlines the proposed approach with discussions on feature computation and classification schemes, Sect. 3 provides details of the dataset and experimental results obtained, Sect. 4 compares the proposed approach with other approaches, while Sect. 5 brings up the overall conclusions and future scope of the research.

2 Proposed Approach

In this paper both the whole and fragmented leaf images are handled using a single texture descriptor. Shape based features would not be reliable and effective for classification of fragmented leaves, hence texture based classification is used. A Color and Edge Directivity Descriptor (CEDD) is used where color information is combined with texture to improve recognition accuracies.

As there is no created dataset of the fragmented leaf, the part of the simple leaf image is cropped from the center, left-top, right-top, left-bottom and right-bottom with different dimensions to make it as fragment leaf.

The block diagram of the proposed approach is shown in Fig. 2.

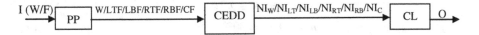

Fig. 2. Major blocks and data flow, I (W/F): input image (whole/fragment), PP: Pre-processing block, W: Whole, LTF: Left-Top Fragmented, LBF: Left-Bottom Fragmented, RTF: Right-Top Fragmented, RBF: Right-Bottom Fragmented, CF: Center Fragmented, CEDD: Feature extraction method, NI_W: Whole feature, NI_{LT}: Left-Top fragmentation feature, NI_{LB}: Left-Bottom fragmentation feature, NI_{RT}: Right-Top fragmentation feature, NI_{RB}: Right-Bottom fragmentation feature, NI_C: Center fragmentation feature, CL: classifier, O: Class output.

2.1 Creation of Fragmented Images from Whole

Since there was no public dataset of fragmented leaves, a new dataset had to be created for performing experimentations. A scheme was designed using which fragmented samples could be generated from whole leaf images in an automated way, keeping sufficient parametric variables for customization and fine tuning. Given an image of size $M \times N$ and a fractional value, say $(1/n)$, a grid of size $M/n \times N/n$ is first superimposed on the image, and then a window of size $(M - 2M/n) \times (N - 2N/n)$ is generated. The image portions within the window boundary is cropped and saved as a fragmented image. If the cropping window is centrally placed on the original window, the extents of the crop window are: $\{M/n : (M-M/n)\}, \{N/n : (N-N/n)\}$. For example if n = 10, then the fragmented image size is $(4M/5 \times 4N/5)$ or $16/25$ of the original image. This is referred to as 36% fragmentation which is the amount of the image missing. The amount of fragmentation F corresponding to the proportion of the leaf area missing, for a fraction $(1/n)$ is thus calculated from the Eq. 1. The process is shown in Fig. 3.

$$F = 1 - (1 - 2/n)^2 \tag{1}$$

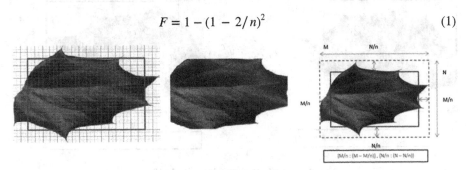

Fig. 3. Fragmented from whole

The dataset into divided into 2 portions: minor fragmentations and major fragmentations. Minor fragmentations corresponds to cases where more than half of the leaf surface is intact i.e. with fragmentations less than 50% and generated as defined in the Eq. 2:

$$n = 18.8, \ F = 20\%$$
$$n = 10, \ F = 30\% \tag{2}$$
$$n = 8.8, \ F = 40\%$$

The second portion of the dataset corresponds to major fragmentations with 50% or more of the leaf surface missing. These are generated as defined in the Eq. 3:

$$n = 6.8, \ F = 50\%$$
$$n = 5.4, \ F = 60\% \tag{3}$$
$$n = 4.4, \ F = 70\%$$

The second parameter adjusted for creating the dataset is the location of the cropping window. By default the window is located over the central region of the image and hence spans over the extents $\{M/n : (M-M/n)\}, \{N/n : (N-N/n)\}$. However recognizing the fact that fragmentations can occur from any portion of the leaf, four variations of the fragmented regions were created by moving the cropping window towards the left-top, right-top, left-bottom, and right-bottom. The extents of the windows as defined in the Eq. 4 and the pictorial representations are shown in Figs. 4 and 5.

$$\begin{aligned}
&\textit{Left-Top}: \{1{:}(M - 2M/n)\}, \{1{:}(N - 2N/n)\} \\
&\textit{Right-Top}: \{2M/n{:}M\}, \{1{:}(N - 2N/n)\} \\
&\textit{Right-Bottom}: \{2M/n{:}M\}, \{2N/n{:}N\} \\
&\textit{Left-Bottom}: \{1{:}2M/n\}, \{2N/n{:}N\}
\end{aligned} \tag{4}$$

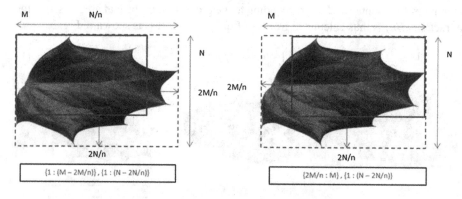

Fig. 4. (left) Left-Top, (right) Right-Top

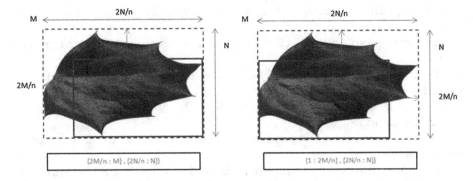

Fig. 5. (left) Right-Bottom, (right) Left-Bottom

2.2 Pre-Processing (PP)

The objective of the pre-processing step is to standardize the translation of the image before feature computation. As we are also handling the fragmented leaf images with the whole leaf images, it is difficult to standardize the proper scale and the orientation angle of a fragmented leaf. That's why only the translation factor is standardizing in this study. The raw image is typically a color image oriented at a random angle and having a random size and translation. To make the features translation-invariant, the background is shrunk until the leaf just fits within the bounding rectangle. The output of the PP block is the translation invariant whole or fragmented image depending on the input image I.

2.3 Color Edge Directivity Descriptor (CEDD)

The CEDD is the combination of the CEDD Color Descriptor and the CEDD Texture Descriptor.

2.3.1 CEDD Color Descriptor
The color descriptor is generated using a 3-step process:

2.3.1.1 Generation of 8 Color Areas
Color of an image is expressed in the HSV (Hue-Saturation-Value) space. Channel H is divided into 8 fuzzy areas based on the response of a set of coordinate logic filters (CLF) on specially constructed artificial images. These areas are: (0) Red to Orange, (1) Orange, (2) Yellow, (3) Green, (4) Cyan, (5) Blue, (6) Magenta and (7) Blue to red.

2.3.1.2 Generation of 10-Bin Color Histogram
Channel S is divided into two fuzzy areas named as 0 and 1, while channel V is divided into three fuzzy areas named as 0, 1 and 2. Based on a set of fuzzy inference rules, the above colors are combined to generate a 10-bin histogram, as specified below.

For any input color if V = 0, output color is black

For any input color if S = 0 and V = 1, output color is gray

For any input color if S = 0 and V = 2, output color is white

If input color is 'red to orange', S = 1, V = 1 or 2, output color is red

If input color is 'orange', S = 1, V = 1 or 2, output color is orange

If input color is 'yellow', S = 1, V = 1 or 2, output color is yellow

If input color is 'green', S = 1, V = 1 or 2, output color is green

If input color is 'cyan', S = 1, V = 1 or 2, output color is cyan

If input color is 'blue', S = 1, V = 1 or 2, output color is blue

If input color is 'magenta', S = 1, V = 1 or 2, output color is magenta

If input color is 'magenta to red', S = 1, V = 1 or 2, output color is red

The output of this stage is a 10-bin histogram, where each bin represents a preset color viz. (0) Black, (1) Gray, (2) White, (3) Red, (4) Orange, (5) Yellow, (6) Green, (7) Cyan, (8) Blue and (9) Magenta.

2.3.1.3 Generation of 24-Bin Color Histogram

In the third stage, two separate fuzzy membership functions divides the S and V channels into 2 fuzzy regions each designated as 0 and 1. Three fuzzy inference rules designate a color as 'pure' if $S = 1$ and $V = 1$, a color as 'light' if $S = 0$ and $V = 1$, and a color as 'dark' if $s = 0$ or 1 and $V = 0$. Using these inference rules the 10-bin histogram is expanded to a 24-bin histogram as follows:

(a) If the input color corresponds to bins 0, 1 or 2 (i.e. black, gray, white), then it is represented as it is in the output bins

(b) If the input color corresponds to bins 3 to 9, then inference rules separates out each color into three variants: pure, light, dark

The output of the third stage is the generation of a 24-bin color histogram as below: (0) black, (1) Gray, (2) White, (3) Dark red, (4) Red, (5) Light red, (6) Dark orange, (7) Orange, (8) Light orange, (9) Dark yellow, (10) Yellow, (11) Light yellow, (12) Dark green, (13) Green, (14) Light green, (15) Dark cyan, (16) Cyan, (17) Light cyan, (18) Dark blue, (19) Blue, (20) Light blue, (21) Dark magenta, (22) Magenta, (23) Light magenta.

2.3.2 CEDD Texture Descriptor

The texture descriptor is generated using the five filters of MPEG-7 Edge Histogram Descriptor (EHD). These are used to define the edges as Horizontal, Vertical, 45° diagonal, 135° diagonal and non-directional. The edge type diagram is shown in Fig. 6.

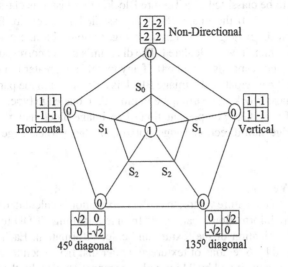

Fig. 6. Edge type diagram

The entire image is divided into a number of image blocks. Each image block is again sub-divided into 4 sub blocks. Let a0, a1, a2, a3 be the average gray levels of the 4 sub-blocks of a specific image block. The filter coefficients for vertical, horizontal, right diagonal, left diagonal and non-directional edges are designated as: Fv, Fh, F45d, F135d and Fnd. For the (i, j)-th image block the edge magnitudes calculated from its constituent sub-blocks are defined as follows:

$$E_v(i,j) = \left| a0(i,j) \times F_v(0) + a1(i,j) \times F_v(1) + a2(i,j) \times F_v(2) + a3(i,j) \times F_v(3) \right| \quad (5)$$

$$E_h(i,j) = \left| a0(i,j) \times F_h(0) + a1(i,j) \times F_h(1) + a2(i,j) \times F_h(2) + a3(i,j) \times F_h(3) \right| \quad (6)$$

$$E_{45d}(i,j) = \left| a0(i,j) \times F_{45d}(0) + a1(i,j) \times F_{45d}(1) + a2(i,j) \times F_{45d}(2) + a3(i,j) \times F_{45d}(3) \right| \quad (7)$$

$$E_{135d}(i,j) = \left| a0(i,j) \times F_{135d}(0) + a1(i,j) \times F_{135d}(1) + a2(i,j) \times F_{135d}(2) + a3(i,j) \times F_{135d}(3) \right| \quad (8)$$

$$E_{nd}(i,j) = \left| a0(i,j) \times F_{nd}(0) + a1(i,j) \times F_{nd}(1) + a2(i,j) \times F_{nd}(2) + a3(i,j) \times F_{nd}(3) \right| \quad (9)$$

The maximum of the magnitudes is calculated from the above edge magnitudes

$$Emax = max\left(E_v, E_h, E_{45d}, E_{135d}, E_{nd}\right) \quad (10)$$

This is subsequently used to normalize the magnitudes

E'v = Ev/Emax,   E'h = Eh/Emax,   E'45d = E45d/Emax,
E'135d = E135d/Emax,   E'nd = End/Emax

The system classifies each Image Block in a two-step process: first, the system calculates the max value. The max value must be greater than the defined threshold for the Image Block to be classified as a Texture Block, otherwise it is classified as a Non Texture Block (Linear). If the Image Block is classified as a Texture Block, each E' value is placed on the pentagonal diagram of Fig. 6 along the line corresponding to digital filter from which it was calculated. The diagram's center corresponds to value 1 and the outer edge corresponds to value 0. If any m value is greater than the threshold on the line where it participates, the Image Block is classified into the particular type of edge. Thus an Image Block can participate in more than one edge type.

The output of this stage is representation of an image block using a 6-bin texture histogram: non-edge, non-directional edge, horizontal edge, vertical edge, 45° diagonal, 135° diagonal.

2.3.3   Feature Vector

To construct the CEDD feature vector, the color information is calculated from the color unit and the texture information is calculated from texture unit. CEDD feature vector is created by the combination of the texture and color information. Each region of the image is constituted by 6 regions of texture and after that from each texture region the color information is constituted by 24 individual regions. That's why the feature vector is of 144 (6 × 24) vector elements.

The CEDD feature from each test image with different orientation angle and scale is calculated. That means the feature vector from fragmented leaf images is calculated which varies in rotation and scale.

2.4   Classification (CL)

For the classification of the whole and fragmented leaf images the Euclidian distance is used. The database of trained images would typically contain leaf samples of varying height and width. The CEDD feature vector is calculated from the trained and test images. The minimum distance of the calculated feature between a test fragment and a train image is obtained. For each test sample, the process is repeated over all training samples and the Euclidian distance values summed up for each class. The test slice is considered a member of that class for which the sum is minimum.

3   Experimentations and Results

Experimentations are done using 700 leaf images divided into 35 classes, collected from [13, 14]. Out of 20 images per class, 10 are used for training and 10 for testing. The images have various orientation angle and scale. Figure 7 shows samples of each class in the dataset.

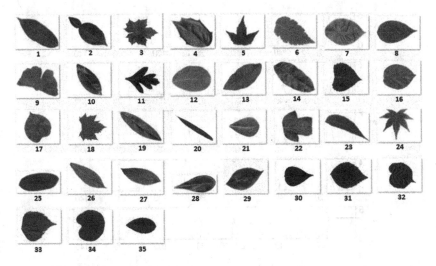

Fig. 7. Samples of 35 classes of the dataset

Five types of fragmented (left-top, right-top, left-bottom, right-bottom and center) images are made from these whole leaf images as described in the Sect. 2.1.

3.1 Pre-processing

The leaf images are first made translation invariant. The pre-processed whole and fragmented image is shown in Fig. 8.

Fig. 8. (Left): original image; (center): pre-processed whole image; (right) pre-processed fragmented image

3.2 Modeling the Texture Feature

Texture based feature using CEDD descriptors is used for classification, as explained above. Figure 9 shows the variations of the 144-element feature vectors averaged for 5 classes of whole (training) images.

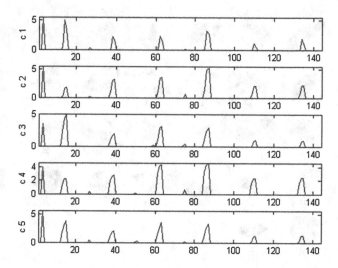

Fig. 9. Variation of CEDD features over 10 classes of whole (training) images.

The CEDD feature extracted from the whole leaf images as well as fragmented from center, left-top, right-top, left-bottom and right-bottom is represented as NI_W, NI_C, NI_{LT}, NI_{RT}, NI_{LB} and NI_{RB}.

3.3 Classification

The classification is done using the Euclidean distance classifier. The accuracies obtained for whole leaf images by applying these features over 35 classes are tabulated in Table 1. The overall accuracy for 35 classes whole leaf image is 90.6% obtained by using Euclidean distances as classification metric. Figure 10 shows the class label output of the test samples.

Table 1. Percent recognition rates of whole leaf images using NI_W

Class	Acc	Class	Acc	Class	Acc	Class	Acc	Class	Acc
1	100	2	90	3	60	4	90	5	100
6	100	7	100	8	70	9	90	10	60
11	100	12	90	13	100	14	90	15	100
16	100	17	100	18	100	19	60	20	90
21	100	22	100	23	90	24	100	25	80
26	100	27	70	28	90	29	100	30	100
31	100	32	90	33	90	34	70	35	100

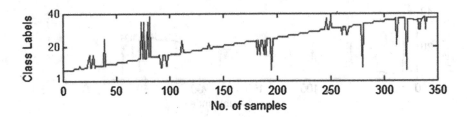

Fig. 10. Class label output of the whole test samples

The whole test samples are cropped in 6 different ways from the center, left-top, right-bottom, left-bottom, right-top creating a total of 350 × 6 types of fragmented images. The fragment percentages are 20%, 30%, 40%, 50%, 60%, and 70%. P% fragmentation means P% of the leaf data is missing in the test sample. NI_C, NI_{LT}, NI_{RT}, NI_{LB} and NI_{RB} features are calculated from the train images and test slices as described before. Each test slice feature is compared with a maximum number of 350 whole train image features before a classification decision can be made.

The overall accuracies of the 6 types of center fragmented leaves are listed in Table 2. Figure 11 shows the Euclidean distance classifier class label outputs for 350 center fragmented (20%) test samples.

Table 2. Percent overall recognition rates for NI_C feature

% of Fragmentation	70%	60%	50%	40%	30%	20%
% of Accuracy	62	63.7	63.8	66.8	76.3	88.3

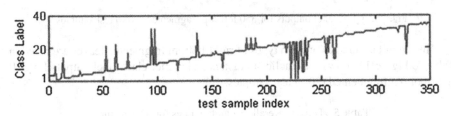

Fig. 11. Class label outputs for 350 center fragmented (20%) test samples

The overall accuracies of the 6 types of right-top fragmented leaves are listed in Table 3. Figure 12 shows the Euclidean distance classifier class label outputs for 350 right-top fragmented (20%) test samples.

Table 3. Percent overall recognition rates for NI_{RT} feature

% of Fragmentation	70%	60%	50%	40%	30%	20%
% of Accuracy	26.6	31.1	33.4	53.4	68.3	77.7

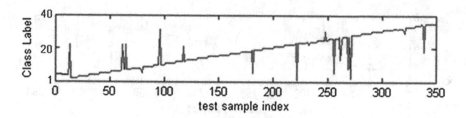

Fig. 12. Class label outputs for 350 right-top fragmented (20%) test samples

The overall accuracies of the 6 types of left-top fragmented leaves are listed in Table 4. Figure 13 shows the Euclidean distance classifier class label outputs for 350 left-top fragmented (20%) test samples.

Table 4. Percent overall recognition rates for NI_{LT} feature

% of Fragmentation	70%	60%	50%	40%	30%	20%
% of Accuracy	24.7	28.5	40.2	58.2	68	74.8

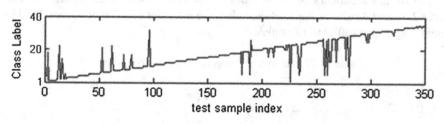

Fig. 13. Class label outputs for 350 left-top fragmented (20%) test samples

The overall accuracies of the 6 types of right-bottom fragmented leaves are listed in Table 5. Figure 14 shows the Euclidean distance classifier class label outputs for 350 right-bottom fragmented (20%) test samples.

Table 5. Percent overall recognition rates for NI_{RB} feature

% of Fragmentation	70%	60%	50%	40%	30%	20%
% of Accuracy	14.5	29.1	40.5	50.8	56.5	75.4

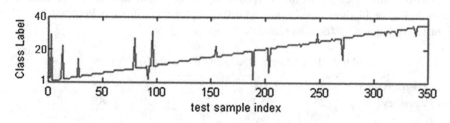

Fig. 14. Class label outputs for 350 right-bottom fragmented (20%) test samples

The overall accuracy of the 6 types of left-bottom fragmented leaves is listed in Table 6. Figure 15 shows the Euclidean distance classifier class label outputs for 350 left-bottom fragmented (20%) test samples.

Table 6. Percent overall recognition rates for NI_{LB} feature

% of Fragmentation	70%	60%	50%	40%	30%	20%
% of Accuracy	12.8	26	42.2	49.1	56.8	73.1

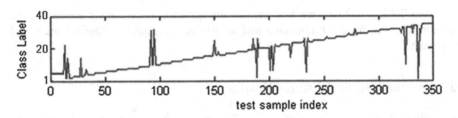

Fig. 15. Class label outputs for 350 left-bottom fragmented (20%) test samples

From Tables 2, 3, 4, 5 and 6 it is clear that when fragmentation amount is 20%, good recognition accuracy can be obtained from the fragmented images. The highest recognition rates for the 20% fragmented image is possibly due to the larger amount of texture information contained within the slice which leads to a better matching performance. Among the 20% fragmented image, the center fragmented image has the highest accuracy due to the highest textural information in the center fragmentation of the leaf.

4 Analysis

To compare the current work vis-à-vis other contemporary works, it should be mentioned that the contemporary approaches have been designed for whole leaf images and none of them seem to have been specifically designed for handling fragmented or partial leaves. Some other texture based methods are applied for the recognition of the fragmented images to compare the efficacy of the current method especially for the recognition of the fragmented images. Three types of texture based methods used here for the recognition of the fragmented leaf images: (1) Using Statistical features: The feature vector is created by using the uniformity, entropy and the third moment calculated from the Ridge filtered image, (2) Moment Invariant: The first invariant moment is used as the feature vector, (3): Gray Level Co-occurrence Matrix (GLCM): The 11 GLCM features such as energy, contrast, correlation, variance, local homogeneity, sum average, sum entropy, sum variance, entropy, information measures of correlation features1 and information measures of correlation measures 2 are calculated from Gabor filtered image. Table 7 shows the comparison of recognition rates when the above said three texture based methods are used for the recognition of the fragmented leaf images. In this experiment the selected fragmentation amount is 80% as most of the leaf texture part is present in this type of fragmentation.

Table 7. Comparison of % of recognition of fragmented leaf images using 3 different texture based methods

Fragmentation	Center	LT	RT	LB	RB
Using statistical features	11.1%	7.4%	8%	7.7%	8.8%
Using sing moment invariant	15.1%	10%	8.2%	10%	10.5%
Using sing GLCM features	13.1%	10%	9.1%	12%	12%
Using sing current approach	88.3%	74.8%	77.7%	73.1%	75.4%

From Table 7 we can see that the current approach is producing the maximum recognition rates for the fragmented leaf images as compared to other texture based approach.

5   Conclusions and Future Scopes

This article discusses a method of automatically characterizing and recognizing of whole leaves as well as the fragmented plant leaves where the entire leaf surface is not available. Here a texture and color based method is used for characterize the feature vector. As for fragmented images, the shape based approaches would not be reliable, the color and texture based technique is used. The Euclidian distance measure is used as the classifier. From the study we can see that the CEDD based approach can efficiently categorize the fragmented images having different orientation angle and scale. From the experimentation results we can see that the center fragmented images are recognized more efficiently as compared to the left-top, right-top, left-bottom and right-bottom type of fragmentations. This is so because the center fragmented images contains the maximum amount of leaf portion as compared to other type of fragmentations.

The future scopes include: (1) Designing an efficient method which can correctly categorize any type of fragmented images where only 10% to 30% leaf data is present, (2) Experimentations with other texture based methodologies, (3) Classification of fragmented images with other classifiers like Neural Network, Neuro fuzzy classifier etc.

References

1. Aakif, M., Khan, F.: Automatic classification of plants based on their leaves. Biosyst. Eng. **139**, 66–75 (2015)
2. Yang, L.-W., Wang, X.-F.: Leaf image recognition using fourier transform based on ordered sequence. In: Huang, D.-S., Jiang, C., Bevilacqua, V., Figueroa, J.C. (eds.) ICIC 2012. LNCS, vol. 7389, pp. 393–400. Springer, Heidelberg (2012). doi:10.1007/978-3-642-31588-6_51
3. Wang, X., Liang, J., Guo, F.: Feature extraction algorithm based on dual scale decomposition and local binary descriptors for plant leaf recognition. Digit. Signal Proc. **34**, 101–107 (2014)
4. Naresh, Y.G., Nagendraswamy, H.S.: Classification of medicinal plants: an approach using modified LBP with symbolic representation. Neurocomputing **173**, 1789–1797 (2016)
5. Zhang, S.W., Wang, X., Zhang, C.: Orthogonal maximum margin discriminant projection with application to leaf image classification. Int. J. Pattern Recognit. Artif. Intell. **28**, 1–20 (2014)

6. Hu, R., Jia, W., Ling, H., Huang, D.: Multiscale distance matrix for fast plant leaf recognition. IEEE Trans. Image Process. **21**, 4667–4672 (2012)
7. Ghasab, M.A.J., Khamis, S., Mohammad, F., Fariman, H.J.: Feature decision-making ant colony optimization system for an automated recognition of plant species. Expert Syst. Appl. **42**, 2361–2370 (2015)
8. Salve, P., Sardesai, M., Manza, R., Yannawar, P.: Identification of the plants based on leaf shape descriptors. In: Satapathy, S.C., Raju, K.Srujan, Mandal, J.K., Bhateja, V. (eds.) Proceedings of the Second International Conference on Computer and Communication Technologies. AISC, vol. 379, pp. 85–101. Springer, New Delhi (2016). doi: 10.1007/978-81-322-2517-1_10
9. Oncevay-Marcos, A., Juarez-Chambi, R., Khlebnikov-Núñez, S., Beltrán-Castañón, C.: Leaf-based plant identification through morphological characterization in digital images. In: Azzopardi, G., Petkov, N. (eds.) CAIP 2015. LNCS, vol. 9257, pp. 326–335. Springer, Cham (2015). doi:10.1007/978-3-319-23117-4_28
10. Liu, H., Coquin, D., Valet, L., Cerutti, G.: Leaf species classification based on botanical shape sub-classifier strategy. In: IEEE International Conference on Pattern Recognition, pp. 1496–1501 (2014)
11. Cerutti, G., Tougne, L., Coquin, D., Vacavant, A.: Leaf margins as sequences: a structural approach to leaf identification. Pattern Recogn. Lett. **49**, 177–184 (2014)
12. Du, J., Zhai, C.M., Wang, Q.P.: Recognition of plant leaf image based on fractal dimension features. Neurocomputing **116**, 150–156 (2013)
13. Flavia Plant Leaf Recognition System. http://sourceforge.net/projects/flavia/files/Leaf %20Image%20Dataset/
14. Plantscan Dataset. http://imedia-ftp.inria.fr:50012/Pl@ntNet/plantscan_v2/
15. Zhao, C., Chan, S.S.F., Cham, W.K., Chu, L.M.: Plant identification using leaf shapes – a pattern counting approach. Pattern Recogn. **48**, 3203–3215 (2015)
16. Chaki, J., Parekh, R., Bhattacharya, S.: Plant leaf recognition using texture and shape features with neural classifiers. Pattern Recogn. Lett. **58**, 61–68 (2015)

K-NN Based Text Segmentation from Digital Images Using a New Binarization Scheme

Ranjit Ghoshal$^{(\boxtimes)}$, Sayan Das, and Aditya Saha

St. Thomas' College of Engineering and Technology, Kolkata 700023, India
ranjit.ghoshal.stcet@gmail.com,
sayandas896@gmail.com, adi96saha@gmail.com

Abstract. Text segmentation in digital images is requisite for many image analysis and interpretation tasks. In this article, we have proposed an effective binarization method towards text segmentation in digital images. This method produces a number of connected components consisting of text as well as non-text. Next, it is required to identify the possible text components from the obtained connected components. Further, to distinguish between text and non-text components, a set of features are identified. Then, during training, we consider the two feature files namely text and non-text prepared by us. Here, K-Nearest Neighbour (K-NN) classifier is considered for the present two class classification problem. The experiments are based on ICDAR 2011 Born Digital Dataset. We have accomplished in binarization and as well as segmenting between text and non-text.

Keywords: Binarization · Connected component · Feature extraction · K-NN classifier · Text segmentation

1 Introduction

Text in images contains a lot of useful information. The text contained in these images are used for various purposes such as optical character recognition (OCR), content-based image and video application etc. Now a days, digital camera is one of the most popular device for capturing images and are often comes with mobile phones and many other hand held devices. Images from these devices contain backgrounds and texts, of non-uniform colors and textures, in natural scene. Extraction of text information from these sources has a useful application in the fields of robotics and image retrieval systems.

Born-digital images are applied in e-mail and web pages. Born digital images can be generated with text superimposed by software. Further, Born-digital images are low resolution in nature. Therefore, segmentation of text from Born digital images is a challenging task. Binarization of image is an important prerequisite to achieve better results towards text segmentation.

J.K. Mandal et al. (Eds.): CICBA 2017, Part II, CCIS 776, pp. 212–225, 2017.
DOI: 10.1007/978-981-10-6430-2_17

Existing methods for scene text detection are generally of four types: sliding window based methods developed by Chen et al. [1] and Kim et al. [2]. Sliding window based methods generally use a fixed sized window which slides over the image, looking for possible text regions and then using machine learning algorithms to detect text. Second is connected component based method [3–5]. In this method text components are extracted by analyzing the connected component in the image, and then grouping of character candidates into text is performed. The third type is hybrid methods [6] which uses region detector to find the text candidates. Finally, Maximally Stable Extremal Regions (MSERs) based methods [7–10].

In recent works, a method based on maximum gradient difference (MGD) values has been proposed by Zeng et al. [11]. In this method identification of strong and weak contrasted text component is done after separating the image into multiple layers based on MGD values.

In the works of Xu et al. [12], a method has been proposed which uses mass estimation technique to identify the text. Exploring of super-pixel information in different color channel, the text atoms in the images are identified. This is similar to spectral Clustering. To identify text candidates from the pixel distribution in a spatial circle, mass estimation concept has been intoduced. The linear linkage graphs help in grouping text elements to obtain full text lines.

Here we have proposed a new binarization technique. Binarization method produces a number of text and non-text connected components. To differentiate between text and non-text components, a number of features are considered. Further, K-Nearest Neighbors (K-NN) classifier is used for the present two class classification problem. Here, we consider ICDAR 2011 Born Digital Dataset [15] for experimental purpose.

The rest of the article is arranged as follows. Our new binarization method is discussed in Sect. 2. Section 3, presents feature extraction and K-NN based text segmentation methodology. Experimental results are presented in Sect. 4. Finally, Sect. 5 represents the summary and future scope.

2 Binarization

An image contains pixels of different intensities. This causes uneven binarization of the image. Hence, using variance, change of pixel intensities can be detected which is useful to identify two distinct regions, i.e., region having similar pixel intensities at surroundings and region having varying pixel intensities at surroundings. These two regions can be separately binarized and merged together to obtain the binarized image. The technique has been represented using block diagram in Fig. 1 and has been discussed below.

The method is illustrated using examples (Fig. 2). First, the color image (Fig. 2(a)) is converted to gray scale image [13] as given in Fig. 2(b). The following formula is used to convert RGB image to gray scale image. Suppose R, G, B denotes pixel the

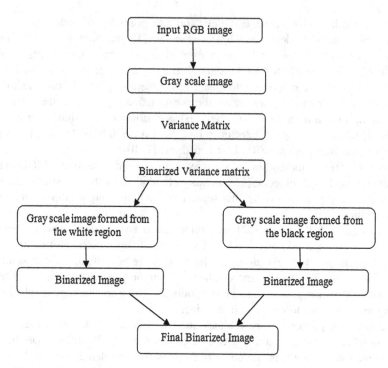

Fig. 1. Block diagram of implementation our binarization method on image

intensity values of the image in red, green, blue plane respectively. Gray scale pixel value is computed as:

$$Gray = 0.2989 \times R + 0.5870 \times G + 0.1140 \times B$$

Now, a window of size 5 × 5 is taken and the variance of the window is calculated. The choice of 5 × 5 is based on experiment such that the change in variation of pixel intensities can be detected to obtain two regions effectively. The calculated variance is replaced at the centre of the window. The process is continued throughout the image. Finally, a resultant matrix is obtained which consist of the variance. Now, applying Otsu's algorithm to the variance matrix, an image (say M) is obtained which consist of two regions (Fig. 2(c)).

Next, it is required to separate two regions as discussed earlier to form two different gray scale images. First, consider the gray pixel intensities from the gray image where the pixels in M are white and form an image (say G_1). Similar operation is performed for black pixels in M to obtain another image (say G_2).

Now, consider any one of the gray image (say G_1). Using Canny algorithm, an edge image is obtained (say E). Also G_1 is binarized again using Otsu's algorithm. Both the binarized image of G_1 and complemented binarized image of G_1 are considered. Now, consider a window of 20 × 20, such that edge pixel in E forms the centre of the window. The choice of 20 × 20 window is done based on experiment to achieve better

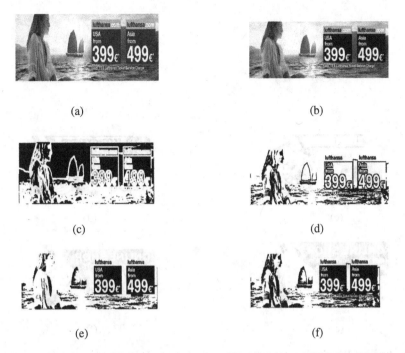

Fig. 2. Steps of Binarization: (a) Input image. (b) Gray scale image of (a). (c) After binarizing variance matrix. (d) After binarizing white region of (c). (e) After binarizing black region of (c). (f) Final binarized image. (Color figure online)

binarization result. This window is mapped both on binarized image and complemented binarized image to form two separate windows, say W_B and W_C respectively. Hence, using W_B and W_C, two separate matrices (say I_B and I_C) are formed by adding W_B and W_C to I_B and I_C respectively. Hence I_B and I_C are defined as follows:

$$I_B(x,y) = \sum \sum W_B(i,j) + I_B(x+i, y+j)$$
$$I_C(x,y) = \sum \sum W_C(i,j) + I_C(x+i, y+j)$$

This process is followed for all edge pixels present in E. Final binarized image for G_1 is formed by comparing I_B and I_C as follows:

$$BW_1(x,y) = 1, \qquad if\ I_B(x,y) > = I_C(x,y)$$
$$= 0, \qquad otherwise$$

Similarly, binarized image for G_2 be BW_2. Figure 2(d) and (e) show the binarized output by our proposed method on two separate regions.

Final binarized image (BW) is obtained by *logical AND* operation between BW_1 and BW_2. Figure 2(f) shows the final binarization output by our proposed method. Another one example is presented in Fig. 3.

(a)

(b)

(c)

(d)

(e)

(f)

Fig. 3. Steps of Binarization: (a) Input image. (b) Gray scale image of (a). (c) After binarizing variance matrix. (d) After binarizing white region of (c). (e) After binarizing black region of (c). (f) Final binarized image.

3   Feature Extraction and Text Segmentation

This section presents a few new shape based features and the K-NN based text segmentation scheme.

3.1   Features Extraction

Image binarization creates a number of connected components. These connected components contain possible text components. In order to separate text components from non-text we have identified the following text specific features.

1. Axial ratio (X_1): It is the ratio of the lengths of the two axes of a connected component. The *Major Axis Length (L_1)* and *Minor Axis Length (L_2)* of a connected component are computed. The X_1 is defined as:

$$X_1 = L_1/L_2.$$

2. Lobes count (X_2): Number of complete lobes or holes can be found using Euler number (N).

$$X_2 = 1 - N.$$

Here, the number of complete lobes in a connected component are used as a feature.

3. Aspect ratio (X_3): For a text connected component it is defined as follows:

$$X_3 = minimum\ of\ ((width/height), (height/width))$$

X_3 lies in a compact range for a text connected component.

4. Elongation ratio (X_4): Generally text connected components are elongated. It is defined as:

$$X_4 = (number\ of\ all\ boundary\ pixels)/(number\ of\ all\ pixels\ in\ the\ connected\ component).$$

5. *Object to background pixels ratio (X_5):* Only a small number of object pixels falls within the text bounding box because of the elongated nature of text component, whereas elongated non-text components are usually straight lines and contribute enough object pixels. It is denoted as:

$$X_5 = (area\ of\ pixels\ in\ the\ CC)/(area\ of\ the\ minimum\ bounding\ box\ -\ area\ of\ pixels\ in\ the\ CC).$$

6. Connected Component Area Ratio (X_6): It is the ratio of the area of the CC and the total area of the image. It is defined as:

$$X_6 = (Number\ of\ pixels\ in\ the\ CC)/(Number\ of\ all\ the\ pixels\ in\ the\ image).$$

7. Length Ratio (X_7): It is the ratio of maximum of the height and width of the CC to the maximum of the height and width of the total image. It is defined as:

$$X_7 = max(height\ of\ CC,\ width\ of\ CC)/max(height\ of\ the\ image,\ width\ of\ the\ image).$$

8. Thickness (X_8): Let v_i and h_i be the vertical and horizontal run lengths of a pixel p_i at the ith position of a connected component CC_j. Now, we calculate the minimum of v_i and h_i and further constitute a set $MIN_j = \{m_i$ such that $m_i = min\ \{(v_i, h_i)\ for\ all\ i\}$. Thus MIN_j represents the set of all the minimum run lengths considering all the pixels of CC_j. The thickness T_j of the component CC_j is defined as the element, having maximum frequency in the set MIN_j.

9. Width Variation (X_9): Width variation of a connected component is the ratio of the variance of the instantaneous thickness and mean thickness. It is defined as:

$$X_9 = (variance(instantaneous\ thickness))/(mean(thickness)).$$

10. Solidity (X_{10}): It is measure of the number of pixels present in the convex hull which are also present in the connected component. It is defined as follows:

$$X_{10} = (Area\ of\ the\ connected\ component)/(Convex\ area).$$

3.2 Text Segmentation Methodology

Considering these features we have created a feature vector denoted as:

$$\alpha = \{X_1, X_2, X_3, X_4, X_5, X_6, X_7, X_8, X_9, X_{10}\}$$

In order to perform text segmentation, K-NN classifier is considered. K-NN classifier is needed to be trained using features vectors of both text class and non-text class.

The ground truth information of the text connected components, provided by the Born Digital dataset, is considered for finding the feature vector. These provide 21700 connected components for texts and hence 21700 feature vectors. Further, to prepare non-text components the following procedure has been followed.

A few sample RGB images from ICDAR Born Digital dataset, their corresponding ground truth images and our constructed non-text images are presented in Table 1.

Table 1. RGB images and Ground Truth (GT) images for text and constructed non-text of the training set

RGB image	GT image for text	Constructed non-text image

First, the training images are binarized using our proposed binarization technique. Next, the ground truth text components are eliminated from that binarized images. Thus we created the images consist only of non-texts. In this way, 78808 non-text components, hence, feature vectors are prepared. Finally, two feature files (text and non-text), are constructed. Using these two feature files the K-NN classifier is trained.

Our next task is to segment the text components from the images. For this, first the image is binarized, then for each connected component the feature vector is obtained. Next, we compare with the trained K-NN classifier model to decide whether the component is text or non-text. Finally, considering only the text component the output image is constructed.

4   Experimental Results

The results are produced using ICDAR 2011 Born Digital Data set, which contains 102 test images and 420 training images. Images are implicitly low-resolution by their nature. Hence, binarization and segmentation of text from Born Digital images is a demanding task now a days. Here, the result section is divided into two parts. First, we present the results of binarization scheme. After that, results of the text segmentation based on K-NN classifier are provided.

To test the results we have used some parameters: *Recall*, *Precision* and *F-measure*. A pixel is considered as TP if it is TRUE in both Ground Truth (GT) and binarized images. A pixel is considered as FP if it is TRUE only in the binarzied image. A pixel is considered as FN if it is TRUE only in the GT image.

Now consider the number of TP pixels, FP pixels and FN pixels are A_{TP}, A_{FP}, A_{FN}. *Recall (RC)*, *Precision (PR)* and *F-measure (FM)* is defined as follows:

$$RC = (A_{TP}/(A_{FN} + A_{TP})) \times 100\%$$
$$PR = (A_{TP}/(A_{FP} + A_{TP})) \times 100\%$$
$$FM = ((2 \times RC \times PR)/(RC + PR)) \times 100\%$$

4.1   Results of Binarization Scheme

Our binarization algorithm is applied on 420 images of ICDAR 2011 Born Digital Dataset. The *Recall*, *Precision* and the *F-measure* value of the binarized images is compared with some other algorithms and it is found that *Precision*, *Recall* and *F-measure* values of our proposed method is higher than the Otsu [16] and Kumar et al. [14] method. The Bhattacharya et al. [13] method has higher value of *Recall* than our method but the *F-measure* and *Precision* values are lower than our method.

The comparison of *Recall*, *Precision* and *F-measure* values in different binarization method is presented in the Table 2. Some output images of these different binarization technique is presented in the Tables 3 and 4.

Table 2. Average values of Recall, Precision and F-measure in different binarization techniques

Binarization techniques	Recall	Precision	F-measure
Our method	89.95	75.91	77.42
Bhattacharya et al. [13]	91.14	47.85	53.81
Kumar et al. [14]	85.56	47.09	46.81
Otsu method [16]	88.98	65.36	65.05

Table 3. Results of various binarization techniques with our proposed method

Input Image	Otsu's Method[16]	Bhattacharya et al.[13]	Kumar et al.[14]	Our Method

Table 4. Few more results of various binarization techniques

Input Image	Otsu's Method[16]	Bhattacharya et al.[13]	Kumar et al.[14]	Our Method

4.2 Results of Text Segmentation

The binarization algorithm produces a number of connected components. These connected components are tested with trained K-NN classifier. In K-NN classification, an object is classified by a majority vote of its neighbors. Here, the object is assigned to the class, most common among its K nearest neighbors (K is a positive integer, typically small).

Finally, we construct an output image using the connected components which are classified as text components by K-NN classifier. Some text segmented images are shown in Tables 5 and 6 and the *Recall, Precession* and *F-measure* values of our text segmentation using K-NN classifier is presented in the Table 7.

Table 5. A few sample images and their corresponding binarized and segmented text images

The evaluation of our text segmentation scheme is performed by comparing with other well known methods. The ICDAR 2011 Robust Reading Competition offered evaluation results of a number of schemes from different participants. In Table 7, some of these methods are compared with our proposed method. Our text segmentation scheme has achieved a *Recall* of 71.64. Our method performs well than other methods considering the *Recall*.

Table 6. Few more sample images and their corresponding binarized and segmented text images

Input Images	Binarized Images	Segmented Text

Table 7. Performance comparison of different methods for text segmentation

Text detection	Recall	Precision	F-measure
Our method	71.64	54.02	56.71
Textorter	65.23	63.63	64.42
SASA	71.28	55.44	62.52

5 Summary and Future Scope

This article presents a K-NN classifier based text segmentation method using a new image binarization technique. The image binarization method is categorized as a local method. This method shows good results in case of low resolution images which is the main advantage of the proposed binarization method. Further for segmentation of text, a number of shape based text specific features are identified. Finally, K-NN classifier is applied to segment the text components from the binarized image. In future, the results can be progressed on, using a number of other distinct features with the existing feature list to distinguish between text and non-text. Other classifiers can be used for the present classification problem.

References

1. Chen, X., Yuille, A.: Detecting and reading text in natural scenes. In: Proceedings of the IEEE Conference on CVPR, Washington, DC, USA, vol. 2, pp. 366–373 (2004)
2. Kim, K., Jung, K., Kim, J.: Texture-base approach for text detection in images using support vector machines and continuously adaptive mean shift algorithm. IEEE Trans. Pattern Anal. Mach. Intell. 25(12), 1631–1639 (2003)
3. Epshtein, B., Ofek, E., Wexler, Y.: Detecting text in natural scenes with stroke width transform. In: Proceedings of the IEEE Conference on CVPR, San Francisco, CA, USA, pp. 2963–2970 (2010)
4. Mancas-Thillou, C., Gosselin, B.: Color text extraction with selective metric-based clustering. Comput. Vis. Image Underst. 107(1–2), 97–107 (2007)
5. Yi, C., Tian, Y.: Localizing text in scene images by boundary clustering, stroke segmentation, and string fragment classification. IEEE Trans. Image Process. 21(9), 4256–4268 (2012)
6. Pan, Y.-F., Hou, X., Liu, C.-L.: A hybrid approach to detect and localize texts in natural scene images. IEEE Trans. Image Process. 20(3), 800–813 (2011)
7. Chen et al., H.: Robust text detection in natural images with edge enhanced maximally stable extremal regions. In: Proceedings of the IEEE International Conference on Image Processing, pp. 2609–2612 (2011)
8. Merino-Gracia, C., Lenc, K., Mirmehdi, M.: A head-mounted device for recognizing text in natural scenes. In: Proceedings of the International Workshop CBDAR, Beijing, China, pp. 29–41 (2011)
9. Neumann, L., Matas, J.: Real-time scene text localization and recognition. In: Proceedings of the IEEE Conference on CVPR, Providence, RI, USA, pp. 3538–3545 (2012)
10. Shi, C., Wang, C., Xiao, B., Zhang, Y., Gao, S.: Scene text detection using graph model built upon maximally stable extremal regions. Pattern Recognit. Lett. 34(2), 107–116 (2013)
11. Zeng, C., Jia, W., He, X.: Text detection in born-digital images using multiple layer images. In: 2013 IEEE International Conference on Acoustics, Speech and Signal Processing (ICASSP), 26–31 May 2013
12. Xu, J., Shivakumara, P., Lu, T.: Text detection in born-digital images by mass estimation. In: 2015 3rd IAPR Asian Conference on Pattern Recognition (ACPR), 3–6 November 2015
13. Bhattacharya, U., Parui, S.K., Mondal, S.: Devanagari and Bangla text extraction from natural scene images. In: Proceedings of the 10th International Conference on Document Analysis and Recognition (2010)

14. Kumar, D., Ramakrishnan, A.G.: OTCYMIST: Otsu-Canny minimal spanning tree for born-digital images. In: 2012 10th IAPR International Workshop on Document Analysis Systems (DAS), 27–29 March 2012
15. Karatzas, D., Mestre, S.R., Mas, J., Nourbakhsh, F., Roy, P.P.: ICDAR 2011 robust reading competition challenge 1: reading text in born-digital images. In: Proceedings of the ICDAR, pp. 1485–1490 (2011)
16. Otsu, N.: A threshold selection method from gray-level histograms. IEEE Trans. Syst. Man Cybern. **9**(1), 377–393 (1979)

Comparative Analysis of Structured and Un-Structured Databases

Anindita Sarkar Mondal[2], Madhupa Sanyal[1], Samiran Chattopadhyay[1], and Kartick Chandra Mondal[1(✉)]

[1] Department of Information Technology, Jadavpur University, Kolkata, India
kartickjgec@gmail.com
[2] School of Mobile Computing, Jadavpur University, Kolkata, India

Abstract. The introduction of relational database systems helped in faster transactions compared to the existing system for handling structured data. However, in course of time the cost of storing huge volume of unstructured data became an issue in traditional relational database systems. This is where some unstructured database systems like NoSQL databases were introduced in the domain to store unstructured data. This paper focuses on four different structured(PostgreSQL) and unstructured database systems(MongoDB, OrientDB and Neo4j). In this paper, we will eventually see the different kind of data models they follow and analyze their comparative performances by experimental evidences.

Keywords: Database systems · Structured data · Un-structured data · Data model · Performance analysis

1 Introduction

Data coming from variant sources in different format is used by applications to yield some analytical result. Hence for proper utilization of this data, an efficient storage system(databases) with proper management principles is essential. The logical structure of a database is defined as data model. Through the data model database management system controls all the working procedure of database.

The earliest data model was hierarchical data model e.g., IBM Information System which was followed by hierarchical database [25]. Further evolution of databases resulted in foundation of relational model [23] where data is represented as tuples or rows which aggregates to form a relation and such systems are called Relational Database Management System (RDBMS). RDBMS uses structured query language (SQL) as its data query language.

Now, the transition from RDBMS to NoSQL is very significant [11]. RDBMS has several advantages [14] like data is stored in a structured way which helps in maintaining the entity relationship. When the data volume is huge and data context is not fixed with time, the demand for incorporation of a new system becomes essential. NoSQL (Not Only Structured Query Language) not only supports the storing of dataset but also supports durability, reliability, availability

© Springer Nature Singapore Pte Ltd. 2017
J.K. Mandal et al. (Eds.): CICBA 2017, Part II, CCIS 776, pp. 226–241, 2017.
DOI: 10.1007/978-981-10-6430-2_18

and scalability [12]. Rather than following the ACID property, NoSQL database follows CAP (Consistency, Availability, Partition Tolerance). With respect to transition-related application, RDBMS is better than NoSQL database.

Considering the NoSQL databases, they have a better management of structured, semi-structured and unstructured data [12,16,20]. There are four types of NoSQL databases like, (a) Key-Value: In this NoSQL database data is stored by forming of a group. This group is identified by a unique identifier known as key. Amazon S3, Azure follow this type of data storage structure to store large voluminous dataset. (b) Document: Here a set of data groups which have variable attributes are stored by forming a document. This document is identified by key value and presented in XML, JSON or BSON format. CouchDB, MongoDB are the examples of document NoSQL database. (c) Graph: In a network-based system, instance of an entity is connected with other instance of another entity and this connection has explicit meaning to the storage dataset. In this situation, graph database stores dataset by holding information about how and in what way an instance is connected with other. OrientDB, Neo4j are the most popular graph based NoSQL database. (d) Column-family: In this storage, data column-wise rather than as a horizontal tuple. This concept makes the data operation (i.e., access, storing) job faster. Cassandra, HBase are the example of Column-family NoSQL database.

This paper presents different data models with sample databases and their architectures. Also, it compares their performance using small dataset on the basis of simple queries. PostgreSQL [7,19] has been chosen as the example of SQL database. For NoSQL databases, Mongodb [8,13], OrientDb [1,24] and Neo4j [18] has been chosen as examples for experiments. Each of the above databases has been discussed with their unique features in Sect. 2. In Sect. 3, practical illustrations are shown as to how data is present in each of the databases followed by performance analysis based on some criteria which has been mentioned in this section. Conclusion is present in Sect. 4.

2 Physical and Logical Structure of Databases

The physical structure of any database follows a n-tier architecture where n represents independent modules and n $>=$ 1. The logical structure of a database is determined by the data models that specify the organization of data in the database. These models provide a layer of abstraction to the database and describes how data is present and link between data. The relational data model is most well known data model where data is stored in tables which in turn is made up of n-ary relation between attributes. Relational model is thus based on first-order predicate logic. RDBMS (SQL databases as commonly referred to) is logically structured on relational model. PostgreSQL which is described later is an example of SQL database modeled on relational model.

No-SQL data modeling techniques are less popular than relational data model. The earliest concept of No-SQL models [15] were introduced in Key-value storage systems where data was present as key-value pairs with no link

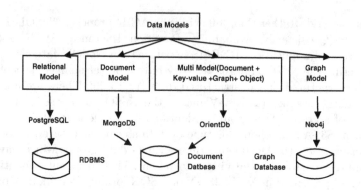

Fig. 1. Classification of different data model and examples databases following them

between keys. A common example of key-value database is Redis [9]. To overcome the difficulty, a new document data model was founded where data was stored as Java Script Object Notation(JSON) objects [17]. Here a collection comprises of a number of documents and each document contains field-value pair. Document-oriented databases follow document models. Examples include MongoDB. Graph-based data model comprises of vertices and edges connecting them. Neo4j is an example of graph database following graph model. OrientDB however is an example of multi-model NoSQL database whose engine supports document, graph, key-value and object data models. However the raw data is stored as documents. In this paper we are actually concentrating on four databases mainly: PostgreSQL, MongoDB, OrientDB, Neo4j which follow four different types of data modeling technique as shown in Fig. 1.

The physical structure of the databases are described below.

PostgreSQL (Example of Relational Model RDBMS): Data is stored as relation in tables in PostgreSQL. Structurally, it comprises of different modules or components which communicates amongst themselves and function to form a complete working unit of the database [7].

As shown in Fig. 2, the components are: Client Process, (Client Application + Client Interface), Server Process(Server+ Postmaster) and back-end or data Storage. The end user communicates with client process via client application. The user might write SQL query or procedural methods to access data in the application. One of the main components of client process is the Interface. It converts procedural code to SQL query which can be understood by the server. Then comes the Server process. Two important components are present here. First is the Postmaster which maps a client process to a server process. Next is Multi version Control System that ensures proper locking mechanism while any server process tries to access innermost component i.e. Data Storage.

MongoDB (Example of Document Model Document-oriented Database): In MongoDB, the complex documents are stored as arrays, hash tables etc. that are supported by JSON Documents [10]. MongoDB stores documents as data in

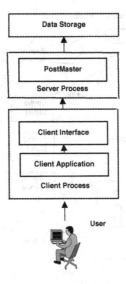

Fig. 2. Working unit of PostgreSQL

binary representation of JSON called BSON [21]. Index is used for ordering the documents in a collection in MongoDB and a unique id is automatically created for that particular index. Index helps in sorting the documents [8,13]. Several documents are integrated into collection. Collections can be compared to tables in RDBMS, and documents to rows and fields to columns. The data is split across numerous shards. The application that needs to access data in shards, connects underlying MongoDB processes. However, small collections need not be split across shards. As given in the Fig. 3, the structural components of MongoDb are:

Shard: Multiple shards are present which holds part of data. Read and write operations are done on the target shard i.e. Primary shard. A replica set is present as a backup to the primary shard. All the changes need to be distributed gradually across replicated secondary shards.

Config Server: Multiple config Servers are present which stores metadata that gives information as to what data is stored in the shard.

Routers: Client directs queries to routers. Routers consult with config server and re-directs to desired shard.

Mongo Client Library: Clients, which are a part of application, issues query to route via the client library.

OrientDB (Example of Multi Model Document-oriented Database): OrientDB is the first multimodel NoSQL database whose engine supports four kinds of data model: document model, graph model, key-value model, object-oriented data model [1]. Generally multi-model databases have got an abstraction layer with API to handle the multiple models. This restricts the performance. But in OrientDB, engine provides direct support to the datamodels. It actually combines

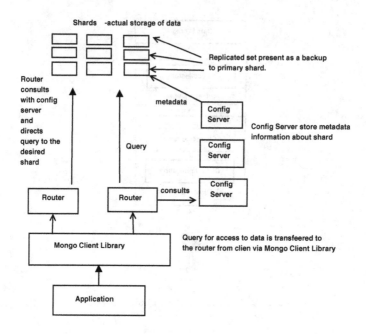

Fig. 3. MongoDB system storage structural components

graph concept in its representation of data as documents. "LINKS" are present between documents which cannot be found in document-oriented databases like MongoDB. The graphical representation of data in OrientDB is almost similar to graph databases. One subtle difference is the property of Inheritance which is applied while defining a "class" (analogous to tables in RDBMS). Class extends Vertex class "V" or edge class "E".

As shown in Fig. 4 OrientDB database supports four kinds of storage namely Paginated Local Storage(plocal), Remote Storage, Memory Storage, Local Storage. plocal comprises of Clusters, Write Ahead log(WAL), Indexes and Index Containers, and File mapping. Cluster is a logical portion of disk space to store records/data. Clusters are split into pages, hence the name "Paginated". .cpm files in cluster maps the cluster location of file data to its actual physical location. WAL is used to record operations/activities. Indexes are necessary to store

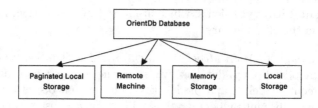

Fig. 4. Data Storage supported by OrientDB

the file and file mapping maps the file name to file id. Remote Storage supports Data storage in remote machines. Memory storage is where data is stored in memory and Local Storage is actually disk storage which has been replaced by plocal now.

Neo4j (Example of Graph Model Graph-oriented Database): It is essentially an open source NoSQL database implemented in Java. It follows the property of Graph Data Model and maintains data in that a way even at storage level [18]. On the top of it maintains additional Cache for implementation of Node-Relationship. The Disk is organized into record based storage assigned to every data structure(node, relationship and property). Each node and relation is identified by id. Now the size of the block depends on type of data structure stored. The representation of data in graph storage system mainly comprises of the following components as shown in Fig. 5.

Node: It contains labels, key-value pair. Pointers are there which points to the first relationship, and to the first property block.

Property: Store information related to node. For example if "Sachin" be the node, its properties may include run, average, noOfMatches etc.

Relationship: Defines the kind of relationship it is. Along with it pointers are present. These point to start and end node; first property block; pointer to previous and next relation of start and end node.

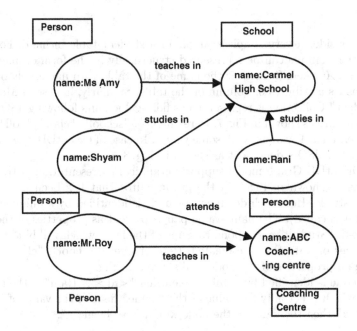

Fig. 5. Graph model of Neo4j

Label: In Fig. 5 these are represented as rectangular boxes. Each node is associated by a label which must be specified at the time of creation. Nodes belonging to different labels may have relationships(edges) between them.

Caches: Implements node or relationship.

3   Experimental Setup and Analysis

We have discussed in the previous section about the structure of four databases. Before going into the example of the sample schema structure we have in hand, let have a look into the Table 1 to get familiarized with the similarity amongst the terminologies of each database components. For instance the term "Table" in PostgreSQL is analogous to "Collection" in MongoDB, "Class" in OrientDB and "Node label" in Neo4j.

Table 1. Analogy of different components between PostgreSQL, MongoDB, OrientDB, Neo4j

PostgreSQL	MongoDB	OrientDB	Neo4j
Table	Collection	Class	Vertex and edge class (node label)
Tuple or row	Document	Vertex	Node
Column	Field	Property	Property

Now, consider a very simple example of a student table in hand. For PostgreSQL, the example can be represented structurally in the form of diagram as shown in Fig. 6 where Student is the name of the table with name, school, class, roll, age as its attributes or column of the table. Similarly, in case of MongoDB the "Student" Collection is represented as field-value pairs following JSON Document structure as shown in Fig. 7. Here "name", "school", "class", "roll", "age" are represented as key along with some values. In case of OrientDB, the raw data is presented as JSON document as shown in Fig. 8.

The OrientDB Graph model supports graphical representation of the JSON documents as shown in Fig. 9 in the graph editor that has been provided by OrientDB studio. Here each document or node is identified by a unique row_id (or rid as it is called). The name-value pair is present as properties of the node.

In Neo4j, "Student" correspond to name of the label which will bind together all the nodes or data that are created. Here "name", "school", "class", "roll", "age" are all properties of the node as displayed in Fig. 10.

Each node is identified by a unique identifier "<id>". "Ram" is the name of the node which is actually the value of the "name" field. If the value of "name" field was "x" then the name of the node would have been "x".

Student
name
school
class
roll
age

```
{
    "_id" : ObjectId("5f"),
    "name" : "Shyam",
    "school" : "CPS",
    "class" : 9.0,
    "roll" : 20.0,
    "age" : 12.0
}
```

```
{
    "@type": "d",
    "@rid": "#45:0",
    "@version": 1,
    "@class": "Student",
    "name": "Ram",
    "school": "DPS",
    "class": "9",
    "roll": "40",
    "age": "13"
}
```

Fig. 6. Table and attributes names for PostgreSQL

Fig. 7. JSON structure for MongoDB

Fig. 8. Raw data format for OrientDB

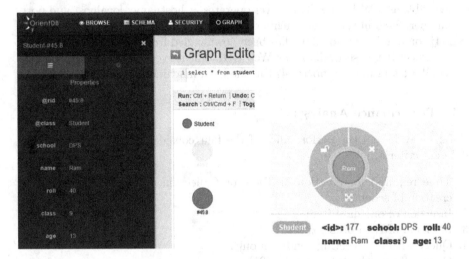

Fig. 9. Image of graph editor showing a node in OrientDB Studio

Fig. 10. Image of a node in Neo4j belonging to label student

3.1 Hardware and Software Specifications

All the databases have been deployed in localhost and not in remote host. The hardware specifications of the machine and the software description are given below.

Hardware Specifications: The hardware configuration of the machine is as follows.

- Processor: Intel(R) Core(TM) i3-4170 CPU @3.70 Ghz 3.70 Ghz
- Installed Memory(RAM): 4.00 GB
- System Type: 64-bit Operating System, X64 based processor
- Operating System: Windows 10

Software Used: Four databases have been installed in the machine as specified above.

PostgreSQL version 9.6 has been used and downloaded from [2]. "pgAdmin 4" is the open source management tool that has been used for PostgreSQL. "pgAdmin 4" provides the graphical interface for management of database objects. The server operates at hostname: localhost and port number: 5432 in the local machine.

MongoDB version 3.4 has been used and downloaded from [3]. "Robomongo 0.9.0" downloaded from [4] is the management tool that has been used in the experiment. The server operates at hostname: localhost and port number: 27017 in the local machine.

OrientDB community version 2.2.13 has been downloaded from [5] and installed as a service. It is actually a java server application and OrientDB Studio is available as a Web GUI. The server operates at hostname: localhost and port number: 2480 in the local machine.

Neo4j community edition 3.0.7 has been downloaded from [6] and is installed as a service. It is also available as Web GUI. The server operates at hostname: localhost and port number: 7474 in the local machine.

3.2 Performance Analysis

We have evaluated the performance of the four considered databases on seven different criteria:

1. Time required for creation of Table or Collection or Class i.e. the initial creation of schema.
2. Insertion of one data item
3. Insertion of N records together.
4. Query with one filtering condition only.
5. Query all records (total count = 21).
6. Delete only one record.
7. Delete all records.

Each of the above cases has been executed in the four databases with their respective query language. Also, they have been represented graphically by bar charts in Figs. 11, 12, 13, 14, 15, 16 and 17. Along X-Axis Time in milliseconds to execute the query has been plotted and along Y-Axis the name of databases are given. For PostgreSQL, the standard Structured Query Processing Language is used and for Neo4j, Cypher Query Language is used [22]. Let us now look into the case studies.

Case 1: Initial creation of outline structure of Table/Collection/Class/ Label. This actually covers the initial creation of Tables (or equivalents) using their respective query language. Figure 11 represents the analysis of performance by four databases. It is evident from the figure that OrientDB takes much greater time than other in this case.

PostgreSQL: The SQL query that is required to create a table is: *create table student_db(name text, school text, class int, roll int, age int)* where "student_db" stands for the name of the table created to accommodate data along with columns "name", "school", "class", "roll" and their respective data types (e.g., text, int). The time taken to execute the query is 100 ms.

MongoDB: To create a database for MongoDB, the query used is *"use student_db"*. Here "student_db" is the name of the database which is the actual container of collections which will holds data. To create collection the query used is *db. createCollection ("Student")* where "Student" is the name of the collection that will hold the documents records. The time taken in this case is 150 ms. It is worth mentioning that if no collection is created separately, MongoDB creates a collection automatically and name it the same as the name of the database.

OrientDB: In case of OrientDB, first a class needs to be created which extends either predefined Vertex class "V" or edge class "E". The query used is *"create class student extends V"* where "student" is the name of the class. The time taken for creating the class is 439 ms. After creating the class, properties need to be created which are actually attributes of the class. The properties can be created using query as well as by using options that are provided by OrientDB Studio. Here query is used to create properties in this paper and the query is: *"create property Student.name string"* where "Student" is the name of class extending vertex class "name" and type is string. The time recorded in this case is 62 ms. In this way other properties like "school", "class", "age", "roll" each of string type has also been created. Time is measured and the total time is 538 ms.

Neo4j: For Neo4j, separate creation of label is not required, since while creating the nodes the label can be specified.

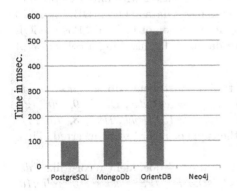

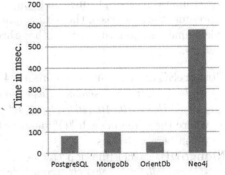

Fig. 11. Initial creation of outine structure of Table/Collection/Class/Label

Fig. 12. Insertion of first data or record

Case 2: Insertion of first data or record. Insertion of first data always takes greater time than the subsequent insertion due to initialization and memory allocation. Case 2 analyses the first insertion of a record in each of the databases. Figure 12 represents the time taken to perform the first insertion operation. Neo4j takes a much greater time in this case to insert first data.

PostgreSQL: The SQL query *"insert into student_db values('Ram', 'DPS', 9, 40, 13)"* inserts a row or tuple in the table "student_db". The entire relation or row represents the data in the database. The query execution takes 81 ms.

MongoDb: The query used to insert data is *"db.student_db.save ([{"name":"Shyam", "school":"CPS","class":9,"roll":20,"age":12}])"*. Also, insert() function could have been used instead of save(). In this case save() and insert() works in the same way. However, when id is passed as a parameter in save(), it performs update if document already exists and inserts if not. insert() will never perform an update operation and it will throw an error. The execution takes 97 ms.

OrientDB: To create a record in OrientDB, class name always need to be mentioned. The query *create vertex Student set name='Ram', school='DPS', class=9, roll=40, age=13* creates data as JSON structure with key and value pair. Since, Student class extends Vertex class hence the data created will be of Vertex type. Graph model features are also available in the studio and the same data can be visualized as a node from graph editor as well. Time required for first insertion in OrientDB is 52 ms.

Neo4j: The Cypher Query Language *"create(ram: Student{name:"Ram", school:"DPS", class:9, roll:40, age:13})"* is used to create a node named "Ram" which belongs to label Student. The key:value pair denotes the properties of the node. Creation of first node takes 580 ms.

Case 3: Insertion of N records together. This case is actually used for analysis of time taken to insert n-records simultaneously, where we assumed n=4. More or less, same query structure is used as case 2 with only exception of a customized javascript function being used to insest data in OrientDB. Figure 13 represents the analysis of the performances for insertion of 4 records. PostgreSQL takes much greater time than other three database for inserting a collection of records.

PostgreSQL: The query to insert 4 tuples in student_db is *"insert into student_db(name, school, class, roll, age) values('abc','CPS', 9, 20, 12), ('def','JPS', 10, 10, 16), ('ghi','HPS', 10, 50, 15), ('jkl','IPS', 8, 70, 14)"* where the value in each "()" denotes the tuple or record to be inserted. Time taken here is 144 ms.

MongoDB: save() function can be used to insert 4 document record like *"db. student_db.   save([{"name":"rita","school":"JPS","class":10,"roll":10, "age":16}, {"name":"mita","school":"HPS","class":10,"roll":50,"age":15}, {"name":"sita","school":"IPS","class":8,"roll":70,"age":14},   {"name": "amy","school":"CPS","class":9,"roll":20,"age":12}])"*. The time taken for MongoDB is 2 ms. In this case, insertMany() function can also be used to insert multiple data.

OrientDB: In this experiment, javascript function is used to create multiple records. The input parameters are specified which takes input and stores it in variables. The variables are passed as values in key-value pair generated for every document record. The time taken is 9 ms.

Neo4j: Like in previous case, the same Cypher Query is used i.e. "*create(shyam:Student {name:"Shyam", school:"CPS", class:9, roll:20, age:12}), (rita:Student {name:"Rita", school:"JPS", class:10, roll:10, age:16}), (mita:Student {name:"mita", school:"HPS", class:10, roll:50, age:15}), (sita:Student {name:"sita", school:"IPS", class:8, roll:70, age:14})*" where the value in each "( )" denotes the node to be created. Since the name of label is mentioned only once this indicates all the nodes belong to same label "Student" and the time required for this operation is 135 ms.

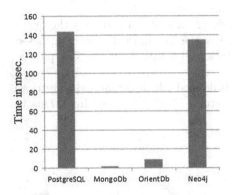 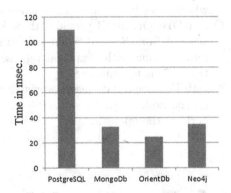

Fig. 13. Insertion of four records together

Fig. 14. Query with one filtering condition only

Case 4: Query with one filtering condition only. In similar way as Case 3, more records have been inserted in the database. The total count of the records here is 21. Figure 14 represents the analysis of the performances for selection on the basis of one filtering condition. It has been seen that PostgreSQL takes a much greater time than others.

PostgreSQL: In PostgreSQL, the query is filtered on basis of names. The query "*select * from student_db where name='Ram'*" retrieves data filtering on attribute name whose value is "Ram". The time taken for this operation is 110 ms.

MongoDB: In this database, find() function is used to retrieve records e.g., "*db.student_db. find ({name:"Ram"})*" is the corresponding query for the required operation. The time taken is 33 ms.

OrientDB: In case of OrientDB, the query is same as that in PostgreSQL. The query "*select * from Student where name='Ram'*" takes 25 ms to execute.

Neo4j: The Cypher Query Language to filter with condition must include the name of label to uniquely identify the node. The query "*match(Ram:Student) where id(Ram) in [177] return Ram*" filters on the basis of id (assigned at the time of creation) which uniquely identifies the node. The query takes 35 ms to execute.

Case 5: Query all records (Total record count is 21). This case analyses the time taken to query all the records present in the database. Figure 15 represents the analysis of the performance for selection of all records and PostgreSQL takes a much greater time than others.

PostgreSQL: SQL Query is same as in Case 4 but only exception is without filtering condition i.e., "*select * from student_db*". This takes 81 ms time to complete the operation.

MongoDB: MongoDB uses find() function for case 5 as "*db.student_db.find()*" which takes just 1 ms to complete its operation.

OrientDB: OrientDB provides three kinds of view of data. It uses the query *select * from Student* where one can view the raw data in document-based format along with graphical representation and tabular view. The process takes 27 ms to complete.

Neo4j: For graph database, a variable x is defined which is required to retrieve all the nodes e.g., "*match(x:Student) return x*" and this requires 27 ms to perform the operation.

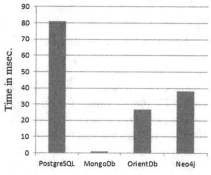

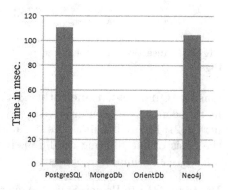

Fig. 15. Query all records(total count=21)

Fig. 16. Delete only one record

Case 6: Delete only one record. This case analyses the time taken to find a particular record and to delete the record. Figure 16 represents the analysis of the performances for deletion of 1 record. PostgreSQL takes much greater time than others for deletion.

PostgreSQL: SQL query for deleting one record is "*delete from student_db where name='Ram'*" and the time taken for this is 111 ms.

MongoDB: For selective deletion we need to pass the name and value pair as parameters to remove() function like "*db.student_ db. remove({name:"Ram"})*" which takes 48 ms time to complete the job.

OrientDB: The query in this case is relatively simple by just mentioning the condition where clause as in case of SQL e.g., "*delete vertex Student where name='Ram'*". It takes 44 ms to perform the operation.

Neo4j: The delete query for Neo4j is "*MATCH (n { name:'Ram'}) DETACH DELETE n*", where Detach Delete is used to delete node irrespective of edges connecting them. Total time required for detaching or deleting is 105 ms.

Case 7: Delete all records. This case demonstrates use of query to delete all records without deleting table or collection or Class. Figure 17 represents the analysis of the performances for deleting all records from the database. PostgreSQL takes a much greater time than others databases.

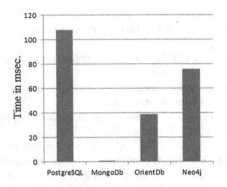

Fig. 17. Delete all records

PostgreSQL: Query in this case is same as in case 6 except the filtering condition e.g., "*delete from student_ db*" which takes 108 ms.

MongoDB: The same remove() function is used to delete all the records. Only difference with the previous case is use of empty which signify that all records need to be deleted i.e., "*db.student_ db.remove({})*". This operation takes 1 ms to complete the job.

OrientDB: The deletion of class Student deletes all records, however the class still remains and the corresponding query is "*delete vertex Student*" which takes 39 ms to execute.

Neo4j: The Cypher query "*MATCH (n:Student) DELETE n*" deletes all the nodes with their properties and the time required for this is 76 ms.

4   Conclusion and Future Scope

This paper actually takes example of four completely different data-model oriented databases. Initial study about physical structure of the databases and comparative study between data models(mainly relational, document, multi model and graph model) reveals that for transactions relational model is important whereas unstructured data can be stored by No-SQL modeling. The basic difference between graph model and document model is the presence of Link between data. Orient DB although being document oriented database, bridges the gap by introduction of link. Small examples have been given to demonstrate the practical example of how data is logically stored in databases. Lastly with the help of small query, performance is evaluated with respect to small data set. From the analysis we see that the initial setup cost of Neo4j is more, yet the cost of select, insert, delete operation is most costly for PostgreSQL. Nowadays object-oriented storages are in uprise for its archival ability. The future scope of the paper would be studying object-oriented database and possibly comparing with these databases.

References

1. OrientDB Manual - version 2.1.x. http://orientdb.com/docs/2.1/. Accessed 7 Jan 2017
2. PostgreSQL: Downloads (1996). https://www.postgresql.org/download/. Accessed 5 Jan 5 2017
3. MongoDB. (2 January 2017). MongoDB Download center. https://www.mongodb.com/download-center#community. 9 Jan 2017
4. Robomongo (2017). https://robomongo.org/download. Acessed 9 January 2017
5. LTD, O. (17 January 2017). Download OrientDB v2.2.17 community and enterprise edition. http://orientdb.com/download/. Accessed 9 Jan 2017
6. Technology, N.: Download neo4j community edition - neo4j graph database (2017). https://neo4j.com/download/community-edition/. Accessed 6 Jan 2017
7. Postgresql: Documentation: 7.1: Architecture (1996). https://www.postgresql.org/docs/7.1/static/arch.html. Accessed 9 Jan 2017
8. Banker, K.: MongoDB in action (2011)
9. Carlson, J.L.: Redis in Action (2013)
10. Crockford, D.: The application/JSON media type for javascript object notation (JSON) (2006)
11. Hadjigeorgiou, C.: RDBMS vs NoSQL: Performance and scaling comparison (2013)
12. Han, J., Haihong, E., Le, G., Du, J.: Survey on nosql database. In: 2011 6th International Conference on Pervasive Computing and Applications (ICPCA), pp. 363–366 (2011)
13. Hawkins, T., Plugge, E., Membrey, P.: The definitive guide to MongoDB: the noSQL database for cloud and desktop computing (2011)
14. Jatana, N., Puri, S., Ahuja, M., Kathuria, I., Gosain, D.: A survey and comparison of relational and non-relational database. Int. J. Eng. Res. Technol. 1(6) (2012)
15. Kaur, K., Rani, R.: Modeling and querying data in nosql databases. In: 2013 IEEE International Conference on Big Data, pp. 1–7 (2013)
16. Leavitt, N.: Will nosql databases live up to their promise? Computer 43(2), 12–14 (2010)
17. Lennon, J.: Introduction to JSON. In: Beginning CouchDB, pp. 87–105 (2009)
18. Miller, J.J.: Graph database applications and concepts with Neo4j. In: Proceedings of the Southern Association for Information Systems Conference, vol. 2324, Atlanta, GA, USA (2013)

19. Momjian, B.: Postgresql performance tuning. Linux J. **2001**(88), 3–9 (2001)
20. Moniruzzaman, A.B.M., Hossain, S.A.: Nosql database: new era of databases for big data analytics-classification, characteristics and comparison. arXiv preprint (2013). arXiv:1307.0191
21. Nayak, A., Poriya, A., Poojary, D.: Type of NOSQL databases and its comparison with relational databases. Int. J. Appl. Inf. Syst. **5**(4), 16–19 (2013)
22. Panzarino, O.: Learning Cypher (2014)
23. Rumbaugh, J., Blaha, M., Premerlani, W., Eddy, F., Lorensen, W.E.: Object-oriented modeling and design, vol. 199 (1991)
24. Tesoriero, C.: Getting Started with OrientDB (2013)
25. Tsichritzis, D., Lochovsky, F.H.: Hierarchical data-base management: a survey. ACM Comput. Surv. (CSUR) **8**(1), 105–123 (1976)

SysML Based Conceptual ETL Process Modeling

Neepa Biswas[1], Samiran Chattopadhyay[1], Gautam Mahapatra[2],
Santanu Chatterjee[2], and Kartick Chandra Mondal[1](✉)

[1] Department of Information Technology, Jadavpur University, Kolkata, India
kartickjgec@gmail.com
[2] Research Centre Imarat DRDO, Ministry of Defence,
Government of India, Kurmalguda, India

Abstract. Data generated from various sources can be erroneous or incomplete which can have direct impact over business analysis. ETL (Extraction-Transformation-Loading) is a well-known process which extract data from different sources, transform those data into required format and finally load it into target data warehouse (DW). ETL performs an important role in data warehouse environment. Configuring an ETL process is one of the key factor having direct impact over cost, time and effort for establishment of a successful data warehouse. Conceptual modeling of ETL can give a high-level view of the system activities. It provides the advantage of pre-identification of system error, cost minimization, scope, risk assessment etc. Some research development has been done for modeling ETL process by applying UML, BPMN and Semantic Web at conceptual level. In this paper, we propose a new approach for conceptual modeling of ETL process by using a new standard Systems Modeling Language (SysML). SysML extends UML features with much more clear semantics from System Engineering point of view. We have shown the usefulness of our approach by exemplifying using a use case scenario.

Keywords: ETL · Data warehouse · Conceptual model · MBSE · SysML

1 Introduction

Data warehouse [13] is a repository of historical data which is consolidated in multidimensional format. In warehouse, data is stored in a standard structure which are obtained by integrating data of different operational sources of an organization. Business analyst [8,30] can access that data, perform analysis, apply business intelligence tool and make prediction as well as take strategic decision. For maintaining a data warehouse, the main focus is to manage large amount of data generated from different type of systems (SAP, ERP, Oracle, Mainframe etc.) and store those data in an uniform structure. For managing the uniformity of data, ETL has a very important role. ETL is a widely used process in business organizations. It identify and extract data from various sources, filter

© Springer Nature Singapore Pte Ltd. 2017
J.K. Mandal et al. (Eds.): CICBA 2017, Part II, CCIS 776, pp. 242–255, 2017.
DOI: 10.1007/978-981-10-6430-2_19

and customize those data according to required format, at last integrate and update it into data warehouse [33].

Data modeling [7] gives an abstract view about how the data will be arranged in an organization and how they will be managed. By applying data modeling techniques, the relationship between different data items can be visualized. The modeling concept has a great benefit over organizational data to manage it in a structural way. At starting phase, it is highly recommended to make an efficient modeling and design of the total workflow. Due to the expensive nature of warehouse implementation, good modeling as well as documentation should be maintained. Based on the report [11], designing a well-established ETL workflow consumes almost one third of cost and effort in a DW implementation. A well designed ETL process is one of the important aspects to accomplish an effective DW. Each vendor provided tool has their own specific methodology for designing the ETL process [9,18]. It requires understanding about functionality, language, standards etc. about that particular tool. Moreover the integrated design is not suitable to execute in other platform.

During the ETL processing, conceptual modeling reflect high-level view of entities and relationship among them. It only provides an abstract view of the workflow instead of the implementation details. Different research work has been done for conceptual modeling of ETL. UML, BPMN and semantic web are commonly used so far for conceptual modeling techniques. We proposed a new way for modeling an ETL process using a system modeling language (SysML). Although there are many contributions towards ETL abstract modeling is done, we think that SysML is a new direction for conceptualizing and validating of ETL workflow. There is a lot of research scope using SysML to practically implement ETL model, validation, simulation, executable code production in a specific way for the sake of both technical and non-technical users.

This paper aims to propose a new technique for designing conceptual model of ETL by using SysML standard supporting Model-based System Engineering (MBSE) approach. SysML is a general purpose system modeling language which facilitates the system by identification, analysis, design, test and validation [14]. It supports system modeling for broad categories of organization like aerospace, automotive, health care etc. SysML is a new modeling language standardize by Object Management Group (OMG) [2] and International Council on Systems Engineering (INCOSE) [15,16]. It can be used to model high-level view of the ETL process and justify the system validation by applying simulation process.

The rest of the paper is structured as follows: Sect. 2 briefly discusses existing work in the area of ETL conceptual modeling. An overview of Model-Based Systems Engineering and SysML notations for requirement and activity diagram with its characteristics are included in Sect. 3. Section 4 explains our proposed work for ETL modeling with a suitable example using SysML diagrams. Finally, in Sect. 5 discuss about the conclusion with probable future direction of this work.

2   Related Work

There are various approaches have been proposed for conceptual designing of ETL process in last few decades. These research work can be classified using the modeling languages they have used like UML, BPMN and Semantic Web based. This section contains a brief discussion about these techniques.

The very first attempt for conceptual ETL modeling was established by Simitsis et al. in [34]. A customizable generic meta-model is proposed and a set of notations is given to represent the ETL activities. Relationship among attributes of source and data warehouse is established through this model. Their module supports customizable template of transformation like primary or foreign key checking, null value checking etc. Finally candidate relationship set is established for updating data in warehouse from multiple source database. The authors further enriched their work [26] by proposing a methodology showing step by step procedure from source selection to warehouse population along with attributes relationship mapping and runtime obstacle handling issues.

J. Trujillo et al. [32] designed the work-flow of ETL based on UML modeling approach. This was the first approach of conceptual model design by using standard UML notations. The author uses UML class diagram to establish database and their attributes relationship. Various transformation process like aggregation, conversion, filter, join etc. is supported by their modeling with zooming in and zooming out facility for different level of design. Another research effort using UML 2.0 was proposed in [19] where authors have highlighted the extraction phase only. They have identified six classes and exhibit class diagram, use case diagram and sequence diagram for extraction phase using standard UML notation. Transformation and loading phase are not included in their work. L. Munoz [20] modeled a complete ETL process by using UML activity diagrams. The activity involved in ETL process are expressed using diagram with control flow sequence supporting various transformation activity. Further, they have enriched their work in [21] proposing automatic code generation from conceptual models by supporting model driven architecture (MDA). A conceptual model based on their previous work [20] is designed by using PIM (Platform Independent Model) supporting UML features. PIM can give a system functional view without bothering about the platform. Different PSM (Platform Specific Model) showing logical model view can be produced from the PIM. Automatic data structure creation code is generated form individual PSM. PIM model to PSM model transformation is done by QVT (Query View Transformation) language.

BPMN stands for Business Process Model and Notation consists of standard graphical notations which helps to understand business processes within a organization. First attempt of using BPMN notations in ETL conceptual modeling was proposed by Akkaoui et al. in [3]. Conceptual model formation process is described and conversion from BPMN to BPEL (Business Process Execution Language) is done to execute the designed model as well as implementing relations with web services. In a sequel of their work [6], a Model-Driven Development (MDD) based vendor independent BPMN meta model is created and automatic code generation for any vendor specific platform is proposed.

Further, they made advancement in their work [5] by proposing model-to-text and model-to-model transformation for code generation. A model updating purpose along with required maintenance factors and designing a BPMN meta model for ETL conceptual view was done in [4]. Oliveira and Belo [22,23] designed a set of generalized ETL meta model for some specific tasks by using BPMN notations. Finally, they have validated their model by case study. Further, they have advanced their work for conceptual to physical model auto-generation process in [10,24].

Skoutas and Simitsis modeled a High-level view of ETL process by using ontologies in literature [27,28]. Use of ontology facilitates to identify the schema of the data source and data warehouse. Automatic transformation and data selection form source to warehouse population is established. Extending their previous work in [29], a framework is proposed by using the feature of ontology with semantic specification of source and the target. A set of graph transformation rules are formulated to guide the flow of ETL operations. In another work, Simitsis converted the conceptual model into natural language explanation in [25] for non technical background people. Hoang Thi and Nguyen proposed a new semantic approach in [17,31] for ETL work-flow using common warehouse meta model (CWM) design standard. CWM support structured, non-structured and multidimensional meta data modeling of object in data warehouse.

The drawback of UML is of having a software centric point of views and having shortfall of clear semantics. Moreover, the relationship within software and hardware are not representable by UML. SysML offer more facilities over UML by adapting some core features and extending many new directions. Whereas BPMN notation is suitable for business users to graphically model complex business processes of an organization. An initial model of the overall process is created by the business users, after that technical developers implement that model. But implementing any SysML model is much more flawless for the technical developers as it is developed from systems engineering view point. SysML is derived from UML model but compared to UML, SysML is very much flexible and expressive which is capable of better requirement analysis and define performance and quantitative parameters of a broad range of system from the perspective of a system engineer and not from software centric views like UML. SysML can efficiently capture continuous nature of system with requirements and parametric relation of a system model.

3   Model Based Systems Engineering (MBSE)

MBSE is an OMG supported new standard for system engineering domain featuring requirement-driven and functional analysis, design, integration, validation and simulation of system design throughout the life-cycle of system development defined by INCOSE [12,15]. MBSE promotes model-based approaches instead of prevalent document-oriented design methods. Model oriented approach helps to capture system architectural descriptions. It promotes better understanding of system construction and its performance. Using model complete system can be visualized with the facilities of system validation in the earlier stage of design. After that model can be mapped into physical implementation. UML or SysML are standard visual modeling language that can be used to describe the system model.

MBSE is gaining popularity in industry for creating complex systems in the scenario of merging multi-disciplinary environment. SysML is one of the key components of MBSE, having properties for capturing requirements, architecture, constraints and hierarchical or multi layered views of system model. It allows linking different types of models that come from different engineering disciplines. MBSE [1] improves system modeling techniques by advanced communication, better system complexity management, standard data management, better quality product, upgraded information capture, risk minimization.

3.1   System Modeling Language (SysML)

SysML is a general purpose graphical modeling language which can be termed as an extended version of UML. Continuous evolution of different visual modeling languages from SA(Structure analysis) SD(Structured design) to SysML are shown in the Fig. 1. SysML 1.0 was standardized by OMG group at 2006.

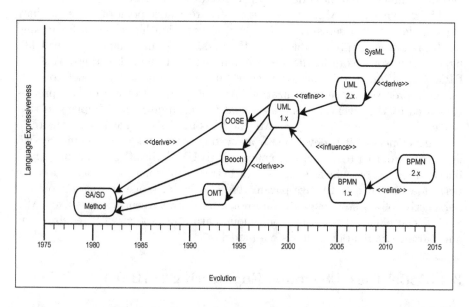

Fig. 1. Evolution of visual modeling languages

For modeling of a system, SysML support requirements, functional and behavioral structure of system and their inter-relationship. As it is originated from UML, it reuses many UML notations with some additional extensions [2]. SysML support various type of diagrams to represent structural and behavioral nature of a system shown in Fig. 2. Activity diagram, Block diagram and internal block diagram indicated by bubble box are modified version of basic UML diagram. Parametric and Requirement diagram indicated by dashed box are introduced in SysML. Other basic diagram of UML can also be drawn using SysML.

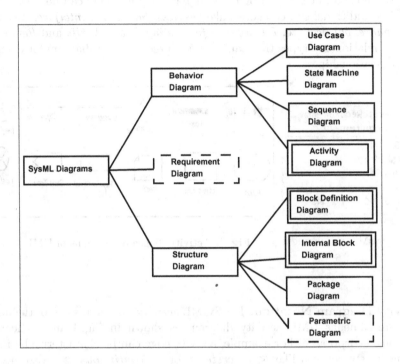

Fig. 2. SysML supported diagrams

3.2 SysML Notation

In this work, we are using SysML requirement diagram and activity diagram for expressing ETL processes. Requirement diagram represents test-based requirement using graphical construct whereas activity diagram explores system behavior by showing flow of control and data within activities. In SysML, each modeling elements can be characterized by their *Stereotype*. There are set of different standard stereotypes available for SysML diagrams. Stereotype notation provide is a new way to define system elements according to user requirements. Stereotypes are expressed by enclosing its type within double chevrons such as ≪ *discrete* ≫, ≪ *continuous* ≫, ≪ *allocated* ≫ etc.

Requirement Diagram Notation. Requirement diagram is a completely new concept compared to UML diagrams. It supports text-based *requirements*, their

relationship and *test cases* to verify the requirements. A basic SysML requirement block is displayed in Fig. 3. A SysML requirement rectangular block contain its stereotype mentioned as ≪ *requirement* ≫, its unique identifier number
Id=RQ1.1 and *Text="#"* for describing textual requirement details. There are
some extended requirement properties such as verification method, source pri-
ority, risk etc. can be selected by the designer. Requirements can be customized
into more additional sub-categories like *business, functional, interface, usability,
performance, physical* etc. *Derive, Satisfy, Nesting, Trace, Verify* and *Refine* are
different relationship types that can be used in requirement diagram for describing the relationship.

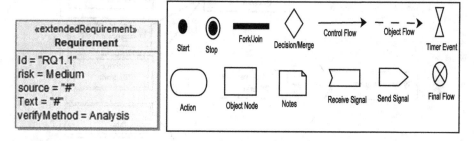

Fig. 3. SysML requirement   **Fig. 4.** Activity diagram notations of UML
block

Activity Diagram Notation. For SysML activity diagram, some of the notations are same as UML activity diagram as shown in Fig. 4 and some new
notations incorporated. For example, activity edge can be characterize by mentioning its stereotypes like ≪ *discrete* ≫ or ≪ *continuous* ≫. Also, actual
rate of the object flow can also be mentioned by using *constraint* notation like
{rate = expression}. Assigning *probability* to any activity edge (mostly control
flow) is another new feature like *{Probability = value%}* in SysML diagram. It
expresses the probability of traversal for any particular edge.

Behavior of any object node can more precisely expressed by using stereotype
≪ *nobuffer* ≫ or ≪ *overwrite* ≫. For the first case, the object node will be
discarded if the next action is not prepared to receive it. For the second case,
the object node will be overwritten if the next action is not prepared to receive
it. Applying *interruptible regions* a group of elements in activity diagram can be
separately identified by a dashed box.

4   Conceptual Modeling of ETL Processes

The main purpose of conceptual ETL modeling is to establish a relationship
between source data schema and the target warehouse data schema. It provides
a high level view of system which does not include any logical or physical implementation details.

We have proposed a design of high-level model of ETL process. At first, we have designed a SysML requirement diagram for the ETL scenario. After that, we have modeled the conceptual ETL process by using SysML activity diagram. Each elements of the SysML model are specified by its simulation specific characteristics.

4.1 Example Scenario

For representing the ETL scenario, we are taking an example of an e-commerce system where a database is maintained for daily transactions. Operational data are stored in relational format. This data needs to be converted and deposited according to the data warehouse format. For the e-commerce system, total sale for each day are calculated and stored in the data warehouse. Moreover, all information related to customer, supplier, website and products are stored in the warehouse.

The structure of the target data warehouse schema is shown in the Fig. 5. The fact table contains key attributes of dimension tables, basic facts and derived facts. Here, the *Fact_Sales* table has six dimensions of *Customer, Supplier, Product, Date_Time, Website* and *Promotion*. Dimension table can have aggregation level hierarchy. Dimension_Website → Dimension_Navigation is an example of hierarchy maintenance. Dimension_Address → Dimension_State → Dimension_City is a three level of hierarchy shared by both Dimension_Customer and Dimension_Supplier.

4.2 Requirement Diagram

Before starting the conceptual modeling, we need to identify the requirement for the ETL process. For this purpose a SysML requirement diagram will help to visualize the requirements and their interrelations. Figure 6 represents an example of the requirement of ETL process for the e-commerce system using MagicDraw.

The operational databases provide data for loading to the data warehouse. Two other data sources are shown here from where data about address and product are derived. The warehouse data are derived from these source databases. The restriction before loading to warehouse is described in the constraint block.

4.3 Activity Diagram

The explanation of the proposed ETL process is shown using SysML activity diagram in Fig. 7 created using MagicDraw. Flow of data as well as control within different activities for loading in an e-commerce sales data warehouse is shown. From starting to ending node, each object flow and control flow stereotypes are indicated for describing their nature of flow. Opaque action and call behavior action are used for describing unit activity and sub-activity as per the

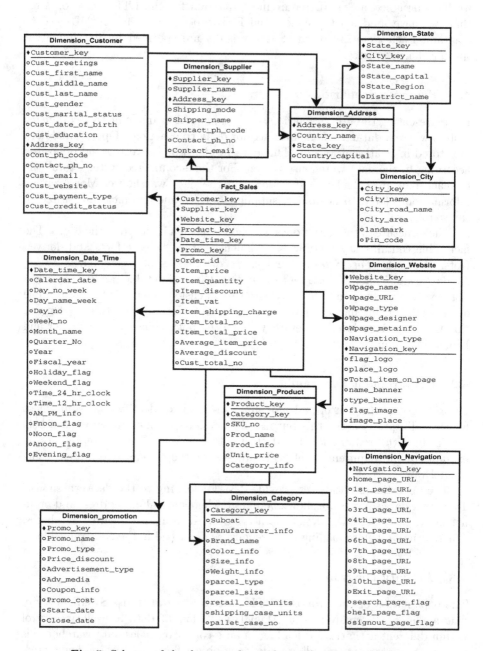

Fig. 5. Schema of the data warehouse for an E-commerce system

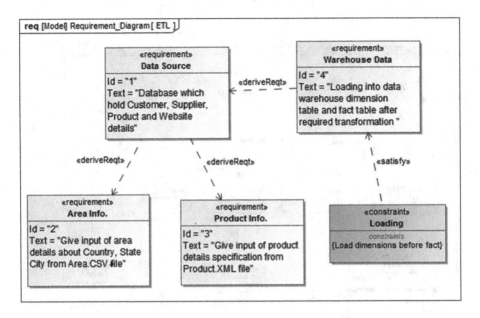

Fig. 6. SysML requirement diagram of the E-commerce system for ETL process

requirement. Value type for each input and output pin of action node is specified. Parallel edges are joined by join node and single paths split into parallel outgoing edges by fork node.

At first source databases are accessed. After verifying the key attributes, list of data about the dimensions are updated by the loader into their respective dimension tables. During dimension loading, aggregation level hierarchy is maintained. For example, Dimension Navigation will be loaded prior to Dimension Website. Data about product is firstly loaded to Dimension Category and then to Dimension Product. Address of Customer and Supplier comes from Area.XML file and list of product catalog fetched from Product.CSV file. Sub activity for loading the Area is given in Fig. 8. After loading the Dimension Address, it is shared and finally loaded by Dimension Supplier and Dimension Customer.

After loading six dimensions, basic facts (price, quantity, discount), derived facts (vat, shipping charge, total price, item total no) and non-additive facts (average item price, average discount) are stored in fact table. The overall ETL process is executed in every 12 h intervals as mentioned in Fig. 7. In this example, extraction and loading processes are shown. Some other common ETL transformation task like Aggregation, Filter, Correction, Conversion, Joining, Splitting, Merging, Log generation can also be represented in the conceptual model.

Post designing the system model, transforming of the SysML model to its corresponding executable code is done. XMI format is the standard platform independent code of a SysML model. This conceptual model can be transformed to its corresponding XMI format. Part of this XMI code is given in Listing 1.1.

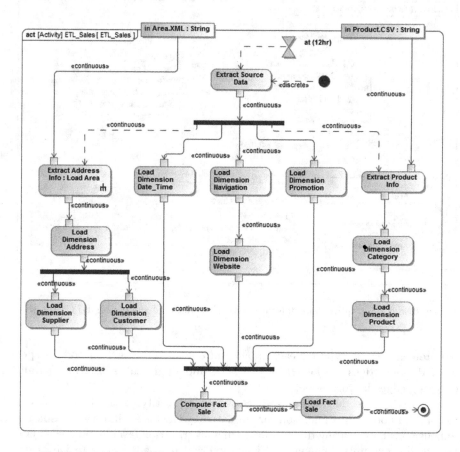

Fig. 7. Example of ETL conceptual model using SysML activity diagram

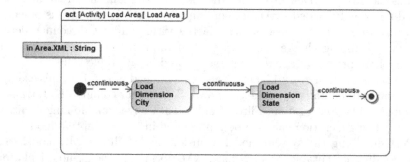

Fig. 8. Sub-activity for loading address using SysML

Listing 1.1. XMI code of SysML diagram

```
1  <?xml version="1.0" encoding="UTF-8"?>
2  −<xmi:XMI xmlns:DSL_Customization="http://www.magicdraw.com/schemas
      /DSL_Customization.xmi" xmlns:MagicDraw_Profile="http://www.omg.
      org/spec/UML/20131001/MagicDrawProfile" xmlns:sysml="http://www.
      omg.org/spec/SysML/20150709/SysML" xmlns:Validation_Profile="
      http://www.magicdraw.com/schemas/Validation_Profile.xmi"
      xmlns:StandardProfile="http://www.omg.org/spec/UML/20131001/
      StandardProfile" xmlns:MD_Customization_for_
3  Requirements__additional_stereotypes="http://www.magicdraw.com/spec
      /Customization/180/Requirements"
      xmlns:MD_Customization_for_SysML__additional_stereotypes="http:
      //www.magicdraw.com/spec/Customization/180/SysML" xmlns:xmi="
      http://www.omg.org/spec/XMI/20131001" xmlns:uml="http://www.omg.
      org/spec/UML/20131001">
4  −<xmi:Documentation>
5     <xmi:exporter>MagicDraw UML</xmi:exporter>
6     <xmi:exporterVersion>18.4 v2</xmi:exporterVersion>
7  </xmi:Documentation>
8  −<xmi:Extension extender="MagicDraw UML 18.4">
9     <plugin pluginVersion="18.4" pluginName="SysML"/>
10    <plugin pluginVersion="18.4" pluginName="Cameo Requirements
         Modeler"/>
11    <req_resource resourceValueName="SysML Activity Diagram"
         resourceName="SysML" resourceID="1440"/>
12    <req_resource resourceValueName="Cameo Requirements Modeler"
         resourceName="Cameo Requirements Modeler" resourceID="1480"/>
13    <req_resource resourceValueName="SysML" resourceName="SysML"
         resourceID="1440"/>
14 </xmi:Extension>
15 −<uml:Model name="Model" xmi:id="eee_1045467100313_135436_1" xmi:type
      ="uml:Model">
16 −<ownedComment xmi:id="_18_4_56101ea_1478679986869_40511_13723"
      xmi:type="uml:Comment" body="Author:Admin. Created:11/9/16 1:56
      PM. Title:. Comment:.">
17    <annotatedElement xmi:idref="eee_1045467100313_135436_1"/>
18 </ownedComment>
19 −<packagedElement name="ETL_Sales" xmi:id="
      _18_4_56101ea_1478679991104_204369_13728" xmi:type="uml:Activity
      ">
20 −<xmi:Extension extender="MagicDraw UML 18.4">
```

5 Conclusion

ETL process is responsible for selection and extraction of data from several sources, then cleaning and transformation according to desired format is done and finally updates into a DW. ETL process modeling is a way to design the orientation of data and establish their relationship throughout the ETL processing activity. In this paper, the main focus is to model an ETL process at conceptual level. Significant number of works has been done for ETL process modeling by UML, BPMN or Semantic web based methods. In this paper, we proposed a MBSE oriented system model for ETL process for data warehouse environment. To do the job, a new modeling language called SysML is used which is gaining popularity for modeling now a days. It is derived from UML by giving some additional facilities to the system engineers. By using SysML, the system model can be designed in more expressive as well as flexible way. An example of e-commerce system for ETL process modeling is discussed in this work. Particularly, propagation of data from sources to DW is explained as an use case of the model. Our developed model is platform Independent by nature and simple to understand by both technical and non-technical users. After designing the ETL model using SysML language, its corresponding executable XMI code is generated. In future, we intend to simulate the proposed model to analyze system behavior and requirements more precisely and to extend the model view at logical and physical level.

References

1. MBSE wiki. http://www.omgwiki.org/MBSE/doku.php
2. OMG systems modeling language. http://www.omgsysml.org/
3. Akkaoui, E.E., Zimányi, E.: Defining ETL worfklows using BPMN and BPEL. In: Proceedings of the ACM Twelfth International Workshop on Data Warehousing and OLAP, pp. 41–48. ACM (2009)
4. El Akkaoui, Z., Mazón, J.-N., Vaisman, A., Zimányi, E.: BPMN-based conceptual modeling of ETL processes. In: Cuzzocrea, A., Dayal, U. (eds.) DaWaK 2012. LNCS, vol. 7448, pp. 1–14. Springer, Heidelberg (2012). doi:10.1007/978-3-642-32584-7_1
5. Akkaoui, Z.E., Zimányi, E., López, J.N.M., Mondéjar, J.C.T., et al.: A BPMN-based design and maintenance framework for ETL processes (2013)
6. Akkaoui, Z.E., Zimànyi, E., Mazón, J.N., Trujillo, J.: A model-driven framework for ETL process development. In: Proceedings of the 14th International Workshop on Data Warehousing and OLAP, pp. 45–52. ACM (2011)
7. Çağıltay, N.E., Topallı, D., Aykaç, Y.E., Tokdemir, G.: Abstract conceptual database model approach. In: Conference on Science and Information, pp. 275–281 (2013)
8. Ayhan, S., Pesce, J., Comitz, P., Sweet, D., Bliesner, S., Gerberick, G.: Predictive analytics with aviation big data. In: Conference on Integrated Communications, Navigation and Surveillance (ICNS 2013), pp. 1–13 (2013)
9. Barateiro, J., Galhardas, H.: A survey of data quality tools. Datenbank-Spektrum 14(15–21), 48 (2005)
10. Belo, O., Gomes, C., Oliveira, B., Marques, R., Santos, V.: Automatic generation of ETL physical systems from BPMN conceptual models. In: Bellatreche, L., Manolopoulos, Y. (eds.) MEDI 2015. LNCS, vol. 9344, pp. 239–247. Springer, Cham (2015). doi:10.1007/978-3-319-23781-7_19
11. Eckerson, W., White, C.: Evaluating ETL and data integration platforms. Report of The Data Warehousing Institute 184 (2003)
12. Estefan, J.A.: Survey of model-based systems engineering (MBSE) methodologies. Incose MBSE Focus Group 25(8) (2007)
13. Franconi, E., Kamblet, A.: A data warehouse conceptual data model. In: Proceedings of 16th International Conference on Scientific and Statistical Database Management, pp. 435–436 (2004)
14. Friedenthal, S., Moore, A., Steiner, R.: A Practical Guide to SysML: The Systems Modeling Language. Morgan Kaufmann, San Francisco (2014)
15. Hart, L.E.: Introduction to model-based system engineering (MBSE) and SysML, 30 July 2015. http://www.incose.org/docs/default-source/delaware-valley/mbse-overview-incose-30-july-2015.pdf
16. Hause, M.: The sysml modelling language. In: 15th European Systems Engineering Conference, vol. 9 (2006)
17. Hoang, A.D.T., Nguyen, B.T.: An integrated use of CWM and ontological modeling approaches towards ETL processes. In: IEEE International Conference on e-Business Engineering (ICEBE 2008), pp. 715–720, October 2008

18. Kherdekar, V.A., Metkewar, P.S.: A technical comprehensive survey of ETL tools. Int. J. Appl. Eng. Res. **11**(4), 2557–2559 (2016)
19. Mrunalini, M., Kumar, T.S., Kanth, K.R.: Simulating secure data extraction in extraction transformation loading (ETL) processes. In: Third UKSim European Symposium on Computer Modeling and Simulation (EMS 2009), pp. 142–147. IEEE (2009)
20. Muñoz, L., Mazón, J.-N., Pardillo, J., Trujillo, J.: Modelling ETL processes of data warehouses with UML activity diagrams. In: Meersman, R., Tari, Z., Herrero, P. (eds.) OTM 2008. LNCS, vol. 5333, pp. 44–53. Springer, Heidelberg (2008). doi:10. 1007/978-3-540-88875-8_21
21. Muñoz, L., Mazón, J.N., Trujillo, J.: Automatic generation of ETL processes from conceptual models. In: Proceedings of the ACM Twelfth International Workshop on Data Warehousing and OLAP, pp. 33–40. ACM (2009)
22. Oliveira, B., Belo, O.: BPMN patterns for ETL conceptual modelling and validation. In: Chen, L., Felfernig, A., Liu, J., Raś, Z.W. (eds.) ISMIS 2012. LNCS, vol. 7661, pp. 445–454. Springer, Heidelberg (2012). doi:10.1007/978-3-642-34624-8_50
23. Oliveira, B., Belo, O.: ETL standard processes modelling - a novel BPMN approach. In: Proceedings of the 15th International Conference on Enterprise Information Systems, pp. 120–127 (2013)
24. Oliveira, B., Santos, V., Belo, O.: Pattern-based ETL conceptual modelling. In: Cuzzocrea, A., Maabout, S. (eds.) MEDI 2013. LNCS, vol. 8216, pp. 237–248. Springer, Heidelberg (2013). doi:10.1007/978-3-642-41366-7_20
25. Simitsis, A., Skoutas, D., Castellanos, M.: Representation of conceptual etl designs in natural language using semantic web technology. Data Knowl. Eng. **69**(1), 96–115 (2010)
26. Simitsis, A., Vassiliadis, P.: A methodology for the conceptual modelling of ETL processes. In: Proceedings of DSE (2003)
27. Skoutas, D., Simitsis, A.: Designing ETL processes using semantic web technologies. In: Proceedings ACM 9th International Workshop on Data Warehousing and OLAP (DOLAP 2006), Arlington, Virginia, USA, pp. 67–74 (2006)
28. Skoutas, D., Simitsis, A.: Ontology-based conceptual design of ETL processes for both structured and semi-structured data. Int. J. Semant. Web Inf. Syst. (IJSWIS) **3**(4), 1–24 (2007)
29. Skoutas, D., Simitsis, A., Sellis, T.: Ontology-driven conceptual design of ETL processes using graph transformations. In: Spaccapietra, S., Zimányi, E., Song, I.-Y. (eds.) Journal on Data Semantics XIII. LNCS, vol. 5530, pp. 120–146. Springer, Heidelberg (2009). doi:10.1007/978-3-642-03098-7_5
30. Snezana, S., Violeta, M.: Business intelligence tools for statistical data analysis. In: Proceedings of the 32nd International Conference on Information Technology Interfaces (ITI 2010), pp. 199–204 (2010)
31. Thi, A.D.H., Nguyen, B.T.: A semantic approach towards CWM-based ETL processes. In: Proceedings of I-SEMANTICS 2008, pp. 58–66 (2008)
32. Trujillo, J., Luján-Mora, S.: A UML based approach for modeling ETL processes in data warehouses. In: Song, I.-Y., Liddle, S.W., Ling, T.-W., Scheuermann, P. (eds.) ER 2003. LNCS, vol. 2813, pp. 307–320. Springer, Heidelberg (2003). doi:10. 1007/978-3-540-39648-2_25
33. Vassiliadis, P.: A survey of extract - transform - load technology. Int. J. Data Warehouse. Min. **5**(3), 1–27 (2009)
34. Vassiliadis, P., Simitsis, A., Skiadopoulos, S.: Conceptual modeling for ETL processes. In: Proceedings DOLAP, pp. 14–21 (2002)

Load Balancing of Unbalanced Matrix with Hungarian Method

Ranjan Kumar Mondal[1(⊠)], Payel Ray[1], Enakshmi Nandi[1],
Biswajit Biswas[2], Manas Kumar Sanyal[2], and Debabrata Sarddar[1]

[1] Department of Computer Science & Engineering,
University of Kalyani, Kalyani, India
ranjan@klyuniv.ac.in, payelray009@gmail.com,
pamelaroychowdhurikalyani@gmail.com,
dsarddar1@gmail.com
[2] Department of Business Administration, University of Kalyani, Kalyani, India
biswajit.biswas0012@gmail.com,
manas_sanyal@rediffmail.com

Abstract. It has been stated that in our real life states, we can find it challenging to balance among tasks and machines, so most of the time we have to look a condition to unbalanced assignment problems. The present paper submits a new technique for solving the unbalanced assignment problems. The method is accomplished by conveying all the jobs to machine optimally. The method is presented in an algorithmic model and implemented on the several sets of input data to investigate the performance and effectiveness of the algorithm. The developed algorithm is coded in Java. An assessment is also prepared with the existing approach, And it is recorded that our algorithm gives better results.

Keywords: Assignment problem · Hungarian method · Machine and jobs and Max-Min

1 Introduction

Load balancing [1] with Task Scheduling is considered to be a major issue in the cloud computing. The demand for effective load balancing with task scheduling increases to achieve high-performance computing. In general, it is not easy to find an optimal resource allocation to minimize the schedule of jobs and effectively utilize the resources. The three most important phases of load balancing are resource finding, collecting resource information and task execution.

Cloud users execute their application as a distributed application. Then the users submit their jobs to cloud resource broker. The resource broker then queries the cloud information service for the availability of resources and to know their properties. The cloud resources are registered within one or more cloud server. The resource servers are responsible for scheduling the jobs on the resources that equivalent job's requirements. After scheduling the resource, provider monitors the execution of jobs, and after completion, it collects the results and sends back to the users.

© Springer Nature Singapore Pte Ltd. 2017
J.K. Mandal et al. (Eds.): CICBA 2017, Part II, CCIS 776, pp. 256–270, 2017.
DOI: 10.1007/978-981-10-6430-2_20

Large numbers of load balancing algorithms are available to minimize the make-span [2–8]. All these algorithms try to find resources to be allocated to the tasks which will reduce the overall completion time of the tasks. Reducing overall execution time of all tasks does not mean that it decreases the actual execution time of the individual task. Two simple, well-known algorithms used for load balancing are Min-Min [4] and LBMM [8]. These two algorithms work by considering the execution and completion time of each task on the each available cloud computing.

The Min-Min algorithm first discovers the minimum execution time from all tasks. Then it chooses the task with the smallest execution time among all current tasks. The algorithm proceeds by assigning the tasks to the resources that generate the minimum execution time. The same method is repeated by Min-Min until all tasks are scheduled.

The limitation of the Min-Min algorithm is that it chooses smallest tasks first which makes use of the resource. Accordingly, the schedule produced by Min-Min is not best when some smaller tasks exceed the large ones.

To stay away from the disadvantages of the Min-Min algorithm, many improved algorithms have been proposed. All the problems discussed in those algorithms are taken and analyzed to give a more efficient schedule. Our proposed algorithm in this paper outperforms all those algorithms both regarding make-span and load balancing. As a result, better load balancing is achieved and the total response time of the cloud system is improved. The proposed algorithm applied the Min-Min strategy in the first stage and then reschedule by allowing for the maximum execution time that is minimum than the make-span obtained from the first phase.

2 Cloud Computing

Cloud Computing (CC) [2] is an Internet-based performance for the fundamental computing servers to retain information and resources. It permits users to utilize resources without installation and access their resources from any connected machine by accessing the Internet. This technique set asides not sufficient the computing resources with storage and bandwidth centralization. CC is a form of Internetwork computing where resources run on attached server rather than on a local machine. As a general client-server model, a client connects to a server to execute task/tasks. The deviation with cloud computing is that the computing procedure may run on more than one linked computers that can be utilized to the perception of virtualization. With virtualization, more than one servers can be put together with virtual servers, and appear to the clients to be a distinct device. The virtual server does not actually remain like existing device and can, therefore, be traveled in all the ways without affecting the end user. CC is a procedure of distributed computing that efforts on conferring an extensive collection of users accessing to virtualized infrastructure over the Internet. It engages distributed computing virtualization, networking, web services, and software. The thought of cloud computing has focused on the attention of the users towards of parallel, distributed and virtualization computing systems nowadays. It has appeared as an attractive solution to supply low-priced and effortless access to externalized IT resources.

2.1   Cloud Computing Characteristics

(1) *Services provide on demand:* - When the user wants to resources, then the cloud provides services upon request.
(2) *Rapid elasticity:* - Number of various resources in the cloud is increasing or decrease smoothly.
(3) *Resource pooling:* - In cloud structure resources are allocated consistent with consumer requirement. The each resource is collective to serve finish users utilizing a model of cloud.
(4) *Broad access to network:* - The cloud resources access is possible throughout the network and used standard methods for the users to the right to use the network.
(5) *Pay per use:* - Every consumer pay charges when it is the usage of computing resources.

Services of CloudCloud computing provide many services to the end users

(1) *Software as a Service:* This service model is a software conveyance model in which every single application is gotten to through web browser. In this SaaS model, the users are not concerned with the cloud structure and also not a concern with the network, servers, storage, operating systems, and platform. Exclusive cloud consumer's applications are naturally organized in a particular logical atmosphere on the SaaS, to achieve optimization regarding security, speed, availability, disaster recovery, and maintenance. There are various services are provide as SaaS like salesforce.com. Google Docs, Google Mail.
(2) *Platform as a Service:* This Service model is a development platform which permits for cloud customers to progress cloud application and services (example SaaS) directly on PaaS cloud. In this Platform as a Service model, the consumers do not control the primary cloud foundation including servers, network, storage and operating system. An example of PaaS is Aneka and Google App Engine.
(3) *Infrastructure as a Service:* This service model provides Infrastructure of servers and different software to the customer on their demand. By using this user now not have to buy any specified hardware and software. Cloud users directly use of IT infrastructure (storage, networks, processing and other computing resources). IaaS provides services like Amazons EC2 [4, 6].

Cloud Deployment Models
The cloud group characterizes four cloud organization models. That represents to various sorts of the cloud [2].

(1) *Public Cloud:* - This cloud is utilized by the general public users and the cloud service provider has the full responsibility for the public cloud with its qualities, policy, costing, profit, and charging model. Many popular cloud services are Google App Engine, Amazon EC2and salesforce.com.
(2) *Private Cloud:* - This cloud will be cloud bases worked for a solitary association and gave security to its resources.

(3) *Community Cloud:* - In community cloud, cloud infrastructure which can be used through several organizations in a private community. This cloud is shared amongst many associations that have comparative cloud prerequisites.

(4) *Hybrid Cloud:* - This cloud it utilizes a combination of no under two clouds where the clouds incorporate a blend of private cloud, public cloud or community cloud.

3 Task Scheduling

Task scheduling [9, 10] is a vital issue in cloud computing. Task Scheduling is used to assign specific tasks to available resources at a precise time. In cloud computing, task scheduling problem is one of the biggest and challenging issues. The first target of task scheduling algorithm is to enhance the presentation and quality of service and at a time retaining the good organization and justice among the jobs and reduce the cost of execution. A proficient task scheduling approach must have a purpose to yield less response time so that the time off offered tasks take a position within a possible minimum time.

In cloud computing systems task scheduling plays a vital role. Scheduling of jobs/tasks cannot be performed on the source of particular factors but under a batch of rules that we can term as a concurrence between consumer and suppliers of the cloud computing. This promise is nothing but the QoS that the consumer desires that from the merchants. According to the agreement providers always try to provide a high quality of services to the users. It is a certain job of the suppliers as at a time there are a huge number of jobs executing on the merchant's part.

The task scheduling difficulty can be analyzed as the discovering a minimal mapping of a set of subtasks of multiple jobs over the current round of application (processors) such that we obtain the expected objectives for tasks. In this paper, we are executing a relevant study of the different algorithms for their correctness, probability, flexibility in the context of cloud scenario, after that we will try to suggest the hybrid approach that can be accepted to improve the presented platform further. So that it can make possible cloud suppliers to supply a better quality of services.

Task Scheduling is the method of begin and end times to a set of tasks. The scheduling algorithm of tasks in cloud means allocating the best appropriate resource available for execution of tasks or to allocate machines to tasks in such a manner so that the completion time is lowest. The primary cause behind the scheduling of the resources by the particular time bound, which involves finding out a complete and the best order in which a variety of tasks can be executed to offer most excellent outcomes to the user. In scheduling algorithm, a list of assignments is created by giving precedence to each task. The tasks are further preferred according to their priorities and will be assigned to the available nodes and machines. We see two fundamental types of scheduling:

- Static scheduling that schedule tasks in a known environment i.e. it already has the information about the complete configuration of jobs and mapping of resources before execution, estimates of task execution time.

- Dynamic scheduling should not be dependent on the allocated tasks to cloud surroundings but also on the existing states of system and machines to make a scheduling decision.

Advantages of Task Scheduling

Maximum resource utilization,
Minimum waiting time,
Minimum response time,
Maximum throughput.

Task Scheduling of Cloud Computing

Scheduling is known as the set of policies for managing the arrange of tasks to be completed by a system. The task or job scheduling in Cloud service center is a set of instructions and factors that determine and decide on the task to be executed on the available resources between gatherings of possible tasks at a particular time. In Cloud service center, the task scheduling algorithms are dependable for allocating the tasks submitted by the consumers to the accessible resources. The major advantage of tasks scheduling algorithm is to achieve a high-performance computing and the best system throughput. Scheduling manages the CPU memory and to accomplish highest resource utilization, requires excellent scheduling policies. In Cloud Computing Environment, Tasks are submitted to the service center broker by the users. The service center broker is an intermediary between the cloud consumers and providers and is responsible for scheduling tasks on Virtual machines (VM). The service center is a virtual infrastructure for housing resources and consists of some hosts. The submitted tasks are scheduled according to the scheduling policies used by the service center Broker. Broker communicates directly with the cloud controller and assigns tasks to VMs in the host of the service center.

4 Types of Load Balancing Algorithms

Load Balancing Algorithms are categorized into three types based on the initiator of the algorithm; Sender-Initiated: Sender identifies that the machines are overwhelmed so that the dispatcher initiates the completing of load balancing algorithm.

Receiver Initiated: The requisite of Load balancing circumstances can be known by the receiver in the cloud, and that server starts the execution of Load Balancing algorithm.

Symmetric: It is the mixture of both the sender initiated, and receiver initiated types. It takes advantages of both types.

- Based on the present state of the server, the two types of load balancing algorithms are used:

Static Schemes- The account does not have the current status machine. Predefine the machines and their properties. Based on this previous information, the algorithm works. Considering as it does not employ current system status information, it is less composite, and it is straightforward to apply.

Dynamic Schemes- This category of algorithms is based on the present system in rank. The algorithm works according to the changes in the state of machines. Dynamic schemes are an expensive one and are very complex to implement, but it balances the load in an efficient manner.

Status Table Status table is a data structure to retain the current status of all the machines in the cloud surroundings. This resources can be used by some of the dynamic scheme algorithms to allocate jobs to the machines that are not heavily loaded.

Need for Load Balancing

To avoid the overload load balancing, if the single machine gets all the jobs, the loads would increase as well as its queue range is increased, and it becomes overloaded. If balance the loads across several machines while every machine is in running state but not in the overloaded state.

The goals are as follows [1]:

- To increase the availability
- To increase satisfaction of client
- To improve the resource consumption
- In queue to reduce the waiting time of tasks as well as to reduce task execution time
- To improve the overall performance of Cloud environment.

5 Related Works

Here we discuss two algorithms one is MM and other is LBMM.

Min-Min algorithm

Min-Min [4] is a static load balancing algorithm wherever the factors related with the jobs are familiar in advance. The jobs with lowest completion time are being assigned first to the processors so that the task is completed in time. But the tasks with the lowest completion need to wait for a given period. As such, all the tasks in the processor must be updated, and the tasks in the queue must be removed. The task with the lowest completion performs better than the highest time execution. The main disadvantage of this algorithm is that it leads to starvation.

Min-min algorithm is based on Minimum Completion Time (MCT) that is used to allocate tasks to the resources to have lowest expected completion time. It would work in two stages, in the first stage; the expected completion time will be calculated for each task in a meta-task list. In the second stage, the task with the overall minimum expected completion time from the meta-task list is selected and assigned to the related resource. Then the current task is removed from the meta-task list, and the process is continued until all tasks in the meta-task list are mapped to the corresponding resources. However, the Min- Min algorithm is unable to balance the load well as it usually does the scheduling of small tasks initially.

Load Balancing with Min-Min Algorithm

One of the important static algorithms called LBMM [8] maintains load balancing among machines to accept it as scheduling issues. This scheduling process searches minimum execution time of all tasks at first. In next stage, it selects job with least execution time among all the jobs this scheduling technique continues with assigning jobs with respective resources that shows the minimum completion time. This process should be repeated up to all jobs are scheduled properly. In this process of execution, this method chooses machines with maximum to make span. It selects tasks corresponding to that machine with minimum execution time. Then completion time of respective task should be calculated for all resources.

In next stage highest completion time of choose task has compared with make span value. If this value is less then selected, the task is assigned to a respective machine which has highest completion time. Otherwise next highest completion time of a respected task is selected and this process has repeated.

If it is less, this schedule will stop if overall machines and tasks are allotted. In the case of Meta task, this schedules gives better performance.

6 Review Work

A. Kumar proposed algorithm [11] as follows:

Author consider a problem in which a set of 5 machines M = {M1, M2, M3, M4, M5}, and a set of 8 jobs J = {J1, J2, J3, J4, J5, J6, J7, J8}. The assignment matrix contains the execution costs of every job to each machine.

Steps-1 to 2: Input: 5, 8.

Step-3 Obtain the sum of each row and column of the matrix, i.e., The sum of each row and each column is as follows:

Sum Row

Sum Column (Table 3)

We partitioned the matrix to define the first sub-problem Part -1 by selecting rows corresponding to J3, J4, J5, J6, J7 and second sub-problem Part -2 by selecting rows corresponding to the jobs J1, J2, J8 and by deleting columns corresponding to M1, M3. Then the modified matrices are as follows:

Sub-Problem-I: Part -1 (Table 4)

and, Sub-Problem-II: Part -2 (Table 5)

Thus, the total assignment cost of the main problem, i.e., 1550. The final optimal assignments are as follows:

Job → Machine	Cost
J3 → M1	180
J4 → M2	180
J5 → M3	190
J6 → M5	140
J7 → M4	180

Total assignment cost = 870

Job → Machine	Cost
J1 → M4	290
J2 → M5	200
J8 → M2	190

Total assignment cost = 680
Final Assignment cost follows:

Job → Machine	Cost
J1 → M4	290
J2 → M5	200
J3 → M1	180
J4 → M2	180
J5 → M3	190
J6 → M5	140
J7 → M4	180
J8 → M2	190

The paper suggested a modified method for solving the unbalanced assignment problems. The Hungarian method gives total assignment cost 870 along with the other three jobs assigned to dummy machine, in other words, that these three jobs are ignored for further processing, while when the original problem is divided into the sub-problems, which are balanced assignment problems in nature.

7 Proposed Method

To find out the matrix cost and a combination of tasks(s) vs. machine(s) of an unbalanced matrix problem, we would focus on a problem which made with a set of 'm' machines $M = \{M_1, M_2,..., M_m\}$. A set of 'n' jobs $J = \{J_1, J_2,..., J_n\}$ is considered to be assigned for completion on the 'm' existing machines and the completion value C_{ij}, where $i = 1, 2,...,m$ and $j = 1,2,...,n$ are mentioned in the matrix where $m > n$. First of all, we calculate the summation of each row and the summation of each column of the matrix, keep the results in the array, named, Row-sum and Column-sum respectively. Then we decide on the first n rows by Row-sum, i.e., starting with lowest to least to the array Row-sum and deleting rows corresponding to the remaining (r) jobs. Keep the outcomes in the new array that should be the array for the first sub-problem. Repeat this progression until remaining jobs become less than all machines when remaining jobs are less than n, then, deleting (c) columns on the based on Column-sum, i.e., corresponding to values highest to higher to consist the last sub-problem. Store the outcome in the new array that shall be the array for the last sub-problem.

To determine the assignment cost of the job(s) vs. machine(s) of an unbalanced assignment problem, we concentrate on a problem which consists of a set of 'n' machines $M = \{M_1, M_2,.., M_n\}$. A set of 'm' jobs $J = \{J_1, J_2,..., J_m\}$ is considered which is to be assigned for execution on the 'n' available machines and the execution cost Cij, where $i = 1,2,..,m$ and $j = 1,2,...,n$ are mentioned in the assignment cost matrix ACM, where $m > n$. First of all, we obtain the sum of each row and each column of the matrix, store the results in the array, namely, summation of row, i.e., **Row_sum** and summation of column i.e. **Column_sum.**

7.1   Problem Definitions

To assign various jobs to different machines, in such a way that the total assignment cost is to be minimum, known as the assignment problem.

If the number jobs are not equal to a number of the machines, then it is known to be unbalanced assignment problem.

Consider a problem which consists of a set of 'm' machines $M = \{M_1, M_2,...,M_n\}$. A set of 'n' jobs $\{J = J_1, J_2,...,J_n\}$ is considered which are to be assigned for execution on 'm' available machines. The execution cost of each job on all the machines is known and mentioned in the matrix of the order of n. The objective is to determine the minimum cost. This problem is solved by well-known a very popular method called Hungarian method [12].

7.2   Hungarian Method

Step 1:   *The input of this algorithm is a n*n square.*

Step 2:   *To find the least value from each row and deduct it from each value in the corresponding row.*

Step 3:   *Similarly, for each column, find the least value and deduct it from each value in the corresponding column.*

Step 4:   *Cover all zeros in the deducted matrix with a lowest value of horizontal and vertical lines. If lines numbers are n then an optimal assignment exists. The algorithm stops. Otherwise, if lines number are less than n then, go to next step.*

Step 5:   *Find the least element that is not covered by a line in Step 4. Deduct with a least uncovered element from all uncovered values, and add a least uncovered value to all value s that are covered twice*

7.3   Algorithm

To give an algorithmic representation of the method, let us consider a problem which consists of a set of 'n' machines $M = \{M_1, M_2,.., M_n\}$. A set of 'm' jobs $J = \{J_1, J_2,..., J_m\}$ is considered which is to be assigned for execution on 'n' available machines and the execution cost Cij, where $i = 1, 2,.., m$ and $j = 1, 2,..., n$, where $m > n$, i.e., the number of jobs is more than a number of machines.

Algorithm:
Step 1: Input: m*n matrix where no. of rows is maximum than no. of columns.
Step 2: It is to add all cost of each job named Row_sum.
Step 3: Eliminate some rows based on maximum Row_sum to do balanced matrix (i.e. delete some number of rows that remaining numbers of the row will be equal to a number of columns.) and named Part 1.
Step 4: Apply Hungarian Method removing Row_sum in part 1.
Step 5: Consist a matrix with deleted number of Rows from the original unbalanced matrix.
Step 6: It is to add all cost of each machine named Column_sum.
Step 7: Eliminate some columns based on maximum Column_sum to do balanced matrix (i.e. delete some number of columns that remaining numbers of the column will be equal to a number of rows.) because of the machines already assigned by corresponding jobs and named Part 2.
Step 8: Apply Hungarian Method removing Column_sum in part 2.
Step 9: Re-arrange the Jobs to corresponding machines.
Step 10: Stop.

8 Example

Let us consider a problem with eight agents and four tasks. Its agent-task assignment cost matrix is as shown in Table 1. This is the original cost matrix:

Step-1: Input: m*n matrix where no. of rows is maximum than no. of columns.

J_mM_n	M_1	M_2	M_3	M_4	M_5
J_1	151	277	185	276	321
J_2	245	286	256	264	402
J_3	246	245	412	423	257
J_4	269	175	145	125	156
J_5	421	178	185	425	235
J_6	257	257	125	325	362
J_7	159	268	412	256	286
J_8	365	286	236	314	279

Step 2: It is to add all cost of each job named **Row_sum**.

J_mM_n	M_1	M_2	M_3	M_4	M_5	$\sum$
J_1	151	277	185	276	321	**1210**
J_2	245	286	256	264	402	**1453**
J_3	246	245	412	423	257	**1583**
J_4	269	175	145	125	156	**870**
J_5	421	178	185	425	235	**1444**
J_6	257	257	125	325	362	**1326**
J_7	159	268	412	256	286	**1381**
J_8	365	286	236	314	279	**1480**

Step 3: Eliminate some rows based on maximum Row_sum to do balanced matrix (i.e. delete some number of rows that remaining numbers of the row will be equal to a number of columns.) and named Part 1.

J_mM_n	M_1	M_2	M_3	M_4	M_5	$\sum$
J_1	151	277	185	276	321	**1210**
J_4	269	175	145	125	156	**870**
J_5	421	178	185	425	235	**1444**
J_6	257	257	125	325	362	**1326**
J_7	159	268	412	256	286	**1381**

Step 4: Apply Hungarian Method removing Row_sum in part 1.

J_mM_n	M_1	M_2	M_3	M_4	M_5
J_1	**151**	277	185	276	321
J_4	269	175	145	**125**	156
J_5	421	**178**	185	425	235
J_6	257	257	**125**	325	362
J_7	159	268	412	256	**286**

Step 5: Consist a matrix with deleted number of Rows from the original unbalanced matrix.

J_mM_n	M_1	M_2	M_3	M_4	M_5
J_2	245	286	256	264	402
J_3	246	245	412	423	257
J_8	365	286	236	314	279

Step 6: It is to add all cost of each machine named **Column_sum**.

J_mM_n	M_1	M_2	M_3	M_4	M_5
J_2	245	286	256	264	402
J_3	246	245	412	423	257
J_8	365	286	236	314	279
$\sum$	856	817	904	1001	938

Step 7: Eliminate some columns based on maximum Column_sum to do balanced matrix (i.e. delete some number of columns that remaining numbers of the column will be equal to a number of rows.) because of the machines already assigned by corresponding jobs and named Part 2.

J_mM_n	M_1	M_2	M_3
J_2	245	286	256
J_3	246	245	412
J_8	365	286	236

Step 8: Apply Hungarian Method removing Column_sum in part 2.

J_mM_n	M_1	M_2	M_3
J_2	**245**	286	256
J_3	246	**245**	412
J_8	365	286	**236**

Thus, the total assignment cost of the main problem 1550. The final optimal assignments are as follows:

Job $\rightarrow$ Machine	Cost
J1 $\rightarrow$ M1	151
J4 $\rightarrow$ M4	125
J5 $\rightarrow$ M2	178
J6 $\rightarrow$ M3	125
J7 $\rightarrow$ M5	286

Total assignment cost = 870

Job $\rightarrow$ Machine	Cost
J2 $\rightarrow$ M1	245
J3 $\rightarrow$ M2	245
J8 $\rightarrow$ M3	236

Total assignment cost = 680.
Step 9: Re-arrange the Jobs to corresponding machines.

Job $\rightarrow$ Machine	Cost
J1 $\rightarrow$ M1	151
J2 $\rightarrow$ M1	245
J3 $\rightarrow$ M2	245
J4 $\rightarrow$ M4	125
J5 $\rightarrow$ M2	178
J6 $\rightarrow$ M3	125
J7 $\rightarrow$ M5	286
J8 $\rightarrow$ M3	236

Step 10: Stop.

9 Final Result

$M_1 \rightarrow$	$J_1 * J_2 \rightarrow$	$151 + 245 = 396$
$M_2 \rightarrow$	$J_3 * J_5 \rightarrow$	$245 + 178 = 423$
$M_3 \rightarrow$	$J_6 * J_8 \rightarrow$	$125 + 236 = 361$
$M_4 \rightarrow$	$J_4 \rightarrow$	125
$M_5 \rightarrow$	$J_7 \rightarrow$	286

10 Result Analysis

Table 1. The execution time (in ms) of every job to each machine.

Ji/Mj	M_1	M_2	M_3	M_4	M_5
J_1	300	290	280	290	210
J_2	250	310	290	300	200
J_3	180	190	300	190	180
J_4	320	180	190	240	170
J_5	270	210	190	250	160
J_6	190	200	220	190	140
J_7	220	300	230	180	160
J_8	260	190	260	210	180

Table 2. Sum of each row of the matrix.

J1	J2	J3	J4	J5	J6	J7	J8
1370	1350	1040	1100	1080	0940	1090	1100

Table 3. Table 2: Sum of each column of the matrix.

M_1	M_2	M_3	M_4	M_5
1990	1870	1960	1850	1400

Table 4. Sub-Problem-I

Ji/Mj	M_1	M_2	M_3	M_4	M_5
J_3	180	190	300	190	180
J_4	320	180	190	240	170
J_5	270	210	190	250	160
J_6	190	200	220	190	140
J_7	220	300	230	180	160

Table 5. Sub-Problem-II

Ji/Mj	M$_2$	M$_4$	M$_5$
J$_1$	290	290	210
J$_2$	310	300	200
J$_8$	190	210	180

The following figure shows execution time (ms) of each task at different computing machines.

Figure 1 shows the execution time for each task at different computing machines. To calculate the performance of our proposed approach is compared with others method by the case shown in Fig. 1. Figure 1 displays the comparison of the execution time of each computing machine among our approach. The execution times for completing all tasks by using proposed algorithm, LBMM and MM are 423, 423 and 555 ms, respectively. Our approach achieves the minimum completion time and better load balancing than MM algorithms.

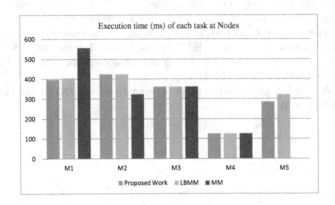

Fig. 1. Execution time (ms) of each task at different computing machines.

11 Conclusion

The present paper proposes a method for solving the unbalanced assignment problems with Hungarian Method. This method is easy to implement. This is an easy method to solve any unbalanced method. This is a very easy process. Our method gives new approach in the case of load balancing of unbalanced assignment problem. In a future study, we want to develop some modification of our approach to give more optimize the result.

References

1. Mondal, R.K., Ray, P., Sarddar, D.: Load balancing. Int. J. Res. Comput. Appl. Inform. Technol. **4**(1), 01–21 (2016). ISSN 2347- 5099, Print: 2348- 0009, DOA: 03012016
2. Mell, P., Grance, T.: The NIST Definition of Cloud Computing (2011)
3. Cybenko, G.: Dynamic load balancing for distributed memory multiprocessors. J. Parallel distrib. Comput. **7**(2), 279–301 (1989)
4. Wang, S.C., Yan, K.Q., Liao, W.P., Wang, S.S.: Towards a load balancing in a three level cloud computing network. In: Computer Science and Information Technology, pp. 108—113 (2010)
5. Ritchie, G., Levine, J.: A fast, effective local search for scheduling independent jobs in heterogeneous computing environments (2003)
6. Dasgupta, K., Mandal, B., Dutta, P., Mandal, J.K., Dam, S.: A genetic algorithm (GA) based load balancing strategy for cloud computing. Procedia Technol. **10**, 340–347 (2013)
7. Armstrong, R., Hensgen, D., Kidd, T.: The relative performance of various mapping algorithms is independent of sizable variances in run-time predictions. In: Proceedings, 1998 Seventh Heterogeneous Computing Workshop, (HCW 1998), pp. 79–87. IEEE, March 1998
8. Kokilavani, T., DI George, A.: Load balanced Min-Min algorithm for static meta-task scheduling in grid computing. Int. J. Comput. Appl. **20**(2), 43–49 (2011)
9. Chen, H., Wang, F., Helian, N., Akanmu, G.: User-priority guided Min-Min scheduling algorithm for load balancing in cloud computing. In: 2013 National Conference on Parallel Computing Technologies (PARCOMPTECH), pp. 1–8. IEEE (2013)
10. Nace, D., Pióro, M.: Max-min fairness and its applications to routing and load-balancing in communication networks: a tutorial. IEEE Commun. Surv. Tutorials **10**(4), 5–17 (2008)
11. Kumar, A.: A modified method for solving the unbalanced assignment problems. Appl. Math. Comput. **176**(1), 76–82 (2006)
12. Kuhn, H.W.: The Hungarian method for the assignment problem. Naval Res. Logistics Q. **2** (1–2), 83–97 (1955)

The Image Recognition System for Terrestrial Reconnaissance

Fuangfar Pensiri[1], Chayute Phupittayathanakorn[2],
and Porawat Visutsak[3(✉)]

[1] Faculty of Science and Technology, Suan Dusit University, Bangkok, Thailand
[2] Military Information Technology Center, Royal Thai Armed Forces
Headquarters, Bangkok, Thailand
[3] Faculty of Applied Science, King Mongkut's University of Technology
North Bangkok, Bangkok, Thailand
porawat.v@sci.kmutnb.ac.th

Abstract. Terrestrial reconnaissance in the border provinces in Thailand is very risky and dangerous mission for troops and government officers. Many of troops were killed and injured by the incendiary bombs buried in the roads. In order to preventing the loss of life and property damages, many inventions of bomb detector have been commercially used such as GPR (Ground Penetration Radar) and REST (Remote Explosive Scent Tracing). Unfortunately, these technologies are expensive and inappropriate in some situations. This paper presents the forthcoming technology of the real-time image recognition for terrestrial reconnaissance. By using the road texture analysis in image analytic, the data set of normal surfaces of the road (e.g. asphalt road and gravel road) will be trained as the prior-knowledge. The system can compare the buried surface with the normal surface of the road and warning the troops beforehand.

Keywords: Image processing · Image detection · Image recognition · Image analytic · Thailand 4.0

1 Introduction

The insurgency in Thailand's three southern border provinces; Pattani, Yala and Narathiwat, is an existing serious problem. It's an ethnic-religious conflict. The evidence varies on time and circumstances. In the past, the government buildings were burned and ruined, people were arrested for ransom while the current situations the violence even more severe. The terrorists attack on the life of innocent civilians such as clergy, teachers, students and government officer, they intend to create a panic situations and their renown. This finally destroyed the mutual trust between citizens and government officers. All government try to solve the problem with measures such as the declaration of martial law, collapse of the Southern Border Provinces Administration Center (SBPAC) of setting up a new government agency to a host of problems such as The Southern Border Provinces Peace Building Command (SBPPBC) but the violence has continued. The following issues are the factors contributing to the violence.

© Springer Nature Singapore Pte Ltd. 2017
J.K. Mandal et al. (Eds.): CICBA 2017, Part II, CCIS 776, pp. 271–283, 2017.
DOI: 10.1007/978-981-10-6430-2_21

1. Education: There are a high proportion of Thai-Muslim citizens in the three Southern provinces. The students study in the Muslim religious school called "Pornor". Some Pornor is the hidden place of the terrorists to form the new generation terrorists by cultivated the negative perception of the country to the students.
2. Economy: The citizens in the three southern provinces are poor. Their income per capita is lower than the other provinces.
3. Politic: There are the conflicts of interest among the influential people in drug, goods smuggling and so on.

Prince of Songkla University, Pattani Campus summarized about the unrest in the three southern provinces since 2004–2015 that there were 15,374 incidents, 1,281 incidents in the annual average. The death toll has reached 6,543 victims, the annual average is 545. There are 11,919 injured people, 993 cases per year caused by arson, explosion or fire correspond to 229, 224 and 59 incidents. Narathiwat has the highest violence rates follows by Yala and Pattani respectively.

Such damage occurs to the life and property of citizens, military/police as well as the other government officers who have the mission in the unsafe areas. These officers face the risk situation at all times particularly being ambushed by another opponent that is likely to happen at any time, for example, the security patrol route of the military, espionage, the clergy and teachers escort.

The patrol route in on the local streets between provincial district and village. Due to the incendiary bombs were often placed to block the way or buried them in roads and wait until the troops patrol in to the area the insurgent group used Remote Control Improvised Explosive Device to command the bomb. Those explosives were destructive power. The attacks in this way undermine the normal mental condition of the people and the military and also affect the daily life of the citizens which can cause health problems. Thus, if the measures are taken to prevent and proactive monitoring it can help reduce the risk of losing. Currently, the technology has brought many types into a tool to work in areas that are vulnerable to threats. Many organizations rely on these technologies into practical tools to create an advantage over its competitors.

Therefore, it is essential that the agencies of the government to maintain order in the three border provinces of Thailand rely on the advancement of the technology application deployment.

The research work is to integrate the communication technology and computer technology to build the system for the military patrol operations and building the prototyping to bring this approach to the real situation. One of the critical processes is to capture the panoramic landscapes and roads. The system will record the details at that moment that the human sight cannot keep all the details. The result can show that, before the troops going into patrol areas, that area has been dug and buried before or not. It may be assumed that the area around is not safe the soldier should not enter that risky area.

This position paper consists of 4 sections: The problem statement and the purpose of this work have been described in the introduction section; Sect. 2 is the literature reviews; the proposed method together with the features extraction and the model will be illustrated in Sect. 3; the future usage and benefits will be discussed in Sect. 5.

2 Literature Reviews

The reconnaissance mission is a specific mission of the nation security operation. This mission is a core component of the military transformation of United States Department of Defense. In order to obtain the information for military decision making process and contribute to the administration, the operation comprises the intelligence, Surveillance and reconnaissance [2]. The management of military and security operations are as follows [5]

- Acquiring the information of military strategy immediately
- Acquiring the photos with accurate details of the areas
- What is around in the critical area including its utilities
- Measurement of distance and time to access the area
- Planning to enter and exit the areas

There are many kinds of the technology brought into use for example radar technology as a tool to support the development of military ordnance which integrated into the GPS technology to collect the images in both ground and air targets. However, it necessary employs the tools with high accuracy. There are cases where no tools are powerful enough to handle the objects in the image; it affects the image detector [15]. In some cases may be leveling photo. This is one more tool to keep in shape and a complex shape. It is very high accuracy. The leveling of the photos can be applied to architecture and archeology [6]. The images used should have the texture and structure obviously. The photo collecting is always a lot to digitize footage more than film [11]. The device is used to collect the photos is the military's unmanned aircraft (Unmanned Aerial Vehicles: UAVs), also known as drones (Drone). The mission of the military drones is to spy or bomb the enemy field. The pictures from military operations are often remote and animated as indicated in the research of Buzasi which is about the automatic aerial Image detection to determine the aircraft's position using The Cellular Neural Network (CNN) theory [1]. The photo is still processing after shooting for several hours; this is the disadvantage in operation since the troops patrol to be continually vigilant. The operation of the drones are moving into the area continuously by controlling from the command center where works with computers and electronics series such as software control, computers, laptops, servers, remote control (RC Controller), GPS, barometric altimeter, etc. [4]. Drones can capture both the bird's eye view photos and the human's eye view photos.

The characteristics of the road surface:

There are three common types of the roads; concrete roads, asphalt roads and gravel roads. The malfunctioning of the road types is different.

1. The gravel road surface has been eroded, destroyed by soil erosion, collapsed by the water and its surface is rough from utilization [12]. See Fig. 1.

Fig. 1. The damages of the gravel roads (Source: Department of Agriculture, United States)

2. Road asphalt, the nature of the damage with 4 factors [13]:

   - Separation of the road surface, the road surface is disappeared, slippery
   - Deformation and distortion of the road surface
   - Fracture of the road produces the liddle pebbles
   - The road was retreated, potholes

3. The concrete surface is very solid. The damage depends on the temperature and the material used to build the road. Nillson, 1993 (cited in [4]) and it can withstand high friction (Fig. 2).

Fig. 2. The damages of the asphalt roads (Source: Walker, 2002)

Recognition

With a digital device, the image data is stored in the pixel which is the smallest unit of the image of. Pixel contains the value of the color, the total of the color values are 256. The research of the Schenk T. found that the smallest is about 5 μm, if the image size is 9 inches or 22.8 cm. An image size of 0.5 GB, there are only few thousand bytes will be used. Therefore, reducing the size of the image can avoid wasting time analyzing results [11]. The first important step is the Feature Extraction; the specific information for analysis will be extracted such as the brightness of the image, the edges of the object in the gray scale images. The next step is to import the features to create natural histogram and spatial frequency spectra [10]. A feature from the extraction process can be colors in the image area [16], weight, diameter, height [3].

Image recognition is an important processing step. It has been developed to be applied to other applications such as capturing infrared to locate the run way in military operations. Image Feature Extraction is discovering the critical line of the image [14]. Libao Zhang's research study on the location of the airport and the airport from remote sensing image. The key features of the images are (1) the edge of the parallel runway (2) the gray scale of the image (3) the structure (shape) and the image size, and (4) the connection of the runway [7].

Pattern Recognition method is the one used for image processing. This approach is based on research like medical and military by considering all possible inductive analysis and show you what is correspond to the imported data. The important task is to define the essential features of the images then convert them to a format that is ready to calculate for example a group of numbers, a series of symbols followed by sorting that data [10] and then analyze the results. In Some cases, the researcher segments the image before performing the procedure Image Feature Extraction [9].

3 The Proposed Method

The main contribution of this work is the image analytic algorithm for road texture analysis, the data set of normal surfaces of the road (e.g. asphalt road and gravel road) will be trained as the prior-knowledge. The system can compare the buried (or digged) surface with the normal surface of the road and warning the troops beforehand. The image recognition for terrestrial reconnaissance consists of two parts:

1. Recognition algorithm: By training the data set of normal surfaces of the road as the prior-knowledge, the recognition algorithm will be used as the road model of the system (step 1–4 in the algorithm).
2. Classification algorithm: The unknown image of the road will be captured and compared with the road model. The system will determine that the surface of the road has been buried or digged. The illustration of the system is shown in Fig. 3 (step 5–10 in the algorithm).

The Algorithm:

1. Training – the data set of normal surfaces of the road

2. Feature extraction – the significant of the road features will be determined

3. Image recognition – the cluster of normal surfaces of the road will be created

4. The road model of the system (clusters: e.g. asphalt road and gravel road)

5. Road images (the normal surfaces) will be taken and the features will be extracted

6. Features analysis

7. The result features will be used as clustering parameters of the road model

8. Unknown image will be taken and passed into the clustering model (the road model)

9-10. Image analytic: unknown image Vs. road image (compare images in step 5 and step 8)

11. System will determine the location of the road in the image that would be changed (compared with the normal sur faces of the road)

In order to build the efficient clustering model (the road model), the researchers have to conduct the survey in the real places in Thailand's three southern border provinces; Pattani, Yala and Narathiwat. All road surface images such as asphalt road and gravel road are needed to be captured in all situations e.g. road surface images in rainy season will have the different texture from summer and winter seasons. The next step after the prototype of the road model has been implemented and tested; the system will be embedded into the smart phone application for the practical use. The result of road image with the pinned location of buried or digged areas will be shown on the smart phone screen. The system implementation on the smart phone is shown in Fig. 4 and the features extraction is also shown in Fig. 5.

The Features Extraction
The edge detection is a feature extraction technique used in this research to detect the short linear sections of the road surface features. Figures 5 and 6 represented the

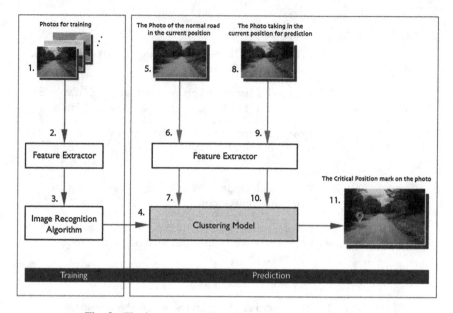

Fig. 3. The image recognition for terrestrial reconnaissance

experiments applying Sobel algorithm to the images which is the approximation of the derivatives in two directions: x and y, then finding their magnitude and direction of edges with the following equation.

$$M = \sqrt{s_x^2 + s_y^2} \qquad (1)$$

Where s_x^2 and s_y^2 are computed by

$$s_x = (a_2 + ca_3 + a_4) - (a_0 + ca_7 + a_6) \qquad (2)$$

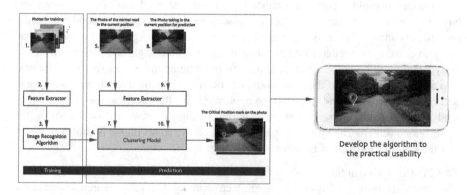

Fig. 4. The smart phone application of the proposed algorithm

Fig. 5. (a) and (b) Feature Extraction on the normal road images

$$s_y = (a_0 + ca_1 + a_2) - (a_6 + ca_5 + a_4) \tag{3}$$

While Constant $c = 2$ and s_x and s_y are the metric masks.

The Feature extraction on the normal road images (Fig. 5) show the repetitive patterns of borders, compare the wide angle image (a) to the close up (b) image, we can see more different edge characteristics on the perspective view (a). In Fig. 6, the various styles of the damaged trails shown by the significant border lines and specific forms in each image (a), (b), (c), (d). This will be the critical information for the next process. However, the features extraction process is ongoing until we get the best result.

4   The Result

There are 15 test images of the three types of the road, (5 images for each type) that were dug and drown; gravel roads, asphalt roads and concrete roads. The experiment provides the threshold values for forming the clustering model for real time terrestrial reconnaissance operation.

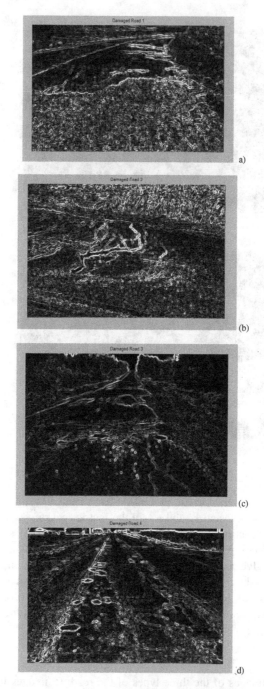

Fig. 6. (a), (b), (c) and (d) Feature Extraction on the damaged roads images

In the area of operation, the drone was assign to collect the normal patrol road surface images ahead in such 1–2 day earlier, those images were sent back to the data storage. In the day of patrol operation, the drone again do the same work in the same route as the day before to collect the images of surface, the images were compare to the image in the data storage by clustering model, for the images of Gravel road if their threshold are reached 25–30%, the soldier should not access in that area because under the road might have the bomb. In the case of the roads are the Asphalt roads or the Concrete roads, their threshold are 15–20% and 7–10% respectively by conducting in the same manner as the Gravel roads.

	Normal Roads (Demonstrate one example of feature extraction)	Damaged Roads (Demonstrate one example of feature extraction)	The Changing Road's Surface Value by **Percentage** (Threshold Range)
Gravel Roads	Normal Gravel Road	Damaged Gravel Road	25 – 30
Asphalt Roads	Normal Asphalt Road	Damaged Asphalt Road	15 - 20
Concrete Roads	Normal Concrete Road	Damaged Concrete Road	7-10

The next step we are dealing the relevant organization to have an experiment in the real operation area, three southern border provinces of Thailand.

5 The Future Usage and Benefits

As mentioned earlier, instead of the procurement of commercial bomb detectors such as GPR (Ground Penetration Radar) and REST (Remote Explosive Scent Tracing) which are expensive and inappropriate in some situations. GPR is a geophysical method that uses radar pulses to detect the changes of soil structures or diffracts buried underneath the surface of the road. This kind of equipment cannot classify the different between rocks and metal (bomb) beneath the surface of the road because the electromagnetic radiation that reflected from rocks and metal (bomb) would be the same. REST is a survey methodology based on scent tracing of bomb, this technology does not suit for the surface with a high relative humidity (e.g. the road after raining; the scent of bomb could be distracted from the moisture in soil) which is the major drawback of REST. Therefore, the smart phone application of the image recognition for terrestrial reconnaissance is suit for this circumstance because it is a handheld device and cost effective compared with GPR and REST.

The benefits of the system can be given in two major areas:

1. Public policy: Reducing the damages of life and property of citizens, military/police as well as the other government officers. Enhancing the security confidence of citizens, military/police/government officers.
2. Economy: Encouraging people to live in the daily life and do their business as their usual. When people can live safely, the mental health problems can be reduced. If the business can run normally therefore the income will increase.

The future work of this study: We have planned to improve the texture mapping algorithm [17] for generating the smooth voxel surface for terrain model; the 3D terrain model of road can be recreating for the later use. The major benefit of the 3D terrain map is the real-time look-like map; this 3D terrain map can be used as the aerial view in some areas where the anti-drone system has already been activated. Figure 7 shows the 3D terrain map with the improved texture mapping algorithm proposed in [17].

Fig. 7. The 3D terrain map with the smooth voxel surface algorithm.

Acknowledgement. "This research was funded by the King Mongkut's University of Technology North Bangkok. Contract no. KMUTNB-GOV-60-53".

References

1. Buzasi, T.: Image processing in the military technology. AARMS **2**(2), 221–231 (2003). Wall Radar Imaging Technology
2. Chizek, J.G.: Military transformation: intelligence, surveillance and reconnaissance. Report for Congress Received through the CRS Web. National Defense Fellow Foreign Affairs, Defense, and Trade Division (2003)
3. Filippidis, A.: Using genetic algorithms and neural networks for surface land mine detection. IEEE Trans. Signal Process. **47**(1), 176–186 (1999). January 2014
4. Geddis, D., Mead, P.: Terrestrial aircraft for reconnaissance applications (Project TARA). B.S. Electrical and Electronics Engineering and Optical Engineering, Norfolk State University (2016)
5. Grenzdorffer, G.J., et al.: Photogrammetric image acquisition and image analysis of oblique imagery-a new challenge for the digital airborne system PFIFF. Wiley Online Libr. **23**(124), 372–386 (2008)
6. Jauregui, L.M., Jauregui, M.: Terrestrial photogrametry applied to architectural restoration and archaeological surveys (2000)
7. Zhang, L.: Airport detection and aircraft recognition based on two-layer saliency model in high spatial resolution remote-sensing images. IEEE J. Sel. Top. Appl. Earth Obs. Remote Sens. (2016)
8. Lofsjogard, M.: Functional properties of concrete roads – development of an optimisation model and studies on road lighting design and joint performance. Doctoral Thesis. Utbildningsservice AB, Stockholm (2003)
9. dos Santos, J.A., et al.: Interactive multiscale classification of high-resolution remote sensing images. IEEE J. Sel. Top. Appl. Earth Obs. Remote Sens. **6**(4), 2020–2034 (2013)
10. Shah, V.V.D.: Image processing and its military applications. Military College of Telecommunication Engineering, Mhow - 453 441.7 (1987)
11. Schenk, T.: Introduction to photogrammetry. Department of Civil and Environmental Engineering and Geodetic Science, The Ohio State University (2005)
12. Department of Agriculture, United States. Environmentally Sensitive Road Maintenance Practices for Dirt and Gravel Road. United States
13. Walker, D.: Pavement surface evaluation and rating asphalt PASER manual. Transportation Information Center. University of Wisconsin-Madison (2002)
14. Wu, W., et al.: Recognition of airport runways in FLIR images based on knowledge. IEEE Geosci. Remote Sens. Lett. **11**(9), 1534–1538 (2014)
15. Wiedemann, A., Moré, J.: Orientation strategies for aerial oblique images. In: International Archives of the Photogrammetry, Remote Sensing and Spatial Information Sciences, vol. XXXIX-B1, 2012 XXII ISPRS Congress, 25 August – 01 September 2012, Melbourne, Australia (2012)
16. Guo, X., Liu, T.: Application of FPGA in high-speed CMOS digital image acquisition and color recognition system. J. Chem. Pharm. Res. **6**(6), 791–798 (2014)
17. Visutsak, P.: Smooth voxel surface for 3D medical models. Research Report, King Mongkut's University of Technology North Bangkok, Bangkok, Thailand (2016)

A Computer Vision Framework for Partitioning of Image-Object Through Graph Theoretical Heuristic Approach

Sourav Saha[1]([✉]), Ankita Mandal[1], Paras Sheth[1], Harshita Narnoli[1], and Priya Ranjan Sinha Mahapatra[2]

[1] Institute of Engineering and Management, University of Kalyani, Kolkata, India
souravsaha1977@gmail.com, mandalankita92@gmail.com,
parasshethiem@gmail.com, harshitanarnoli18@gmail.com
[2] Department of Computer Science and Engineering, University of Kalyani,
Kolkata, India
priya_cskly@yahoo.co.in

Abstract. The aim of this work is to develop a graph theoretical computer vision framework to partition shape of an image object into parts based on a heuristic approach such that the partitioning remains consistent with human perception. The proposed framework employs a special polygonal approximation scheme to represent a shape suitably in simpler graph form where each polygonal side represents a graph-edge. The shape-representative graph is explored to determine vertex-visibility graph by a simple algorithm presented in this paper. We have proposed a heuristic based iterative clique extraction strategy to decompose the shape-representative graph depending on its vertex-visibility graph. This proposed framework considers MPEG-7 shape data set for probing the acceptability of the proposed framework and according to our observation, the performance of the framework is comparable with existing schemes.

Keywords: Shape partitioning · Polygonal approximation · Visibility graph

1 Introduction

Cognitive experimental evidence suggests that human vision organizes object-shape in terms of its constituent parts along with their mutual spatial relationships for visual processing [3,8]. From computational perspective, partitioned view of a shape is useful as many objects are consisting of parts that move non-rigidly with respect to each other. A part-based description allows one to decouple the constituent parts of a shape based on the spatial relationships between the parts and thereby offers a natural way to represent and recognize

This work has been supported by DST Purse Scheme, University of Kalyani.

J.K. Mandal et al. (Eds.): CICBA 2017, Part II, CCIS 776, pp. 284–296, 2017.
DOI: 10.1007/978-981-10-6430-2_22

articulated objects. Moreover, in reality the view of an object may be variably or partially visible due to occlusion with other objects or under various transformations of its flexible object-parts. Representing shapes by parts allows the recognition process to proceed with the view which may undergo different transformations of flexible parts or partial occlusion with other objects. From pragmatic perspective, it is commonly experienced that the shape of individual flexible component of an object-body is less likely to be influenced under different natural shape-transformations. Human observers mostly perceive an object-body as a combination of various non-flexible parts. From computational perspective, algorithms satisfying certain principles for partitioning may turn out meaningful as well as useful if they produce partitioning which closely matches with the perception of human observers. As fundamental principles, each meaningful partitioning must be stable over small generic perturbations of viewpoint, and over small generic transformations in object shape specially around the junction of flexible parts. Keeping the above mentioned principles as primary focus, we have proposed a graph theoretic computer vision framework using a heuristic graph partitioning algorithm to obtain partitioning of a shape which is coherent with human perception based partitioning.

1.1 Related Work

Shape partitioning is a fundamental step towards shape analysis and understanding. Such representation method is widely used in shape recognition, shape retrieval, skeleton extraction and motion planning. In recent years, partitioning of image objects into meaningful regions has been drawing attention of many researchers to address various computer vision problems. Primarily, researchers have adopted two strategies for shape partitioning: (a) bottom up strategy where small shape-parts are grouped into a large shape parts, and (b) top down strategy which is decomposing large shape into meaningful parts [3]. Bottom-up grouping method is used to form hierarchical shape vocabularies from a large number of shape instances. Top down approach exploits perceptual cues to decompose shapes. Based on various cues, various optimized shape decomposition algorithms have been developed by the computer vision scientists. There are some rules from cognitive science which are the basis for meaningful partitioning. Hoffman et al. [8] showed that the human visual system perceives region boundaries at negative minima of principal curvature which is known as the minima-rule. The minima-rule is an elegant theory that defines a framework for how human perception might decompose an object into its constituent parts. This rule only defines boundary points at which to parse but does not tell how to use these points to cut shapes. On the other hand, short-cut rule as proposed by Singh et al. [14] is basically is its complement which states that human vision prefers to use the shortest possible cut-lengths to decompose shapes into parts. They proposed methods to decompose polygons into approximately convex parts and reported that approximate convex decomposition usually results insignificantly smaller number of parts and can be computed more efficiently. Gopalan et al. [6] proposed another algorithm based on convexity for producing approximated convex decomposition. Liu et al. [10] considered both convexity and the short-cut rule to obtain near-optimal shape decomposition. Based on their work, Ren et al. [12] further used minima-rule along with the number of shape-parts in the objective function during optimization. Jiang et al. [9] used a combination of convexity, short-cut and minima-rule while focusing on minimizing the number of shape-parts primarily to preserve natural visual interpretation of various parts. Unfortunately, existing schemes still fail to provide a rigorous way to obtain an effective shape-partitioning consistent with the natural visual interpretation of various parts of an object.

In our paper, we primarily explore graph theory as a tool to obtain partitioning heuristically based on some perception based criteria. The proposed framework employs a special polygonal approximation to represent a shape suitably as a simpler graph form where each polygonal side represents an edge. Such graph-representation of shape facilitates us to apply graph theoretic approaches. The shape-representative graph is explored to determine vertex-visibility graph by a simple algorithm presented in this paper. We have proposed a heuristic based iterative clique extraction strategy to decompose the shape depending on its vertex-visibility graph. According to our observation, the performance of the framework is coherent with human observation to a large degree and comparable with existing schemes. The organization of the rest of the paper is as follows. Section 2 discusses our proposed shape partitioning framework. In Sect. 3, we show results of our experiments and finally we summarize the contribution of this work and identify areas for further work in the conclusion section.

2   Proposed Framework

This section discusses our proposed framework comprehensively. As mentioned earlier the proposed scheme for partitioning shape works on graph based shape representation of an object through a special polygonal approximation of closed curve. It is observed that most of the popular shape partitioning schemes fail

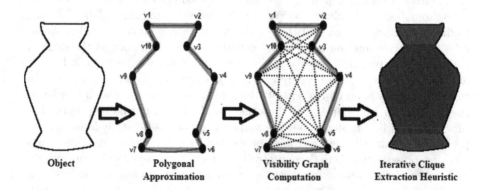

Fig. 1. Overall flow of the proposed scheme

to address the presence of bumpy irregularities along the contour effectively. Our proposed framework attempts to handle such noisy curve using a thick-edge polygonal approximation (Fig. 1d) reported in [13]. Figure 1 outlines the overall flow of the proposed strategy. The proposed algorithm takes a sequence of boundary points as input which is obtained through tracing contour of an object by adopting Moore's strategy [5]. Below, we discuss in detail each step of the proposed strategy as mentioned in Fig. 1.

2.1   Thick-Edge Polygonal Approximation

Extracting meaningful information and features from the contour of 2-D digital planar curves has been widely used for shape modeling. Detection of dominant points (DP) along the contour to represent visual characteristics of a shape has always been a challenging aspect for effective shape modeling. Polygonal approximation of a closed digital curve has always been considered as an effective techniques for detection of DPs as the vertices of the shape representative polygonal form. In this proposed work, we have used polygonal approximation of an object to interpret its shape in graph representative form where each graph-node corresponds to a vertex of the polygon. The merit of such a strategy depends on how closely a polygon can represent a shape with minimal number of DP without loss of significant visual characteristics. Most of the traditional polygonal approximation schemes fail to address the presence of bumpy irregularities along the contour effectively as they sometimes tend to produce misleading polygonal representation either with too many sides (Fig. 2b) or with too few sides (Fig. 2c). In [13], Sourav et al. proposed a framework which attempts to handle such noisy curve using a thick-edge polygonal approximation (Fig. 2d) based on digital geometric approach wherein each edge can have reasonably varied thickness. Vertices of such a shape-approximating polygon are extracted through a novel heuristic strategy and these vertices are considered as dominant points (DP). The proposed framework as presented in [13] allows us to approximate a polygonal representation of the contour with each polygonal-side having a thickness derived sensibly to handle contour curvatures with irregular bumps. Figure 2 intuitively demonstrates suitability of the proposed strategy.

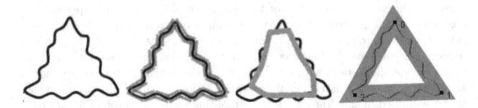

Fig. 2. a. Object b. & c. traditional polygonal approximation d. proposed scheme

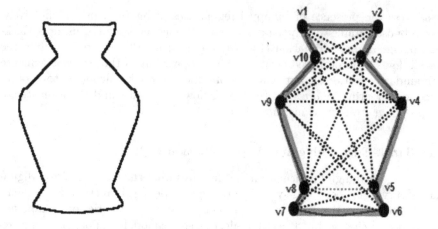

Fig. 3. a. Object b. visibility graph of polygonal approximation

2.2 Visibility Graph Computation

The visibility graph is a fundamental geometric structure useful in many applications. In computational geometry, two nodes are said to be visible adjacent pair in the vertex-visibility graph of a polygon if and only if the line segment joining the associated vertices is at no point exterior to the polygon. Figure 3b diagrammatically depicts vertex-visibility graph of a polygonal approximation of the shape Fig. 3a. Any adjacent pair of vertices forming an edge is always mutually visible and in Fig. 3b, the connection between this kind of edge representative vertex-pair is shown by a solid line segment whereas connections betweeen other mutually visible pair of vertices are shown by dotted line segment. Understandably, the connection between visible adjacent pair is equivalent to the line of sight. A non-convex polygonal shape can be partitioned into several convex parts based on its visibility graph as explained later. In this framework, we have explored the concept of visibility graph for partitioning a non-convex polygonal shape. The visibility graph computation problem has been solved for some special classes of polygons called spiral polygons and tower polygons [4]. Researchers notably Hershberger et al. [7] contributed algorithms in generalized sense for checking the visibility of two points in planar region in presence of obstacles. In the proposed framework, a simple polygon with no holes is considered as an approximated representative of a shape as discussed in previous section. For such specific hole-free simplar polygonal shape, Bose et al. [1] computed the visibility graph with $O(n^3 \lg n)$ time complexity. Below, we present an algorithm (namely ConstructVisibilityMatrix) along with an illustration which we have applied in this framework for computing visibility graph of an approximated polygonal shape.

Illustration of the Proposed Visibility Graph Computation Algorithm: Here, we illustrate basic principle of the proposed algorithm for computation of visibility

---

Algorithm 1: CONSTRUCTVISIBILITYMATRIX

Input: *polygonVertexList*: An ordered list of polygon-vertices obtained through clockwise traversal of edges

Output: Global *visibilityMatrix*: If a vertex-pair (v_i, v_j) is mutually visible then the cell(i, j) and cell(j, i) are set to true otherwise both the cells are set to false. Initially, cells corresponding the edges are set as true since any vertex-pair forming an edge always constitutes a visible pair.

1   **for** *each vertex v_i in polygonVertexList* **do**
2   **for** *each vertex v_j in polygonVertexList* **do**
3   **if** $v_i \neq v_j$ ***OR*** $\overline{v_i v_j}$ *is not an edge* **then**
4   *intersectFlag* ← **false**
5   **for** *each edge with end vertices (v_p, v_q)* **do**
            `/* check whether line segment` $\overline{v_i v_j}$ `intersects edge` $\overline{v_p v_q}$
              `depending on clockwise or counter-clockwise`
              `orientation of an ordered triplet of points     */`
6   *orientation1* ← orientation of point-triplet (v_i, v_j, v_p)
7   *orientation2* ← orientation of point-triplet (v_i, v_j, v_q)
8   *orientation3* ← orientation of point-triplet (v_p, v_q, v_i)
9   *orientation4* ← orientation of point-triplet (v_p, v_q, v_j)
10   **if** *orientation1* $\neq$ *orientation2* ***AND***
            orientation3 $\neq$ *orientation4* **then**
11   *intersectFlag* ← **true**
12   **break**
13   **end**
14   **end**
15   **end**
16   **if** *intersectFlag* = ***true*** **then**
        `/*` $\overline{v_i v_j}$ `intersects an edge                    */`
17   *visibilityMatrix*$[i, j]$ ← **false**
18   **end**
19   **else**
        `/*` $\overline{v_i v_j}$ `does not intersect any edge          */`
20   **if** *mid-point of* $\overline{v_i v_j}$ *is inside polygon* **then**
21   *visibilityMatrix*$[i, j]$ ← **true**
22   **end**
23   **end**
24   **end**
25 **end**
26 **return** *visibilityMatrix*

---

graph. Algorithm 1: Construct VisibilityMatrix computes visibility graph by checking whether any two vertices v_i and v_j are visible pair of a polygon depending on whether line segment $\overline{v_i v_j}$ intersects any edge of the polygon. The decision of intersection is made based on the notion of clockwise or counter-clockwise orientation of an ordered triplet of points in a plane. For example, in Fig. 3b vertices v_1 and v_8 do not form visible pair as $\overline{v_1 v_8}$ intersects edge $\overline{v_9 v_{10}}$. The deciding criteria of intersection is based on the satisfaction of following two conditions– a) The orientation of point-triplet (v_1, v_8, v_9) is clockwise but the orientation of point-triplet (v_1, v_8, v_{10}) is counter-clockwise and b) The orientation of point-triplet (v_9, v_{10}, v_1) is counter clockwise but the orientation of point-triplet (v_9, v_{10}, v_8) is clockwise. On the contrary, none of the vertex-pairs namely (v_1, v_3) or (v_1, v_9) intersects any edge of the polygon. Among these two candidate pairs, only (v_1, v_3) forms visible pair because the mid-point of $\overline{v_1 v_3}$ lies inside the polygon whereas the mid-point of $\overline{v_1 v_9}$ lies outside the polygon. The notable fact is that a pair (v_i, v_j) would not form a visible pair if any other vertex v_k falls on the line of sight between v_i and v_j. For example, pair (v_1, v_5) fails to form a visible pair since the vertex v_{10} falls on the line of sight joining v_1 and v_5. The proposed algorithm constructs a two-dimensional visibility matrix based on the formation of visible vertex-pair. Understandably, the three nested loops in the proposed algorithm cause a time complexity of $O(n^3)$.

2.3   Shape Partitioning Through Iterative Maximal Clique Extraction

A clique is a complete sub-graph of a graph. A maximal complete sub-graph is called a maximal clique which is not contained in any other complete subgraph i.e. it can not be extended by including any more adjacent vertices. In Fig. 3, polygonal vertices namely v_3, v_4, v_5, v_8, v_9, and v_{10} construct a maximal clique. The most popular technique to find all the maximal cliques of a given undirected graph was presented by Coen Bron et al [2]. The basic form of the Bron-Kerbosch algorithm is a recursive backtracking algorithm that searches for all possible maximal cliques in a given graph. Interestingly, it is most likely that a maximal clique corresponds to non-flexible part of a shape. On the basis of this idea, we have developed a heuristic strategy based on the principle concept of Bron–Kerbosch algorithm [2] to iteratively extract maximal clique from the visibility graph of a polygonal shape. The proposed heuristic algorithm is presented as Algorithm 2: GetShapePartition.

Illustration of the Proposed Shape Partitioning Algorithm–GetShapePartition: The main objective of Algorithm 2:GetShapePartition is to find a suitable clique-partitioning of polygonal shape based on some heuristic. The proposed algorithm solely considers maximal cliques and henceforth for the sake of simplicity, a maximal clique is sometimes referred as clique in following sections. In this framework, we explored various optimal criteria like (a) Maximize {Area(clique)}, (b) Minimize $\{\frac{1}{N} \sum boundary\text{-}cut\text{-}length\}$ (c) Maximize $\{\frac{Area(clique)}{\frac{1}{N} \sum boundary\text{-}cut\text{-}length}\}$ as heuristics for selecting a clique-partition from the graph-representation of a

---

Algorithm 2: GetShapePartition

Input: G : A graph in terms of adjacency matrix; R : A set of vertices, Initially it is set as empty; P: VertexSet(G); X: A set of vertices, Initially it is set as empty;

Output: Global *PartitioningList*: A list partitioning of G

1 **Function** *GetShapePartition (G, R, P, X)*

2   **if** *G is null-graph* **then**

     /* terminate since no more partition is required   */

3   **return**;

4   **end**

5   **if** *P is empty AND X is empty* **then**

     /* R is a maximal clique. Apply heuristic to obtain current most suitable maximal clique.   */

6      $heuristicCost \leftarrow$ GetHeuristicCost(R);

7   **if** $currentMinHeuristicCost > heuristicCost$ **then**

8        $suitableMaximalClique \leftarrow R$;

9        $currentMinHeuristicCost \leftarrow heuristicCost$;

10   **end**

11      $S \leftarrow S \cup R$;

12   **if** $S = VertexSet(G)$ **then**

       /* all possible maximal cliques are generated for current G */

13   Output most suitable partition described by $suitableMaximalClique$;

14   Add $suitableMaximalClique$ to $PartitioningList$;

15        $MaximalCliqueAdjMat \leftarrow GetAdjacencyMatrix(suitableMaximalClique)$;

16   **for** *each edge described by pair (i, j) in G* **do**

         /* Update G: Remove an edge from G if it belongs the sub-complete graph stored as current $suitableMaximalClique$ such that it is not a boundary-cut   */

17   **if** $edge(i, j) \neq boundary\text{-}cut$ **then**

18            $G(i, j) \leftarrow \{G(i, j) - MaximalCliqueAdjMat(i, j)\}$;

19   **end**

20   **end**

21   **end**

22   **end**

23    $u \leftarrow$ a pivot vertex $\in P \cup X$;

24   **for** *each vertex $v \in P \setminus NeighboSet(u)$* **do**

25   GetShapePartition($G, R \cup \{v\}, P \cap NeighborSet(v), X \cap NeighborSet(v)$);

26      $P \leftarrow P \setminus \{v\}$;

27      $X \leftarrow X \cup \{v\}$;

28   **end**

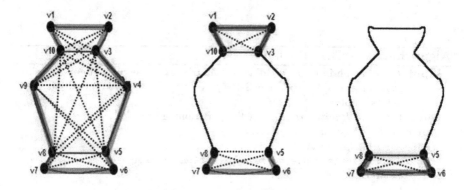

Fig. 4. GetShapePartition iterative steps: a. Step 1b. Step 2c. Step 3

polygonal shape. In experimental result section, we have discussed about all the criteria in detail.

Here, we illustrate the flow of Algorithm 2:GetShapePartition based on the heuristic criteria which maximizes {Area(clique)}. It will help in basic understanding of overall working principle of the proposed algorithm. Area of a maximal clique in the visibility graph can be computed as the convex-polygonal area covered by it. At every step, the objective would be to obtain a clique from the residual graph which covers maximal polygonal area. With reference to Fig. 4a, there can be seven possible maximal cliques that can be extracted from the initial original graph. These seven maximal cliques are **clique-1**:$\{v_3, v_4, v_5, v_8, v_9, v_{10}\}$, **clique-2**:$\{v_5, v_6, v_7, v_8\}$, **clique-3**:$\{v_1, v_2, v_3, v_{10}\}$, **clique-4**:$\{v_5, v_6, v_8, v_9\}$, **clique-5**:$\{v_4, v_5, v_7, v_8\}$, **clique-6**:$\{v_1, v_3, v_4, v_{10}\}$, and **clique-7**:$\{v_2, v_3, v_9, v_{10}\}$. Out of these cliques, **clique-1**:$\{v_3, v_4, v_5, v_8, v_9, v_{10}\}$ contains largest polygonal area and therefore it is selected at first iteration-step. Removal of **clique-1** results in a residual graph with nodes $\{v_1, v_2, v_3, v_{10}, v_5, v_6, v_7, v_8\}$ as shown in Fig. 4b. Similarly at second iteration, maximal clique $\{v_1, v_2, v_3, v_{10}\}$ being the largest area holder would be selected and its removal generates a residual graph with nodes $\{v_5, v_6, v_7, v_8\}$ as shown in Fig. 4c. Lastly, maximal clique $\{v_5, v_6, v_7, v_8\}$ would be selected resulting in a null residual graph which leads to termination of the algorithm.

3   Experimental Results and Analysis

Evaluation of performance is a crucial issue for the proposed framework, mainly due to the subjectivity of human vision based judgment. The merit of such a scheme depends on how closely the partitioning of an approximated polygonal shape matches with the human perception based partitioning. The most intuitive criteria, for estimating effectiveness of the scheme would be to examine the similarity between the partitioning obtained through the proposed framework and the partitioning based on human perception. In this framework, we explored

Table 1. Result: Shape Partitioning

Max-Area Heuristic	Min-Cut-Length Heuristic	Combined Heuristic

Table 2. Comparative Result: Shape Partitioning

Perception Based Partitioning	Gopalan et. al. [6] Partitioning	Liu et. al.[10] Partitioning	Proposed Partitioning

following optimal criteria as heuristics for selecting a clique-partition through the proposed algorithm.

- Criteria (a) Heuristic Based on Maximizing {Area(clique)}: It is the convex-polygonal area covered by a maximal clique of a visibility graph. At every step, the objective would be to obtain a clique from the residual graph which covers maximal polygonal area.
- Criteria (b) Heuristic Based on Minimizing $\{\frac{1}{N} \sum boundary\text{-}cut\text{-}length\}$: For any pair of vertices (v_i, v_j) in clique, if the line of sight connecting v_i and v_j is shared between two area-wise disjoint maximal cliques inside the polygonal shape, then the edge (v_i, v_j) in visibility graph forms a boundary-cut and the distance between v_i and v_j is called boundary-cut-length. As shown in Fig. 3, red dotted-lines connecting the pair (v_3, v_{10}) and the pair (v_5, v_8) can be treated as boundary-cuts of the maximal clique: $\{v_3, v_4, v_5, v_8, v_9, v_{10}\}$. Natural partitioning of an object normally attempts to decompose a part with boundary-cuts as small as possible. The average boundary-cut-length of a clique can be calculated by computing mean-length considering all of its boundary-cuts. Mathematically, for N boundary-cuts of a clique, the average boundary-cut-length can be computed as $\{\frac{1}{N} \sum boundary\text{-}cut\text{-}length\}$. At every step, the objective can be set so as to obtain a clique with minimal average boundary-cut-length.
- Criteria (c) Combined Heuristic using both of the above criteria: Here, we have used both of the above mentioned heuristic criteria and at every step, the objective is set so as to obtain a clique which maximizes $\{\frac{Area(clique)}{\frac{1}{N} \sum boundary\text{-}cut\text{-}length}\}$.

This proposed framework considers well-known MPEG-7 shape dataset [11] for probing the acceptability of our proposed framework. The results are listed in Table 1 wherein first column correponds to criteria-(a), second column correponds to criteria-(b) and third column correponds to criteria-(c). Based on our obseravtion, it appears that the third column corresponding to the criteria-(c) is more consistent with the human perception based partitioning as compared to other criteria. Table 2 compares some of the notable outcomes of the proposed framework with the results obtained by Gopalan et al. [6] and Liu et al. [10] and one can verify that the performance of the proposed framework is qualitatively comparable and acceptable with reference to the perception based partitioning.

4   Conclusion

This paper attempts to develop a graph theoretical heuristic based computer vision framework to decompose shape of an image-object into meaningful parts similar to the perception based partitioned-view of an object. The proposed framework employs a special thick-edged polygonal approximation to represent a shape suitably as simpler graph form which is later explored to compute vertex-visibility graph. We have proposed a heuristic based iterative clique extraction strategy to partition the shape-representative graph based on its vertex-visibility graph. The proposed partitioning relies on the notion that there is a high probability of finding correspondence between a non-flexible part of a shape and a fully-connected sub-graph i.e. a clique belonging to the polygonal shape approximated graph. This proposed framework considered several criteria as heuristics for selecting a suitable partition and according to our observation, the performance of the framework using the heuristic criteria based on both area and cut-length of a maximal clique with an objective of maximizing $\{\frac{Area(clique)}{\frac{1}{N}\sum boundary\text{-}cut\text{-}length}\}$ appears impressive and comparable with existing schemes. However, there is a scope of further research towards possibility of merging or splitting of decomposed parts to make the partitioning more aligned with the natural visual interpretation.

References

1. Bose, P., Lubiw, A., Munro, J.I.: Efficient visibility queries in simple polygons. Comput. Geom. Theory Appl. **23**(3), 313–335 (2002)
2. Bron, C., Kerbosch, J.: Algorithm 457: finding all cliques of an undirected graph. Commun. ACM **16**(9), 575–577 (1973)
3. Felzenszwalb, P.F., Girshick, R.B., McAllester, D., Ramanan, D.: Object detection with discriminatively trained part-based models. IEEE Trans. Pattern Anal. Mach. Intell. **32**, 1627–1645 (2010)
4. Ghosh, K.S.: Visibility Algorithms in the Plane. Cambridge University Press, New York (2007)
5. Gonzalez, R.C., Woods, R.E.: Digital Image Processing, 3rd edn. Prentice-Hall Inc., Upper Saddle River (2006)
6. Gopalan, R., Turaga, P., Chellappa, R.: Articulation-invariant representation of non-planar shapes. In: Daniilidis, K., Maragos, P., Paragios, N. (eds.) ECCV 2010. LNCS, vol. 6313, pp. 286–299. Springer, Heidelberg (2010). doi:10.1007/978-3-642-15558-1_21
7. Hershberger, J.: An optimal visibility graph algorithm for triangulated simple polygons. Algorithmica **4**(1), 141–155 (1989)
8. Hoffman, D.D., Richards, W.A.: Parts of recognition. Cognition **18**, 65–96 (1985)
9. Jiang, T., Dong, Z., Ma, C., Wang, Y.: Toward perception-based shape decomposition. In: Lee, K.M., Matsushita, Y., Rehg, J.M., Hu, Z. (eds.) ACCV 2012. LNCS, vol. 7725, pp. 188–201. Springer, Heidelberg (2013). doi:10.1007/978-3-642-37444-9_15
10. Liu, H., Liu, W., Latecki, L.J.: Convex shape decomposition. In: 2010 IEEE Computer Society Conference on Computer Vision and Pattern Recognition, pp. 97–104, June 2010
11. Ralph, R.: Mpeg-7 core experiment (1999). http://www.dabi.temple.edu/shape/MPEG7/dataset.html
12. Ren, Z., Yuan, J., Liu, W.: Minimum near-convex shape decomposition. IEEE Trans. Pattern Anal. Mach. Intell. **35**(10), 2546–2552 (2013)
13. Saha, S., Roy, S., Dey, P., Soumya, P., Chakraborty, T., Mahapatra, P.R.S.: A computer vision framework for detecting dominant points on contour of image-object through thick-edge polygonal approximation. In: Mandal, J., Satapathy, S., Sanyal, M., Bhateja, V. (eds.) Proceedings of the First International Conference on Intelligent Computing and Communication. AISC, vol. 458, pp. 188–201. Springer, Singapore (2017). doi:10.1007/978-981-10-2035-3_54
14. Singh, M., Seyranian, G., Hoffman, D.: Parsing silhouettes: the short-cut rule. Percept. Psychophys. **61**, 636–660 (1999)

Segmentation of Bengali Handwritten Conjunct Characters Through Structural Disintegration

Rahul Pramanik$^{(\boxtimes)}$ and Soumen Bag

Department of Computer Science and Engineering,
Indian Institute of Technology (ISM) Dhanbad,
Dhanbad 826004, Jharkhand, India
rahul.wbsu@gmail.com, bagsoumen@gmail.com

Abstract. Substantial size of convoluted conjunct characters in Bengali language makes the recognition process burdensome. In this paper, we propose a structural disintegration based segmentation technique that fragments the conjunct characters into discernible shapes for better recognition accuracy. We use a set of structure based segmentation rules that bifurcates the characters into discernible shape components. The bifurcation is done by finding the *touching region* where two basic shapes coincide to form a conjunct character. The proposed method has been tested on a data set of Bengali handwritten conjunct characters efficiently. In future, we will continue our work to incorporate it as a prominent preprocessing step for Bengali optical character recognition system.

Keywords: Bengali · Handwritten · Segmentation · OCR

1 Introduction

Character segmentation is one of the most important preprocessing step in optical character recognition (OCR). The accuracy of recognition strictly depends on the correctness of the segmentation output. Several work on character segmentation have been published on Arabic [1,2], Chinese [3], English [4,5] scripts. But there exist very few work on regional Indian scripts [6], even more so for Bengali script [7,8]. Research work on handwritten Bengali character segmentation is limited not only due to its cursive nature but also due to the presence of a large sized conjunct character (also known as compound) set. Pal *et al.* [9] have introduced a technique that uses directional information as features and modified quadratic discriminant function (MQDF) to recognize conjunct character classes. Das *et al.* [10] have proposed a method that recognizes 55 handwritten conjunct character classes using quadtree-based longest run feature and multi-layer perceptron (MLP). Later, they [11] have broadened their research by proposing a technique that uses shadow and quadtree-based longest run features with MLP and support vector machine (SVM) to recognize 93 character classes that incorporates 50 basic and 43 conjunct handwritten Bengali characters. Subsequently, Das *et al.* [12] have presented a multi-stage classification based on combined

© Springer Nature Singapore Pte Ltd. 2017
J.K. Mandal et al. (Eds.): CICBA 2017, Part II, CCIS 776, pp. 297–306, 2017.
DOI: 10.1007/978-981-10-6430-2_23

genetic algorithm (GA) and SVM for handwritten Bengali conjunct characters. Multiple feature set such as shadow, octant centroid, quadtree-based longest run, and different topological attributes are combined to form the overall feature set.

Present classifiers are not very effective in tackling the complicated shape of a conjunct character. Now-a-days, structural feature set have become the center of attention for researchers to overcome this problem. But unsheathing the proper structural features from a convoluted conjunct character is itself a substantial challenge. Reduction in the structural intricacy of conjunct characters should improve the recognition accuracy of such characters. Our work is based on the premise that classification and recognition of two basic characters instead of a complex-shaped conjunct character would be much simpler and should provide better recognition rate. To the best of our knowledge no work has been published on this aspect for Bengali handwritten complex-shaped conjunct characters. In this paper, we propose a structural disintegration based strategy to segment the conjunct characters which would provide better classification and recognition accuracy for existing Bengali OCR systems in future.

The remaining paper is organized as follows. Section 2 describes the proposed methodology. The experimental results are discussed in Sect. 3. Finally, a brief conclusion is presented in Sect. 4.

2   Proposed Methodology

We propose a structural disintegration based strategy to segment 71 conjunct characters for better classification and recognition accuracy. The 71 characters represents nearly 80% of the conjunct characters that can be found in a normal Bengali text. The proposed methodology is divided into two parts: group formation and shape decomposition. At first we detect the group of each conjunct character and then we perform sequential steps to decompose the conjunct characters into prominent shapes.

2.1   Group Formation

We divide the conjunct character set into four groups based on their structural shapes and patterns with respect to their *touching region*. A *touching region* is defined as the region where two basic characters converge to form a conjunct character. A decision tree based representation of these grouping is shown in Fig. 1. A set of structural rules corresponding to each group is given below.

Group 1: If the *touching region* of the conjunct character contains a vertical line and the consonants forming the conjunct character lie on opposite sides of the vertical line.

Group 2: If the *touching region* of the conjunct character contains a vertical line and the consonants forming the conjunct character lie on the same side of the vertical line.

Group 3: If the *touching region* of the conjunct character does not contain a vertical line and the image window height (W_h) is greater than the image window width (W_d).

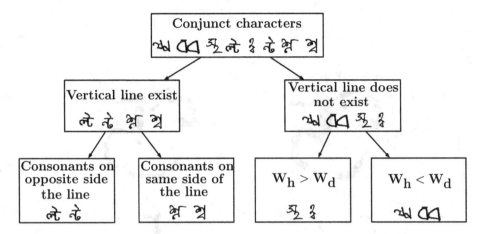

Fig. 1. Decision tree to determine the group of a conjunct character. In this figure, each rectangle box contains the structural property of character set (with few sample images) based on which the decisions are made in our proposed method.

Group 4: If the *touching region* of the conjunct character does not contain a vertical line and the image window height (W_h) is less than the image window width (W_d).

2.2 Shape Decomposition

After the grouping, the proposed method is illustrated in the following steps.

1. We perform image binarization of character images using a global threshold method [13] (Fig. 2a). As in our proposed method we deal with isolated character images with less noisy background, so this global thresholding method gives the expected binarized results.
2. We observe that the skeletonization of character images with more than one iteration produce over-thinned junction points comparing with our basic need. As the junction points are one of the important feature in structure shape analysis, so these over-thinned junction points cannot preserve the true structural shape of the character images. To overcome this problem, we perform partial thinning of the conjunct characters by a single iteration of a parallel thinning method [14] (Fig. 2b).
3. We use a 8-neighbourhood structural element to erode the image which results in splitting the image into a number of components. Next, we apply the Rosenfeld and Kak component labelling algorithm [15] to label all the components in the eroded image as $\mathcal{R} = <r_1, r_2, \cdots, r_n>$ (Fig. 2c). Then we sort $\mathcal{R}$ in decreasing order of pixel values of these components to get a descending ordered set $\mathcal{R}'$. We infer from our observation that the junction point which connects the two consonants would be among the top five components with the highest pixel values. So, we keep the first five components (Fig. 2d) from

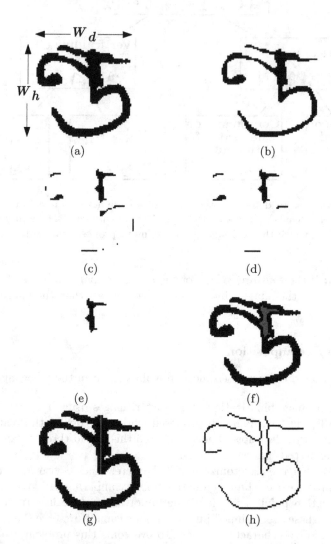

Fig. 2. Stepwise illustration of the proposed method. (a) After image binarization; (b) After partial thinning; (c) After erosion and component labelling; (d) Top 5 components with highest pixel values; (e) The closest connected component from the centroid of the whole image; (f) Detected *touching region* in the original image marked by red colour; (g) After the segmentation where the segmented area is marked with red colour; (h) Final thinned result with proper decomposition of conjunct characters into basic structural shapes. (Color figure online)

$\mathcal{R}'$ while discarding all the others. We calculate centroid of each of these components as well as that of the whole image. The centroid of the image (δ_C^x, δ_C^y) is shifted by $+10$ rightwards, owing to our observation that the *touching region* lies a little right from the centroid of the image.

4. We employ *Manhattan* distance measure technique as detailed in Eq. 1 to calculate the distance between the centroid of the image and that of each of the component. Shifting the centroid rightwards makes certain that the *touching region* is the closest component to the centroid.

$$d_i = |\delta_C^x - \delta_i^x| + |\delta_C^y - \delta_i^y| \tag{1}$$

where, (δ_C^x, δ_C^y) is the centroid of the entire image and (δ_i^x, δ_i^y), $i \in [1,5]$ is the centroid of the considered component.

The component with minimum distance is the *touching region* that connects the two consonants. The closest component which we consider to be the *touching region* is extracted (Fig. 2e) and its position in the original image is determined (Fig. 2f). Once we determine the location, a threshold of ± 10 (particular to our experimentation) is used to find if a vertical line exists on either side of the centroid or not.

5. Now, we check to which of these four groups does each of the conjunct character belongs. The grouping is done as per the structural properties of each group as discussed above. Based on the group, we perform horizontal/vertical cut for the proper decomposition of conjunct characters.

    i: If a character belongs to Group 1, then we perform vertical cut.
    ii: If a character belongs to Group 2, then we perform horizontal cut.
    iii: If a character belongs to Group 3, then we perform vertical cut.
    iv: If a character belongs to Group 4, then we perform horizontal cut. In Fig. 2g, we perform vertical cut as the given input belongs to Group 1.

6. We further thin the resultant image using the same parallel thinning method as discussed in Step 2 to get the final decomposed thinned image (Fig. 2h) that can be further used for classification and recognition.

3 Experimental Results and Analysis

3.1 Dataset

We have taken the Cmaterdb [16] dataset for our experimental purposes. 40 samples for each of the 71 conjunct characters are chosen randomly from the dataset. A total of 2840 sample images of conjunct characters are used to carry out the experiment. A Core i7 machine with 4 GB RAM and 500 GB HDD is used to carry out the experiments. All the programs are written in MATLAB on the Windows 7 platform.

3.2 Experimental Analysis

In this section we present the experimental results of our proposed work. We evaluate the correctness of segmentation through visual perspective only. Table 1 provides a detailed analysis of the performance achieved by each group of conjunct characters. As we can see from the tabulated results, Group 3 provides the most precise result providing an accuracy of 88.19% while Group 4 provides the least precise result with an accuracy of 77.04%. Tables 2 and 3 provides a character wise assessment of the performance of the most and least accurate characters. The character অ provided an accuracy of 100% highest among all the characters. The character � was the least accurate. An overall accuracy of 83.46% was achieved. Some of the results that we obtained has been reported in Fig. 3.

Table 1. Detailed statistics of each group of conjunct characters.

Group	Subset of Conjunct Characters	Total no. of samples	No. of samples correctly detected	Accuracy (%)
1	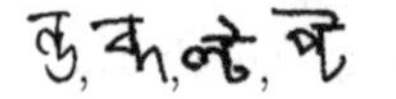 ঙ, ঞ, ঞ, ঞ	800	648	81.00
2	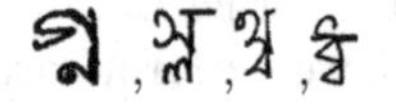 ঞ, ঞ, ঞ, ঞ	880	771	87.61
3	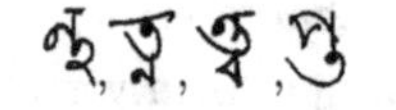 ঞ, ঞ, ঞ, ঞ	720	635	88.19
4	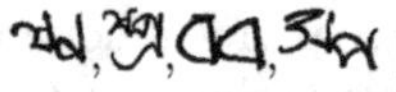 ঞ, ঞ, ঞ, ঞ	440	339	77.04

Table 2. List of conjunct characters with higher accuracy rates in prominent shape decomposition.

Conjunct character	 অ	 ঞ	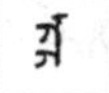 ঞ	 ঞ	 ঞ	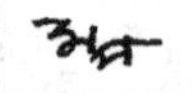 ঞ	 ঞ	 ঞ	 ঞ	 ঞ
Total # Samples	40									
# Samples correctly detected	40	38	38	38	38	38	38	38	38	36
Accuracy (%)	100	95	95	95	95	95	95	95	95	90

Table 3. List of conjunct characters with lower accuracy rates in prominent shape decomposition.

Conjunct character	 ঞ	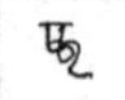 ঞ	 ঞ	 ঞ	 ঞ	 ঞ	 ঞ	 ঞ	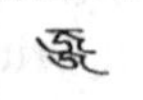 ঞ	 ঞ
Total # Samples	40									
# Samples correctly detected	14	16	16	16	18	18	18	22	22	24
Accuracy (%)	35	40	40	40	45	45	45	55	55	60

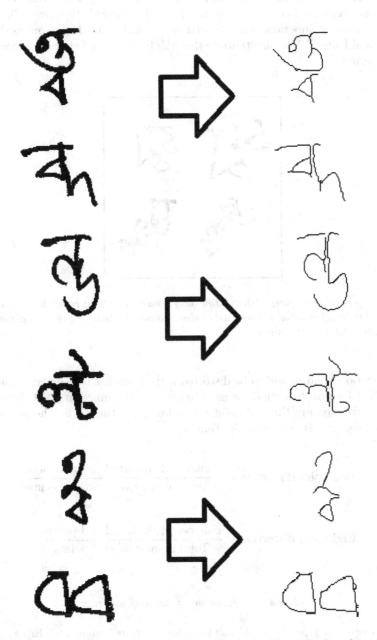

Fig. 3. Test results on Bengali handwritten conjunct characters: **Left column:** input images; **Right column:** the corresponding thinned and segmented basic structural shapes.

In order to extract the structural features from the segmented conjunct characters, the segmented characters are needed to be thinned. We have utilised the measures namely, junction point distortion and end point distortion, as defined by Bag and Harit [17] to substantiate that the final thinned characters are much less distorted.

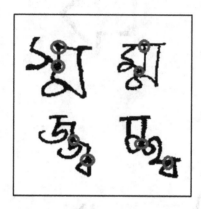

Fig. 4. Top row: characters with two *touching regions*; **Bottom row:** three characters connected by two *touching regions*. Red circles indicate the *touching regions* of conjunct characters. (Color figure online)

A junction point is said to be distorted if the branches that emerges out of it is locally deformed. Equation 2 is used to measure the junction point distortion. Similarly, we measure the end point distortion using the Eq. 3. The percentage of distortion error is delineated in Table 4.

$$\text{Junction point distortion} = \frac{\text{Number of distorted junction points}}{\text{Total number of junction points}} \quad (2)$$

$$\text{End point distortion} = \frac{\text{Number of distorted end points}}{\text{Total number of end points}} \quad (3)$$

Table 4. Measurement of thinning accuracy.

Distortion type	Total number	Distorted number	% Error
Junction point distortion	6120	1899	31.03
End point distortion	9658	632	6.54

3.3   Failure Cases

Despite the flexibility of our proposed approach, it fails at some instances. This algorithm has been designed to detect only one *touching region*. So, if there are two or more *touching regions* that connect the characters, this algorithm fails to appropriately segment the complex-shaped character. The algorithm also fails when the conjunct character is formed by three or more basic characters which is in turn an extension of the first problem. An example for both the cases is shown in Fig. 4.

4   Conclusion

The recognition task is strenuous due to the cursive nature of Bengali handwritten characters. The presence of large number of conjunct characters makes the task much more harder. Reducing the structural intricacy of these conjunct characters would make the recognition accuracy more precise. In the current work, we have developed a structural disintegration based approach to segment the convoluted conjunct characters into two simple, basic, and prominent shapes. In future, we will continue our work to incorporate this methodology as a prominent preprocessing step for Bengali OCR system.

References

1. Omidyeganeh, M., Azmi, R., Nayebi, K., Javadtalab, A.: A new method to improve multi font Farsi/Arabic character segmentation results: using extra classes of some character combinations. In: Cham, T.-J., Cai, J., Dorai, C., Rajan, D., Chua, T.-S., Chia, L.-T. (eds.) MMM 2007. LNCS, vol. 4351, pp. 670–679. Springer, Heidelberg (2006). doi:10.1007/978-3-540-69423-6_65

2. Wshah, S., Shi, Z., Govindaraju, V.: Segmentation of Arabic handwriting based on both contour and skeleton segmentation. In: International Conference on Document Analysis and Recognition, pp. 793–797 (2009)

3. Tan, J., Lai, J.H., Wang, C.D., Wang, W.X., Zuo, X.X.: A new handwritten character segmentation method based on nonlinear clustering. Neurocomputing **89**, 213–219 (2012)

4. Khan, A.R., Mohammad, Z.: A simple segmentation approach for unconstrained cursive handwritten words in conjunction with the neural network. Int. J. Image Process. **2**(3), 29–35 (2008)

5. Lee, H., Verma, B.: Binary segmentation algorithm for English cursive handwriting recognition. Pattern Recogn. **45**(4), 1306–1317 (2012)

6. Kumar, M., Jindal, M.K., Sharma, R.K.: Segmentation of isolated and touching characters in offline handwritten Gurmukhi script recognition. Int. J. Inf. Technol. Comput. Sci. **6**(2), 58–63 (2014)

7. Bag, S., Bhowmick, P., Harit, G., Biswas, A.: Character segmentation of handwritten Bangla text by vertex characterization of isothetic covers. In: Proceedings of the National Conference on Computer Vision, Pattern Recognition, Image Processing and Graphics, pp. 21–24 (2011)

8. Sarkar, R., Das, N., Basu, S., Kundu, M., Nasipuri, M., Basu, D.K.: A two-stage approach for segmentation of handwritten Bangla word images. In: Proceedings of the International Conference on Frontiers in Handwriting Recognitions, pp. 403–408 (2008)

9. Pal, U., Wakabayashi, T., Kimura, F.: Handwritten Bangla compound character recognition using gradient feature. In: Proceedings of the International Conference on Information Technology, pp. 208–213 (2007)

10. Das, N., Basu, S., Sarkar, R., Kundu, M., Nasipuri, M., Basu, D.K.: Handwritten Bangla compound character recognition: potential challenges and probable solution. In: Proceedings of the Indian International Conference on Artificial Intelligence, pp. 1901–1913 (2009)

11. Das, N., Das, B., Sarkar, R., Basu, S., Kundu, M., Nasipuri, M.: Handwritten Bangla basic and compound character recognition using MLP and SVM classifier. J. Comput. **2**(2), 109–115 (2010)

12. Das, N., Acharya, K., Sarkar, R., Basu, S., Kundu, M., Nasipuri, M.: A novel GA-SVM based multistage approach for recognition of handwritten Bangla compound characters. In: Satapathy, S.C., Avadhani, P.S., Abraham, A. (eds.) Proceedings of the InConINDIA 2012. AISC, vol. 132, pp. 145–152. Springer, Heidelberg (2012). doi:10.1007/978-3-642-27443-5_17

13. Otsu, N.: A threshold selection method from gray-level histograms. IEEE Trans. Syst. Man Cybern. **9**(1), 62–66 (1979)

14. Zhang, T.Y., Suen, C.Y.: A fast parallel algorithm for thinning digital patterns. Commun. ACM **27**(3), 236–239 (1984)

15. Rosenfeld, A., Kak, A.: Digital Picture Processing, vol. 1 and 2, 2nd edn. Academic Press, New York (1982)

16. Das, N., Acharya, K., Sarkar, R., Basu, S., Kundu, M., Nasipuri, M.: A benchmark image database of isolated Bangla handwritten compound characters. Int. J. Doc. Anal. Recogn. **17**(4), 413–431 (2014)

17. Bag, S., Harit, G.: Skeletonizing character images using a modified medial axis-based strategy. Int. J. Pattern Recognit. Artif. Intell. **25**(7), 1035–1054 (2011)

Rank Order Reduction Based Fast Pattern Matching Algorithm

Himanshu Jaiswal[1], Deep Suman Dev[2], and Dakshina Ranjan Kisku[1(✉)]

[1] Department of Computer Science and Engineering, National Institute of Technology Durgapur, Durgapur 713209, West Bengal, India
hims.jais@gmail.com, drkisku@cse.nitdgp.ac.in
[2] Department of Information Technology, Neotia Institute of Technology, Management and Science, South 24 Paragana, Kolkata, West Bengal, India
deepsumandev@yahoo.co.in

Abstract. This paper reports a fast pattern matching algorithm which makes use of K-NN (K-nearest neighbor) based rank order reduction approach to detect a pattern or object in a given image efficiently. Initially, the given image is divided into several candidate windows, each of size the input pattern. In the next step, both the input pattern and the candidate windows are characterized by Haar transform. From the characterization, Haar Projection Values (HPV) is determined. Further, rectangle sum on both input pattern and candidate windows is computed using integral image technique. Subsequently, by using sum of absolute difference (SAD) correlation distance between the input pattern and candidate windows is determined. In order to detect the pattern, rank order approach using K-NN is applied to determine the first k number of most similar candidate windows containing the input pattern. To reduce the computational complexity of selecting a perfectly matched window, again sum of absolute differences (SAD) is applied and this leads to select the best match pattern having the total object. Decoupling correlation measures also increase the accuracy of matching pattern. Finally, the input pattern is detected and localized in the given image. The pattern matching accuracy proves the efficacy of the proposed algorithm.

Keywords: Pattern matching · Haar transform · Sum of absolute difference · K-NN approach

1 Introduction

Pattern Matching [1] is a high level machine vision technique which finds a pattern in a given image. The pattern is usually a 2D image lump which is found much smaller in size than the scene image delineated in Fig. 1 where matched face pattern is being detected. This technique has found its application in wide areas like image based rendering [6], image compression [7], object detection [8], super resolution [9], texture synthesis [10], motion estimation [11], image de-noising [12, 13], road tracking [14], mouth tracking [15], image matching [16, 18, 19] and action recognition [17, 20]. The pattern matching approaches [1] may be classified into four groups, such as (a) Feature-dependent approach, (b) Template-dependent approach, (c) Model-dependent approach

© Springer Nature Singapore Pte Ltd. 2017
J.K. Mandal et al. (Eds.): CICBA 2017, Part II, CCIS 776, pp. 307–322, 2017.
DOI: 10.1007/978-981-10-6430-2_24

and (d) Template-dependent convolution approach. In feature-based approach, template image having strong features and based on those features matching is performed. In template-based approach, template may not provide direct match and there could be more than one match. Model-based approach incorporates the shape or structure of the object during the detection process. Template-based convolution uses a convolution mask which contains a specific feature for matching.

Fig. 1. An Example of Pattern Matching Technique where Input Pattern is compared with all the Candidate Windows and later, best match Candidate Window is determined.

Pattern matching requires rigorous computations as the search space is found to be very large. To relieve this burden, full search algorithms are generally divided into non-equivalent and equivalent algorithms [1]. For example, the paper [2] reports pattern matching approach which finds the exact best match in images. Another work [3] proposes fast pattern matching algorithm which makes use of orthogonal Haar transforms and integral image. An object matching algorithm is presented in [8] which makes use of linear programming concept and geometric constraint.

Pattern matching or template matching [1] refers to locating pattern in a given image which is based either on total matching or partial matching. In case of total template matching, a template can be matched with other template as a complete template, whereas in case of partial matching, part of another pattern is matched with the given pattern. In other words, partial pattern matching is explained as transforming one pattern so that a pattern becomes a part of other pattern. However, in case of scaling, this definition generates unwanted results. In terms total pattern matching, partial matching can be defined in several ways.

1.1   Approach

This paper primarily deals with two novel total pattern matching algorithms, namely, rank order reduction – first pattern matching (ROR-FPM) and rank order reduction – covariance of Haar transform and fusion (ROR-CHF) algorithms. This paper proposes an algorithm where Haar transform [3] is used. Haar Transform is applied on the candidate windows whose size is similar to that of given input pattern. After applying Haar transform, Haar Projection Values (HPVs) are obtained and later, integral image [3] is applied for generating cumulative sum values. This is required for calculating the rectangle sum, followed by K-NN [1], which limits the number of windows and contribute to the selection of perfectly matched window using decoupling correlation measure sum of absolute differences (SAD).

1.2 Objectives and Contributions

Main objective of pattern matching is to detect the pattern specified in the pattern image in the large image. Pattern matching problem can be thought as the matching of the feature points representing an object or pattern to an instance of that object given in a scene. It has an extensive application in object tracking and detection, shape matching, image retrieval and industrial automotive machine design. In these applications, a priori information about the target pattern is determined in the form of deformable shape, texture, boundary information, etc. Therefore, the responsibility of pattern matching is to check for the presence of the pattern in the scene with some priori information. Moreover, the features which constitute the target pattern make the correspondence with features determine from a candidate window in a scene by maximizing the similarity function. Main objective is to detect the pattern as far as it is possible. There are some varying constraints which may easily degrade the performance of pattern matching problems. For example, rotation of pattern or background noise may create negative impact on pattern matching. So, these problems need to be taken care of and correct pattern is to be detected. After detection, localization has to be performed for finding the location of pattern, is given in the image. Proposed algorithms take care of both these varying constraints. Key contributions are summarized as follows.

- The pattern matching algorithms proposed in this paper are rotation invariant.
- Second contribution makes use of covariance matrix as well as the fusion of Haar coefficients to escalate the accuracy and pace of the pattern matching algorithm.
- Algorithms are able to detect object independently in presence of background noise.

The paper is structured as follows. Section 2 reports review of existing algorithms. Section 3 presents the proposed algorithms ROR-FPM and ROR-CHF. Experimental evaluations are given in Sect. 4 and the Sect. 5 states concluding remarks.

2 Literatures Review

Pattern matching [5] is one of the popular research areas in machine vision where it is usually executed by skimming the scene image and measuring the deviation between input pattern and each window and then finds an appropriate candidate window as instance of the input pattern. In this section, some existing pattern matching algorithms and approaches are briefly discussed.

Template matching algorithm with full search criteria [23] measures distortion at each pixel position in the image by checking the whole image. This algorithm also measures the matching proximity between a given pattern and the image sub-window. To locate the pattern in the scene image, a maximum-correlation or minimum-distortion need to be examined. A good number of statistical and correlation-based distance measures are available to accomplish pattern matching. As full search algorithm is found considerably slow with many applications, therefore faster algorithms have been developed and later it has replaced the earlier in literature. However, non-exhaustive algorithms take less time by lessening the search space [24] or by decomposing the scene image into rectangular sectors and approximating each sector as a polynomial [25]. Further, when normalized cross correlation (NCC) function is used for pattern matching, a faster exhaustive algorithm can be achieved in the frequency domain by computing correlation [26, 27]. In signal domain, this approach yields computational cost low with respect to full search algorithm in the given conditions. Moreover, in order to skip unmatched image positions based on upper bounding functions, NCC-based pattern matching is made faster by installing adequate ailments and this approach is known as Bounded Partial Correlation (BPC). A novel algorithm [23] is called Enhanced Bounded Correlation (EBC), can be used for exhaustive NCC based pattern matching and it relies on bounding the NCC. The BPC algorithms [21, 22] involve more operative bounding scheme which is based on the deployment of a sequence of progressively tighter upper bounds. EBC approach [23] can skip many unmatched positions in the image without deriving any part of the cross-correlation term. However, BPC algorithms are deployed by entities for which the bounding functions are found to be rigid. Another advantage of this scheme is that to allow a parameter-free EBC implementation, it is necessary to estimate all parameters of the algorithm. The work reported in [3] requires computing the features of the segments for pattern matching. In order to compute Haar Projection Values (HPV), the sum of squares measure is used and in this case, rectangle sum is needed three computations including additions and subtractions. This fast algorithm uses strip sum to compute the sum of pixels in a rectangle in terms of one addition [3]. Strip sum is used for computing Orthogonal Haar Transform thereby reducing the number of computations by two per pixel. Orthogonal Haar Transform requires $O(log\ u)$ additions per pixel when computed on sliding windows, to map input data onto u basis vectors using strip sum.

3   Proposed Algorithms

3.1   Pattern Matching Algorithm – Type 1: ROR-FPM

This work proposes a fast pattern matching algorithm which makes use of K-NN [1] based rank order reduction approach to detect a pattern or object in a given image efficiently. Initially, the given image is divided into several candidate windows, each of size the input pattern. In the next step, both the input pattern and the candidate windows are characterized by Haar transform. From the characterization, Haar projection values (HPV) [3] is determined. Further, rectangle sum on input pattern and candidate windows is computed using integral image technique. Subsequently, sum of absolute difference (SAD) [3] correlation is used to find the distance between the input pattern and sliding candidate windows. In order to detect the pattern, rank order approach using K-NN is applied to determine the first k number of most similar candidate windows containing the input pattern. To reduce the computation complexity of selecting a perfectly matched window, again SAD is applied and this acts increase the accuracy of matching pattern. Finally, the input pattern is detected and localized in the given image.

The main objective is to search for a fragmented pattern in an input image. An image of size $N1 \times N2$ is given and a pattern $N3 \times N4$ is given where $N3$ is much less than $N1$ and $N4$ is much less than $N2$. In order to perform the search operation the input pattern need to be localized in the given image. To accomplish the task, the algorithm is divided into two sections, viz. detection and localization.

For pattern matching, an original input image of size $N_1 \times N_2$ is divided into a set of candidate windows whose size is $N_3 \times N_4$. Candidate window set set_{can} will contain all the sets of candidate windows and these candidate windows starts from top-left of the image i.e. pixel position (1, 1) and each window will be moved horizontally pixel wise. After the completion of first row, it will start from next row i.e. pixel position (2, 1) and this will keep going till the end of the input image. Let, the input pattern be represented by X_t which is also called as template and candidate window be represented by X_w. For example, if original image is of size 64×64 and input pattern is of 16×16, then set_{can} will contain $(64 - 16 + 1)^2$ number of windows. In Fig. 1, an example of candidate window matched with pattern is shown.

Initially each candidate window and input pattern is transformed into Haar Transform [5]. This transformation is done to compute Haar features as Haar Projection Values (HPVs) based on which similarity of pattern with image depends on. This similarity and dissimilarity is governed by the threshold.

3.1.1 Computation of HPV

For two-dimensional image, the Haar wavelet [3] can be defined as a system consists of mutually orthogonal wavelet scaling function $h_0(v, t)$ and the mother wavelet functions $h_1(v, t)$, $h_2(v, t)$ and $h_3(v, t)$. Further, the individual functions can be characterized which are coming next.

$$h_0(v, t) = \begin{cases} 1, & (v, t) \quad in \quad [0, 1)I[0, 1) \\ 0, & otherwise \end{cases} \tag{1}$$

$$h_1(v, t) = \begin{cases} 1, & (v, t) \quad in \quad [0, 1)I[0, 1/2) \\ -1 & (v, t) \quad in \quad [0, 1)I[1/2, 1) \\ 0, & otherwise \end{cases} \tag{2}$$

$$h_2(v, t) = \begin{cases} 1, & (v, t) \quad in \quad [0, 1/2)I[0, 1/2) \\ -1 & (v, t) \quad in \quad [1/2, 1)I[0, 1/2) \\ 0, & otherwise \end{cases} \tag{3}$$

$$h_3(v,t) = \begin{cases} 1, & (v,t) \quad in \quad [0,1/2)I[1/2,1) \\ -1 & (v,t) \quad in \quad [1/2,1)I[1/2,1) \\ 0, & otherwise \end{cases} \tag{4}$$

Similarly, the pth $(p>3)$ wavelet basis function can be explained as

$$h_p(v,t) = h_3(2^k v - i, 2^k t - \frac{2^k - 1 + j}{2})$$
$$for \quad p = (3.2^k + i) \cdot 2^k + j (k \geq 1; \quad i,j = 0,1,2,\dots,2^k - 1), \tag{5}$$

An image with dimension $N = 2^l \times 2^l = 4$ and the analogous four 2D Haar wavelet basis functions can be exhibited as in Fig. 2 and from concatenation of their rows they can also be represented as vectors $B_4^{(0)}, B_4^{(1)}, B_4^{(2)}$ and $B_4^{(3)}$ as follows,

$$B_4^{(0)} = \left(h_0(\frac{0}{2},\frac{0}{2}), h_0(\frac{1}{2},\frac{0}{2}), h_0(\frac{0}{2},\frac{1}{2}), h_0(\frac{1}{2},\frac{1}{2}) \right)^T = (1,1,1,1)^T \tag{6}$$

$$B_4^{(1)} = \left(h_1(\frac{0}{2},\frac{0}{2}), h_1(\frac{1}{2},\frac{0}{2}), h_1(\frac{0}{2},\frac{1}{2}), h_1(\frac{1}{2},\frac{1}{2}) \right)^T = (1,1,-1,-1)^T \tag{7}$$

$$B_4^{(2)} = \left(h_2(\frac{0}{2},\frac{0}{2}), h_2(\frac{1}{2},\frac{0}{2}), h_2(\frac{0}{2},\frac{1}{2}), h_2(\frac{1}{2},\frac{1}{2}) \right)^T = (1,-1,0,0)^T \tag{8}$$

$$B_4^{(3)} = \left(h_3(\frac{0}{2},\frac{0}{2}), h_3(\frac{1}{2},\frac{0}{2}), h_3(\frac{0}{2},\frac{1}{2}), h_3(\frac{1}{2},\frac{1}{2}) \right)^T = (0,0,1,-1)^T \tag{9}$$

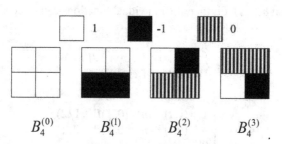

$$B_4^{(0)} \qquad B_4^{(1)} \qquad B_4^{(2)} \qquad B_4^{(3)}$$

Fig. 2. 2×2 Haar basis functions

In Eqs. (6)–(9), T is a vector transposition.

Generally, for an images of size $N = 2^n \times 2^n$, the corresponding 2D Haar wavelet basis function can be referred to as $B_N^{(0)}, B_N^{(1)}, \dots, B_N^{(N-1)}$. These basis vectors are found mutually orthogonal to each other and constructing the following Haar wavelet basis matrix.

$$H_N = B_N^{(0)}, B_N^{(1)}, \dots, B_N^{(N-1)} \tag{10}$$

Let, $z_t^{(p)}$ and $z_{w,j}^{(p)}$ be the pth Haar Projection Values (HPVs) of N – Dimensional pattern vector X_t and candidate window vector X_w^j respectively. Then, HPVs can be formulated as follows.

$$z_t^{(p)} = (B_N^{(p)})^T X_t \qquad (11)$$

$$z_{w,j}^{(p)} = (B_N^{(p)})^T X_w^j \qquad (12)$$

Thus, the HPV vectors of X_t and X_w^j can be represented as

$$Z_t = (z_t^{(0)}, z_t^{(1)}, z_t^{(2)}, \ldots, z_t^{(N-1)})^T = H_N X_t \qquad (13)$$

$$Z_w^j = (z_{w,j}^{(0)}, z_{w,j}^{(1)}, z_{w,j}^{(2)}, \ldots, z_{w,j}^{(N-1)})^T = H_N X_w^j \qquad (14)$$

3.1.2 Rectangle Sum Calculation and Similarity Measurement

Transforming into HPVs [3], both the input pattern and input candidate window is converted into integral image. Integral Image is nothing but the sum of pixels present left to it and above to it corresponding to a particular pixel. Let $g(x, y)$ be the gray scale value at pixel (x, y) of an image. The integral image $I(x, y)$ is nothing but the sum of all gray values present left of (x, y) and above (x, y) and can be represented with the equation:

$$I(x,y) = \sum_{i=0}^{x-1} \sum_{j=0}^{y-1} g(i,j) \qquad (15)$$

where image is size of $x \times y$ pixels, $I(x, y)$, where $0 \le i \le x - 1$ and $0 \le j \le y - 1$.

Let, W and H refer the width and height of an image. The integral image can be determined with $2WH$ additions. From upper left coordinate (x, y) to lower right coordinate $(x + w, y + h)$ of any rectangle area in an image, is shown in the Fig. 3. The rectangle sum can be formulated by using integral image procedure as follows:

$$RS(rect) = I(x + w, y + h) - I(x + w, y) - I(x, y + h) + I(x, y) \qquad (16)$$

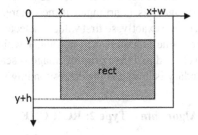

Fig. 3. Formulation of rectangle sum using integral image.

After applying integral image to the candidate window X_w and template X_t, the distance between the candidate window and input window is calculated. This distance determines how much the similarity between the input pattern and candidate window is. To find the similarity between candidate window and the input pattern, correlation based technique sum of absolute differences (SAD) [3] is used. Threshold is determined heuristically, and it is the necessary and sufficient condition to discard the candidate window. Windows which are satisfying the threshold condition are taken as valid windows and others are discarded.

3.1.3   Rank Order Reduction Using K-NN

Rank order statistics selects the *k-th* ranked object in sample of objects space arranged in a particular order. In general, the *k-th* order statistics is either *k-th* smallest or *k-th* largest value depends on how it is being ordered as per requirement. In this work, Rank order statistics is used, where sample is based on Euclidean distance of the two images. After applying the threshold for matching, matching windows are taken into consideration which may contain matched windows, non-matched windows and partially matched windows. Now main objective is to select perfectly matched window. For this, firstly Euclidean distance is calculated between the input pattern and those matching which are taken into consideration. This distance vector is arranged in ascending order and minimum value is assumed to be rank 1 and maximum value is assumed to be last rank. To apply K-nearest neighbor (K-NN), first *k* distances are selected using *L1* norm because matching window and pattern would have minimum distance between them. Here, *k* windows are selected because it is possible that window corresponding to minimum distance may not match perfectly that's why *k* distances and corresponding windows are selected.

3.1.4   Localization

Localization denotes the tracking of object in the original image means drawing the boundary across the pattern being detected. Rank order reduction statistics is applied after applying K-NN to select perfectly matched window. After applying K-NN, *k* Euclidean distance and their corresponding windows are given as a result. Now the task is to select one Euclidean distance and its corresponding window which matches the object completely. For this, sum of absolute differences (SAD) is calculated between *k* windows and input pattern and this is arranged in non-increasing order. SAD gives output 1 when two images match exactly, so first value is selected because it is maximum and in this case maximum value is assumed to be rank 1 which is perfectly matched window. This window is selected and then original image is scanned once again till the selected window and boundary is drawn at the corresponding window.

3.2   Pattern Matching Algorithm – Type 2: ROR-CHF

In addition to the first algorithm this paper proposes another pattern matching algorithm dealing with total pattern matching problem which makes use of Haar transform [3], HPVs [3] and Integral Image [3]. However, it decouples Haar coefficients values by computing directional Haar projection components determined from vertical, horizontal and diagonal directions along with an approximation matrix. All these directional components are determined after computing Integral Image and HPVs. Further, the proposed algorithm finds the covariance matrices of all four components and fuse them together. Finally, it is then followed by K-NN which gives ranking to the matched windows and also limits the number of windows which is helpful in reducing the number of computation and it helps to find the best matched window.

After computation of HPVs, further two-dimensional discrete wavelet transform (2D DWT) [1] is used to achieve the single level two-dimensional wavelet decomposition and it decomposes each HPVs matrix into four components, viz. horizontal (CH), vertical (CV), diagonal (CD) and approximation (CA) components. Approximation component is known as approximation coefficients of HPVs and others are generally known as detail coefficients of HPVs. In case of 2D DWT, first 1D filter bank is applied to the columns of the HPV matrix and then it is applied to the rows of the HPVs. Let us consider, each HPV matrix has M numbers of rows and N number of columns. Then after applying 1D filter bank to the each column, two subband images would be created, each having $M/2$ rows and N columns. Again, after applying 1D filter bank to each row of both the two subband images, four subband images would be created, each subband having $M/2$ number of rows and $N/2$ number of columns. This is illustrated in Fig. 4.

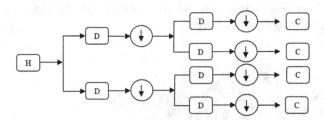

Fig. 4. 2D DWT decomposition of HPVs.

In covariance matrix, an element at the position (i, j) refers the covariance between the ith and j^{th} elements of a random vector and the random vector can be defined in multiple dimensions. Each element in a vector is a scalar quantity where each element has either a finite value or a finite or infinite number of values. The values are quantified by a joint probability distribution function. In this step, covariance matrices of all four directional and approximation matrices are computed and later, they are fused together by using 'minimum' fusion technique. This fusion rule makes use of minimum component value of the corresponding points from both the covariance matrices and it results the fused feature vector. The 'minimum' fusion rule is described as follows.

$$F(i,j) = \sum_{i=1}^{M} \sum_{j=1}^{N} \min\{A(i,j), B(i,j)\} \tag{17}$$

where A and B are any two covariance matrices obtained from decoupled HPVs in the form of three directional components and one approximation component.

Now, we apply threshold so that mismatched windows can be eliminated and only matched windows are taken into consideration. We follow the same approach for measuring the similarity which is discussed in Sect. 3.1.2. Then K-NN is applied to limit the number of windows so that appropriate k number of windows can be selected for further computation as it is explained in detail in Sect. 3.1.3. Finally, localization is done. It refers to give the perfect location of the object, if present in the given original image which means drawing boundary or changing the contrast, etc. So that object tracked should be highlighted, which makes easy for the user to know whether object is present or not in the given image. It is already discussed in Sect. 3.1.4.

4   Evaluation

The experiment is conducted on a publicly available dataset COIL-100 (Columbia Object Image Library) [4] containing 7200 color images of 100 objects. To capture the objects photographs, a motorized turntable is used and objects are kept on the table against a black background. In order to vary the objects pose, the turntable is rotated through 360° with respect to camera position. Then objects are photographed at posture intervals of 5°. The dataset containing the images each of size 256 × 256 and the pattern is given of size 64 × 64. The Fig. 5 shows a sample image and an input pattern. The input pattern is present in the image and the proposed algorithm detects and localizes the pattern in the image shown in Fig. 5.

(a) Input Image   (b) Input Pattern

Fig. 5. An input image and an input pattern are shown from COIL-100 database.

After applying Haar transform and integral image and rank order based K-NN, four candidate windows from Fig. 6(a) through Fig. 6(d) are obtained from Fig. 5(a) and two of them contain partial pattern and rest of two contain complete pattern. To select the perfectly matched window again SAD is applied and finally, the candidate window shown in Fig. 8(e) is selected. This window contains the complete pattern. Thereafter, Localization [7] is performed and boundary is drawn over the detected input pattern shown in Fig. 6(f). One of the data sets used for this pattern matching consists of 8 patterns which are given as input and the input patterns are figured in Fig. 7.

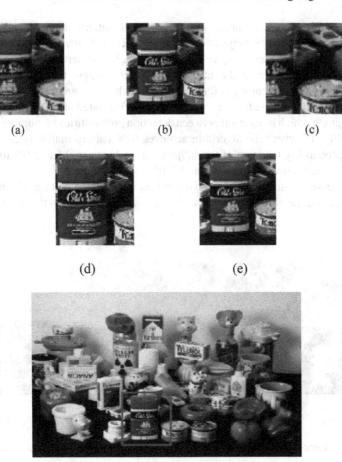

(a)   (b)   (c)

(d)   (e)

(f) Localization of input pattern

Fig. 6. Output for the given input image and input patten.

Fig. 7. One of the input pattern in different angle from dataset is shown.

For determining the accuracy of the proposed pattern matching algorithm, 20 subjects are taken and each subject contains 8 instances which are rotated to some angle with respect to as it is present in the original image. It is observed while testing that if the pattern object is twirled in the interval between 80° to 280° then the accuracy of the algorithm decreases. Accuracy is found minimum when it is around 180°. So the work can be extended to increase the accuracy if the object is rotated in the mentioned interval. Accuracy graph which is trade-off between detection probabilities vs. number of subjects shown in Fig. 10 where the algorithm achieves 64% pattern matching accuracy. The detection probability for most of the subjects varies between 0.5 and 0.9 for the input pattern which is rotated between 80° and 280°.

The proposed Algorithm (ROR-CHF) makes use of input pattern which is present in the image and the algorithm detects and localized the pattern in the image shown in Fig. 8.

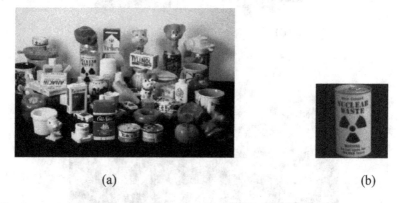

(a)   (b)

Fig. 8. Example of an image and an input pattern from COIL-100 database are shown.

After applying fusion and rank order based K-NN, six candidate windows are obtained by applying proposed Algorithm ROR–CHF, based on the value of k, which is taken as six, from Fig. 9(a) through Fig. 9(f) are obtained from Fig. 8(a) in which some contains partial object, some contains full object and it could be possible that some may not contain the object to be traced. Further, a window is selected having complete object which has to be traced, i.e., perfectly matched window. To select the completely matched window, SAD is applied again and finally window containing the complete object is taken as shown in Fig. 9(g). Thereafter, localization is performed means drawing boundary over the selected input pattern as shown in the Fig. 9(h). One of the data sets used for this pattern matching consists of 8 patterns which are given as input and input patterns are displayed in Fig. 10.

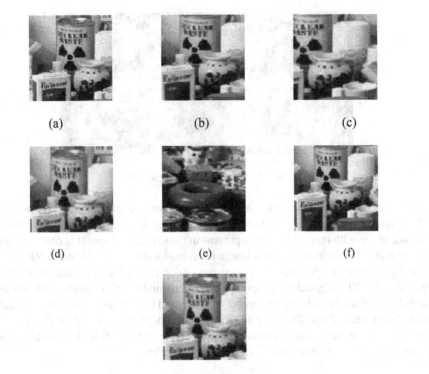

(a)   (b)   (c)

(d)   (e)   (f)

(g) Perfectly matched candidate window

(h) Localization of input pattern.

Fig. 9. First six detected candidate windows are shown from 9(a) through 9(f), 9(g) shows perfectly matched window and 9(h) shows localization of input pattern.

Fig. 10. Dataset of 8 input patterns.

For determining the accuracy of the proposed pattern matching algorithm (ROR-CHF), again 20 subjects are taken and each subject contains 8 instances which are rotated to some angle with respect to as it is present in the original image. It is observed while testing that if the object in pattern image is pivoted with interval between 80° to 280° then the accuracy of the algorithm decreases. Accuracy is found minimum when it is around 180°. The algorithm achieves 70% pattern matching accuracy. The detection probability of all the subjects varies between 0.5 and 0.9 for the input pattern which is rotated between 80° and 280° and no other subjects degrade pattern detection performance by varying detection probability below 0.5. Henceforth, this algorithm proves to be an efficient one in compared to ROR-FPM algorithm.

5   Conclusion

In this paper, two efficient and fast pattern matching algorithms have presented. To accomplish this task, Haar transform and image integral technique has been used. Haar transform is used for feature representation of both candidate windows and the input pattern. Image integral is then used to compute the rectangle sum of input pattern and candidate windows. To find the similarity between candidate windows and the input pattern, correlation based SAD metric is applied. To discard the large number of mismatch windows rank order based K-NN is used and reduced the candidate windows to k number of windows containing either most of the parts of the pattern or the complete pattern. In order to obtain the perfectly matched window, again SAD is applied and k is reduced to one window which contains the complete pattern. In the second algorithm, in addition to Haar transform, HPVs and Integral Image, decompositions of HPVs are used and further they are fused together. Later, K-NN and SAD are used for detecting the most relevant contestant window within the scene image and thus pattern matching is performed.

As object in original image could be present in frontal view but the input pattern could be given in rotated position, therefore it would be difficult to detect the objects that are given in rotated positions more than 30° and the number of mismatch windows would increase. So, the reducing the number of mismatch windows will also be done as a future work.

References

1. Brunelli, R.: Template Matching Techniques in Computer Vision: Theory and Practice, p. 348. Wiley, New York (2009)
2. Alkhansari, M.G.: A fast globally optimal algorithm for template matching using low-resolution pruning. IEEE Trans. Image Process. **10**(4), 526–533 (2001)
3. Ouyang, W., Zhang, R., Cham, W.K.: Fast pattern matching using orthogonal Haar transform. In: IEEE Conference on Computer Vision and Pattern Recognition (2010)
4. http://www.cs.columbia.edu/CAVE/databases/
5. Iain, E.G.R.: H.264 and MPEG-4 Video Compression: Video Coding for Next-generation Multimedia. Wiley, Chichester (2003)
6. Hart, P.E.: The condensed nearest neighbor rule. IEEE Trans. Inf. Theory **18**, 515–516 (1968)
7. Shapiro, L.G., Stockman, G.C.: Computer Vision. Prentice Hall, Englewood Cliffs (2001)
8. Li, H., Kim, E., Huang, X., He, L.: Object matching with a locally affine-invariant constraint. In: International Conference on Computer Vision and Pattern Recognition, pp. 1641–1648 (2010)
9. Fitzgibbon, A., Wexler, Y., Zisserman, A.: Image-based rendering using image-based priors. Int. J. Comput. Vision **63**(2), 141–151 (2005)
10. Luczak, T., Szpankowski, W.: A suboptimal lossy data compression based on approximate pattern matching. IEEE Trans. Inform. Theory **43**(5), 1439–1451 (1997)
11. Dufour, R.M., Miller, E.L., Galatsanos, N.P.: Template matching based object recognition with unknown geometric parameters. IEEE Trans. Image Process. **11**(12), 1385–1396 (2002)
12. Freeman, W.T., Jones, T.R., Pasztor, E.C.: Example-based super-resolution. IEEE Comput. Graph. Appl. **22**(2), 56–65 (2002)
13. Efros, A.A., Leung, T.K.: Texture synthesis by non-parametric sampling, in Computer Vision. In: IEEE International Conference on The Proceedings of the Seventh, vol. 2, pp. 1033–1038. IEEE (1999)
14. Mak, C.-M., Fong, C.-K., Cham, W.-K.: Fast motion estimation for H.264/AVC in Walsh-Hadamard domain. IEEE Trans. Circ. Syst. Video Technol. **18**(6), 735–745 (2008)
15. Buades, A., Coll, B., Morel, J.-M.: A non-local algorithm for image denoising. In: IEEE Computer Society Conference on Computer Vision and Pattern Recognition, CVPR 2005, vol. 2, pp. 60–65. IEEE (2005)
16. Dabov, K., Foi, A., Katkovnik, V., Egiazarian, K.: Image denoising by sparse 3-D transform domain collaborative altering. IEEE Trans. Image Process. **16**(8), 2080–2095 (2007)
17. Alon, Y., Ferencz, A., Shashua, A.: Off-road path following using region classification and geometric projection constraints. In: IEEE Computer Society Conference on Computer Vision and Pattern Recognition, vol. 1, pp. 689–696. IEEE (2006)
18. Shin, Y., Ju, J.S., Kim, E.Y.: Welfare interface implementation using multiple facial features tracking for the disabled people. Pattern Recogn. Lett. **29**(13), 1784–1796 (2008)
19. Wang, Q., You, S.: Real-time image matching based on multiple view kernel projection. In: IEEE Conference on Computer Vision and Pattern Recognition, CVPR 2007, pp. 1–8. IEEE (2007)
20. Wu, X.: Template-based action recognition: classifying hockey players' movement. PhD thesis, The University of British Columbia (2005)
21. Di Stefano, L., Mattoccia, S.: A sufficient condition based on the Cauchy-Schwarz inequality for efficient template matching. In: Proceedings, 2003 International Conference on Image Processing, ICIP 2003, vol. 1. IEEE (2003)
22. Di Stefano, L., Mattoccia, S.: Fast template matching using bounded partial correlation. Mach. Vis. Appl. **13**(4), 213–221 (2003)

23. Mattoccia, S., Tombari, F., Stefano, L.D.: Fast full-search equivalent template matching by enhanced bounded correlation. IEEE Trans. Image Process. **17**(4), 528–538 (2008)

24. Goshtasby, A.A.: 2-D and 3-D Image Registration: for Medical, Remote Sensing, and Industrial Applications. Wiley, New York (2005)

25. Briechle, K., Hanebeck, U.D.: Template matching using fast normalized cross correlation. In: Aerospace, Defense Sensing, Simulation, and Controls, pp. 95–102. International Society for Optics and Photonics (2001)

26. Lewis, J.P.: Fast template matching. Vision Interface **95**, 15–19 (1995)

27. Kadyrov, A., Petrou, M.: The invaders' algorithm: range of values modulation for accelerated correlation. IEEE Trans. Pattern Anal. Mach. Intell. **28**(11), 1882–1886 (2006)

3D MRI Brain Image Segmentation:
A Two-Stage Framework

Sayan Kahali[1], Sudip Kumar Adhikari[2], and Jamuna Kanta Sing[1(✉)]

[1] Department of Computer Science and Engineering,
Jadavpur University, Kolkata, India
`sayankahaliiway@gmail.com, jksing@ieee.org`
[2] Department of Computer Science and Engineering,
Cooch Behar Government Engineering College, Cooch Behar, India
`sudipadhikari@ieee.org`

Abstract. Image Segmentation is a process of delineating an image into some meaningful regions. It has the significant impact on the computer guided medical image diagnosis and research. The Magnetic Resonance Imaging (MRI) brain data are severely affected by the noise and inhomogeneity artifacts which lead to blurry edges in the intersection of the intra-organ soft tissue regions. This paper presents a novel two stage framework for segmenting the 3D brain MR image data. The first stage consists of modified fuzzy c-means algorithm (MoFCM) which incorporates the spatial neighborhood information of the volume data to define the new local membership function along with the traditional fuzzy c-means (FCM) membership function. The cluster prototypes obtained from the first stage are fed into the modified spatial fuzzy c-means (MSFCM) algorithm which includes 3D spatial information of the 3D brain MR image volume to generate the final prototypes. Our main endeavor is to address the shortcomings of the traditional FCM which is highly sensitive to noise as it solely depends on the intensity values of the image and develop a new method which performs well in noisy environment. The method is validated on several simulated and *in-vivo* 3D brain MR image volumes. The empirical results show the supremacy of our method than the other FCM based algorithms devised in the past.

Keywords: Fuzzy C-means · 3D image clustering · 3D spatial information · 3D image segmentation

1 Introduction

Segmentation is an essential preprocessing step in computer guided medical image research and diagnosis [1]. This helps doctors to extract soft tissue regions from the respective organs of the human body for surgical decisions, abnormality detection and therapy management. The brain MR images are severely affected by the noise and

© Springer Nature Singapore Pte Ltd. 2017
J.K. Mandal et al. (Eds.): CICBA 2017, Part II, CCIS 776, pp. 323–335, 2017.
DOI: 10.1007/978-981-10-6430-2_25

intensity inhomogeneity artifacts due to radio frequency coil non-uniformity, patient movement etc. This makes the segmentation process more challenging as the boundaries are foggy in nature. It may be noted that the manual segmentation is very difficult to achieve as it is error prone. In this case, successful segmentation mainly depends on the expertise of the physician. In past few decades, several investigators have presented different image segmentation techniques [2–5]. Several segmentation methods are presented in the literature based on edge-, region- and classification.

Among the different segmentation techniques devised in the past, the fuzzy c-means has proved its efficacy. FCM is unsupervised clustering algorithm which calculates membership values for each voxel against each class. So, unlike hard clustering techniques one voxel can be a part of multiple clusters with different membership values. The main disadvantage of the FCM is that it is sensitive to the noise and inhomogeneity which leads to erroneous segmentation results and undesired visual quality in case of brain MR image data. Moreover, the cluster prototypes are trapped to the local minimum and thereby produce lower convergence rate.

Bezdek [6] incorporated the fuzzy criterion to the hard clustering and proposed the FCM algorithm. Some investigators claim that the FCM algorithm can efficiently perform clustering but fails to give high convergence as hard clustering algorithm. Wei et al. [7] developed rival checked fuzzy c-means (RCFCM) technique to eliminate the slow convergence problem. Later, the limitations of RCFCM are addressed and eliminated by a new suppressed FCM clustering algorithm (SFCM) [8]. Chuang et al. [9] introduced a new variant of FCM clustering algorithm by incorporating the spatial information of the image into the membership function. To overcome the problems of traditional FCM algorithm many scientists modified the objective function by considering different criteria and presented more efficient and robust clustering algorithm [10–12].

Pedrycz [13] devised a FCM algorithm based on auxiliary variable also known as conditional variable. The structure with in the pattern family is exposed by considering the neighborhood information in the feature space along with the similarity values obtained by the use of conditional variable. Mohamed et al. proposed automatic modified fuzzy c-means clustering technique inspired from the Markov Random Field (MRF). It incorporates the spatial information for computing the similarity measure [14]. Ahmed et al. presented a fuzzy segmentation technique which allows the labeling of pixel (voxel) subjective to the labels in its immediate neighborhood. It can also be used to estimate the intensity inhomogeneity from the brain MR image [15].

Qiu et al. [16] developed a modified interval type-2 fuzzy c-means algorithm. This algorithm uses two fuzzifiers in interval type-2 FCM and a spatial criterion in the membership function. Recently, Sanchez et al. [17] effectively compared the new Fuzzy Granular Gravitational Clustering Algorithm (FGGCA) with other existing FCM techniques.

Most of the methods discussed so far faced difficulty in segmenting the image with high noise density and intensity inhomogeneity. Intensity inhomogeneity is nothing but an artifact that is mainly caused by improper image acquisition process, patient movement or imperfection in magnet manufacturing.

In this paper, we propose a new two-stage framework for segmenting the 3D brain MR image volumes which can efficiently be performed in the presence of high noise and inhomogeneity density. This algorithm comprises of two stages, namely (i) MoFCM and (ii) MSFCM. The MoFCM uses the spatial information to calculate the local membership grades and it is integrated with the global membership function *i.e.* membership defined in traditional FCM to calculate the cluster centers. The cluster prototypes are obtained by this algorithm and taken as the initial cluster center as input in the MSFCM algorithm. The final cluster prototypes are estimated by this algorithm. In order to calculate this, we have incorporated the spatial neighborhood information of the 3D image.

The remainder of this paper is structured as follows. In Sect. 2 we have described each stage of the proposed two-stage framework for 3D brain MR image clustering. The results are discussed in Sect. 3. Finally, the concluding remarks are elucidated in Sect. 4.

2   Proposed Algorithm

In this study, the segmentation process is characterized by the classification of the voxel intensities into some meaningful non-overlapping homogeneous regions. In case of brain MR image the neighboring voxels are highly correlative in nature. However, this is more significant at the edges of soft tissue regions as the boundary regions are not prominent. The degree of belongingness of the neighboring voxels to the same cluster is high as the neighboring voxels share similar characteristics. The proposed algorithm consists of two stages to compute the final prototypes and final partition matrix. The two stage architecture of the entire segmentation algorithm is illustrated in Fig. 1.

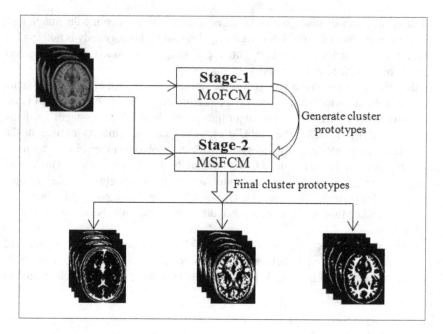

Fig. 1. The complete work-flow of the proposed two-stage 3D image segmentation framework.

The description of Stage-1 and Stage-2 of the 3D brain MR image segmentation algorithm is elucidated below:

2.1 Stage 1: Modified Fuzzy C-means Algorithm (MoFCM)

We have modified the objective function of the FCM algorithm where a local spatial membership grade (u_{ixyz}) is incorporated along with the traditional membership grade or global membership (μ_{ixyz}). In the objective function, we have introduced a probability criterion ξ_{ixyz} to incorporate the local spatial information of the region $(3 \times 3 \times 3)$. It defines the probability of the belongingness to the ith cluster of the neighboring voxels of voxel centering (x,y,z). ξ_{ixyz} can be defined as follows:

$$\xi_{ixyz} = \frac{\sum_{i=1}^{C} \sum_{j \in N_{xyz}} \mu_{ij} I_{ij}}{\sum_{i=1}^{c} \sum_{j \in N_{xyz}} I_{ij}} \tag{1}$$

where N_{xyz} is the number of voxels in the 3D neighborhood of the voxel centering (x,y,z). In this study we have used neighborhood size of $3 \times 3 \times 3$ as it results superior to the other window size. In this research work, we have included this probability distribution in the local spatial membership function to calculate new membership values which have the influence of local information of the volume data. In this regard, if the characteristics of the neighboring voxels are similar, the probability of belongingness to the same cluster of the centering voxel is high. As mentioned earlier, we have introduced a new membership (u_{ixyz}) which incorporates this spatial probability criterion (ξ_{ixyz}) to exploit the local information of the 3D MRI image.

The modified objective function can be expressed as follows:

$$J_{MoFCM} = \sum_{i=1}^{C}\sum_{z=1}^{P}\sum_{x=1}^{M}\sum_{y=1}^{N} \mu_{ixyz}^{m}\|I_{xyz} - v_i\|^2$$

$$+ \alpha \sum_{i=1}^{C}\sum_{z=1}^{P}\sum_{x=1}^{M}\sum_{y=1}^{N} \xi_{ixyz}u_{ixyz}^{m}\|\bar{I}_{xyz} - v_i\|^2 \tag{2}$$

where $\{v_i\}_{i=1}^{c}$ represents the cluster prototypes; $U_1 = [\mu_{ixyz}]$ and $U_2 = [u_{ixyz}]$ denotes the global and local partition matrix, respectively each satisfying $U_1, U_2 \in [0 \quad 1]$ and $0 < \sum_{l=1}^{P}\sum_{j=1}^{M}\sum_{k=1}^{N} \mu_{ixyz}, \sum_{l=1}^{P}\sum_{j=1}^{M}\sum_{k=1}^{N} u_{ixyz} < 1$; $\|\cdot\|$ is the norm and m is the degree of fuzziness, generally $m > 1$, $\bar{I}_{xyz}$ represents the mean intensity value of the neighborhood of the voxel (x,y,z), α provides the influence of the neighboring voxels in the objective function J_{MoFCM}. However, the objective function mutates to the original FCM algorithm when $\alpha = 0$. u_{ixyz} values are large at $\alpha > 0$ when the membership values of the neighboring voxels which belongs to the other clusters are small. In this work, we have obtained superior results at $\alpha = 0.1$.

The partition matrix (μ_{ixyz}) used as it appears in the traditional FCM algorithm. The equations for μ_{ixyz} and u_{ixyz} can be stated as follows:

$$\mu_{ixyz} = \frac{1}{\sum_{c=1}^{C} \frac{\|I_{xyz}-v_i\|^{\frac{2}{m-1}}}{\|I_{xyz}-v_c\|^{\frac{2}{m-1}}}} \tag{3}$$

$$u_{ixyz} = \frac{1}{\sum_{c=1}^{C} \left(\frac{\xi_{ixyz}\|\bar{I}_{xyz}-v_i\|}{\xi_{cxyz}\|\bar{I}_{xyz}-v_c\|}\right)^{\frac{2}{(m-1)}}} \tag{4}$$

Subject to the constraints mentioned below:

$$\sum_{i=1}^{C} \mu_{ixyz} = 1, \sum_{i=1}^{C} u_{ixyz} = 1 \text{ and } \xi_{ixyz} > 0$$

The MoFCM algorithm is epitomized as below:

Algorithm 1: MoFCM

Input: Image X $(x_1, x_2, \ldots, x_N)$ with N voxels, number of clusters (C), degree of fuzziness (m).
Output: cluster centers

    Step 1. Randomly initialize the cluster centers (v_i).
    Step 2. $l = 0$
    ***Step 3.* Repeat**
        i. $l = l + 1$
      ii. **Calculate** the membership matrix $U_1^{(l)}$ using the cluster centers $v_i^{(l-1)}$.

$$\mu_{ixyz} = \frac{1}{\sum_{c=1}^{C} \frac{\left\| I_{xyz} - v_i \right\|^{\frac{2}{m-1}}}{\left\| I_{xyz} - v_c \right\|^{\frac{2}{m-1}}}}$$

      iii. **Calculate** $U_2^{(l)}$ using the cluster centers $v_i^{(l-1)}$.

$$u_{ixyz} = \frac{1}{\sum_{c=1}^{C} \left(\frac{\xi_{ixyz} \left\| \bar{I}_{xyz} - v_i \right\|}{\xi_{cxyz} \left\| \bar{I}_{xyz} - v_c \right\|} \right)^{\frac{2}{(m-1)}}}$$

    where,

$$\xi_{ixyz} = \frac{\sum_{i=1}^{C} \sum_{j \in N_{xyz}} \mu_{ij} I_{ij}}{\sum_{i=1}^{C} \sum_{j \in N_{xyz}} I_{ij}}$$

      iv. **Update** the centers $v_i^{(l)}$ using $U_1^{(l)}$ and $U_2^{(l)}$ as,

$$v_i = \frac{\sum_{z=1}^{P} \sum_{x=1}^{M} \sum_{y=1}^{N} (\mu_{ixyz}^m I_{xyz} + \alpha \, \xi_{ixyz} \, u_{ixyz}^m \, \bar{I}_{xyz})}{\sum_{z=1}^{P} \sum_{x=1}^{M} \sum_{y=1}^{N} (\mu_{ixyz}^m + \alpha \, \xi_{ixyz} \, u_{ixyz}^m)}$$

***Step 4.* Until** $\left\| v_i^{(l)} - v_i^{(l-1)} \right\| < \varepsilon$
***Step 5.* Return** the cluster centers v_i; $i = 1, 2, \ldots, C$.

The cluster centers retuned by this algorithm are given as the input with the 3D image matrix in *Stage 2* to calculate the final cluster centers.

2.2 Stage 2: Modified Spatial C-means Algorithm (MSFCM)

The cluster prototypes calculated in MoFCM are influenced by the local spatial information of the 3D brain MR image data and newly introduced probability distribution discussed in Sect. 2. A. In this stage, these values are used to define the trivial cluster centers for this algorithm. It may be noted that the performance of the fuzzy c-means algorithm is predominantly governed by the initial cluster values. The pursuit of finding the good cluster centers motivates us to design MoFCM. It enables the proposed MSFCM algorithm to converge faster. The traditional FCM algorithm in case of high dimensional data sometimes converges to the local minimum. This may lead to different cluster prototype values for different initialization. Hence, the cluster centers obtained from the MoFCM also helps us to avoid the selection of cluster centers to its local minima. We again iteratively refined the cluster centers with this algorithm to obtain the final prototypes. The objective function of MSFCM can be expressed as follows:

$$J_{MSFCM} = \sum_{i=1}^{C} \sum_{z=1}^{P} \sum_{x=1}^{M} \sum_{y=1}^{N} z_{ixyz}^{m} \left\| \bar{I}_{xyz} - w_i \right\|^2 \tag{5}$$

The MSFCM algorithm is summarized as follows:

Algorithm 2: MSFCM

Input: Image X $(x_1, x_2, \ldots, x_N)$ with N voxels, number of clusters (C), degree of fuzziness (m).

Output: Final cluster centers, segmented tissue volumes and 3D image after segmentation.

Step 1. initialize the cluster centers (w_i) with the prototypes obtained from *Algorithm 1.*

Step 2. $l = 0$

Step 3. **Repeat**

    i. $l = l + 1$

    ii. **Calculate** the membership matrix $V^{(l)}$ using the cluster centers $w_i^{(l-1)}$.

$$z_{ixyz} = \cfrac{1}{\cfrac{\left\| \bar{I}_{xyz} - w_i \right\|^{\frac{2}{m-1}}}{\sum_{c=1}^{C} \left\| \bar{I}_{xyz} - w_c \right\|^{\frac{2}{m-1}}}}$$

    iii. **Update** the centers $w_i^{(l)}$ using $V^{(l)}$ as,

$$w_i = \frac{\sum_{i=1}^{C} \sum_{z=1}^{P} \sum_{x=1}^{M} \sum_{y=1}^{N} z_{ixyz}^{m} \bar{I}_{xyz}}{\sum_{i=1}^{C} \sum_{z=1}^{P} \sum_{x=1}^{M} \sum_{y=1}^{N} z_{ixyz}^{m}}$$

Step 4. **Until** $\left\| w_i^{(l)} - w_i^{(l-1)} \right\| < \varepsilon$

Step 5. **Return** the final cluster centers $w_i;\ i = 1, 2, \ldots, C$.

---

3 Results and Discussion

The performance of the proposed technique is evaluated on the Brainweb simulated 3D brain MR image volumes and in-vivo human brain image volume. The simulated brain MR image volumes are provided by the McConnell Brain Imaging Center of the Montreal Neurological Institute, McGill University [18]. We have tested the performance on T1-weighted volumes with different combinations of noise and inhomogeneity such as, 7% noise 20% inhomogeneity, 7% noise 40% inhomogeneity, 9% noise 20% inhomogeneity and 9% noise 40% inhomogeneity. The resolution of each MRI volume considered in this study is $181 \times 217 \times 181$ with voxel spacing $1 \times 1 \times 1$ mm^3.

The real images are acquired at the EKO X-RAY & IMAGING INSTITUTE, Kolkata, India with the 1.5-Tesla MRI machine. The resolution of real patient image volume is $181 \times 181 \times 25$.

We have investigated the performance of the proposed method in terms of qualitative and quantitative evaluation in both for simulated and real patient images. The quantitative investigation involves calculation of tissue segmentation accuracy and different cluster validity functions (V_{pc}, V_{pe} and similarity index).

3.1 Qualitative Evaluation

In this section, we have shown qualitative outputs of our algorithm. It involves cross-sectional view of original 3D brain MR image volume, corresponding segmented soft tissue volumes such as Cerebrospinal fluid (CSF), Gray matter (GM) and White matter (WM) produced from our algorithm. Furthermore, we have also included the segmented image volume. Figure 2 illustrates the qualitative outputs of proposed algorithm. Figure 2(a) represents the cross-sectional view of original T1 weighted brain MR image volume. Figures 2(b)-(d) show the soft tissue regions i.e. CSF, GM and WM of 3D brain MR image volume. In this case also we have presented the cross-sectional view of the entire tissue volumes. Figure 2(e) illustrates the cross-sectional view of the total segmented 3D MR image volume.

3.2 Quantitative Evaluation

To validate our claim we also have compared the performance of our method with the FCM and sFCM [9] method in terms of tissue segmentation accuracy. Furthermore, we also have calculated cluster validity function for comparing our method with the aforementioned methods. The cluster validity functions include partition coefficient (Vpc), partition entropy (Vpe) and similarity index. The functions are described as follows:

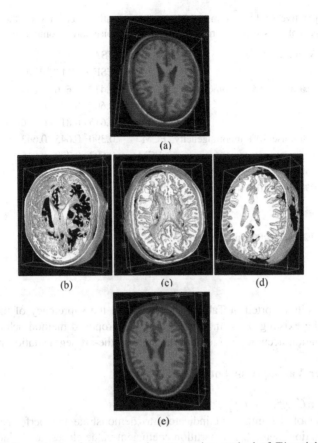

Fig. 2. Qualitative outputs of the proposed segmentation method of T1-weighted brain MR image volume. (a): Original brain MR image volume; (b-d): Segmented soft tissue regions *i.e.* CSF, GM and WM; (e) Segmented image volume.

3.2.1 Tissue Segmentation Accuracy

To assess the performance of the proposed segmentation algorithm we have calculated the tissue segmentation accuracy of each volume [18]. This can be defined as follows:

$$TSA = \frac{2N_{CTK}}{N_{CITK} + N_{GTK}} \tag{6}$$

where N_{CTK} represents the voxels which are correctly classified to tissue K which is inside the ground truth mask by the proposed method, N_{CITK} describes the total number of voxels of tissue K which includes inside and outside of the ground truth mask, N_{GTK} represents total number of voxels of tissue K in the discrete anatomical model.

Table 1 illustrates the performance of the proposed method in terms of tissue segmentation accuracy for each soft tissue regions. In this regard, we have calculated the same by considering the discrete anatomical model or ground truth volume. Furthermore, we have compared our experimental outcome with the existing similar

Table 1. Comparative study in terms of Tissue Segmentation Accuracy on the T1-weighted MRI brain image volumes with different combination of noise and inhomogeneity

Volume	Method	TSA		
		CSF	GM	WM
7% noise 20% inhomogeneity	FCM	0.417	0.660	0.694
	sFCM	0.602	0.795	0.822
	Proposed	0.615	0.819	0.856
7% noise 40% inhomogeneity	FCM	0.390	0.645	0.693
	sFCM	0.592	0.778	0.815
	Proposed	0.605	0.811	0.848
9% noise 20% inhomogeneity	FCM	0.377	0.621	0.666
	sFCM	0.558	0.762	0.808
	Proposed	0.591	0.807	0.842
9% noise 40% inhomogeneity	FCM	0.361	0.610	0.671
	sFCM	0.552	0.751	0.792
	Proposed	0.588	0.796	0.832

works. The results reported in Table 1 clearly stated the supremacy of the proposed method than the existing ones. In all the cases the proposed method achieves higher tissue segmentation accuracy value than the state-of-the-art segmentation methods.

3.2.2   Cluster Validity Function

(i)   *Partition Coefficient (V_{pc})*

It is one of the important indicators to demonstrate the performance of the segmentation method. The partition coefficient value closest to '1' indicates best clustering result. This can be eressed as follows [6, 9, 16]:

$$V_{pc} = \frac{\sum_{i=1}^{C} \sum_{z=1}^{P} \sum_{x=1}^{M} \sum_{y=1}^{N} z_{ixyz}^2}{M \times N \times P} \tag{7}$$

(ii)   *Partition Entropy (V_{pe})*

The partition entropy value nearer to '0' indicates superior segmentation result. The equation is stated below [6, 9, 16]:

$$V_{pe} = \frac{-\sum_{i=1}^{C} \sum_{z=1}^{P} \sum_{x=1}^{M} \sum_{y=1}^{N} \left[z_{ixyz} \log \left(z_{ixyz} \right) \right]}{M \times N \times P} \tag{8}$$

(iii) *Similarity Index (ρ)*

The equation for the similarity index can be stated as follows [16]:

$$\rho = \frac{1}{C} \sum_{i=1}^{C} \frac{2|S_i \cap G_i|}{|S_i| + |G_i|} \times 100\% \tag{9}$$

where S_i and G_i denotes the voxels of ith cluster in the segmented image and the ground truth, respectively. The range of ρ is in between 0 and 100. The value closer to 100 indicates optimal clustering.

Table 2 shows the comparison between the proposed method over existing methods in terms of cluster validity functions such as V_{pc}, V_{pe} and ρ. The results reported in the Table 2 illustrates that in all four cases the proposed method outperforms the other methods as it produces maximum V_{pc}, minimum V_{pe}. Moreover, the similarity index value depicts the superiority of the proposed segmentation algorithm.

Table 2. Comparative study in terms of Cluster Validity Functions on the T1-weighted MRI brain image volumes with different combination of noise and inhomogeneity.

Volume	Method	V_{pc}	V_{pe}	ρ (%)
7% noise 20% inhomogeneity	FCM	0.782	0.321	67.27
	sFCM	0.915	0.155	76.72
	Proposed	0.951	0.046	78.66
7% noise 40% inhomogeneity	FCM	0.786	0.294	66.10
	sFCM	0.908	0.148	75.68
	Proposed	0.946	0.049	77.61
9% noise 20% inhomogeneity	FCM	0.795	0.328	64.21
	sFCM	0.892	0.175	74.29
	Proposed	0.942	0.052	76.42
9% noise 40% inhomogeneity	FCM	0.793	0.327	63.61
	sFCM	0.890	0.171	73.57
	Proposed	0.940	0.054	75.33

The quantitative investigation of *in-vivo* 3D brain MR image data involves the estimation of partition coefficient and partition entropy. In this context, the ground truth or discrete anatomical model of the aforementioned volume is absent. So, we are not able to calculate the other parameters such as, tissue segmentation accuracy and similarity index for the same.

Table 3 shows the empirical results in terms of partition coefficient and partition entropy. We have compared the result obtained from the proposed method with FCM and sFCM method to evaluate the supremacy of our method. The result reported in Table 3 demonstrates that the proposed method effectively segments the volume than other competent methods.

Table 3. Comparative study in terms of different validity functions on the in-vivo human MRI brain image volumes

Volume	Method	V_{pc}	V_{pe}
Real patient	FCM	0.7912	0.2526
	sFCM	0.8351	0.0736
	Proposed	0.9176	0.0167

4 Conclusion

This paper aims at proposing a new 3D brain image segmentation algorithm based on the fuzzy c-means algorithm. The proposed technique consists of two stages namely, MoFCM and MSFCM. The first stage of the algorithm yields the cluster prototypes which are given as the initial cluster values of the second stage along with the 3D brain MR image data.

We have incorporated spatial information of the image volume and introduced a new membership function called local membership. This membership grade is combined with the traditional FCM membership named as global membership. To calculate the local partition matrix we again have introduced a new probability distribution parameter to exploit the spatial information which estimates the belongingness of a voxel depending on the neighborhood information. The output i.e. the cluster centers obtained from MoFCM algorithm are fed in to the MSFCM algorithm to generate the final cluster values.

The proposed method has been tested on several 3D simulated brain MR image volumes with different combination of noise and inhomogeneity. Furthermore, we also have performed the proposed method on one real patient image volume. The performance of the proposed method is compared with other competent methods to validate our claim. The result of the qualitative and quantitative evaluation of the presented method collectively indicates that the proposed method outperforms the other methods.

Acknowledgement. Authors would like to express their profound indebtedness to the EKO X-RAY & IMAGING INSTITUTE, Jawaharlal Neheru Road, Chowrangee, Kolkata, for providing 3D brain MR image data. Authors are thankful to Dr. Amitabha Bhattacharyya for his invaluable suggestion and ardent support.

References

1. Duncan, J.S., Ayache, N.: Medical image analysis: progress over two decadesand the challenges ahead. IEEE Trans. Pattern Anal. Mach. Intell. **22**(1), 85–106 (2000)
2. Pham, D.L., Xu, C., Prince, J.L.: A survey of current methods medical image segmentation. Technical reports JHU/ECE 99-01, Annual Review of Biomedical Engineering (2000)
3. Balafar, M.A., Ramli, A.R., Saripan, M.I., Mashohor, S.: Review of brain MRI image segmentation methods. J. Artif. Intell. **33**(3), 261–274 (2010)
4. Olabarriaga, S.D., Smeulders, A.W.M.: Interaction in the segmentation of medical images: a survey. Med. Image Anal. **5**(2), 127–142 (2001)
5. Nayak, J., Naik, B., Behera, H.S.: Fuzzy c-means (FCM) clustering algorithm: a decade review from 2000 to 2014. Comput. Intell. Data Min. **2**, 133–149 (2015)
6. Bezdek, J.C.: Pattern Recognition with Fuzzy Objective Function Algorithms. Plenum Press, New York (1981)
7. Wei, L.M., Xie, W.X.: Rival checked fuzzy c-means algorithm. ACTA Eletronica Sinica **28**(7), 63–66 (2000)
8. Fan, J.L., Zhen, W.Z., Xie, W.X.: Suppressed fuzzy c-means clustering algorithm. Pattern Recogn. Lett. **24**(9), 1607–1612 (2003)

9. Chuang, K.S., Tzeng, H.L., Chen, S., Wu, J., Chen, T.J.: Fuzzy c-means clustering with spatial information for image segmentation. Computerized Med. Imag. Graphics **30**(1), 9–15 (2006)
10. Liew, A.W., Leung, S., Lau, W.: Fuzzy image clustering by incorporating spatial continuity. IEE Proc. Vision Image Signal Process. **147**(2), 185–192 (2000)
11. Pham, D.L.: Spatial models for clustering. Comput. Vis. Image Underst. **84**(2), 285–297 (2000)
12. Liew, A.W., Yan, H.: An adaptive spatial fuzzy clustering algorithm for 3D MR image segmentation. IEEE Trans. Med. Imag. **22**(9), 1063–1075 (2003)
13. Pedrycz, W.: Conditional fuzzy c-means. Pattern Recogn. Letters **17**(6), 625–631 (1996)
14. Mohamed, N.A., Ahmed, M.N., Farag, A.A.: Modified fuzzy c-means in medical image segmentation. In: Proceeding of Engineering in Medicine and Biology Society, vol. 20, no. 3, pp. 1377–1380 (1998)
15. Ahmed, M.N., Yamany, S.M., Mohamed, N., Farag, A.A., Moriarty, T.: A modified fuzzy c-means algorithm for bias field estimation and segmentation of MRI data. IEEE Trans. Med. Imag. **21**(3), 193–199 (2002)
16. Qiu, C., Xio, J., Yu, L., Han, L., Iqbal, M.N.: A modified interval type-2 fuzzy c-means algorithm with application in MR image segmentation. Pattern Recogn. Letters **34**(12), 1329–1338 (2013)
17. Sanchez, M.A., Castillo, O., Castro, J.R., Melin, P.: Fuzzy granular gravitational clustering algorithm for multivariate data. Inf. Sci. **279**, 498–511 (2014)
18. Wang, Z., Song, Q., Soh, Y.C., Sim, K.: An adaptive spatial information-theoretic fuzzy clustering algorithm for image segmentation. Comput. Vis. Image Underst. **117**(10), 1412–1420 (2013)

A Novel Intelligent Modeling of Storage and Bandwidth Constraints in Distributed Storage Allocation

Hindol Bhattacharya[1], Samiran Chattopadhyay[2]([✉]),
Matangini Chattopadhyay[1], and Avishek Banerjee[3]

[1] School of Education Technology, Jadavpur University,
Kolkata 700032, India
hindolbhattacharjee12@gmail.com, matanginic@gmail.com
[2] Department of Information Technology, Jadavpur University,
Kolkata 700098, India
samirancju@gmail.com
[3] Department of Information Technology, Asansol Engineering College,
Asansol 713305, India
avishekbanerji@gmail.com

Abstract. The distributed storage allocation problem is an important optimization problem in reliable distributed storage, which aims to minimize storage cost while maximizing error recovery probability by optimal storage of data in distributed storage nodes. A key characteristics of distributed storage is that data are stored in remote servers across a network. Thus, network resources especially communication links are an expensive and non-trivial resource which should be optimized as well. In this paper, we present a simulation based study of the network characteristics of a distributed storage network in the light of several allocation patterns. By varying the allocation patterns we have demonstrated the interdependence between network bandwidth, defined in terms of link capacity and allocation pattern using network throughput as a metric. Recognizing the importance of network resources as an important cost metric, we intend to solve an optimization problem based on minimizing both the storage cost and the cost of network resources. The results of this optimization problem will determine how both storage and network optimization can be performed jointly so that a highly robust yet cost effective storage solution could be developed.

Keywords: Distributed Storage Allocation · Genetic algorithm · Network and storage optimized storage system

1 Introduction

Reliability is the basic demand for any form of storage. Reliability in the context of data storage entails to preserve the original form of data as it has been stored in the system by the subscriber. Loss of integrity of stored data leads

© Springer Nature Singapore Pte Ltd. 2017
J.K. Mandal et al. (Eds.): CICBA 2017, Part II, CCIS 776, pp. 336–346, 2017.
DOI: 10.1007/978-981-10-6430-2_26

to data corruption and hence low reliability. Data corruption can be attributed to both malicious as well as inadvertent corruption due to unavoidable reasons. Separate mechanisms are in place in the domain of information security to deal with malicious corruption of data. However, even in the absence of malicious attacks, data is likely to get corrupt over a period of time. Thus, error correction codes are used to recover from such eventual data corruption and to maintain high reliability. However, error correction codes occupy considerable storage; and hence contributes to storage overhead. A naive error correction mechanism would require excessive amount of storage just to store such codes. Thus, efficient error correction codes are required to achieve high reliability with low cost of storage.

In distributed storage systems, apart from clever error correction codes; reliable low cost storage can be achieved by exploiting numerous other parameters, unique to such systems. Distributed storage requires data to be stored in a set of storage nodes distributed across a network. In such systems storage options such as changing allocation pattern in nodes, option to locally or globally repair a problem, etc. becomes available. These options can be intelligently exploited to improve reliability without having to incur excessive storage cost.

Distributed Storage Allocation is one such option available in distributed storage systems; that may ensure high reliability in storage systems while optimizing on the storage cost. In this paper we look into this aspect of reliability improvement scheme in distributed storage systems.

The rest of the work is organized as follows. Section 2 discusses the basic concepts required for understanding this work. Section 3 lists down the problems and limitations of the existing work in literature that we would like to address in this work. Section 4 contains a discussion of the related works in the field. Section 5 focuses on the network simulation experiment which forms the first part of our work. Network simulation experiment measures network performance by varying storage allocation patterns and spread of data on a distributed storage network. Section 6 deals with the optimization problem for minimization of storage and link capacity costs jointly. Section 7 concludes our study and includes a broad outline on the future direction of research.

2   The Basic Concepts

The key concept in distributed storage allocation problem is to distribute data across a set of available storage nodes in such a way that probability of data recovery from errors can be maximized; while keeping storage cost as low as possible. In absence of optimization criteria such as limited network bandwidth, minimizing required storage space, etc. the problem of maintaining high reliability is trivial. We can simply store the entire data at every node.

However, when optimization is required, the naive solution referred to above ceases to be effective. The most common optimization criteria is the limitation in storage space, more formally called total storage budget constraint.

Definition 1. *Total storage budget is the limit on the total amount of data that can be stored across a set of distributed storage nodes.*

Individual nodes can store any amount of data; however, the sum total of data stored in each node cannot exceed the total storage budget allocated.

It is evident with low total storage budget, less storage cost has to be borne. However, the consequence of defining total storage budget is that allocation and access of data is now no more trivial. Data have to be optimally allocated and accessed to achieve the goal of maximum error recoverability while remaining within budget limits.

An allocation pattern may be either symmetric or non-symmetric and maximal or minimal spread. Thus, according to the allocation pattern following possibilities arise which are given in the following.

- Symmetric maximal spread
- Non-symmetric maximal spread
- Symmetric minimal spread
- Non-symmetric minimal spread

Maximal spreading means that most of the available nodes are used for storage while minimal spread means that data allocations are concentrated on a few available nodes. Symmetric allocation means that all nodes chosen for allocation store equal amount of data while non-symmetric means that unequal amount of data is stored in each node chosen for allocation. For symmetric allocation, the allocation and access model can be of either probabilistic or deterministic. Therefore, four allocation-access models are possible as follows:

- Probabilistic Allocation Probabilistic Access
- Probabilistic Allocation Deterministic Access
- Deterministic Allocation and Probabilistic Access
- Deterministic Allocation Deterministic Access

Further classification can be made on the type of nodes, which may be either homogeneous or heterogeneous in nature. These are given in the following.

Definition 2. *Homogeneous nodes are those which exhibit similar network, IO and failure characteristics.*

Definition 3. *Heterogeneous nodes are those which exhibit different network, IO and failure characteristics.*

The distributed storage allocation problem attempts to find the best possible allocation pattern and spread which maximizes error recovery probability while maintaining optimal total storage budget.

3   Problem Statement

The definition of total storage budget is based on the core assumption that the communication links between the nodes are able to support the amount of data on the respective storage nodes. In cases where the communication link capabilities are not sufficient, total storage budget is limited and defined in terms of the communication link capacity. The limitations of this work is that it chooses between two equally important cost factors viz. storage and link capacities. Ideally a storage network administrator would like to minimize both the storage and communication costs together, if possible. An optimization problem which would consider them both as costs and work towards their minimization would be a novel work to the problem.

To the best of our knowledge no work has been done to study the network performance while varying the storage allocation pattern and spread. Our intuition is that network performance will vary noticeably with change in network allocation pattern and spread. A simulation based study to study the network performance by varying storage pattern and spread is in our opinion a novel venture.

3.1 Proposed Work

Based on the discussions above we enumerate the following problems that we would like to address in this paper:

- Study network performance by varying the network allocation pattern. We check whether symmetric or non-symmetric patterns gives better performance. We also investigate whether maximal or minimal spread is best in terms of network performance.
- Formulate an optimization problem which would jointly optimize the essential cost factors viz. required storage and link capacity; while maintaining high reliability.

4 Related Works

The distributed storage allocation problem was first presented in [4]. The four allocation-access model was presented in this paper and the symmetric vs unsymmetric model was investigated vis-a-vis the allocation-access model keeping in mind the storage budget constraint and the goal of high probability in error recovery. The storage allocation problem was further expanded and the analyzed in respect of data spreading in [6]. The paper considered three cases - Independent probabilistic access to each node, Access to a random fixed size subset of nodes and Probabilistic symmetric allocation. The conclusion reached by the them is that, for high reliability, spread minimally for small storage budget while spread maximally for large storage budget. [5] discusses in details about the symmetric allocation pattern. The intuitive idea that symmetric allocation is always the optimal allocation pattern is not always true. This work addresses the question of under which conditions, symmetric allocation becomes optimal.

Repair bandwidth cost and its trade-offs with storage space has also been discussed in various works. [11] established the repair-bandwidth trade-off. The authors established the trade-oof by formulating a bi-objective linear programming problem.

Distributed storage system in view of constrained memory has been accounted for in [1]. They concluded that in case of memory constrained distributed storage systems symmetric allocation is not always an optimal one. This held true even for large network size and in cases where all nodes had uniform amount of available storage memory. They also concluded that similar observations can be made in case of memory constrained heterogeneous distributed storage systems as well.

Studies cited so far considered mainly homogeneous nodes. Distributed storage allocation problem in heterogeneous nodes has been studies in [7,8].

One of the recent works addressing reliability-bandwidth trade-off. in terms of heterogeneous nodes is [3]. However, these works does not provide an interdependence study between network throughput (bandwidth requirement) and allocation pattern or data spreading.

5 Network Simulation Study

This section addresses the first part of our work, which is to investigate the performance of the storage network by varying the allocation patterns.

5.1 Simulation Software

The simulation experiment has been carried out using the NTU implementation of DCN in NS-3 simulator [10]. Among the choice of DCN topology, we have chosen the Fat-tree topology implemented in the framework.

5.2 Data Center Network

In distributed storage systems, data are stored in data centers, which are specialized facilities for reliable storage of data. Thus, data center network has been found suitable for simulating distributed storage system. Data Center Network architecture are of many types such as 3-tier, Fat-tree, Dcell, Bcube etc. to name a few. The Fat-tree network architecture has been considered for our simulation study because of its proven capability of delivering high throughput with low-latency [2]. This characteristic is useful since our simulation study concerns performance comparison in terms of throughput by varying data storage allocation patterns. The NTU-DCN framework provides a data center framework where two data center topologies are implemented viz. BCube and Fat-tree.

5.3 Simulation Setup

The simulation is essentially modification of the Fat-tree implementation of the NTU-DCN framework of NS-3. The essential simulation parameters are as follows (Table 1):

In our Simulation, throughput is considered as a measurement metric, which computes the amount of data transferred per unit time. Throughput determines

Table 1. Table of essential simulation parameters

Total number of nodes	50
Maximum no of access nodes	16
No of access nodes	1, 8 and 16
Topology	Fat-tree
Links	Edge-host:CSMA Rest:P2P
Data rate	1 Gbps
Delay	0.001 ms
Application	On-Off
Packet size	1024 bytes
On-Off data rate	Default
Total data transferred	125 MB
Total client nodes	5

the performance level that can be expected for a given bandwidth of the network. Thus, throughput at a constant network bandwidth determines which allocation patterns are the most suitable for higher network performance.

5.4   Simulation Results

Network throughput has been measured by varying the spread of data. The following data spread has been considered for both symmetric and non-symmetric allocation patterns: accessing data from all 16 nodes or from 8 nodes out of 16 nodes. The 8 nodes have been chosen in the following manner. 8 nodes towards

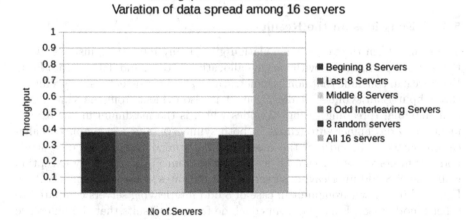

Fig. 1. Results of non-symmetric allocation

the beginning are chosen first; middle 8 nodes are chosen next; 8 nodes towards the end, 8 nodes with odd interleaving and 8 random nodes are chosen successively. The symmetric allocation also has an additional single node access case.

Figure 1 measures network throughput under varying spread when data is allocated in a non-symmetric manner. Figure 2 measures network throughput under varying spread when data is symmetrically allocated. Figure 3 provides a comprehensive picture considering both allocation patterns - symmetric and non-symmetric under varying spread.

The discussion and interpretation of results follows in the next subsection.

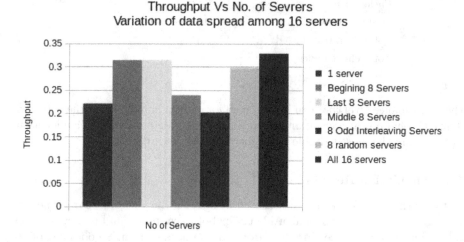

Fig. 2. Results of symmetric allocation

5.5   Discussions on the Results

The results from the network simulation gives many interesting insights about the network performance with varying allocation pattern and data spread. From Fig. 3 we can conclude that non-symmetric allocation consistently shows a higher throughput than symmetric allocation. It is also evident from the same figure that maximal spreading (using 16 nodes which is the maximum in our experiment) provides higher throughput in both symmetric and non-symmetric allocation patterns. In most of the cases minimal spreading (i.e., use of a single node) exhibits worse throughput as is evident from Fig. 2. The only exception is in case of 8 odd interleaving servers which indicates worse performance. Also, Fig. 1 exhibits low throughput in case of 8 odd interleaving servers compared to other 8-node cases. Finally we can conclude from the results that the difference of throughput between spreads is more pronounced in case of non-symmetric allocation than symmetric allocation.

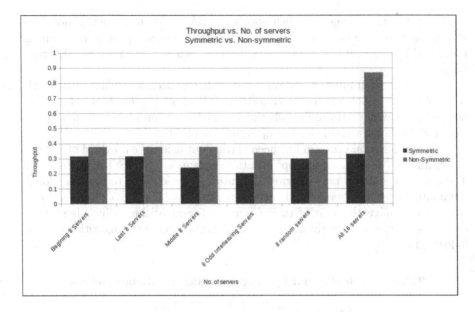

Fig. 3. Consolidated results

6   Constraint Optimization Problem

The constraint optimization problem constitutes the second part of our work. In this work we perform a constraint optimization on the objectives of minimizing the storage cost and link capacity requirement. Through our solution of the optimization problem we seek to find the answer to the question of whether and upto what extent the two objectives can be optimized together. This will provide a foundation on which future distributed storage system could be developed.

6.1   Problem Formulation

Thus optimization problem with the new cost function for a probability-1 recovery regime can be written as:

$$Minimize \; T = \sum_{i=1}^{n} x_i + \sum_{i=1j=1}^{n} y_{ij}$$

$$subject \; to$$

$$x_i >= 0 \quad and \quad y_{ij} >= 0 \quad and \quad i \neq j$$

$$\sum_{i \in r} x_i >= 1 \quad and \quad \sum_{ij \in r} y_{ij} >= 1 \quad \forall r \in R$$

where

$$R = \binom{n}{r} \quad and \quad r \subset \{1, 2, ..., n\}$$

T is total storage budget which now is a composite cost function of both the storage and link capacity. For each node allotted storage space is represented by x_i and link capacity between two nodes is y_{ij} where i and j are two different nodes.

We consider that out of n nodes the data collector accesses each r-subset with probability p_r. r belongs to the collection of R of all $\binom{n}{r}$ r-subsets of storage nodes. In our work we try to find whether symmetric or non-symmetric allocation would yield the best result for our optimization problem.

The optimization problem has been carried out using the a hybrid of genetic algorithm and particle swam optimization known as GA-PSO algorithm [9]. The genetic algorithm part explores the entire solution space to find the global minimum instead of being stuck in a local minima. The PSO part has been added to enhance the rate of convergence of the algorithm, which is slow in case of pure genetic algorithm. The essential parameters of the algorithms are as follows (Table 2):

Table 2. Table of essential parameters for the optimization problem

Parameters	Value
Population size	150
Maximum generation	100
Probability of crossover	0.85
Probability of mutation	0.15
Beta (model coefficient)	1.5
No. of storage nodes	5
No. of nodes selected for retrieval	2
No. of runs	50

6.2   Results

The optimization problem has been run for the best value of minimization case and the following results have been obtained (Table 3 and Fig. 4):

6.3   Discussions on the Results

From the solution of the constraint optimization problem, some conclusions can be drawn on the feasibility of joint optimization of storage and network resources in distributed storage allocation problem. We find from the solution that non-symmetrical allocation is the best allocation method for composite cost reduction. Hence it will serve us better to follow non-symmetrical allocation approach. This is consistent with our findings in network simulation results as discussed in Sect. 5.5. Further we find that best storage and network resource cost allocation are similar.

Table 3. Table of results for the best values of minimization

Node no.	Storage allocation	Link capacity allocation
Node 1	0.34448	0.38848
Node 2	0	0.022
Node 3	0.1207977	0.121977
Node 4	0.999965	1.039
Node 5	0.246705	0.241605

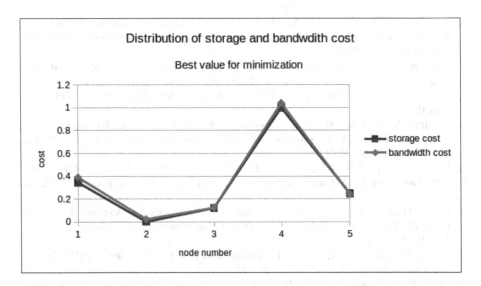

Fig. 4. Graphical view of the best value of minimization

7 Conclusion and Future Scope

Our work consists of two interconnected parts. In the first part we have tried to establish the importance of network parameters in distributed storage allocation problems through NS3 simulation study. Through simulation results we have shown that throughput is highly dependent on the allocation pattern and spread of allocation among storage nodes. Thus, the importance of network parameters in case of Distributed Storage Allocation problem is hopefully well established and it needs to be duly considered. Interestingly it has also observed that the non-symmetric distribution yields better result in terms of throughput. In the second part we have formulated a new optimization problem where the objective function is a redefinition of the total storage budget in terms of storage space and link capacity required. Our aim here is to identify the allocation pattern - symmetric or nonsymmetric, which would minimize he cost function, while maintaining high reliability. Like the result of the network simulation, non-symmetric allocation also gives the best minimization values. Moreover, it has been found that both the metrics can be optimized jointly.

The results of this work are very encouraging. In future we intend to study which allocation models minimizes the joint objectives for storage and bandwidth. Introduction of heterogeneous nodes with independent failure probabilities will also be considered in our model.

References

1. Andriyanova, I., Olmos, P.M.: On distributed storage allocations for memory-limited systems. In: 2015 IEEE Global Communications Conference (GLOBE-COM), pp. 1–6. IEEE (2015)
2. Bilal, K., Khan, S.U., Zhang, L., Li, H., Hayat, K., Madani, S.A., Min-Allah, N., Wang, L., Chen, D., Iqbal, M., et al.: Quantitative comparisons of the state-of-the-art data center architectures. Concurr. Comput. Pract. Exp. **25**(12), 1771–1783 (2013)
3. Brahma, S., Mercier, H.: Reliability-bandwidth tradeoffs for distributed storage allocations. In: 2016 IEEE International Symposium on Information Theory (ISIT), pp. 1013–1017. IEEE (2016)
4. Leong, D., Dimakis, A.G., Ho, T.: Distributed storage allocation problems. In: 2009 Workshop on Network Coding, Theory, and Applications, pp. 86–91. IEEE (2009)
5. Leong, D., Dimakis, A.G., Ho, T.: Symmetric allocations for distributed storage. In: 2010 IEEE Global Telecommunications Conference, GLOBECOM 2010, pp. 1–6. IEEE (2010)
6. Leong, D., Dimakis, A.G., Ho, T.: Distributed storage allocations. IEEE Trans. Inf. Theory **58**(7), 4733–4752 (2012)
7. Li, Z., Ho, T., Leong, D., Yao, H.: Distributed storage allocation for heterogeneous systems. In: 2013 51st Annual Allerton Conference on Communication, Control, and Computing (Allerton), pp. 320–326. IEEE (2013)
8. Ntranos, V., Caire, G., Dimakis, A.G.: Allocations for heterogenous distributed storage. In: 2012 IEEE International Symposium on Information Theory Proceedings (ISIT), pp. 2761–2765. IEEE (2012)
9. Sahoo, L., Banerjee, A., Bhunia, A.K., Chattopadhyay, S.: An efficient GA-PSO approach for solving mixed-integer nonlinear programming problem in reliability optimization. Swarm Evol. Comput. **19**, 43–51 (2014)
10. Wong, D., Seow, K.T., Foh, C.H., Kanagavelu, R.: Towards reproducible performance studies of datacenter network architectures using an open-source simulation approach. In: 2013 IEEE Global Communications Conference (GLOBECOM), pp. 1373–1378. IEEE (2013)
11. Yu, Q., Shum, K.W., Sung, C.W.: Tradeoff between storage cost and repair cost in heterogeneous distributed storage systems. Trans. Emerg. Telecommun. Technol. **26**(10), 1201–1211 (2015)

Integrating Multi-view Data: A Hypergraph Based Approach

Saif Ayan Khan$^{(\boxtimes)}$ and Sumanta Ray

Department of Computer Science and Engineering, Aliah University, Kolkata, India
saifayankhan@gmail.com, sumanta.ray@aliah.ac.in

Abstract. In this paper, we have proposed a novel framework to integrate multiple views of data using hypergraph based partitioning approach. Representing each view as separate graphs, we partitioned them into clusters using standard clustering technique. Each clustering solution is represented as a separate hypergraph in which a hyperedge encodes a cluster. Concatenating all these hyperedges result to an adjacency matrix (H) of a hypergraph with n vertices which is equal to the number of objects in each data, and E edges which is equal to total number of clusters in the representative clustering solutions. A similarity matrix (S) is compiled from the adjacency (H) by taking entry wise average. Each entry of S merely denotes the fraction of clustering in which two objects are members of the same group/cluster. Clustering the S matrix results in meta-clusters which essentially inherit the characteristics of all data views in the original data. We have performed a simulation study on three data views to validate the framework. For each view, we tune the parameter of data, and investigate whether the results conform the changes. We have also applied the proposed framework in a real life dataset to identify meta-clusters. Moreover, we have analyzed the resulting meta-clusters to validate our proposed method.

Keywords: Hypergraphs · Clustering · Meta-clusters · Multi-view data · Gene expression · Gene ontology · Protein-protein interaction

1 Introduction

Integrating multiple data sources has been found in various fields such as in multi-sensor data fusion [2,8], in econometrics [4], in bioinformatics [7,10,12,13], in social networks studies [1] etc. The main task of integration merely depends on a effective multi-learner system which generates ensemble of each component learner which tries to solve the same task [14]. Naturally, there exists several different ways to define data of same objects. This opens onto multiple representation of same data objects or patterns. The problem is to make an ensemble of all the representations and check which one describes all the patterns in the best possible way [5]. The patterns are either entirely compatible where same patterns exist in all views or incompatible, where significant difference exists

© Springer Nature Singapore Pte Ltd. 2017
J.K. Mandal et al. (Eds.): CICBA 2017, Part II, CCIS 776, pp. 347–357, 2017.
DOI: 10.1007/978-981-10-6430-2_27

between data views. A good data integration approach should identify the differences, find common patterns while preserving the unique characteristics of each view.

Early studies in this area involves combining multiple rankings [11], integrating different biological data sources to detect perturbation of coexpressed modules [12], non-negative matrix factorization based integration to predict protein-protein interactions [12], multi-view data integration for performing cluster analysis on heterogeneous social network data [6].

In this work, we have developed a novel framework based on hypergraph partitioning to integrate multiple views of same object. First, each view is mapped into a network structure, where nodes represent objects and weights of edges represent the particular characteristics of each view. The constructed networks are then partitioned using standard partitional clustering algorithm to group the similar objects of each view. Each of the clustering results is viewed as a separate hypergraph, in which nodes correspond to objects and hyperedges encode each cluster. Thus all the clustering results of each view can be represented using multiple hypergraphs. All the hypergraphs are then concatenated to build an adjacency of a single hypergraph in which hyperedges represent all the identified clusters. A similarity matrix is then constructed by computing the entry-wise average of the adjacency matrix. Each entry of the similarity matrix signifies a fraction of clustering where two objects are belonging to the same cluster. Partitioning the similarity matrix yields meta-clusters which inherit the characteristics of all the data views. For partitioning the similarity matrix we have utilized a widely used clustering algorithm, Metis [9]. To validate the proposed methodology we have performed a simulation study described in Subsect. 3.1. Moreover, we have also applied the proposed methodology in a real life biological dataset and described it in Subsect. 3.2. Here, the identified gene meta-clusters inherits three biological source of information. Gene expression data, protein-protein interaction data and gene ontology data are extracted for a set of genes. These three biological sources are serve as three different views of the gene set. The identified meta-clusters are analyzed to investigate the correctness of the proposed framework.

2   Proposed Method

In this section we describe the proposed method of the data integration technique. Here, each representative clustering is mapped into hypergraph representation. A widely used algorithm, Metis [9] is utilized here to partition the constructed hypergraph into meta-clusters. The whole framework is described in Fig. 1. The figure describes the framework for three views of data. It may be extended to more views for integration.

2.1   Data Views as Network

In nature there exists several distinct representations of the same objects. This leads to different views of same data which have distinct perspectives in the

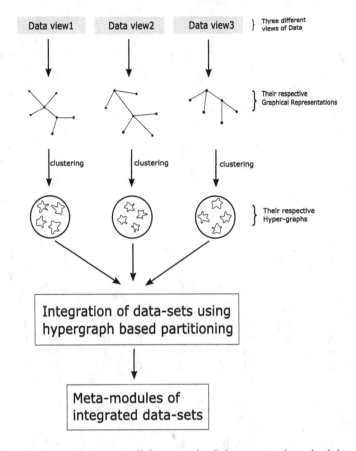

Fig. 1. Figure shows overall framework of the proposed methodology.

respective domains. The major challenge is to integrate this different views by extracting the cocoon patterns or preserve the unique patterns which characterizes the perspective. To integrate them, it is necessary to represent each view in a common format that could be integrated by applying any machine learning algorithm. Here, we represent each view of the data in a graph/network structure, where data objects are represented as nodes and the inter-relationship between the nodes are represented as edges.

2.2 Partitioning the Network

In this step each representative network of each view is clustered using a partitional clustering algorithm. As we know the best representative for the network is that module, so clustering of each data view merely represents a prototype of the respective view. Here we utilize k-means to partition each network of different views. However, other clustering techniques can be applicable here to

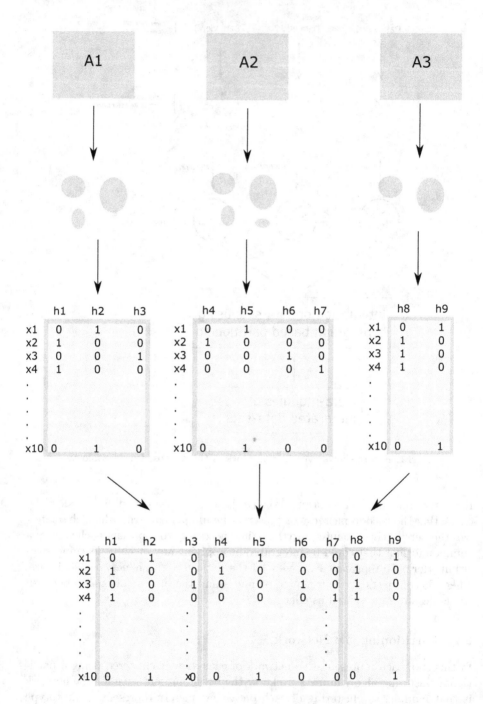

Fig. 2. Figure shows hypergraph representation of clustering results. Here three adjacency matrix of three views are clustered and represented as hypergraphs.

partition the data view. Each representative clustering solutions are mapped into a distinct hypergraph.

2.3   Hypergraph Representation of Partition

Clustering technique on a network yields different clusters which can be represented as a hypergraph. A hypergraph consists of a set of nodes and hyperedges. Unlike regular graph which defines a relation between two nodes as edges, hypergraph generalizes it by defining relation among more than two nodes termed as hyperedge. So a hyperedge can connect any set of vertices. It is very intuitive to represent a clustering solution of network in terms of a hypergraph. In particular, the nodes correspond to the nodes of the representative hypergraph, whereas the hyperedges encodes the clusters.

2.4   Partitioning the Hypergraph

Each hyperedge encodes a cluster. The hypergraph representation of a whole clustering solution can be modeled as an adjacency matrix as follows: assume there are three views $V1$, $V2$ and $V3$ of n objects. Each of the data views is represented as network adjacency matrices $A1$, $A2$ and $A3$ of same dimensions. After partitioning let $A1$ is partitioned into 3 clusters, $A2$ is partitioned into 4 clusters and $A3$ is partitioned into 2 clusters. Each of the partitioning results can be represented as a matrix of dimension $n \times k$, where n corresponds to the number of objects whereas k represents the number of clusters. This matrix can be assumed as an adjacency matrix of a hypergraph. We have created a model view of the whole scenario in Fig. 2. From the figure it can be noticed that 10 objects are clustered in 2 clusters for $A1$, 4 clusters for $A2$ and 3 clusters for $A3$. Each clustering result is represented as a 0–1 adjacency matrix D_i with the following assumptions: entry $D_i(i,j)$ is equal to 1 if data object x_i is belonging to cluster j and is equal to 0 otherwise. Here each cluster may be assumed as a hyperedge. From Fig. 2 it can be noticed that the clusters are represented as adjacency matrices of hypergraphs. For example the hypergraph which represents the clustering solution of the network adjacency $A1$, has three hyperedges h_1, h_2 and h_3. Similarly, h_4 to h_7 encodes the four clusters of $A2$, and h_8 and h_9 represents the two clusters of $A3$. Concatenating these hyperedges yields a hypergraph H, with nine hyperedges and ten nodes. In Fig. 2, 3rd step, it can noticed that all the nine hyperedges are concatenated to construct a single hypergraph. Please note that here an object can belong to multiple hyperedges. Thus an integrated representation of different views of same data are arranged. For partitioning the constructed hypergraph, we first compute an overall similarity matrix S by computing entry-wise average. This can be achieved by performing the following operation: $S = \frac{1}{m}HH^T$, where m corresponds to the number of views. Thus the similarity matrix S signifies an ensemble of three-cluster similarity matrix of three views. Figure 3 shows heatmaps of the three cluster similarity matrices and the ensemble similarity matrix S. For partitioning S a widely used

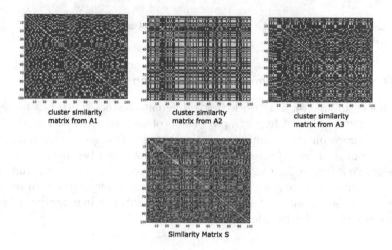

Fig. 3. Figure shows heatmaps of three cluster similarity matrix constructed from three clustering results and the ensemble (S) of these three matrices.

clustering algorithm, Metis, is utilized here. The resulting meta-clusters inherit all the characteristics of the different views.

3   Results

In this section we performed a simulation study to validate the proposed framework and then applied it in a real life data to find meta-clusters.

3.1   Simulation Study

Before running our proposed framework on real-life data-sets, we perform a simulation study using randomly generated artificial datasets. We take three views of 100 objects for this purpose. The data views are created randomly by varying properties of each view. Particularly, we create a network with a fixed property for each view, and adjust the property to make a set of networks. For data view-1 we create networks with varying densities, (property-1) from 0.1 to 0.9. Thus nine networks are created with increasing density values. Similarly, for data view-2 the networks with average weights (property-2) varying from −0.8 to +1 with an increment of 0.2 are created. For data view-3 nine networks are built by varying the average weights (property-3) between 0.1 to 0.9 with an increment of 0.1. Thus, for each view we have nine networks; each of which have a fixed property. We take each network separately from three views at a time, and make partitions using clustering technique. Here we use simple K-means algorithm for partitioning the networks. The obtained partitions are represented as hypergraphs where an hyperedge encode an individual cluster. The hyperedges are concatenated to form an adjacency of an overall hypergraph which represents

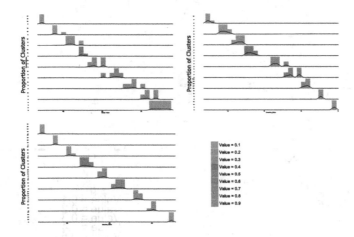

Fig. 4. Figure shows distribution of meta-clusters with three properties. Panel-(a) shows the distribution with varying density property, whereas panel (b) and panel (c) show the same for other two properties.

an intermediate representation of three views of the data. From the hypergraph thus formed, is converted to a similarity matrix S by performing the procedure mentioned in the Subsect. 2.4. By clustering the similarity matrix we get meta-clusters which inherit the properties of the original data views. Thus we get nine sets of meta-clusters each of which combines the characteristics of the three views.

To investigate whether the obtained meta-clusters are carrying the characteristics of individual data views, we plot the distributions of meta-clusters for the three mentioned properties. Particularly, we check how the three properties are distributed in the obtained meta-clusters which are basically a consensus of all clusters identified in each data view. In Figs. 4 and 5, (a), (b) and (c) we show the distribution of nine sets of meta-clusters with the three properties. In Fig. 4(a), (b) and (c) the distribution of meta-clusters with their average densities are shown. From the figures it can be noted that when we adjust or increase the properties of each data view the meta-clusters also inherits the increasing properties. From each of the Fig. 4 we can see that the distribution of the meta-clusters are gradually shifted towards right with the increasing properties. Similarly, from Fig. 5, we can see the distribution shift upwards. Thus our framework performs correctly to combine the three characteristics of each of the data views.

3.2 Application on a Real Life Data

Genomic relationships can be represented as graphs. The vertices will be representing every node and the edges between them, the relationship we want to map. We take three biological data sources, gene expression data, protein-protein interaction data and Gene Ontology data of same set of genes. We downloaded

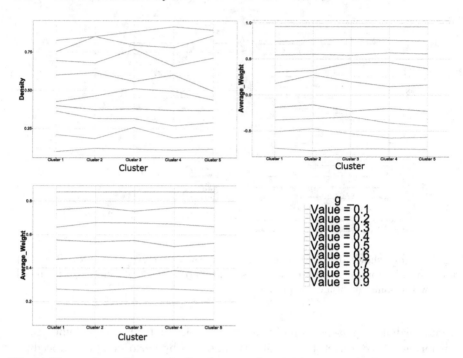

Fig. 5. Figure shows line-graph distribution of meta-clusters with three properties. Panel-(a) shows the distribution with varying density property, whereas panel (b) and panel (c) show the same for other two properties.

the gene expression dataset (GSE6740 series) from GEO database (http://www.ncbi.nlm.nih.gov/geo). The expression data consists of expression values of CD4+ and CD8+ cells of three HIV infection stages. From this, we have taken expression data of acute stage infection. We select 2828 most varying genes among the total 22,284 genes by performing variance cutoff. Next, We have prepared a correlation matrix of dimension 2828 × 2828, where each entry signifies the Pearson correlation between two gene expression profiles. We also collected protein-protein interaction (PPI) data from HPRD [3] database. We took PPI information of the selected 2828 genes from whole human PPI database. We have also collected Gene Ontology information of these selected genes from Gene Ontology consortium (http://www.geneontology.org/). We compute functional similarity between two genes by measuring semantic similarity between set of GO-terms associated with these genes. Thus we construct three matrices which represents three different views of same set of genes. PPI adjacency matrix represents interaction information, correlation matrix represents similarity between each pair of gene expression profiles whereas semantic similarity matrix signifies functional similarity of the same set of selected genes.

Our primary objective is to represent these in form of hypergraphs and integrating them into one single similarity matrix which would be a graph of genes with a mixture of properties. The creation of the hypergraphs is achieved by partitioning each matrix and representing them as a separate hypergraph. Next we have applied our proposed framework to integrate the hyperedges and got 30 meta-clusters. The obtained meta-clusters consists of set of genes which essentially inherits the PPI information, gene expression information as well as gene ontology information. It is observed that all the meta-clusters have high density, average correlation and average semantic similarity. Most of the meta-clusters have density greater than 0.6, while preserving a good average correlation value (≥ 0.5) and average semantic similarity value (≥ 0.6). In Table 1 we show some of the meta-clusters having high density, average correlation and average semantic similarity value. It can be seen from the table that average value of all three properties is seemingly high. Average of all density values of identified meta-clusters is higher than 0.6, which signifies most of the meta clusters have preserved density properties of original data. Moreover, the average of all correlations and semantic similarity value are also high for the meta-clusters. This also signifies the meta-clusters not only inherit one property, but are also carrying the same properties form other two views of data.

Table 1. Table shows density, average correlation and average semantic similarity of some meta-clusters.

Meta-clusters	Average density	Average correlation	Average semantic similarity
Meta-cluster-2 (# genes 89)	0.8	0.76	0.81
Meta-cluster-5 (# genes 120)	0.71	0.68	0.73
Meta-cluster-19 (# genes 180)	0.75	0.71	0.88
Meta-cluster-13 (#genes 123)	0.85	0.62	0.78

4 Conclusions

In this article, we have proposed a novel framework to integrate data with multiple views through hypergraph based partitioning method. Here, we represent each view of the data in a network format and cluster them to get modules. The clustering solutions are represented as hypergraphs in which hyper-edges encode individual clusters. Concatenating all the hyper-edges yield an adjacency of hypergraphs which combine all the views of the dataset. The hypergraph is then partitioned by using a well known algorithm Metis to obtain meta-clusters, which inherit all the properties of each view. From the results we noticed that the meta-clusters carry the proteins of each view. Moreover adjusting the parameters of individual view also change the characteristics of the meta-clusters. In other words the change in individual properties of views leads to the change in meta-clusters' properties. This is also reflected while we apply our algorithm in real life data. The identified gene meta-clusters have high density, correlation and semantic similarity. The biological significance of the identified gene meta-clusters are yet to be investigated. This work opens a whole new possibility for representing data and integrating them with the characteristics being inherited by the next generations flawlessly. Multiple perspectives of the same data values can be analyzed to check which views compliment each other and which do not. Thus resulting in the acquirement of more useful data and pruning unnecessary data from the same data values, with just different views/perspectives. This can be used in finding trends, patterns and also increase the efficiency of predictions for machine learning algorithms and the like.

References

1. Cai, D., Shao, Z., He, X., Yan, X., Han, J.: Mining hidden community in heterogeneous social networks. In: Proceedings of the 3rd International Workshop on Link Discovery, LinkKDD 2005, NY, USA, pp. 58–65 (2005). doi:10.1145/1134271. 1134280

2. Dasarathy, B.: Decision Fusion. IEEE CS Press, Los Alamitos (1994)

3. Fu, W., Sanders-Beer, B., Katz, K., Maglott, D., Pruitt, K.: Human immunodeficiency virus type-1, human protein interaction database at NCBI. Nucl. Acids Res. (Database Issue) 37, D417–D422 (2009)

4. Granger, W.J.: Combining forecasts twenty years later. Eur. Conf. Mach. Learn. 8(3), 167–173 (1989)

5. Green, D., Cunningham, P.: A matrix factorization approach for integrating multiple data views. In: Berlin, S.V. (ed.) Proceedings in ECML PKDD 2009, Proceedings of the European Conference on Machine Learning and Knowledge Discovery in Databases, pp. 423–438 (2009)

6. Greene, D., Cunningham, P.: Multi-view clustering for mining heterogeneous social network data. In: Workshop on Information Retrieval over Social Networks, 31st European Conference on Information Retrieval, ECIR 2009 (2009)

7. Hecker, M., Lambeck, S., Toepfer, S., van Someren, E., Guthke, R.: Gene regulatory network inference: data integration in dynamic models? A review. BioSystems 96, 86–103 (2009)

8. Hull, R., Zhou, G.: A framework for supporting data integration using the materialized and virtual approaches. In: Proceedings of the 1996 ACM SIGMOD International Conference on Management of Data, vol. 25, pp. 481–492, June 1996

9. Karypis, G., Kumar, V.: A fast and high quality multilevel scheme for partitioning irregular graphs. SIAM J. Sci. Comput. 20(1), 359–392 (1998). doi:10.1137/S1064827595287997

10. Lapatas, V., Stefanidakis, M., Jimenez, R., Via, A., Schneider, M.V.: Data integration in biological research: an overview. J. Biol. Res. Thessalon. 2, 9 (2015)

11. Liu, Y.T., Liu, T.Y., Qin, T., Ma, Z.M., Li, H.: Supervised rank aggregation. In: Proceedings of the 16th International Conference on World Wide Web, WWW 2007, NY, USA, pp. 481–490 (2007). doi:10.1145/1242572.1242638

12. Ray, S., Bandyopadhyay, S.: A NMF based approach for integrating multiple data sources to predict HIV-1-human PPIs. BMC Bioinform. 17(1), 121 (2016). doi:10. 1186/s12859-016-0952-6

13. Smith, B., Ashburner, M., Rosse, C., Bard, J., Bug, W., Ceusters, W., Goldberg, L., Eilbeck, K., Ireland, A., Mungall, C., Leontis, N., Rocca-Serra, P., Ruttenberg, A., Sansone, S., Scheuermann, R., Shah, N., Whetzel, P., Lewis, S.: The OBO foundry: coordinated evolution of ontologies to support biomedical data integration. Nat. Biotechnol. **25**, 1251–1255 (2007)
14. Strehl, A., Ghosh, J.: Cluster ensembles a knowledge reuse framework for combining multiple partitions. J. Mach. Learn. Res. **3**(12), 583–617 (2002)

Chemical Graph Mining for Classification of Chemical Reactions

Shreya Ghosh, Ankita Samaddar[(⊠)], Trishita Goswami, and Somnath Pal

Indian Institute of Engineering Science and Technology, Shibpur, Howrah, India
shreya.cst@gmail.com, anki.samaddar@gmail.com, trstgsm@gmail.com,
sp@iiests.ac.in

Abstract. The first step of prediction of product(s) of unknown chemical reactions by a computer is to classify known chemical reactions. Several authors came up with various reaction templates or reaction classes by studying (mostly) organic chemical reactions. This paper presents an algorithm that automates the process of finding reaction classes from known chemical reaction graphs. The algorithm presented here is sufficiently general to cover both organic and inorganic chemical reactions and can be applied to wider varieties of reactions. This graph mining algorithm derives all the reaction classes obtained from earlier schemes and thus earlier schemes are subsets of the present algorithm. The new reaction classes can also be derived from the algorithm presented in this paper.

Keywords: Chemoinformatics · Chemical graph · Graph mining · Ugi's scheme · Classification

1 Introduction

Chemical compounds can be represented as molecular graphs, where the nodes represent the atoms and the edges between any two nodes represent the bonds between the two atoms. The number of parallel edges between any two nodes represent the bond order [1]. The prediction of unknown chemical reactions calls for classification of known chemical reactions. Since, there are a large number of chemical reactions that are in existence, classification of existing chemical reactions needs to be done by computer. The computer generates template for the representation of a reaction class. There are two types of methods for chemical reaction classification: (i) Model Driven approach, (ii) Data Driven approach. In model driven approach, a chemical graph [2] is represented in a form that is suitable for processing using computer. One such method was proposed by Ugi and his co-workers [3] that represents a chemical graph using Bond Electron matrix (BE matrix) [4]. They studied 1900 organic chemical reactions and came up with 30 reaction classes [5]. In this paper, a general algorithm for obtaining reaction classes from wide varieties of chemical reactions (both organic and inorganic) has been proposed. In the next section, Ugi's scheme is discussed in

© Springer Nature Singapore Pte Ltd. 2017
J.K. Mandal et al. (Eds.): CICBA 2017, Part II, CCIS 776, pp. 358–370, 2017.
DOI: 10.1007/978-981-10-6430-2_28

some detail along with its extensions. In Sect. 3, an internal computer representation of chemical graph in the form of Extended Bond Electron matrix (EBE matrix) is described. The algorithm for obtaining reaction templates from EBE matrix is given with discussions and examples in Sect. 4. In the final section, the conclusion summarizes the contribution of this paper.

2   Background

2.1   Ugi's Scheme

Ugi's scheme, a model driven approach, was developed in the year 1970. The Scheme mainly deals with representation of chemical structures by Bond-Electron matrix or B-E matrix. Bond-Electron matrix of a molecule consisting of n atoms is a (n * n) symmetric matrix where each entry represents the existing bonds between corresponding atoms. It also stores information about valence electrons residing on an atom. The diagonal cells in a Bond-Electron matrix stores the free radical information existing on an atom. B-E matrix represents not only a chemical compound, but it is also used to represent a chemical reaction. Representation of a chemical reaction with the help of a Bond-Electron matrix is shown in Tables 1 and 2 [6]. B-E matrix has few properties such as -

- The sum over all the entries of a row or a column indicates the number of valence electrons on the atom
- The sum over all the entries of a B-E matrix indicates the number of valence electrons in the molecule

   Bond-Electron matrix on the Educt side is the Educt matrix (represented by E) and that on the product side is the Product matrix (represented by P). The reaction matrix denoted by R can be obtained by subtracting Educt matrix (E) from Product matrix (P), i.e., $R = P - E$. Each cell entry (r_{ij}) in this

Table 1. BE matrix for the educts of the reaction $C + O = O \rightarrow O = C = O$

	C	O	O
C	0	0	0
O	0	0	2
O	0	2	0

Table 2. BE matrix for the products of the reaction $C + O = O \rightarrow O = C = O$

	C	O	O
C	0	2	2
O	2	0	0
O	2	0	0

Reaction matrix (R) represents the number of bonds broken and the number of bonds made in the course of the reaction. Based on making and breaking of bonds, a reaction can be classified under a particular reaction class called reaction template. Ugi's Scheme consists of 30 reaction classes.

2.2   Extension of Ugi's Scheme

Ugi's Scheme has been efficiently implemented in [7]. But, when tested with The Chemical Thesaurus [8] (a chemical reaction database), it has been found that some of the reactions cannot be classified under Ugi's scheme. An extension of Ugi's scheme has been proposed in [9] where 24 new reaction classes has been developed in addition to 30 reaction classes of Ugi's scheme by studying 3096 chemical reactions from [8].

3   A General Graphical Representation of Chemical Reactions

3.1   Extended Bond Electron Matrix

An extended B-E matrix (EBE matrix) representation was suggested in [11] to include chemical reactions involving both organic and inorganic compounds by adding two extra columns at the end of B-E matrix. These facilitated to store additional information about chemical compounds like:

- Charge information(cation/anion information) to denote charge present on a particular atom in a chemical reaction
- Co-ordinate bond information to denote the positions of atoms between which co-ordinate bond exists.

Unlike, B-E matrix, proposed by Ugi, this Extended B-E matrix (denoted by EBE) has dimension $n \times (n + 2)$. Further, EBE matrix can also represent addition compounds. Since charge information are stored in EBE matrix, so the rule followed by B-E matrix (i.e., the sum of all the rows and columns is zero) may not be applicable in EBE matrix if either of Charge information column or Co-ordinate bond information column has non zero entries.

3.2   Rules Used in EBE Matrix

B-E matrix represents the bond existing between atoms which are participating in a chemical reaction. Apart from bond representation, EBE matrix represents some extra information as discussed in the previous section. Some conventions used in EBE matrix are as follows:

- **Addition Compounds-** An addition compound contains two or more simpler compounds that can be packed in a definite ratio into a crystal. A dot is used to separate the compounds in the formula. In EBE matrix representation, an asterisk sign (*) is placed at the intersecting point between which the dot exists. For example, $MgCl_2.H_2O$ is an addition compound. The EBE matrix representation of this compound is as in Table 3.

Table 3. EBE matrix of addition compound $MgCl_2.H_2O$

	Mg	Cl	Cl	H	O	H	Charge	CoBond
Mg	0	1	1	*	0	0	0	0
Cl	1	0	0	0	0	0	0	0
Cl	1	0	0	0	0	0	0	0
H	0	0	0	0	1	0	0	0
O	0	0	0	1	0	1	0	0
H	0	0	0	0	1	0	0	0

- **Co-ordinate Compounds-** Co-ordinate compounds is represented in EBE matrix by a double marker/single marker (??/?) in the index where the co-ordinate bond exists. The extra Co-ordinate bond information column contains the corresponding index where co-ordinate bond exists. The double marker/single marker denotes that co-ordinate bond is from double marker atom to single marker atom. For example, HNO_3 is a co-ordinate compound and its EBE matrix representation is as in Table 4.

Table 4. EBE matrix for HNO_3

	H	N	O	O	O	Charge	CoBond
H	0	0	0	0	1	0	0
N	0	0	2	??	1	0	4
O	0	2	0	0	1	0	0
O	0	?	0	0	1	0	2
O	1	1	0	0	1	0	0

- **Cations/Anions-** Cations/Anions are charged atoms. In EBE matrix representation, the extra column (Charge Information) contains the charge value with sign (e.g., +1 for single positive charge, −1 for single negative charge) in the index corresponding to the atom on which the charge resides. For example, in Hydronium ion $(H_3O)+$ charge resides on oxygen atom and this compound is represented in EBE representation as shown in Table 5.

Table 5. EBE matrix for hydronium ion $(H_3O)+$

	H	H	H	O	Charge	CoBond
H	0	1	0	0	0	0
H	1	0	1	??	0	4
H	0	1	0	0	0	0
O	0	?	0	0	1	2

Table 6. EBE matrix of educts of the reaction $\{HCl\} + \{H - O - H\} \to \{Cl - 1\} + \{O + 1H2 \sim H\}$

	H	Cl	H	O	H	Charge	CoBond
H	0	1	0	0	0	0	0
Cl	1	0	0	0	0	0	0
H	0	0	0	1	0	0	0
O	0	0	1	0	1	0	0
H	0	0	0	1	0	0	0

Table 7. EBE matrix of products of the reaction $\{HCl\} + \{H - O - H\} \to \{Cl - 1\} + \{O + 1H2 \sim H\}$

	Cl	O	H	H	H	Charge	CoBond
Cl	0	0	0	0	0	-1	0
O	0	0	1	1	??	+1	5
H	0	1	0	0	0	0	0
H	0	1	0	0	0	0	0
H	0	?	0	1	0	0	2

- **Representation of a complete chemical reaction with the help of EBE matrix-** A complete chemical reaction can be represented by the Educt matrix (E) and the Product matrix (P). The Reaction matrix (R) is obtained by subtracting the Educt matrix (E) from the Product matrix (P). In EBE matrix representation, we do not consider the last two columns of the E and P matrix for getting the R matrix. The last two columns of EBE matrix are used only to store the extra information about a compound. The EBE matrix representation of a complete chemical reaction with Educt and Product matrix is shown in Tables 6 and 7 respectively.

4   An Algorithm to Obtain Reaction Template from Extended Bond Electron Matrix

4.1   Algorithm Description

To obtain class or template for a given chemical reaction, the bond information of the chemical reaction including breaking of bonds and making new bonds is needed to be known. In this paper, a general classification algorithm has been proposed which can generate template of a given chemical reaction by computing the bond information. The proposed algorithm is a generalised algorithm and the Ugi's scheme [3] with its 30 templates or its extension [9] with its 24 additional templates can be obtained as subsets of the proposed algorithm. Additionally, the proposed algorithm covers inorganic compounds along with addition compounds, co-ordinate compounds and cations/anions, which [3,9] do not. Thus, wider varieties of new reaction template (class) can be obtained from the proposed algorithm.

Our proposed algorithm consists of main two phases:

- Generate extended reaction matrix (R matrix) which captures all breaking and making bond information along with additional information of coordinate bonds, addition compound and all other types of reaction features. Algorithm 1 generates R matrix of a reaction.
- Create corresponding reaction template by extracting necessary information from EBE matrix of educt, product and R matrix. Algorithm 2 defines the procedure to create reaction template.

In the proposed algorithm (Algorithm 1), EBE matrices (discussed earlier in Sect. 3) of educt(s) and product(s) are taken as input. Reaction matrix (R matrix) is obtained by subtracting Educt matrix from product matrix excluding the main diagonal and last two columns. If there is "*" in the first row of educt EBE which represents presence of an addition compound, then 100 is placed (to backtrack addition compound while generating class of the reaction) in that place and subtraction is performed. If there is single/double marker (?/??), which represents co-ordinate bond information then it is marked as 1 and the subtraction is performed to get the R matrix. Therefore, the R matrix stores all bond related information, i.e. breaking and making of bonds. All information related with free radicals, charge is kept in Educt and Product EBE matrix without any modification so that such information can be obtained while generating the class.

Then, Upper triangular matrix of R is scanned. All bond breaking information (negative value in R matrix) are stored in BREAK_BOND list and new bond making information (positive value in R matrix) are stored in MAKE_BOND list. To obtain the class of the reaction, each entry in the BREAK_BOND list is taken and a new entity (name is given in alphabetic order starting from A to Z) is formed in the template. Corresponding entry in Educt EBE matrix is checked and the bond is associated with other entities in template accordingly. Thus, left hand side of the template is formed. An '=' sign is placed at the end of the left-hand side. Just like above, with MAKE_BOND list and Product EBE matrix, right-hand side of the template is generated as newly formed bond information can be obtained from MAKE_BOND list and EBE matrix of the product. If any value of EBE matrix contains -99 or $+99$, then it implies there is an addition compound. Since, 100 was put in place of addition compound in EBE matrix of educt and product matrices, therefore after subtraction it yields a value of -99 or $+99$ while bond making or breaking respectively. Then a "." is appended at the end of the template whose Educt/Product matrix contains $-99/+99$ to indicate the addition compound. After obtaining all the bond information, information of free radicals, charge and co-ordinate bonds are just appended with the corresponding entity in template by scanning EBE matrix of Educt and Product matrices as described in step 6 of the algorithm. The complete algorithm (Algorithms 1 and 2) are shown below.

Algorithm 1. Generate R Matrix of a given reaction

Data: EBE matrix of educt(s)(E)and product(s)(P) of a chemical reaction.

Result: R matrix the reaction

Form a reaction matrix (R) of size n*n where n = number of atoms in educt(s)
and initialize it to 0

Make two lists of dimension n; MAKE_BOND: each entry in the list is (i,j)
which represents i is making new bond with j, BREAK_BOND: each entry in
the list is (i,j) which represents i is breaking bond with j;

while *Check for Addition compound* **do**

    if *E[1,j]== "*"* **then**

        E[1,j]=100;

        R=P-E (excluding the main diagonal and last two columns)

end

while *Check for co-ordinate compounds* **do**

    if *E[i,j]==? or E[i,j]==??* **then**

        E[i,j]=1;

        R=P-E;

end

4.2   Algorithm Description with Chemical Reaction

Figure 1 shows chemical reaction between Methanol and Hydrogen Cyanide to
form Cyanohydrin. ESMILES [10] represents the reaction as

$$H-(C=O)-H + H-C\#N \rightarrow H-(C(-O-H)(-H)(-C\#N))$$

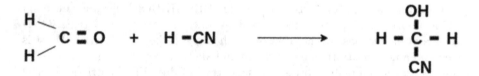

Fig. 1. Chemical reaction between methanol and hydrogen cyanide

Input to the system is given as Tables 8 and 9.

Different steps of Algorithms 1 and 2 are shown as following:

- Reaction matrix (R) is generated and initialized to 0.
- MAKE_BOND and BREAK_BOND lists are created. Tables 10 and 11 show
  initial BREAK_BOND and MAKE_BOND lists respectively.
- Reaction Matrix(R) is created as per Algorithm 1. Table 12 represents newly
  created Reaction Matrix (R).
- In the next phase of the framework, EBE matrices of educts, products
  and reaction matrix are inputs. Tables 13 and 14 show BREAK_BOND and
  MAKE_BOND of the reaction respectively.
- Bonds are created from EBE matrices and lists. Figures 2, 3 and 4 shows
  different steps of template generation.

Algorithm 2. Generate Template Class of a given reaction

Scan the upper triangle of R matrix.

Take the -ve values and store the corresponding (i,j)th index in BREAK_BOND
list

Take the +ve values and store the corresponding (i,j)th index in MAKE_BOND
list

for *(i=1 to n from BREAK_BOND[n])* **do**

    Make a new entity in Template list with a new letter (starting from A)
provided it is not already in the Template list

    j = 1 **while** *((i != j) and (j < i))* **do**

        Take each entry in BREAK_BOND list and obtain bond information
between ith and jth entry corresponding to the ith row of EBE matrix
of Educts

        if *(entry == + 99 or entry == - 99)* **then**

        | Place a dot between ith and jth entry of the EBE matrix

        else

            Place the bond information in Template between ith and jth entry
of the EBE matrix of Educts.

            j=j+1

        end

    end

end

Place "=" sign at the end of the Template. //Processing Educt Part of the
Template is complete.

Repeat step 4 replacing BREAK_BOND[n] by MAKE_BOND[n] and Educt
Matrix by Product Matrix

for *(i=1 to n)* **do**

    if *(there is (are) non zero value(s) in the main diagonal(excluding the part
of the matrix containing the last two columns of EBE matrix of educt and
product matrix))* **then**

    | Then append the non-zero value as free radical(s)with the
corresponding entity in the Template list

    if *the (n+1) th column of EBE matrices of Educt and Product matrix has a
non-zero value* **then**

    | Then append the value as Charge with the corresponding entity.

    if *the (n+2)th column of EBE matrices of Educt and Product matrix has a
non-zero value, if there is a double marker in any entry* **then**

    | place "—>" sign in the corresponding entity accordingly to denote
co-ordinate bond

end

$$A \equiv B \quad + \quad C - D$$

Fig. 2. Template generation (Step 1)

$$A \equiv B \quad + \quad C - D \quad =$$

Fig. 3. Template generation (Step 2)

Table 8. EBE matrix of educts of the reaction in Fig. 1

	O	C	H	H	H	C	N	Charge	CoBond
O	4	2	0	0	0	0	0	0	0
C	2	0	1	1	0	0	0	0	0
H	0	1	0	0	0	0	0	0	0
H	0	1	0	0	0	0	0	0	0
H	0	0	0	0	0	1	0	0	0
C	0	0	0	0	1	0	3	0	0
N	0	0	0	0	0	3	2	0	0

Table 9. EBE matrix of products of the reaction in Fig. 1

	O	C	H	H	H	C	N	Charge	CoBond
O	4	1	0	0	1	0	0	0	0
C	1	0	1	1	0	1	0	0	0
H	0	1	0	0	0	0	0	0	0
H	0	1	0	0	0	0	0	0	0
H	1	0	0	0	0	1	0	0	0
C	0	1	0	0	0	0	3	0	0
N	0	0	0	0	0	3	2	0	0

Table 10. Initialization of BREAK_BOND

O	C	H	H	H	C	N
(0,0)	(0,0)	(0,0)	(0,0)	(0,0)	(0,0)	(0,0)

Table 11. Initialization of MAKE_BOND

O	C	H	H	H	C	N
(0,0)	(0,0)	(0,0)	(0,0)	(0,0)	(0,0)	(0,0)

Table 12. Reaction matrix (R)

	O	C	H	H	H	C	N
O	0	−1	0	0	1	0	0
C	−1	0	0	0	0	1	0
H	0	0	0	0	0	0	0
H	0	0	0	0	0	0	0
H	1	0	0	0	0	−1	0
C	0	1	0	0	−1	0	0
N	0	0	0	0	0	0	0

Table 13. Final BREAK_BOND list

O	C	H	H	H	C	N
(1,2)	(0,0)	(0,0)	(0,0)	(5,6)	(0,0)	(0,0)

Table 14. Final MAKE_BOND list

O	C	H	H	H	C	N
(1,5)	(2,6)	(0,0)	(0,0)	(0,0)	(0,0)	(0,0)

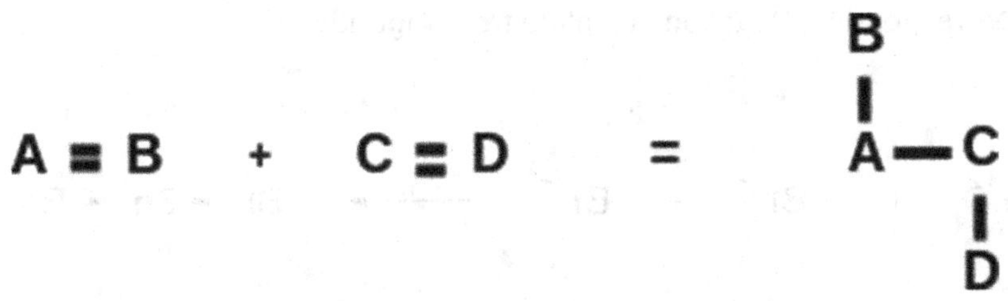

$$A \equiv B \quad + \quad C \equiv D \quad = \quad \begin{matrix} B \\ | \\ A\!-\!C \\ | \\ D \end{matrix}$$

Fig. 4. Template generation (Step 3)

4.3   Examples

Figure 5 illustrates three different categories of chemical reactions involving co-ordinate compound, anions-cations and addition compound and their corresponding reaction templates obtained by applying Algorithms 1 and 2.

4.4   Experiments and Results

The above algorithms are implemented in Java. Our input consists of a chemical reaction in the form of an EBE-matrix which is stored in a .txt file. Our output consists of the template of the given chemical reaction. The template generated is also stored in an output file in .txt format. Some of the results generated by Algorithms 1 and 2 are shown in Table 15.

Table 15. Examples of reactions with templates

Chemical reaction	Template
$H - H + Br - Br \rightarrow H - Br + H - Br$	$A - B + C - D = A - C + B - D$
$CH2 = CH2 + H - H \rightarrow CH3 - CH3$	$A = B + C - D = C - A - B - D$
$N(.2)H3 + H - Cl \rightarrow NH3 \sim HCl$	$A(.2)B + C = A - B \rightarrow C$
$H^+ + Cl^- \rightarrow H - Cl$	$A+1 + B-1 = A - B$
$H^+ + H^+ + S(= O)(= O)(-O^-)(-O^-) \rightarrow$ $S(= O)(= O)(-O - H)(-O - H)$	$A+1 + B+1 + C - (D-1)(E-1) =$ $C(D-A)(E-B)$
$Fe - S + H - Cl + H - Cl \rightarrow$ $Cl - Fe - Cl + H - S(.4) - H$	$A - B + C - D + E - F =$ $D - A - F + C - B(.4) - E$

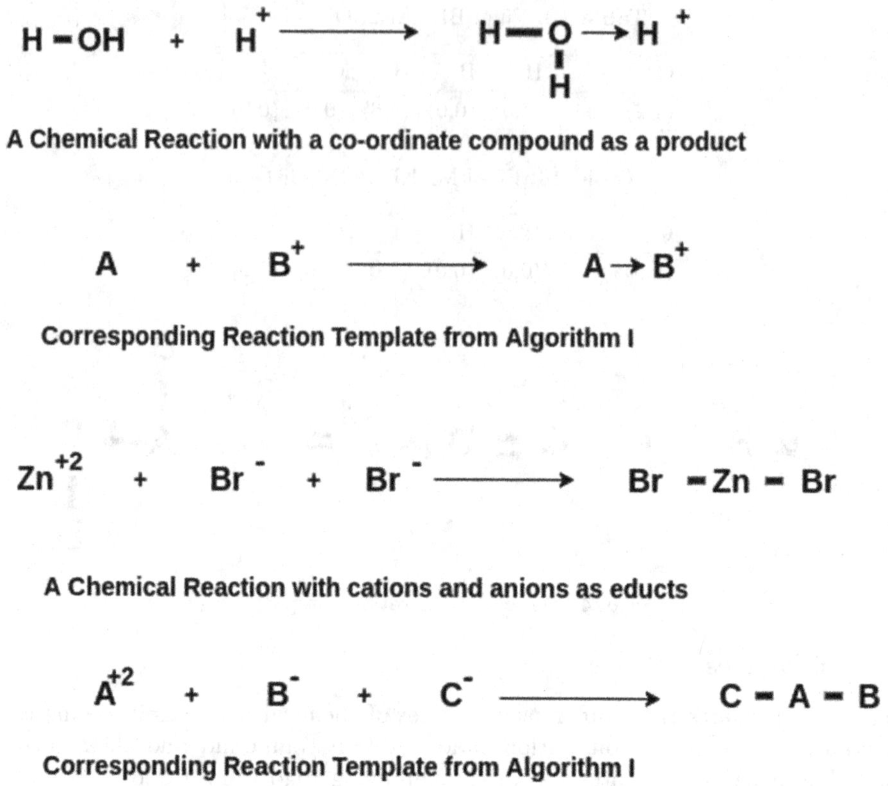

$$H - OH \quad + \quad H^+ \quad \longrightarrow \quad H - \underset{\underset{H}{|}}{O} \rightarrow H^+$$

A Chemical Reaction with a co-ordinate compound as a product

$$A \quad + \quad B^+ \quad \longrightarrow \quad A \rightarrow B^+$$

Corresponding Reaction Template from Algorithm I

$$Zn^{+2} \quad + \quad Br^- \quad + \quad Br^- \quad \longrightarrow \quad Br - Zn - Br$$

A Chemical Reaction with cations and anions as educts

$$A^{+2} \quad + \quad B^- \quad + \quad C^- \quad \longrightarrow \quad C - A - B$$

Corresponding Reaction Template from Algorithm I

Fig. 5. Some new reaction classes derived by Algorithm 1.

4.5   Time Complexity of the Algorithm

The algorithm to generate the reaction template consists of two main parts -

- generation of R matrix from a given chemical reaction
- generation of reaction template of the given chemical reaction

The first step of R matrix generation algorithm takes $O(n^2)$ time to initialise the R matrix. The MAKE_BOND and BREAK_BOND lists take $O(n)$ time to initialise. Checking for the presence of addition compound needs to scan only the first row of the matrix which requires for only $O(n)$ comparisons. Checking whether a co-ordinate compound is present in a chemical reaction requires to scan only the upper/lower triangular matrix, and if a (?/??) is found in the $(i, j)^{th}$ entry, then the corresponding $(j, i)^{th}$ entry is to be filled up with (??/?). This step requires $O(n^2)$ comparisons approximately. So, Algorithm 1 takes approximately $O(n^2)$ time. The second part of the algorithm, i.e., the generation of template class of a reaction, takes approximately $O(n^2)$ for scanning the upper triangular matrix in order to fill up the MAKE_BOND and BREAK_BOND lists in the educt part of the reaction. Similarly, the template for the product part is generated in $O(n^2)$ time. The diagonal elements are scanned in $O(n)$ time and the free radical information (if present) is appended on the template. Finally, the extra information are appended on the template according to the last two column information, i.e., (co-ordinate bond, cation/anion) information. So, the overall time complexity for template generation is $2 * O(n^2)$, i.e., $O(n^2)$.

5   Conclusion

In this paper, a Model Driven approach to obtain chemical reaction templates (classes) has been proposed by mining chemical reactions represented in the form of a chemical graph. There are many methods to obtain reaction classes using model driven classification approach, such as Hendrickson's scheme [10], Ugi's scheme [3], and extended Ugi's scheme [9]. Hendrickson's scheme consists of 7 reaction classes. The previous other approaches like Ugi's scheme and extended Ugi's scheme came up with 30 reaction classes and 24 additional classes respectively. Both these approaches use Bond Electron matrix and Ugi's scheme was obtained by studying organic chemical reactions. The present approach covers both organic and inorganic chemical reactions and is a general reaction template eliciting algorithm. The algorithm uses a more elaborate computer representation of chemical graph namely Extended Bond Electron matrix. Specifically, this algorithm can obtain reaction classes for chemical reactions involving cations/anions, co-ordinate compounds and addition compounds, which are not possible in Ugi's scheme and extended Ugi's scheme. The proposed algorithm is sufficiently general in that all reaction templates obtained from Ugi's scheme and extended Ugi's scheme are also obtained by the algorithm. The proposed algorithm can be used to derive to newer reaction classes.

References

1. Balban, A.T.: Chemical graphs: Looking back and a glimpsing ahead. J. Chem. Inf. Comput. Sci. **35**(3), 339–350 (1995). doi:10.1021/ci00025a0021
2. Ivanciuc, O.: Representing two-dimensional (2D) chemical structures with molecular graphs. In: Foulon, J.L., Bender, A. (eds.) Handbook of Chemoinformatics Algorithms, pp. 1–36. CRC Press (2010)
3. Ugi, I., Brandt, J., Friedrich, J., Gasteiger, J., Jochum, C., Lemmen, P., Schubert, W.: The deductive solution of chemical problems by computer programs on the basis of a mathematical model of chemistry. Pure Appl. Chem. **60**(11), 1573–1586 (1988). Wiley, Chichester
4. Dugundji, J., Ugi, I.: An algebraic model of constitutional chemistry as a basis for chemical computer programs. In: Computers in Chemistry-Topics in Current Chemistry, pp. 19–64. Springer, Heidelberg (1973)
5. Gasteiger, J., Engel, T.: Chemoinformatics: A Textbook. Wiley-VCH, KgaA, Weinheim (2003)
6. Maity, S., Ganguli, M.: Elements of Chemistry, Part - II, 7th edn. Kolkata Publishing Syndicate, Kolkata (2003)

7. Ram, S., Pal, S.: An efficient algorithm for automating classification of chemical reactions into classes in ugis reaction scheme. Int. J. Chemoinformatics Chem. Eng. **2**(2), 1–14 (2012)
8. Cousins, K.R.: The chemical thesaurus 4.0. J. Am Chem. Soc. **123**(35), 8645–8646 (2001)
9. Maiti, S., Ram, S., Pal, S.: Extension of Ugis scheme for model-driven classification of chemical reactions. Int. J. Chemoinformatics Chem. Eng. **4**(1), 26–51 (2015)
10. Hendrickson, J.B., Chen, L.: Reaction classification. In: Schleyer, P.V.R., Allinger, N.L., Clark, T., Gasteiger, J., Kollman, P.A., Schaefer, H.F., Schreiner, P.R. (eds.) Encyclopedia of Computational Chemistry, pp. 2381–2402. Wille, Chichester (1998)
11. Samaddar, A., Goswami, T., Ghosh, S., Pal, S.: An algorithm to input and store wider classes of chemical reactions for mining chemical graphs. In: International Advanced Computing Conference 2015, pp. 1082–1086. IEEEXplorer (2015)

Moving Object Detection in Video Under Dynamic Background Condition Using Block-Based Statistical Features

Amlan Raychaudhuri[1(✉)], Satyabrata Maity[2], Amlan Chakrabarti[2], and Debotosh Bhattacharjee[3]

[1] Department of Computer Science and Engineering, B.P. Poddar Institute of Management & Technology, 137, VIP Road, Kolkata 700 052, India
amlanrc@gmail.com

[2] A.K. Choudhury School of Information Technology, University of Calcutta, JD-2, JD Block, Sector-III, Kolkata 700 098, India
satyabrata.maity@gmail.com, amlanc@ieee.org

[3] Department of Computer Science and Engineering, Jadavpur University, 188, Raja S.C. Mallick Road, Kolkata 700 032, India
debotoshb@hotmail.com

Abstract. In this paper, an efficient technique has been proposed to detect moving objects in the video under dynamic background condition. The proposed method consists block-based background modeling, block processing of current frame and elimination of background using bin histogram approach. Next, enhanced foreground objects are obtained in the post-processing stage using morphological operations. The proposed approach effectively minimizes the effect of dynamic background to extract the foreground information. We have applied our proposed technique on Change Detection CDW-2012 dataset and compared the results with the other state-of-the-art methods. The experimental results prove the efficiency of the proposed approach compared to the other state-of-the-art methods in terms of different evaluation metrics.

Keywords: Moving object detection · Dynamic background · Background modeling · Block processing · Background elimination · Bin histogram

1 Introduction

Moving object detection from a given video sequence under dynamic background condition is a very challenging task in video processing and has been an active research area in the field of computer vision for the last few decades [1, 2]. It has wide application in video surveillance, event detection, dynamic scene analysis, activity recognition and activity based human recognition [1, 2]. To detect moving objects from a given video sequence, the object regions which are moving are needed to be identified with respect to their background [2]. Moving object detection is done mainly using three different kinds of approaches [3]: background subtraction [6, 7], temporal differencing [5] and optical flow [4]. Two important steps for background subtraction approaches are: proper

© Springer Nature Singapore Pte Ltd. 2017
J.K. Mandal et al. (Eds.): CICBA 2017, Part II, CCIS 776, pp. 371–383, 2017.
DOI: 10.1007/978-981-10-6430-2_29

generation and updation of reference background model, and then application of an appropriate elimination technique to eliminate the background model from the current frame. Over the years, numerous different techniques have been proposed by various researchers. For all these methods, the most important steps are generation of background model and how it is updated over time.

Detection of moving objects remains an open research problem even after research of several years in this field. To obtain an accurate, robust and high-performance approach is still a very challenging job. Shaikh et al. [3] mentioned some of the challenges of background subtraction related to video surveillance in their work. The challenges are - (a) Illumination changes: for a video sequence, illumination may change gradually or in some cases rapidly. To detect a moving object accurately from these kinds of videos, the background model should take this into consideration. (b) Dynamic background: in some videos, the background is not static. It contains movement (a fountain, wave of water, movement of tree leaves, etc.) in some regions of the background. To eliminate these kinds of movement is a challenging task. (c) Camouflage: some portion of the objects' intensity is very much similar to that of the background intensity in the same region. To classify objects and background correctly under this scenario is a huge challenging task. (d) Presence of shadows: shadows are created mainly due to presence of foreground objects; removal of shadows occurring due to foreground objects is a very challenging task.

Background subtraction is a popularly used method for motion segmentation in static scenes [8]. Heikkila and Silven [9] used the simple version of this scheme. They have tried to detect moving regions by pixel-wise subtraction of the current frame from a background reference frame. The pixels will be treated as foreground if the corresponding difference is above a threshold. The generation of the background image by applying some technique is known as background modeling. After creating a foreground pixel mask, some morphological operations are used such as erosion, dilation and closing for noise reduction and to enhance the detected foreground regions in the post-processing step. The reference background is updated over time to handle the dynamic scene changes.

Some authors used temporal differencing to detect moving regions by taking the pixel-by-pixel difference between consecutive two or three frames in a video sequence. Lipton et al. [10] proposed a two-frame differencing method where the pixel-by-pixel difference is calculated for two consecutive frames. If that difference is above some threshold value, then the corresponding pixel is marked as foreground. In [11], the authors have used three frames differencing in order to overcome the shortcomings of two frames differencing. For instance, Collins et al. [12] developed a hybrid method which combines three frames differencing with an adaptive model for background subtraction. The hybrid algorithm successfully discriminates moving regions from the background region in the video without the limitations of temporal differencing and background subtraction.

Stauffer and Grimson [13] proposed a statistical method based on an adaptive background mixture model for real-time tracking. There, every pixel is separately modeled by a mixture of Gaussians which are updated using incoming image data. For detection of a pixel belongs to a foreground or background, the Gaussian distributions of the mixture model for that pixel are evaluated.

In [14], the authors proposed a system which uses a statistical background model. In their work, each pixel is represented by its minimum (*min*) intensity value, maximum (*max*) intensity value and maximum difference (*diff*) of intensity values between any two consecutive frames. These features are used during initial training period where no moving objects are present in the scene. A pixel in the current frame is classified as foreground if the absolute difference between *max* and the pixel intensity value is greater than *diff* value or the absolute difference between *min* and the pixel intensity value is greater than *diff* value of the corresponding pixel. After thresholding, morphological erosion and dilation are applied to get the final foreground object.

In [3], the authors proposed a low-cost background subtraction method for detecting moving objects under dynamic background conditions. They have created a background model by computing the median of corresponding pixels of a certain number of frames. Then through block processing and using statistical method, background is eliminated from the current frame. After that in the post processing step, some morphological operations are applied to obtain the foreground object.

In [4, 15, 16], the authors have used optical flow methods to make use of the flow vectors of the objects which are moving over time for detection of moving objects in an image. In this approach, they have computed the apparent velocity and the direction of every pixel. It is an effective but time-consuming method.

In our research work, we have detected moving objects in a video under dynamic background condition. After generating a background model, efficiently the background is eliminated from the current frame using block processing and thresholding of bin histogram. Finally at the post-processing step, we applied some morphological operations to eliminate very small wrongly detected foreground regions and enhance the original foreground regions. The remainder of this paper is presented as follows: Sect. 2 yields the details of proposed method. The experimental results and analysis are discussed in Sect. 3. Finally, the conclusion is given in Sect. 4.

2   Proposed Method

In this research work, we have proposed a new technique to detect moving objects in a video under dynamic background condition. Here, we have worked on gray-scale frames. Thus, at first, all the frames of a video sequence are extracted, and they are converted into gray-scale images. The brief sketch of our proposed method is shown in Fig. 1. The proposed method has the following important steps: (a) background modeling with block processing, (b) block processing of the current frame and background elimination and (c) post-processing operations.

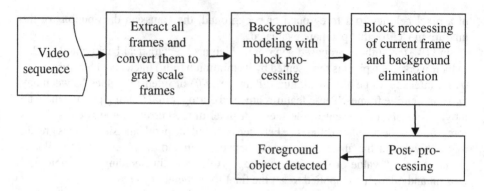

Fig. 1. A brief sketch of the proposed method

2.1 Background Modeling with Block Processing

To detect the moving objects in the current frame, we have generated a background model consisting of previous n frames where the objects are not present. The value of n should be large enough as to generate a realistic background model for the dynamic background. We have taken recent frames for consideration of background model to cater the recent changes in the scene.

At first, each frame (*frame size = r × c*) of these n frames is divided into a number of equal sized logical blocks bg_{ij} (*block size = m × m*), resulting $i × j$ number of blocks, where $i = 1$ *to r/m* and $j = 1$ *to c/m*. Block-wise we gather the statistical features of the background. For block processing, bin histogram is used here for each of the blocks. The pixels, whose intensity values are close to each other, belong to the same bin depending on the bin size. By using bin histogram, we efficiently handle the dynamic nature of the background. There are total 256 intensity values (0 to 255) in a gray-scale image. Depending on the bin size (*bs*), a total number of bins (*bn*) are calculated using Eq. (1).

$$bn = 256/bs \tag{1}$$

Thus, total bn number of bins are considered for each block and corresponding to those bins, a bin histogram is computed which is shown in Fig. 2. A block bg_{ij} of a frame is shown in Fig. 2(a) and its corresponding bin histogram is shown in Fig. 2(b). In Fig. 2(b), $bs = 16$ is considered, so as a result the value of bn is also 16. A bin histogram represents the frequency of bins in a block. If the intensity of a pixel x_t is represented by *intensity*(x_t), then the bin at which pixel x_t will be mapped is given by Eq. (2). This computation is done for all the blocks of these n frames. Thereafter, a background model is generated by averaging the bin histogram values corresponding to each block of these n frames, which is shown in Eq. (3).

$$x_t \in bn_l, \quad if\ bn_l = int\,(intensity(x_t)/bs) + 1$$
$$\{\forall t = 1\ to\ m \times m,\ 1 \le l \le bn\} \tag{2}$$

where x_t pixel maps to bin bn_l, bs is the bin size and bn represents the total number of bins in the bin histogram, total $(m \times m)$ number of pixels are present in each block.

$$bin\_hist(bg_{ij})_{bg} = average \{bin\_hist(bg_{ij})_1, bin\_hist(bg_{ij})_2, \ldots, bin\_hist(bg_{ij})_n\}$$
$$\{\forall i = 1 \ to \ r/m, \ \forall j = 1 \ to \ c/m\}$$
(3)

where $bin\_hist(bg_{ij})_k$ means bin histogram of block bg_{ij} (size $= m \times m$) of k-th frame and $bin\_hist(bg_{ij})_{bg}$ represents bin histogram of block bg_{ij} of the background model, n represents the total number of frames considered for generating background model, r and c denote the number of rows and the number of columns of a frame.

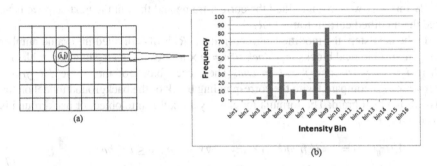

Fig. 2. (a) Block bg_{ij} of a frame. (b) Corresponding bin histogram

In the next step, a background image (BG) is created with the help of same n number of frames. The pixel intensity of each position of BG is calculated by averaging the intensity values of the corresponding position for the n number of frames, which is shown in Eq. (4).

$$BG(i,j) = \sum_{k=1}^{n} B_k(i,j)/n \qquad \{\forall i = 1 \ to \ r, \ \forall j = 1 \ to \ c\}$$
(4)

$BG(i, j)$ and $B_k(i, j)$ represent the (i, j)-th pixel intensity of the background image (BG) and the k-th frame respectively.

2.2 Block Processing of the Current Frame and Background Elimination

Before block processing of the current frame, some pre-processing is done on the current frame. Here we have worked on the video sequences under dynamic background condition. Background is not static; it is changing over time due to various causes. Under this situation, it is very difficult to extract accurate moving objects from the video sequence. It may be happened that, the intensity values are also changed due to illumination changes. So, to handle these kinds of situations, the current frame (TR) is modified with the Eq. (5).

$$TR(i,j) = BG(i,j), \quad if \ |TR(i,j) - BG(i,j)| \ < \ th_1$$
$$= TR(i,j), \quad otherwise \quad \{\forall i = 1 \ to \ r, \forall j = 1 \ to \ c\} \tag{5}$$

For the current frame (TR), the intensity value of a pixel is modified by the corresponding background pixel intensity, if the absolute difference between these two pixels intensity is less than a threshold value (th_1). Otherwise, no change for the pixel value of the current frame. Here computation of th_1 value is shown in Eq. (6).

$$th_1 = std(TR)/2 - 5 \tag{6}$$

where $std(TR)$ means the standard deviation of the current frame (TR).

By this way we have modified the current frame and then in the next step we have used the modified current frame (TR).

In the next step, the modified current frame (TR) is also divided into same number of equal-sized logical blocks tr_{ij} (block size $= m \times m$), resulting $i \times j$ number of blocks, where $i = 1$ to r/m and $j = 1$ to c/m. Then, each block of the frame TR (frame size $= r \times c$) is compared with the corresponding block of the background model on the basis of bin histogram. The formula for classify a pixel x_t into object or background is given in Eq. (7).

$$I_1(tr_{ij}(x_t)) = 1, \quad if \ freq(bn_l) < th_2 \quad \{\forall x_t \in bn_l, \ 1 \le l \le bn\}$$
$$= 0, \quad otherwise \quad \{\forall i = 1 \ to \ r/m, \forall j = 1 \ to \ c/m\} \tag{7}$$

A pixel x_t of a particular block tr_{ij} of the modified current frame will be treated as foreground pixel, if its corresponding bin's frequency $freq(bn_l)$ is less than a threshold value th_2 in the bin histogram of the corresponding block bg_{ij} of the background model. Otherwise, the pixel x_t will be treated as background. In this way, after processing all the pixels of each block of the modified current frame, a new binary image I_1 is created, where all the foreground pixels are assigned with value '1' and background pixels are with '0'.

We have compared the bin histogram of a block of the current frame with the bin histogram of the corresponding block of the background model using a threshold th_2 for all the blocks. The threshold value th_2 is dependent on the video sequences. In this way, we have efficiently eliminated the dynamic nature of the background information from the current frame.

2.3   Post-processing Operations

After background elimination by the above mentioned method, a binary image I_1 is generated. This image contains some noises outside the foreground region and some foreground pixels are misclassified as background pixels. So in the post-processing step, we have applied two morphological operations – *open* and *close* to reduce noises and misclassifications.

The morphological *open* operation is applied on the binary image I_1 to reduce noises outside the foreground region. In this case, very small regions which are misclassified as foreground regions are eliminated from the image I_1. In the resultant image, some portion of the foreground region may be misclassified as background. Thus to obtain enhanced foreground object regions, the morphological closing operation is applied on the resultant image.

In this way, the desired binary image is obtained. Where white pixels represent foreground object and black pixels represent background. Figure 3 shows the result on a sample frame.

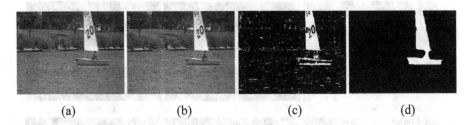

| (a) | (b) | (c) | (d) |

Fig. 3. Result on a sample frame. (a) Sample frame in RGB color. (b) Corresponding gray-scale image. (c) Output after background elimination. (d) Final output after post-processing.

3 Experimental Results and Analysis

To evaluate the effectiveness of our approach, we performed our experiments on the Change Detection CDW-2012 (dynamic background) [17] dataset. This is a standard benchmark dataset consisting of six video categories with a dynamic background. The threshold value th_2 which is described in Sect. 2.2, is chosen based on experimental testing. Here for this dataset we have considered the th_2 value in the range from 5 to 10 to obtain the best results. For effectiveness of our research work, we have compared our results with the readily available ground truth data in the above mentioned dataset. Figure 4 shows a sample color frame from each category of videos, its corresponding ground truth and output of our proposed method.

To evaluate the performance of our proposed method, different evaluation measures techniques [17] have been applied here. The evaluation measures are based on the following parameters: TP = true positives; the number of foreground pixels correctly classified as foreground. TN = true negatives; the number of background pixels correctly classified as background. FP = false positives; the number of background pixels misclassified as foreground. FN = false negative; the number of foreground pixels misclassified as background. The different metrics are described below.

Recall: It is defined as the ratio of true positive to true positive and false negative. A high value of recall is desired.

$$Recall = TP/(TP + FN) \tag{8}$$

Specificity: It is defined as the ratio of true negative to true negative and false positive. A high value of this metric is desired.

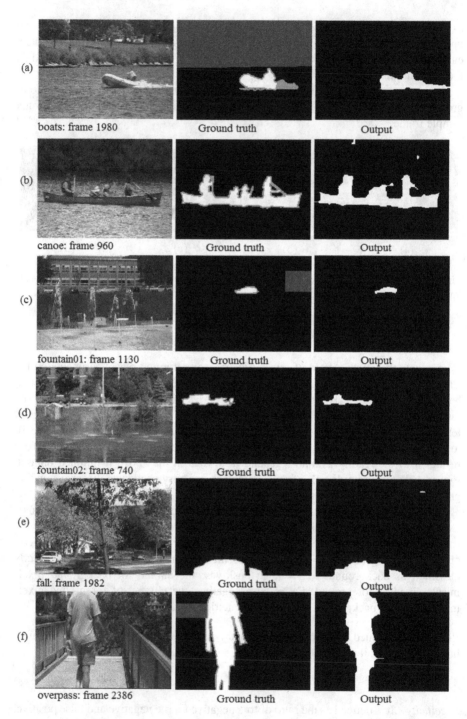

Fig. 4. Sample frames, corresponding ground truths and outputs of the proposed method for six video categories (a–f)

$$Specificity = TN/(TN + FP) \tag{9}$$

False Positive Rate (FPR): It is the ratio of false positive to false positive and true negative. A low value of FPR is desired.

$$FPR = FP/(FP + TN) \tag{10}$$

False Negative Rate (FNR): It is the ratio of false negative to false negative and true positive. A low value of FNR is desired.

$$FNR = FN/(FN + TP) \tag{11}$$

Percentage of the Wrong Classification (PWC): It is 100 times the ratio of false positive and false negative to all the detected pixels. It is better if the PWC value is lower.

$$PWC = 100 * (FP + FN)/(TP + TN + FP + FN) \tag{12}$$

F-measure: It is based on recall and precision both. A high value of F-measure is desired.

$$F - measure = 2 * Recall * Precision/(Recall + Precision) \tag{13}$$

Precision: It is the ratio of true positive to true positive and false positive. A high value of Precision is desired.

$$Precision = TP/(TP + FP) \tag{14}$$

Figure 4 shows sample frames for each category of videos, their corresponding ground truth and outputs by applying our proposed method. Table 1 shows the average results of the proposed method for all the six video categories based on the above mentioned seven metrics.

Table 1. Average results on all the videos

Videos	Recall	Specificity	FPR	FNR	PWC	F-measure	Precision
Boats	0.9333	0.9979	0.0021	0.0667	0.4798	0.9419	0.9507
Canoe	0.9363	0.9923	0.0077	0.0637	1.1530	0.9173	0.8990
Fountain01	0.5730	0.9998	0.0002	0.4270	0.3650	0.5888	0.6055
Fountain02	0.5647	0.9990	0.0010	0.4353	0.6406	0.6881	0.8804
Fall	0.7602	0.9899	0.0101	0.2398	2.1632	0.7794	0.7996
Overpass	0.8506	0.9931	0.0069	0.1494	1.4059	0.8583	0.8661
Average	0.7697	0.9953	0.0047	0.2303	0.9798	0.7956	0.8336

In Table 2, the comparison results of our method with the other state-of-the-art methods using an average of all seven evaluation metrics are shown. It can be seen that, in the case of five metrics (*Specificity, FPR, PWC, F-measure and Precision*) out of seven, our proposed method is superior to that of the other methods. Thus it validates

380   A. Raychaudhuri et al.

the efficiency of our proposed method. Figure 5 presents graphically the comparison results based on all the seven metrics.

Table 2. Comparison results with the other state-of-the-art methods

Methods	Recall	Specificity	FPR	FNR	PWC	F-measure	Precision
Stauffer and Grimson [13]	0.7108	0.9860	0.0140	0.2892	3.1037	0.6624	0.7012
PBAS [18]	**0.7840**	0.9898	0.0102	**0.2160**	1.7693	0.7532	0.8160
CDPS [19]	0.7769	0.9848	0.0152	0.2231	2.2747	0.7281	0.7610
Proposed	0.7697	**0.9953**	**0.0047**	0.2303	**0.9798**	**0.7956**	**0.8336**

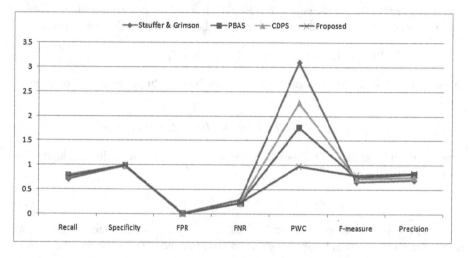

Fig. 5. Comparisons based on all the seven evaluation metrics

Figure 6 illustrates the graphical analysis of our method compared to the other state-of-the-art methods [13, 18, 19] in respect to all the seven metrics for each video sequence. It clearly proves the efficiency of our proposed technique compared to the other techniques.

We have also applied our proposed method to the *Office* [17] video sequence. In that video sequence, the movement of foreground object is very slow. The results obtained here for the sequence are very impressive. Figure 7 shows sample frame, its corresponding ground truth and the output of our proposed method.

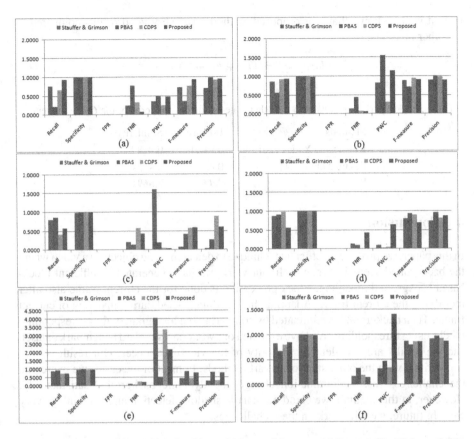

Fig. 6. Comparison analysis for six videos: (a) boats, (b) canoe, (c) fountain01, (d) fountain02, (e) fall, and (f) overpass

frame 690   Ground Truth   Output

Fig. 7. Sample frame, corresponding ground truth and output of the *Office* sequence

The comparison results of our method with the other state-of-the-art methods for the *Office* sequence are shown in Table 3. Here comparison is done with respect to two metrics – *F-measure* and *Similarity*. The computation of *F-measure* is already mentioned in Eq. (13) and the metric *Similarity* is computed by the Eq. (15). From the table it is also shown that, our proposed method gives very good results compared to the other methods.

$$Similarity = TP / (TP + FP + FN) \tag{15}$$

Table 3. Comparison results with the other state-of-the-art methods for the *Office* sequence

Methods	F-measure	Similarity
Kumar and Yadav [20]	0.9129	0.8189
Rahman et al. [21]	0.6545	0.4864
Proposed	**0.93**	**0.8691**

4 Conclusion

In this paper, we propose an efficient technique to detect moving objects in a video where the background scene is dynamic. In our work, we have generated an efficient block-based background modeling. Block processing is done for the current frame also after modifying the current frame. Adapting thresholding is used during updating of current frame. Then background is eliminated by comparing bin histogram of the corresponding blocks using thresholding. We have executed our work on a standard benchmark dataset, and the results are excellent for majority of the video sequences. Our result is very competitive with the other state-of-the-art methods. In most of the cases, we overcome the challenges like – illumination change and dynamic background satisfactorily. However, in this method, we could not handle shadow detection and camouflage very well. In future, we will work on these challenges.

References

1. Bovik, A.C.: Hand Book on Image and Video Processing. Academic Press, New York (2000)
2. Tekalp, A.M.: Digital Video Processing. Prentice Hall, New Jersey (1995)
3. Shaikh, S.H., Saeed, K., Chaki, N.: Moving object detection using background subtraction. In: Shaikh, S.H., et al. (eds.) Moving Object Detection Using Background Subtraction. SCS, pp. 15–23. Springer, Cham (2014). doi:10.1007/978-3-319-07386-6_3
4. Paragios, N., Deriche, R.: Geodesic active contours and level sets for the detection and tracking of moving objects. IEEE Trans. Pattern Anal. Mach. Intell. **22**(3), 266–280 (2000)
5. Fejes, S., Davis, L.S.: Detection of independent motion using directional motion estimation. Comput. Vis. Image Underst. (CVIU) **74**(2), 101–120 (1999)
6. Piccardi, M.: Background subtraction techniques: a review. In: Proceedings of the IEEE International Conference on Systems, Man and Cybernetics (SMC), vol. 4, pp. 3099–3104 (2004)
7. Elhabian, S., El-Sayed, K., Ahmed, S.: Moving object detection in spatial domain using background removal techniques — state-of-art. Recent Pat. Comput. Sci. **1**, 32–54 (2008)
8. McIvor, A.M.: Background subtraction techniques. In: Proceedings of Image and Vision Computing (2000)

9. Heikkila, J., Silven, O.: A real-time system for monitoring of cyclists and pedestrians. Proc. Image Vis. Comput. **22**(7), 563–570 (2004)

10. Lipton, A.J., Fujiyoshi, H., Patil, R.S.: Moving target classification and tracking from real time video. In: Proceedings of the 4th IEEE Workshop on Applications of Computer Vision (WACV 1998), pp. 129–136 (1998)

11. Wang, L., Hu, W., Tan, T.: Recent developments in human motion analysis. Pattern Recogn. **36**(3), 585–601 (2003)

12. Collins, R.T., Lipton, A.J., Kanade, T., Fujiyoshi, H., Duggins, D., Tsin, Y., Tolliver, D., Enomoto, N., Hasegawa, O., Burt, P., Wixson, L.: A system for video surveillance and monitoring. In: Technical report CMU-RI-TR-00-12, The Robotics Institute, Carnegie Mellon University (2000)

13. Stauffer, C., Grimson, W.E.L.: Adaptive background mixture models for real-time tracking. In: Proceedings of the IEEE Computer Society Conference on Computer Vision and Pattern Recognition (CVPR), vol. 2 (1999)

14. Haritaoglu, I., Harwood, D., Davis, L.S.: W^4: real-time surveillance of people and their activities. IEEE Trans. Pattern Anal. Mach. Intell. **22**(8), 809–830 (2000)

15. Wixson, L.: Detecting salient motion by accumulating directionally - consistent flow. IEEE Trans. Pattern Anal. Mach. Intell. **22**(8), 774–780 (2000)

16. Pless, R., Brodsky, T., Aloimonos, Y.: Detecting independent motion: the statistics of temporal continuity. IEEE Trans. Pattern Anal. Mach. Intell. **22**(8), 768–773 (2000)

17. Goyette, N., Jodoin, P.-M., Porikli, F., Konrad, J., Ishwar, P.: Changedetection.net: a new change detection benchmark dataset. In: Proceedings of the IEEE Workshop on Change Detection (CDW-2012) at CVPR (2012)

18. Hofmann, M., Tiefenbacher, P., Rigoll, G.: Background segmentation with feedback: the pixel-based adaptive segmenter. In: Proceedings of the IEEE Workshop on Change Detection, pp. 38–43 (2012)

19. Francisco, J., Lopez, H., Rivera, M.: Change detection by probabilistic segmentation from monocular view. Proc. Mach. Vis. Appl. **25**(5), 1175–1195 (2014)

20. Kumar, S., Yadav, J.S.: Video object extraction and its tracking using background subtraction in complex environments. Perspect. Sci. **8**, 317–322 (2016)

21. Rahman, A.Y.F., Hussain, A., Zaki, W., Zaman, B., Tahir, M.: Enhancement of background subtraction techniques using a second derivative in gradient direction filter. J. Electr. Comput. Eng. **2013**, 1–12 (2013)

A Fuzzy Based Hybrid Hierarchical Clustering Model for Twitter Sentiment Analysis

Hima Suresh[1(✉)] and S. Gladston Raj[2]

[1] School of Computer Sciences, M.G University, Kottayam, Kerala, India
himasuresh@gmail.com
[2] Department of Computer Science, Government College, Nedumangadu, Kerala, India
gladston@rediffmail.com

Abstract. The increasing popularity of Twitter allows users to share target information as well as to express their own opinions on concerned subjects. Though the Twitter based information gathering techniques enable collecting direct responses from the target audience, not much by the way of research has been done to predict, model and forecast user behavior using the already existing and often abundant supply of personal data housed by the social network. This ready and continuous stream of social media information could be analyzed with the use of an Unsupervised learning technique to predict social behavior. In this research work, a novel fuzzy based hybrid hierarchical clustering model has been proposed to analyze Unsupervised techniques on Twitter samples. The efficiency of the model was measured based on the performance metrics namely accuracy, precision and recall. The model not only provides higher quality of results for dynamic users and tweet sentiment analysts, but also improves the performance of the clustering techniques in terms of accuracy with approximately 79.8%.

Keywords: Clustering · Unsupervised · Hierarchical clustering · Machine learning

1 Introduction

Human beings are fairly sophisticated when it comes to understanding the complicated meanings beneath the written words. With the help of Machine learning techniques computers could read between the lines of tweets, resulting in a new technology called Sentiment Analysis.

Sentiment analysis is the process of identifying and extracting opinion, which in turn, could guide the strategy as well as help in decision making. In the current business scenario, it is increasingly necessary that we know what the competitors, employees or the customers think about the particular brand and product. Sentiment Analysis would help us do this often relatively inexpensively.

The Interest in Sentiment Analysis methods stems from two different techniques namely Supervised and Unsupervised techniques. Unsupervised techniques draw inferences from the dataset without any labeled response or prior known output. An approach to such technique is clustering. Clustering techniques are of two different types such as

© Springer Nature Singapore Pte Ltd. 2017
J.K. Mandal et al. (Eds.): CICBA 2017, Part II, CCIS 776, pp. 384–397, 2017.
DOI: 10.1007/978-981-10-6430-2_30

Partition based clustering and Hierarchical clustering. We adopted the Hierarchical clustering based Unsupervised technique instead of Partition based clustering technique since; it is more versatile, no prior knowledge about the number of clusters is required, method could give different partitioning depending on the level of resolution. In order to deal with uncertainty in the tweet information gathered for Sentiment Analysis of a product brand "Samsung Galaxy S6", fuzzy logic has been employed with our hybrid hierarchical clustering technique.

The major contributions of our proposed work are as follows:

(1) The Twitter samples of 1500 real datasets were taken from the Twitter Application Programming Interface (TAPI) that was collected over a time period of 14 months.
(2) We have made a comparative analysis of the modern hierarchical clustering techniques in our domain of Twitter Sentiment Analysis.
(3) Designed and implemented a new method to achieve prominent results in analyzing the brand impact of the smart phone; Samsung Galaxy S6.

The rest of the paper is organized as follows. The related studies of most relevant research papers were presented in Sect. 2. The methodology of the proposed work was described in Sect. 3. The experimental results were discussed in Sect. 4. Finally the concluding remarks were made in Sect. 5.

2   Related Studies

Previous works related to the domain of Sentiment Analysis is analyzed and discussed in this section. The related concepts and terms are described below:

2.1   Unsupervised Machine Learning

Unsupervised machine learning is the task of drawing inference of a function from data set containing input without labeled data or target value to describe hidden patterns from unlabeled data. The most common Unsupervised machine learning method is hierarchical cluster analysis. It is used for exploratory data analysis in order to find the hidden patterns.

2.2   Hierarchical Clustering

Hierarchical clustering is a type of cluster analysis technique which attempts to create a hierarchy of clusters. The two main strategies of hierarchical clustering are Agglomerative and Divisive clustering. The Agglomerative clustering is a bottom up approach and each observance starts in its own cluster, and the pairs of clusters are merged as one up the hierarchy where as Divisive clustering is a top down approach. In this approach, the entire observances start in individual cluster and then divide the clusters recursively as one move down the hierarchy. The findings of hierarchical clustering are usually represented in a dendrogram [1].

Jeevanandan et al. [2] proposed a method that uses the methodology to base the threshold measure on Manhattan hierarchical cluster and the information gain. The accuracy obtained with the method was quite good.

Bhavna [3] discussed various types of clustering techniques and suggested that the performance of existing hierarchical clustering techniques may be improved by using a hybrid approach. In our work we have proved that the efficiency of hierarchical clustering methods could be improved by employing a hybrid hierarchical algorithm with fuzzy logic.

Muqtar et al. [4] proposed an Unsupervised learning technique to overcome the problems of domain dependency and to limit the requirement of annotated training data for the Sentiment Analysis of movie reviews.

Sneha et al. [5] provided the overall survey regarding the challenges and about some of the existing clustering algorithms used for Sentiment Analysis. The experimental results and the source of data taken were missing.

Abeed et al. [6] presented a Supervised model to find the sentiments using centroid, clusters as well as sentiment lexicons. The method only achieved moderate results on the practical Sem Eval Sentiment Analysis task.

Karel et al. [7] presented the Sentiment Analysis of existing datasets collected from web using the already existing hierarchical clustering algorithms and observed the results. The overall clarity about the contribution in the work was missing.

Dario et al. [8] presented a model for finding the social hotspot from Twitter streaming data. The Hierarchical clustering method was used for Sentiment Analysis. Even though the enhancement of existing hierarchical clustering method is mentioned but the details were not specified to ensure the credibility.

Pravesh et al. [9] presented the review of existing Unsupervised and Supervised methods for Sentiment Analysis. The researcher in this work mentioned that the clustering techniques were good for consumer service but the paper lacks the practical aspects and the experimental results.

Li et al. [10] proposed a new Unsupervised clustering based Sentiment Analysis approach for analyzing the opinions in blogs and reviews. The researcher says that the proposed approach was better for recognizing neutral opinions.

Luiz et al. [11] presented a new method C3ESL to combine both the clustering methods and classifiers. The method was employed on existing datasets available on website and observed that it shows comparatively good results.

Maria et al. [12] proposed a novel robust hierarchical algorithm. The algorithm achieved better performance and was based on the bottom up agglomerative hierarchical clustering.

Soni et al. [13] proposed a hybrid approach to analyze the sentiment of a product by extracting tweets and classified based on two class positive and negative sentiments. The proposed approach combines an unsupervised learning K-means cluster and Decision Trees with SVM for classification. The result shows an overall accuracy of 72.33%.

Cambaria et al. [14] attempted to make use of an ensemble hierarchical clustering approach for identifying the primitives for the two different types of parts of speech namely the noun and the verb in sentic net. The analytical result shows comparatively better efficiency than the previous version of the strategy.

Stojonovski et al. [15] presented an overview of the process of identifying hotspots from social media, Twitter and applying the data for Sentiment Analysis. The hierarchical algorithm and DBSCAN algorithms were used to analyze the performance of spatial clusters. They have also proposed an approach based on deep learning to identify the user's attitude while participating in hotspots.

Sanjay et al. [16] attempted a survey of opinion mining and discussed about the challenges in the domain and also made an analysis with Twitter data on the existing algorithms; K Means and DBSCAN hierarchical clustering algorithms.

Emil et al. [17] proposed a model for aspect based Sentiment Analysis with a neural network which is a modified growing hierarchical clustering technique called Self Organizing Map. The sentences in the review documents were classified based on the proposed model. The researchers say that the model has been tested on review corpus regarding the photo cameras and has achieved good results.

Lawrence et al. [18] presented and demonstrated the need for considering neutral sentiment category while using clustering techniques and also described the usage of fuzzy logic in clustering aspects.

3 Methodology

See Fig. 1.

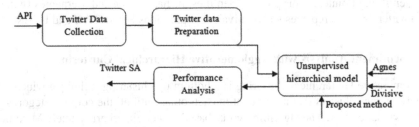

Fig. 1. Conceptual diagram of the proposed model

3.1 Twitter Data Collection

The tweets were extracted from the official Application Programming Interface of Twitter; a token based authentication system that indexes tweets that match a given search string and the response would be in json format that could be easily read by the program. The datasets used in this work is approximately 1500 real tweet samples acquired over a time period of 14 months. The server side programming language used for tweet extraction was an open source tool called R of version 3.3.2. The tweets collected are then processed based on Data Processing Task. It is depicted in the Sect. 3.2 below.

3.2 Twitter Data Preparation

The gathered raw Twitter feeds were parsed into a tweet corpus for Sentiment Analysis. After this step, the succeeding tasks were executed to filter and prepare the tweets for further analysis. It involves the tasks; Removing URL, Removing stop words, Word Stemming, Word Compression, Removing meaningless words, Removing irrelevant punctuation and Identifying pointers.

1. Removing URL: The tweets contain hyper links and it would be replaced with alternate keyword URL.
2. Removing Stop words: Stop words are the commonly used English words with no specific meaning. Such words would be identified and removed from each tweet samples by matching the stop word list in the text mining package of the open source data mining tool R.
3. Word Stemming: Stemming process reduces the derived words to their word stem. In our work we have used an open source library Snowball for tweet word stemming.
4. Word Compression: This process compresses words that express strong emotions. The occurrence of such word would be limited to two. Example- I am happyyyyy.
5. Removing meaningless words: This process eliminates all the irrelevant and meaningless words that do not serve any purpose in the corresponding tweets.
6. Removing irrelevant punctuation: Punctuations were identified and replaced with an alternative keyword PUNCT.
7. Identifying Pointers: This process identifies the hash tags # and usernames @ in the Twitter data and replaces with equivalent expressions HASHTAG and USER.

3.3 Sentiment Analysis with Agglomerative Hierarchical Clustering

Agglomerative Hierarchical clustering is a bottom up clustering technique which iteratively merges clusters that are nearest to each other until all the corpus categorize to an individual cluster. The algorithm works based on certain criteria namely Maximum Linkage clustering, Minimum Linkage clustering, Average Linkage clustering and Centroid Linkage clustering. The pseudo code for Agglomerative Hierarchical Clustering to perform Twitter Sentiment Analysis is as follows:

Algorithm:
Input – Set of data points $\{d_1, d_2, d_3 \ldots \ldots d_n\}$

1. Start with n number of clusters each holds one object
2. Compute the least distance pair of clusters.
3. Compute the most like pairs of clusters
4. Update the distance matrix
5. Repeat from step 2 until there is only one cluster left.

Output- Dendrogram

The Agglomerative hierarchical clustering was used in our domain to group the Twitter data one by one on the basis of the closest distance measure of all the pair wise distance between the tweet data point. The methods such as Simple, Complete, Average and Ward's method were tried for this algorithm in our Twitter Sentiment Analysis using 1500 tweet samples. The algorithm starts with n number of clusters where each one comprises of one object. Then the least distance pair and the most like pairs of clusters were computed. After that the distance matrix was updated accordingly. The process was repeated from step 2 until there is only one cluster left. The clusters obtained were grouped as Positive, Negative and Neutral sentiments of the popular brand of smart phone; Samsung Galaxy S6.

3.4 Sentiment Analysis with Divisive Hierarchical Clustering

The Divisive hierarchical algorithm is a top down clustering approach. The algorithm begins with all tweet data in one cluster. Then the cluster would be split using a flat clustering algorithm. This process will be applied recursively until each tweet is in its own singleton cluster. The algorithm steps are described as follows:

Input: Set of data points $\{d_1, d_2, d_3.....d_n\}$

1. Place all the data objects in one cluster
2. The process should be repeated until all clusters are singletons
   (a) Identify the cluster to split
   (b) Replace the selected cluster with sub clusters

Output - Dendrogram

The Divisive hierarchical algorithm was employed in our work to perform Sentiment Analysis of a popular Smart phone brand. This method is conceptually more complex than the Agglomerative hierarchical clustering method since we require a flat clustering algorithm as a sub routine. The algorithm begins by putting all the data objects in the tweets in one cluster. The process would be iterated until all the clusters are singletons.

3.5 Sentiment Analysis with Proposed Method

Many of the existing works for Sentiment Analysis were based on either Agglomerative or Divisive hierarchical clustering techniques. Both hierarchical algorithms have drawbacks such as; in the case of Agglomerative algorithm it lacks the interpretability concerning the cluster descriptors, it is not possible to make corrections once the merging and splitting decision is already made. Also this method is expensive for high dimensional and large datasets. Divisive hierarchical algorithm on the other hand is a complex method since it required second flat clustering algorithm. Moreover this method is less blind to the global structure of the Twitter data. In order to overcome these shortcomings we have proposed a Fuzzy based Hybrid Hierarchical Clustering model (FHHC) which is based on both the top down and bottom up clustering. The pseudo code of the proposed method is described below.

Input- Set of data points $\{d_1, d_2....d_n\}$

1. Estimate the mutual clusters using the bottom up approach.
2. Execute a constrained top down approach so that each mutual cluster stays intact.
3. Separate each mutual cluster by executing yet another top down clustering approach.
4. Compute the correlation between the trees
5. Check whether the membership ≥ 0 for all data objects i = 1 to n and clusters c_1 to c_k
6. Do minimize the objective function and estimate fuzziness coefficients
7. Compute the membership coefficient

Output- (i) Clustered instances
        (ii) Nearest crisp clustering

The proposed method works as: First it would estimate the mutual clusters with the bottom up approach. Then executes a constrained top down approach to allow the mutual clusters stay intact. After this step, each mutual cluster would be separated by executing another top down approach and the correlation between the trees was computed. Finally the fuzzy logic would be employed to the hybrid hierarchical approach to deal with the uncertainty. The membership function used in our work is a cyclic triangular membership function. Our proposed method aims to minimize the objective function which is nothing other than a function that should be optimized using certain constrains so that it need to be minimized. The following fuzzy constrains shows the conditions to which the chosen membership functions subjected to:

1. Membership $m \geq 0$ for all data object i = 1 ... n and all clusters c_1 to c_k.
2. $\sum_{c=1}^{c} m = 1$, for all data object i = 1 ... n.

The clusters obtained using the proposed method is three that is to say Positive, Negative and Neutral sentiment clusters. The pictorial representation showing the fuzzy hybrid hierarchical cluster plot is depicted in Fig. 2 below.

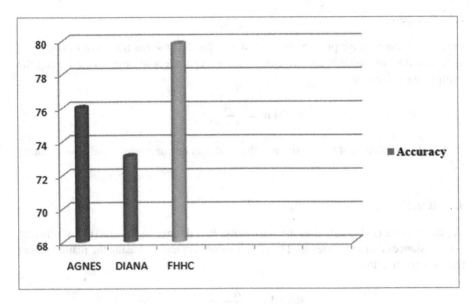

Fig. 2. The plot representing accuracy values of clustering methods

4   Experimental Results

In this section we describe our experimental setup for analyzing the sentiments of a popular Smart phone brand; Samsung Galaxy S6. The whole experiment was carried out with real world Twitter data feeds taken over a time period of 14 month's gap. The experimental analysis was conducted on Intel R core processor with 2 GB memory using the data mining software R, version 3.3.2. The external validation measures adopted to perform comparative analysis of the existing methods over the proposed method were accuracy, precision and recall. The following subsections describe the definition of above mentioned external validation methods.

4.1   Accuracy

Accuracy is defined as the measure of the predictive data model that reflects the proportionate number of times that the algorithm is correct when applied to the Twitter data. The Accuracy could be calculated by using the following mathematical formula:

$$Accuracy = \frac{A + B}{A + B + C + D} \tag{1}$$

The letter "A" represents the true positive value, "B" represents true negative, "C" represents the false negative and "D" shows the false positive value.

4.2   Precision

Precision is the positive predictive value. It is defined as the fraction of retrieved tweet instances that are suitable for the query. The Precision could be estimated using the mathematical formula:

$$\text{Precision} = \frac{A}{A+C} \tag{2}$$

It is the proportion of true positive to the total sum of true positive and false negative values.

4.3   Recall

Recall measure is also called as the sensitivity. It is defined as the fraction of relevant tweet instances that are retrieved. The Recall value is calculated using the mathematical formula given below:

$$\text{Recall} = \frac{A}{A+D} \tag{3}$$

That is, the proportion of true positive "A" to the sum of true positive "A" and false positive values "D".

To determine the efficiency of clustering algorithms we first evaluated the accuracy values of existing clustering methods and also the accuracy of our proposed method. It is observed that our method surpasses the other clustering methods with an overall accuracy of 79.8% where as Agglomerative clustering algorithm produced 76% and Divisive hierarchical algorithm produced 73.1% accuracy. Furthermore we have compared the existing algorithms with the proposed method using other two external validation measures namely precision and recall. The precision values of Agglomerative hierarchical cluster, Divisive hierarchical cluster and the proposed Fuzzy Hybrid Hierarchical Cluster (FHHC) methods were 0.51, 0.47, and 0.56 approximately. Likewise the recall measures obtained by the algorithms were 0.31, 0.31 and 033 respectively. The Table 1 shows the values obtained by corresponding hierarchical clustering methods. The graphical representation of the metric values obtained by the algorithms is depicted in the Figs. 2 and 3 respectively.

Table 1.   Accuracy values obtained by the hierarchical clustering algorithms

Methods	Accuracy	Precision	Recall
Agglomerative	76%	0.51	0.31
Divisive	73.1%	0.47	0.31
FHHC	79.8%	0.56	0.33

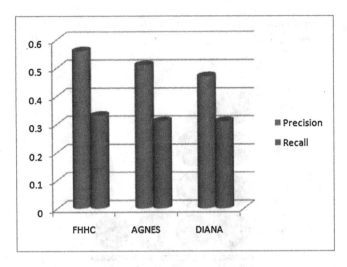

Fig. 3. The precision-recall metric plot for clustering methods

The result of Agglomerative hierarchical clustering is shown in Fig. 4, in the dendrogram below. This graphical representation depicted all the tweet samples and indicated the level of similarity when any two clusters would bring together. The clusters obtained were three in this case, depending on the desired degree of similarity. Here each line shown in the dendrogram shows a group that was distinguished when the objects were combined together into clusters. The dissimilarities between the clusters of given objects would be determined using different criterion and are represented in Fig. 5 below.

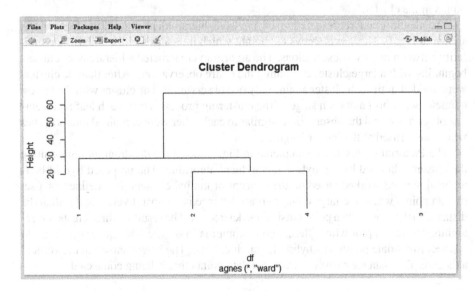

Fig. 4. Graphical representation of dendogram obtained by Agglomerative hierarchical cluster

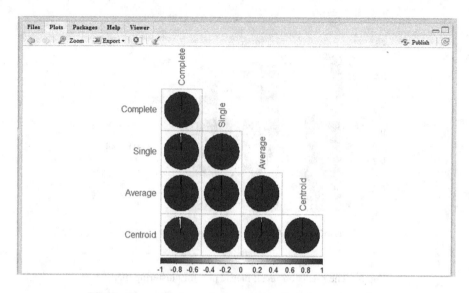

Fig. 5. Hierarchical correlation matrix criterion representation

The figure below shows the dissimilarity criterion such as Single, Average, Centroid and Complete Linkage clustering. Here the Single Linkage clustering merged the two closest members of clusters possessing the smallest distance. The Complete Linkage cluster merged two clusters with the smallest diameter. The Centroid cluster defined the similarity of centroids as the similarity of any two clusters. Whereas the Average Linkage cluster in the figure given below represents the average distance between the points in the cluster.

The dendrogram representation of Divisive hierarchical algorithm (DIANA) is shown in Fig. 6. The y axis shows the height which indicates the dissimilarity or similarity between any two observations. The algorithm constructed a hierarchy of clusters beginning with a large cluster containing the entire observations. After that the clusters were divided until each cluster attains only one observation. The cluster with the largest diameter was chosen at each stage of the clustering process. Here, each leaf represents one observation and the observations similar to each other were combined into branches which were fused at the higher height.

The Pictorial representation depicted in Fig. 7 shows the dendrogram representing the clusters obtained by the hybrid hierarchical algorithm. The proposed hybrid hierarchical method worked based on the concept of mutual clusters. It is defined as a set of data points where the largest inner group distance is comparatively smaller than the distance to the closest data point outside the desired set. The resulting three clusters were highlighted in the plot with different color combinations. The lines in the dendrogram connect tweet data points in a hybrid hierarchical tree. The height shown in the vertical axis gives the distance between two tweet data points that is being connected.

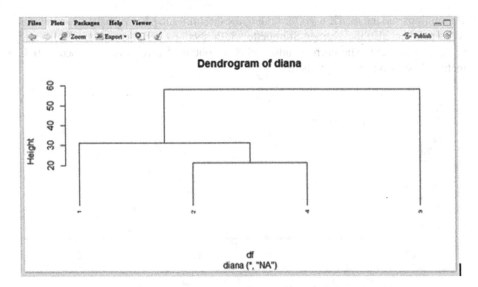

Fig. 6. Graphical representation of dendogram obtained by Divisive hierarchical cluster

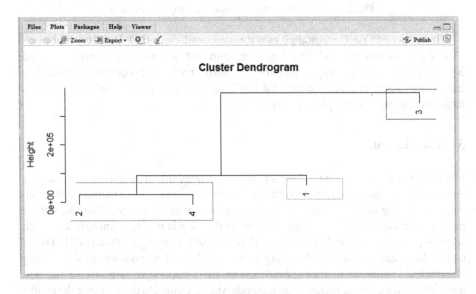

Fig. 7. Graphical representation of dendogram obtained by proposed hierarchical method

The idea of fuzzy contributed by Dr. Lotfi Zadeh [19] was being employed here along with our hybrid hierarchical model to ensure more robust results with better accuracy and to head off uncertainness. The matrix with the level to which the observation belongs to a particular cluster was chosen as non negative values and was summed up to 1 for each fixed observation. The fuzziness coefficients were measured using Dunn's and Normalized coefficients with 0.872 and 0.744 scores. There were a total number of

10 iterations and the metric used for finding the dissimilarities between the observations was Euclidean also the average Silhouette width obtained per clusters were 0.916 and 0.783 respectively. The corresponding clusters obtained using our proposed FHHC method is shown in the Fig. 8 below.

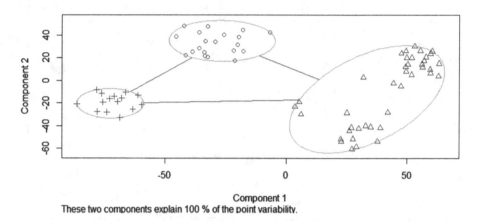

Fig. 8. Cluster plot obtained using the proposed method

The proposed FHHC method gives promising results with 55% Positive sentiments, 25% Neutral sentiments and 20% Negative sentiments for the popular product brand; Samsung Galaxy S6. The experimental results show that the our proposed method gives interesting results based on the external validation measures and it is suitable to handle large datasets with pretty good accuracy values.

5   Conclusion

The Hierarchical clustering method is actually a framework to deal with the shortcomings of partition based clustering methods. However the hierarchical method still suffers major clustering problems such as the vagueness of termination criterion, inability to make corrections once the merging or splitting decision is made. In our research work, we have proposed a Fuzzy based Hybrid Hierarchical Clustering method (FHHC) based on top down and bottom up clustering to address these short comings of the existing hierarchical clustering methods. Furthermore the comparative analysis of the new method with the existing hierarchical methods was performed to demonstrate the quality of Sentiment Analysis results and to highlight the effectiveness of our proposed work.

References

1. Rokach, L., Maimon, O.: Clustering methods. In: Maimon, O., Rokach, L. (eds.) Data Mining and Knowledge Discovery Handbook, pp. 321–352. Springer, US (2005)
2. Jotheeswaram, J., Kumaraswamy, Y.S.: Opinion mining using decision tree based feature selection through Manhattan hierarchical technology. J. Theor. Appl. Inf. Technol. **58**(1), 72–79 (2013)
3. Bharadwaj, B.: Text mining, its utilities, challenges and clustering techniques. Int. J. Comput. Appl. **135**(7), 22–24 (2016)
4. Unnisa, M., Ameen, A., Raziuddin, S.: Opinion mining on Twitter data using unsupervised learning technique clustering. Int. J. Comput. Appl. **148**(12), 12–19 (2016)
5. Sneha, G., Vidhya, C.T.: Algorithm for opinion mining and sentiment analysis: an overview. Int. J. Adv. Res. Comput. Sci. Softw. Eng. 455–459 (2016)
6. Sarkar, A., Gonzallez, G.: DiegoLab 16 at SemEval-2016 task 4: sentiment analysis in Twitter centroids, clusters and sentiment lexicons. In: Proceedings of SemEval-2016, pp. 214–219 (2016)
7. Gutierrez Batista, K., Campana, J.R., Martinez-Folgoso, S., Vila, M.A: About the effects of sentiments on topic detection in social networks. In: European Hand Book of Crowd Sourced Geographic Information, pp. 224–235 (2015)
8. Stojanovski, D., Chorbev, I., Dimitrovski, I., Madjarov, G.: Social networks VGI: Twitter sentiment analysis of social hotspots. Procedia Comput. Sci. 183–190 (2015). Elsevier
9. Singh, P.K., Husain, M.S.: Methodological study of opinion mining and sentiment analysis techniques. Int. J. Soft Comput. **5**, 1586–1592 (2014)
10. Li, G., Liu, F.: Sentiment analysis based on clustering: a framework in improving accuracy and recognizing neutral opinions. Appl. Intell. **40**, 441–452 (2014). Springer
11. Coletta, L.F.S., da Silva, N.F.F., Hruschka, E.R., Hruschka, E.R.: Combining classification and clustering for tweet sentiment analysis, pp. 210–215. IEEE (2014)
12. Balcon, M.F., Liang, Y., Gupta, P.: Robust hierarchical clustering. J. Mach. Learn. Res. 4011–4051 (2014)
13. Soni, R., Mathai, K.J.: Improved Twitter sentiment prediction through cluster then predict model. Int. J. Comput. Sci. Netw. 559–563 (2015)
14. Cambaria, E., Poria, S., Bajpai, R., Schuller, B.: SenticNet 4: a semantic resource for sentiment analysis based on conceptual primitives. In: Proceedings of the 26th International Conference on Computational Linguistics (COLING 2016), pp. 2666–2677, December 2016
15. Stojanovski, D., Chorbev, I., Dimitrovski, I., Madjarov, G.: Social networks VGI: Twitter sentiment analysis of social hotspots. In: Capiner, C., Haklay, M., Huang, H., Antoniou, V., Kettunen, J., Ostermann, F., Purves, R. (eds.) European Handbook of Crowd Sourced Geographic Information, pp. 223–235 (2016)
16. Lulla, S., Bhatia, V., Hemwani, R., Bhatia, G.: Social media analytics for E-commerce organization. Int. J. Comput. Sci. Inf. Technol. **7**(6), 2431–2435 (2016)
17. Chifu, E.S., Letia, T.S., Chifu, V.R.: Un-supervised aspect level sentiment analysis using ant clustering and self organizing maps. In: IEEE International Conference on Speech Technology and Human Computer Dialogue (2015)
18. Ndene, L., Jouandeau, N., Akdag, H.: Importance of the neutral category in fuzzy clustering of sentiments. Int. J. Fuzzy Log. Syst. **4**, 1–6 (2014)
19. Kirsci, M.: Integrated and differentiated spaces of triangular fuzzy numbers. Math. Subj. classif. 1–14 (2017)

Road-User Specific Analysis of Traffic Accident Using Data Mining Techniques

Prayag Tiwari[1(✉)], Sachin Kumar[2], and Denis Kalitin[1]

[1] Department of Computer Science and Engineering,
National University of Science and Technology Misis, Moscow, Russia
prayagforms@gmail.com, kalitindv@gmail.com
[2] Centre for Transportation Systems, Indian Institute of Technology Roorkee,
Roorkee, India
sachinagnihotri16@gmail.com

Abstract. Analysis of road accident is very important because it can expose the relationship between the different types of attributes that contributes to a road accident. Attributes that affect the road accident can be road attribute, environment attributes, traffic attributes etc. Analyzing road accident can provide the information about the contribution of these attributes which can be utilized to overcome the accident rate. Nowadays, Data mining is a popular technique for examining the road accident dataset. In this study, we have performed the classification of road accident on the basis of road user category. We have used Self Organizing map (SOM), K-modes clustering technique to group the data into homogeneous segments and then applied Support vector machine (SVM), Naive Bayes (NB) and Decision tree to classify the data. We have performed classification on data with and without clustering. The result illustrates that better classification accuracy can be achieved after segmentation of data using clustering.

Keywords: Data mining · Accident analysis · Clustering · Classification

1 Introduction

Road accident have been the major reason for untimely death as well as damage to property and economic losses around the world. There are a lot of people die every year in a traffic or road accident. Hence, traffic authority devotes substantial endeavor to lessen the road accident but still, there is no such reduction in accident rate since in these analyzed years. Road accident is unpredictable and undetermined. Hence, analysis of traffic accident requires the understanding of circumstance which is influencing them. Data Mining [4, 6, 19, 20, 26–30] has pulled in a lot of consideration in the IT industries as well as in public arena because of the extensive accessibility of vast quantity of data. So, it's necessary to transform these data into applicable knowledge and information. These applicable knowledge and information may be utilized to

© Springer Nature Singapore Pte Ltd. 2017
J.K. Mandal et al. (Eds.): CICBA 2017, Part II, CCIS 776, pp. 398–410, 2017.
DOI: 10.1007/978-981-10-6430-2_31

implement in different areas such as marketing, road accident analysis [11, 12, 15], fraud detection and so on.

Lee C [1] stated that statistical pattern was a better option to determine the connection between traffic, accident, and other geometric circumstances. Data mining [3, 23] is a mutative method which has been utilizing in the area of transportation. Although Barai [2] stated that there is the diverse approach of data mining in the engineering field of transportation such as pavement analysis, road surface analysis and so on. Data mining comprises many techniques such as preprocess, clustering, association, prediction, classification and etc. Clustering [5] is the errand of categorizing a heterogeneous quantity into various more homogeneous clusters or subgroups. What makes a contrast between clustering and classification is that in classification, every record allocated a pre-defined class in according to an enhanced model along with training on the pre-classified examples as well as clustering does not depend on pre-defined classes. Karlaftis and Tarko [7] utilized analysis to cluster the data and then categorized that dataset of the accident into individual categories and moreover cluster results of analyzed data by utilizing Negative Binomial (NB) to determine the reason of road accident by focusing age of driver which may demonstrate some results. Ma and Kockelman [9] utilized clustering techniques as their initial level to group the dataset into individual division and moreover, they utilized Probit model to determine the connection between individual accident features. In this paper, we used Self organizing map (SOM) and k-modes clustering techniques.

Classification comprises of analyzing the characteristics of a recently introduced object and appointing this to one of the predetermined set of classes. The classified objects are to be demonstrated by the record in the table of the file for the database, and the demonstration of classification comprises of including another segment with a class code of some type. To classify the dataset, we used support vector machine (SVM), Naïve bays and J48. Kwon OH [10] utilized decision tree and naive bays classification techniques to analyze aspect dependencies associated with road safety. Young Sohn [17] used a different algorithm to enhance the accuracy of different classifiers for two severity categories of a traffic accident and each classifier used neural network and decision tree. Tibebe [18] developed a classification model that could assist the traffic officers at Addis Ababa Traffic office for taking the decision to control traffic activities in Ethiopia. S. Kuznetsov et al. [21, 22, 24, 25] used an algorithm based on FCA for numerical data mining and provided more efficient results. The organization of the paper is as follows: Sect. 2 will describe the data set used and methodology adopted in the study. Section 3 will present the results and discuss the findings. Finally, Sect. 4 will conclude with a future scope.

2 Materials and Methods

This research work focuses on casualty class based or road user-based classification of a road accident. The paper describes the Self Organizing Map (SOM) and K-modes clustering techniques for cluster analysis of the dataset. Moreover, Support Vector Machine (SVM), Naïve Bays and Decision tree are used in this paper to classify the accident data.

2.1   Clustering Techniques

Self Organizing Map (SOM)

Self-organizing maps (SOMs) [13] is a method for visualizing data and this method is given by Professor Teuvo Kohonen, the primary objective of this technique is to convert multidimensional data into the lower dimension data or one or two-dimensional data. It is also known as vector quantization or data compression because it reduces the dimension of vectors. The major goal of this study is to entrench different fragments of the neural network to respond similarly to some identified input pattern. When a training set has been imposed to the neural networks then their Euclidean distance to final weight vectors are computed. Now the neuron weight is approximately similar to the weight of input. So, this is called by the winner or Best Matching Neuron (BMN). The neuron and weight of BMN which are adjacent in the lattice of SOM are moved towards the input vector. The weight of changes reduces with distance and time from the BMN. The estimated formula for neuron n with having weight vector $W_n(s)$ is given as

$$W_n(s+1) = W_n(s) + \theta(i, n, s) \cdot \alpha(s) \cdot (F(t) - W_n)) \tag{1}$$

In this given formula, s is step index, t is an index in training example, i is an index of BMN for $F(t)$, $\alpha(s)$ is decreasing coefficient and input vector is $F(t)$. $\theta(i, n, s)$ is the district function which provides the space between neuron i and n in s step. As upon the execution, t may analyze dataset consistently (t = 0, 1, 2, 3, 4 ... T−1 and T is the size of training example).

K-modes clustering

Clustering is an unsupervised data mining method whose major objective is to categorize the data objects into a distinct type of clusters in such a way that objects inside a group are more alike than the objects in different clusters. K-means [3] algorithm is a very famous clustering technique for large numerical data analysis. In this, the dataset is grouped into k clusters. There are diverse clustering algorithms available but the assortment of appropriate clustering algorithm relies on type and nature of data. Our major objective of this work is to differentiate the accident location on their frequency occurrence. Let's assume that X and Y is a matrix of m by n matrix of categorical data. The straightforward closeness coordinating measure amongst X and Y is the quantity of coordinating quality estimations of the two values. The more noteworthy the quantity of matches is more the comparability of two items. K-modes [14, 16, 20] algorithm can be explained as:

$$d(X_i, Y_i) = \sum_{i=1}^{m} \delta(Xi, Yi) \tag{2}$$

$$Where\ \delta(Xi, Yi) = \begin{cases} 1,\ if\ Xi = Yi \\ 0,\ if\ Xi \neq Yi \end{cases} \tag{3}$$

2.2   Classification Techniques

Support Vector Machine
SVM is supervised learning method with an analogous algorithm which analyzes data for regression and classification analysis. SVM works on the basis of decision planes which explain decision boundary. Decision planes are something which differentiates across a set of objects with having distinct classes. It's a classifier technique that executes classification task by making hyper planes in n- dimensional space which differentiates the level of classes. SVM assist classification task as well as regression task also and can manage multiple categorical as well as continuous variables.

For the classification type of SVM, minimize the error function: $(V^T V/2) + C \sum_{i=1}^{n} \beta_i$

Subjects to the limitations: $Y_i (V^T \theta(X_i) + b) >\ = 1 - \beta_i, \beta_i >\ = 0, i = 1, 2, 3, \ldots N$

$$(4)$$

Here v is vector coefficient, c which is known as capacity constant, β explain the boundary for managing non separable data which is input data and here b is constant. Here i is the index for level T cases of training set, X_i and Y_i describe the class labels and independent variables. α is generally using for transmuting data from the input data to the space feature. If C is greater than more error proscribed so C must be chosen properly.

It's the second type to reduce error function for classification type: $(V^T V/2) + v\alpha + \frac{1}{N} \sum_{i=1}^{N} \beta_i$

Subjects to the limitations: $Y_i (V^T \theta(X_i) + b) >\ = \alpha - \beta_i, \beta_i >\ = 0, i = 1, 2, 3, \ldots N$ *and* $\alpha >\ = 0$ *always*

$$(5)$$

You need to evaluate the dependent function of the y dependent factor on an arrangement of independent factors x. It accepts as other regression issues that the connection across the independent and dependent factors is provided by a deterministic function which is f in addition to the expansion of some extra noise

$Y = f(x) +$ some noises

For the regression type of SVM : $(V^T V/2) + C \sum_{i=1}^{n} \beta_i + C \sum_{i=1}^{n} \beta'_i$ (6)

These reduce subjects to $V^T \theta(X_i) - bY_i =\ <\varepsilon + \beta'_i$

$$Y_i - V^T \theta(X_i) - b =\ <\varepsilon + \beta_i$$
$$\beta_I \beta'_I >\ = 0, i = 1, 2, 3, \ldots N$$

It's the second type to reduce error function for classification type:
$$(V^T V/2) - C \left(v\varepsilon + \frac{1}{N} \sum_{i=1}^{N} (\beta i + \beta' i) \right)$$ (7)

$$(V^T \theta(X_i) + b) - Y_i = \; < \varepsilon + \beta_i$$
$$Y_i - (V^T \theta(X_i) + b) = \; < \varepsilon + \beta_i'$$

$$\beta_I \beta_I' > \; = 0, \; i = 1, 2, 3, \dots N, \varepsilon > 0$$

Naïve Bayes

This classifier is on the basis on Bayes' hypothesis with autonomy suspicions across indicators. This model is easier to design, with no astonishing iterative measure approximation which makes it primarily precious for large datasets. Despite its smoothness, this classifier often works very well and which is generally utilized on the grounds that it regularly outflanks more complex order techniques. Given a class variable x and element vector y_1 through y_n, Bayes' hypothesis expresses the accompanying relationship:

$$P(x|y_1, \dots \dots y_n) = \frac{P(x)P(y_1, \dots \dots \dots y_n|x)}{P(y_1 \dots \dots \dots y_n)} \qquad (8)$$

By using the Naive Bayes assumption that

$$P(y_i|x, y_1 \dots \dots, y_{i-1}, \dots \dots, y_n) = P(y_i|x) \qquad (9)$$

for all i, this relationship is streamlined to

$$P(x|y_1, \dots \dots y_n) = \frac{P(x) \prod_{i=1}^{n} P(y_i|x)}{P(y_1 \dots \dots \dots y_n)} \qquad (10)$$

Since $P(y_1, \dots y_n)$ is steady given the information, we can utilize the accompanying classification run the show:

$$P(x|y_1, \dots \dots y_n) \propto P(x) \prod_{i=1}^{n} P(y_i|x)$$
$$x^\wedge = arg \; max = P(x) \prod_{i=1}^{n} P(y_i|x) \qquad (11)$$

What's more, we can utilize Maximum A Posteriori (MAP) estimation to gauge P (x) and P (y_i|x); the previous is then the relative recurrence of class x in the preparation set. Regardless of their clearly over-improved suppositions, credulous Bayes classifiers have worked great in some genuine circumstances, broadly record classification and spam separating. They require a little measure of preparing information to gauge the fundamental parameters.

Decision Tree

J48 is an augmentation of ID3. The additional elements of J48 are representing missing data. In the WEKA, J48 is a Java platform open source of the C4.5 calculation. The WEKA gives various alternatives connected with tree pruning. If there should arise an occurrence of possible overfitting pruning may be utilized as a tool for accuracy. In different calculations, the classification is executed recursively till each and every leaf is clean or pure, that is the order of the data ought to be as impeccable as would be prudent. The goal is dynamically speculation of a choice tree until it picks up the balance of adaptability and exactness. This technique utilized the 'Entropy' that is the computation of disorder data. Here Entropy $\vec{X}$ is measured by:

$$\text{Entropy } (\vec{X}) = -\sum_{i=1}^{n} \frac{|Xi|}{\overrightarrow{|X|}} \log\left(\frac{|Xi|}{\overrightarrow{|X|}}\right) \tag{12}$$

$$\text{Entropy } (i|\vec{X}) = \frac{|Xi|}{\overrightarrow{|X|}} \log\left(\frac{|Xi|}{\overrightarrow{|X|}}\right) \tag{13}$$

Hence,

$$\text{Total Gain} = \text{Entropy } (\vec{X}) - \text{Entropy } (i|\vec{X}) \tag{14}$$

Here the goal is to increase the total gain by dividing total entropy because of diverging arguments $\vec{X}$ by value i.

2.3   Description of Data Set

The traffic accident data is obtained from the online data source for Leeds UK [8]. This data set comprises 13062 accident that occurred during 2011 to 2015. Initial preprocessing of the data results in 11 attributes that found to be suitable for further analysis. The attributes selected for analysis are a number of vehicles, time of the accident, road surface, weather conditions, lightening conditions, casualty class, sex of casualty, age, type of vehicle, day and month of the accident. The accident data is illustrated in Table 1.

Table 1. Road accident attribute description

S. No.	Attribute	Code	Value	Total	Casualty class		
					Driver	Passenger	Pedestrian
1	No. of vehicles	1	1 vehicle	3334	763	817	753
		2	2 vehicle	7991	5676	2215	99
		3+	>3 vehicle	5214	1218	510	10
2	Time	T1	[0–4]	630	269	250	110
		T2	[4–8]	903	698	133	71
		T3	[6–12]	2720	1701	644	374
		T4	[12–16]	3342	1812	1027	502
		T5	[16–20]	3976	2387	990	598
		T6	[20–24]	1496	790	498	207

(continued)

Table 1. (*continued*)

S. No.	Attribute	Code	Value	Total	Casualty class		
					Driver	Passenger	Pedestrian
3	Road surface	OTR	Other	106	62	30	13
		DR	Dry	9828	5687	2695	1445
		WT	Wet	3063	1858	803	401
		SNW	Snow	157	101	39	16
		FLD	Flood	17	11	5	0
4	Lightening condition	DLGT	Day Light	9020	5422	2348	1249
		NLGT	No Light	1446	858	389	198
		SLGT	Street Light	2598	1377	805	415
5	Weather condition	CLR	Clear	11584	6770	3140	1666
		FG	Fog	37	26	7	3
		SNY	Snowy	63	41	15	6
		RNY	Rainy	1276	751	350	174
6	Casualty class	DR	Driver		7657	0	0
		PSG	Passenger		0	3542	0
		PDT	Pedestrian		0	0	1862
7	Sex of casualty	M	Male	7758	5223	1460	1074
		F	Female	5305	2434	2082	788
8	Age	Minor	<18 years	1976	454	855	667
		Youth	18–30 years	4267	2646	1158	462
		Adult	30–60 years	4254	3152	742	359
		Senior	>60 years	2567	1405	787	374
9	Type of vehicle	BS	Bus	842	52	687	102
		CR	Car	9208	4959	2692	1556
		GDV	Goods Vehicle	449	245	86	117
		BCL	Bicycle	1512	1476	11	24
		PTV	PTWW	977	876	48	52
		OTR	Other	79	49	18	11
10	Day	WKD	Weekday	9884	5980	2499	1404
		WND	Weekend	3179	1677	1043	458
11	Month	Q1	Jan–March	3017	1731	803	482
		Q2	April–June	3220	1887	907	425
		Q3	Jul-Sep	3376	2021	948	406
		Q4	Oct-Dec	3452	2018	884	549

2.4   Measurement of Accuracy

The classification accuracy is one of the important measures of how correctly a classifier classifies a record to its class value? The confusion matrix is an important data structure that helps in calculating different performance measures such as precision, accuracy, recall and sensitivity of classification technique on some data.

Table 2. Confusion matrix sample

	Negative	Positive
Negative	TN (True negative)	FN (False negative)
Positive	FP (False positive)	TP (True positive)

Table 2 provides a sample confusion matrix table and Eqs. 1–4 illustrates the formulas to calculate different performance measures.

$$Accuracy = \frac{TN + TP}{TP + TN + FP + FN} \tag{15}$$

$$False\ Positive\ Rate = \frac{FP}{TN + FP} \tag{16}$$

$$Precision = \frac{TP}{FP + TP} \tag{17}$$

$$Sensitivity = \frac{TP}{FN + TP} \tag{18}$$

3   Results and Discussion

In this section, the experimental analysis and the obtained results will be discussed.

3.1   Classification Analysis

We utilized different approaches to classifying this bunch of dataset on the basis of casualty class using SVM (support vector machine), Naïve bays and Decision tree. The classification accuracy achieved is shown in Fig. 1. It can be seen that decision tree obtained the highest accuracy of 70.7% in comparison to other two classifiers.

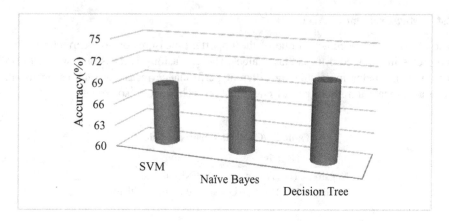

Fig. 1. Classification accuracy of different classifiers on accident data

3.2   Classification Followed by Clustering of Accident

In this analysis, we utilized two clustering techniques which are SOM (Self organizing map) and K-modes techniques. We achieved better results by using k-modes as compared to SOM technique and therefore we are describing the performance of classifiers on clusters obtained by k-modes only.

Performance evaluation of SVM

In this study, we applied SVM to classify dataset on the basis of casualty class and this classifier classified data into 3 classes. The output of this classifier are determined on the basis of their precision, recall, error rate and other factors and we achieved accuracy which is *75.5838%* and it's increased approximately 7% and it is better than earlier when we analyzed our dataset without clustering. Table 3 provides the performance of SVM on clusters obtained from k-modes.

Table 3. Performance of SVM

Rate of error = 0.1628								
Predicted values					Confusion matrix			
Class	Precision	Recall	TPR	FPR	Class	DR	PSG	PDT
DR	0.779	0.909	0.90	0.36	DR	6958	153	546
PSG	0.824	0.375	0.37	0.03	PSG	1828	1330	384
PDT	0.630	0.851	0.85	0.083	PDT	146	132	1584

Performance evaluation of Naïve Bayes

In this study, we applied Naïve Bays to classify our dataset on the basis of casualty class and this classifier classified dataset into 3 classes. Here again, we can see that our output are determined on the basis of precision, recall, error, error rate, TPR and other various factors which play a really important role. Our accuracy reached to *76.4583%* which is approximately better than earlier without clustering as we achieved *68.5375%*. Table 4 provides the performance of Naïve Bayes on clusters obtained from k-modes.

Table 4. Performance of naive bayes

Rate of error = 0.2352								
Predicted values					Confusion matrix			
Class	Precision	Recall	TPR	FPR	Class	DR	PSG	PDT
DR	0.788	0.86	0.86	0.33	DR	6649	515	493
PSG	0.697	0.43	0.43	0.07	PSG	1624	1535	383
PDT	0.742	0.828	0.828	0.078	PDT	170	151	1541

Performance evaluation of Decision Tree

In this study, we used Decision Tree classifier which improved the accuracy better than earlier which we achieved without clustering. We achieved accuracy *81%* which is better than earlier. Table 5 provides the performance of decision tree on clusters obtained from k-modes.

Table 5. Performance of decision tree

Rate of error = 0.1628								
Predicted values					Confusion matrix			
Class	Precision	Recall	TPR	FPR	Class	DR	PSG	PDT
DR	0.784	0.893	0.893	0.348	DR	6841	422	394
PSG	0.724	0.457	0.457	0.065	PSG	1649	1620	273
PDT	0.683	0.770	0.770	0.060	PDT	231	197	1434

We achieved error rate, precision, TPR (True positive rate), FPR (False positive rate), Precision, recall for every classification techniques as shown in given tables and also achieved different confusion matrix for different classification techniques and we can see the performance of different classifier techniques by the help of confusion matrix.

Here in the next table, we have shown the overall accuracy of analysis with clustering with the help of Tables 3, 4 and 5 and as we can observe from these tables classification accuracy increased for each classification technique after doing clustering.

Figure 2 illustrates the classification accuracy of SVM, Naïve Bayes and decision tree on clusters obtained from k-modes and SOM. It can be seen that classification accuracy is better for clusters obtained from k-modes clustering rather than obtained from SOM. It can be concluded that k-modes clustering technique provides better clustering than SOM on data with categorical road accident attributes.

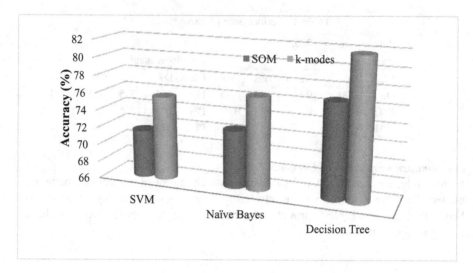

Fig. 2. Classification accuracy on clusters obtained from k-modes and SOM

4 Conclusion

In this research work, we analyzed accident dataset by using clustering techniques which are SOM (Self Organizing Map), K-modes, as well as classification techniques which are Support Vector Machine (SVM), Naïve Bays and Decision Tree to find pattern on road user specific and we, achieved better accuracy by using clustering techniques. We achieved better accuracy from this way on the basis of casualty class so we can see clearly that what circumstances affect and who is involved more in an accident between the driver, passenger or pedestrian. In this result, k-modes provided us better clustering results as compared to SOM and classification accuracy of SVM, Naïve Bays, and Decision Tree is found better on clusters obtained from k-modes. It indicates that clustering certainly improves the classification accuracy of classifiers and k-modes clustering would be a better option to cluster road accident data with categorical attributes.

References

1. Lee, C., Saccomanno, F., Hellinga, B.: Analysis of crash precursors on instrumented freeways. Transp. Res. Rec. (2002). doi:10.3141/1784-01
2. Barai, S.: Data mining application in transportation engineering. Transport **18**, 216–223 (2003). doi:10.1080/16483840.2003.10414100
3. Kumar, S., Toshniwal, D.: A data mining approach to characterize road accident locations. J. Mod. Transp. **24**(1), 62–72 (2016)
4. Han, J., Kamber, M.: Data Mining: Concepts and Techniques. Academic Press, San Francisco (2000). ISBN 1-55860-489-8

5. Berry, M.J.A., Linoff, G.S.: Data Mining Techniques: For Marketing, Sales, and Customer Relationship Management, 2nd edn. Wiley, New York (1997)
6. Witten, I.H., Frank, E., Hall, M.A.: Data Mining: Practical Machine Learning Tools and Techniques. Morgan Kaufmann Publishers, San Francisco (2005)
7. Karlaftis, M., Tarko, A.: Heterogeneity considerations in accident modeling. Accid. Anal. Prev. **30**(4), 425–433 (1998)
8. Data source: https://data.gov.uk/dataset/road-traffic-accidents. Accessed 24 Oct 2016
9. Ma, J., Kockelman, K.: Crash frequency, and severity modeling using clustered data from Washington state. In: 2006 IEEE Intelligent Transportation Systems Conference, Toronto, Canadá (2006)
10. Kwon, O.H., Rhee, W., Yoon, Y.: Application of classification algorithms for analysis of road safety risk factor dependencies. Accid. Anal. Prev. **75**, 1–15 (2015). doi:10.1016/j.aap.2014.11.005
11. Geurts, K., Wets, G., Brijs, T., Vanhoof, K.: Profiling of high-frequency accident locations by use of association rules. Transp. Res. Rec. (2003). doi:10.3141/1840-14
12. Kumar, S., Toshniwal, D.: A novel framework to analyze road accident time series data. J. Big Data **3**(8), 1–11 (2016). Springer
13. Kohonen, T.: Self-Organizing Maps, 2nd edn. Springer, Heidelberg (1995)
14. Kumar, S., Toshniwal, D.: A data mining framework to analyze road accident data. J. Big Data **2**(26), 1–18 (2015)
15. Kumar, S., Toshniwal, D.: Analysis of hourly road accident counts using hierarchical clustering and cophenetic correlation coefficient (CPCC). J. Big Data **3**(13), 1–11 (2016)
16. Kumar, S., Toshniwal, D., Parida, M.: A comparative analysis of heterogeneity in road accident data using data mining techniques. Evol. Syst. **8**(2), 147–155 (2016)
17. Sohn, S.Y., Lee, S.H.: Data fusion, ensemble and clustering to improve the classification accuracy for the severity of road traffic accidents in Korea. Saf. Sci. **41**(1), 1–14 (2003)
18. Tibebe, B.T., Abraham, A., Grosan, C.: Rule mining and classification of road traffic accidents using adaptive regression trees. Int. J. Simul. **6**, 10 (2005)
19. Tiwari, P., Mishra, B.K., Kumar, S., Kumar, V.: Implementation of n-gram methodology for rotten tomatoes review dataset sentiment analysis. Int. J. Knowl. Discov. Bioinform. (IJKDB) **7**(1), 30–41 (2017). doi:10.4018/IJKDB.2017010103
20. Kumar, S., Toshniwal, D.: Analyzing road accident data using association rule mining. In: ICCCS-2015, Mauritius. IEEE-Xplore (2015). doi:10.1109/CCCS.2015.7374211
21. Kaytoue, M., Kuznetsov, S.O., Napoli, A., Duplessis, S.: Mining gene expression data with pattern structures in formal concept analysis. Inf. Sci. Int. J. **181**(10), 1989–2001 (2011). Information Science, Special Issue on Information Engineering Applications Based on Lattices. Elsevier, New York (2011)
22. Tiwari, P., Dao, H., Nguyen, G.N., Kumar, S.: Performance evaluation of lazy, decision tree classifier and multilayer perceptron on traffic accident analysis. Informatica **41**(1), 39 (2017)
23. Poelmans, J., Kuznetsov, S.O., Ignatov, D.I., Dedene, G.: Formal Concept Analysis in knowledge processing: A survey on models and techniques. Expert Syst. Appl. **40**(16), 6601–6623 (2013)
24. Tiwari, P.: Comparative analysis of big data. Int. J. Comput. Appl. **140**(7), 24–29 (2016). Foundations of Computer Science (FCS)
25. Kuznetsov, Sergei O.: Fitting pattern structures to knowledge discovery in big data. In: Cellier, P., Distel, F., Ganter, B. (eds.) ICFCA 2013. LNCS, vol. 7880, pp. 254–266. Springer, Heidelberg (2013). doi:10.1007/978-3-642-38317-5_17
26. Kuznetsov, S.O., Poelmans, J.: Knowledge representation and processing with formal concept analysis. Wiley Interdisc. Rev. Data Min. Knowl. Discov. **3**(3), 200–215 (2013)

27. Sachin, K., Semwal, V.B., Tiwari, P., Solanki, V., Denis, K: A conjoint analysis of road accident data using K-modes clustering and bayesian networks. Ann. Comput. Sci. Inf. Syst. 10, 53–56 (2017)
28. Tiwari, P.: Improvement of ETL through integration of query cache and scripting method. In: 2016 International Conference on Data Science and Engineering (ICDSE). IEEE (2016)
29. Tiwari, P.: Advanced ETL (AETL) by integration of PERL and scripting method. In: 2016 International Conference on Inventive Computation Technologies (ICICT), Coimbatore, India, pp. 1–5 (2016). doi:10.1109/INVENTIVE.2016.7830102
30. Tiwari, P., Kumar, S., Mishra, A.C., Kumar, V., Terfa, B.: Improved performance of data warehouse. In: International Conference on Inventive Communication and Computational Technologies (ICICCT-2017), Coimbatore, 10–11 March 2017. Proceeding will be published IEEE-Xplore

Detection of Liver Tumor in CT Images Using Watershed and Hidden Markov Random Field Expectation Maximization Algorithm

Amita Das[1], S.S. Panda[2], and Sukanta Sabut[3($\boxtimes$)]

[1] Department of Electronics and Communication Engineering,
Siksha'O'Anusandhan University, Bhubaneswar, Odisha, India
[2] Department of Surgical Oncology IMS & SUM Hospital, Siksha'O'Anusandhan University,
Bhubaneswar, Odisha, India
[3] Department of Electronics and Instrumentation Engineering, Siksha'O'Anusandhan University,
Bhubaneswar, Odisha, India
sukantsabut@soauniversity.ac.in

Abstract. Precisely segmenting liver from computed tomography (CT) scan images is a challenging task of computer aided diagnosis. The first and crucial step for diagnosis is automatic liver segmentation. In this paper, the watershed transform, Hidden Markov Random Field- Expectation Maximization (HMRF-EM) and threshold algorithms have been used for visualizing and measuring the tumor area which is a part of liver which is segmented from CT abdominal images. The proposed process was tested on a series of CT scan images of liver. The segmentation and area estimation images are obtained by the study of 2D images. To validate the proposed approach tumor area, MSE and PSNR values are measured from the segmented region which helps the physician for a successful treatment and diagnosis procedure.

Keywords: Liver · Tumor · Image segmentation · Computed tomography (CT) · Watershed · HMRF-EM

1 Introduction

Liver cancer is the third major cause of death within all cancer diseases [1–3]. Metastatic diseases like primary cancer or hepatocellular carcinoma are the common diseases in advance countries. To improve the patient condition from the diseases, early and accurate detection of tumor and an effective approach to monitor the treatment procedure is required. Normally before surgery, computed tomography or magnetic resonance imaging (MRI) techniques are used for assessing primary or secondary hepatic tumor [4]. Computer aided segmentation and measurements of target object required for surgical planning and monitoring the disease. The manual segmentation which performs by medical genius is expensive and time consuming therefore automatic segmentation algorithm are developed in past literature.

© Springer Nature Singapore Pte Ltd. 2017
J.K. Mandal et al. (Eds.): CICBA 2017, Part II, CCIS 776, pp. 411–419, 2017.
DOI: 10.1007/978-981-10-6430-2_32

An interactive method combination of watershed transform and SVM classifier is proposed on CT volume to demonstrate the efficiency and accuracy of the segmentation [5]. A liver tumor segmentation method using local constraint based level set method was proposed to separate the tumors from abdominal structures and the results were compared to geodesic level set method and manual segmentation having a better jacquard distance error, relative volume difference and maximum surface distance [6]. An automatic liver region segmentation method founded on watershed MLP neural network was presented which deals with the over segmentation problem of watershed and the results were compared with an active contour algorithm having higher jacquard coefficient [7]. The combined process of adaptive thresholding and Kernelized fuzzy clustering was used to visualize the tumor region in an abdominal CT image and the PSNR and MSE values shows the affectivity of the method [8]. Fang et al. proposed a combine marker-control watershed and fuzzy algorithm for the delineation of liver metastasizes and the results are compared with manual segmentation [9]. Zhang *et al.* proposed a HMRF-EM model based stochastic process generated by MRF where the state sequence are estimated through observations rather than directly and it also avoids the limitation of finite mixture (FM) model by taking the spatial information of an image into account [10]. Smeets *et al.* proposed the fuzzy clustering based pixel classification accompanied by an edge based LSM to segment the liver tumor. A nonlinearly filtered probabilistic distribution was implemented for speed function in fuzzy clustering for detecting liver tumor [11]. A learning-based algorithm which combines auto–context model (ACM), multi-atlases, and mean-shift techniques are found to be an efficient and accurate method in segmenting the liver from 3-D CT images [12]. Banerjee et al. proposed an unsupervised MRF based segmentation technique for synthetic aperture radar (SAR) images and the results shows that the inclusion of optimized parameter clearly enhance the performance of clustering [13]. Huang et al. proposes an approach that segment nasopharyngeal carcinoma from the MRI images of brain. The tumor contour was obtained from level set method and HMRF-EM is used to refine the method and it achieves good results [14]. Zhanpeng *et al.* proposes segmentation based on watershed and region merging to extract liver area. The experimental result shows that the algorithm can accurately extract the liver region [15]. Sethi *et al.* proposes a region separation, region enhancement and distance regularized level set evolution (DRLSE) for detecting low contrast boundaries and the results are compared with two active contours and it proves the superiority of the proposed method [16]. Lin et al. proposes a collaborative model to formulate the tumor segmentation from region partition and boundary presence. They present an inference algorithms using augmented Lagrangian method to propagate the segmentation across the image sequences. The proposed system for segmenting liver tumor achieved very promising results [17].

In this work a hidden Markov random field with expectation maximization (HMRF-EM) with watershed transform have been proposed to segment the CT images of the liver to detect the tumor inside the liver. The rest of the paper is organized as follows; Sect. 2 includes different segmentation methods i.e. watershed, HMRF-EM algorithm. Section 3 defines the result of our proposed methodology and Sect. 4 includes the conclusion.

2 Methods

2.1 Watershed Transform

Liver is a metabolic organ that performs various functions like production of protein, bile acid and cholesterol [18]. It also filter the blood and pass it to the rest of the body. Liver segmentation from the abdominal CT or MRI images is a challenging task. For early disease detection and surgical planning segmentation provide most important information. So for accurate separation of liver from the clinical images like MRI and CT scan a marker control watershed segmentation is deployed. Watershed transform is a combination of edge detection and region growing method for producing stable results with connected boundaries. The main purpose of watershed transform is that if a point belongs to one minimal then the point is merge with it else the point is taken as a boundary in-between the two minimal. Morphological dilation is used to perform this operation in binary images. Morphological gradient of each band of the image is calculated using Eq. (1)

$$G(f) = (f \oplus B) - (f \ominus B) \tag{1}$$

where G(f) = Morphological color gradient

f = input image, B = structuring element

The multi-scale morphological color gradient is then calculated using the formula given in Eq. (2).

$$MG(f) = \frac{1}{n} \sum_{i=1}^{n} [G(f) \ominus B_{i-1}] \tag{2}$$

Where B_{i-1} = Structuring element of size $(2i + 1)*(2i + 1)$.

The final gradient image, $FG(f)$ is obtained by reconstructing the multi-scale gradient image, $MG(f)$ with its dilated image used reference image.

$$FG(f) = \phi^{rec}((MG(f) \oplus B) + h, MG(f)) \tag{3}$$

The markers are extracted using morphological Laplacian, which can be defined as:

$$L(f) = g^{+}(f) - g^{-}(f) \tag{4}$$

Where $g^{+}(f)$ = white top hat transform

$g^{-}(f)$ = black top hat transform.

A marker-controlled watershed approach [19] is used to control the over segmentation problem. Generally markers are the connected components that belongs to an image. A binary image having a single marker point or a large marker region is considered as a marker image. Initially each marker is placed inside an object that is surrounded by watershed lines. Markers are taken as local minima of the gradient of image. Algorithm

(1) describes the different steps of finding ROIs from a CT image of liver using marker controlled watershed transform.

Algorithm (1): Liver segmentation using watershed approach.

1: Calculate the minima of an image by determining the marker matrix using the gradient.

2: Verify each and every pixel related to a minimal and add the point to the related minimal.

3: If a pixel belongs to more than one minimal then considerate as an boundary.

4: The resultant image will have boundaries in zero values and regions as numeric labels.

2.2 Hidden Markov Random Field Model

Zhang *et al.* [20] proposed a HMRF-EM method for image segmentation. In this paper HMRF-EM method is applied to a CT scan image of liver to segment the tumor. The theory of Hidden Markov Random Field (HMRF) representation is generated from Hidden Markov Model. This is a process of Markov Chain and its state sequence are observed through a sequence of observation. HMRF is a graph based model where the true states are predicted from an observation field. In HMRF approach there is an observable sequence known as $y = (y_1, \dots y_N)$, where y_i = featurevalueofonepixel. Aim is to induce a hidden random field i.e. $x = (x_1, \dots x_N)$, where $x_i \in L$. In image segmentation point of view, $x_i = configurationoflabels$ and $L = setofallpossiblelabels$.

So the conditional dependency between x and y is derived in Eq. (5).

$$P(y|x) = \underset{i \in s}{\pi} \, p(y_i|x_i) \tag{5}$$

where s is a neighborhood system. L wise the joint probability is defined in Eq. (6).

$$P(x_1, x_2, \dots x_n, y_1, y_2, \dots y_n) = P(y_1)P(x_1|y_1) \underset{k=2}{\overset{n}{\pi}} P(y_k|y_{k-1})P(x_k|y_k) \tag{6}$$

2.2.1 Estimation of HMRF from EM Algorithm

The EM algorithm is generally used to find the class level x and to estimate θ which is a model parameter of each pixel. This algorithm defines two steps: first one is to estimate the total amount of unobservable data required to form the data set and second one is to maximize likelihood function for this data set.

Depending on MAP criterion, we define the label x^* in Eq. (7)

$$x^* = \arg\max_{x} \{P(y|x, \Theta p(x))\} \tag{7}$$

2.2.2 MAP Estimation

The parameters that are obtained from the EM algorithm are utilized for the MAP segmentation. Initially k-means segmentation has been performed and it will serve for the evaluation of the segmentation process. The total amount of posterior energy required for MAP estimate is defined in Eq. (8).

$$x^* = \arg\min_{x \in X} \{U(y|x, \Theta) + U(x)\} \tag{8}$$

The posterior energy has two constitutions. First one is the likelihood of energy and second one is the prior of energy function U(x) i.e. defined in Eq. (9).

$$U(x) = \sum_{c \in C} V(x)_c \tag{9}$$

It produces a sum of clique potentials $V_{c(x)}$ through all cliques C. In image segmentation clique potential is used to indicate the impact of adjacent pixels on the pixel i. The clique potential for each pixel i is describe as the total number of adjacent pixels having different labels which explained in Eq. (10)

$$V_C(x_i) = \frac{1}{2}(1 - I_{x_i,x_j}) \tag{10}$$

where $x_j \in N_i$, and

$$I_{x_{i,x_j}} = \begin{cases} 0 & x_i \neq x_j \\ 1 & x_i \neq x_j \end{cases} \tag{11}$$

To resolve an iterative algorithm, we first estimate $x_{(0)}$, that appear from the EM algorithm and provide $x_{(k)}$, for all $1 \leq i \leq N$, we obtained in Eq. (12)

$$x_i^{(k+1)} = \arg\min_{l \in L} \left\{ U(y_i|l) + \sum_{j \in N_i} V_c(l, x_j^{(k)}) \right\} \tag{12}$$

This Eq. (12) continues until

$$U(y|x, \Theta) + U(x) \tag{13}$$

3 Result and Discussion

A. *Proposed Methodology*

The proposed methodology of segmentation and visualization has been applied to the CT images of liver to extract tumor region. The images are collected from department of radiology, IMS and SUM hospital, Bhubaneswar. A framework of liver tumor segmentation procedure is illustrated in Fig. (1). The suitable slice having clear indication of tumor is selected from a number of images of CT volume. Initially the images are de-noises with Gaussian filter to enhance the performance of the algorithm.

B. *Watershed Algorithm*

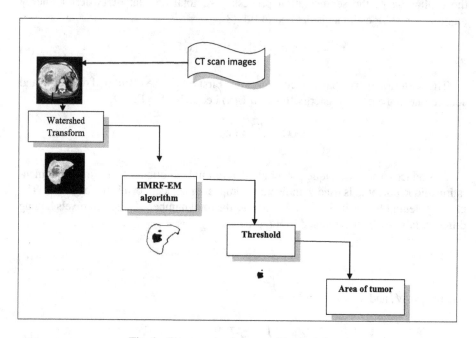

Fig. 1. Framework of proposed methodology

Initially a marker control watershed transform is applied to the CT scan image of liver. This method separate the liver from the CT image and the resultant image is shown in Fig. (1).

C. *HMRF-EM Algorithm*

A Gaussian blur or a type of image blurring filter is applied at the resultant image of watershed. The Gaussian operator G(x, y) is calculated in Eq. (14) to smoothen the image

$$G(x, y) = \frac{1}{\sqrt{2\pi\sigma^2}} e^{\frac{x^2 + y^2}{2\sigma^2}} \qquad (14)$$

Initially K-means clustering is used for segmentation before the application of HMRF-EM algorithm to the segmented liver region. The initial labels $X_{(0)}$ are chosen from the K-means clustering which is used for the MAP algorithm and initial parameter $\Theta^{(0)}$ is used in EM algorithm. A canny edge detection algorithm is applied on the segmented liver image and the edge map that is obtained and is presented in Fig. (2). From Fig. (2) it is observed that the initial label generated from the K-means algorithm are not clear and smooth. So to overcome this disadvantage HMRF will refine the labels. The final results were obtained with 5 classes and 10 iteration of EM algorithm. The area of the identified tumor has been estimated by applying thresholding at the final results of the HMRF-EM algorithm. Figure 3. shows the output results of the processed images.

D. *Validation of the proposed method*

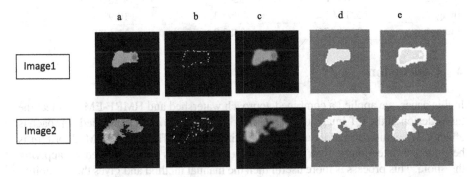

Fig. 2. (a) Original image (b) canny edge detection (c) blurred image output (d) initial labels from k-means (e) final segmentation from HMRF-EM algorithm.

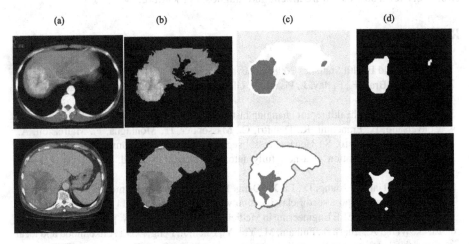

Fig. 3. (a) Original image (b) watershed image(c) images from HMRF-EM (d) final result obtained from threshold negative

The total no of pixels located in the tumor region and also the area of the region is calculated from the resultant images of threshold method. The PSNR, MSE values are calculated for the final segmented liver tumor images and the results are given in Table 1.

Table 1. Results of area, PSNR, MSE of segmented tumor in proposed method.

Image	Proposed method area (in pixel)	PSNR (peak signal to noise ratio)	MSE (mean square error)
Image1	3131.4	10009	8.1269
Image2	1105.56	5241.3	9.2636
Image3	5219.9	4993.3	10.9364
Image4	3304.435	3483.9	11.1469

4   Conclusion

In this paper, we applied a combined approach watershed and HMRF-EM to detect the tumor lesion in the CT image of liver. Firstly the marker control watershed approach is effectively segmented the liver from abdominal organs. The HMRF-EM algorithm is help for the detection of liver tumor and the final results were obtained by applying threshold. This process is more useful then the manual method and gives the possibility for calculating the area and location of the liver tumor. Particularly the proposed approaches help the physician to visualize and detect the liver tumor accurately and effectively for a successful treatment and diagnosis procedure.

References

1. WHO, World Health Statistics 2008. Geneva, Switzerland. WHO Press (2008)
2. Parkin, M., Bray, F., Ferlay, J., Pisani, P.: Global cancer statistics, 2002. CA-Cancer J. Clin. **55**, 74–108 (2005)
3. WHO. The world health report changing history (2004)
4. Conversano, F., Franchini, R., Demitri, C., Massoptier, L., Montagna, F., Maffezzoli, A., Malvasi, A., Casciaro, S.: Hepatic vessel segmentation for 3-D planning of liver surgery: experimental evaluation of a new fully automatic algorithm. Acad. Radiol. **18**, 461–470 (2011)
5. Zhang, X., Tian, J., Xiang, D., Li, X., Deng, K.: Interactive liver tumor segmentation from CT scans using support vector classification with watershed. In: 2011 Annual International Conference of the IEEE Engineering in Medicine and Biology Society, pp. 6005–6008 (2011)
6. Li, C., Wang, X., Eberl, S., Fulham, M., Yin, Y., Chen, J., Feng, D.D.: A likelihood and local constraint level set model for liver tumor segmentation from CT volumes. IEEE Trans. Biomed. Eng. **60**(10), 2967–2977 (2013)
7. Masoumi, H., Behrad, A., Pourmina, M.A., Roosta, A.: Automatic liver segmentation in MRI images using an iterative watershed algorithm and artificial neural network. Biomed. Signal Process. Control **7**, 429–437 (2012)
8. Das, A., Sabut, S.K.: Kernelized fuzzy C-means clustering with adaptive thresholding for segmenting liver tumors. Procedia Comput. Science. **92**, 389–395 (2016)
9. Yan, J., Fang, J.Q.: Segmentation of liver metastasis on CT images using the marker-controlled watershed and fuzzy connectedness algorithms. In: 2015 International Symposium on Bioelectronics and Bioinformatics (ISBB), pp. 47–50 (2015)
10. Zhang, Y., Brady, M., Smith, S.: Segmentation of brain MR images through a hidden markov random field model and the expectation-maximization algorithm. IEEE Trans. Med. Imaging **20**(1), 45–57 (2001)

11. Smeets, D., Loeckx, D., Stijnen, B., Dabbler, D., Vandermeulen, D., Suetens, P.: Semi-automatic level set segmentation of liver tumors combining a spiral-scanning technique with supervised fuzzy pixel classification. Med. Image Anal. **14**, 13–20 (2010)

12. Pham, M., Susomboon, R., Disney, T., Raicu, D., Furst, J.: A comparison of texture models for automatic Liver segmentation. In: Proceedings of SPIE Medical Imaging Conference, San Diego, CA, USA. 65124E (2007)

13. Banerjee, B., De, S., Manickam, S., Bhattacha, A.: An unsupervised hidden markov random field based segmentation of polarimetric SAR images. In: IEEE International Geosciences and Remote Sensing Symposium (IGARSS), pp. 1536–1539 (2016)

14. Huang, K.W., Zhao, Z.Y., Gong, Q., Zha, J., Chen, L., Yang, R.: Nasopharyngeal carcinoma segmentation via HMRF-EM with maximum entropy. In: 37 Annual International Conference of the IEEE Engineering in Medicine and Biology Society (EMBC), pp. 2968–2972 (2015)

15. Zhanpeng, H., Qi, Z., Shizhong, J., Guohua, C.: Medical image segmentation based on watershed and region merging. In: 3rd International Conference on Information Science and Control Engineering (ICISCE), pp. 1011–1014 (2016)

16. Sethi, G., Saini, B.S., Singh, D.: Segmentation of cancerous region in liver using an edge-based and phase congruent region enhancement method. Comput. Electr. Eng. **53**, 244–262 (2016)

17. Lin, L., Yang, W., Li, C., Tang, J., Cao, X.: Inference with collaborative model for interactive tumor segmentation in medical image sequences. IEEE Trans. Cybern. **46**(12), 2796–2809 (2016)

18. Chen, H.Y., Wang, J.R., Lu, K.Y., Wen, K.L.: The evaluation of liver function via gray relational analysis. In: 2009 IEEE International Conference on Systems, Man and Cybernetics, pp. 767–770 (2009)

19. Zidan, A., Ghali, N.I., Hassamen, A., Hefny H.H.: Level set-based CT liver image segmentation with watershed and artificial neural network. In: 12th International Conference on Hybrid Intelligent Systems (HIS), pp. 96–102 (2012)

20. Abdulbaqi, H.S., Jafri, M.Z.M., Omar, A.F., Muttor, K.N., Abood, L.K., Mustafa, I.S.B.: Segmentation and estimation of brain tumor volume in computed tomography scan using hidden markov random field expectation maximization algorithm. In: IEEE Student Conference on Research and Developments (SCOReD), pp. 55–60 (2015)

Computational Intelligence

Modelling Multiobjective Bilevel Programming for Environmental-Economic Power Generation and Dispatch Using Genetic Algorithm

Debjani Chakraborti[1], Papun Biswas[2], and Bijay Baran Pal[3(✉)]

[1] Narula Institute of Technology, Agarpara, West Bengal, India
debjani_333@yahoo.co.in
[2] JIS College of Engineering, Kalyani, West Bengal, India
papunbiswas@gmail.com
[3] University of Kalyani, Kalyani, West Bengal, India
bbpal18@hotmail.com

Abstract. This article describes a multiobjective bilevel programming (MOBLP) model to solve environmental-economic power generation and dispatch (EEPGD) problem through genetic algorithm (GA) based fuzzy goal programming (FGP) in a thermal power plant operational system. In MOBLP approach, first the objectives of problem are divided into two sets of objectives, and they are separately included at two hierarchical decision levels (top-level and bottom-level), where each level contains one or more controls variables associated with power generation decision system. Then, optimization problems of both the levels are described fuzzily to accommodate the impression arises with regard to optimizing them. In FGP model formulation, the membership functions associated with defined fuzzy goals are designed, and then they are converted into membership goals by assigning highest membership value (unity) as achievement level and introducing under- and over-deviational variables to each of them. In achievement function, minimization of under-deviational variables of membership goals according to weights of importance is considered to achieve optimal solution in decision environment. In the process of solving FGP model, a GA scheme is adopted at two stages, direct optimization of individual objectives at the first stage for fuzzy representation of them and, at the second stage, evaluation of goal achievement function to reach optimal power generation decision. The use of the proposed method is demonstrated via IEEE 30-bus system.

Keywords: Bilevel programming · Environmental-economic power generation · Fuzzy goal programming · Genetic algorithm · Membership function · Transmission-loss

1 Introduction

The major sources for electric power generation are thermal power plants, where more than 75% of them use coal to generate power with regard to meeting power demand in society. But, burning of fossil-fuel coal to generation power produces various pollutants, namely oxides of carbon, nitrogen and sulphur and others.

© Springer Nature Singapore Pte Ltd. 2017
J.K. Mandal et al. (Eds.): CICBA 2017, Part II, CCIS 776, pp. 423–439, 2017.
DOI: 10.1007/978-981-10-6430-2_33

It may be pointed out here that such by-products affect the entire living beings on earth. Therefore, the problem of EEPGD is essentially needed, where optimization of real-power generation cost and environmental pollution subject to various operational constraints have to be considered simultaneously to run thermal power plants.

Actually, a thermal power plant problem in [1] is optimization problem with multiplicity of objectives in power generation decision environment. The mathematical programming (MP) model in power generation system was first studied by Dommel and Tinney in [2]. Thereafter, MP model for control of emission was discussed by Gent and Lament in [3]. Then, study on the field was further made by Sullivan and Hackett in [4] and others to solve EEPGD problems.

However, the modelling aspect of minimizing both power generation cost and environmental-emission was initially introduced by Zahavi and Eisenberg in [5], and then the study on MP models for EEPGD problems was made in [6, 7] in the past.

A survey on the study of EEPGD problems made in the past was presented in [8] in 1977. Also, various MP models studied to solve EEPGD problems have been surveyed in [9–11] in the past.

During 1990s, controlling of power plant emissions were considered seriously and different optimization methods in [12–17] were presented with due consideration of 1990's Clean Air Amendment Act in [18] to make a pollution free environment. It is worthy to note here that the approaches of solving an EEPGD problem with multiple objectives made previously are classical ones on the line of transforming multiobjective models into single objective problems. As a matter of fact, decision troubles are frequently raised owing to the difficulty of taking individual optimality of objectives in decision making horizon.

Now, GP as efficient tool for multiobjecive decision analysis and based on satisficing philosophy in [19] has been employed to EEPGD problem in [20] to obtain goal oriented solution in crisp decision environment.

However, in most of the cases to model EEPGD problems, it may be noted that the parameters associated with objectives are not exact in nature due to imprecise nature of setting parameter values in real practice. To overcome the shortcoming, fuzzy programming (FP) approaches in [21] have been introduced in [22, 23] to EEPGD problems in the past. Further, stochastic programming (SP) methods to EEPGD problems have also been discussed in [24, 25] previously. But, extensive study on solving such problems is yet to circulate widely in literature.

Now it is worthy to mention that uses of classical approaches to MODM problems often leads to achieving suboptimal solution to owing to competing in nature of objectives in optimizing them as well as involvement of nonlinearity in objectives/constraints of a real-world problem. To avoid such a situation, GAs as a prominent tool in the area of evolutionary computing can be used to solve MODM problems. The potential use of GAs to EEPGD problems have been discussed in [26–28] in the past.

Now, it is worth noting that the objectives of EEPGD problems are often conflicted regarding optimization of them in decision environment. As such, optimization of objectives in a hierarchical order can be taken into account and which is based on decision maker's (DM's) needs to generate thermal power. Therefore, optimization of them on the basis of hierarchical importance, and the use of bilevel programming (BLP) in [29] could be effective to reach optimal decision. Although, such a problem has been discussed in [30] in the recent past, study in the area is at initial stage. Again, MOBLP method to solve EEPGD problem within the framework of FGP by using GA is not circulated widely in literature.

In this article, an FGP method to solve MOBLP formulation of an EEPGD problem using GA is considered. In model formulation, *minsum* FGP in [31] as the simplest version of FGP is addressed to make power generation decision in fuzzy environment. In decision process, individual decisions for optimizing objectives are computed first by using a GA scheme towards fuzzy goal description of objectives. Then, evaluation of goal achievement function as a second stage problem regarding minimization of weighted under-deviational variables of membership goals defined for fuzzy goals is considered. The effective use of the method is illustrated via IEEE 6-generator 30-bus system.

The paper is organized as follows. The description of problem is presented in Sect. 2. Section 3 shows MOBLP formulation of EEPGD problem. In Sect. 4, a GA scheme for modelling and solving EEPGD problem is discussed. Section 5 provides the proposed FGP model of the problem. An illustrative case example is provided in Sect. 6. Finally, concluding remarks and scope for future research are highlighted in Sect. 7.

Now, objectives and constraints of the problem are presented in the Sect. 2.

2 Problem Description

Let P_{gi} be decision variables defined for power generation (in p.u) from ith generator of the system, $i = 1, 2, ..., n$. Then, let P_D be total demand of power, T_L be total transmission- loss (in p.u) and P_L be real power-loss in power generation context.

The objectives and constraints involved with EEPGD problem are presented in the following sect.

2.1 Description of Objective Functions

The two types of objectives that are inherent to the problem are presented as follows.

2.1.1 Economic Power Generation Objectives

(a) **Fuel-cost Function:**

The total fuel-cost ($/h) incurred for power generation is expressed as:

$$F_C = \sum_{i=1}^{n} (a_i P_{gi}^2 + b_i P_{gi} + c_i), \tag{1}$$

where a_i, b_i and c_i are cost-coefficients concerned with generation of power from ith generator.

(b) Transmission-loss function:

The function associated with power transmission lines involves certain parameters which directly affect the ability to transfer power effectively. Here, the transmission-loss (T_L) (in p.u.) occurs during power dispatch is modelled as a function of generator output and that can be obtained as:

$$T_L = \sum_{i=1}^{n} \sum_{j=1}^{n} P_{g_i} B_{ij} P_{g_j} + \sum_{i=1}^{n} B_{0i} P_{g_i} + B_{00}, \tag{2}$$

where B_{ij}, B_{0i} and B_{00} are B-coefficients in [23] associated with ith generator in power transmission network.

2.1.2 Pollution Control Functions

In a thermal power generation system, the most harmful pollutants that are discharged separately to earth's environment are NO_x, SO_x and CO_x. The pollution control functions are quadratic in nature and they are expressed in terms of generators' output P_{gi}, $i = 1,2,..., n$.

The functional expression of total quantity of NO_x emissions (kg/h) is of the form:

$$E_N = \sum_{i=1}^{n} d_{N_i} P_{gi}^2 + e_{N_i} P_{gi} + f_{N_i}, \tag{3}$$

where d_{N_i}, e_{N_i}, f_{N_i} represent NO_x emission-coefficients concerned with power generation from ith generator.

Similarly, the pollution control functions arise for SO_x- and CO_x-emissions appear as:

$$E_S = \sum_{i=1}^{n} d_{Si} P_{gi}^2 + e_{Si} P_{gi} + f_{Si}, \tag{4}$$

$$E_C = \sum_{i=1}^{n} d_{Ci} P_{gi}^2 + e_{Ci} P_{gi} + f_{Ci}, \text{ respectively}, \tag{5}$$

where the emission-coefficients associated with respective expressions can be defined in an analogous to the expression in (3).

2.2 Description of System Constraints

The constraints associated with generation of power are defined as follows.

2.2.1 Generator Capacity Constraints

The constraints on generators' take the form:

$$
\begin{aligned}
P_{gi}^{min} &\leq P_{gi} \leq P_{gi}^{max}, \\
V_{gi}^{min} &\leq V_{gi} \leq V_{gi}^{max}, \quad i = 1, 2, \ldots, n
\end{aligned}
\tag{6}
$$

where P_{gi} and V_{gi} represent active power and generator-bus voltage of ith generator, respectively.

2.2.2 Power Balance Constraint

The generation of total power from the system is always equal to total demand (P_D) and total transmission-loss in thermal power generation system.

The power balance constraint is of the form:

$$\sum_{i=1}^{n} P_{gi} - (P_D + T_L) = 0 \tag{7}$$

Now, formulation of MOBLP model of the problem is discussed in the Sect. 3.

3 MOBLP Formulation

In MOBLP formulation, the objectives concerning environmental-emission control are considered leader's optimization problems and that concerned with economic-power generation are included to follower's problem in hierarchical structure of EEPGD problem.

The MOBLP model is presented in the Sect. 3.1.

3.1 MOBLP Model

In the context of designing the proposed model, the vector of decision variables is divided into two distinct vectors with regard to control them separately by DMs of two hierarchical levels.

Let X be the vector of decision variables in power generation system. Again, let X_L and X_F be the subsets of X that are controlled by leader and follower, respectively, where L and F are used to denote leader and follower, respectively.

Then, MOBLP model appears as [29]:

Find $X(X_L, X_F)$ so as to:

$$\underset{X_L}{Minimize} \ E_N = \sum_{i=1}^{n} d_{N_i} P_{gi}^2 + e_{N_i} P_{gi} + f_{N_i},$$

$$\underset{X_L}{Minimize} \ E_S = \sum_{i=1}^{n} d_{S_i} P_{gi}^2 + e_{S_i} P_{gi} + f_{S_i},$$

$$\underset{X_L}{Minimize} \ E_C = \sum_{i=1}^{n} d_{C_i} P_{gi}^2 + e_{C_i} P_{gi} + f_{C_i},$$

(leader's problem)

and, for given X_L, X_F solves

$$\underset{X_F}{Minimize} \quad F_C = \sum_{i=1}^{n}(a_i P_{gi}^2 + b_i P_{gi} + c_i),$$

$$\underset{X_F}{Minimize} \, T_L = \sum_{i=1}^{n}\sum_{j=1}^{n} P_{gi} B_{ij} P_{gj} + \sum_{i=1}^{n} B_{0i} P_{gi} + B_{00},$$

$$(8)$$

(follower's problem)

subject to the constraints in (6) and (7),

where $X_L \cap X_F = \varphi$, $X_L \cup X_F = X$ and $X \in P(\neq \varphi)$, where P indicates feasible solution set, $\cap$ and $\cup$ stand for 'intersection' and 'union', respectively.

Now, the GA scheme adopted to search solution is described in the Sect. 4.

4 GA Scheme

There is a variety of GA schemes in [32, 33] for generating new population by employing 'selection', 'crossover' and 'mutation' operators.

In genetic search process, binary coded solution candidates are considered where initial population is generated randomly. The fitness of each chromosome (individual feasible solution) at each generation is justified with a view to optimizing objectives of the problem.

Now, formulation of FGP model of the problem in (8) is described in the Sect. 5.

5 FGP Model Formulation

In the structural framework of a BLP problem, it is conventionally considered that DM at each level is motivated to cooperative each other regarding achievement of objectives in decision environment. In the decision search process, since leader is with the power of making decision first, relaxation on his/her decision is needed to make decision by follower to certain satisfactory level. Consequently, relaxation on individual objective values and components of X_L need be given to certain tolerance levels for benefit of follower. Therefore, use of the notion of fuzzy set to solve the problem in (8) would be effective one to reach overall satisfactory decision.

The fuzzy version of the problem is discussed in the Sect. 5.1.

5.1 Fuzzy Goal Description

In fuzzy environment, objective functions of the problem are expressed as fuzzy goals by means of incorporating imprecise target values to them.

In the decision making context, since minimum value of an objective of a DM is highly acceptable, solutions achieved for minimization of objectives of individual DMs can be considered the best solutions, and they are determined as $(X_L^{lb}, X_F^{lb}; E_N^{lb}, E_S^{lb}, E_C^{lb})$

and $(X_L^{fb}, X_F^{fb}; F_C^{fb}, T_L^{fb})$, respectively, by employing GA scheme, where lb and fb indicate the best for leader and follower, respectively.

Then, the successive fuzzy goals take the form:

$$E_N \lesssim E_N^{lb}, \ E_S \lesssim E_S^{lb} \text{ and } E_C \lesssim E_C^{lb}$$
$$F_C \lesssim F_C^{fb} \text{ and } T_L \lesssim T_L^{fb}, \tag{9}$$

where '$\lesssim$' indicates softness of $\leq$ restriction and signifies 'essentially less than' in [34].

Again, since most dissatisfactory solutions of DMs correspond to maximum values of objectives, the worst solutions of leader and follower are obtained by using the GA scheme as $(X_L^{lw}, X_F^{lw}; E_N^{lw}, E_S^{lw}, E_C^{lw})$ and $(X_L^{fw}, X_F^{fw}; F_C^{fw}, T_L^{fw})$, respectively, where lw and, fw indicate worst cases for leader and follower, respectively.

As a matter consequence, E_N^{lw}, E_S^{lw}, E_C^{lw}, F_C^{fw} and T_L^{fw} could be taken as upper-tolerance values towards achieving the respective fuzzy target levels E_N, E_S, E_C, F_C and T_L.

Again, fuzzy goal representation of control vector X_L can be reasonably taken as:

$$X_L \lesssim X_L^{lb} \tag{10}$$

Now, it may be mentioned that an increase in value of a goal defined by goal vector in (10) would never be more than upper-bound of corresponding generator capacity defined in (6).

Let $X_L^t, (X_L^t < X_L^{max})$, be the vector of upper-tolerance values to achieve the associated vector of fuzzy goal levels defined in (10).

Now, characterization of membership functions of fuzzy goals is described in the Sect. 5.2.

5.2   Characterization of Membership Function

The membership function of fuzzy objective goal E_N can be algebraically presented as:

$$\mu_{E_N}[E_N] = \begin{cases} 1, & \text{if } E_N \leq E_N^{lb} \\ \frac{E_N^{lw} - E_N}{E_N^{lw} - E_N^{lb}}, & \text{if } E_N^{lb} < E_N \leq E_N^{lw} \\ 0, & \text{if } E_N > E_N^{lw} \end{cases} \tag{11}$$

where $(E_N^{lw} - E_N^{lb})$ represents tolerance range concerning achievement fuzzy goal defined in (9).

Again, membership functions associated with other two objectives, E_s and E_c of leader as well as objectives of follower can be obtained.

The membership function associated with X_L is obtained as:

$$\mu_{X_L}[X_L] = \begin{cases} 1, & \text{if } X_L \leq X_L^{lb} \\ \frac{X_L^t - X_L}{X_L^t - X_L^{lb}}, & \text{if } X_L^{lb} < X_L \leq X_L^t \\ 0, & \text{if } X_L > X_L^t \end{cases} \tag{12}$$

where $(X_L^t - X_L^{lb})$ represents vector of tolerance ranges regarding achievement of vector of decision variables defined in (10).

Now, *minsum* FGP model is presented in the Sect. 5.3.

5.3   *Minsum* FGP Model

To formulate FGP model of the problem, membership functions are converted into membership goals by introducing unity (highest membership value) as target level and incorporating under- and over-deviational variables to them. In achievement function, minimization of sum of weighted under-deviational variables associated with membership goals is taken into account.

The model appears as [31]:

Find $X(X_L, X_F)$ so as to:

Minimize: $Z = \sum_{k=1}^{5} w_k^- d_k^- + w_6^- d_6^-$

and satisfy

$$\frac{E_N^{lw} - E_N}{E_N^{lw} - E_N^{lb}} + d_1^- - d_1^+ = 1, \quad \frac{E_S^{lw} - E_S}{E_S^{lw} - E_S^{lb}} + d_2^- - d_2^+ = 1,$$

$$\frac{E_C^{lw} - E_C}{E_C^{lw} - E_C^{lb}} + d_3^- - d_3^+ = 1, \quad \frac{F_C^{fw} - F_C}{F_C^{fw} - F_C^{fb}} + d_4^- - d_4^+ = 1, \tag{13}$$

$$\frac{T_L^{fw} - T_L}{T_L^{fw} - T_L^{fb}} + d_5^- - d_5^+ = 1, \quad \frac{X_L^t - X_L}{X_L^t - P_{GL}^{lb}} + d_6^- - d_6^+ = \mathbf{I}$$

subject to the constraints in (6) and (7)

where d_k^-, $d_k^+ \geq 0$, $(k = 1,...,5)$ represent under- and over-deviational variables, respectively. $d_6^-, d_6^+ \geq 0$ indicate vector of under- and over-deviational variables, respectively, and where I is a column vector. Z is goal achievement function, $w_k^- > 0$, $k = 1, 2, 3, 4, 5$ are relative numerical weights of importance of achieving target levels of goals, and $\mathbf{w_6^-} > \mathbf{0}$ represents vector of numerical weights associated with $\mathbf{d_6^-}$, and where weights are inverse of the respective tolerance ranges in [31] concerning achievement of target levels of goals.

The use of the model in (13) is illustrated through a case example in the Sect. 6.

6 Case Example

The IEEE 30-bus 6-generator test system in [15] is taken into account to demonstrate the proposed method.

The system is with 41 transmission lines and total power demand for 21 load buses is 2.834 p.u. The generator capacity limits and load data were discussed in [15] previously. The different coefficient sets associated with the model are given in Tables 1, 2, 3 and 4.

Table 1. Power generation cost-coefficients.

Generator→	g_1	g_2	g_3	g_4	g_5	g_6
Cost-coefficients						
a	100	120	40	60	40	100
b	200	150	180	100	180	150
c	10	12	20	10	20	10

Table 2. NO_x emission-coefficients.

Generator→	g_1	g_2	g_3	g_4	g_5	g_6
NO_x emission-coefficients						
d_N	0.006323	0.006483	0.003174	0.006732	0.003174	0.006181
e_N	−0.38128	−0.79027	−1.36061	−2.39928	−1.36061	−0.39077
f_N	80.9019	28.8249	324.1775	610.2535	324.1775	50.3808

Table 3. SO_x emission-coefficients.

Generator→	g_1	g_2	g_3	g_4	g_5	g_6
SO_x emission-coefficients						
d_S	0.001206	0.002320	0.001284	0.000813	0.001284	0.003578
e_S	5.05928	3.84624	4.45647	4.97641	4.4564	4.14938
f_S	51.3778	182.2605	508.5207	165.3433	508.5207	121.2133

Table 4. CO_x emission-coefficients.

Generator→	g_1	g_2	g_3	g_4	g_5	g_6
CO_x emission-coefficients						
d_S	0.265110	0.140053	0.105929	0.106409	0.105929	0.403144
e_S	−61.01945	−29.95221	−9.552794	−12.73642	−9.552794	−121.9812
f_S	5080.148	3824.770	1342.851	1819.625	13.42.851	11381.070

The *B-coefficients* in [20] are presented as follows:

$$B = \begin{bmatrix} 0.1382 & -0.0299 & 0.0044 & -0.0022 & -0.0010 & -0.0008 \\ -0.0299 & 0.0487 & -0.0025 & 0.0004 & 0.0016 & 0.0041 \\ 0.0044 & -0.0025 & 0.0182 & -0.0070 & -0.0066 & -0.0066 \\ -0.0022 & 0.0004 & -0.0070 & 0.0137 & 0.0050 & 0.0033 \\ -0.0010 & 0.0016 & -0.0066 & 0.0050 & 0.0109 & 0.0005 \\ -0.0008 & 0.0041 & -0.0066 & 0.0033 & 0.0005 & 0.0244 \end{bmatrix}_{(6\times6)}$$

$$B_0 = [-0.0107 \quad 0.0060 \quad -0.0017 \quad 0.0009 \quad 0.0002 \quad 0.0030]_{(1\times6)},$$
$$B_{00} = 9.86E - 04$$

Now, to formulate MOBLP model, it is considered that $X_L(P_{g3}, P_{g5})$ is under the control of leader, and $X_F(P_{g1}, P_{g2}, P_{g4}, P_{g6})$ is that of follower.

Using the data presented in Tables 1, 2, 3 and 4, the executable MOBLP model for EEPGD problem is stated as follows.

Find $X(P_{g1}, P_{g2}, P_{g3}, P_{g4}, P_{g5} \, P_{g6})$ so as to:

$$\underset{X_L}{Minimize}\, E_N(X) = (0.006323P_{g1}^2 - 0.38128P_{g1} + 80.9019 + 0.006483P_{g2}^2 - 0.79027P_{g2} + 28.8249$$

$$+ 0.003174P_{g3}^2 - 1.36061P_{g3} + 324.1775 + 0.006732P_{g4}^2 - 2.39928P_{g4} + 610.2535$$

$$+ 0.003174P_{g5}^2 - 1.36061P_{g5} + 324.1775 + 0.006181P_{g6}^2 - 0.39077P_{g6} + 50.3808)$$

$$(14)$$

$$\underset{X_L}{Minimize}\, E_S(X) = (0.001206P_{g1}^2 + 5.05928P_{g1} + 51.3778 + 0.002320P_{g2}^2 + 3.84624P_{g2} + 182.2605$$

$$+ 0.001284P_{g3}^2 + 4.45647P_{g3} + 508.5207 + 0.000813P_{g4}^2 + 4.97641P_{g4} + 165.3433$$

$$+ 0.001284P_{g5}^2 + 4.45647P_{g5} + 508.5207 + 0.003578P_{g6}^2 + 4.14938P_{g6} + 121.2133)$$

$$(15)$$

$$\underset{X_L}{Minimize}\, E_C(X) = (0.265110P_{g1}^2 - 61.01945P_{g1} + 5080.148 + 0.140053P_{g2}^2 - 29.95221P_{g2} + 3824.770$$

$$+ 0.105929P_{g3}^2 - 9.552795P_{g3} + 1342.851 + 0.106409P_{g4}^2 - 12.73642P_{g4} + 1819.625$$

$$+ 0.105929P_{g5}^2 - 9.552794P_{g5} + 1342.851 + 0.403144P_{g6}^2 - 121.9812P_{g6} + 11381.070)$$

$$\text{(leader's objectives)}$$

$$(16)$$

and, for given X_L; X_F solve

$$\underset{X_F}{Minimize}\, F_C(X) = (100P_{g1}^2 + 200P_{g1} + 10 + 120P_{g2}^2 + 150P_{g2} + 10 + 40P_{g3}^2$$

$$+ 180P_{g3} + 20 + 60P_{g4}^2 + 100P_{g4} + 10 + 40P_{g5}^2 + 180P_{g5} \qquad (17)$$

$$+ 20 + 100P_{g6}^2 + 150P_{g6} + 10)$$

$$\underset{X_F}{\text{Minimize}}\, T_L(X) = 0.1382 P_{g1}^2 + 0.0487 P_{g2}^2 + 0.0182 P_{g3}^2 + 0.0137 P_{g4}^2 + 0.0109 P_{g5}^2 + 0.0244 P_{g6}^2$$

$$- 0.0598 P_{g1} P_{g2} + 0.0088 P_{g1} P_{g3} - 0.0044 P_{g1} P_{g4} - 0.0020 P_{g1} P_{g5} - 0.0016 P_{g1} P_{g6}$$

$$- 0.0050 P_{g2} P_{g3} + 0.0008 P_{g2} P_{g4} + 0.0032 P_{g2} P_{g5} + 0.0082 P_{g2} P_{g6} - 0.140 P_{g3} P_{g4}$$

$$- 0.0132 P_{g3} P_{g5} - 0.0132 P_{g3} P_{g6} + 0.010 P_{g4} P_{g5} + 0.0066 P_{g4} P_{g6} + 0.0010 P_{g5} P_{g6}$$

$$- 0.0107 P_{g1} + 0.0060 P_{g2} - 0.0017 P_{g3} + 0.0009 P_{g4} + 0.0002 P_{g5} + 0.0030 P_{g6} + 9.8573 X 10^{-4}$$

$$\text{(follower's objectives)}$$

(18)

subject to,

$$0.05 \leq P_{g1} \leq 0.50, \quad 0.05 \leq P_{g2} \leq 0.60,$$

$$0.05 \leq P_{g3} \leq 1.00, \quad 0.05 \leq P_{g4} \leq 1.20,$$

$$0.05 \leq P_{g5} \leq 1.00, \quad 0.05 \leq P_{g6} \leq 0.60,$$

$$\text{(generator capacity constraints)}$$

(19)

and

$$P_{g1} + P_{g2} + P_{g3} + P_{g4} + P_{g5} + P_{g6} - (2.834 + L_T) = 0,$$

$$\text{(Power balance constraint)}$$

(20)

Now, in solution search process, 'Roulette-wheel selection' and 'single point crossover' with population size 50 are initially introduced. The parameter values adopted to execute the problem are crossover-probably = 0.8 and mutation-probability = 0.07.

The computer program developed in MATLAB and GAOT (GA Optimization Toolbox) in MATLAB-Ver. R2010a is employed to execute the problem. The execution is made in Intel Pentium IV with 2.66 GHz. Clock-pulse and 4 GB RAM.

The individual best solutions of leader and follower are found as:

$$(P_{g1}, P_{g2}, P_{g3}, P_{g4}, P_{g5}, P_{g6}; E_N^{lb})$$
$$= (0.05, 0.05, 0.5177, 1.20, 1.00, 0.05\ ; 1413.708)$$

$$(P_{g1}, P_{g2}, P_{g3}, P_{g4}, P_{g5}, P_{g6}; E_S^{lb})$$
$$= (0.05, 0.60, 0.8379, 0.05, 0.7320, 0.60\ ; 1549.535)$$

$$(P_{g1}, P_{g2}, P_{g3}, P_{g4}, P_{g5}, P_{g6}; E_C^{lb})$$
$$= (0.50, 0.60, 0.05, 1.0985, 0.05, 0.60\ ; 24655.09)$$

$$(P_{g1}, P_{g2}, P_{g3}, P_{g4}, P_{g5}, P_{g6}; F_C^{fb})$$
$$= (0.1220, 0.2863, 0.5832, 0.9926, 0.5236, 0.3518\ ; 595.9804)$$

$$(P_{g1}, P_{g2}, P_{g3}, P_{g4}, P_{g5}, P_{g6} ; T_L^{fb})$$
$$= (0.0861, 0.0978, 0.9764, 0.5001, 0.8533, 0.3373 \; ; 0.0170).$$

Further, worst solutions of leader and follower are obtained as:

$$(P_{g1}, P_{g2}, P_{g3}, P_{g4}, P_{g5}, P_{g6} ; E_N^{lw})$$
$$= (0.50, 0.60, 0.6036, 0.05, 0.5269, 0.60 \; ; 1416.167)$$

$$(P_{g1}, P_{g2}, P_{g3}, P_{g4}, P_{g5}, P_{g6} ; E_S^{lw})$$
$$= (0.50, 0.05, 0.1002, 1.2, 1.00, 0.05 \; ; 1551.043)$$

$$(P_{g1}, P_{g2}, P_{g3}, P_{g4}, P_{g5}, P_{g6} ; E_C^{lw})$$
$$= (0.05, 0.05, 1.00, 0.7040, 1.00, 0.05 ; 24752.86)$$

$$(P_{g1}, P_{g2}, P_{g3}, P_{g4}, P_{g5}, P_{g6} ; F_C^{fw})$$
$$= (0.500, 0.600, 0.1397, 0.05, 1.00, 0.600 ; 705.2694)$$

$$(P_{g1}, P_{g2}, P_{g3}, P_{g4}, P_{g5}, P_{g6} ; T_L^{fw})$$
$$= (0.50, 0.05, 0.05, 1.20, 1.00, 0.1036 \; ; 0.0696)$$

Then, the fuzzy objective goals are obtained as:

$$E_N \lesssim 1413.708, \; E_S \lesssim 1549.535, \; E_C \lesssim 24655.09, \; F_C \lesssim 595.9804, \; T_L \lesssim 0.0170.$$

The fuzzy goals for power generation decisions under the control of leader appear as:

$$P_{g3} \lesssim 0.15 \text{ and } P_{g5} \lesssim 0.15.$$

The upper-tolerance limits of E_N, E_S, E_C, F_C and T_L are obtained as $(E_N^{lw}, E_S^{lw}, E_C^{lw}, F_C^{fw}, T_L^{fw}) = (1416.167, 1551.043, 24752.86, 705.2694, 0.0696,)$.

Again, upper-tolerance limits of decision variables associated with X_L are considered $(P_{g3}^t, P_{g5}^t) = (0.6, 0.6)$.

Then, the membership functions are constructed as follows:

$$\mu_{E_N} = \frac{1416.167 - E_N}{1416.167 - 1413.708}, \; \mu_{E_S} = \frac{1551.043 - E_S}{1551.043 - 1549.535},$$

$$\mu_{E_C} = \frac{24752.86 - E_C}{24752.86 - 24655.09}, \; \mu_{F_C} = \frac{705.2694 - Z_1}{705.2694 - 595.9804},$$

$$\mu_{T_L} = \frac{0.0696 - T_L}{0.0696 - 0.0170}, \; \mu_{P_{g3}} = \frac{0.60 - P_{g3}}{0.60 - 0.40}, \; \mu_{P_{g5}} = \frac{0.60 - P_{g5}}{0.70 - 0.40}$$

Then, the *minsum* FGP model is constructed as follows.
Find $X\,(P_{g1},\ P_{g2},\ P_{g3},\ P_{g4},\ P_{g5},\ P_{g6})$ so as to:

$$Minimize\ Z = 0.4067d_1^- + 0.6631d_2^- + 0.0102d_3^- + 0.0092d_4^- + 19.0114d_5^- + 2.5d_6^- + 2.5d_7^-$$

and satisfy

$$\frac{1416.167 - \sum_{i=1}^{n} d_{Ni}P_{gi}^2 + e_{Ni}P_{gi} + f_{Ni}}{1416.167 - 1413.708} + d_1^- - d_1^+ = 1$$

$$\frac{1551.043 - \sum_{i=1}^{n} d_{Si}P_{gi}^2 + e_{Si}P_{gi} + f_{Si}}{1551.043 - 1549.535} + d_2^- - d_2^+ = 1$$

$$\frac{24752.86 - \sum_{i=1}^{n} d_{Ci}P_{gi}^2 + e_{Ci}P_{gi} + f_{Ci}}{24752.86 - 24655.09} + d_3^- - d_3^+ = 1 \qquad (21)$$

$$\frac{705.2694 - \sum_{i=1}^{n} (a_i P_{gi}^2 + b_i P_{gi} + c_i)}{705.2694 - 595.9804} + d_4^- - d_4^+ = 1$$

$$\frac{0.0696 - \sum_{i=1}^{n}\sum_{j=1}^{n} P_{gi}B_{ij}P_{gj} + \sum_{i=1}^{n} B_{0i}P_{gi} + B_{00}}{0.0696 - 0.0170} + d_5^- - d_5^+ = 1$$

$$\frac{0.60 - P_{g3}}{0.60 - 0.40} + d_6^- - d_6^+ = 1, \frac{0.60 - P_{g5}}{0.60 - 0.40} + d_7^- - d_7^+ = 1$$

subject to the constraints in (19) and (20)
The function Z in (21) acts as evaluation function in solution search process.
The function to evaluate fitness of a chromosome takes the form:

$$Eval\ (E_v) = (Z)_v = \left(\sum_{k=1}^{5} w_k^- d_k^- + \sum_{k=6}^{7} w_k^- d_k^-\right)_v, \quad v = 1, 2, \ldots, PS, \qquad (22)$$

where PS stands for population-size, and where $(Z)_v$ denotes achievement function (Z) to measure fitness value of vth chromosome.
The best objective value (Z^*) at any solution stage is obtained as:

$$Z^* = min\ \{eval\,(E_v)\,|\,v = 1, 2, \ldots, PS\} \qquad (23)$$

The resultant objective values are found as:

$$(E_N,\ E_S,\ E_C,\ F_C,\ T_L) = (1414.69,\ 1550.38,\ 24669.95,\ 629.73,\ 0.0522)$$

with the respective membership values:

$$\left(\mu_{E_N}, \mu_{E_S}, \mu_{E_C}, \mu_{F_C}, \mu_{T_L}\right) = (0.5978, 0.4357, 0.8479, 0.6912, 0.0255).$$

The power generation decision is obtained as:

$$(P_{g1}, P_{g2}, P_{g3}, P_{g4}, P_{g5}, P_{g6}) = (0.1821, 0.4197, 0.40, 0.9885, 0.40, 0.47737).$$

The bar-diagram to represent power generation decision is depicted in Fig. 1.

The result indicates that the solution is a satisfactory one, and sequential executions

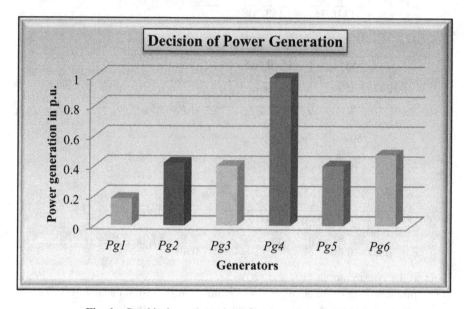

Fig. 1. Graphical representation of power generation decision.

of decision powers of DMs are preserved in hierarchical order for optimizing objectives of the problem.

7 Performance Comparison

To highlight more the effectiveness of the proposed method, a comparison of resultant solution is made with the solution achieved by employing general *minsum* FGP method in [35].

Here, values of the objectives are found as:

$$(E_N, E_S, E_C, F_C, T_L) = (1414.847, 1550.01, 24719.38, 631.60, 0.0175).$$

The resultant power generation decision is:

$(P_{g1}, P_{g2}, P_{g3}, P_{g4}, P_{g5}, P_{g6}) = (0.05, 0.1409, 0.9898, 0.4379, 0.8938, 0.3389)$.

The above result indicates that reduction of 49.43 kg/h of CO_x emission and reduction of 1.87 \$/h fuel cost are made here by using the proposed method without sacrificing total units of power demand.

8   Conclusions and Future Research Direction

The main advantage of using BLP to EEPGD problem is that optimization of objectives in the order of hierarchy is obtained here in inexact environment. Again, hierarchical order of objectives as well as fuzzy descriptions of objectives/ constraints can easily be rearranged under the proposed FGP method in decision making context. Furthermore, computational burden arises with linearization of objectives by using conventional technique does not involve here owing to use of bio-inspired tool to make power generation decision. Here, it may be claimed that the GA based FGP method presented here may open up future research for thermal power generation decision and to make pollution free living environment on earth. However, the proposed model can be extended to formulate multilevel programming (MLP) [36] problem with multiplicity of objectives in power plant operation and management system, which is a problem in future research.

Acknowledgements. The authors are thankful to the Reviewers and CICBA-2017 Program chairs for providing constructive suggestions to improve quality of presentation of the paper.

References

1. Zhu, J.: Optimization of Power System Operation. Wiley, Hoboken (2009)
2. Dommel, H.W., Tinney, W.F.: Optimal Power Flow Solutions. IEEE Trans. Power Appar. Syst. **PAS-87**(10), 1866–1876 (1968)
3. Gent, M.R., Lament, J.W.: Minimum-emission dispatch. IEEE Trans. Power Appar. Syst. **PAS-90**(6), 2650–2660 (1971)
4. Sullivan, R.L., Hackett, D.F.: Air quality control using a minimum pollution-dispatching algorithm. Environ. Sci. Technol. **7**(11), 1019–1022 (1973)
5. Zahavi, J., Eisenberg, L.: Economic-environmental power dispatch. IEEE Trans. Syst. Man Cybern. **SMC-5**(5), 485–489 (1975)
6. Cadogan, J.B., Eisenberg, L.: Sulfur oxide emissions management for electric power systems. IEEE Trans. Power Appar. Syst. **96**(2), 393–401 (1977)
7. Tsuji, A.: Optimal fuel mix and load dispatching under environmental constraints. IEEE Trans. Power Appar. Syst. **PAS-100**(5), 2357–2364 (1981)
8. Happ, H.H.: Optimal power dispatch - a comprehensive survey. IEEE Trans. Power Appar. Syst. **96**(3), 841–854 (1977)
9. Chowdhury, B.H., Rahman, S.: A review of recent advances in economic dispatch. IEEE Trans. Power Syst. **5**(4), 1248–1259 (1990)
10. Talaq, J.H., El-Hawary, F., El-Hawary, M.E.: A summary of environmental/ economic dispatch algorithms. IEEE Trans. Power Syst. **9**(3), 1508–1516 (1994)

11. Momoh, J.A., El-Hawary, M.E., Adapa, R.: A review of selected optimal power flow literature to 1993. II. Newton, linear programming and interior point methods. IEEE Trans. Power Syst. **14**(1), 105–111 (1999)

12. Hobbs, B.F.: Emission dispatch under the underutilization provision of the 1990 U.S. Clean air act amendments: models and analysis. IEEE Trans. Power Syst. **8**(1), 177–183 (1993)

13. El-Keib, A.A., Ma, H., Hart, J.L.: Economic dispatch in view of the clean air act of 1990. IEEE Trans. Power Syst. **9**(2), 972–978 (1994)

14. Srinivasan, D., Tettamanzi, A.G.B.: An evolutionary algorithm for evaluation of emission compliance options in view of the clean air act amendments. IEEE Trans. Power Syst. **12**(1), 336–341 (1997)

15. Abido, M.A.: A novel multiobjective evolutionary algorithm for environmental/economic power dispatch. Electr. Power Syst. Res. **65**(1), 71–81 (2003)

16. AlRashidi, M.R., El-Hawary, M.E.: Pareto fronts of the emission-economic dispatch under different loading conditions. Int. J. Electr. Electron. Eng. **2**(10), 596–599 (2008)

17. Vanitha, M., Thanushkodi, K.: An efficient technique for solving the economic dispatch problem using biogeography algorithm. Eur. J. Sci. Res. **5**(2), 165–172 (2011)

18. Congressional Amendment to the Constitution, H.R. 3030/S.1490 (1990)

19. Simon, H.A.: Administrative Behavior. Fress Press, New York (1957)

20. Nanda, J., Kothari, D.P., Lingamurthy, K.S.: Economic-emission load dispatch through goal programming techniques. IEEE Trans. Energy Convers. **3**(1), 26–32 (1988)

21. Zadeh, L.A.: Fuzzy sets. Inf. Control **8**(3), 338–353 (1965)

22. Basu, M.: An interactive fuzzy satisfying-based simulated annealing technique for economic emission load dispatch with nonsmooth fuel cost and emission level functions. Electr. Power Compon. Syst. **32**(2), 163–173 (2004)

23. Wang, L.F., Singh, C.: Environmental/economic power dispatch using a fuzzified multi-objective particle swarm optimization algorithm. Electr. Power Syst. Res. **77**(12), 1654–1664 (2007)

24. Dhillon, J.S., Parti, S.C., Kothari, D.P.: Stochastic economic emission load dispatch. Electr. Power Syst. Res. **26**(3), 179–186 (1993)

25. Yokoyama, R., Bae, S.H., Morita, T., Sasaki, H.: Multiobjective optimal generation dispatch based on probability security criteria. IEEE Trans. Power Syst. **3**(1), 317–324 (1988)

26. Abido, M.A.: Multiobjective evolutionary algorithms for electric power dispatch problem. IEEE Trans. Evol. Comput. **10**(3), 315–329 (2006)

27. Basu, M.: Dynamic economic emission dispatch using nondominated sorting genetic algorithm-II. Int. J. Electr. Power Energy Syst. **30**(2), 140–149 (2008)

28. Gong, D., Zhang, Y., Qi, C.: Environmental/economic power dispatch using a hybrid multi-objective optimization algorithm. Electr. Power Energy Syst. **32**, 607–614 (2010)

29. Pal, B.B., Chakraborti, D.: Using genetic algorithm for solving quadratic bilevel programming problems via fuzzy goal programming. Int. J. Appl. Manage. Sci. **5**(2), 172–195 (2013)

30. Zhang, G., Zhang, G., Gao, Y., Lu, J.: Competitive strategic bidding optimization in electricity markets using bilevel programming and swarm technique. IEEE Trans. Industr. Electron. **58**(6), 2138–2146 (2011)

31. Pal, B.B., Moitra, B.N., Maulik, U.: A goal programming procedure for fuzzy multiobjective linear fractional programming problem. Fuzzy Sets Syst. **139**(2), 395–405 (2003)

32. Goldberg, D.E.: Genetic Algorithms in Search, Optimization and Machine Learning. Addison-Wesley, Reading (1989)

33. Michalewicz, Z.: Genetic Algorithms + Data Structures = Evolution Programs', 3rd edn. Springer, Heidelberg (1996)

34. Zimmermann, H.-J.: Fuzzy Sets, Decision Making and Expert Systems. Kluwer Academic Publisher, Boston, Dordrecht, Lancaster (1987)
35. Ignizio, J.P.: Goal Programming and Extensions. D.C. Health, Lexington (1976)
36. Anandaligam, G.: Multi-level programming and conflict resolution. Eur. J. Oper. Res. **51**(2), 233–247 (1991)

An Opposition Based Differential Evolution to Solve Multiple Sequence Alignment

Sabari Pramanik[1(✉)] and S.K. Setua[2]

[1] Department of Computer Science, Vidyasagar University, Midnapore, West Bengal, India
sabari.pramanik@mail.vidyasagar.ac.in
[2] Department of Computer Science and Engg, University of Calcutta, Kolkata, West Bengal, India
sksetua@gmail.com

Abstract. Multiple Molecular sequence alignment is a problem of utmost concern in bioinformatics. The prime intension of this paper is to maximize the similitude among the molecular sequences by inserting gaps in the sequences. In this article we present an evolutionary technique to solve the alignment multiple molecular sequences. Differential evolutions are well known optimization techniques for solving complex problems. Here we use opposition based differential evolution technique with a new chromosome representation. We also use sum of product scoring function to calculate the fitness of chromosomes. Point Accepted Mutation matrix is used as scoring matrix. The results we get are verified with the BAliBASE 1.0 benchmark dataset and conventional differential evolution. Simulation result exhibits better performance in terms of SOP score.

Keywords: Multiple sequence alignment (MSA) · Differential evolution (DE) · Opposition based learning · Opposition based differential evolution · Computational biology · Bioinformatics

1 Introduction

It is very interesting to see that the researchers often look into the nature for finding methods/techniques to solve complex computational problems. They are exploring natures for inspiration, both as the form of model and as metaphor. According to Darwinian Principle, to survive, every living organism tries to optimize their journeys in the complicated condition of life. Optimization is the soul of many native processes. Since 1950, Darwinian Principle has been used as a powerful optimization tool for solving complex search and optimization problems. Such types of optimization processes are known as Evolutionary Computation [1].

Evolutionary Computation is an important field of computational intelligence that solves continuous optimization and combinatorial optimization problems. In the early 1950s, the idea of evolutionary computation originated with the initiation of developing automatic problem solver with the help of Darwinian Principle. Later Genetic Algorithm (GA) was developed at the University of Michigan by John Henry Holland to solve native optimization problems. Since then GA is successfully used for optimization for scientific problems.

© Springer Nature Singapore Pte Ltd. 2017
J.K. Mandal et al. (Eds.): CICBA 2017, Part II, CCIS 776, pp. 440–450, 2017.
DOI: 10.1007/978-981-10-6430-2_34

In the middle of 90s, R. Storn and K.V. Price proposed a very aggressive form of evolutionary computation called Differential Evolution (DE) [2]. The next year in Nagoya, Japan, the First International Contest on Evolutionary Optimization (1st ICEO) was held and Differential Evolution algorithm stood third in this competition. The main supremacy of DE algorithm is that it requires a very few control parameters. In its present status, [3, 4, 5, 6] the performance of DE is more superior than other optimization methods regarding robustness and speed of convergence. DE needs large computational times like other population based algorithm and this drawback is only for its evolutionary nature. Opposition-based DE (ODE) has been brought into use to defeat this limitation [7]. The convergence rate of DE has been accelerated by using ODE.

Sequential alignment is very common in Computational Biology. It performs an important role in observing regions of resemblance among molecular sequences. If the sequences are highly alike, then they have similar there dimensional structures or they can share similar functional properties. The sequence alignment is broadly classified into pair wise alignment and multiple sequence alignment (MSA). The problem domain of MSA is very challenging its computational cost is massive. The computational complexity of MSA is $O(M^P)$, where M is the sequence length and P is the no. of sequences [8]. The value of M may be in the order of hundreds for DNA, order of thousands in case of RNA and for protein it can be millions. So, for a few number of sequences the complexity is very large [9].

In this work we propose an Opposition-based Differential evolution algorithm with a different form of chromosome representation. We compare our results with BAliBASE benchmark datasets. We also compare our results with normal differential evolution technique and show that opposition based differential evolution gives a better results.

The paper is structured as follows: the Sect. 2 analysis literatures and related works; Sect. 3 shows the opposition-based DE algorithm. The proposed algorithms are written in Sect. 4. In Sect. 5 the datasets and results of the experiments are discussed. The paper concludes at Sect. 6.

2 Literature Survey

In principle the multiple sequence alignment is a optimizing problem with a exponential time complexity [10]. There exist various methods to solve MSA problem. We can broadly divide the methods into progressive methods and iterative methods [11]. All of these algorithms are based on local alignments or global alignments techniques [12]. A local alignment is one, which looks for the best matching substring within the sequences. Whereas global alignment tries to align the sequences from end to end point [13].

Smith-Waterman algorithm [14] and Needleman-Wunsch algorithms [15] are commonly used dynamic programming techniques for solving MSA problem. The dynamic programming techniques are good to find optimal alignment but only for two sequences [16]. As the no. of sequences and the sequence length increases the complexity to solve MSA also increase in exponential order. This leads the problem to NP hard problem.

Feng and Doolittle [17] have proposed a tree based progressive alignment technique which constructs an evolutionary tree [18] to predict the relationship among the sequences using Needleman-Wunsch algorithm. In general, at the beginning the progressive alignment method aligns identical sequences and then incorporates more divergent sequences till end. CLUSTALW [19] is a popular method that uses progressive alignment method. There exist other algorithms that use progressive alignment techniques such as DiAlign [20] or Match-Box [21], which arrange the alignment in a sequence-independent manner by incorporating segment pairs in an order prescribed by their alignment score until the end of all residues and sequences. Progressive alignment methods are considered to be very fast and deterministic, but it suffers from getting trapped into local optima [22]. It also suffers from a problem in which if any mistake takes place in initial alignment, it gets propagated to the end of the alignment and cannot be corrected in later stage. To avoid such type of problems some literatures propose stochastic or iterative procedure for good alignments [23].

An iterative method does not depend on initial alignment. It begins with a random alignment and gradually improves this alignment in each iteration until no more improvement is possible. Some researchers have proposed a few iterative and stochastic approaches to solve multiple sequence alignment process using simulated annealing [24, 25] or Hidden Markov model [26] based approach. The problem with these methods is they may be stuck into local optima.

In population based evolutionary algorithm the initial populations are generated randomly. Then some operators are used to modify the initial generation into the next successive generation. This process is continued until we find the global optima [27–29]. There exist several methods which are used genetic algorithm for solving MSA problem, such as SAGA [30], MSA-GA [31], RBT-GA [32], GA-PAM [33], Steady state GA [34] etc. The drawbacks of these methods are also the sticking in local optima [35].

3 Opposition Based Differential Evolution

Differential Evolution (DE) came out as a simple but powerful evolutionary algorithm more than a decade ago and has now developed into a very promising research area in the field of evolutionary computation.

Originally DE was first introduced by Storn and Price (1995). The DE algorithm started with an initial population vector, which is generated randomly using a uniform distribution function. At each generation, an individual u_i is created using three mutually separated individual u_r, u_s and u_t. The new candidate solution u_{off} is created by mutation operator as:

$$u'_{off} = u_t + F(u_r - u_s) \tag{1}$$

where F takes the value randomly from 0 to 1. The parameter F controls the difference between the candidate solution and u_i. The mutation operator shown in Eq. (1) is conventionally known as DE/rand/1. There are other types of the mutation operator, that have been proposed in literature [3]:

$$\text{DE/best/1: } u'_{off} = u_{best} + F(u_s - u_t) \qquad (2)$$

$$\text{DE/cur-to-best/1: } u'_{off} = u_i + F(u_{best} - u_i) + F(u_s - u_t) \qquad (3)$$

$$\text{DE/best/2: } u'_{off} = u_{best} + F(u_s - u_t) + F(u_m - u_n) \qquad (4)$$

$$\text{DE/rand/2: } u'_{off} = u_r + F(u_s - u_t) + F(u_m - u_n) \qquad (5)$$

$$\text{DE/rand-to-best/2: } u'_{off} = u_t + F(u_{best} - u_i) + F(u_r - u_s) + F(u_m - u_n) \qquad (6)$$

where u_{best} denotes the best individual among population, and u_m and u_n are two randomly selected individuals.

The opposition-based learning was first conceptualized by Tizhoosh [7]. It has been seen that the performance of conventional DE is growing significantly by introducing opposition based learning concept into DE. This idea was added in two stages of conventional DE, population initialization stage and generation jumping stage. Generally, every evolutionary algorithm starts with a random guess, because no prior information about the actual optima is known. So in this case, we upgrade our initial random value by concurrently checking the fitness of the opposite solution. This concept is applied to each solution in each population. We first discuss here the opposite number,

Definition 1. We assume m is a real number and m $\in$ [x,y]. Then the opposite number O(m) of m can be explained as,

$$O(m) = x + y - m \qquad (7)$$

The Opposition based Differential evolution (ODE) alters the normal DE using the idea of opposite numbers at the following two different phases:

Opposition based population initialization: First an consistently distributed non uniform population P(NP) is created and after that the opposite number OP(NP) is determined. The pth opposite individual similar to pth parameter vector of P(NP) is $OP_{p,j} = x_{p,j} + y_{p,j} - P_{p,j}$, where p is an integer from 1 to NP and j is from 1,2,...D, $x_{p,j}$ and $y_{p,j}$ indicate the difference boundaries of jth parameter of the pth vector. Finally, NP number of suitable individuals are adopted from the set {P(NP), OP(NP)} as the opening population.

Opposition based generation jumping: In this phase, following every iteration, without generating fresh population, the opposite population is generated with a previously fixed probability JR. The value of JR is from the range of 0 to 0.5. Then NP fittest individuals are chosen from the present population and the opposite population [7].

4   Proposed Algorithm

Here we explore our proposed method for resolving multiple sequence alignment problems using Opposition-based Differential Evolution. This algorithm uses DE/cur-to-best/1 [Eq. (3)] version of Differential Evolution. It also uses a divergent characterization of chromosome which helps us to produce better population so that a comparatively better alignment could be found. The overall algorithm is shown in Fig. 1.

```
Msa_ode( )
{
// Initialize uniformly distributed arbitrary population of individual
        initialize_population q(t);
//For the opposition based population initialization find the opposition of q(t), i.e. oq(t)
        oq(t) = a + b - q(t)
// evaluation of fitness for all opening individuals in population
        evaluate q(t);          evaluate oq(t);
//Select best np no. of individual from q(t) and oq(t)
        nq(t) = {q(t) U oq(t)}
//checking for stopping criteria or (maximum no. of generation)
while (maximum_generation is not achieved) {
Find best chromosome Best(t) from np(t)
  for all population nq(t)    {
      // select two parents U and V randomly from nq(t) where U ≠V
          U=random_value(nq(t));          V=random_value(nq(t))
          for ith individual, find
              Xᵢ = nqᵢ(t) + F(Best(t) − nqᵢ(t)) + F(U-V)
          for all dimension D (j=0 to D)      {
                  if (random_value(0,1) < CR)
                      Yᵢ,ⱼ = Xᵢ,ⱼ
                  else
                      Yᵢ,ⱼ = nqᵢ,ⱼ(t)      }
          evaluate Yᵢ
          if (fitness of (Xᵢ) greater than fitness of (nqᵢ(t)))
                  nqpᵢ(t+1) = Xᵢ
          else
                  nqpᵢ(t+1) = nqᵢ (t)  }
// Opposition based Generation jumping find the opposition of nqᵢ(t+1), i.e. onq(t+1)
for (random_value(0,1) < JR{
      onq(t+1) = a + b − nqp(t+1)
// evaluation of fitness of all initial individuals in population
      evaluate nq(t+1);        evaluate onq(t+1);
//Select best nq no. of individual from q(t) and oq(t)
      nq(t+1) = {nq(t+1) U onq(t+1)}
  }  // end for
} // end while
} // end msa_ode
```

Fig. 1. Algorithm for ODE

4.1 Chromosome Representation

The main idea behind the chromosome representation is to retain the solution hint inside it. Each column of every chromosome is considered as gene. In this proposed algorithm each chromosome represents a candidate solution to the MSA problem. Each chromosome is represented by a two dimensional integer valued matrix, where number of rows is equal to the number of input sequences. Each element in the matrix represents the position of gap in the corresponding sequence. If the chromosome matrix contains 5 in (i,j) position then 5th element of ith sequence in the alignment contains a gap.

4.2 Fitness Function

To find the fitness value, at first the sequences are created from each chromosome. Then using the sum of pair scoring function the alignment score is calculated. We calculate the sum of pair score (SOP score) using a scoring matrix known as PAM matrix. PAM is point accepted mutation matrix and it works as a substitution matrix. This matrix is created and evaluated by calculating the differences in highly related proteins.

The fitness value is computed for l sequences using equation, as in (8),

$$\text{Fitness\_value} = \sum_{m=1}^{l-1} \sum_{n=i+1}^{l} \text{ScoringMatrix}\left(A_m, A_n\right) \tag{8}$$

4.3 Parameters

Three parameters are used in opposition based differential evolution. CR is the crossover rate. JR is the jumping rate for selecting opposite value and F is the mutation constant.

4.4 BAliBASE

The BAliBASE 1.0 [36] dataset accommodates 142 references multiple sequence alignment, which are derived from the known structures of protein. There are five reference sets in BAliBASE 1.0. Small numbers of equidistant sequences are incorporated in reference 1. Reference 2 contains totally unrelated data. Reference 3 incorporated sequences from divergent sub families. Long terminal sequence contains in reference 4. Reference 5 contains huge internal insertions and deletions.

5 Experimental Verification

To verify our proposed ODE algorithm, we take nine datasets from the Reference 1 alignments from BAliBASE 1.0 [36] benchmark dataset. We take three sequences each from short, medium and long sequences subgroups (Table 1). We select the sequences according to their identity percentage for each subgroup. We have also used PAM (Point Accepted Mutation) 350 scoring matrix to calculate the sum-of-pair value.

Table 1. Dataset description

Type	Name	Number	Longest	Shortest	Identity
Short	1ubi	4	94	76	<25%
	1tgxA	4	64	57	20%–40%
	1fmb	4	104	98	>35%
Medium	1bbt3	5	192	149	<25%
	1aym3	4	244	219	20%–40%
	1ar5A	4	203	192	>35%
Long	1ped	3	374	327	<25%
	1gowA	4	481	451	20%–40%
	actin	5	395	379	>35%

In our experimental setup, the population size for all iteration is 30. After a large number of simulations, we have calculated the average of sum-of-pair score for each dataset. We have taken the gap penalty as -10. We compare our results with BAliBASE 1.0 datasets and normal differential evolution algorithm.

Table 2 shows the comparison among the sum-of-pair score of our proposed opposition based differential evolution algorithm (ODE), BAliBASE Score and normal differential evolution (DE) algorithm.

Table 2. Comparision of Results (Best Fitness Value)

Type	Name	ODE	DE	BAliBASE
Short	1ubi	−301	−320	−1074
	1tgxA	587	333	558
	1fmb	1687	1168	1607
Medium	1bbt3	−1651	−4461	−3180
	1aym3	1762	−52	1719
	1ar5A	1997	1538	0
Long	1ped	−523	−1186	−814
	1gowA	2485	−2360	1601
	actin	4231	608	610

From Table 2, it is clear that comparing with normal DE and BAliBASE, ODE gives the results better than other two methods. It means that ODE algorithm is more accurate than DE and BAliBASE. It also found that for long sequences it gives a very good result. Figures 2, 3 and 4 shows the convergence rate of ODE and DE. Here we consider the average fitness value.

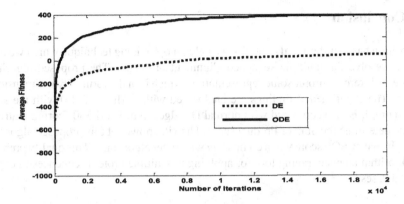

Fig. 2. Average Fitness value of 1tgxA data

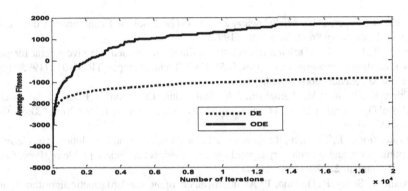

Fig. 3. Average Fitness value of 1aym3 data

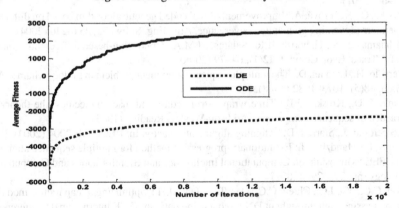

Fig. 4. Average Fitness value of 1gowA data

6   Conclusion

Opposition based differential evolution is a global optimizing technique which we have used to resolve the multiple sequence alignment problems. The proposed algorithm deduces a different chromosome representation, which is in the form of two dimensional matrix. The experimental findings are analogized with BAliBASE 1.0 with the same SOP score. It is also compared with normal DE algorithm. PAM 350 scoring matrix is used to determine the Sum of Product score. The vital power of this proposed algorithm is a high quality SOP score when comparing with other algorithms. This quality prepares the algorithm an encouraging tool for applying to multiple protein sequences in experimental cases.

References

1. Back, T., Fogel, D.B., Michalewicz, Z. (eds.): Handbook of Evolutionary Computation. Oxford University Press, New York (1997)
2. Storn, R., Price, K.V.: Differential evolution: a simple and efficient adaptive scheme for global optimization over continuous spaces, ICSI, USA, Technical report TR-95-012 (1995). http://icsi.berkeley.edu/~storn/litera.html
3. Price, K., Storn, R.M., Lampinen, J.A.: Differential Evolution: A Practical Approach to Global Optimization. Natural Computing Series, 1st edn. Springer, New York (2005). ISBN 3540209506
4. Vesterstroem, J., Thomsen, R.: A comparative study of differential evolution, particle swarm optimization, and evolutionary algorithms on numerical benchmark problems. Proc. Congr. Evol. Comput. 2, 1980–1987 (2004)
5. Andre, J., Siarry, P., Dognon, T.: An improvement of the standard genetic algorithm fighting premature convergence in continuous optimization. Advance in Engineering Software 32, 49–60 (2001)
6. Hrstka, O., Kučerová, A.: Improvement of real coded genetic algorithm based on differential operators preventing premature convergence. Adv. Eng. Softw. 35, 237–246 (2004)
7. Rahnamayan, S., Tizhoosh, H.R., Salama, M.M.A.: Opposition-based differential evolution. IEEE Trans. Evol. Comput. 12(1), 64–79 (2008)
8. Carrillo, H., Lipman, D.: The multiple sequence alignment problem in biology. Siam J. Appl. Math. 48(5), 1073–1082 (1988)
9. Sankoff, D., Kruskal, J.B.: Time wraps, string edits, and macromolecules: the theory and practice of sequence comparison. Addison-Wesley, Reading (1983)
10. Kececioglu, J., Starrett, D.: Aligning alignments exactly. In: RECOMB 2004 (2004)
11. Kupis, P., Mandziuk, J.: Evolutionary-progressive method for multiple sequence alignment. In: IEEE Symposium on Computational Intelligence and Bioinformatics and Computational Biology, pp. 291–297 (2007)
12. Wei, C.C., Yu, J.C., Chien, C.C., Der, T.L., Jan, M.H.: Optimizing a map reduce module of preprocessing high throughput DNA sequencing data. In: IEEE International Conference on Bid Data, pp. 6–9 (2013)
13. Carrillo, H., Lipman, D.: The multiple sequence alignment problem in biology. Siam J. Appl. Math. 48(5), 1073–1082 (1988)

14. Haoyue, F., Dingyu, X., Zhang, X., Cangzhi, J.: Conserved secondary structure prediction for highly group of related RNA sequences. In: Control and Decision Conference, pp. 5158–5163 (2009)
15. Needleman, S.B., Wunsch, C.D.: A general method applicable to the search for similarities in the amino acid sequence of two proteins. J Mol Biol. **48**, 443–453 (1970)
16. Zhimin, Z., Zhong, W.C.: Dynamic programming for protein sequence alignment. In: International BioScience BioTechnology, p. 5 (2013)
17. Feng, D.F., Dolittle, R.F.: Progressive sequence alignment as a prerequisite to correct phylogenetic trees. J. Mol. Evol. **25**, 351–360 (1987)
18. Bhattacharjee, A., Sultana, K.Z., Shams, Z.: Dynamic and parallel approaches to optimal evolutionary tree construction. In: Canadian Conference on Electrical and Computer Engineering, pp. 119–112 (2006)
19. Thompson, J.D., Higgins, D.G., Gibson, T.J.: CLUSTAL W: Improving the sensitivity of progressive multiple sequence alignment through sequence weighting, position-specific gap penalties and weight matrix choice. Nucleic Acids Res. **22**, 4673–4680 (1994)
20. Morgenstern, B., Frech, K., Dress, A., Werner, T.: DIALIGN: finding local similarities by multiple sequence alignment. Bioinformatics **14**(3), 290–294 (1998)
21. Depiereux, E., Feytmans, E.: MATCH-BOX: a fundamentally new algorithm for the simultaneous alignment of several protein sequences. Comput. Appl. Biosci. CABIOS **8**(5), 501–509 (1992)
22. Naznin, F., Sarker, R., Essam, D.: Progressive alignment method using genetic algorithm for multiple sequence alignment. IEEE Trans. Evol. Comput. **16**(5), 615–631 (2012)
23. El-Nahas, A.R., Shokeir, A.A., El-Assmy, A.M., Mohsen, T., Shoma, A.M., Eraky, I., El-Kappany, H.A.: Post-percutaneous nephrolithotomy extensive hemorrhage: a study of risk factors. J. Urol. **177**(2), 576–579 (2007)
24. Kim, J., Pramanik, S., Chung, M.J.: Multiple sequence alignment using simulated annealing. Comput. Appl. Biosci. CABIOS **10**(4), 419–426 (1994)
25. Lukashin, A.V., Engelbrecht, J., Brunak, S.: Multiple alignment using simulated annealing: branch point definition in human mRNA splicing. Nucleic Acids Res. **20**(10), 2511–2516 (1992)
26. Eddy, S.R.: Multiple alignment using Hidden Markov Models. ISMB **3**, 114–120 (1995)
27. Cai, L., Juedes, D., Liakhovitch, E.: Evolutionary computation techniques for multiple sequence alignment. In: Proceedings of the 2000 Congress on Evolutionary Computation, vol. 2, pp. 829–835. IEEE (2000)
28. Chellapilla, K., Fogel, G.B.: Multiple sequence alignment using evolutionary programming. In: Proceedings of the 1999 Congress on Evolutionary Computation, CEC 1999, vol. 1. IEEE (1999)
29. Horng, J.T., Lin, C.M., Liu, B.J., Kao, C.Y.: Using genetic algorithms to solve multiple sequence alignments. In: Proceedings of the 2nd Annual Conference on Genetic and Evolutionary Computation, pp. 883–890. Morgan Kaufmann Publishers Inc., July 2000
30. Notredame, C., Higgins, D.G.: SAGA: sequence alignment by genetic algorithm. Nucleic Acids Res. **24**(8), 1515–1524 (1996)
31. Gondro, C., Kinghorn, B.P.: A simple genetic algorithm for multiple sequence alignment. Genet. Mol. Res. **6**(4), 964–982 (2007)
32. Taheri, J., Zomaya, A.Y.: RBT-GA: a novel metaheuristic for solving the multiple sequence alignment problem. BMC Genom. **10**(1), 1 (2009)
33. Naznin, F., Sarker, R., Essam, D.: Progressive alignment method using genetic algorithm for multiple sequence alignment. IEEE Trans. Evol. Comput. **16**(5), 615–631 (2012)

34. Pramanik, S., Setua, S.K.: A steady state genetic algorithm for multiple sequence alignment. In: International Conference on Advances in Computing, Communications and Informatics (ICACCI, 2014), pp. 1095–1099. IEEE, September 2014

35. Yadav, R.K., Banka, H.: GSAMSA: Gravitational search algorithm for multiple sequence alignment. Indian J. Nat. Sci. **6**(33) (2015)

36. Thompson, J.D., Plewniak, F., Poch, O.: BAliBASE: a benchmark alignment database for the evaluation of multiple alignment programs. Bioinformatics **15**(1), 87–88 (1999)

Swarm Intelligence Algorithms for Medical Image Registration: A Comparative Study

D.R. Sarvamangala[1](✉) and Raghavendra V. Kulkarni[2]

[1] REVA University, Bengaluru, India
sarvamangaladr@reva.edu.in
[2] M.S. Ramaiah University of Applied Sciences, Bengaluru, India
arvie@ieee.org

Abstract. The search for transformation parameters for image registration has been treated traditionally as a multidimensional optimization problem. Non-rigid registration of medical images has been approached in this paper using the particle swarm optimization algorithm and the artificial bee colony algorithm (ABC). Brief introductions to these algorithms have been presented. Results of Matlab simulations of medical image registration approached through these algorithms have been analyzed. The results show that the ABC algorithm results in higher quality of image registration; but, takes longer to converge. The tradeoff issue between the quality of registration and the computing time has been brought forward. This has a strong impact on the choice of the most suitable algorithm for a specific medical application.

Keywords: Artificial bee colony algorithm · Medical image registration · Particle swarm optimization algorithm · Swarm intelligence

1 Introduction

Image registration targets at aligning of structures or regions accurately across multiple, related images acquired under different times, or at various conditions, or using different modalities [1]. This important problem in medical image processing is an active area of research. Image registration has a multitude of applications in medical image processing. Image registration is essential for image-guided surgery [2,3], image guided intervention [4], radiotherapy planning [5], cardiac perfusion [6] and monitoring of disease progression. Analysis of efficiency of treatments, such as radiotherapy, chemotherapy requires the registration of pre-treatment and post-treatment images taken from scans. Also, structural and functional information obtained from different imaging modalities need to be combined for efficient determination of abnormalities which requires accurate registration [7]. Medical image registration may involve any number of images.

This paper focuses on medical image registration of two images. The first image is called as reference image and the second image as the sensed image.

© Springer Nature Singapore Pte Ltd. 2017
J.K. Mandal et al. (Eds.): CICBA 2017, Part II, CCIS 776, pp. 451–465, 2017.
DOI: 10.1007/978-981-10-6430-2_35

The reference image is kept unchanged and sensed image is transformed until it aligns properly with reference image. The former is aligned with the sensed image and the similarity between the two is measured. If they are not similar, the sensed image is re-transformed with different set of parameters and similarity between the two is measured again. This process is repeated until the two images are similar. This process has been illustrated in Fig. 1.

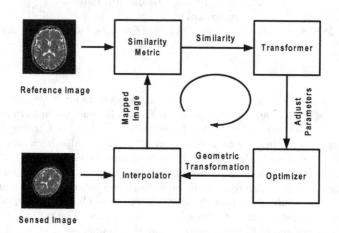

Fig. 1. The process of image registration

1.1   Image Registration

Image registration is used to determine the transformation between the images. The images are either 2- or 3-dimensional; hence, the transformation can be from 2-D to 2-D, from 2-D to 3-D, or from 3-D to 3-D. Intensity-based methods are widely used for a variety of applications involving registering images having same or different number of dimensions, rigid or nonrigid transformations and deformable transformations, same modality or different modality images. The reference image I_1 is fixed and does not undergo transformation; whereas, the sensed image I_2, undergoes series of transformations until it matches with the reference image. Consider the sets of voxels in these images as $I_1(i)$ and $I_2(i)$, respectively, and let the transformation be denoted by T. The transformed image $I_2' = T(I_2)$. The objective of registration is to determine the transformation T^* that results in maximum $I_1 \cap I_2'$. Image registration involves four major aspects: similarity metric, transformation, optimization and interpolation.

Similarity Metric. The similarity metrics include the sum of squared intensity difference, the correlation coefficient, the mutual information (MI), the normalized MI (NMI) and the regional MI (RMI) [8]. MI is the measure of dependence between images and is a powerful metric to determine the similarity between multimodal images. MI is maximum for perfectly matched images. MI M is calculated using entropy and joint entropy, where $H(I)$ is the entropy of an image I and determined using (1), and joint entropy of the two images X and Y, given by $H(X, Y)$ is calculated using (2) and M is calculated using (3). Entropy is calculated using the probability distribution function p.

$$M(X, Y) = H(X) + H(Y) - H(X, Y) \qquad (1)$$

The NMI N is also a very powerful similarity metric for multimodal image registration. When the images are perfectly matched, then the value of $N = 1$. The NMI is determined using (2).

$$N(X, Y) = \frac{H(X) + H(Y)}{H(X, Y)} \qquad (2)$$

MI and NMI are the most preferred similarity metrics for intensity-based multimodal image registration and the other metrics are typically used for monomodal image registration.

Transformation. A transformation function T is used to estimate the geometric relationship between the sensed and the referenced images. The estimate is then used to transform the sensed image. Transformation can be broadly classified as

Rigid Transformation: Rigid transformation involves translation and rotation of the image. This is determined using (3) and (4).

$$X = x \cos \theta - y \sin \theta + a \qquad (3)$$
$$Y = x \sin \theta + y \cos \theta + b \qquad (4)$$

Here, a and b denote translations in x and y dimension, and θ is angle of rotation. X and Y are the transformation parameters.

Non-rigid Transformations: Non-rigid transformations involve translation, rotation and scaling [9]. Non-rigid transformation are determined using (5) and (6), where s denotes the scaling factor.

$$X = xs \cos \theta - ys \sin \theta + a \qquad (5)$$
$$Y = xs \sin \theta + ys \cos \theta + b \qquad (6)$$

Optimization. Medical image registration involves finding the right transformation parameters from a huge set. Since the set is very huge, process of optimization is essential. An optimization algorithm takes a series of intelligent guesses of the parameters of transformation, applies them on sensed image and uses the similarity metric as the optimization objective function. This metric denotes the degree of accuracy of image registration. Image registration is performed by applying the guessed transformation parameters to the sensed image and determining the objective function on the obtained images. The registration process continues by either guessing or obtaining new parameters and recalculating the objective function. This process is repeated until the desired objective function value is reached. An optimization algorithm updates the transformation parameters until the similarity metric between two input images reaches maximum. There are multiple optimization algorithms available in the literature. They include gradient descent, quasi-Newton, downhill simplex and simulated annealing. In addition, there are many bio-inspired heuristic algorithms, such as genetic algorithm (GA) [10], particle swarm optimization (PSO) [11], ABC [12] and bacterial foraging algorithm (BFA) [9]. Many hybrids of these bio-inspired algorithms, such as PSO+GA, PSO+BFA, PSO+neural networks (NN), GA+NN and ABC+NN have been developed to achieve faster convergence and to minimize the computation time. They are popular in medical image processing as well.

To best of author's understanding, there is no comparative performance analysis of modern bio-inspired algorithms applied to nonrigid image registration. Authors aim to bridge this gap by performing a comparative analysis of the performances of two efficient bio-inspired algorithms, ABC and PSO in non rigid medical image registration. It is hoped that it benefits researchers and doctors in deciding the best suiting algorithm according to patients' requirements. The primary contribution of the paper are as follows:

- Medical image registration has been recaptured as a continuous optimization problem.
- Bio-inspired algorithms, PSO and ABC, have been used as the tools to approach non-rigid medical image registration.
- Results of PSO- and ABC-based medical image registration have been presented.
- A comparative investigation of these algorithm has been presented in terms of accurateness and computing time for implementation of image registration.
- A trade off issue between the quality of registration and computing time has been brought to fore which helps doctors in choosing an appropriate approach.

The remainder of this paper has been structured as follows: A survey of literature on medical image registration using bio-inspired techniques has been presented in Sect. 2. SI algorithms, PSO and ABC, have been introduced in Sect. 3. Implementation of medical image registration and MATLAB-based numerical simulations using PSO and ABC have been explained in Sect. 4. Simulation results are presented and discussed in Sect. 5. Finally, conclusions and suggestions for future extension of this research have been presented in Sect. 6.

2   Related Work

Image registration has been tackled using multiple approaches. A common among them is the information theoretic approach MI which was proposed in

[13]. It has been proved as the best deterministic method [8]. When two images are properly aligned, their MI is maximum. The MI approach is robust against noise and it generates sharper peaks at the more correct registration values than other correlation metrics requirement in accurate registration [14]. MI has been used as the similarity criteria for clinical image alignment [15].

Image registration is considered as an ill-posed optimization problem and has been solved using various optimization methods, such as gradient descent, conjugate gradient, quasi-Newton, Gauss-Newton, stochastic gradient descent, Levenberg-Marquardt algorithm, graph-based methods, belief programming, linear programming and evolutionary methods [16]. Evolutionary computation and other heuristic optimization approaches are more sturdy than the commonly used gradient-based approaches, as they are not dependent on initial solution. In addition, these approaches give specific plans to escape from local minima or maxima. These approaches have been widely used in different kinds of optimization tasks in image registration [17]. Image registration is a high dimensional problem, computationally very intense, and involves a lot of local minima. Traditional optimization methods are likely to get trapped in local minima. Therefore, researchers have proposed metaheuristic methods to achieve good results [18]. According to a comparative study of evolutionary algorithms for image registration by [16], the best performance has been delivered by a PSO implementation. Multimodal image registration using PSO as optimization technique and NMI as similarity metric has been implemented by [19]. He illustrates the substantial potential of PSO in solving image registration. Also, PSO has proven itself as an efficient optimization algorithm in several areas [20]. The ABC algorithm has been used to solve various constrained, unconstrained, single and multiple objective optimization problems [12,21–23]. ABC's performance has been proved to be very efficient in other areas of research [21].

3 Bio-inspired Algorithms for Medical Image Registration

Nature, an affluent source of novel ideas and techniques, inspires scientists and researchers to solve many problems. The fame of nature inspired algorithm has been attributed to their efficiency, accurate results, simple and humble computation. Two biologically inspired algorithms, namely PSO and ABC, are explained in the following subsections.

3.1 The PSO Algorithm

The PSO algorithm is population based [11]. The algorithm is inspired by the social behavior of bird flocking and fish schooling. It consists of a swarm of multiple n-dimensional candidate solutions called particles (n is the number of optimal parameters to be determined). Particles explore the search space for a global solution. Each particle has an initial position and moves towards the global solution with some initial velocity. Each particle is evaluated through a fitness formula. The fitness value of every particle becomes its personal best, and the minimum (or maximum) of all particles becomes the global best. All particles try to move towards global best by changing their position and velocities iteratively. This process is repeated till an acceptable global best is achieved or for a determined number of iteration. The PSO algorithm has been used to solve various optimization problems and has found to be efficient. It has been applied in wireless sensor networks [20], image registration [24] and segmentation [25], power systems [26] and antenna engineering [27].

3.2 The ABC Algorithm

The ABC algorithm is an optimization algorithm which draws inspiration from the honey bees foraging behaviour [23,28,29]. The algorithm involves three different kinds of bees, namely onlooker bees, employed bees and scout bees. The employed bees perform exploitation of food sources and load the nectar of the source to the hive. The employed bees dance to communicate information about the food source that is being exploited currently. The number of employed bees is equal to the of number food sources. The onlooker bees look at the dance of the employed bees and based on the dance, find out the amount of nectar in the food source. The exploration of newer food source is by the scout bees. In the process of exploitation, some food sources nectar might become empty, and the bees which are employed and exploiting these food source become scout. The algorithm considers each food source position as a solution to an optimization problem, and the nectar amount as the fitness of the solution. The exploration for the food is done by the scout bees and the exploitation by the employed bees. ABC has been applied to solve multiple optimization problem and a survey on its applications in image, signal and video processing has been presented in [18,21].

Medical image registration is treated as an optimization problem, and the parameters of optimization are the transformation parameters namely, translation along x and y axes, rotation, and scaling along x and y axes. Thus, the dimensionality of the problem equals five. These parameters are obtained using PSO and ABC and the parameters thus obtained are checked for efficiency using the objective function NMI using (2). Implementations of image registration approached using PSO and ABC algorithms are described below.

4   Implementation and Numerical Simulation

4.1   Implementation

PSO-Based Image Registration. The PSO-based image registration algorithm has been presented in Algorithm 1.

4.2   Numerical Simulation

The algorithms presented in this paper have been verified using MATLAB R2012a numeric simulations, on computer having an Intel CORE i5 processor.

Algorithm 1. Pseudocode for the PSO algorithm

1: Initialize maximum allowable iterations r_{max}, target fitness function s to zero and global best value G to maximum value.
2: Set the values of V_{min}, V_{max}, X_{min}, X_{max} where V denotes velocity and X denotes position
3: **for** every particle j **do**
4:   **for** every dimension d **do**
5:     Randomly initialize X_{jd} such that: $X_{min} \leq X_{jd} \leq X_{max}$
6:     Initialize the Personal best values P
7:     $P_{jd} = X_{jd}$
8:     Initialize v_{jd} randomly: $V_{min} \leq v_{jd} \leq V_{max}$
9:   **end for**
10:   Determine $f(X_j)$ using (2)
11:   **if** $f(X_j) < f(G)$ **then**
12:     **for** every dimension d **do**
13:       $G_d = X_{jd}$
14:     **end for**
15:   **end if**
16: **end for**
17: loop $i = 1$
18: **while** $(i \leq r_{max})$ AND $(f(G) > s)$ **do**
19:   **for** every particle j **do**
20:     **for** every dimension d **do**
21:       Calculate velocity $V_{jd}(k)$
22:       $i_1 = c_1 r_{1jd}(k)(Xpbest_{jd}(k) - X_{jd}(k))$
23:       $i_2 = c_2 r_{2jd}(k)(Xgbest_{jd}(k) - X_{jd}(k))$
24:       $V_{jd}(k) = wV_{jd}(k-1) + i_1 + i_2$
25:       Restrict V_{jd} to $V_{min} \leq v_{jd} \leq V_{max}$
26:       Determine position using $X_{jd}(k)$
27:       $X_{jd}(k) = X_{jd}(k) + V_{jd}(k)$
28:       Restrict X_{jd} to $X_{min} \leq X_{jd} \leq X_{max}$
29:     **end for**
30:     Determine $f(X_j)$ using (2)
31:     **if** $f(X_j) < f(G)$ **then**
32:       **for** each dimension d **do**
33:         $G_d = X_{jd}$
34:       **end for**
35:     **end if**
36:   **end for**
37:   $i = i + 1$
38: **end while**

Algorithm 2. Pseudocode for the ABC algorithm

1: Initialize food sources m, Dimensions dim, iterations i_{max}, abandonment limit of food source l
2: **for** $i = 1$ to m **do**
3:    **for** $j = 1$ to dim **do**
4:       Randomly initialize food source $s_i^j = s_{min}^j + r(0,1) \times (s_{max}^j - s_{min}^j)$,
5:    **end for**
6:    Trial of each food source $t_i = 0$
7: **end for**
8: $k = 1$
9: **while** $k \leq i_{max}$ **do**
10:    Compute $f(s_i)$ using (2) //Employed bees phase of ABC algorithm
11:    **for** $i = 1$ to m **do**
12:       **for** $j = 1$ to dim **do**
13:          Exploit novel food source $z_i = s_{ij} + \phi_{ij}(s_{ij} - s_{kj})$
14:       **end for**
15:       Compute n0vel food fitness value $f(z_i)$ using (2)
16:       **if** $f(z_i) < f(s_i)$ **then**
17:          $s_i = z_i$, $t_i = 0$ //Make the trial t of the new food source as zero
18:       **else**
19:          $t_i = t_i + 1$
20:       **end if**
21:    **end for**
22:    Determine the probability for onlooker bees $P_i = \dfrac{F_i}{\sum\limits_{j=1}^{n} F_i}$

23:    $t = 0$, $i = 1$ //Onlooker bees phase of ABC algorithm
24:    **repeat**
25:       $r \sim (0,1)$
26:       **if** $r < P_i$ **then**
27:          $t = t + 1$
28:          **for** $j = 1$ to D **do**
29:             Exploit novel food source $z_i = s_{ij} + \phi_{ij}(s_{ij} - s_{kj})$
30:          **end for**
31:          **if** $f(s_i) > f(z_i)$ **then**
32:             $s_i = z_i$, $t_i = 0$
33:          **else**
34:             $t_i = t_i + 1$
35:          **end if**
36:       **end if**
37:       $i = i + 1 \ mod(n + 1)$
38:    **until** $t = n$
39:    **for** $i = 1$ to n **do**
40:       **if** $t_i \geq l$ **then**
41:          $s_i = s_{min}^j + r(0,1) \times (s_{max}^j - s_{min}^j)$, $t_i = 0$
42:       **end if**
43:    **end for**
44:    $k = k + 1$
45: **end while**

Numerical vales pertaining to case study 1 and 2 are presented in the following subsections:

Case Study 1: PSO Algorithm Based Medical Image Registration. In the study, parameters of PSO are initialized as follows. These are the standard recommended parameters for the PSO algorithm.

– Dimensions $d = 5$
– Acceleration constants $c_1 = c_2 = 2.0$
– Inertia weight $w=0.8$

Case Study 2: ABC Based Medical Image Registration. In this case study, ABC algorithm parameters are set as follows.

– Dimension $d= 5$
– Abandonment Limit $= 0.6 \times D \times P$
– Acceleration Coefficient Upper Bound $a = 1$

The reference image shown in Fig. 2(a) is an MRI image subjected to transformation using randomly generated parameters to obtain the sensed image shown in Fig. 2(b). Bio-inspired algorithms, ABC and PSO, have been used to register these two images to approximately calculate parameters of transformation and the obtained transformation parameters has been applied to sensed image to obtain the registered images. Registered images shown in Fig. 2(c) and (d) have been obtained using the transformation parameters derived using ABC and PSO, respectively.

The study has been conducted with various population sizes (20, 30, 50, 100) and different iteration values (500, 1000). 30 trial simulations have been done, with randomly generated initial population. Mean of the results of 30 trials has been calculated for inference. Since both algorithms are stochastic, the solutions produced are not the same in all trials and therefore, the results of multiple trials have been averaged.

5   Results and Discussion

The parameters for transformation namely T_x, T_y, θ, Sx and Sy were randomly generated (referred to as the expected optimization parameters) and applied to the reference image shown in Fig. 2(a) to obtain the sensed image shown in Fig. 2(b). The proposed algorithms had to determine these transformation parameters given both the reference and sensed image as inputs. The obtained parameters of the proposeds were used to transform the sensed image to obtain the registered image. It can be observed that the reference image of Fig. 2(a) and the registered images obtained using PSO shown in Fig. 2(c) and obtained using ABC Fig. 2(d) have aligned properly.

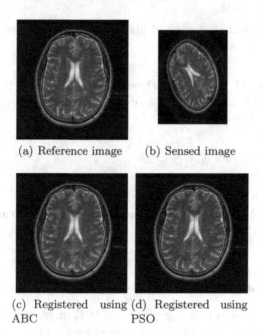

(a) Reference image   (b) Sensed image

(c) Registered using (d) Registered using
ABC   PSO

Fig. 2. Image registration using ABC and PSO algorithms

The expected optimization parameters, the obtained optimization parameters, the time taken for convergence and the best fitness obtained and the number of iterations taken for convergence for both ABC and PSO are shown in the Tables 1 and 2, respectively. The results of these tables are for 10 trials with a population of 30. It can be observed from the Tables 1 and 2, the expected optimization parameters are almost the same as the obtained optimization parameters and hence the fitness value is very close to zero, and also the time taken for convergence is in terms of seconds, rather than hours which is generally the case with traditional optimization problems.

The plot of best fitness values obtained versus iterations for population size of 20 and maximum iteration value of 10000 are shown in the Figs. 3 and 4 for PSO and ABC, respectively. It can be observed that the best fitness value reaches very close to zero, and also converges after 2000 iterations in both the cases. This denotes both the algorithms yield good results for determination of transformation parameters in image registration.

The mean results of 30 trial runs for varying population size of 20, 30, 50 and 100 and maximum iterations of 1000 for the PSO and the ABC algorithm are given in the Table 1 and the mean results of 30 trial runs for varying population size of 20, 30, 50 and 100 and maximum iterations of 500 for PSO and ABC are given in the Table 2. These tables contain the mean best solution obtained, standard deviation of the best solution, mean convergence time and the mean iterations of convergence. From these two tables, it can be observed that the

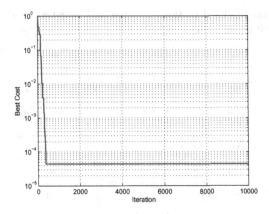

Fig. 3. NMI values obtained from 10000 iterations for PSO

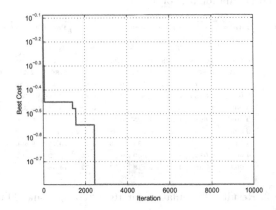

Fig. 4. NMI values obtained from 10000 iterations for ABC

obtained optimization transformation parameters are nearly the same as the expected transformation parameters and also the standard deviation is very close to 0 which denotes that the obtained optimization parameters using both the proposed algorithm are yielding very good solutions close to the mean. The standard deviation of the algorithms becomes better with the increase in the population size.

Tables 1 and 2 has presented the statistical summary of 30 trials for different population sizes for both the algorithms. These tables contain the mean best solution obtained, standard deviation of the best solution, mean convergence time and the mean iterations of convergence. It can be observed that as the population size reaches 100, the efficiency of both the algorithms in terms of convergence and accuracy has been increased.

It can be observed from both the Tables 1 and 2, that ABC requires more computing time when compared to PSO to obtain the optimum results. But,

Table 1. Simulation results depicting expected and obtained parameters using PSO for 10 trial runs and population size of 30

Trial	Time (sec)	Iterations	Fitness	Expected parameters					Parameters obtained by PSO				
				T_x	T_y	θ	S_x	S_y	T_x	T_y	θ	S_x	S_y
1	390.66	500	0.019	4.559	0.261	0.521	0.522	1.12	4.561	0.261	0.521	0.512	1.23
2	375.25	500	0.558	0.983	9.895	7.855	1.333	0.665	0.597	10.125	7.742	1.343	0.765
3	177.64	240	0.006	8.91	7.49	0.34	1.63	2.06	8.91	7.49	0.31	2.06	1.53
4	413.17	500	0.505	2.529	7.847	5.722	1.95	0.885	2.631	7.526	5.610	1.85	0.985
5	382.89	500	0.544	1.828	2.162	0.419	1.76	0.652	1.726	2.366	0.747	1.576	0.752
6	352.19	500	0.349	8.267	4.180	0.918	0.321	1.23	8.230	4.099	0. 843	0.42	1.120
7	341.39	500	0.562	1.226	3.121	0.798	0.632	1.326	1.150	2.6182	0.593	0.732	1.216
8	344.78	500	0.056	6.347	9.452	9.607	0.032	0.065	6.347	9.452	9. 614	0.023	0.051
9	298.93	429	0.008	9.530	0.237	1.185	0.005	0.0465	9.531	0.2372	1. 184	0.006	0.065
10	336.47	500	0.361	8.153	6.718	6.848	0.36	0.51	8.147	6.848	6.848	0.236	0.451

Table 2. Simulation results depicting expected and obtained parameters using ABC for 10 trial runs and population size of 30.

Trial	Time (sec)	Iterations	Fitness	Expected parameters					Parameters obtained by ABC				
				T_x	T_y	θ	S_x	S_y	T_x	T_y	θ	S_x	S_y
1	1053.4	500	0.010	16.378	4.228	3.611	1.522	0.12	16.371	4.288	3.661	1.532	0.143
2	71.70	32	0.007	2.80	2.23	5.47	0.25	1.12	2.80	2.23	5.47	0.26	1.31
3	1080.1	500	0.001	6.047	12.59	7.053	0.81	0.34	6.047	12.594	7. 052	0.82	0.35
4	650.72	305	0.004	14.766	3.744	0.893	0.76	0.64	14.766	3.744	0.893	0.72	0.621
5	559.33	264	0.009	16.18	4.208	4.634	0.343	0.98	16.18	4.21	4.64	0.435	0.91
6	749.62	350	0.009	3.668	8.040	10.75	0.522	1.12	3.668	8.040	10. 76	0.522	1.02
7	467.99	223	0.008	5.459	16.59	6.09	0.985	0.892	5.459	16.592	6. 094	0.887	0.781
8	1045.0	500	0.030	19.15	9.855	7.138	0.635	0.75	19.157	9.856	7. 137	0.623	0.656
9	474.775	226	0.008	6.073	13.07	10.39	0.567	0.65	6.072	13.071	10.39	0.522	0.52
10	1023.2	481	0.009	14.68	1.00	2.118	0.27	0.72	14.68	1.00	2.12	0.23	0.76

Table 3. Results of simulation for 1000 iterations and 30 trials

Algorithm	ABC				PSO			
Population size	20	30	50	100	20	30	50	100
Mean fitness	0.3119	0.1404	0.0140	$8.105e-05$	0.425	0.3661	0.1040	0.0085
Std deviation of fitness	0.0575	0.0193	0.0016	$2.111e-05$	0.33	0.2436	0. 2088	0.0019
Mean convergence at iteration	1000	1000	1000	181	549	744	537.4	216
Mean computing time (in second)	818	$1.26e+03$	$2.03e+03$	921.28	403	871	$1. 26e+0.3$	827.92

however in terms of accuracy of the result, the ABC has an upper hand over the PSO. The results conclude in a bargain between accuracy and computing time. Also, as population size increases, the accuracy of the ABC improves, but at the cost of increased computing time (see Tables 3 and 4).

Table 4. Results of simulation for 500 iterations and 30 trials

Algorithm	ABC				PSO			
Population size	20	30	50	100	20	30	50	100
Mean fitness	0.2113	0.2012	0.0603	$2.63e-05$	0.3087	0.3966	0.135	0. 0097
Std deviation of fitness	0.1007	0.0936	0.0231	$3.61e-05$	0.2260	0.228	0. 183	0.0027
Mean Convergence at iteration	500	500	500	131.800	433.75	465	378	270
Mean Computing time (in second)	875.45	925	$2.18e+03$	$6.19e+03$	329.25	335.9	748	$1.02e+03$

6 Conclusion and Future Work

The research reported in this paper has been inspired by the success of bio-inspired, population based search algorithms to solve the medical image registration problem. The medical image registration problem has been treated as n-dimensional continuous optimization problem. And the optimization parameters are determined using two bio-inspired algorithms namely ABC and PSO algorithm. A brief introduction to ABC and PSO algorithm has been provided. A statistical analysis of the results obtained has been presented. The results obtained using both the methods are compared.

The results show that both ABC and PSO can handle the image registration successfully. However, there are some tradeoff issues. While ABC gives higher quality results, it suffers from longer convergence time, whereas PSO results are not as higher quality as ABC, but the convergence is fast. Also, with the increase in population size, better fitness value is obtained but again at the cost of computing time in both the cases. The computational complexity of ABC is higher than PSO due to the greater emphasis on exploitation in the search space.

Medical image registration is a one-time exercise. Since medical image registration helps a doctor in decision making, higher quality of results is desirable. Therefore, ABC algorithm is a better choice than PSO in situations in which higher precision is needed. However, a dialectical choice between these two algorithm depend on the availability of desired computational speed, computing resources and accuracy.

This research can be extended further in multiple directions. Variants and hybrids of the bio-inspired algorithms can be developed to achieve improved quality of results and resource efficiency. These algorithms can also be applied to solve three-dimensional medical image registration, deformable image registration and medical image fusion. Bio-inspired algorithms can also be used to address several unresolved research issues in medical image processing.

Acknowledgment. Authors acknowledge with gratitude the support received from REVA University, Bengaluru, and M.S. Ramaiah University of Applied Sciences, Bengaluru. They also express sincere thanks to the anonymous reviewers of this paper for their constructive criticism.

References

1. Rueckert, D., Schnabel, J.A.: Registration and segmentation in medical imaging. In: Cipolla, R., Battiato, S., Farinella, G.M. (eds.) Registration and Recognition in Images and Videos. SCI, vol. 532, pp. 137–156. Springer, Heidelberg (2014). doi:10.1007/978-3-642-44907-9_7
2. Xu, R., Athavale, P., Nachman, A., Wright, G.A.: Multiscale registration of real-time and prior MRI data for image-guided cardiac interventions. IEEE Trans. Biomed. Eng. **61**(10), 2621–2632 (2014)
3. Peressutti, D., Gómez, A., Penney, G.P., King, A.P.: Registration of multiview echocardiography sequences using a subspace error metric. IEEE Trans. Biomed. Eng. **64**(2), 352–361 (2017)
4. Kang, X., Armand, M., Otake, Y., Yau, W.-P., Cheung, P.Y.S., Hu, Y., Taylor, R.H.: Robustness and accuracy of feature-based single image 2-D to 3-D registration without correspondences for image-guided intervention. IEEE Trans. Biomed. Eng. **61**(1), 149–161 (2014)
5. Li, B., Tian, L., Ou, S.: Rapid multimodal medical image registration and fusion in 3-D conformal radiotherapy treatment planning. In Proceedings of the 4th International Conference on Bioinformatics and Biomedical Engineering (iCBBE), pp. 1–5, June 2010
6. Ebrahimi, M., Kulaseharan, S.: Deformable image registration and intensity correction of cardiac perfusion MRI. In: Camara, O., Mansi, T., Pop, M., Rhode, K., Sermesant, M., Young, A. (eds.) STACOM 2014. LNCS, vol. 8896, pp. 13–20. Springer, Cham (2015). doi:10.1007/978-3-319-14678-2_2
7. Shenoy, R., Shih, M.-C., Rose, K.: Deformable registration of biomedical images using 2-D hidden Markov models. IEEE Trans. Image Process. **25**(10), 4631–4640 (2016)
8. Tagare, H.D., Rao, M.: Why does mutual-information work for image registration? A deterministic explanation. IEEE Trans. Pattern Anal. Mach. Intell. **37**(6), 1286–1296 (2015)
9. Yang, F., Ding, M., Zhang, X., Hou, W., Zhong, C.: Non-rigid multi-modal medical image registration by combining L-BFGS-B with cat swarm optimization. Inf. Sci. **316**, 440–456 (2015)
10. Mitchell, M.: An Introduction to Genetic Algorithms. MIT Press, Cambridge (1998)
11. Kennedy, J., Eberhart, R.: Particle swarm optimization. In: Proceedings of the IEEE International Conference on Neural Networks, vol. 4, pp. 1942–1948 (1995)
12. Karaboga, D., Akay, B.: A modified artificial bee colony (ABC) algorithm for constrained optimization problems. Appl. Soft Comput. **11**(3), 3021–3031 (2011)
13. Wells, W.M., Viola, P.A., Atsumi, H., Nakajima, S., Kikinis, R.: Multi-modal volume registration by maximization of mutual information. Med. Image Anal. **1**(1), 35–51 (1996)
14. Cole-Rhodes, A.A., Johnson, K.L., Le Moigne, J., Zavorin, I.: Multiresolution registration of remote sensing imagery by optimization of mutual information using a stochastic gradient. IEEE Trans. Image Process. **12**(12), 1495–1511 (2003)

15. Pradhan, S., Patra, D.: Enhanced mutual information based medical image registration. IET Image Proc. **10**(5), 418–427 (2016)
16. Sotiras, A., Davatzikos, C., Paragios, N.: Deformable medical image registration: a survey. IEEE Trans. Med. Imaging **32**(7), 1153–1190 (2013)
17. Bermejo, E., Cordón, O., Damas, S., Santamaría, J.: A comparative study on the application of advanced bacterial foraging models to image registration. Inf. Sci. **295**, 160–181 (2015)
18. Damas, S., Cordon, O., Santamaria, J.: Medical image registration using evolutionary computation: an experimental survey. IEEE Comput. Intell. Mag. **6**(4), 26–42 (2011)
19. Schwab, L., Schmitt, M., Wanka, R.: Multimodal medical image registration using particle swarm optimization with influence of the data's initial orientation. In: Proceedings of the IEEE Conference on Computational Intelligence in Bioinformatics and Computational Biology (CIBCB), pp. 1–8 (2015)
20. Kulkarni, R.V., Venayagamoorthy, G.K.: Particle swarm optimization in wireless-sensor networks: a brief survey. IEEE Trans. Syst. Man Cybern. Part C Appl. Rev. **41**(2), 262–267 (2011)
21. Akay, B., Karaboga, D.: A survey on the applications of artificial bee colony in signal, image, and video processing. SIViP **9**(4), 967–990 (2015)
22. Brajevic, I.: Crossover-based artificial bee colony algorithm for constrained optimization problems. Neural Comput. Appl. **26**(7), 1587–1601 (2015)
23. Kulkarni, V.R., Desai, V., Kulkarni, R.V.: Multistage localization in wireless sensor networks using artificial bee colony algorithm. In: Proceedings of the IEEE Symposium Series on Computational Intelligence (SSCI), pp. 1–8, December 2016
24. Damas, S., Cordón, O., Santamaria, J.: Medical image registration using evolutionary computation: an experimental survey. IEEE Comput. Intell. Mag. **6**(4), 26–42 (2011)
25. Kulkarni, R.V., Venayagamoorthy, G.K.: Bio-inspired algorithms for autonomous deployment and localization of sensor nodes. IEEE Trans. Syst. Man Cybern. Part C Appl. Rev. **40**(6), 663–675 (2010)
26. De Leon-Aldaco, S.E., Calleja, H., Aguayo Alquicira, J.: Metaheuristic optimization methods applied to power converters: a review. IEEE Trans. Power Electron. **30**(12), 6791–6803 (2015)
27. Pi, Q., Ye, H.: Survey of particle swarm optimization algorithm and its applications in antenna circuit. In: Proceedings of the IEEE International Conference on Communication Problem-Solving (ICCP), pp. 492–495, October 2015
28. Karaboga, D., Basturk, B.: A powerful and efficient algorithm for numerical function optimization: artificial bee colony (ABC) algorithm. J. Glob. Optim. **39**(3), 459–471 (2007)
29. Brajevic, I., Tuba, M.: An upgraded artificial bee colony (ABC) algorithm for constrained optimization problems. J. Intell. Manuf. **24**(4), 729–740 (2013)

Rough Kernelized Fuzzy C-Means Based Medical Image Segmentation

Amiya Halder$^{(\boxtimes)}$ and Siddhartha Guha

St. Thomas' College of Engineering and Technology,
Kolkata 700023, West Bengal, India
amiya.halder77@gmail.com, siddharthaguha18@gmail.com

Abstract. This paper presents a rough kernelized fuzzy c-means clustering (RKFCM) based medical image segmentation algorithm. It is a combination of rough set and kernelized FCM clustering (KFCM). KFCM
introduced new technique of clustering using kernel induced distance and
improved its robustness towards noise. However, it is failed to remove the
vagueness and uncertainty of the clustering technique. In this paper, we
use rough set with KFCM for removal of uncertainty by introduction of
higher and lower estimation of rough set theory. The objective function
derived from KFCM is merged with rough set to get better segmentation results. Experiments performed on numerous medical image data
sets and its resulting validity index values have proved this algorithm to
be more efficient in comparison to existing algorithms.

Keywords: Fuzzy c-means · Rough set · Image segmentation

1   Introduction

Medical imaging stands for pictorial representation of interior parts of the body
for clinical analysis. With the increasing use of medical images for diagnosis purposes image segmentation algorithms have played a vital role for study of the
nature of anatomical structure. Image segmentation is subdividing an image into
various regions or segments. It is usually done so that the resulting image formed
is easier to analyze and its characteristics can be judged more meaningfully. The
process should be terminated once the area of interest in an image is achieved.
Initially, the segmentation algorithm that is used K-means algorithm [1]. However one of the widely used algorithms is FCM [2]. In 2008, Wang, Kong and
Lu proposed MRI brain image segmentation using modified FCM algorithm [3].
In 2005, Pal and Pal proposed a possibilistic FCM algorithm [4]. The removal
of incompleteness and vagueness in the clustering technique was introduced by
Lingras and Peters [5]. In 2007, Majhi and pal proposed a rough set based FCM
algorithm (RFPCM) [6,7]. Still both FCM and RFCM gives poor performance
in noisy environment. In 2003, Zhang and Chen proposed Kernel-based fuzzy
and PCM algorithm [9]. The concept of distance in FCM is substituted by
kernel function. Several other kernel based algorithms have been proposed

© Springer Nature Singapore Pte Ltd. 2017
J.K. Mandal et al. (Eds.): CICBA 2017, Part II, CCIS 776, pp. 466–474, 2017.
DOI: 10.1007/978-981-10-6430-2_36

[8,10,11]. In 2011, Kaur Soni and Gosain proposed a kernel based intuition-istic FCM algorithm (KiFCM) [12]. Our paper proposes an algorithm where we modeled the membership function knowledge of kernel based FCM and clus-tering technique knowledge of rough set theory which both serves the purpose of robustness towards noise and helps in overcoming the problem of vagueness among patterns in between the higher and lower estimation.

2   The FCM Algorithm

In the FCM clustering, a set of randomly generated clusters partition a set of N data set $\{p_1, p_2, .., p_N\}$ by assigning each data set to a particular cluster and calculate membership grades of each data points. The algorithm targets to minimize the function:

$$M = \sum_{k=1}^{c} \sum_{\alpha=1}^{N} \tau_{k\alpha}^m * ||p_\alpha - \rho_k||^2 \qquad (1)$$

The m ($m > 1$) controls the fuzziness and $\tau_{k\alpha}$ is the membership value of the kth cluster and α_{th} data value ρ_k is the k_{th} centroid. Easily derive the membership value and new cluster centre formula by differentiating the objective function both with respect to $\tau_{k\alpha}$ and ρ_k given as follows:- $\frac{dM}{d\tau_{k\alpha}} = 0$ and $\frac{dM}{d\rho_k} = 0$. This gives:-

$$\tau_{k\alpha} = \frac{1}{\sum_{j=1}^{c} \frac{||p_\alpha - \rho_k||^{\frac{2}{m-1}}}{||p_\alpha - \rho_j||^{\frac{2}{m-1}}}} \qquad (2)$$

$$\rho_k = \frac{\sum_{p_\alpha \in \rho_k} p_\alpha * \tau_{k\alpha}^m}{\sum_{\alpha=1}^{N} \tau_{k\alpha}^m} \qquad (3)$$

3   Kernelized FCM Clustering

The main drawback of FCM is its sensitivity to noisy environment. This issue is resolved by KFCM with the introduction of the Kernel trick. The idea of the kernel based method is that a set of input data $\{p_1, p_2, ..., p_N\} \subseteq P$ is mapped to a feature space with a high dimension G. The basic mapping procedure is given by $\gamma : P \to G(p \to \gamma(p))$. The KFCM objective function is:

$$M = \sum_{k=1}^{c} \sum_{\alpha=1}^{N} \tau_{k\alpha}^m \star ||\gamma(p_\alpha) - \gamma(\rho_k)||^2 \qquad (4)$$

From the kernel concept we get the equation:

$$||\gamma(p_\alpha) - \gamma(\rho_k)||^2 = (\gamma(p_\alpha) - \gamma(\rho_k))^T (\gamma(p_\alpha) - \gamma(\rho_k)) \qquad (5)$$

$$= \gamma(p_\alpha)^T \gamma(p_\alpha) + \gamma(\rho_k)^T \gamma(\rho_k) - \gamma(p_\alpha)^T \gamma(\rho_k) - \gamma(\rho_k)^T \gamma(p_\alpha) \qquad (6)$$

$$= \kappa(p_\alpha, p_\alpha) + \kappa(\rho_k, \rho_k) - 2\kappa(p_\alpha, \rho_k) \tag{7}$$

Obviously $\kappa(x, x) = 1$ Hence Eqs. 4 and 5 is reduced to

$$M = 2 * \sum_{k=1}^{c} \sum_{\alpha=1}^{N} \tau_{k\alpha}^m * (1 - k(p_\alpha, \rho_k)) \tag{8}$$

After the first derivative of M with respect to $\tau_{k\alpha}$ and ρ_k and zeroing them we get:-

$$\tau_{k\alpha} = \frac{(1 - \kappa(p_\alpha, \rho_k))^{-\frac{1}{m-1}}}{\sum_{j=1}^{k}(1 - \kappa(p_\alpha, \rho_j))^{-\frac{1}{m-1}}} \tag{9}$$

$$\rho_k = \frac{\sum_{\alpha=1}^{N} \tau_{k\alpha}^m * (\kappa(p_\alpha, \rho_k)) * p_\alpha}{\sum_{\alpha=1}^{N} \tau_{k\alpha}^m * (\kappa(p_\alpha, \rho_k))} \tag{10}$$

$$\kappa(p_1, q_1) = exp(\frac{-||p_1 - q_1||^2}{\epsilon^2}) \tag{11}$$

4   Rough Fuzzy C-Means Clustering

Rough set theory deals with the classification of incomplete information and knowledge. The fundamental concepts behind rough set is the estimation of lower and higher spaces of a set. The rough set algorithm proposes to assign data value to upper and lower approximation of a set [6]. In RFCM, we use rough set theory with FCM by integrating the higher and lower estimation of rough set with the membership function. Thus RFCM deals with the insufficient factor in class definition and efficiently handles overlapping partitions. The RFCM algorithm is given below:

4.1   Algorithm

Data set: $P = \{p_1, p_2, ..p_N\}$
Randomly generated cluster: ρ_k, for k = 1 to c
for $\alpha = 1.....N$ do
   Calculate $d_{min} = min_{1 \leq j \leq k} d(p_\alpha, \rho_j)$
   for $i = 1.....c$ do
    $S = \frac{d(p_\alpha, \rho_j)}{d(p_\alpha, \rho_i)}, \forall i \neq j$
   if $S \leq threshold$ then
     $S = 1$
   end if
  end for
  if $S = 0$ then
   $p_\alpha \in \overline{U}(\rho_i)$ and $p_\alpha \in \underline{U}(\rho_i)$
  else
   $p_\alpha \in \overline{U}(\rho_i)$ and $p_\alpha \in \overline{U}(\rho_j)$
  end if

end for
calculate new cluster:
if $\underline{U}(\rho_i) \neq 0$ and $(\overline{U}(\rho_i) - \underline{U}(\rho_i) = 0)$ **then**
$$\rho_i = \frac{\sum_{p_\alpha \in \underline{U}(\rho_i)} p_\alpha}{\underline{U}(\rho_i)}$$
else
    if $\underline{U}(\rho_i) = 0$ and $(\overline{U}(\rho_i) - \underline{U}(\rho_i)) \neq 0$ **then**
$$\rho_i = \frac{\sum_{p_\alpha \in (\overline{U}(\rho_i) - \underline{U}(\rho_i))} p_\alpha}{|(\overline{U}(\rho_i) - \underline{U}(\rho_i))|}$$
    else
$$\rho_i = \frac{\sum_{p_\alpha \in \underline{U}(\rho_i)} p_\alpha}{\underline{U}(\rho_i)} * w_{low} + \frac{\sum_{p_\alpha \in (\overline{U}(\rho_i) - \underline{U}(\rho_i))} p_\alpha}{|(\overline{U}(\rho_i) - \underline{U}(\rho_i))|} * w_{high}, \text{ where } \{0 \leq w_{low} \leq$$
    0.5 and $w_{high} = 1 - w_{low}\}$
    end if
end if

5 Proposed Method

In the proposed method we first randomly generate c clusters. Initially each data set is assigned to a particular cluster. For each data set, find the maximum membership value corresponding to c clusters. Then the maximum membership value is divided by other membership values corresponding to (c-1) clusters. If the result is less than the threshold value then the execution is immediately stopped. If the result is not equal to zero the data belongs to higher estimation of both the clusters else the data set belongs to the higher and lower estimation of the cluster for which the membership value is maximum. Once all data set values are assigned to particular clusters we calculate new cluster values. The method is iterative and will continue until the entire cluster values do not change. The results are effective and the clustering is more robust to noise. The membership value and the new cluster values will be calculated as according to that of kernel. We incorporate Gaussian radial basis function given by Eq. (10). The upper and lower bounds ensure removal of uncertainty of belongingness of data set values to only one cluster or more than one cluster. Hence the algorithm is more precise and definite. Here, m measures fuzziness of the classification. Hence the algorithm is more precise and definite.

5.1 Algorithm

for $\alpha = 1, .., N$ **do**
  calculate $max_{1 \leq j \leq c}(\tau_{j\alpha}) = A$
  $pos1 = j$
  for $f = 1.....c$ **do**
    $S = \frac{A}{\tau_{j\alpha}}, \forall f \neq pos1$
    if $S \leq threshold$ **then**
      $S = 1$
      $pos2 = f$
    end if
  end for

if $S = 0$ **then**

    $p_\alpha \in \overline{U}(\rho_{pos1})$ and $p_\alpha \in \underline{U}(\rho_{pos1})$

else

    $p_\alpha \in \overline{U}(\rho_{pos1})$ and $p_\alpha \in \overline{U}(\rho_{pos2})$

end if

end for

Centroid calculation:

for $k = 1, .., c$ **do**

    if $\underline{U}(\rho_k) \neq 0$ and $(\overline{U}(\rho_k) - \underline{U}(\rho_k) = 0)$ **then**

$$\rho_k = \frac{\sum_{\alpha=1}^{N} \tau_{k\alpha}^m * p_\alpha * \kappa(p_\alpha, \rho_k)}{\sum_{\alpha=1}^{N} \tau_{k\alpha}^m * \kappa(p_\alpha, \rho_k)}, \forall p_\alpha \in \underline{U}(\rho_k)$$

    else

        if $\underline{U}(\rho_i) = 0$ and $(\overline{U}(\rho_i) - \underline{U}(\rho_i)) \neq 0$ **then**

$$\rho_k = \frac{\sum_{\alpha=1}^{N} \tau_{k\alpha}^m * p_\alpha * \kappa(p_\alpha, \rho_k)}{\sum_{\alpha=1}^{N} \tau_{k\alpha}^m * \kappa(p_\alpha, \rho_k)}, \forall p_\alpha \in (\overline{U}(\rho_k) - \underline{U}(\rho_k))$$

        else

$$\rho_k = w_{lo}\rho_1 + w_{up}\rho_2, \text{ where } \{0 \leq w_{lo} \leq 0.5 \text{ and } w_{up} = 1 - w_{lo}\}$$

$$\rho_1 = \frac{\sum_{\alpha=1}^{N} \tau_{k\alpha}^m * p_\alpha * \kappa(p_\alpha, \rho_k)}{\sum_{\alpha=1}^{N} \tau_{k\alpha}^m * \kappa(p_\alpha, \rho_k)}, \forall p_\alpha \in (\overline{U}(\rho_k) - \underline{U}(\rho_k))$$

$$\rho_2 = \frac{\sum_{\alpha=1}^{N} \tau_{k\alpha}^m * p_\alpha * \kappa(p_\alpha, \rho_k)}{\sum_{\alpha=1}^{N} \tau_{k\alpha}^m * \kappa(p_\alpha, \rho_k)}, \forall p_\alpha \in \underline{U}(\rho_k)$$

        end if

    end if

    and $\tau_{k\alpha} = \dfrac{(1 - \kappa(p_\alpha, \rho_k))^{-\frac{1}{m-1}}}{\sum_{j=1}^{c}(1 - \kappa(p_\alpha, \rho_j))^{-\frac{1}{m-1}}}$

end for

6 Experimental Results

Performance of the proposed algorithm is compared with existing methods K-means, FCM, RFCM, KFCM, KiFCM. The weighted T1 and T2 MR scan images have been used from the IXI-dataset [13] to check the effectiveness of the proposed method. For experiment purpose, we apply this proposed algorithm on more than 100 images. Efficiency of this proposed method measure using validity index [14] of the segmented images, calculated by Eq. (12).The segmented output (using the above five different method and proposed algorithm) are shown in Figs. 1 and 2 for Gaussian noise and mixed noise T2-type medical images. Segmented images for normal medical images is shown in Fig. 3. From the above results analysis, the proposed method gives improved results than the K-means, FCM RFCM, KFCM, KiFCM and it constantly locate a result within the optimal range of cluster. In this experiment, we consider $m = 2$, $threshold = 0.4$, $c = 2$ for noisy medical images and $c = 5$ for normal medical images. Also, we compare validity index of these segmentation methods which is shown in Fig. 4, and it gives the better results than K-means, FCM RFCM, KFCM, KiFCM methods. The cluster validity index is measured by the given equation:

$$CV = g * \frac{intra}{inter} \tag{12}$$

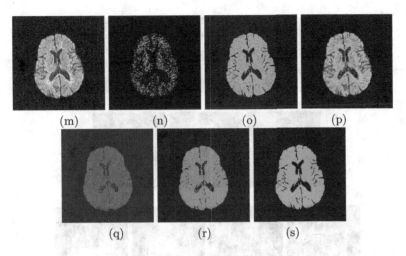

Fig. 1. Comparison of segmented images using K-means (n), FCM (o), RFCM (p), KFCM (q), KiFCM (r) and proposed methods (RKFCM) (s). The original Gaussian noisy image (m).

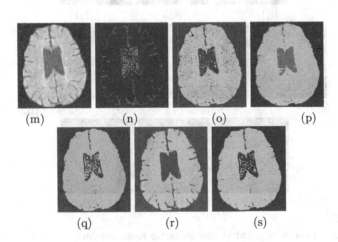

Fig. 2. Comparison of segmented images using K-means (n), FCM (o), RFCM (p), KFCM (q), KiFCM (r) and proposed methods (RKFCM) (s). The original mixed noisy image (m).

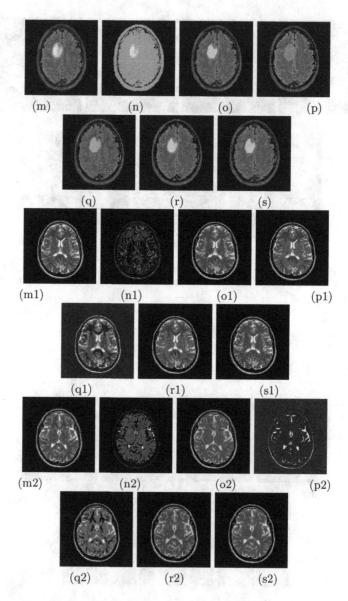

Fig. 3. Comparison of segmented images using K-means (n, n1 and n2), FCM (o, o1 and o2), RFCM (p, p1 and p2), KFCM (q, q1 and q2), KiFCM (r, r1 and r2) and proposed methods (RKFCM) (s, s1 and s2). (m), (m1) and (m2) are normal brain images.

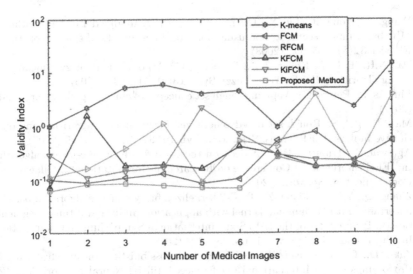

Fig. 4. Comparison of validity index using K-means, FCM, RFCM, KFCM, KiFCM and proposed methods (RKFCM).

$$intra = \frac{1}{X} \sum_{k=1}^{c} \sum_{p \in \rho_k} ||p - \rho_k||^2 \tag{13}$$

$$inter = min(||\rho_l - \rho_k||^2) \tag{14}$$

Here, $l = 1$ to c, $k = 1$ to c, and $l \neq k$ and

$$g = b * M(2,1) + 1 \tag{15}$$

Here, b is a value given explicitly by the user and $M(2,1)$ represents Gaussian Distribution with standard deviation of 1, mean 2.

7   Conclusion

In this paper, a combination of rough set and kernelized FCM based medical image segmentation is proposed for the segmented of medical images that are corrupted with various noise and normal brain images. This proposed method gives better results especially for a noisy image than other existing image segmentation methods.

References

1. Na, S., Xumin, L., Yong, G.: Research on k-means clustering algorithm. In: 3rd International Symposium on Intelligent Information (2010)
2. Suganya, R., Shanthi, R.: Fuzzy c-means algorithm-a review. Int. J. Sci. Res. Publ. **2**(11) (2012)

3. Wang, J., Kong, J., Lu, Y., Qi, M., Zhang, B.: A modified FCM algorithm for MRI brain image segmentation using both local and non-local spatial constraints. Elsevier **32**(8), 685–698 (2008)

4. Pal, N.R., Pal, K., Keller, J.M., Bezdek, J.C.: A possibilistic fuzzy c-means clustering algorithm. IEEE Trans. Fuzzy Syst. **13**(4), 517–530 (2005)

5. Lingras, P., Peters, G.: Applying rough set concepts to clustering. Springer, London (2012)

6. Maji, P., Pal, S.: Rough set based generalized fuzzy c-means algorithm and quantitative indices. IEEE Trans. Syst. Man Cybern. **37**(6), 1529–1540 (2007)

7. Agrawal, S., Tripathy, B.K.: A decision theoretic rough fuzzy c-means algorithm. In: IEEE International Conference on Research in Computational Intelligence and Communication Networks (2015)

8. Zhang, Q., Yue, Y., Jiang, Z.: Type-2 kernelized fuzzy c-means algorithm based on uncertain width of Gaussian kernel with applications in liver and tumor segmentation. In Proceedings of the 2013 Sixth International Symposium on Computational Intelligence and Design, vol. 1, pp. 289–292 (2013)

9. Zang, D., Chen, S.: Kernel-based fuzzy and possibilistic c-means clustering. In: Proceedings of the International Conference Artificial Neural Network, pp. 122–125 (2003)

10. Zang, D., Chen, S.: A novel kernelized fuzzy c-means algorithm with application in medical image segmentation. Artif. Intell. Med. **32**(1), 37–50 (2004)

11. Zang, D., Chen, S.: Clustering incomplete data using kernel-based fuzzy c-means algorithm. Neural Process. Lett. **18**(3), 155–162 (2003)

12. Kaur, P., Soni, A.K., Gosain, A.: A robust kernelized intuitionistic fuzzy c-means clustering algorithm in segmentation of noisy medical images. Elsevier (2012)

13. http://brain-development.org/ixi-dataset/

14. Turi, R.H.: Clustering-based color image segmentation, Ph.D. thesis, Monash University (2001)

A Hybrid PSO-Fuzzy Based Algorithm for Clustering Indian Stock Market Data

Somnath Mukhopadhyay[1(✉)], Tamal Datta Chaudhuri[2], and J.K. Mandal[3]

[1] Department of Information Technology, Calcutta Business School,
Kolkata 743503, India
som.cse@live.com
[2] Department of Finance, Calcutta Business School, Kolkata 743503, India
tamalc@calcuttabusinessschool.org
[3] Department of Computer Science and Engineering, University of Kalyani,
Kalyani 713248, India
jkm.cse@gmail.com

Abstract. Partitioning data points into several homogeneous sets is known as clustering. This paper proposes a hybrid clustering algorithm based on Different Length Particle Swarm Optimization (DPSO) algorithm and is applied to a study of Indian stock market volatility. The heterogeneous data items of stock market are fuzzified to homogeneous data items for efficient clustering. Each data item has 7 attributes. Three evaluation criteria are used for computing the fitness of particles of the clustering algorithm. Different length particles are encoded in the PSO to minimize the user interaction with the program hence also the running time. The single point crossover operator of Genetic Algorithm is used here for differencing between two particles. The performance of the proposed algorithm is demonstrated by clustering stock market data of size 2014 × 7. The results are compared with some well known existing algorithms.

Keywords: Crisp clustering · Euclidean distance · Fuzzification · Implied volatility · Mean Square Error · Quantization error · Different length particle swarm optimization · Single point cross over · Historic volatility

1 Introduction

Clustering is a process of making groups of set of samples or data points so that they become similar within each group. The groups are called clusters [5]. The applications of clustering are in varied fields of pattern recognition, such as image processing, object recognition, data mining, patterns in financial sector variables, etc. The algorithms always try to minimize or maximize certain objective or fitness functions.

A popular partitioning clustering algorithm is K-means [20]. The algorithm clusters the data based on Euclidean distance as similarity/dissimilarity measure.

© Springer Nature Singapore Pte Ltd. 2017
J.K. Mandal et al. (Eds.): CICBA 2017, Part II, CCIS 776, pp. 475–487, 2017.
DOI: 10.1007/978-981-10-6430-2_37

The algorithm can cluster large data set and it is easy to implement. In any fixed length clustering algorithm, like K-means algorithm, clustering is obtained by iteratively minimizing a fitness function that is dependent on the distance of the data points to the cluster centers. However, the K-means algorithm, like most of the existing clustering algorithms, assume a priori knowledge of the number of clusters, K, while in many practical situations, this information cannot be determined in advance. It is also sensitive to the selection of the initial cluster centers and may converge to the local optima. Finding an optimal number of clusters is usually a challenging task and several researchers have used various combinatorial optimization methods to solve the problem. Some other fixed length image clustering algorithms [11, 12, 18, 21] are present in the literature.

Various approaches [8–10, 17, 19] toward the image clustering based on variable length chromosome genetic algorithm and variable length particle swarm optimization have also been proposed in the recent years for clustering. Some cluster validity indices [15, 16] have also been proposed for fuzzy and crisp clustering.

In a recent contribution, Datta Chaudhuri and Ghosh [1] addressed the issue of predicting stock market volatility in a clustering framework. The essence of the paper was that if time series data on market volatility can be shown to fall in certain specific clusters, then the data points are in some sense homogenous, and hence can be used for prediction. If the number of clusters is small, then prediction using this data makes sense. If, on the other hand, the number of clusters is large, then the time series data is truly random, and hence prediction would be inefficient. It was emphasized in the paper that the method clustering provided a way of understanding the nature of the data and should be undertaken before executing any prediction exercise.

For predicting future values of a variable, either lagged values of the same variable can be used, or a set of predictors need to be identified. The other purpose of the above mentioned paper was to identify an efficient set of predictors of stock market volatility using the clustering method. It was postulated that if a set of predictors, along with the variable to be predicted, falls in specific clusters, and if efficiency of clustering rises with the inclusion of predictors, then these set of predictors will give efficient prediction, within the cluster. Thus the paper mapped predictors against clusters to find the optimal mix.

The dependent variable in the paper was historic volatility of market returns in India defined by volatility of *NIFTY returns*, and the predictors were *India VIX* (implied volatility measure), *CBOE VIX*, *volatility of gold returns, volatility of crude oil returns, volatility of DJIA returns, volatility of DAX returns, volatility of Hang Seng returns* and *volatility of Nikkei returns*. The variables reflect both historic volatility and expected volatility at home and abroad and also other sources of volatility. The study on predicting volatility is important as

1. It helps in intra-day trading.
2. Is the basis of neutral trading in the options market.
3. Affects portfolio rebalancing by fund managers.
4. Helps in hedging.

5. Affects capital budgeting decisions through timing of raising equity from the market and its pricing and also.
6. Affects policy decisions relating to the financial market.

In this paper, a new approach termed as *hybrid PSO-Fuzzy based algorithm* is proposed for clustering *Indian stock market data* on seven attributes namely volatility of NIFTY returns (HISTORIC VOLATILITY), India VIX, CBOE VIX, volatility of crude oil returns (CRUDEV), volatility of DJIA returns (DJIARV), volatility of DAX returns (DAXV), volatility of Hang Seng returns (HANGSENGV). The time series data on the variables is from 04/03/2008 to 26/05/2016 and the data set is of size 2014 × 7.

In Particle Swarm Optimization [3,7], the solution parameters are encoded in the form of strings called particles. A collection of such strings is called a swarm. Initially a random population of swarm is created, which represents random different points in the search space. An objective or fitness is associated with each string that represents the degree of goodness of the solution encoded in the particles. In the proposed algorithm, a swarm of particles of different lengths, automatically determines the number of clusters and simultaneously clusters the data set with minimal user interference. Similarity/dissimilarity between each pair of data is measured by using intra cluster distance, inter cluster distance and an error minimizer function. Euclidean distance function is used as distance function between two data points. The algorithm terminates when the *(gBest)* converges to optimal solution or it meets a finite number of iterations. Since the actual number of clusters is unknown, the string of different particles in the same swarm population are allowed to contain different number of clusters. As a consequence, the different particles have different lengths having different number of cluster centers. Since all these values are different in size and types we have fuzzified these values to homogeneous set of values. These fuzzyfied values are given for clustering using different length particle swarm optimization. As particles are of different length, we have incorporated the single point cross over technique of Genetic Algorithm (GA) [2,6] for making a binary operation between two parent particles to generate a child particle.

The rest of the paper is organized as follows. The standard PSO algorithm is described in Sect. 2. Section 3 describes the proposed hybrid model of clustering of stock market data. Experimental results and discussions are provided in Sect. 4 and Sect. 5 concludes the paper.

2   Particle Swarm Optimization

Particle Swarm Optimization (PSO) is a population based stochastic optimization technique modeled on the social behavior of bird flocks [7]. It maintains a population of particles, where each particle represents a potential solution of the optimization problem. Each particle is assigned a velocity. The particles then flow through the problem space. The aim of PSO is to find the particle position that results the best fitness value. A fitness function is associated with a given optimization problem, which gives a fitness value for each particle. Each particle keeps track of the following information in the problem space: x_i, the current position of the particle; v_i, the current velocity of the particle; and y_i, the personal best position of the particle which is the best position that it has achieved so far. This position yields the best fitness value for that particle. The fitness value of this position is called *pBest*. There is another parameter in PSO, called global best *(gBest)*. *(gBest)* is the best particle determined from the entire swarm. The PSO changes the velocity and position of each particle at each time step so that it moves toward its personal best and global best locations, using (1) and (2) respectively. The process is repeated for maximum iterations or sufficient good fitness value.

$$v_p(i+1) = h(i) * v_p(i) + \Psi_p * r_p * (x_{pB}(i) - x_p(i)) + \Psi_g * r_g * ((x_{gB}(i) - x_p(i)) \quad (1)$$

$$x_p(i+1) = x_p(i) + v_p(i+1) \quad (2)$$

In Eqs. 1 and 2, Ψ_p and Ψ_g are the positive learning factors (or acceleration constants). r_p and r_g are random numbers in $[0, 1]$. i is the generation number in $[1, I_{MAX}]$. I_{MAX} is the maximum number of iterations. $h(i) \in [0, 1]$ is the inertia factor. $f_{pB}(i)$ and $f_{gB}(i)$ are the fitness values known as *(pBest)* value and *(gBest)* at i^{th} generation, respectively. $x_{pB}(i)$ and $x_{gB}(i)$ are respectively the personal and global best positions of pth particle at i^{th} generation.

3   Proposed Hybrid PSO-Fuzzy Based Clustering Algorithm

3.1   Fuzzyfication

The 7 attributes of each day stock market data are fuzzyfied using (3) to make a homogeneous data set for efficient clustering. Here x is the value which is fuzzyfied, min and max are the minimum and maximum values in vector A. The fuzzyfication technique here is used for simplification of the data set and done one time only as the preprocessing method.

$$A = \{(x, \mu_A(x)) : x \in A, \mu_A(x) \in [0, 1]\} \quad (3)$$

where

$$\mu_A(x) = \frac{x - min}{max - min} \quad (4)$$

3.2   Different Length PSO (DPSO) Based Clustering

In this paper, a hybrid PSO-Fuzzy based clustering algorithm has been proposed for clustering stock market data. In this algorithm, after fuzzyfication of data set, a hybrid PSO based clustering algorithm is done. The algorithm of different length particles automatically determines the number of clusters and simultaneously clusters the data set with minimal user interference. It starts with random partitions of the data set, encoded in each particle of the swarm.

The fitness function proposed by Omran and Salman [12,14,18] has been used in the proposed clustering. The proposed fitness function defined in (9), contains three evaluation criteria such as intra cluster distance measure, inter cluster distance and the quantization error minimization function. These criteria are defined respectively in (6), (7) and (8). We consider the same weight of all these three criteria to the fitness of the corresponding particle. The *Euclidean* distance function [12], given in (5), is used to compute the distance between two data points, which is used for computing intra cluster distance measure, inter cluster distance and the quantization error. The proposed Euclidean distance function between the i-th data and j-th data in the stock market is computed using (5), where the values of i and j lie between 1 and 7.

$$d(x) = \sqrt{\Sigma_{i,j}(x_i - x_j)^2} \tag{5}$$

Let $Z = (z_1, z_2, z_3, ..., z_{N_p})$ be the fuzzified data for the time period. The DPSO maintains a swarm of particles, where each particle represents a potential solution to the clustering problem and each particle encodes partition of the stock market data Z. DPSO tries to find the number of clusters, N_c. The proposed clustering method has various parameters:

N_p: Number of data points to be clustered.
N_c: Number of clusters.
z_p: p-th data vector of the data.
m_j: Mean or center of cluster j.
C_j: Set of data points in cluster j.
$|C_j|$: Number of data points in cluster j.

Each particle can be represented by $\{m_{i1}, ..., m_{ij}, ..., m_{iN_c}\}$, where m_{ij} refers to the j-th cluster center vector of the i-th particle. In this algorithm, particles have different lengths since the number of clusters is unknown. The particles are initialized with random number of cluster centers in the range $[K_{min}, K_{max}]$, where K_{min} is usually 2 and K_{max} describes the maximum particle length, which represents the maximum possible number of clusters. K_{max} depends on the size and type of data set. The proposed algorithm for stock market data clustering using different length particle swarm optimization is presented in Algorithm 1.

The intra-cluster distances of all the clusters are measured and the maximum one among all the clusters is selected in d_{max} which is defined in (6), where Z is a partition matrix representing the assignment of data points to clusters of particle i. A smaller value of d_{max} means that the clusters are more compact.

$$d_{max}(Z, x_i) = \max_{j=1 \text{ to } N_c} \left\{ \sum_{\forall z_p \in C_{ij}} d(z_p, m_{ij}) / |C_{ij}| \right\} \tag{6}$$

Inter-cluster separation distances for all clusters are measured and the minimum distance between any two clusters is calculated using (7). A large value of d_{min} means that the clusters are well separated.

Algorithm 1. DPSO Algorithm

Input: 2014 × 7 Stock market data
Output: Partition Matrix
 1: **begin**
 2: Initialize the maximum number of cluster centers K_{max} and all the constant parameters
 3: Initialize each particle with K randomly selected cluster centers
 4: Initialize each particle x_i with the $pBest_i$ and also the *(gBest)*
 5: **while** gen $< I_{max}$ **do**   ▷ I_{max} is the maximum number iterations
 6: **for** i=1 to NOP **do**   ▷ Number of particles
 7:     **for** x=1 to rows **do**   ▷ Number of rows of the data set
 8:         Let x be the data point in the pth day
 9:         Find Euclidean distance between p^{th} data point and all centers of ith particle
10:         Assign p^{th} data point to j^{th} center of ith particle
11:     **end for**
12:     Compute Intra cluster distance of ith particle using (6)
13:     Compute Inter cluster distance of ith particle using (7)
14:     Compute Quantization error of ith particle using (8)
15:     Compute the fitness value of ith particle using (9), which uses (6), (7) and (8)
16:     Update *(pBest)* position $x_{pB}(i)$ and *(pBest)* value $f_{pB}(i)$ of ith particle
17: **end for**
18: Update *(gBest)* from all the particles in the swarm
19: **for** i=1 to NOP **do**
20:     **if** lop(gBest) = lop($particle_i$) **then**
21:         Compute velocity and then update position of particle i using (1) and (2).
22:     **else**
23:         Do Single point crossover (algorithm 2) to find the updated position of particle i
24:     **end if**
25: **end for**
26: Update inertia weight
27: **end while**
28: **end**

$$d_{min}(x_i) = \min_{\forall j1,j2,j1 \neq j2}\{d(m_{ij_1}, m_{ij_2})\} \qquad (7)$$

The quantization error function [4,12] is proposed in the clustering of stock market data points which calculates the average distance of the data points of a cluster to its cluster centers, followed by the average distances of all clusters and hence calculates new average. The problem of Esmin *et al.* [4] is that any cluster with one data point would affect the final result with another cluster containing many data points. Suppose for i^{th} particle in a cluster which has only data point and very close to the center and there is another cluster that has many data points which are not so close to the center. The problem has been resolved by assigning less weight to the cluster containing only one data point than with cluster having many data points. The weighted quantization error function is given in (8), where N_0 is the total number of data vectors to be clustered. The fitness function is constructed by intra-cluster distance d_{max}, inter-cluster distance d_{min}, along with the quantization error Q_e function. The fitness function used to minimize $f(x_i, Z)$ [21] is given in (9). Here z_{max} is a big value assumed. In the optimization function, equal weights are assigned to the three distance functions. The fitness function is given in the optimization technique and which minimizes the value of f in each generation to make the stock market data well clustered.

$$Q_e = \{ \sum_{\forall j=1 \ to \ N_c} [(\sum_{\forall z_p \in c_{ij}} d(z_p, m_{ij})/ |C_{ij}|.(N_0/ |C_{ij}|)]\} \qquad (8)$$

$$f(x_i, Z) = d_{max}(z, x_i) + (z_{max} - d_{min}(x_i)) + Q_e \qquad (9)$$

The single point cross over technique is given in Algorithm 2. The reason behind using the single point cross over technique of genetic algorithm is that the particles are of different length. If two particles are of same length, then they can be used for a binary operation to generate a child particle. Since we are dealing with different length particles, it becomes difficult to subtract between them to find the child particle. If gBest particle and the particle i have same length then they can be subtracted easily to find the velocity for particle i. In case of different lengths of the gBest particle and particle i we have incorporated the Single Point Cross over technique of Genetic Algorithm for computing the updated position of particle i.

Algorithm 2. Single point Cross over technique

1: **begin**
2: Let p_1 and p_2 represents the gBest and current particles respectively
3: Say, pt_1 and pt_2 are generated randomly in ranges [2,lop(p_1)-1] and [2,lop(p_2)-1], respectively   ▷ lop(p_1) is Length of p_1 particle
4: Current particle gets updated position as $p_2=[p_1(1:pt_1),p_2(pt_2:end)]$
5: Delete repetition of any cluster center in p_2, if any
6: Change lop(p_2) of current particle

---

4   Results and Comparisons

The proposed algorithm is applied to 2014 × 7 stock market data set. The performance of the proposed algorithm is measured by three evaluation metrics namely *intra cluster distance*, *inter cluster distance* and *quantization error*. The performance of the algorithm is compared with five existing algorithms, viz, *K-means, Man et al.* [21], *FPSO* [12], *DPSO* [13] and *VPSO* [18] algorithms. For comparison purpose, the following parameter values are used for the algorithms:

- Data set resolution = 2014 × 7
- Number of particles (NOP) = 20
- Maximum number of clusters = 25
- maximum number of iterations = 200

Number of iterations for Man et al., FPSO, DPSO, VPSO and the proposed hybrid model are set to 200. For K-means, the number of iterations will be 200 × number of particles, because in each iteration the fitness of 20 particles are computed in PSO based clustering algorithms. The inertia factor is set to 1 initially and decreased linearly with the number of iterations. Both the acceleration constants are set to 2. For FPSO, DPSO, VPSO and proposed hybrid algorithm, minimum (K_{min}) and maximum (K_{max}) number of clusters are set to 2 and 25 respectively. For K-means algorithm, only Mean Square Error (MSE) is used as fitness function. For Man et al., FPSO, DPSO, VPSO and proposed algorithm, the same fitness function is used for evaluation which is given in (9).

Table 1 shows the intra cluster distance d_{max}, inter cluster distance d_{min}, weighted quantization error Q_e and fitness value by the existing and proposed algorithms. The intra cluster distance and quantization error values are minimized in each generation by the proposed algorithm whereas the inter cluster distance is maximized. The fitness value is also minimized as a whole. For K-means algorithm, we observe that all the three performance metrics like intra cluster distance, inter cluster distance, weighted quantization error are very poor compared to all other algorithms. Man et al. performs much better than the K-Means algorithm in terms of all performance metrics, whereas FPSO and DPSO obtain similar results.

The VPSO performs much better than the other earlier algorithms. Proposed hybrid model of PSO and GA is best with respect to all those metrics. It obtains a significant less quantization error value compared all other algorithms in the table. The last column of the table shows the fitness values of all the algorithms. We can see from the table that the proposed hybrid algorithm outperforms all the other algorithms in all respects.

Table 1. Clustering results using Intra distance (d_{max}), quantization error (Q_e), inter distance (d_{min}) and fitness value.

Algorithm	d_{max}	Q_e	d_{min}	Fitness value
(1.) K-Means	0.9678	0.4531	0.0471	1.4680
(2.) Man et al.	0.8793	0.1202	0.1892	1.1887
(3.) FPSO	0.8102	0.0955	0.2167	1.1224
(4.) DPSO	0.7201	0.0676	0.2822	1.0699
(5.) VPSO	0.4954	0.0207	0.5043	1.0204
(6.) **Proposed**	0.1998	0.0036	0.7093	0.9127

Table 2. Partition matrix/tabulation of cluster center, counts and percentages of the data points

Cluster center	Count	Percent
1	31	15.93%
2	449	22.31%
3	51	2.53%
4	54	2.68%
5	126	6.26%
6	343	17.04%
7	63	3.13%
8	103	5.12%
9	75	3.73%
10	83	4.12%
11	57	2.63%
12	12	0.60%
13	566	28.12%

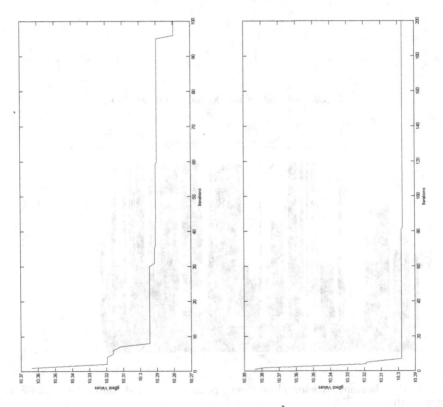

Fig. 1. gBest values in 100 and 200 generations

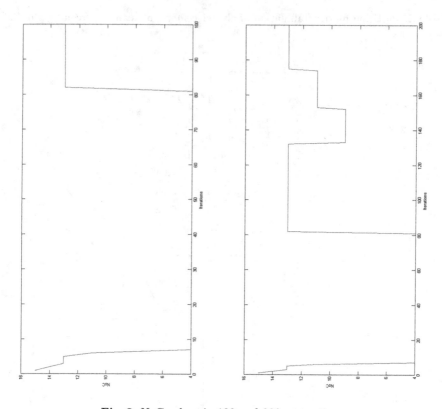

Fig. 2. NoC values in 100 and 200 generations

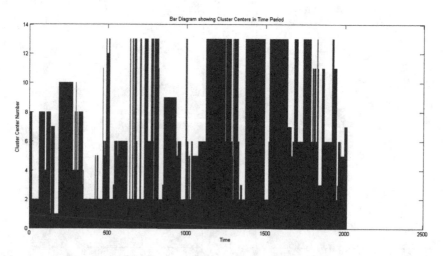

Fig. 3. Bar diagram showing cluster centers in time period during 04/03/2008 to 26/05/2016

The proposed hybrid PSO-fuzzy based algorithm for clustering of stock market data has been executed for 100 and 200 number of generations. In Fig. 1, we have shown the *gBest* values when the algorithm iterates for 100 and 200 number of generations. We can see from these figures that the proposed algorithm minimizes the global best fitness values in successive iterations. The *gBest* values are scaled in above 10 in these figures. In Fig. 2, we have shown the number of cluster centers which are obtained by the algorithm after executing it 100 and 200 number of generations.

The results shown in Fig. 1 are obtained after executing the algorithm for 200 number of generations. We can notice the fact that after iterating the proposed algorithm for 100 and 200 number of generations, it converges to and produces similar kind of results. The *gBest* values are marginally different in those two cases. So we can conclude that after iterating for 100 generations it produces a result which can outperform the other algorithms.

The results of the PSO algorithm provide us with the following insights:

1. Table 2 indicates the total number of fuzzified variable in each cluster, and also that the entire data set is captured in 13 clusters. Five clusters namely, second, fifth, sixth, eighth and thirteen contains 73.73 % of observations. That is, the seven attributes per day tend to be together most of the times, and hence can be used as predictors of historic volatility.
2. Since there are a few clusters with large number of members, prediction is possible, and the data is not truly random.
3. It is interesting to observe from Fig. 3, that large values of the fuzzified variable are followed by periods of low values of the variable up possibilities of volality trading.

5   Conclusion

This paper proposes a hybrid technique for clustering Indian stock market volatility. The algorithm is based on variable length Particle Swarm Optimization with fuzzified data set. The Single Point crossover operator of Genetic Algorithm is incorporated in the PSO based clustering algorithm for measuring the distance between a pair of particles of different length. This algorithm uses a fitness function which has three evaluation criteria such as intra cluster distance, quantization error and inter cluster distance. The results show that the proposed hybrid architecture performs better than five other algorithms in the literature, viz. K-Means algorithm, Man *et al.*, FPSO, DPSO and VPSO algorithms. The algorithm can minimize the user intervention during the program run as it can find the number of cluster centers automatically in a specified range.

In future, cluster validity indices will be used in the fitness function of the algorithm and attempts will be made to use *Multi-objective evolutionary algorithm (MOEA)* to get a set of optimal solutions where the three criteria used in proposed algorithm will be used as objective functions.

References

1. Chaudhuri, T.D., Ghosh, I.: Using clustering method to understand indian stock market volatility. Commun. Appl. Electron. (CAE) **2**(6), 35–44 (2015). Foundation of Computer Science FCS, New York, USA
2. Goldberg, D.E.: Genetic Algorithm in Search, Optimization and Machine Learning. Addison-Wesley, Boston (1989)
3. Eberhart, R., Kennedy, J.: A new optimizer using particle swarm theory. In: Proceedings of the Sixth International Symposium on Micro Machine and Human Science, MHS 1995, pp. 39–43. IEEE (1995). http://ieeexplore.ieee.org/xpls/abs_all.jsp?arnumber=494215
4. Esmin, A.A.A., Pereira, D.L., de Arajo, F.P.A.: Study of different approach to clustering data by using particle swarm optimization algorithm. In: Proceedings of the IEEE World Congress on Evolutionary Computation (CEC 2008), Hong Kong, China, pp. 1817–1822, June 2008
5. Gose, E., Johnsonbough, R., Jost, S.: Pattern Recognition and Image Analysis. Prentice-Hall, Upper Saddle River (1996)
6. Holland, J.H.: Adaptation in Natural and Artificial Systems. MIT Press, Cambridge (1992)
7. Kennedy, J., Eberhart, R.C.: Particle swarm optimization. In: IEEE International Conference on Neural Network, Perth, Australia, pp. 1942–1948 (1995)
8. López, J., Lanzarini, L., Giusti, A.: VarMOPSO: multi-objective particle swarm optimization with variable population size. In: Kuri-Morales, A., Simari, G.R. (eds.) IBERAMIA 2010. LNCS (LNAI), vol. 6433, pp. 60–69. Springer, Heidelberg (2010). doi:10.1007/978-3-642-16952-6_7
9. Katari, V., Ch, S., Satapathy, R., Ieee, M., Murthy, J., Reddy, P.P.: Hybridized improved genetic algorithm with variable length chromosome for image clustering abstract. Int. J. Comput. Sci. Netw. Secur. **7**(11), 121–131 (2007)
10. Maulik, U., Bandyopadhyay, S.: Fuzzy partitioning using a real-coded variable-length genetic algorithm for pixel classification. IEEE Trans. Geosci. Remote Sens. **41**(5), 1075–1081 (2003)
11. Mukhopadhyay, S., Mandal, J.K.: Adaptive median filtering based on unsupervised classification of pixels. In: Handbook of Research on Computational Intelligence for Engineering, Science and Business. IGI Global, 701 E. Chocolate Ave., Hershey, PA 17033, USA (2013)
12. Mukhopadhyay, S., Mandal, J.K.: Denoising of digital images through pso based pixel classification. Central Eur. J. Comput. Sci. **3**(4), 158–172 (2013). Springer Vienna
13. Mukhopadhyay, S., Mandal, P., Pal, T., Mandal, J.K.: Image clustering based on different length particle swarm optimization (DPSO). In: Satapathy, S.C., Biswal, B.N., Udgata, S.K., Mandal, J.K. (eds.) Proceedings of the 3rd International Conference on Frontiers of Intelligent Computing: Theory and Applications (FICTA) 2014. AISC, vol. 327, pp. 711–718. Springer, Cham (2015). doi:10.1007/978-3-319-11933-5_80
14. Omran, M., Engelbrecht, A., Salman, A.: Particle swarm optimization method for image clustering. Int. J. Pattern Recognit Artif Intell. **19**, 297–322 (2005)
15. Pakhira, M.K., Bandyopadhyay, S., Maulik, U.: Validity index for crisp and fuzzy clusters. Pattern Recogn. **37**(3), 487–501 (2004). http://www.sciencedirect.com/science/article/pii/S0031320303002838

16. Pakhira, M.K., Bandyopadhyay, S., Maulik, U.: A study of some fuzzy cluster validity indices, genetic clustering and application to pixel classification. Fuzzy Sets Syst. **155**(2), 191–214 (2005). http://www.sciencedirect.com/science/article/pii/S0165011405001661

17. Qiu, M., Liu, L., Ding, H., Dong, J., Wang, W.: A new hybrid variable-length ga and pso algorithm in continuous facility location problem with capacity and service level constraints. In: IEEE/INFORMS International Conference on Service Operations, Logistics and Informatics, SOLI 2009, pp. 546–551, July 2009

18. Somnath Mukhopadhyay, J.K.M., Pal, T.: Variable length PSO-based image clustering for image denoising. In: Handbook of Research on Natural Computing for Optimization Problems. IGI Global, 701 E. Chocolate Ave., Hershey, PA 17033, USA (2016)

19. Srikanth, R., George, R., Warsi, N., Prabhu, D., Petry, F., Buckles, B.: A variable-length genetic algorithm for clustering and classification. Pattern Recogn. Lett. **16**(8), 789–800 (1995). http://www.sciencedirect.com/science/article/pii/016786559500043G

20. Tan, P., Steinbach, M., Kumar, V.: Introduction to Data Mining. Pearson Education, Boston (2006)

21. Wong, M.T., He, X., Yeh, W.C.: Image clustering using particle swarm optimization. In: 2011 IEEE Congress on Evolutionary Computation (CEC), pp. 262–268, June 2011

Application of Artificial Immune System Algorithms for Intrusion Detection

Rama Krushna Das[1(✉)], Manisha Panda[2], Sanghamitra Dash[3], and Rabindra Kishore Mishra[3]

[1] National Informatics Centre, Berhampur, India
ramdash@yahoo.com
[2] Parala Maharaja Engineering College, Berhampur, India
manishapanda2013sai@gmail.com
[3] Department of Electronic Science, Berhampur University, Berhampur, India
smdash71@gmail.com, prof.r.k.mishra@gmail.com

Abstract. Intrusion Detection (ID) is one of the most challenging problems in today's era of computer security. New innovative ideas are used by the hackers to break the security, hence the challenge for developing better ID systems are increasing day-by-day. In this paper, we applied the Artificial Immune System (AIS) based classifiers for intrusion detection. Each classifier is evaluated based on high accuracy and detection rate with low false alarm rate. The results are compared using percentage split (80%) and cross validation (10 fold) test options basing on two nominal target attributes i.e. type of attacks and protocol types having 5 and 3 sub-classes respectively. The experimental results indicate that the performance of CSCA (clonal selection classification algorithm) is better AIS based classifier for network based Intrusion Detection.

Keywords: AIS · AIRS1 · AIRS2 · AIRS2Parallel · CLONALG · CSCA · Immunos1 · Immunos2 · Immunos99 · Intrusion detection · Intrusion detection system · NSL-KDD · KDD · False alarm rate · Detection rate

1 Introduction

The most essential and important challenges with computer security are determining the difference between normal and malicious activity. An intrusion can be defined as "any set of actions that attempt to compromise the integrity, confidentiality or availability of a resource".

Data mining is the process of using datasets of inventing patterns in datasets involving certain methods at the intersection of artificial intelligence, machine learning, statistics and database systems [9]. In this paper, a brief study of intrusion detection is made on the clean KDDcup 99 dataset (NSL-KDD) [1] and the Artificial Immune System based classifiers are used for the evaluation on the NSL-KDD dataset. The NSL-KDD dataset is evaluated using AIRS1, AIRS2, AIRS2Parallel, CLONALG, CSCA, Immunos1, Immunos2 and Immunos99 algorithms and from the performance and experiment comparisons were made upon each classifiers. Two test options

© Springer Nature Singapore Pte Ltd. 2017
J.K. Mandal et al. (Eds.): CICBA 2017, Part II, CCIS 776, pp. 488–503, 2017.
DOI: 10.1007/978-981-10-6430-2_38

(percentage split and cross validation) are used for the evaluation basing on two class attributes (types of attacks and protocol types) having 5 and 3 sub classes respectively.

There are several intrusion detection based approaches which were employed using KDD Cup 99 dataset. In [1], the authors statistically evaluated the entire KDD Cup 99 data set. The analysis showed that there are two important issues in the data set which highly affects the performance of evaluated systems, and results in a very poor evaluation of anomaly detection approaches. To solve these issues, they have proposed a new data set, NSL-KDD [8], which consists of selected records of the complete KDD data set. In [2], the authors analyzed the classifier problem of network intrusion detection by applying anomaly based approach has been taken into consideration. To classify the problem dataset, clonal selection classification algorithm, which is worked on the basis of negative selection through artificial immune system, has been applied. The classifier has been evaluated on the basis of various performance measures like precision, sensitivity, specificity and accuracy. The proposed algorithm has been tested on KDD CUP'99. In [3], authors considered intrusion detection process by using the supremacy of data mining in its effective use of information. They found that this is a method that can automatically generate accurate and applicable intrusion patterns from enormous scrutiny data, which makes intrusion detecting system compatible to any computer environment.

2 Intrusion Detection

Intrusion detection is a problem related with the field of computer security where in the computer systems are guarded against malicious activities and attacks. An IDS gathers and analyses information from various areas within a computer or a network to identify possible security breaches, which include both intrusions (attacks from outside the organisation) and misuse (attacks from within the organization) [15]. An Intrusion Prevention System (IPS) is also known as Intrusion Detection and Prevention System (IDPS). It is mainly considered as a software application that monitors a network or system for mischievous activity or policy ignorance and damage [11]. The function of IDS is mainly to recognise malicious activity, log information about the activity, account it and shot to stop it. IDS can be broadly classified into four different types, they are: Network-based intrusion detection system (NIPS), Wireless Intrusion Prevention Systems (WIPS), Network Behavior Analysis (NBA), Host-based Intrusion Prevention System (HIPS).

3 Artificial Immune System (AIS)

AIS is a complex system with the facility of self-adapting, self-learning, self-organizing, parallel processing and distributed coordinating. It also has the basic function to distinguish self and non-self. Some of the basic AIS models are: Negative selection algorithm [5, 12], Artificial immune network [14], Clonal selection algorithm [6, 7, 10] and Danger theory inspired algorithms [4].

4 KDD CUP 99 Dataset

Several Groups of special interest on Knowledge Discovery and Data mining (SIGKDD) has introduced an annual conference ACM SIGKDD conference on Knowledge Discovery and Data mining (KDD) since 1995. Conference papers of each proceedings of the SIGKDD international conference on KDD are published through Association for Computing Machinery (ACM). KDD dataset fully focuses on ID [16]. It contains 41 attributes and is labelled as either normal or an attack type. The KDD Cup 99 dataset contains 22 different attack types [17]. The NSL-KDD dataset also has 41 attributes, where these were constructed for each network connection. These attributes have either discrete values or continuous values [12]. The stimulated attack fall in one of the following four categories: Denial of Service Attack (DoS), User to Root Attack (U2R), Remote to Local Attack (R2L) or Probing attack. There are also three types of internet protocols to which all instances fall and they are [13]: Internet Control Message Protocol (ICMP), Transmission Control Protocol (TCP) or User Datagram Protocol (UDP).

5 Experiment

Nowadays many tools and software are known for data mining and knowledge discovery such as Waikato Environment for knowledge Analysis (WEKA), RapidMiner, Orange, KNIME, NLTK, etc. These tools and software provide us various set of methods and algorithms that help us in superior evaluation of data and information available to us, which include methods and algorithms for data analysis, cluster analysis, genetic algorithms, nearest neighbour, etc. The major part of this paper has provided detail overview of NSL-KDD dataset [8] which contains 125973 number of instances and 41 number of attributes. This dataset is implemented on several artificial immune inspired algorithms like CLONALG, CSCA, AIRS1, AIRS2, AIRS2parallel, IMMUNOS-1, IMMUNOS-2 and IMMUNOS-99.

Percentage Split: It randomly split your dataset into a training and a testing partitions each time you evaluate a model. This gives a very rapid evaluation of performance. This test option is preferable only when you have a large dataset. Default split value is taken as 66% to 34% for train and test sets respectively. Here in this paper, we have used 80% percentage split. This splits the dataset into 80% train and 20% test set. The user can set manually the percentage split value according to choice.

Cross Validation: Split the dataset into k-partitions or folds. Train a model on all of the partitions except the one that is taken out as the test set, then the process is repeated which creates k-different models and each fold is given a chance of being held out as the test set. Then the average performance of all k models are calculated. The default test option is right to be used when you are not sure. Common values for k are 5 and 10, depending on the size of the dataset. Here in this paper, we have used 10 fold cross validation.

There are eight tables in this experiment which is divided into 2 groups. Group 1 comprises of Tables 1, 2, 3 and 4, which consists of the values and analysis of the dataset using the test option percentage split 80% (Tables 1 and 2) and cross validation 10 fold (Tables 3 and 4) taking target attribute as types of attacks whereas Group 2 comprises of Tables 5, 6, 7 and 8, which consists of the values and analysis of the dataset using the test option percentage split 80% (Tables 5 and 6) and cross validation 10 fold (Tables 7 and 8) taking target attribute as protocol types.

Confusion Matrix: It is a visualization tool typically used in supervised learning (in unsupervised learning it is typically called a matching matrix). A confusion matrix that summarizes the number of instances predicted correctly or incorrectly by a classification model.

Table 1. Classifier output using percentage split 80% taking types of attacks as target attribute

Classifier	Values	Attacks					Confusion matrix				
		Normal	DoS	R2L	Probes	U2R					
AIRS1	TP	13232	8057	0	166	0	13232	191	1	0	0
	TN	9322	14731	25000	22801	25186	1120	8057	0	29	0
	FP	2449	1258	4	29	0	182	9	0	0	0
	FN	192	1149	191	2199	9	1138	1058	3	166	0
							9	0	0	0	0
AIRS2	TP	12907	8250	35	15	0	12907	159	310	48	0
	TN	9085	15060	24679	22782	25186	950	8250	6	0	0
	FP	2686	929	325	48	0	154	2	35	0	0
	FN	517	956	156	2350	9	1575	768	7	15	0
							7	0	2	0	0
AIRS2PARALLEL	TP	11478	8242	177	807	3	11478	27	1220	61	638
	TN	10336	15599	23687	22743	23927	775	8242	21	26	142
	FP	1435	390	1317	87	1259	12	0	177	0	2
	FN	1946	964	14	1558	6	644	363	74	807	477
							4	0	2	0	3
CLONALG	TP	12582	7450	0	533	0	12582	194	0	648	0
	TN	9807	14920	25004	21233	25194	807	7450	0	949	0
	FP	1964	1069	0	1597	0	191	0	0	0	0
	FN	842	1756	191	1832	1	958	874	0	533	0
							8	1	0	0	0
CSCA	TP	12917	9023	98	1692	0	12917	215	28	264	0
	TN	11335	15363	24975	22456	25186	77	9023	0	106	0
	FP	436	626	29	374	0	87	2	98	4	0
	FN	507	183	93	673	9	263	409	1	1692	0
							9	0	0	0	0
IMMUNOS1	TP	9789	8255	123	1293	7	9789	183	2588	185	679
	TN	11764	14810	21597	22454	24427	0	8255	761	190	0
	FP	7	1179	3407	376	759	2	0	123	0	66
	FN	3635	951	68	1072	2	4	996	58	1293	14
							1	0	0	1	7
IMMUNOS2	TP	13420	6787	0	0	0	13420	4	0	0	0
	TN	6818	15954	25004	22830	25186	2419	6787	0	0	0
	FP	4953	35	0	0	0	191	0	0	0	0
	FN	4	2419	191	2365	9	2334	31	0	0	0
							9	0	0	0	0

(continued)

Table 1. (*continued*)

Classifier	Values	Attacks					Confusion matrix				
		Normal	DoS	R2L	Probes	U2R					
IMMUNOS99	TP	9635	8265	117	1257	7	9635	189	2717	203	680
	TN	11767	14808	21428	22446	24417	2	8265	759	180	0
	FP	4	1181	3576	384	769	2	0	117	0	72
	FN	3789	941	74	1108	2	0	992	99	1257	17
							0	0	1	1	7

From Table 1, the values of true positive (TP), false positive (FP), true negative (TN) and false negative (FN) is calculated using the test option percentage split 80% for each attack from the confusion matrix of the corresponding algorithm for the NSL KDD dataset, where TP = number of true positives, TN = number of true negatives, FP = number of false positives, FN = number of false negatives.

Let's take the confusion matrix of AIRS1 classifier in percentage split test option (Table 1) taking types of attack as target attribute:

$\frac{predicted}{actual}$	normal	DoS	R2L	probes	U2R
normal	13232	191	1	0	0
DoS	1120	8057	0	29	0
R2L	182	9	0	0	0
R2L	1138	1058	3	166	0
R2L	9	0	0	0	0

In the above matrix rows represent the actual values and the columns represent the predicted values for the five attacks i.e. normal, DoS, R2L, probes and U2R respectively. From this confusion matrix: TP, TN, FP and FN are calculated for each attack.

For class normal:

TP is the actual normal attacks and also predicted as normal attacks. i.e. 13232.

FP is the non actual normal attacks but predicted as normal attacks. i.e. 2449 (1120 + 182 + 1138 + 9).

TN is the non actual normal attacks and also predicted as non normal attacks. i.e. 9322 (8057 + 29 + 9 + 1058 + 3 + 166).

FN is the actual normal attacks that are predicted as non normal attacks. i.e. 192 (191 + 1).

And the above process is repeated for other 4 attacks and respectively for each AIS classifier of other features and test options taken in the experiment. The same procedure is also repeated while calculating the values for target attributes.

In Table 2, the values of accuracy, specificity, detection rate and false alarm rate for the corresponding classifier is shown. The AIRS2 classifier takes more time to build model (128582.13 s) and the classifier CSCA gives more accuracy (97.70%) than other classifier using the test option percentage split at 80%. By using the Table 1, we found out the values of TP, FP, TN and FN from the confusion matrix, from these values we found the values of accuracy, sensitivity and specificity.

Table 2. Accuracy, specificity, detection rate and false alarm rate in percentage split (for types of attacks).

Classifiers	Accuracy	Specificity	Detection rate	False alarm rate
AIRS1	0.94	0.94	0.85	0.14
AIRS2	0.93	0.93	0.84	0.14
AIRS2PARALLEL	0.93	0.94	0.82	0.08
CLONALG	0.92	0.93	0.81	0.12
CSCA	0.97	0.98	0.94	0.03
IMMUNOS1	0.91	0.94	0.77	0.03
IMMUNOS2	0.92	0.92	0.80	0.22
IMMUNOS99	0.91	0.94	0.76	0.03

Accuracy can be defined as the probability that the algorithms can correctly predict positive and negative examples.

$$\text{Accuracy} = \frac{TP + TN}{(TP + TN + FP + FN)} \tag{1}$$

Detection rate (DR) measures the proportion of positives that are correctly identified as such.

$$DR = \frac{TP}{(TP + FN)} \tag{2}$$

Specificity means probability that the algorithms can correctly predict negative examples.

$$\text{Specificity} = \frac{TN}{(TN + FP)} \tag{3}$$

False alarm rate (FPR) is calculated as the ratio between false positives and the total number of actual negative events (regardless of classification).

$$FPR = \frac{FP}{(FP + TN)} \tag{4}$$

Table 3. Classifier output using cross validation 10 fold taking protocol types as target attribute

Classifier	Values	Attacks					Confusion matrix				
		Normal	DoS	R2L	Probes	U2R					
AIRS1	TP	62797	43805	22	8410	0	62797	3917	258	370	1
	TN	52929	75581	124718	113806	125919	1985	43805	0	137	0
	FP	5701	4465	260	511	2	961	7	22	4	1
	FN	4546	2122	973	3246	52	2706	539	1	8410	0
							49	2	1	0	0

(*continued*)

Table 3. (*continued*)

Classifier	Values	Attacks					Confusion matrix				
		Normal	DoS	R2L	Probes	U2R					
AIRS2	TP	53187	44523	162	10388	6	53187	12366	743	1044	3
	TN	55311	67562	124229	113167	125916	1296	44523	2	106	0
	FP	3319	12484	749	1150	5	831	0	162	0	2
	FN	14156	1404	833	1268	46	1150	118	0	10388	0
							42	0	4	0	6
AIRS2PARALLEL	TP	59264	45094	689	10839	15	59264	5953	1689	414	23
	TN	56874	73882	123278	113887	125895	818	45094	0	15	0
	FP	1756	6164	1698	430	26	302	2	689	1	3
	FN	8079	833	308	817	37	607	209	1	10839	0
							29	0	8	0	15
CLONALG	TP	56918	40263	0	5268	0	56918	4715	0	5710	0
	TN	52313	71000	124978	106156	125921	3565	40263	0	2099	0
	FP	6317	9046	0	8161	0	547	99	0	349	0
	FN	10425	5664	995	6388	52	2158	4230	0	5268	0
							47	2	0	3	0
CSCA	TP	64648	44641	561	8509	0	64648	630	218	1847	0
	TN	56201	77551	124751	111854	125921	692	44641	0	594	0
	FP	2429	2495	227	2463	0	414	0	561	20	0
	FN	2695	1286	434	3147	52	1280	1865	2	8509	0
							43	0	7	2	0
IMMUNOS1	TP	49417	41231	883	6493	50	49417	895	12845	1044	3142
	TN	58603	74407	108018	112380	122585	0	41231	3804	892	0
	FP	27	5639	16960	1937	3336	4	4	883	0	104
	FN	17926	4696	112	5163	2	22	4740	311	6493	90
							1	0	0	1	50
IMMUNOS2	TP	67326	33846	0	0	0	67326	17	0	0	0
	TN	34003	79872	124978	114317	125921	12081	33846	0	0	0
	FP	24627	174	0	0	0	995	0	0	0	0
	FN	17	12081	995	11656	52	11499	157	0	0	0
							52	0	0	0	0
IMMUNOS99	TP	48366	41298	742	6884	48	48366	948	13536	1095	3398
	TN	58584	75040	107026	112396	122211	6	41298	3798	825	0
	FP	46	5006	17952	1921	3710	7	4	742	0	242
	FN	18977	4629	253	4772	4	31	4054	617	6884	70
							2	0	1	1	48

From Table 3, the various values of true positive (TP), false positive (FP), true negative (TN) and false negative (FN) is calculated using the test option cross validation 10 fold for each attack from the confusion matrix of the corresponding algorithm for the NSL KDD dataset.

Table 4. Accuracy, specificity, detection rate and false alarm rate in cross validation (for types of attacks).

Classifiers	Accuracy	Specificity	Detection rate	False alarm rate
AIRS1	0.965	0.967	0.91	0.07
AIRS2	0.944	0.952	0.85	0.08
AIRS2PARALLEL	0.968	0.974	0.92	0.04
CLONALG	0.925	0.935	0.81	0.10
CSCA	0.975	0.980	0.93	0.03

(*continued*)

Table 4. (*continued*)

Classifiers	Accuracy	Specificity	Detection rate	False alarm rate
IMMUNOS1	0.911	0.939	0.77	0.02
IMMUNOS2	0.921	0.915	0.80	0.22
IMMUNOS99	0.909	0.940	0.77	0.02

In Table 4, the values of accuracy, specificity detection rate and false alarm rate for the corresponding classifier is shown. The IMMUNOS99 classifier takes more time to build model (120666.35) and the classifier CSCA gives more accuracy (97.50%) than other classifier using the test option percentage split at 80%.

Table 5. Classifier output using percentage split 80% taking protocol type as target attribute

Classifiers	Values	Protocol type			Confusion matrix		
		TCP	UDP	ICMP			
AIRS1	TP	20527	0	0	20527	0	0
	TN	0	110980	117682	3041	0	0
	FP	23284	0	0	1627	0	0
	FN	0	14993	8291			
AIRS2	TP	20527	0	0	20527	0	0
	TN	0	110980	117682	3041	0	0
	FP	23284	0	0	1627	0	0
	FN	0	14993	8291			
AIRS2PARALLEL	TP	18345	562	855	18345	2156	26
	TN	1815	19763	23379	2316	562	163
	FP	2853	2391	881	537	235	855
	FN	2182	2479	772			
CLONALG	TP	22077	3400	0	22077	12883	0
	TN	4089	24124	40095	1735	3400	0
	FP	3782	13572	0	2047	689	0
	FN	12883	1735	2736			
CSCA	TP	23456	650	848	23456	32	4
	TN	1591	24380	24178	40	650	52
	FP	112	73	852	72	41	848
	FN	36	92	113			
IMMUNOS1	TP	14405	3005	1394	14405	5804	318
	TN	4668	16117	23214	0	3005	36
	FP	0	6037	1712	0	233	1394
	FN	6122	36	233			

(*continued*)

Table 5. (*continued*)

Classifiers	Values	Protocol type			Confusion matrix		
		TCP	UDP	ICMP			
IMMUNOS2	TP	20527	0	0	20527	0	0
	TN	0	110980	117682	3041	0	0
	FP	23284	0	0	1627	0	0
	FN	0	14993	8291			
IMMUNOS99	TP	14501	3015	1459	14501	5752	199
	TN	4743	16159	23268	0	3015	36
	FP	0	5985	1658	0	233	1459
	FN	5951	36	233			

From Table 5, the various values of true positive (TP), false positive (FP), true negative (TN) and false negative (FN) is calculated using the test option percentage split 80% for each protocol type from the confusion matrix of the corresponding algorithm for the NSL KDD dataset.

Table 6. Accuracy, specificity, detection rate and false alarm rate in percentage split (for protocol types)

Classifiers	Accuracy	Specificity	Detection rate	False alarm rate
AIRS1	0.87	0.66	0.81	0.81
AIRS2	0.87	0.66	0.81	0.81
AIRS2PARALLEL	0.84	0.74	0.78	0.51
CLONALG	0.72	0.71	0.59	0.43
CSCA	0.98	0.96	0.91	0.03
IMMUNOS1	0.81	0.88	0.74	0.03
IMMUNOS2	0.87	0.66	0.81	0.81
IMMUNOS99	0.81	0.88	0.85	0.11

In Table 6, the values of accuracy, specificity, detection rate and false alarm rate for the corresponding classifier is shown. The classifier CSCA gives more accuracy (98.50%) than other classifier using the test option percentage split at 80%.

Table 7. Classifier output using cross validation 10 fold taking protocol type as target attribute

Classifiers	Values	Protocol type			Confusion matrix		
		TCP	UDP	ICMP			
AIRS1	TP	102331	12867	7184	102331	315	43
	TN	20722	110148	117485	1972	12867	154
	FP	2562	832	7227	590	517	7184
	FN	358	2126	1107			

(*continued*)

Table 7. (*continued*)

Classifiers	Values	Protocol type			Confusion matrix		
		TCP	UDP	ICMP			
AIRS2	TP	102331	12867	7184	102331	315	43
	TN	20722	110148	117485	1972	12867	154
	FP	2562	832	7227	590	517	7184
	FN	358	2126	1107			
AIRS2PARALLEL	TP	100976	0	0	100976	2	3
	TN	27	110351	116571	15593	0	0
	FP	24965	29	3	9372	27	0
	FN	5	15593	9399			
CLONALG	TP	75343	6603	2615	75343	22518	4828
	TN	13069	86460	111005	6541	6603	1849
	FP	10215	24520	7443	3674	2002	2615
	FN	27346	8390	5676			
CSCA	TP	103920	12674	8597	103920	298	27
	TN	21374	112898	116892	0	12674	103
	FP	354	298	8624	354	0	8597
	FN	325	103	354			
IMMUNOS1	TP	72215	14780	7099	72215	28899	1575
	TN	23284	80889	115894	0	14780	213
	FP	0	30091	8674	0	1192	7099
	FN	30474	213	1192			
IMMUNOS2	TP	102689	0	0	102689	0	0
	TN	0	110980	117682	14993	0	0
	FP	23284	0	0	8291	0	0
	FN	0	14993	8291			
IMMUNOS99	TP	72215	14780	7099	72215	28899	1575
	TN	23284	80889	115894	0	14780	213
	FP	0	30091	8674	0	1192	7099
	FN	30474	213	1192			

From Table 7, the various values of true positive (TP), false positive (FP), true negative (TN) and false negative (FN) is calculated using the test option cross validation 10 fold for each protocol type from the confusion matrix of the corresponding algorithm for the NSL KDD dataset.

Table 8. Accuracy, specificity, detection rate and false alarm rate in cross validation (for protocol types)

Classifiers	Accuracy	Specificity	Detection rate	False alarm rate
AIRS1	0.96	0.94	0.97	0.09
AIRS2	0.96	0.94	0.97	0.09

(*continued*)

Table 8. (*continued*)

Classifiers	Accuracy	Specificity	Detection rate	False alarm rate
AIRS2PARALLEL	0.86	0.66	0.33	0.33
CLONALG	0.77	0.75	0.67	0.33
CSCA	0.97	0.97	0.98	0.02
IMMUNOS1	0.81	0.88	0.74	0.03
IMMUNOS2	0.87	0.66	0.81	0.81
IMMUNOS99	0.81	0.88	0.74	0.03

In Table 8, the values of accuracy, specificity, detection rate and false alarm rate for the corresponding classifier is shown. The classifier CSCA gives more accuracy (97.50%) than other classifier using the test option cross validation 10 fold.

6   Discussion

Although we know that the test option cross validation is not used for large datasets, but the use of this test option gives more accuracy, sensitivity and specificity irrespective of time taken to build the model. Other than using percentage split as test option we can use cross validation option for better results. We also came to know from the above experiment, that the CSCA AIS classifier is better classifier in both the cases of test option, may be in percentage split or in cross validation basing on two target attribute (types of attack and protocol types). The above tables in the experiment shows that the CSCA classifier gives better result in accuracy, specificity, detection rate and false alarm rate.

There are six figures shown below, first three figures (Figs. 1, 2 and 3) shows values basing on types of attacks as target attribute last three figures (Figs. 4, 5 and 6) shows values basing on protocol types as target attributes. Figure 1 shows the accuracy

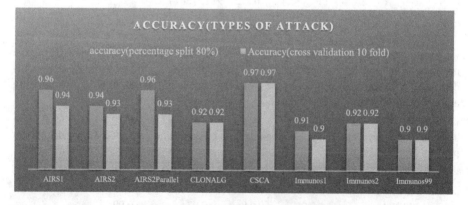

Fig. 1. Accuracy for NSL-KDD-train dataset against percentage split (80% P.S) and cross validation (10 fold C.F) for AIS algorithms taking types of attacks as a target attribute.

of NSL-KDD-train dataset in both the test option i.e. percentage split (p.s) and cross validation (c.f) for all AIS based classifiers. It is clearly seen that the CSCA classifier have the highest accuracy in the case of both the test option. Figure 2 shows the detection rate of NSL-KDD-train dataset using both the test option, the CSCA classifier have the highest detection rate against other AIS based classifier. Figure 3 shows the comparison of FAR among all the AIS classifiers against both test option. It is seen that the CSCA classifier have the lowest FAR in both the test option. Figure 4 is for the comparison of accuracy for the taken dataset. The accuracy value of both the test option is taken against each AIS classifier. The CSCA classifier has the highest value of accuracy among all the AIS classifiers. In Fig. 5, the detection rate is represented against percentage split and cross validation test option. The detection rate is seen to be highest in the case of CSCA classifier. Figure 6 shows the comparison of FAR of the taken dataset against both the test option using all the AIS methods. As from above figures, here also CSCA classifier have the lowest FAR and is the best classifier for intrusion detection.

In the above figure, the accuracy of NSL-KDD-train dataset against each and every AIS classifier for both the test option i.e. percentage split (represented in P.S) and cross validation (represented in C.F) taking types of attacks as target attribute is shown. Here in the experiment done we took percentage split as 80% train and 20% test whereas in the case of cross validation 10 fold is taken. The CSCA classifier has the highest classification accuracy against both the test option. The accuracy value for CSCA classifier under percentage split (80%) test option is seen to be 97.19% and the accuracy value of CSCA classifier under cross validation (10 fold) test option is seen to be 97.96%.

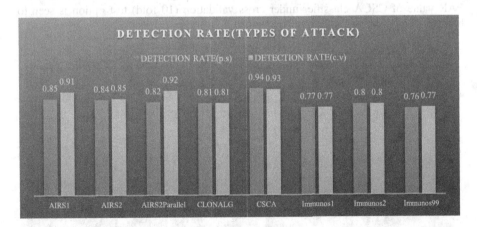

Fig. 2. Detection rate for NSL-KDD-train dataset against percentage split (80% P.S) and cross validation (10 fold C.F) for AIS algorithms taking types of attacks as a target attribute.

In the above figure, the detection rate of NSL-KDD-train dataset against each and every AIS classifier for both the test option i.e. percentage split (represented in P.S) and cross validation (represented in C.F) taking types of attacks as target attribute is shown.

The detection rate for CSCA classifier under percentage split (80%) test option is seen to be 94.19% and the detection rate of CSCA classifier under cross validation (10 fold) test option is seen to be 93.96%.

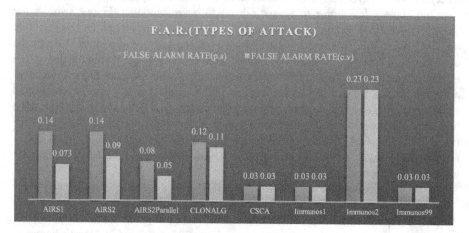

Fig. 3. F.A.R. for NSL-KDD-train dataset against percentage split (80% P.S) and cross validation (10 fold C.F) for AIS algorithms taking types of attacks as a target attribute.

In the above figure, the False alarm rate (FAR) of NSL-KDD-train dataset. The CSCA classifier has the lowest FAR against both the test option. The FAR value for CSCA classifier under percentage split (80%) test option is seen to be 3% and the FAR value of CSCA classifier under cross validation (10 fold) test option is seen to be 3%.

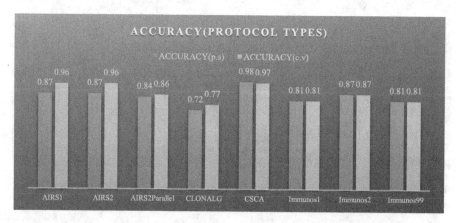

Fig. 4. Accuracy for NSL-KDD-train dataset against percentage split (80% P.S) and cross validation (10 fold C.F) for AIS algorithms taking protocol types as a target attribute.

In the above figure, the accuracy of NSL-KDD-train dataset taking protocol types as target attribute is shown. The CSCA classifier has the highest classification accuracy against both the test option. The accuracy value for CSCA classifier under percentage split (80%) test option is seen to be 98.19% and the accuracy value of CSCA classifier under cross validation (10 fold) test option is seen to be 97.96%.

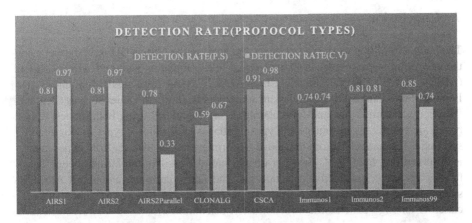

Fig. 5. Detection rate for NSL-KDD-train dataset against percentage split (80% P.S) and cross validation (10 fold C.F) for AIS algorithms taking protocol types as a target attribute.

In the above figure, the detection rate of NSL-KDD-train dataset taking protocol types as target attribute is shown. The CSCA classifier has the highest detection rate against both the test option. The detection rate for CSCA classifier under percentage split (80%) test option is seen to be 91.19% and the detection rate of CSCA classifier under cross validation (10 fold) test option is seen to be 98.96%.

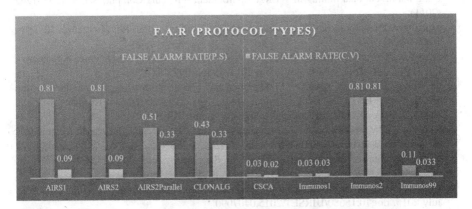

Fig. 6. F.A.R for NSL-KDD-train dataset against percentage split (80% P.S) and cross validation (10 fold C.F) for AIS algorithms taking protocol types as a target attribute.

In the above figure, the False alarm rate (FAR) of NSL-KDD-train dataset taking protocol types as target attribute is shown. The CSCA classifier has the lowest FAR against both the test option. The FAR for CSCA classifier under percentage split (80%) test option is seen to be 3% and the FAR of CSCA classifier under cross validation (10 fold) test option is seen to be 2%.

7 Conclusion

The main aim of this work is to evaluate and analyse the NSL-KDD-train dataset using the test options percentage split and cross fold validation with the AIS classifiers (AIRS1, AIRS2, AIRS2Parallel, CLONALG, CSCA, Immunos1, Immunos2 and Immunos99). Using all the AIS classification models, different values such as accuracy, specificity, detection rate and false alarm rate are calculated using both the test option basing on two target attributes i.e. Types of attacks and protocol types having 5 and 3 subclasses respectively. From the above performance of the dataset from experiment it is observed that the CSCA classifier of AIS based classifiers performed better classification accuracy, specificity, detection rate and false alarm rate among all AIS classifiers. So, it can be concluded from the experiment that CSCA classifier is a better classifier among AIS classifiers for intrusion detection.

References

1. Tavallaee, M., Bagheri, E., Lu, W., Ghorbani, A.A.: A detailed analysis of the KDD CUP 99 data set. In: CISDA 2009 (2009)
2. Chan, F.T.S., Prakash, A., Tibrewal, R.K., Tiwari, M.K.: Clonal selection approach for network intrusion detection. In: Proceedings of the 3rd International Conference on Intelligent Computational Systems, ICICS 2013, Singapore, 29–30 April 2013
3. Mohammad, M.N., Sulaiman, N., Muhsin, O.A.: A novel intrusion detection system by using intelligent data mining in WEKA environment. Procedia Comput. Sci. **3**, 1237–1242 (2011)
4. Matzinger, P.: Tolerance, danger and the extended family. Annu. Rev. Immunol. **12**, 991–1045 (1994)
5. Jain, Y.K., Upendra: Intrusion detection using supervised learning with feature set reduction. Int. J. Comput. Appl. **33**(6), November 2011. ISSN: 0975-8887
6. de Castro, L.N., Von Zuben, F.J.: Learning and optimization using the clonal selection principle. IEEE Trans. Evol. Comput. **6**(3), 239–251 (2002). doi:10.1109/tevc.2002. 1011539. Special Issue on Artificial Immune Systems. IEEE
7. Kalyani, G., Jaya Lakshmi, A.: Performance assessment of different classification techniques for intrusion detection. IOSRJCE **7**(5), 25–29 (2012). ISSN: 2278-0661, ISBN: 2278-8727
8. NSL-KDD data set for network-based intrusion detection systems, March 2009. http://nsl.cs. unb.ca/NSL-KDD/. Accessed 05 Dec 2016
9. Dutt, I., Borah, S.: Some studies in intrusion detection using data mining techniques. **4**(7), July 2015. doi:10.15680/IJIRSET.2015.0407090
10. Burnet, F.M.: A modification of Jerne's theory of antibody production using the concept of clonal selection. CA Cancer J. Clin. **26**(2), 119–121 (1976). doi:10.3322/canjclin.26.2.119. PMID 816431

11. Nguyen, H.A., Choi, D.: Application of data mining to network intrusion detection: classifier selection model. In: Ma, Y., Choi, D., Ata, S. (eds.) APNOMS 2008. LNCS, vol. 5297, pp. 399–408. Springer, Heidelberg (2008). doi:10.1007/978-3-540-88623-5_41

12. Modi, U., Jain, A.: A survey of IDS classification using KDD CUP 99 dataset in WEKA. Int. J. Sci. Eng. Res. **6**(11), 947–954 (2015)

13. Siddiqui, M.K., Naahid, S.: Analysis of KDD CUP 99 dataset using clustering based data mining. Int. J. Database Theory Appl. **6**(5), 23–34 (2013)

14. Jerne, N.K.: Towards a network theory of the immune system. Ann. Immunol. (Inst. Pasteur) **125C**, 373–389 (1974)

15. Debar, H.: An Introduction to Intrusion-Detection Systems. IBM Research, Zurich Research Laboratory, Säumerstrasse 4, CH–8803 Rüschlikon, Switzerland

16. KDD Cup 1999 data. https://kdd.ics.uci.edu/databases/kddcup99/kddcup99.html. Accessed 05 Dec 2016

17. SIGKDD. https://en.wikipedia.org/wiki/SIGKDD. Accessed 05 Dec 2016

Genetic Algorithm-Based Matrix Factorization for Missing Value Prediction

Sujoy Chatterjee$^{(\boxtimes)}$ and Anirban Mukhopadhyay

Department of Computer Science and Engineering,
University of Kalyani, Nadia 741235, India
{sujoy,anirban}@klyuniv.ac.in

Abstract. Sparsity is a major problem in the areas like data mining and pattern recognition. In recommender systems, predictions based on these few observations lead to avoidance of inherent latent features of the user corresponding to the item. Similarly, in different crowdsourcing based opinion aggregation models, there is a minimal chance to obtain opinions from all the crowd workers. Even this sparsity problem has an extensive effect in predicting actual rating of a particular item due to limited and incomplete observations. To deal with this issue, in this article, a genetic algorithm based matrix factorization technique is proposed to estimate the missing entries in the response matrix that contains workers' responses over some questions. We have created three synthetic datasets and used one real-life dataset to show the efficacy of the proposed method over the other state-of-the-art approaches.

Keywords: Matrix factorization · Sparsity · Genetic algorithm · Judgment analysis

1 Introduction

Over the last decade, taking user input for the prediction of rating to recommend item to other similar users has been used extensively. In order to solve any real-life problem in a time efficient way, non expert public opinions (crowd opinions) by outsourcing the problem to crowd are also taken as input instead of hiring experts [11]. In this crowdsourcing settings, there are some questions posted online to collect opinions from online crowd workers and the opinions of crowd workers (question-wise) are stored in a response matrix. In most of the cases due to the large scale data, it is often noticed that the response matrix containing crowd opinions over various questions is very much sparse. The same sparsity problem is common in recommender systems also [1,5]. One of the fundamental issues lies in appropriate representation of the data that does not consider the latent features explicitly. Therefore to mitigate this problem non-negative matrix factorization [8,10,15] is widely used as an useful tool.

Although non-negative matrix factorization [9] (NMF) has been widely used to produce lower rank matrix approximation, due to the random initialization of

© Springer Nature Singapore Pte Ltd. 2017
J.K. Mandal et al. (Eds.): CICBA 2017, Part II, CCIS 776, pp. 504–516, 2017.
DOI: 10.1007/978-981-10-6430-2_39

the initial matrices, the final result can be heavily dependent on the initialization. These methods also incur a large amount of time if the matrix factorization method is used repeatedly on the same matrix in order to extract the best result. Moreover, the matrix generated randomly for different executions on the same dataset can make the results mutually independent. Thus it motivates us to boost up the performance of the NMF methods along with a future scope to apply this in crowdsourcing domains to resolve decision problem due to sparsity.

In crowdsourcing domain, it is well established that instead of hiring expert, a large task can be solved very efficiently by involving non-experts [3,7,11,20]. In crowdsourcing environment, as it is not mandatory that all the annotators attempt all the questions, therefore the response matrix becomes very much sparse. In this response matrix, for a single question, multiple opinions are obtained but the main problem lies in finding an accurate aggregated judgment from those sparse opinions. Additionally, there are numerous annotators providing their opinions for a very few number of questions. So it is not always possible to assign a task depending upon the accuracy of worker who have attempted a very few questions. However, if the missing opinions of the workers are predicted based on the other similar workers then for few cases the accuracy of them can be estimated properly. Therefore prediction of missing value can be helpful to get more accurate estimate for further task assignment as well as to predict better judgment.

In this paper, the problem of missing value prediction is treated as an optimization problem and a genetic algorithm based approach is proposed to predict the missing values. Here the functions are optimized based on the measure closeness of RMSE (Root Mean Squared Error) values of non-zero elements of original matrix and the estimated matrix. The method is applied on various synthetic datasets as well as one real-life dataset. The performance of the proposed algorithm is compared with that of state-of-the-art approaches and the results demonstrate the effectiveness of it over the others.

2 Matrix Factorization

The primary objective of Matrix Factorization [6,13] is in reducing the error due to the large scale of sparsity and extracting the latent features that are kept hidden in the original matrix. This model tries to map the user and the items into a latent space so that the user-item is modeled as the inner product.

Suppose, there is a set of users U, and a set of items I. Let R be the rating matrix that contains users' interests over the items and the dimension of R (whose all elements are non-negative) is $|U \times I|$. Now to capture the latent feature, the objective of the matrix factorization method is to find the two matrices for an integer $K \leq \min\{U, I\}$ and $P \in \mathbb{R}^{|U \times K|}$, $Q \in \mathbb{R}^{|I \times K|}$, such that the product of P and Q^T is approximately equal to R. Mathematically it is denoted by

$$R \approx P \times Q^T = \hat{R}. \tag{1}$$

Now to measure the goodness of the solution the common measures used are Frobenius norm and Kullback-Leibler divergence [13]. To illustrate this, suppose for a non-negative matrix V, the objective of NMF is to compute non-negative matrix factor W and H so that $V \approx WH$. The aim is to minimize $J(W, H)$ as defined in the following equation.

$$\min_{W \geq 0, H \geq 0} J(W, H) = \frac{1}{2} ||V - WH||_F^2. \tag{2}$$

In the above equation both the matrices should have non-zero elements.

2.1   Related Work

Non-negative matrix factorization is widely adopted in various domains such as information retrieval, data mining and computer vision [4,21]. Although a lot of research has been accomplished to make better algorithm in terms of accuracy or convergence guarantee, still there is much space in the room for further improvement. There are plenty of algorithms proposed over the years to make a solution of Eq. 1. Paatero and Tapper first introduced the NMF problem [18,19] but they did not take into account of negativity constraints at that time. Since then this problem has received attention of researchers from different viewpoints.

Multiplicative update algorithm is one of the most popular method that are mostly used by majority of the NMF algorithm. But there are some limitations in the convergence guarantee of the method (LEE) [13]. Another method namely hierarchical alternating least squares (HALS) algorithm has been introduced with convergence proof.

Several methods inspired from ANLS framework [14] have been put forward for solutions of matrix factorization problem and for solving Eq. 2. In this framework, the variables are kept into two subgroups and those groups are updated iteratively. The steps of this method are described below.

– Fill up the matrix $H \in \mathbb{R}$ with non-negative elements.
– The following equation is solved iteratively until the convergence criteria are met.
  • $\min_{W>0} ||H^T W^T - A^T||_F^2$, when H is kept fixed and
  • $\min_{H>0} ||WH - A||$, when W is fixed.
  • Normalize the columns of W and the rows of H are scaled accordingly.

In this method, to solve the original problem, primarily two problems are solved. A classical solution to solve the problem is active set method. Here exchanges of variables between two working sets happen and the two-block coordinate decent algorithm is used. The major limitation of the algorithm is that it performs slower when the number of unknown parameters becomes large. However, it shows the convergence proof. In recent years, block principal pivoting method [9,10] has been developed that can speed up the search process by exchanging multiple variables instead of one variable between two working sets. In this article, we propose a genetic algorithm based method that provides stable good solution accross all the time for any point K.

3 Proposed Genetic Algorithm-Based Method

This section describes the use of genetic algorithm [16,17] for producing near-optimal solutions for matrix factorization. The proposed approach is discussed in detail below.

3.1 Encoding of Chromosomes

Suppose a matrix with dimension $M \times N$ is being factorized into two matrices P and Q with dimensions $M \times K$ and $K \times N$, respectively. As these matrices are initialized randomly, therefore to encode the information of each solution into a chromosome, the length of it should be $M \times K + K \times N$. Each part of the chromosome should be floating point coded that represents the values of the matrices for a fixed division point K. As this chromosome contains the information about two matrices P and Q with dimension $M \times K$ and $K \times N$, respectively, therefore the first $M \times K$ positions of it should represent the matrix P, whereas the positions from $M \times K + 1$ to $M \times K + K \times N$ represents the matrix Q. Note that, in this problem we have considered that all the chromosomes should have same length, i.e., the division point K is fixed for all the matrices. In this problem, primarily the matrix is made normalized (to make the values between 0 and 1) that requires the cells of the chormosomes to be floating point values (see Fig. 1).

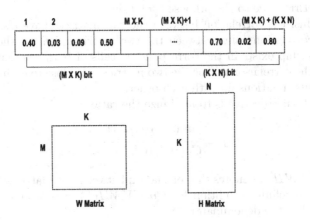

Fig. 1. Encoding scheme of chromosomes.

3.2 Initial Population

In the initial population, we take the whole set of solutions containing information for different random matrices (with same dimensions) for which an optimal solution is to be generated.

3.3 Local Refinement

After the generation of initial population a local refinement step is carried out on the initial population with an aim to reduce the search time in finding the objective solution. In this local refinement step, a gradient descent algorithm is used once in the starting phase and the elements of the chromosomes are revised by a certain amount. The multiplicative update is used for revising the elements of the matrix and it is illustrated below.

Using Lagrange multiplier method, the rules of updation are defined as follows:

$$H_{a\mu} \leftarrow H_{a\mu} \frac{(W^T)a\mu}{(W^TWH)a\mu}, \quad W_{a\mu} \leftarrow W_{a\mu} \frac{(VH^T)a\mu}{(WHH^T)a\mu} \tag{3}$$

3.4 Objective Function

The prime goal here is minimization of the difference between the non-zero entries of the original matrix V and estimated matrix generated after multiplying the two matrices W and H. Let us consider the dimension of V, W and H are $|W \times H|$, $|W \times K|$ and $|K \times H|$, respectively. Here K is chosen an integer and $K \leq min\{W, H\}$ as it is the rank of the matrix V. The distance between the non-zero cell values of the matrix is denoted by $||V - WH^T||^2$. The simple measure is termed as Error due to the proposed solution.

Besides this, the correlation between the two matrices have also been compared. The correlation value between the two matrices denotes the amount of linear relationship exists in the corresponding cells of both the matrices. Thus maximizing the correlation means the two matrices are close to each other maintaining a robust relationship with each other.

Thus the final objective is to minimize the ratio

$$f = \frac{||V - WH^T||^2}{Corr(V, WH^T) + c}, \tag{4}$$

where $Corr(V, WH^T)$ denotes the correlation between two matrices V and WH. To avoid the indefinite condition for $Corr(V, WH^T) = 0$, a nominal value of $c = 1$ is added in the denominator.

3.5 Selection

This process picks individuals for later breeding incorporated by the notion of "survival of the fittest" often practised as natural selection. In binary tournament selection strategy, it involves running several "tournaments" among a few individuals that are chosen randomly from the initial population. In this current context, the selection is based on binary tournament selection strategy.

3.6 Crossover

Crossover is a probabilistic process in which genetic information between two parent chromosomes are exchanged to produce two child chromosomes. In this article crossover with a "fixed" crossover probability of k_c is used. In traditional GA based algorithms crossover is generally single point or multipoint crossover. In this problem multipoint crossover with a binary mask is performed.

3.7 Mutation

Each chromosome undergoes mutation with a small mutation probability pm. In the mutation operator we have used to add some float value ranging between $0-1$ to each cell value being mutated in a chromosome.

3.8 Elitism

To preserve the best solution of current generation in the search space, the elitism method is used. Thus the current best solution is retained for future generation in order to produce near-optimal solution in reduced time.

4 Empirical Analysis

In this section, we first describe the datasets that we have used for experimental purpose. We have performed experiments on three artificial datasets and one real-life dataset (with different dimensions) to evaluate the performance of the proposed algorithm. The algorithm is compared with various well-known existing NMF methods, namely alternating least square non-negativity matrix with block principle pivoting (ANLS-BPP) [9,10], alternating least square (ANLS) [2], hierarchical least square (HALS) [6], multiplicative update method (MU) [13], and another EM based method (LEE) [12]. The adopted performance metric is the squared error measure between the non-zero elements of original matrix and predicted matrix.

Experiments are performed in MATLAB 2008a and the running environment is an Intel (R) CPU 1.6 GHz machine with 4 GB of RAM running Windows XP Professional.

4.1   Datasets

Three artificial datasets are used for experiments. A short description of the datasets in terms of the dimension and the sparseness is provided in Table 1. The artificial datasets are created with uniformly distributed random values between 0 and 1. Then some of the cells of this matrix are replaced by zeros using a threshold value 0.5. Any threshold value (between 0 and 1) can be chosen to perform the discretization to create the missing entries. Thus in this way the artificial datasets with different dimensions are produced.

One real-life gene expression dataset is used to perform the experiments. This dataset contains gene expression values for samples of prostate tumors. It contains 50 normal tissues and 52 prostate tumor samples. The expression matrix consists of 12,533 number of genes and 102 number of samples. It is publicly available in this website: http://www.biolab.si/supp/bi-cancer/projections/. For our current experimental purpose, we have arbitrarily taken a subset of genes from the dataset that contains 29 genes and 102 number of samples. Some of the gene expression values have been made zeros randomly to make the missing entries. After that, the matrix is made normalized (to make the values between 0 and 1) and the experiment is performed on it. A brief description of the dataset in terms of the dimension and the sparseness is provided in Table 2.

Table 1. Description of the artificial datasets

Dataset	Dimension	Sparsity
Dataset 1	10×20	48.50%
Dataset 2	20×30	47.33%
Dataset 3	50×100	55.16%

Table 2. Description of the real-life dataset

Dataset	Dimension	Sparsity
Dataset 4	102×29	50.98%

4.2   Parameter Settings

In this experimental setting, the length of the chormosomes is fixed for a particular dataset. For the proposed algorithm, the crossover rate is 0.9, mutation rate is 0.01, population size is 40 and number of generations is 1000.

4.3   Comparative Results

For the three artificial datasets and one real-life dataset, the Error values obtained by different matrix factorization methods along with the proposed

method are plotted in Figs. 2, 3, 4 and 5, respectively. To evaluate the result
we have executed all the methods by varying the value of K. It is evident that
in most of the cases, the proposed genetic algorithm based matrix factorization
consistently provides good performance. Moreover, it performs better in all K
values, which demonstrates the utility of the evolutionary framework for developing such type of methods.

It is seen for initial value of K the proposed method is far better than the
other methods. Although the margins of differences decrease if the value of K

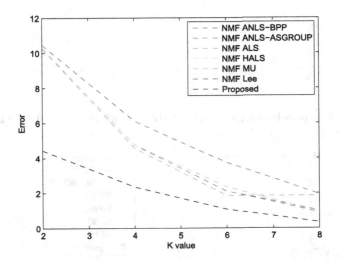

Fig. 2. Comparative plot with other NMF methods are shown for dataset 1.

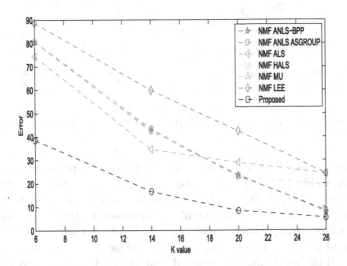

Fig. 3. Comparative plot with other NMF methods are shown for dataset 2.

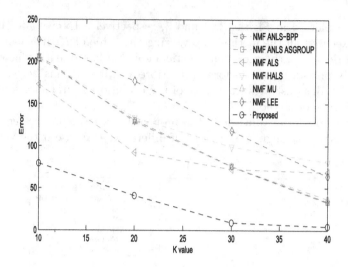

Fig. 4. Comparative plot with other NMF methods are shown for dataset 3.

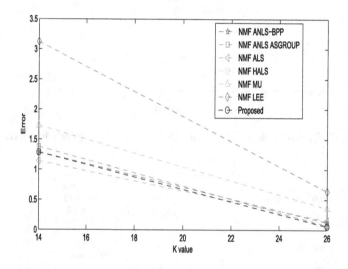

Fig. 5. Comparative plot with other NMF methods are shown for real-life dataset.

is increased further. But it is easily observed that the proposed approach is consistently yielding the best result for most of the K values and it produces more accurate result if the number of generations is allowed to be increased further. In Fig. 5 the graphical plot of the proposed method is shown for the real-life dataset. Here although initially the NMF-LEE method is good for the lower value of K but as K increases the proposed method performs better. With respect to all the methods, it is realized that the performance of NMF-ANLS-BPP is competitively close to that of the proposed method.

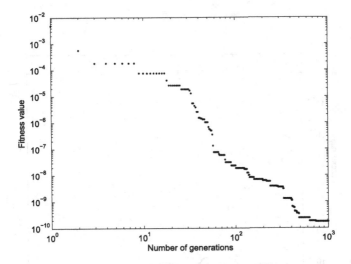

Fig. 6. Generation-wise fitness value for dataset 1.

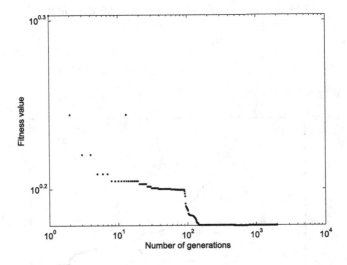

Fig. 7. Generation-wise fitness value for dataset 2.

In Figs. 6, 7, 8, 9 and 10, the generation wise best fitness value of the proposed method is plotted. As elitism is incorporated, therefore it is seen that there is always a tendency to reduce the error in each generation. On the other hand, these curves show the stability of the method as it produces same fitness values for few generations. This also nullifies the condition of premature convergence of the proposed method.

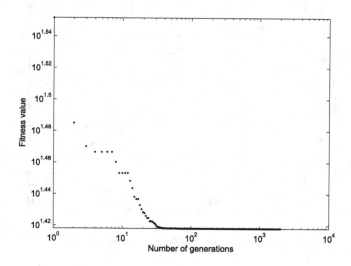

Fig. 8. Generation-wise fitness value for dataset 3.

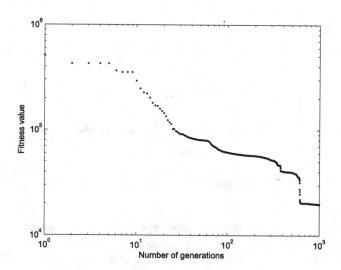

Fig. 9. Generation-wise fitness value for real-life dataset. Here the K value is chosen as 26.

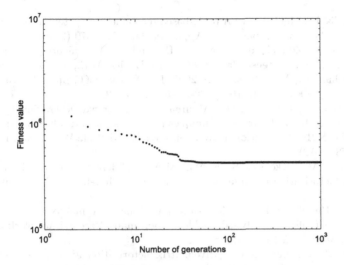

Fig. 10. Generation-wise fitness value for real-life dataset. Here the K value is chosen as 14.

5   Conclusion

In this article, an evolutionary matrix factorization algorithm has been proposed to remove the sparsity problem that arises in the recommender system and crowdsourcing based annotation system. The objectives are to minimize the distance between the non-negative elements of the original matrix and the predicted matrix whereas maximizing the correlations of the non-zero elements between the two matrices. The performance of the proposed method has been compared with that of other existing matrix factorization methods on some artificial and real-life datasets. The results demonstrate the utility of the proposed technique over other existing approaches. In future study, this method can be extended in multi-objective evolutionary framework. Moreover, how quality of the final aggregated crowd opinions is improved further can be investigated by removing sparseness with this method.

References

1. Adomavicius, G., Tuzhilin, A.: Toward the next generation of recommender systems: a survey of the state-of-the-art and possible extensions. IEEE Trans. Knowl. Data Eng. **6**, 734–749 (2005)
2. Berry, M., Browne, M., Langville, A., Pauca, V., Plemmons, R.: Algorithms and applications for approximate nonnegative matrix factorization. Comput. Stat. Data Anal. **52**(2), 155–173 (2007)
3. Brabham, D.C.: Detecting stable clusters using principal component analysis. Methods Mol. Biol. **224**(10), 159–182 (2013)
4. Brunet, J., Tamayo, P., Golub, T., Mesirov, J.: Metagenes and molecular pattern discovery using matrix factorization. Proc. Nat. Acad. Sci. **101**, 1464–1469 (2004)

5. Christidis, K., Mentzas, G.: A topic-based recommender system for electronic marketplace platforms. Expert Syst. Appl. **40**(11), 4370–4379 (2013)
6. Cichocki, A., Zdunek, R., Amari, S.: Hierarchical ALS algorithms for nonnegative matrix and 3D tensor factorization. In: Davies, M.E., James, C.J., Abdallah, S.A., Plumbley, M.D. (eds.) ICA 2007. LNCS, vol. 4666, pp. 169–176. Springer, Heidelberg (2007). doi:10.1007/978-3-540-74494-8_22
7. Demartini, G., Difallah, D.E., Mauroax, C.: Zencrowd: leveraging probabilistic reasoning and crowdsourcing techniques for large scale entity linking. In: Proceedings of the 21st International Conference on World Wide Web, Lyon, France, pp. 469–478 (2012)
8. Friedman, A., Berkovsky, S., Kaafar, M.A.: A differential privacy framework for matrix factorization recommender systems. User Model. User-Adap. Inter. **26**(5), 425–458 (2016)
9. Kim, J., He, Y., Park, H.: Algorithms for nonnegative matrix and tensor factorizations: a unified view based on block coordinate descent framework. J. Global Optim. **58**(2), 285–319 (2014)
10. Kim, J., Park, H.: Fast nonnegative matrix factorization: an active-set-like method and comparisons. SIAM J. Sci. Comput. (SISC) **33**(6), 3261–3281 (2011)
11. Kittur, A., Nickerson, J.V., Bernstein, M., Gerber, E., Shaw, A., Zimmerman, J., Lease, M., Horton, J.: The future of crowd work. In: Proceedings of the CSCW, pp. 1301–1318 (2013)
12. Lee, D., Seung, H.: Learning the parts of objects by non-negative matrix factorization. Nature **401**, 788–791 (1999)
13. Lee, D., Seung, H.: Algorithms for non-negative matrix factorization. Proc. Adv. Neural Inf. Process. Syst. **13**, 556–562 (2001)
14. Lin, C.J.: Projected gradient methods for nonnegative matrix factorization. Neural Comput. **19**(10), 2756–2779 (2007)
15. Luo, X., Liu, H., Gou, G., Xia, Y., Zhu, Q.: A parallel matrix factorization based recommender by alternating stochastic gradient decent. Eng. Appl. Artif. Intell. **25**(7), 1403–1412 (2012)
16. Maulik, U., Bandyopadhyay, S.: Genetic algorithm based clustering technique. Pattern Recogn. **32**, 1455–1465 (2000)
17. Mukhopadhyay, A., Maulik, U., Bandyopadhyay, S.: A survey of multiobjective evolutionary clustering. ACM Comput. Surv. **47**(4), 61:1–61:46 (2015)
18. Paatero, P.: Least squares formulation of robust non-negative factor analysis. Chemometr. Intell. Lab. Syst. **37**(1), 23–35 (1997)
19. Paatero, P., Tapper, U.: Positive matrix factorization: a non-negative factor model with optimal utilization of error estimates of data value. Environmetrics **5**(2), 111–126 (1994)
20. Ross, J., Irani, L., Silberman, M., Zaldivar, A., Tomilson, B.: Who are the crowdworkers? Shifting demographics in mechanical turk. In: Proceedings of the SIGCHI Conference on Human Factors in Computing Systems, pp. 2863–2872 (2010)
21. Xu, W., Liu, X., Gong, Y.: Document clustering based on non-negative matrix factorization. In: Proceedings of the 26th Annual International ACM SIGIR Conference on Research and Development in Information Retrieval, vol. 101, pp. 267–273. ACM Press (2003)

Genetic Algorithm-Based Association Rule Mining Approach Towards Rule Generation of Occupational Accidents

Sobhan Sarkar[1(✉)], Ankit Lohani[2], and Jhareswar Maiti[1]

[1] Department of Industrial and Systems Engineering,
Indian Institute of Technology Kharagpur, Kharagpur, India
sobhan.sarkar@gmail.com
[2] Department of Chemical Engineering,
Indian Institute of Technology Kharagpur, Kharagpur, India

Abstract. Occupational accident is a grave issue for any industry. Therefore, proper analysis of accident data should be carried out to find out the accident patterns so that precautionary measures could be undertaken beforehand. Association rule mining (ARM) technique is mostly used in this scenario to find out the association (i.e., rules) causing accidents. But, among the rules generated by ARM, all are not useful. To handle this kind of problem, a new model ARM and genetic algorithm (GA) has been proposed in this study. The model automatically selects the optimal *Support* and *Confidence* value to generate useful rules. Out of 1285 data obtained from a steel industry in India, eleven useful rules are generated using this proposed method. The findings from this study have the potential to help the management take the better decisions to mitigate the occurrence of accidents.

Keywords: Occupational accidents · Steel industry · Association rule mining · Genetic algorithm

1 Introduction

In today's world, advancements in industrialization has led to the establishment of industries and workplaces. In this highly competitive atmosphere, every industry has a number of problems, one of them being industrial accidents. Various circumstances and events lead to occupational accidents in the industry. From prior study, it has been realized that most of these accidents are due to poor safety standards, non—compliance/availability of the standard operating procedures, health of workers and poor machine conditions. Advancements in technology and automations in industries have promoted different types of accidents. Thus, it is required to address the loss of lives and economic resources caused by these occupational accidents. Various studies have been conducted to study the nature of occupational accidents to suggest the ways of preventing

© Springer Nature Singapore Pte Ltd. 2017
J.K. Mandal et al. (Eds.): CICBA 2017, Part II, CCIS 776, pp. 517–530, 2017.
DOI: 10.1007/978-981-10-6430-2_40

them. With proper analysis of past data, these accidents can be controlled if they can be predicted.

At steel plants, the nature of work pattern, tasks and environment are complex and diverse in nature. Additionally, the transitory nature of factory workforce and workplace makes it more dangerous and prone to accidents. The steel manufacturing process involves the use of high technology and physical labor, making safety management a complicated task. Safety performance has largely been measured and driven by lagging indicators (including injuries, illnesses and fatalities). Different strategies to study the pattern of accidents have been implemented in industries with a view to reduce the number of accidents. This has been very helpful in designing safety standards for the industries. The basis of this analysis is collecting of facts, classifying them, and reporting them precisely in a timely manner. Usually, incident occurs as a culmination of various factors. Some events in the past might also lead to an accident. Hence, various machine learning approach used to identify key association rules between relevant factors is useful to deal with this kind of problem. The association rules can relate various factors which are significant in the occurrence of accidents. One can derive safety measures from this relation to reduce the accidents in future.

In this work, association rule analysis is applied using Genetic Algorithm (GA) to determine a strong level of association among various influencing factors. ARM can give many rules that are irrelevant and needs a manual input of threshold values of *Support* and *Confidence*. But, when implemented with GA, ARM outputs only significant rules with less time complexity and without manually putting any threshold values. The result of this analysis can be used to provide managarial suggestions to the steel plants to take preventive measures from the rules for a safer working environment.

The rest of the paper is organized as follows: Sect. 2 presents a brief literature review on occupational accident analysis using ARM approach, which is followed by research gap and contribution of the present study. In Sect. 3, the methods(i.e. ARM and GA) have been briefly described. A case study from a steel plant has been considered for implementation of the proposed method and is described in Sect. 4. Results and Discussions are illustrated in Sect. 5. Finally, in Sect. 6, conclusion with future scopes is presented.

2   Literature Review

In occupational accident analysis, various methods have been proposed, most of them being parametric models like multivariate models - logistic regression in [1,2]. [3] used the Poisson regression, segmental point process [17], and negative binomial regression techniques in traffic accident analysis. Since there are predetermined assumptions in these models, they give low prediction accuracy. Therefore, researchers developed various non - parametric models like classification and regression tree (CART) model in [4]. A tree-based logistic regression approach for the work zone casualty risk assessment is presented by Cheng et al. [5]. However, these non - parametric models suffer from a great disadvantage of over-fitting. Some studies recently introduced optimization techniques used for parameter tuning of the base algorithm like grid search-based support vector machines (GS-SVM), GA-based SVM [14], GA-CART [15] in occupational accident analysis scenario. Along with these studies, some text mining based approaches have been developed for accident occurrence prediction [16, 18].

Association Rule Mining is another famous non-parametric model for safety analysis overcoming the aforementioned problem. Verma et al. worked on finding the accident patterns in a steel plant using association rule mining of incident parameters derieved from investigation reports [6]. Using 10 features it proposed safety actions to be implemented by the company. They pointed out that SOP (Standard Operating Procedure) non-compliance was an important reason for property damage cases. Dehuri et al. in a similar vein, made a similar identification that the root causes of accidents in steel industries are slip/trip/fall (STF), collision/dashing, inadequacy of standard operating procedures (SOPs) and unsafe acts by workers in the workplaces [7].

In case of association rule mining (ARM), there are too many rules generated for a given threshold of parameters. Hence, the analysis becomes cumbersome for management and some major problems are not provided significant importance. Optimization of the model hence becomes a necessity. [8] proposed a rule mining method called multi objective genetic algorithm (MOGA). However, they concentrated only on developing the algorithm and tested it on various datasets. The outcomes of the algorithm were a set of non-dominated solutions. But this method was slow, so, they improved the performance by parallel processing GA (genetic algorithm). In 2008, Dehuri et al., used crossover and mutation methods to modify the solutions using their elitist multi-objective genetic algorithm (EMOGA) [11]. They used Pareto-based rank for fitness evaluation of chromosomes. Some researches were carried out on developing algorithms for rule mining that was based on GA without providing the value of minimum *Support* [9,10]. They used relative *Confidence* as their fitness function and implemented it using frequent pattern (FP) tree. Qodmanan et al. proposed multi objective ARM with GA without specifying threshold values for *Support* and *Confidence* which worked faster than other heuristic approaches [12]. In one of the latest works, Cococcioni et al. presented a semi-supervised learning-aided evolutionary method in [13]. Consistency constraint has te be met in the pair of classifiers designed, between a worker's risk perception with respect to a task and the level of caution of the same worker for the same task.

In all the aforementioned works, ARM technique has been successfully used as a tool in the analysis of accidents. Some of the researchers used variety of optimization techniques to enhance the process. However, to the best of authors' knowledge, similar work in safety analysis has not been done till date. Thus, our present work aims to bridge this gap in occupational accident literature to ensure a safer working environment for the workers.

2.1 Challenge

Based on the review of literature, it has been identified that the research using association rule mining approach on occupational accident domain is very less. Moreover, some studies have also reported the difficulty and have imposed a challenge in handling the huge number of rules generated from ARM approach as this method is more sensitive towards the selection of parameters like *Support* and *Confidence*. Therefore, optimal rule generation is required through proper optimization of parameters of ARM, which is not reported in occupational accident research so far.

2.2 Proposed Work

The present study proposed a new method i.e., GA optimized ARM for the rule generation of incident cases in steel industry. To the best of the authors' knowledge, none of the previous studies have reported this kind of analysis so far in occupational accident domain.

3 Methods Used

In this section, the methods ARM and GA have been described briefly. The proposed methodological flowchart is depicted in Fig. 1. It shows the steps from collection of raw data, pre-processing, feature selection to final analysis. Thereafter, in ARM, which parameters are optimized by GA, has been implemented on the pre-processed data which gives the optimal rules describing the incident outcomes. The entire process of ARM and GA is described below.

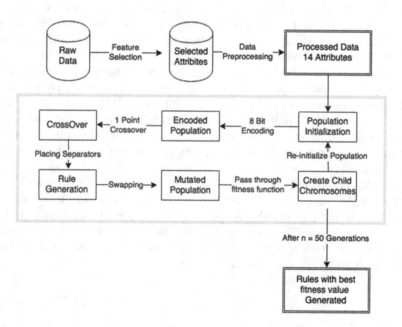

Fig. 1. Proposed methodological flowchart of GA-ARM approach.

3.1   Association Rule Mining

Introduced as an unsupervised approach, Association rule mining (ARM) was used to find patterns in large data sets. The method derived gets its identity from a method where there is a set of transactions from a shop and each transaction is considered a market basket consisting a set of items purchased. A particular item may or may not be a part of the transaction. So, there lies a pattern of rules in the form of a transaction. Apriori algorithm is used to mine these rules from the data set. Let I be a universe of items. A data set D is a set of transactions $T_1, \ldots, T_n$, where each transaction is a set of items from I. An item set X is a subset of I. The frequency of X, freq(X), is the number of transactions T in D for which X is a subset of T, then the *Support* can be calculated from the Eq. (1):

$$Supp(X) = \frac{freq(X)}{|D|} \tag{1}$$

An association rule has two parts- antecedent (denoted by X) and consequent (denoted by Y). Former part is an item found in the data while latter is an item that is found in combination of the earlier one. The intersection of the two parts is a null set. The *Support* of the rule is denoted by supp(X U Y). The *Confidence* of the rule is a ratio of how often it is correct to how often it applies and can be expressed as Eq. (2):

$$Conf(XUY) = \frac{supp(XUY)}{supp(X)} \tag{2}$$

Lift is the ratio of *Confidence* to Expected *Confidence*. It can be expressed as Eq. (3). Among association rules if the value of *Lift* is greater than 1.0, it implies that the relationship between the antecedent and the consequent is more significant than would be expected if the two parts were independent. Higher value of *Lift* denotes higher significance.

$$Lift = \frac{supp(XUY)}{supp(X) * supp(Y)} \tag{3}$$

Association rule mining algorithm is used to find a set of rules which are above a minimum value of *Support* and *Confidence* also known as threshold values. Firstly, all item sets having a *Support* value greater than the threshold value are enlisted as frequent. Then, association rules are generated from these item sets and only those rules are kept that have a *Confidence* value greater than the threshold *Confidence* value. The principle behind apriori is that if an item set is frequent, then all of its subsets must also be frequent. The total of $2^I - 1$ item sets can be generated from I items in the dataset, hence, the step to find the frequent item sets is the more complex than other parts.

3.2 Genetic Algorithm

A genetic algorithm (GA) is a heuristic search algorithm that is inspired from the process of natural selection proposed by Charles Darwin. It is used to generate useful solution to optimization and search problems to find a global optimum in a defined phase space. Before we proceed to apply GA, it is necessary to *encode* the dataset in any format, such as the bit encoding. The three fundamental principles of the algorithm are: **(a) Selection** - In this primary step, individual genomes are chosen from the population for further steps; An *initial population* is generated in the beginning of the procedure. The selection for further generations are done on the basis of their fitness; **(b) Crossover** - This genetic operator is used to generate the next generation of population based of the fitness calculated using the fitness function. This *fitness function* measures the quality of the solution. Since the best chromosomes from the earlier generation is used, the average fitness is greater than the last generation; and **(c) Mutation** - This operator maintains genetic diversity among various generations. In mutation, the solution may entirely change from previous solution. This step overcome the problem if the fitness value at some point is stuck at the local minima.

A combination of these two algorithms is used in this paper for occupations accident analysis in steel industry as described in the next section.

4 Case Study

4.1 Problem Statement and Motivation

The case company is facing a serios issue of occupation accidents occuring at its workplaces. The cost of human live is immense and of utmost importance. Instead of having all precautionary measures, the incidents have been taking place in an uncontrolled way. Cause-effect analyses, though carried out, has not been successful enough to check the occurrences of accidents. Thus, accident patterns in terms of association rules are necessary to be identified so that it can be used to take several precautionary steps. Under these circumstances, application of ARM is realized to be of great value to provide the best managerial suggestions.

4.2 Data Collection and Data Types

The data set for analysis has been collected from a steel plant in India from 24 different divisions in the span of three years (2010–2013). For our analysis, we have used 1285 data points or observations from a particular department of a certain division of the plant.

The data set consists of categorical attributes and each of them has multiple classes. The attributes used in analysis have been enlisted in Table 1 along with the number of classes each feature possesses. They are -

Table 1. Attributes and their corresponding number of classes in the data set used in the study.

Attribute	Number of classes
Injury Type	8
Primary Cause	21
Status	6
Working Condition	3
Machine Condition	3
Observation Type	4
Employee Type	3
Serious Process Incident Score (SPI)	3
Injury Potential Score(IP)	3
Equipment Damage Score(EDS)	3
Safety Standards	18
Incident Category	2
Incident Type	6
Standard Operating Procedure (SOP)	3

(i) **Primary Cause** - This attribute implies the causes behind the accident. There are 21 possible causes of any incident described in the dataset - Crane Dashing, Dashing/Collision, Derailment, Electrical Flash, Energy Isolation, Equipment Machinery Damage, Fire/Explosion, Gas Leakage, Hot Metals, Hydraulic/Pneumatic, Lifting Tools Tackles, Material Handling, Medical Ailment, Occupational Illness, Process Incidents, Rail,Road Incident, Run Over, Skidding, Slip/Trip/Fall, Structural Integrity.

(ii) **Status** - This represents the current state of the investigation of incident case. It may be either close or open.

(iii) **Working Condition** - This attribute implies the condition of work which may be Single Working(SW), Group Working(GW) or Not applicable (Napp).

(iv) **Machine Condition** - Machine failure is a signicant cause of accidents which can be avoided. It represents the machine condition after the incident, i.e. if Idle machine condition(MI), the machine was working while accident occured or Not applicable(Napp) if the accident was not around any machine

(v) **Incident Type** - The accident can occur because of human error or as a reason of an inherent problem with the process. Thus, it can be classified as - Behavorial (Beh); Process (Pro)

(vi) **Employee Type** - There are two types of workers in the workplaces. They have different roles and any accident depends on the work they are performing. On site, Contractor, Employee are the two employee types;

(vii) **Serious Process Incident Score (SPI)** - The incident observed is scored on the basis of severity in three levels, namely - lowspi, mediumspi and highspi

(viii) **Injury Potential Score(IP)** - The injury caused to the causalitites are also categorized in three levels - lowip, mediumip and highip to classify the seriousness of the accident

(ix) **Equipment Damage Score(EDS)** - Many accidents involve damage to machines and equipments too. Based on the level of damage caused to these machines, every accident is associated with an equipment damage score as - loweds, mediumeds and higheds

(x) **Observation Type** - Various safety standards are defined for every activity in these workplaces to maintain a definite protocol of safety. These are categorized as - Unsafe act unsafe condition(UAUC), Unsafe Act(UA), Unsafe condition(UC)

(xi) **Injury Type** - This attribute indicates the type of injury incurred. It has following types - Fatal, First Aid, IOW, No injury, Normal, Injury, Serious Injury.

(xii) **Incident Category** - The incident has been reported as - Property Damage(PrDm), NearMiss(NM) or Injury (Inj) with their meaning as their name depicts;

(xiii) **Standard Operating Procedure (SOP)** - Every process and activity in an industry has a SOP associated with it and are categorized as available but not followed (SANF), available and followed (SF) while in some cases it might mot be required or cannot be proposed like SOP not required (SNR), SOP not available (SNA).

(xiv) **Safety Standards** - Industries follow wide range of safety techniques but still incidents occur. So they form an important criterion in the study to identify how resourceful they have been in preventing accidents. There could be various practices like - barricading, confined space, dismantling, electrical safety, excavation, fire safety, gas cutting & welding, material handling, mines safety, positive isolations, personal protective equipment (PPE), process safety, road safety, wiring, tools & equipment and work permit system.

4.3   Data Pre-processing

In this stage, data cleaning involving missing data handling, outlier detection, and data reduction by feature selection have been done. Due to the limitation of the page, total steps of data pre-processing task have not been included in the scope of the present study. Once data has been pre-processed, it was encoded for application of GA.

4.4   Encoding

First of all, dataset is encoded to initiate the experimentation of GA. This encoding is used in our solution is binary encoding scheme. Any rule, that is treated

Table 2. Schematic arrangement of a chromosome.

A1	A2	A3	A4	A5	A6	A7	A8	A9	A10	A11	A12	A13	A14

as chromosome, is encoded in the format as in Table 2, containing 14 genes per chromosome per rule.

A list of 15 items can be used to describe a rule. Out of this 15, 14 genes are classes from the different features enlisted in Table 1 and the last one is a separator that is placed somewhere in between. This separator will separate antecedent from consequent. Any attribute can either be a part of the rule or not. If it is a part of the rule then it can have one out of the multiple classes it has over the whole dataset. Table 1 shows the list of 14 attributes that has been used in the analysis and different classes each attribute can have.

For example, injury potential is one of the features. It has three different classes namely lowip, mediumip, highip. Say, 3 bits are used to encode this feature. Then, we have $2^3 = 8$ combinations of bits. We use three of them to encode the classes of injury potential, namely 000 (lowip), 001 (mediumip), 010 (highip) respectively. In any rule, it can have one of the three values encoded in binary form, or it might be a null value, i.e., it is not a part of the rule. The remaining 5 combination of 3 bits 100, 110, 101, 011, and 111 are assigned a value phi (meaning - null). The class phi signifies that this feature will not be a part of the generated rule during Roulette Wheel selection. The probability of selection of a particular class is depicted in Table 3.

Table 3. Selection Probability of various classes.

Injury Potential Score	Probability of selection for rule
Lowips	1/8
Mediumips	1/8
Highips	1/8
Phi	5/8

Once the data has been encoded, it is ready to implement with the three fundamental steps of GA. Initially, a random set of initial population is chosen from the dataset.

4.5   Initial Population Generation

The 14 genes or attributes are individually encoded using the schematic described in the previous section. We select the size of initial population for our analysis. Hence, our initial population consists of 500 rules/chromosomes. Value of each attribute in every chromosome is selected using Roulette Wheel

Selection; for example, Injury Potential Score depicted in Table 3. Each gene in a chromosome has a significant probability of not being a part of the rule. These probabilities have been decided by the number of bits used for its encoding. If there are more values for an attribute, it has less *Support* and it will be a part of less frequent itemset. For example, primary cause can take 21 different values and its *Support* will be less as compared to an attribute with less diversity. Hence, probability of its existence in the rule will be less as compared to the other one. This population undergoes crossover among itself and a new population or rules are generated.

4.6 Crossover

It is one of the three operators used in genetic algorithm. After generation of initial population, we have 14 genes in each chromosome denoted by respective number of bits as shown in Table 4. There can be two strategies for crossover. We can use *point crossovers* over the whole chromosome. This method has a drawback. Every gene will not have proper crossover and a particular combination of gene is retained and it is simply repositioned in the list. Thus, after few generations, offsprings similar to the parents are generated and the whole point of having diversity in genetic algorithm fails. Hence, we opted for strategy two. In this, we take two chromosomes and operate a 1-point crossover for every gene. This method ensures proper diversity and creation of new rules over every iteration. The two strategies can be explained through Tables 4, 5 and 6.

Table 4. Before crossover of a selected rule.

1001	100010	1100	010	011	000	111	101	110	011	101101	10	1101	110

Table 5. Crossover strategy 1: About middle point of chromosome.

101	110	011	101101	10	1101	110	1001	100010	1100	010	011	000	111

Table 6. Crossover strategy 2: about mid-point of each gene in chromosome.

110	101	011	011110	01	0111	011	0110	100001	0011	001	011	000	111

Placing Separators for Rule Generation: In this step, a separator is placed at one of the random positions in the chromosome generated after crossover. All the attributes which got a value phi after crossover, are dropped at this stage and a rule showing (antecedent → consequent) is left. Thus, rules generated from the previous population are ready. The unfit rules are then segregated from them using the fitness function (see Eq. (4)).

Selection of Population for Next Generation: Association rule mining using genetic algorithm gives many rules. Many of them are insignificant because they have less *Support* for the itemset or less *Confidence* for the rule. We eliminate these weak offsprings by defining a new fitness function that has been described in the paper Qodmanan et Nasiri [12]. The function is

$$fitness = \frac{(1 + supp(XUY))^2}{1 + supp(X)} \tag{4}$$

In this equation, sup(X U Y) is the *Support* of X Y and supp(X) is the *Support* of antecedent part of it. We move toward the third fundamental step of GA - mutation, to prevent the algorithm from stucking at any local optima.

4.7 Mutation

This operator is used to create diversity in the population from the initial population, with the use of this method, such as swapping, we can change the *Confidence* of the rule. We can do the same by swapping the position of separators in the two genes. The algorithm was applied taking an initial population of 1000 chromosomes and rules over 50 generations were generated.

Table 7. Rules generated using GA-ARM approach.

Antecedent	Consequent	Confidence	Lift
PRI, SW, lowspi	NM	1	1.46
SW, UAUC	highip	0.705	0.867
MI, mediumip	Loweds	0.1	19.32
SI	Beh	0.625	0.761
UAUC, contractor	Mediumip	0.33	2.9
Close, SW, MI, mediumip	SANF	0.625	1.6309
UAUC, mediumspi	SNR	0.25	1.98
EI, Pro	SNR	0.14	1.133
Mediumip, loweds	PrDm	1.0	35.69
MI, UA, Contractor	Lowspi, beh	1.0	1.221
Napp	Mediumip	0.117	1.02

5   Results and Discussion

In the present study, GA-based ARM method has been applied in order to generate rules for the occurrence of occupational accidents in steel plant. To start with GA, encoding of the data set has been performed which is followed by the sequential steps i.e., initial population generation, crossover, mutation, and finally ARM. The average of fitness values of all rules for a given generation is calculated and plotted against the iteration number. The average fitness value of all rules in a particular generation has been plotted against the generation number. Figure 2 clearly depicts the output. The best among the 50 generations is selected for analysis. For a particular run, the fifth generation showed the best fitness value for the given generation. The following rules (see Table 7) were deduced.

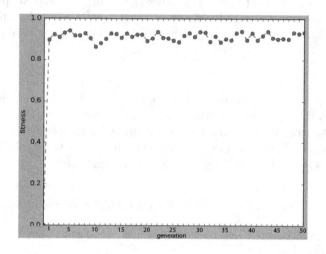

Fig. 2. Graph of generations vs average fitness obtained from GA-ARM approach.

The generated rule [MI, mediumip → loweds] signifies that for accidents that occurred in case of idle machine condition (MI) with average injury potential (mediumip), the equipment damage score (loweds) was also less. From the rule [mediumip, loweds → PrDm], it can be concluded that there are high chances that accidents involving average injury potential (mediumip) and low equipment damage score (loweds) will have high property damage (PrDm). One of the rules, [SI → Beh] depicts the higher risk of having behavioral (beh) accidents with primary cause being structural integrity (SI). Next rule, [Close, SW, MI, mediumip → SANF], tells that in single working conditions (SW) and idle machine (MI) conditions has significant injury potential index (mediumip) even though the cases are closed because of non-availability of SOPs (SANF).

6   Conclusion

From the analysis of rules, it can be inferred that steel industry under study is still not capable of handling hazards successfully to avoid major accidents. The rules that have been derived after this analysis depicts that injury potential of accidents is significant. Cases of unsafe act and unsafe condition (UAUC) are found to be the reason for most of cases.

This work can be further extended to a comprehensive comparision with various other state of art optimization methods, like particle swarm optimization (PSO), ant colony optimization (ACO) etc. The proposed method can be further tuned for a few more values of crossover and mutation probabilities for a intuitive analysis of GA over ARM. Another important future direction can be prediction-based collective class classification rule mining. Structured association map (SAM), another powerful visualization technique, could be used for better visualization of the association rules. Another future direction can be the generation of high-utility item sets from the occupational accident database which could provide potential benefit to the safety manager of any organization.

Acknowledgement. The authors are thankful to the safety personnel for their kind support from the collection of data to the final evaluation phase of the project.

References

1. Bedard, M., Guyatt, G.H., Stones, M.J., Hirdes, J.P.: The independent contribution of driver, crash, and vehicle characteristics to driver fatalities. Accid. Anal. Prev. **34**(6), 717–727 (2002)
2. Li, Y., Bai, Y.: Development of crash-severity-index models for the measurement of work zone risk levels Accid. Anal. Prev. **40**(5), 1724–1731 (2008)
3. Wong, S.C., Sze, N.N., Li, Y.C.: Contributory factors to traffic crashes at signalized intersections in Hong Kong Accid. Anal. Prev. **39**(6), 1107–1113 (2007)
4. Chang, L., Wang, H.: Analysis of traffic injury severity: an application of nonparametric classification tree techniques. Accid. Anal. Prev. **34**(5), 1019–1027 (2006)
5. Weng, J., Meng, Q., Wang, D.Z.: Tree-Based logistic regression approach for work zone casualty risk assessment. Risk Anal. **33**(3), 493–504 (2013)
6. Verma, A., Khan, S.D., Maiti, J., Krishna, O.B.: Identifying patterns of safety related incidents in a steel plant using association rule mining of incident investigation reports. Saf. Sci. **70**, 89–98 (2014)
7. Cheng, C.-W., Yao, H.-Q., Wu, T.-C.: Applying data mining techniques to analyze the causes of major occupational accidents in the petrochemical industry. J. Loss Prev. Process Ind. **26**, 1269–1278 (2013)
8. Dehuri, B., Ghosh, A.: Muti objective association rule mining using genetic algorithm. Inf. Sci. **163**, 123–133 (2004)
9. Yan, X., Zhang, C., Zhang, S.: Genetic algorithm-based strategy for identifying association rules without specifying actual minimum support. Expert Syst. Appl. **36**(2), 3066–3076 (2009)
10. Cheng, C.W., Lin, C.C., Leu, S.S.: Use of association rules to explore cause effect relationships in occupational accidents in the Taiwan construction industry. Saf. Sci. **48**(4), 436–444 (2010)
11. Dehuri, S., Patnaik, S., Ghosh, A., Mall, R.: Application of elitist multiobjective genetic algorithm for classification rule generation. Soft Comput. **8**(1), 477–487 (2008)
12. Qodmanan, H.R., Nasiri, M., Minaei-Bidgoli, B.: Multi objective association rule mining with genetic algorithm without specifying minimum support and minimum confidence. Expert Syst. Appl. **38**(1), 288–298 (2011)

13. Cococcioni, M., Lazzerini, B., Pistolesi, F.: A semi-supervised learning-aided evolutionary approach to occupational safety improvement. In: IEEE Congress on Evolutionary Computation (2016)
14. Sarkar, S., Vinay, S., Pateshwari, V., Maiti, J.: Study of optimized SVM for incident prediction of a steel plant in India. In: 2016 IEEE Annual India Conference (INDICON), pp. 1–6. IEEE, December 2016
15. Sarkar, S., Patel, A., Madaan, S., Maiti, J.: Prediction of occupational accidents using decision tree approach. In: 2016 IEEE Annual India Conference (INDICON), pp. 1–6. IEEE, December 2016
16. Sarkar, S., Vinay, S., Maiti, J.: Text mining based safety risk assessment and prediction of occupational accidents in a steel plant. In: 2016 International Conference on Computational Techniques in Information and Communication Technologies (ICCTICT), pp. 439–444. IEEE, March 2016
17. Gautam, S., Maiti, J., Syamsundar, A., Sarkar, S.: Segmented point process models for work system safety analysis. Saf. Sci. **95**, 15–27 (2017)
18. Brown, D.E.: Text mining the contributors to rail accidents. IEEE Trans. Intell. Transp. Syst. **17**(2), 346–355 (2016)

Intelligent Generation of Flavor Preserving Alternative Recipes for Individuals with Dietary Restrictions

Somosmita Mitra[1]($\boxtimes$) and Pabitra Mitra[2]

[1] Department of Computer Science and Engineering,
Institute of Engineering and Management, Kolkata 700091, India
somosmita.mitra@gmail.com
[2] Department of Computer Science and Engineering,
Indian Institute of Technology, Kharagpur, India
pabitra@cse.iitkgp.ernet.in

Abstract. Many diseases lead to treatments which bring forth certain restrictions in diet and quantity of consumption of the patients. Our target has been to work around these restrictions to generate a novel approach for creating a balance in taste and flavor while maintaining the nutritional properties within the given upper bound. The resulting product is not only a flavor-wise approximate supplement of the item to be replaced but is also created from ingredients which are derived from the list of food items permitted for consumption by a particular patient suffering from a certain disease. There is a two layer selection procedure which chooses the substitutes from the given list based on the flavor profile of the item whose supplement is to be found, with the cut-off being designed on the basis of the calories, carbohydrates, sugars and fats permitted for the patient being considered to consume. Our results have shown to predict near-identical flavor profiles with significantly lower values of calories, fats, sugars or carbohydrates as per the requirement of the patient. The output has been validated by experienced food technologist.

Keywords: Flavor prediction · Forward selection · Stepwise regression · Food supplement generation · Machine learning

1 Introduction

Advancement of medication and knowledge has led to tremendous progress in the fields of disease discovery and treatment. From the early onset of time nutrition has played an important role throughout society in shaping the longevity period and health of individuals. Diseases which were life threatening and sometimes fatal have now been reduced to being easily controllable through the use of appropriate medication and following of a healthy diet. As human beings we are inclined to crave for all things forbidden. Hence, once a person is diagnosed with

© Springer Nature Singapore Pte Ltd. 2017
J.K. Mandal et al. (Eds.): CICBA 2017, Part II, CCIS 776, pp. 531–539, 2017.
DOI: 10.1007/978-981-10-6430-2_41

a diet restrictive disease it often leads to a certain degree of dissatisfaction in taste and appetite. The patient wants to taste something which he/she did enjoy previously, but now due to the restrictive measures, is unable to do so.

The proposed algorithm is an intelligent, new approach which utilizes forward stepwise regression [1] at its base to develop a unique combination of items permitted for consumption, depending on the flavor profile of the item being replaced, to generate the best possible approximate flavor profile while keeping in memory the nutritional data. An important part of machine based substitute detection is using statistical methods to create new ingredient combinations which mimic the essential flavor properties of the initial item to be replaced. Human flavor perception is very complicated, involving a variety of external sensory stimuli and internal states. The taste of a particular item at a given time depends not only on the five basic flavor properties but also the surrounding conditions, sensation of smell, texture, memories associated with a certain dish and more such features which differ from individual to individual. These are nearly impossible for a different individual to predict, let alone a machine.

What is important to highlight here is that the paper does not offer a method for individuals to taste their grandmother's special casserole without the ingredients which made it special in the first place. The aim is to offer an alternative to people suffering from dietary restrictions. For example a diabetic wanting to taste a particular sweet dish A, can be helped by generating a flavor profile as similar to that of A without exceeding the calorie and sugar specifications which could potentially wreak havoc in the blood glucose level and invoke unsolicited damage.

Research in related areas have been reported in literature. Recipe recommendation system has been developed [2] using combination of ingredient networks and nutrition information, with the network capturing the relationship between the ingredients. A method for finding replaceable materials in cooking recipe texts was designed [3] by extraction of cooking actions followed by measurement of their similarity. A data-driven analysis of recipes from Medieval Europe was undertaken [4] to investigate the flavor pairing hypothesis and generate inferences about the evolution of culinary arts. A flavor network was introduced [5] to capture the flavor compounds shared by culinary ingredients, towards a systematic understanding of culinary practice.

Our approach, on the other hand, uses forward selection in the stepwise regression search mechanism of machine learning to generate the design. It works on the initial set of data with a specific flavor profile, consisting of sweet, sour, bitter, salt and savory (henceforth known as X), along with the health detrimental properties of calories, carbohydrates, sugars and fats (referred to as Y, from here onwards). We select each item from the list of permissible items and check if its addition to the generated substitution chain maintains the Y properties of the chain to be less than or equal to the Y properties of the item being replaced. We add it to our list if it upholds all criteria, compare with the X properties of the item being substituted and progress. Working with forward stepwise selection we replace items using the X properties and check for the most near approximate between the Y feature approved items using the X properties as parameters. The resulting combination is the best suitable approximate substitute chain of the product we want to replace, as validated by experienced food technologist.

The rest of the article is organized as follows. Section 2 outlines the problem which has motivated us to work on this algorithm. The data used in this experiment was hard to procure in our required format, and the sources used are described in Sect. 3. The proposed algorithm for the problem is presented in Sect. 4, along with a step by step analysis of procedure. The case study in Sect. 5 serves to demonstrate the efficacy of our approach, along with some results. Finally Sect. 6 concludes the paper and discusses the applications of the implementation of the proposed algorithm.

2   Problem Description

Mortality rates have declined at a relatively constant rate of approximately 1 to 2 percent per year since 1900. Medical care and improvement in living conditions are attributed as the prime factors responsible for the changes in the ability to avoid and withstand infectious diseases; which ultimately lead to reducing mortality. With the advent of time the number of people suffering from disease leading to a restrictions-imposed lifestyle has increased to the extent that approximately one in every three people are found to suffer from some form of an ailment.

Even though lifestyle changes are mandated by the physician, we as human beings tend to be drawn towards certain dishes which have been our favorites for a long time, yet are unable to consume due to the prognosis. Modern technology permits the production of gluten free, dairy free, sugar free food items which cater to the health conscious, people with specific religious beliefs and those diagnosed with diet-restrictive diseases. What is observable in these products is that most of them do not taste the same way as the prototype they have been modeled after. This leads to the building of an emotional discontentment and craving for what the physician has essentially prescribed to avoid.

It is at such a junction that our proposed algorithm comes into play. We utilize the fundamental properties of flavor to find that product combination which, while necessarily lying within the limits of calories, carbohydrates, sugars and fats, permissible for consumption, generates the best fit flavor profile. On entering the products suitable for consumption, the algorithm fetches each product's flavor profile and nutritional values profile in its standard volume. The food item to be substituted has its own specific nutrient data and flavor data, which on being fed into the algorithm, generates and displays its replacement. We, however, cannot ignore the fact that human beings associate taste and flavor perceived with surrounding conditions, sensation of smell, texture, memories associated with a certain dish along with the fundamental flavors being considered here. The machine based approach may not be the perfect replacement of the human based method of physically generating all combinations of permissible ingredient of various quantities. On varying the weights of the initial dataset from a small quantity to larger values, one can generate all possible concoctions using the machine learning based approach. Considering the involvement of time and the physical stamina involved in each process, the machine learning based approach is found to be more convenient and converges to the best suitable result faster. Thereby, the result produced may not always be the perfect substitute for a product but as far as feasibility and taste goes, the best approximate replacement will be generated in all cases.

3   Data Sources

This study uses two different datasets which deal with the various aspects of food flavor and properties. The first chart is an ingredient-wise break-up consisting of calories, carbohydrates, fats and sugars, while the second is a flavor profile which consists of fractional values ranging from 0 to 5 in each column of sweet, sour, bitter, salt and savory. Each level corresponds to a particular degree of presence, 1 signifies "very little", 2 stands for "somewhat present", 3 is used to represent "present", 4 shows the flavor is "pronounced", 5 signifies the "bold and intense" sensation of the particular flavor. An excerpt of the ingredient nutrient statistic chart is shown. All data values, except for calories, specified in the nutrient charts used throughout this paper are measured in grams (see Table 1).

Table 1. A sample Ingredient Nutrient statistic chart

Ingredient	Calories	Carbohydrates	Fats	Sugars
RED APPLE	130	34	0	25
AVOCADO	50	3	4.5	0
BANANA	110	30	0	19
BLUE-CRAB	100	0	1	0
ICEBERG-LETTUCE	10	2	0	2
TOMATOES	25	5	0	3
TUNA	130	0	1.5	0

The data has been taken from the food charts present in www.marshallsplan.com and standardized over specific quantities. In this case, the Red Apple quantity considered is 242 g/8 oz, for Banana it is 126 g/4.5 oz, Blue Crab and Tuna nutrition values have been measured at 34 g/3 oz, Iceberg lettuce at 89 g/3.2 oz and finally Tomatoes at 148 g/5.3 oz. The flavor profile, although sourced from www.cooksmarts.com/articles/study-flavor-profiles/, is harder to obtain and simplify. The flavor approximate value is taken as a weighted average of ingredient quantities used to identify the flavor features, so that it generates a uniform distribution with better suitability for approximation. At each stage the flavor level perceived in an ingredient also depends on the particular product and, thus, the generalized flavor specific level value occurs in ranges. The ranges are then utilized to calculate the weighted average range values, and the final data set is generated. An example of the flavor profile lies below (see Table 2).

Table 2. A sample flavor profile

Item	Sweet	Sour	Salt	Bitter	Savory
CHENIN-BLANC WHITE WINE	1–2	3–4	1–2	1	2–3
SYRAH RED WINE	2.3–3.4	2–3	3–4	3	1–2

Calculations of similarity of flavor profiles are done using this final dataset.

4 Proposed Approach

We use the theory of the second best where the best product, being which the patient has been clinically advised to avoid, fails to satisfy the optimality conditions of calories, carbohydrates, fats and sugars. Thus, it is to be substituted with the second best item or a combination of items flavor-wise. This principle is utilized to generate a flavor profile which falls within the limit of permitted calories, carbohydrates, fats and sugars while maintaining as similar a taste palette as deemed feasible.

Our algorithm deals with two data sets which are inbuilt in the model. The first data set deals with the nutrient information, while the second deals with the sweet, sour, bitter, salty and savory scores from 0 to 5 for a specific taste. When the product whose substitutes are sought is entered, the algorithm utilizes the flavor scores of the product to generate a chain of items from the inherent data sets which has the best approximate flavor profile to that of the product being replaced.

The approach of our algorithm is to keep adding all ingredients until the element whose addition to the substitute ingredients chain exceeds the specified optimality bounds of calories, carbohydrates, fats and sugars. For that element, we look from the beginning of the chain to find all those elements which when replaced by the new element can generate a better flavor score. The element with the least contribution in generating a comprehensive flavor profile, averaged over standardized weights, is replaced from the chain with the new element. This process continues until the best substitute chain is developed and displayed.

The implementation of the algorithm is done using arrays to store the data values of the flavor and ingredient tables, while a linked list is used to generate and develop the chain of substitute ingredients. It can be summarized as:

Algorithm
Step 1: Initialize flavor and nutrient profile and input item to be replaced
Step 2: Repeat Step 3 to Step 10 until end of ingredients is reached, then go to

Step 12.

Step 3: Get next element.

Step 4: If the addition of the element does not exceed total nutrient values of the item, then go to Step 6, else go to Step 7.

Step 5: Add the element to the list of replacement ingredients. Go to Step 2.

Step 6: Go to the origin point of the replacement element list. Replace variable worst with new element.

Step 7: Check if the replacement ingredient pointed to in list compared with worst variable's element gives a better approximate flavor profile with comparable nutrient components. If true then go to Step 9, else go to Step 8.

Step 8: Change worst variable with element pointed in list.

Step 9: Get next element. Go to Step 7. If no more elements in list then go to Step 10.

Step 10: If the worst variable is not new element then change new and worst.

Step 11: Display replacement ingredients list.

5   Case Study

We demonstrate the working of the proposed methodology by the use of three cases which have generated convincing results. The most trivial case solution arises when we are substituting a single food item and we get a singular ingredient as result.

For example, consider the fruit Banana (see Table 3):

Table 3. Nutrient profile of banana

Ingredient	Calories	Fats	Carbohydrates	Sugars
BANANA	110	0	30	19

The nutrient values of Banana have been measured over 126 g/4.5 oz in quantity. Here the patient has restrictions on calories set at 60, fats at 7, carbohydrates at 10 and sugars at 0. Our algorithm works around this data and fetches the flavor profile statistics from the database to output a combination of ingredients (in this case a single item result), which is generated as the best suitable flavor substitute for the ingredient in question. There exists a scarcity of exhaustive data, and hence the result generated by the algorithm depends on the database it is linked with. In this case the result is: It is seen that avocado has a higher fat content than banana, however it may be accepted due to the value lying below the patient's fat consumption measure. The avocado nutrient statistic is measured at 30 g/1.1 oz in quantity (see Table 4).

A different aspect of our algorithm lies in the hiding of food items restricted by the physician. In this scenario, the patient is assumed to have certain allergic

Table 4. Nutrient profile of avocado

Ingredient	Calories	Fats	Carbohydrates	Sugars
AVOCADO	50	4.5	3	0

restrictions and requires a substitute ingredients chain to be generated. Let us flag Bell Pepper from the database, assuming the user wants to avoid consuming it. After the item has been flagged and hidden from the database, the input is set as: Bell Pepper quantity is specified as 148 g/5.3 oz. Our method substitutes it with Cucumber, matching it with the flavor profile while maintaining the nutrient content values as the upper bound. The physician's restriction limits have been set to that of the nutrient specifications of Bell Pepper. Cucumber calories, fats, carbohydrates and sugars values have been measured at 99 g / 3.5 oz. Here, the physician recommended calories, fats, carbohydrates and sugar values are set the same as those that of Bell Pepper. However the food item BELL PEPPER is hidden when the dataset is being read, so that a substitute chain with a similar flavor profile may be generated but a direct correspondence with BELL PEPPER in the original dataset is not made. Another case studied has the input as: The nutrient statistics have been specified for 148 g/5.3 oz of Potato. The physician's restrictions have been set as 100 calories, 20 g in fat, 0 g of carbohydrates and 10 g in sugars. While there exists many varied combinations for generating the substitute for potatoes, our proposed methodology predicts the best result as cauliflower, measured over 99 g/3.5oz in quantity. On observing the values we see that this is a special case of the substitution chain where there exists the concept of multiplicity. As mentioned earlier, the quantity or volume of the ingredient specified in the dataset defines the nutrient and flavor statistic. In a similar way, the substitute ingredient in the above example, when multiplied by four, generates the nutrient statistic of the food item to be substituted. This is the best approximate constant and depends on the data provided in the dataset. Our results have been generated using a self created nutrient and flavor profile gathered from various data sources. The nature of the output is thus seen to directly depend on the profiles the method runs on. It is also to be noted that the quantity or volume of ingredients vary from one another and are specified in a separate column in the actual dataset (and are mentioned here in the corresponding text) (see Tables 5, 6, 7 and 8).

Table 5. Nutrient profile of bell pepper

Ingredient	Calories	Fats	Carbohydrates	Sugars
BELL PEPPER	25	0	6	4

Table 6. Nutrient profile of cucumber

Ingredient	Calories	Fats	Carbohydrates	Sugars
CUCUMBER	10	0	2	1

Table 7. Nutrient profile of potato

Ingredient	Calories	Fats	Carbohydrates	Sugars
POTATO	110	26	0	8

Table 8. Nutrient profile of cauliflower

Ingredient	Calories	Fats	Carbohydrates	Sugars
CAULIFLOWER	25	5	0	2

6   Conclusion and Future Scope

Generation of flavor based approximation algorithms using Machine Learning is a new direction in the classification of food ingredients. Our research is based on generating the most similar flavor profile consisting of weighted sweet, sour, bitter, salt and savory values. While many people argue that no two individuals can have the same flavor palette, this work has been specifically designed for individuals with dietary restrictions and require the best substitute feasible to remind them of what that particular item tasted like.

In this paper, we have utilized the disease specific optimality conditions of calories, carbohydrates, fats and sugars to deduce the most suitable flavor profile to that of the item being replaced. The research articles that exist in related domains use complex time-consuming procedures which involve chemical compositions or relationships between ingredients, and may not always best describe the real scenario. Instead of controlling how much oil or water to add to an item, we use blanched, fried item specific nutrient and flavor statistics so that the algorithm is able to learn the values and utilize them when required. Our algorithm has shown to predict feasible solutions which generate the most similar flavor combination to that of the item which the patient wants to replace. The results have been validated by an experienced food technologist.

The shortage of data is the primary reason why this algorithm may not be as effective if globally implemented. We do not create flavor databases as we know that they may never be perfect. Due to the advancement of medication and improvement in living conditions, the aged population is on the rise. This leads to the manifestation of innumerable diseases which bring forth strict lifestyle restrictions and leads to dissatisfaction among the aged. Our algorithm if implemented globally will benefit these individuals. However, for that to happen, we need to create an accessible database with food ingredients which under standard volumes have generalized flavor approximations. These values when taken from such databases and applied to our algorithm will help each individual get a taste of what they crave for.

References

1. Efroymson, M.A.: Multiple regression analysis. In: Ralston, A., Wilf, H.S. (eds.) Mathematical Methods for Digital Computers. Wiley, New York (1960)
2. Teng, C., Lin, Y., Adamic, L.A.: Recipe recommendation using ingredient networks. In: Proceedings of the 4th Annual ACM Web Science Conference, pp. 298–307 (2012)
3. Shidochi, Y., Takahashi, T.: Finding replaceable materials in cooking recipe texts considering characteristic cooking actions. In: Proceedings of CEA 2009, pp. 9–14 (2009)
4. Varshney, K.R., Varshney, L.R., Wang, J., Myers, D.: Flavor pairing in Medieval European cuisine: a study in cooking with dirty data. In: Proceedings of IJCAI (2013)
5. Ahn, Y.Y., Ahnert, S.E., Bagrow, J.P., Barabasi, A.L.: Flavor network and the principles of food pairing. Scientific Reports, 1, Article number: 196 (2011)

Intuitionistic Multi-fuzzy Convolution Operator and Its Application in Decision Making

Amalendu Si[1($\boxtimes$)] and Sujit Das[2]

[1] Department of CSE, Mallabhum Institute of Technology,
Bishnupur 722122, India
amalendu.si@gmail.com
[2] Department of C.S.E, Dr. B.C. Roy Engineering College,
Durgapur 713206, India
sujit_cse@yahoo.com

Abstract. Intuitionistic multi-fuzzy set (IMFS) is a generalization of multi-fuzzy set, where the elements are having multiple numbers of membership and non-membership values instead of a single membership and non-membership value. Here we develop intuitionistic multi-fuzzy convolution (IMFC) operator for information aggregation using IMFS. This paper introduces harmonic average method to degenerate IMFS to intuitionistic fuzzy set (IFS). Then we present a decision making approach applying the proposed IMFC operator, where harmonic average, Hamming distance, and Euclidean distance measures are used for the decision making purpose. Finally, we have given a real life example to show the applicability of the proposed operator.

Keywords: Decision making · Convolution operator · Intuitionistic multi-fuzzy set · Intuitionistic fuzzy set

1 Introduction

Intuitionistic fuzzy set (IFS) [1, 2] has been using as an efficient tool to handle uncertainties, where each element is assigned a membership degree and a non-membership degree. IFS is considered as an generalization of Zadeh's [3] fuzzy set, where only a membership degree is allocated to each element. Since the appearance of IFS in 1986, contributions of many researchers can be found for the advancement of IFS theory and its applications [23–29] both in theoretical and application point of view. Recently, information aggregation in IFS theory has become a significant research area especially in group decision making (GDM) problems. In [10], Atanassov [10] defined various operations of IFSs such as intersection, union, complement, algebraic sum, algebraic product, etc., which were extended in [11], where the authors [11] further defined some new operations and proved them. Szmidt and Kacprzyk [12] proposed Hamming distance and Euclidean distance measures between two IFSs. Combining multi-set [4] and fuzzy set [3], Yager [5] introduced multi-fuzzy set (MFS),

© Springer Nature Singapore Pte Ltd. 2017
J.K. Mandal et al. (Eds.): CICBA 2017, Part II, CCIS 776, pp. 540–551, 2017.
DOI: 10.1007/978-981-10-6430-2_42

where an element may appear multiple times with probably the similar or dissimilar membership values. MFS can be considered as an extension of fuzzy sets, L-fuzzy sets [6], and IFSs. Sebastian and Ramakrishnan [7] studied the relation between IFS and MFS, and presented multi-fuzzy mappings. Shinoj and John [8] introduced intuitionistic multi-fuzzy set (IMFS) and Das et al. [9] applied it in decision making problems.

In GDM, several methods are considered to aggregate the opinions of different experts. Yager [13] proposed ordered weighted averaging (OWA) operator, where the items are aggregated according to their order in the set. As an extension of OWA operator, Yager and Filev [14] developed induced ordered weighted averaging (IOWA) operator, where order inducing variable manages the ordering of the arguments. Xu and Yager [15] initially proposed intuitionistic fuzzy weighted geometric (IFWG) and intuitionistic fuzzy ordered weighted geometric (IFOWG) aggregation operators. Combining IFWG and IFOWG, the authors [15] proposed intuitionistic fuzzy hybrid geometric (IFHG) operator. Similarly, Xu [16] firstly offered intuitionistic fuzzy weighted averaging (IFWA) and intuitionistic fuzzy ordered weighted averaging (IFOWA) operator, and then as a hybridization of IFWA and IFOWA, the authors [16] proposed intuitionistic fuzzy hybrid aggregation (IFHA) operator. Wei [17] generalized these operators using inducing variables [14] and developed some induced geometric aggregation operators. Generalized IFWA, generalized IFOWA, and generalized IFHA operator were defined by Zhao et al. [18]. A series of intuitionistic fuzzy point operations and generalized intuitionistic fuzzy point aggregation operators were defined by Xia and Xu [19]. Wang and Liu [20] used Einstein operations to implement intuitionistic fuzzy information aggregation. Li and He [21] defined intuitionistic fuzzy prioritized "or" (PRI-OR) and prioritized "and" (PRI-AND) aggregation operators. Recently, Das et al. [9] has focused on IMFS and presented intuitionistic multi-fuzzy weighted averaging operator (IMFWA) in the context of IMFS. The authors also proposed Hamming distance and Euclidean distance measures in the framework of IMFS and studied IMFS based score and accuracy functions in order to compare two intuitionistic multi-fuzzy values (IMFVs). Finally, they developed a decision making approach and applied IMFWA operator in decision making problems.

Preceding discussion narrates that the researchers have developed many aggregation operators using IFSs to solve the real life decision making problems. However, a few research works can be found, where the researchers have considered IMFS to solve decision making problems using information aggregation. In this era of uncertainty, when a single membership and non-membership value alone is not sufficient to represent an object, rather the object can be well represented by multiple number of membership and non-membership values, IMFS is used for reasoning such kind of situations. This paper proposes IMFC operator to aggregate intuitionistic multi-fuzzy information and then apply it in decision making problems.

The rest of this paper is arranged as follows. Section 2 presents some basic ideas correlated to this work. In Sect. 3, we propose IMFS based convolution operator followed by the algorithmic approach in Sect. 4. The real life example is demonstrated in Sect. 5. The conclusions are discussed in Sect. 6.

2 Preliminaries

In this section, we recall some basic ideas relevant to this paper.

Definition 1 [1, 2]. Let X be the initial universe. An intuitionistic fuzzy set in X is defined by $A = \{\langle x, \mu_A(x), v_A(x)\rangle | x \in X\}$, where $\mu_A : X \to [0, 1], v_A : X \to [0, 1]$ and $0 \leq \mu_A(x) + v_A(x) \leq 1, \forall x \in X$. Here $\mu_A(x)$ and $v_A(x)$ respectively denote the degree of membership and non-membership of the element x in the set A. For each intuitionistic fuzzy set A in X, the hesitation margin or intuitionistic fuzzy index is defined as $\pi_A(x) = 1 - \mu_A(x) - v_A(x), x \in X$, which expresses the lack of information whether $x \in A$ or $x \notin A$. Also for each $x \in X, 0 \leq \pi_A(x) \leq 1$.

Definition 2 [5]. Let k be a positive integer. A multi-fuzzy set (MFS) $\widehat{A}$ over X is a set of ordered sequence $\widehat{A} = \left\{ x / \left(\mu_{\widehat{A}}^1(x), \mu_{\widehat{A}}^2(x), \ldots, \mu_{\widehat{A}}^i(x), \ldots, \mu_{\widehat{A}}^k(x) \right) : x \in X \right\}$, where $\mu_{\widehat{A}} = (\mu_{\widehat{A}}^1, \mu_{\widehat{A}}^2, \ldots, \mu_{\widehat{A}}^k)$ is the multi-membership function of MFS $\widehat{A}$ and the dimension of $\widehat{A}$ is defined by k.

Definition 3 [8]. An IMFS $\widehat{A}$ is defined by $\widehat{A} = x / \left(\mu_{\widehat{A}}^1(x), \mu_{\widehat{A}}^2(x), \ldots, \mu_{\widehat{A}}^k(x) \right)$, $\left(v_{\widehat{A}}^1(x), v_{\widehat{A}}^2(x), \ldots, v_{\widehat{A}}^k(x) \right) : x \in X$, where $0 \leq \mu_{\widehat{A}}^i(x) + v_{\widehat{A}}^i(x) \leq 1$, $\pi_{\widehat{A}}^i(x) = 1 - \left(\mu_{\widehat{A}}^i(x) + v_{\widehat{A}}^i(x) \right) \forall x \in X$, $i = 1, 2, \ldots, k$, and $k > 0$. Intuitionistic multi-fuzzy value (IMFV) or intuitionistic multi-fuzzy number (IMFN) is defined by $\{\mu_A^i(x), v_A^i(x)\}$, where $x \in X$ is fixed.

Let $\widehat{A} = \left\{ x / \left(\mu_{\widehat{A}}^1(x), \mu_{\widehat{A}}^2(x), \ldots, \mu_{\widehat{A}}^k(x) \right), \left(v_{\widehat{A}}^1(x), v_{\widehat{A}}^2(x), \ldots, v_{\widehat{A}}^k(x) \right) : x \in X \right\}$ and $\widehat{B} = \left\{ x / \left(\mu_{\widehat{B}}^1(x), \mu_{\widehat{B}}^2(x), \ldots, \mu_{\widehat{B}}^k(x) \right), \left(v_{\widehat{B}}^1(x), v_{\widehat{B}}^2(x), \ldots, v_{\widehat{B}}^k(x) \right) : x \in X \right\}$ be two IMFSs of dimension k. In addition $\left(\widehat{A} \oplus \widehat{B} \right)$ operation of $\widehat{A}$ and $\widehat{B}$, the membership and non-membership values are respectively computed as $\mu_{\widehat{A} \oplus \widehat{B}}^j(x) = \mu_{\widehat{A}}^j(x) + \mu_{\widehat{B}}^j(x) - \mu_{\widehat{A}}^j(x) \cdot \mu_{\widehat{B}}^j(x)$ and $v_{\widehat{A} \oplus \widehat{B}}^j(x) = v_{\widehat{A}}^j(x) \cdot v_{\widehat{B}}^j(x), j = 1, 2, \ldots, k, x \in X$. Similarly, in multiplication $\left(\widehat{A} \otimes \widehat{B} \right)$ operation, the membership and non-membership values are computed as $\mu_{\widehat{A} \otimes \widehat{B}}^j(x) = \mu_{\widehat{A}}^j(x) \cdot \mu_{\widehat{B}}^j(x)$ and $v_{\widehat{A} \otimes \widehat{B}}^j(x) = v_{\widehat{A}}^j(x) + v_{\widehat{B}}^j(x) - v_{\widehat{A}}^j(x) \cdot v_{\widehat{B}}^j(x)$, $j = 1, 2, \ldots, k, x \in X$.

Multiplication and power of IMFS $\widehat{A}$ of dimension k with real value $\lambda > 0$ are respectively defined as $\lambda \widehat{A} = \left\{ 1 - \left(1 - \mu_{\widehat{A}}^i \right)^\lambda, \left(v_{\widehat{A}}^i \right)^\lambda \right\}$ and $\widehat{A}^\lambda = \left\{ \left(\mu_{\widehat{A}}^i \right)^\lambda, \left(1 - \left(1 - v_{\widehat{A}}^i \right) \right)^\lambda \right\}$, where $i = 1, 2, \ldots, k, x \in X$.

Definition 4 [9]. Score function $S(x)$ and accuracsy function $H(x)$ of the IMFV $x = \left\{ (\mu_x^1, \mu_x^2, \ldots, \mu_x^k), (v_x^1, v_x^2, \ldots, v_x^k) \right\}$ are respectively defined as $S(x) = \sum_j \left\{ \mu^j(x) - v^j(x) \right\}$ and $H(x) = \sum_j \left\{ \mu^j(x) + v^j(x) \right\}, j = 1, 2, \ldots, k.$

If $x = \left\{ (\mu_x^1, \mu_x^2, \ldots, \mu_x^k), (v_x^1, v_x^2, \ldots, v_x^k) \right\}$ and $y = \left\{ (\mu_y^1, \mu_y^2, \ldots, \mu_y^k), (v_y^1, v_y^2, \ldots, v_y^k) \right\}$ are IMFVs, then x and y are compared as follows:

(1) *if* $S(x) < S(y)$, x is smaller than y
(2) *if* $S(x) = S(y)$, then
    (a) *if* $H(x) < H(y)$, x is smaller than y
    (b) *if* $H(x) = H(y)$, x and y represent the same information.

Definition 5 [9]. Hamming Distance measurements $d^H(\widehat{A}, \widehat{B})$ between IMFSs $\widehat{A}$ and $\widehat{B}$ in $X = (x_1, x_2, \ldots, x_m)$ of dimension k is defined as follows:

$$d^H(\widehat{A}, \widehat{B}) = \frac{1}{2k} \left(\sum_{j=1}^m \sum_{p=1}^k \left(|\mu_{\widehat{A}}^p(x_j) - \mu_{\widehat{B}}^p(x_j)| + |v_{\widehat{A}}^p(x_j) - v_{\widehat{B}}^p(x_j)| + |\pi_{\widehat{A}}^p(x_j) - \pi_{\widehat{B}}^p(x_j)| \right) \right), x \in X.$$

Normalized Hamming distance $l^H(\widehat{A}, \widehat{B})$ between IMFSs $\widehat{A}$ and $\widehat{B}$ in $X = (x_1, x_2, \ldots, x_m)$ of dimension k is defined as

$$l^H(\widehat{A}, \widehat{B}) = \frac{1}{2mk} \left(\sum_{j=1}^m \sum_{p=1}^k \left(|\mu_{\widehat{A}}^p(x_j) - \mu_{\widehat{B}}^p(x_j)| + |v_{\widehat{A}}^p(x_j) - v_{\widehat{B}}^p(x_j)| + |\pi_{\widehat{A}}^p(x_j) - \pi_{\widehat{B}}^p(x_j)| \right) \right), x \in X.$$

Definition 6 [9]. Euclidean Distance measurements $d^E(\widehat{A}, \widehat{B})$ between IMFSs $\widehat{A}$ and $\widehat{B}$ in $X = (x_1, x_2, \ldots, x_m)$ of dimension k is defined below.

$$d^E(\widehat{A}, \widehat{B}) = \left(\frac{1}{2k} \sum_{j=1}^m \sum_{p=1}^k \left((\mu_{\widehat{A}}^p(x_j) - \mu_{\widehat{B}}^p(x_j))^2 + (v_{\widehat{A}}^p(x_j) - v_{\widehat{B}}^p(x_j))^2 + (\pi_{\widehat{A}}^p(x_j) - \pi_{\widehat{B}}^p(x_j))^2 \right) \right)^{\frac{1}{2}}, x \in X.$$

Normalized Euclidean distance $l^E(\widehat{A}, \widehat{B})$ between IMFSs $\widehat{A}$ and $\widehat{B}$ in $X = (x_1, x_2, \ldots, x_m)$ of dimension k can be defined as

$$l^E(\widehat{A}, \widehat{B}) = \left(\frac{1}{2mk} \sum_{j=1}^m \sum_{p=1}^k \left((\mu_{\widehat{A}}^p(x_j) - \mu_{\widehat{B}}^p(x_j))^2 + (v_{\widehat{A}}^p(x_j) - v_{\widehat{B}}^p(x_j))^2 + (\pi_{\widehat{A}}^p(x_j) - \pi_{\widehat{B}}^p(x_j))^2 \right) \right)^{\frac{1}{2}}, x \in X.$$

3 Intuitionistic Multi-fuzzy Convolution Operator

Convolution [22] is a formal mathematical operation like addition, multiplication, and integration. Intuitively, convolution is a mathematical manner of combining two signals to develop a third signal which is used in digital signal processing. Normally, convolution is used in probabilities and statics. However, it has many applications in engineering like signal processing and analysis. Let $\alpha_j = (\mu_{\alpha_k}, v_{\alpha_k}), j = 1, 2, \ldots, n$ be a collection of IMFNs of dimension k, Θ represents an IMFN, and $IMFC : \Theta^n \to \Theta$. The intuitionistic multi-fuzzy convolution (IMFC) operator is defined as

$$IMFC(\alpha_1, \alpha_2, \ldots, \alpha_n)$$

$$= \left(\frac{1 - \prod\limits_{i=1}^{n} \prod\limits_{l=1}^{k} \left(1 - \mu_{\alpha_i}^l\right)}{1 + \prod\limits_{i=1}^{n} \prod\limits_{l=1}^{k} \left(1 - \mu_{\alpha_i}^l\right)}, \frac{1 - \prod\limits_{i=1}^{n} \prod\limits_{l=1}^{k} \left(1 - v_{\alpha_i}^l\right)}{1 + \prod\limits_{i=1}^{n} \prod\limits_{l=1}^{k} \left(1 - v_{\alpha_i}^l\right)}, \frac{1 - \prod\limits_{i=1}^{n} \prod\limits_{l=1}^{k} \left(1 - \pi_{\alpha_i}^l\right)}{1 + \prod\limits_{i=1}^{n} \prod\limits_{l=1}^{k} \left(1 - \pi_{\alpha_i}^l\right)} \right).$$

Example 1. Let α_1 and α_2 be two IMFNs of dimension 3, where

$$\alpha_1 = \{(0.7, 0.6, 0.5), (0.1, 0.2, 0.4), (0.2, 0.2, 0.1)\},$$
$$\alpha_2 = \{(0.4, 0.4, 0.3), (0.3, 0.4, 0.6), (0.3, 0.2, 0.1)\}$$

Using convolution operator over α_1 and α_2, we get

$$\left\{ \begin{array}{l} \left(\frac{1 - (1 - 0.7)(1 - 0.4)}{1 + (1 - 0.7)(1 - 0.4)} = \frac{1 - 0.18}{1 + 0.18} = 0.70, \frac{1 - (1 - 0.6)(1 - 0.4)}{1 + (1 - 0.6)(1 - 0.4)} = \frac{1 - 0.24}{1 + 0.24} = 0.61, \frac{1 - (1 - 0.5)(1 - 0.3)}{1 + (1 - 0.5)(1 - 0.3)} = \frac{1 - 0.35}{1 + 0.35} = 0.48 \right) \\ \left(\frac{1 - (1 - 0.1)(1 - 0.3)}{1 + (1 - 0.1)(1 - 0.3)} = \frac{1 - 0.63}{1 + 0.63} = 0.27, \frac{1 - (1 - 0.2)(1 - 0.4)}{1 + (1 - 0.2)(1 - 0.4)} = \frac{1 - 0.48}{1 + 0.48} = 0.35, \frac{1 - (1 - 0.4)(1 - 0.6)}{1 + (1 - 0.4)(1 - 0.6)} = \frac{1 - 0.24}{1 + 0.24} = 0.61 \right) \\ \left(\frac{1 - (1 - 0.2)(1 - 0.3)}{1 + (1 - 0.2)(1 - 0.3)} = \frac{1 - 0.56}{1 + 0.56} = 0.28, \frac{1 - (1 - 0.2)(1 - 0.2)}{1 + (1 - 0.2)(1 - 0.2)} = \frac{1 - 0.64}{1 + 0.64} = 0.22, \frac{1 - (1 - 0.1)(1 - 0.1)}{1 + (1 - 0.1)(1 - 0.1)} = \frac{1 - 0.81}{1 + 0.81} = 0.1 \right) \end{array} \right\}$$
$$= \{(0.70, 0.61, 0.48), (0.27, 0.35, 0.61), (0.28, 0.22, 0.1)\}$$

Transformation of IMFS to IFS using harmonic average method

An IMFS $\widehat{A} = \{x/(\mu_{\widehat{A}}^1(x), \mu_{\widehat{A}}^2(x), \ldots, \mu_{\widehat{A}}^k(x)), (v_{\widehat{A}}^1(x), v_{\widehat{A}}^2(x), \ldots, v_{\widehat{A}}^k(x)) : x \in X\}$ can be transformed to a IFS $A^G = \{x/(\mu_A^G(x), (v_A^G(x)) : x \in X\}$ based on harmonic average method, where

$$\mu_A^G(x) = k / \left(1 / \sum_{l=1}^{k} \mu_A^l\right), v_A^G(x) = k / \left(1 / \sum_{l=1}^{k} v_A^l\right) \quad \text{and} \quad 0 \le \mu_A^G(x) + v_A^G(x) \le 1,$$
$$\pi_A^G(x) = 1 - (\mu_A^G(x) + v_A^G(x)) \text{ for every } x \in X.$$

4 Decision Making Using IMFC Operator

This section presents a decision making algorithm using the proposed IMFC operator. Let the set of decision makers, alternatives, and attributes are respectively denoted by

$DM = \{DM_1, DM_2, \ldots, DM_l\}, X = \{x_1, x_2, \ldots, x_m\}$, and $E = \{e_1, e_2, \ldots, e_n\}$. Decision makers $DM_i, i = 1, 2, \ldots, l$ provide their opinions regarding the attributes $e_t, t = 1, 2, \ldots, n$ of various alternatives $x_j, j = 1, 2, \ldots, m$ using intuitionistic multi-fuzzy matrices (IMFMs). Opinion of decision maker $DM_i, i = 1, 2, \ldots, l$ is expressed as IMFM given below.

$$R^{(i)} = \left[r_{jt}^{(i)} \right]_{mxn} = \begin{bmatrix} r_{11}^{(i)} r_{12}^{(i)} & \cdots & r_{1n}^{(i)} \\ r_{21}^{(i)} r_{22}^{(i)} & \cdots & r_{2n}^{(i)} \\ \vdots & \ddots & \vdots \\ r_{m1}^{(i)} r_{m2}^{(i)} & \cdots & r_{mn}^{(i)} \end{bmatrix}$$

Here $r_{jt}^{(i)} = \{(\mu_{jt}^{(i1)}(x), \mu_{jt}^{(i2)}(x), \ldots, \mu_{jt}^{(ik)}(x)), (v_{jt}^{(i1)}(x), v_{jt}^{(i2)}(x), \ldots, v_{jt}^{(ik)}(x), (\pi_{jt}^{(i1)}(x),$ $\pi_{jt}^{(i2)}(x), \ldots, \pi_{jt}^{(ik)}(x)) : x \in X\}$, k be the dimension of IMFS. For experimentation purpose, a reference knowledge base matrix (S) is considered, where the information about the alternatives and attributes are given using intuitionistic fuzzy numbers.

Step 1:   Opinions of individual decision makers $DM_i, i = 1, 2, \ldots, l$ are represented using intuitionistic multi-fuzzy matrices $R^{(i)}, i = 1, 2, \ldots, l$, where $R^{(i)} = \left[r_{jt}^{(i)} \right]_{mxn}$.

Step 2:   Intuitionistic multi-fuzzy convolution operator is used to combine the opinions of various decision makers. The combined matrix $\widehat{R}^{(i)} = \left[\widehat{r}_{jt}^{(i)} \right]_{mxn}$ is computed using the IMFC operator as given below.

$$\widehat{r}_{jt} = IMFC(r_{jt}^1, r_{jt}^2, \cdots, r_{jt}^l), j = 1, 2, \ldots, m, t = 1, 2, \ldots, n$$

Step 3:   The combined IMFM is normalized as given below.

$$\mu_{jt}^p(x) = \frac{\mu_{jt}^p(x)}{\mu_{jt}^p(x) + v_{jt}^p(x) + \pi_{jt}^p(x)}, v_{jt}^p(x) = \frac{v_{jt}^p(x)}{\mu_{jt}^p(x) + v_{jt}^p(x) + \pi_{jt}^p(x)}, \pi_{jt}^p(x)$$
$$= \frac{\pi_{jt}^p(x)}{\mu_{jt}^p(x) + v_{jt}^p(x) + \pi_{jt}^p(x)}$$

where $p = 1, 2, \ldots, k$ and k be the dimension of IMFS.

Step 4:   Normalised Hamming and Euclidean distances are computed over the normalized combined matrix $(\widehat{R})$ and reference matrix (S) to construct the distant matrix, which is constructed using the following two steps.

Step 4.1:   If both of the combined matrix $(\widehat{R})$ and reference matrix (S) are represented as IMFM, then normalised Hamming distance $l^H(\widehat{R}, S)$ and Euclidean distance $l^E(\widehat{R}, S)$ between $(\widehat{R})$ and S can be defined with c_{ij} where

$$c_{ij}^H = l^H(\widehat{R}, S) = \frac{1}{2mk} \sum_{j=1}^{m} \sum_{i=1}^{k} (|\mu_{\widehat{R}}^i(x_j) - \mu_S^i(x_j)| + |v_{\widehat{R}}^i(x_j) - v_S^i(x_j)| + |\pi_{\widehat{R}}^i(x_j) - \pi_S^i(x_j)|).$$

$$c_{ij}^E = l^E(\widehat{R}, S) = \left(\frac{1}{2mk} \sum_{j=1}^{m} \sum_{i=1}^{k} ((\mu_{\widehat{R}}^i(x_j) - \mu_S^i(x_j))^2 + (v_{\widehat{R}}^i(x_j) - v_S^i(x_j))^2 + (\pi_{\widehat{R}}^i(x_j) - \pi_S^i(x_j))^2) \right)^{\frac{1}{2}}.$$

Step 4.2: Here the combined matrix $(\widehat{R})$ is represented as IMFM and reference matrix (S) is represented by intuitionistic fuzzy matrix (IFM), where IFM is the matrix form of intuitionistic fuzzy set. Hence

$$c_{ij}^H = l^H(\widehat{R}, S) = \frac{1}{2mk} \sum_{j=1}^{m} \sum_{i=1}^{k} (|\mu_{\widehat{R}}^i(x_j) - \mu_S(x_j)| + |v_{\widehat{R}}^i(x_j) - v_S(x_j)| + |\pi_{\widehat{R}}^i(x_j) - \pi_S(x_j)|).$$

$$c_{ij}^E = l^E(\widehat{R}, S) = \left(\frac{1}{2mk} \sum_{j=1}^{m} \sum_{i=1}^{k} ((\mu_{\widehat{R}}^i(x_j) - \mu_S(x_j))^2 + (v_{\widehat{R}}^i(x_j) - v_S(x_j))^2 + (\pi_{\widehat{R}}^i(x_j) - \pi_S(x_j))^2) \right)^{\frac{1}{2}}.$$

Step 4.3: When the combined matrix $(\widehat{R})$ is degenerated to IFM and reference matrix (S) is represented as IFM, then

$$c_{ij}^H = l^H(\widehat{R}, S) = \frac{1}{2m} \sum_{j=1}^{m} (|\mu_{\widehat{R}}(x_j) - \mu_S(x_j)| + |v_{\widehat{R}}(x_j) - v_S(x_j)| + |\pi_{\widehat{R}}(x_j) - \pi_S(x_j)|).$$

$$c_{ij}^E = l^E(\widehat{R}, S) = \left(\frac{1}{2m} \sum_{j=1}^{m} ((\mu_{\widehat{R}}(x_j) - \mu_S^i(x_j))^2 + (v_{\widehat{R}}^i(x_j) - v_S^i(x_j))^2 + (\pi_{\widehat{R}}^i(x_j) - \pi_S^i(x_j))^2) \right)^{\frac{1}{2}}.$$

Step 5: Attribute with minimum distances are selected for each alternative

5 Real Life Example

Recently heart disease has become a major health concern in the world. Proper diagnosis and treatment is essential to recover from the disease. In this example, we categorize the heart disease into four different stages $D = \{D_1, D_2, D_3, D_4\} = \{$Stage I, Stage II, Stage III, Stage IV$\}$ based on a common set of symptoms $S = \{S_1, S_2, S_3, S_4, S_5\} = \{$chest pain, palpitation, dizziness, fainting, fatigue$\}$. Stage I specifies that the patient is in initial stage of heart disease, which can be cured if diagnosis and treatment are initiated earlier. Stage II is more unsafe and less curable. Stage III patients are more insecure than that of Stage II, while the patient belongs to Stage IV not recoverable. This example considers the inspections of four medical consultants $E = \{E_1, E_2, E_3, E_4\}$ for a set of four patients $P = \{P_1, P_2, P_3, P_4\}$, which are respectively given in Tables 1, 2, 3, and 4. Table 7 represents a reference value of the symptoms $S = \{S_1, S_2, S_3, S_4, S_5\}$ corresponding to the different stages $D = \{D_1, D_2, D_3, D_4\}$. In this example, the consultants prescribe their opinions using intuitionistic multi-fuzzy sets, where the consultants visit the patients at regular intervals to monitor their conditions. Here three intervals are considered, i.e., three membership degree, three non-membership degree, and three hesitation margins are considered.

Below, we give the steps of the proposed algorithm step wise.

Step 1: Inspections of the consultants $E = \{E_1, E_2, E_3, E_4\}$ are represented using IMFMs (R^1, R^2, R^3, and R^4) which are respectively shown in Tables 1, 2, 3, and 4.

Step 2 & Step 3: Convolution operator is used to combine the IMFMs (R^1, R^2, R^3, and R^4). The normalized combined intuitionistic multi-fuzzy matrix is shown in Table 5.

Step 4 & Step 5: Since the given reference matrix is intuitionistic fuzzy matrix, the resultant intuitionistic multi-fuzzy matrix is degenerated into intuitionistic fuzzy matrix using harmonic average method which is shown in Table 6. Next normalized Hamming and normalized Euclidean distance measurements are performed between the reference matrix and the degenerated combined matrix, shown in Table 8. As lowest distance shows proper diagnosis, Table 8 shows that patient P_1 is in Stage I, P_2 and $P4$ are in Stage II, and P_3 is in Stage IV of heart disease

Table 1. Inspection of consultant I

Patients/Symptoms	Chest Pain	Palpitations	Dizziness	Fainting	Fatigue
P_1	(0.6,0.5,0.7)	(0.6,0.3,0.5)	(0.2,0.2,0.2)	(0.6,0.6,0.6)	(0.3,0.4,0.5)
	(0.2,0.2,0.2)	(0.3,0.5,0.4)	(0.7,0.7,0.7)	(0.3,0.3,0.2)	(0.6,0.3,0.3)
	(0.2,0.3,0.1)	(0.1,0.2,0.1)	(0.1,0.1,0.1)	(0.1,0.1,0.2)	(0.1,0.3,0.2)
P_2	(0.4,0.5,0.6)	(0.7,0.5,0.7)	(0.7,0.4,0.6)	(0.4,0.6,0.4)	(0.6,0.5,0.6)
	(0.4,0.3,0.2)	(0.3,0.3,0.2)	(0.2,0.4,0.3)	(0.5,0.2,0.3)	(0.1,0.3,0.2)
	(0.2,0.2,0.2)	(0.0,0.2,0.1)	(0.1,0.2,0.1)	(0.1,0.2,0.3)	(0.3,0.2,0.2)
P_3	(0.4,0.6,0.2)	(0.4,0.4,0.1)	(0.7,0.7,0.6)	(0.5,0.3,0.2)	(0.6,0.4,0.4)
	(0.3,0.2,0.7)	(0.5,0.1,0.7)	(0.1,0.1,0.3)	(0.4,0.6,0.6)	(0.2,0.6,0.5)
	(0.3,0.2,0.1)	(0.1,0.5,0.2)	(0.2,0.2,0.1)	(0.1,0.1,0.2)	(0.2,0.0,0.1)
P_4	(0.6,0.4,0.3)	(0.7,0.6,0.6)	(0.4,0.6,0.2)	(0.6,0.5,0.4)	(0.2,06,0.7)
	(0.2,0.3,0.3)	(0.1,0.2,0.3)	(0.4,0.2,0.6)	(0.2,0.3,0.5)	(0.6,0.3,0.3)
	(0.2,0.3,0.4)	(0.2,0.2,0.1)	(0.2,0.2,0.2)	(0.2,0.2,0.1)	(0.2,0.1,0.0)

Table 2. Inspection of consultant II

Patients/Symptoms	Chest Pain	Palpitations	Dizziness	Fainting	Fatigue
P_1	(0.5,0.7,0.5)	(0.4,0.5,0.5)	(0.5,0.6,0.7)	(0.7,0.2,0.6)	(0.5,0.7,0.8)
	(0.2,0.2,0.3)	(0.4,0.3,0.3)	(0.2,0.2,0.2)	(0.1,0.6,0.2)	(0.3,0.2,0.2)
	(0.3,0.1,0.2)	(0.2,0.2,0.2)	(0.3,0.2,0.1)	(0.2,0.2,0.2)	(0.2,0.1,0.0)
P_2	(0.6,0.4,0.6)	(0.7,0.4,0.4)	(0.6,0.5,0.5)	(0.4,0.4,0.3)	(0.4,0.3,0.4)
	(0.2,0.4,0.3)	(0.2,0.5,0.4)	(0.3,0.3,0.2)	(0.5,0.5,0.6)	(0.3,0.4,0.4)
	(0.2,0.2,0.1)	(0.1,0.1,0.2)	(0.1,0.2,0.3)	(0.1,0.1,0.1)	(0.3,0.3,0.2)

(continued)

Table 2. (*continued*)

Patients/Symptoms	Chest Pain	Palpitations	Dizziness	Fainting	Fatigue
P_3	(0.4,0.5,0.6)	(0.4,0.2,0.5)	(0.8,0.4,0.5)	(0.5,0.4,0.2)	(0.5,0.2,0.3)
	(0.5,0.2,0.2)	(0.5,0.2,0.2)	(0.1,0.2,0.2)	(0.3,0.6,0.6)	(0.3,0.2,0.5)
	(0.1,0.3,0.2)	(0.1,0.6,0.3)	(0.1,0.4,0.3)	(0.2,0.0,0.2)	(0.2,0.8,0.2)
P_4	(0.5,0.7,0.4)	(0.5,0.6,0.4)	(0.4,0.6,0.4)	(0.4,0.7,0.6)	(0.0,0.2,0.1)
	(0.2,0.2,0.4)	(0.3,0.3,0.4)	(0.2,0.2,0.5)	(0.3,0.2,0.2)	(0.6,0.4,0.5)
	(0.3,0.1,0.2)	(0.2,0.1,0.2)	(0.4,0.2,0.1)	(0.3,0.1,0.2)	(0.4,0.4,0.4)

Table 3. Inspection of consultant III

Patients/Symptoms	Chest Pain	Palpitations	Dizziness	Fainting	Fatigue
P_1	(0.4,0.6,0.8)	(0.4,0.7,0.5)	(0.5,0.2,0.3)	(0.4,0.4,0.6)	(0.0,0.3,0.6)
	(0.4,0.3,0.2)	(0.6,0.2,0.3)	(0.3,0.5,0.7)	(0.4,0.5,0.2)	(0.7,0.4,0.3)
	(0.2,0.1,0.0)	(0.0,0.1,0.2)	(0.2,0.3,0.0)	(0.2,0.1,0.2)	(0.3,0.3,0.1)
P_2	(0.6,0.5,0.7)	(0.4,0.5,0.6)	(0.6,0.4,0.3)	(0.4,0.6,0.2)	(0.7,0.6,0.5)
	(0.3,0.2,0.2)	(0.4,0.3,0.2)	(0.3,0.5,0.4)	(0.2,0.3,0.7)	(0.1,0.2,0.3)
	(0.1,0.3,0.1)	(0.2,0.2,0.2)	(0.1,0.1,0.3)	(0.4,0.1,0.1)	(0.2,0.2,0.2)
P_3	(0.6,0.2,0.5)	(0.4,0.5,0.3)	(0.7,0.6,0.7)	(0.5,0.4,0.3)	(0.5,0.6,0.4)
	(0.2,0.4,0.3)	(0.4,0.2,0.4)	(0.2,0.2,0.2)	(0.3,0.4,0.4)	(0.2,0.2,0.3)
	(0.2,0.4,0.2)	(0.2,0.3,0.3)	(0.1,0.2,0.1)	(0.2,0.2,0.3)	(0.3,0.2,0.3)
P_4	(0.7,0.5,0.6)	(0.6,0.4,0.2)	(0.8,0.3,0.5)	(0.5,0.6,0.5)	(0.3,0.4,0.5)
	(0.2,0.2,0.2)	(0.2,0.3,0.4)	(0.1,0.3,0.2)	(0.3,0.3,0.2)	(0.4,0.2,0.2)
	(0.1,0.3,0.2)	(0.2,0.3,0.4)	(0.1,0.4,0.3)	(0.2,0.1,0.3)	(0.3,0.4,0.3)

Table 4. Inspection of consultant IV

Patients/Symptoms	Chest Pain	Palpitations	Dizziness	Fainting	Fatigue
P_1	(0.4,0.6,0.5)	(0.7,0.5,0.4)	(0.5,0.4,0.5)	(0.6,0.5,0.5	(0.3,0.3,0.4)
	(0.2,0.1,0.3)	(0.3,0.4,0.4)	(0.3,0.5,0.4)	(0.3,0.2,0.2)	(0.6,0.5,0.4)
	(0.4,0.3,0.2)	(0.0,0.1,0.2)	(0.2,0.1,0.1)	(0.1,0.3,0.3)	(0.1,0.2,0.2)
P_2	(0.4,0.3,0.6)	(0.0,0.2,0.4)	(0.3,0.2,0.3)	(0.7,0.6,0.3)	(0.2,0.4,0.0)
	(0.4,0.5,0.2)	(0.6,0.3,0.2)	(0.2,0.6,0.1)	(0.2,0.4,0.1)	(0.2,0.1,0.8)
	(0.2,0.2,0.2)	(0.4,0.5,0.4)	(0.5,0.2,0.6)	(0.1,0.1,0.6)	(0.6,0.5,0.2)
P_3	(0.5,0.4,0.3)	(0.6,0.3,0.3)	(0.7,0.6,0.4)	(0.4,0.6,0.3)	(0.2,0.3,0.4)
	(0.2,0.2,0.3)	(0.2,0.1,0.3)	(0.1,0.2,0.2)	(0.4,0.2,0.3)	(0.4,0.5,0.3)
	(0.3,0.2,0.4)	(0.2,0.6,0.4)	(0.2,0.2,0.4)	(0.2,0.2,0.4)	(0.4,0.2,0.3)
P_4	(0.5,0.6,0.4)	(0.3,0.6,0.3)	(0.4,0.3,0.2)	(0.3,0.4,0.2)	(0.4,0.5,0.0)
	(0.2,0.2,0.2)	(0.3,0.2,0.4)	(0.4,0.4,0.2)	(0.4,0.2,0.3)	(0.2,0.1,0.6)
	(0.3,0.2,0.4)	(0.4,0.2,0.3)	(0.2,0.3,0.6)	(0.3,0.4,0.5)	(0.4,0.4,0.4)

Table 5. Combined IMFM

Patients/ Symptoms	Chest Pain	Palpitations	Dizziness	Fainting	Fatigue
P_1	(0.44,0.53,0.55)	(0.49,0.47,0.45)	(0.40,0.37,0.44)	(0.51,0.41,0.51)	(0.32,0.41,0.51)
	(0.27,0.23,0.30)	(0.42,0.37,0.36)	(0.39,0.44,0.48)	(0.32,0.40,0.23)	(0.49,0.35,0.34)
	(0.39,0.24,0.15)	(0.09,0.16,0.19)	(0.21,0.19,0.08)	(0.17,0.19,0.26)	(0.20,0.24,0.15)
P_2	(0.46,0.41,0.55)	(0.46,0.37,0.47)	(0.36,0.38,0.32)	(0.34,0.43,0.24)	(0.45,0.42,0.38)
	(0.35,0.36,0.27)	(0.34,0.31,0.27)	(0.34,0.39,0.29)	(0.46,0.38,0.49)	(0.19,0.27,0.42)
	(0.19,0.24,0.18)	(0.19,0.33,0.26)	(0.30,0.23,0.39)	(0.20,0.20,0.26)	(0.37,0.31,0.20)
P_3	(0.44,0.43,0.38)	(0.43,0.37,0.31)	(0.63,0.51,0.49)	(0.45,0.42,0.26)	(0.42,0.33,0.37)
	(0.32,0.27,0.38)	(0.40,0.16,0.39)	(0.17,0.20,0.25)	(0.36,0.44,0.44)	(0.29,0.33,0.39)
	(0.24,0.30,0.23)	(0.16,0.46,0.31)	(0.20,0.29,0.26)	(0.19,0.14,0.29)	(0.29,0.33,0.24)
P_4	(0.51,0.49,0.40)	(0.48,0.49,0.37)	(0.46,0.43,0.32)	(0.43,0.49,0.40)	(0.25,0.41,0.35)
	(0.23,0.25,0.29)	(0.25,0.28,0.36)	(0.30,0.29,0.37)	(0.31,0.28,0.31)	(0.42,0.26,0.37)
	(0.26,0.25,0.31)	(0.27,0.23,0.26)	(0.24,0.29,0.31)	(0.26,0.23,0.29)	(0.33,0.33,0.28)

Table 6. Transformed IFM

Patients/Symptoms	Chest Pain	Palpitations	Dizziness	Fainting	Fatigue
P_1	(0.42,0.30,0.17)	(0.43,0.39,0.17)	(0.34,0.46,0.19)	(0.44,0.29,0.23)	(039,0.36,0.20)
P_2	(0.38,0.33,0.26)	(0.43,0.30,0.25)	(0.35,0.34,0.29)	(0.32,0.44,0.22)	(0.39,0.25,0.31)
P_3	(0.36,0.40,0.22)	(0.35,0.23,0.21)	(0.49,0.24,0.23)	(0.32,0.45,0.12)	(0.27,0.40,0.30)
P_4	(0.47,0.28,0.25)	(0.34,0.39,0.24)	(0.24,0.41,0.33)	(0.41,0.35,0.19)	(0.32,0.37,0.30)

Table 7. Reference matrix

Symptoms/Stage	Stage I	Stage II	Stage III	Stage IV
Chest Pain	(0.7,0.2,0.1)	(0.6,0.2,0.2)	(0.7,0.2,0.1)	(0.1,0.8,0.1)
Palpitations	(0.2,0.6,0.2)	(0.7,0.1,0.2)	(0.2,0.6,0.2)	(0.2,0.7,0.1)
Dizziness	(0.1,0.8,0.1)	(0.3,0.3,0.4)	(0.7,0.2,0.1)	(0.4,0.4,0.2)
Fainting	(0.6,0.2,0.2)	(0.5,0.1,0.4)	(0.3,0.1,0.6)	(0.1,0.8,0.1)
Fatigue	(0.7,0.2,0.1)	(0.1,0.1,0.8)	(0.5,0.2,0.3)	(0.3,0.4,0.3)

Table 8. Distance matrix

Patients/Diseases	Hamming distance				Euclidean distance				Diagnosis result
	Stage I	Stage II	Stage III	Stage IV	Stage I	Stage II	Stage III	Stage IV	
P_1	**0.40**	0.48	0.45	0.47	**0.56**	0.86	0.64	0.92	Stage I
P_2	0.48	**0.46**	0.47	0.47	0.77	**0.72**	0.75	0.79	Stage II
P_3	0.57	0.52	0.48	**0.40**	0.52	0.47	0.46	**0.42**	Stage IV
P_4	0.51	**0.45**	0.48	0.47	0.85	**0.74**	0.77	0.92	Stage II

6 Conclusion

In this paper, we have proposed IMFC operator for decision making using IMFS and apply it in decision making problems. We have also introduced harmonic average method to degenerate IMFS to IFS. The real life example is related to diagnosing the various stages of heart disease based on a set of symptoms. The symptoms of each of the patients are represented using IMFVs. A group of four experts have been used to monitor the set of symptoms for a set of four patients. The convolution operator has been used to aggregate the opinions of those four experts. This study has done distance measurement between the combined matrix and reference matrix to determine the collective decision of the experts. Since convolution of two functions represents the amount overlap between the two functions, IMFC operator will provide good result when the decision makers don't differ much in their opinions. In future, the convolution operator may be extended to decision making in uncertainties using the various extensions of fuzzy sets.

References

1. Atanassov, K.T.: Intuitionistic fuzzy sets. Fuzzy Sets Syst. **20**, 87–96 (1986)
2. Atanassov, K.T.: Intuitionistic Fuzzy Sets: Theory and Applications. Physica-Verlag, Heidelberg/New York (1999)
3. Zadeh, L.A.: Fuzzy sets. Inf. Control **8**, 338–353 (1965)
4. Blizard, W.D.: Real-valued multisets and fuzzy sets. Fuzzy Sets Syst. **33**(1), 77–97 (1989)
5. Yager, R.R.: On the theory of bags. Int. J. General Syst. **13**(1), 23–37 (1986)
6. Goguen, J.A.: L-fuzzy sets. J. Math. Anal. Appl. **18**(1), 145–174 (1967)
7. Sebastian, S., Ramakrishnan, T.: Multi-fuzzy sets. Int. Math. Forum **5**, 2471–2476 (2010)
8. Shinoj, T., John, S.J.: Intuitionistic fuzzy multisets and its application in medical diagnosis. World Acad. Sci. Eng. Technol. **61**, 1178–1181 (2012)
9. Das, S., Kar, M.B., Kar, S.: Group multi-criteria decision making using intuitionistic multi-fuzzy sets. Journal of Uncertainty Analysis and Applications **10**(1), 1–16 (2013)
10. Atanassov, K.T.: New operations defined over the intuitionistic fuzzy sets. Fuzzy Sets Syst. **61**(2), 137–142 (1994)
11. De, S.K., Biswas, R., Roy, A.R.: Some operations on intuitionistic fuzzy sets. Fuzzy Sets Syst. **114**(3), 477–484 (2000)
12. Szmidt, E., Kacprzyk, J.: Distances between intuitionistic fuzzy sets. Fuzzy Sets Syst. **114**(3), 505–518 (2000)
13. Yager, R.R.: On ordered weighted averaging aggregation operators in multi-criteria decision making. IEEE Trans. Syst. Man Cybern. **18**(1), 183–190 (1988)
14. Yager, R.R., Filev, D.P.: Induced ordered weighted averaging operators. IEEE Trans. Syst. Man Cybern. B Cybern. **29**(2), 141–150 (1999)
15. Xu, Z., Yager, R.R.: Some geometric aggregation operators based on intuitionistic fuzzy sets. Int. J. Gen Syst **35**(4), 417–433 (2006)
16. Xu, Z.: Intuitionistic fuzzy aggregation operators. IEEE Trans. Fuzzy Syst. **15**(6), 1179–1187 (2007)
17. Wei, G.: Some induced geometric aggregation operators with intuitionistic fuzzy information and their application to group decision making. Appl. Soft Comput. **10**(2), 423–431 (2010)

18. Zhao, H., Xu, Z., Ni, M., Liu, S.: Generalized aggregation operators for intuitionistic fuzzy sets. Int. J. Intell. Syst. **25**(1), 1–30 (2010)
19. Xia, M., Xu, Z.: Generalized point operators for aggregating intuitionistic fuzzy information. Int. J. Intell. Syst. **25**(11), 1061–1080 (2010)
20. Wang, W., Liu, X.: Intuitionistic fuzzy information aggregation using einstein operations. IEEE Trans. Fuzzy Syst. **20**(5), 923–938 (2012)
21. Li, B., He, W.: Intuitionistic fuzzy pri-and and pri-or aggregation operators. Inform. Fusion **14**(4), 450–459 (2013)
22. Theodoridis, T., Hu, H.: A fuzzy-convolution model for physical action and behaviour pattern recognition of 3D time series. In: Proceedings of the 2008 IEEE International Conference on Robotics and Biomimetics Bangkok, Thailand, 21–26 February 2009
23. Das, S., Kar, S.: The Hesitant Fuzzy Soft Set and Its Application in Decision-Making. In: Chakraborty, M., Skowron, A., Maiti, M., Kar, S. (eds.) Facets of Uncertainties and Applications. Springer Proceedings in Mathematics & Statistics, vol. 125, pp. 235–247. Springer, New Delhi (2013). doi:10.1007/978-81-322-2301-6_1
24. Das, S., Kar, S., Pal, T.: Group decision making using interval-valued intuitionistic fuzzy soft matrix and confident weight of experts. J. Artif. Intell. Soft Comput. Res. **4**(1), 57–77 (2014)
25. Das, S., Kar, M.B., Pal, T., Kar, S.: Multiple attribute group decision making using interval-valued intuitionistic fuzzy soft matrix. In: Proceeding of IEEE International Conference on Fuzzy Systems (FUZZ-IEEE), Beijing, pp. 2222–2229 (2014). doi:10.1109/FUZZ-IEEE.2014.6891687
26. Das, S., Kar, S.: Group decision making in medical system: an intuitionistic fuzzy soft set approach. Appl. Soft Comput. **24**, 196–211 (2014)
27. Das, S., Kar, S.: Intuitionistic multi fuzzy soft set and its application in decision making. In: Maji, P., Ghosh, A., Murty, M.N., Ghosh, K., Pal, S.K. (eds.) PReMI 2013. LNCS, vol. 8251, pp. 587–592. Springer, Heidelberg (2013). doi:10.1007/978-3-642-45062-4_82
28. Das, S., Kar, S., Pal, T.: Robust decision making using intuitionistic fuzzy numbers, granular computing (2016). doi:10.1007/s41066-016-0024-3
29. Das, S., Rani, M., Pal, T., Kar, S. :Interval-valued induced averaging aggregation operator and its application in group decision making with intuitionistic fuzzy information. In: Proceedings of the Seventh International Joint Conference on Computational Sciences and Optimization (CSO), Beijing, pp. 307–311 (2014) doi:10.1109/CSO.2014.64

Bengali-to-English Forward and Backward Machine Transliteration Using Support Vector Machines

Kamal Sarkar[⊠] and Soma Chatterjee

Department of Computer Science and Engineering,
Jadavpur University, Kolkata, India
jukamal2001@yahoo.com, somadey05@gmail.com

Abstract. Name transliteration is an area which deals with transliteration of out-of-vocabulary (OOV) words. It plays an important role in developing automatic machine translation and cross lingual information retrieval system because these systems cannot directly translate out-of-vocabulary (OOV) words. In this article, we present SVM based name transliteration approach that considers transliteration task as a multi-class problem of pattern classification, where the input is a source transliteration unit (chunks of source grapheme) and the classes are the distinct transliteration units (chunks of target grapheme) in the target language. Our proposed approach deals with Bengali-to-English forward and backward name transliteration. Our proposed method has also been compared with some existing transliteration model that uses a modified version of Joint-Source channel model. After the systems have been evaluated, the obtained results show that our proposed SVM based model gives the best results among the others.

Keywords: Name transliteration · Support Vector Machines (SVM) · KNN · Modified joint-source channel model · Machine Transliteration (MT) · Machine translation

1 Introduction

Transliteration is a process of mapping a source language phoneme or grapheme to its approximate representation in a target language [1]. The process of transforming a source language word represented as a phone sequence or grapheme sequence into an equivalent representation in a target language is called forward transliteration, while the reverse is called Backward Transliteration. For example, if the input name in Bengali is "অনিন্দিতা," the output of the Bengali-to-English MT system should be "anindita". Transliteration is mainly useful in Statistical Machine Translation (SMT), and Cross Language Information Retrieval (CLIR) where OOV words are transliterated because the system has no translation for OOV words. A SMT system which is usually trained with a very large parallel corpora consisting of several million words may not have a complete coverage over highly productive word classes like proper names. When a SMT system translates a new sentence from a source language to a target language and

© Springer Nature Singapore Pte Ltd. 2017
J.K. Mandal et al. (Eds.): CICBA 2017, Part II, CCIS 776, pp. 552–566, 2017.
DOI: 10.1007/978-981-10-6430-2_43

the system sees any unknown word (not present in the training corpora), it will either leave it un-translated or fail.

The performance of CLIR system can also be improved by incorporating an additional module for transliterating unknown words and proper names [2, 3]. MT assists in translation of queries submitted to a CLIR system.

Due to information explosion on the web, increasing number of new terms are being added to the web. Since most of the new terms are out-of-vocabulary terms, translations of these terms are not also available. So, MT is also necessary for handling these new terms.

Major MT models which have been proposed by several researchers are grapheme-based transliteration model [4–12], phoneme-based transliteration model [13–15] and hybrid model [7, 16, 17]. These models are categorized in terms of the units to be transliterated. Sometimes the grapheme based transliteration model is called the *direct method* because it directly maps source language graphemes into the equivalent target language graphemes without using any phonetic knowledge of the source language words. The phoneme based model has two important steps: (1) maps source language graphemes to source language phonemes, (2) maps source phonemes to target language graphemes. The hybrid model exploits the knowledge of both source language graphemes and source language phonemes in the transliteration process.

Our proposed MT method is a grapheme based transliteration model that uses direct mapping from source language graphemes into the equivalent target language graphemes. In our approach, a machine learning algorithms SVM and KNN are trained to learn to map source language graphemes into the corresponding target language graphemes. To do this, source language grapheme is represented as a sequence of meaningful units called transliteration units (TUs) [1] where a TU is a meaningful chunk of the source grapheme. Accordingly, the target grapheme is also represented as sequence of TUs. Here, MT problem is reduced to a machine learning problem where the task is to learn the function f that maps a sequence of source TU sequence to the best possible target TU sequence. We have simplified this learning problem as reading the source TU sequence one by one from the left of a source name and assigning the best possible target TU to the source TU under consideration. For a source TU, there may have several possible transliterations in the target language, for example, for the Bengali TU "ল", there are three English representations in our training data like "l", "la" and "lo". So, this problem is analogous to sense disambiguation problem where there may exist several senses of a source TU under the different contexts. We attach the contextual information with the source TU to disambiguate its sense. We consider the surrounding TUs of a source TU as its context. Then a source is represented by a pattern vector using the TUs in the context window which is set up by keeping the source TU under consideration at the center of the window. Thus, the learning function f can be symbolically written as:

$$f : x \rightarrow y$$

Where x is the pattern vector representing a source TU and y is the set of possible target classes (TUs). Y is basically the set of all possible distinct TUs in the target language.

If there are m number of distinct TUs in the target language, y can take any one value from set of m values. The contributions of our work are summarized below:

(1) We address the problems of Bengali- to- English forward and backward transliteration of proper names in a unified frame work
(2) We view the MT problem as a pattern classification problem
(3) Contextual window based features are used to represent each source TU
(4) We apply Support Vector Machines (SVM) and K nearest neighbour (KNN) classifiers for solving MT problem.

The organization of the rest of this paper is as follows. Previous work related to our study has been presented in Sect. 2. A brief description of the data set has been presented in Sect. 3. Our proposed method has been described in Sect. 4. The experiments, evaluation and results has been described Sect. 5. The conclusion of this paper with a summary and a look at future enhancements of our work has been described Sect. 6.

2   Related Work

Transliteration process takes a character string in source language as input and generates a character string in the target language as output.

So, depending on how the input words can be decomposed into units for mapping them to the corresponding units in the target language, the major approaches of MT can be broadly classified as (1) grapheme based approach, (2) phoneme based approach and (3) hybrid approach. Most researchers have used machine learning technique for aligning the source language unit sequence with the target language unit sequence. Few researchers have used rule based algorithm for such alignment.

The previous works on MT can be differentiated based on three important dimensions-(1) which approach used (i.e., whether grapheme based approach or phoneme based approach or hybrid approach), (2) for which language pair (i.e., Bengali-English or Hindi-English or Japanese-English etc.) and (3) which algorithm is used (rule based or generative learning like HMM, Naïve Bayes or discriminative learning like CRF, SVM, Logistic Regression). We have shown in Fig. 1 a Multi-dimensional view of MT. In the following subsections, we review previous work related to the three major transliteration approaches.

2.1   Phoneme Based Approaches

The phoneme based approach broadly has two important steps- (1) grapheme to phoneme transformation and (2) phoneme to target language graphemes transformation.

The MT systems that uses phoneme based approach and generative learning based algorithm and that have been applied for the Japanese to English language pair have presented in [13, 18], English to Korean [14].

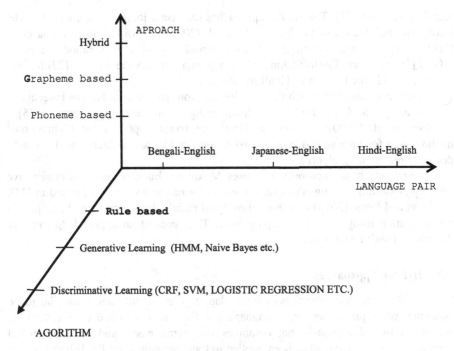

Fig. 1. Multi-dimensional view of MT

Other phoneme based MT approaches that use SVM have been applied for transliteration of the language pairs English - Kannada [19], Hindi-English and Marathi–English [20].

Hindi-to-English MT of named entities using CRF as a statistical probability tool and n-gram as feature set has been presented in [21].

Phoneme based MT system that uses Pronunciation and Contextual Rules for English-Korean Transliteration has been presented in [22].

2.2   Grapheme Based Approaches

The grapheme based approach directly transforms source language graphemes into the equivalent target language graphemes without using any intermediate phonetic representation.

The grapheme based MT approaches that use a set of hand crafted rules for transliterating from English to Punjabi have been presented in [23, 24].

Ekbal et al. (2006) [1] and Das et al. (2010) [25], present a framework that uses direct orthographical mapping between two languages that are of different origins It uses the linguistic knowledge of possible conjuncts and diphthongs in Bengali and their equivalents in English. The generative learning algorithm called joint source channel model and its variants have been used for transliterating from English-to-Bengali and backward. Since the work presented in Ekbal et al. (2006) [1] is mostly similar to our work, we have compared our proposed models with the best model presented in

Ekbal et al. (2006) [1]. The similar approaches that use a joint source channel model have also been presented in [26, 27]. Li et al. (2004) [26] differs from Rama et al. (2009) [27] in which language pair they considered for transliteration. Li et al. (2004) [26] considers English-Chinese language pair whereas the work in [27] focuses the task of MT, for English-to-Hindi transliteration.

A grapheme based approach that transliterates foreign words in Korean language to English using HMM based generative learning algorithm has been presented in [5].

Kang et al. (2000) [8] presents Grapheme based approach for bi-directional methodology for English-to-Korean transliteration and back-transliteration. They used decision tree learning algorithm.

A grapheme based approach that uses Maximum Entropy based discriminative learning algorithm for English to Japanese transformation has been presented in [11].

Josan and Lehal (2010) [28] have considered mainly direct grapheme-to-grapheme transformation using a set of mapping rules. They present an approach to improve Punjabi to Hindi transliteration.

2.3   Hybrid Approaches

The hybrid approach combines both source language graphemes and source language phonemes when producing target language transliterations. Lee and Choi (1998) [4] presents a hybrid approach that combines Grapheme based and phoneme based approaches. This approach has been applied to transliteration from English to Korean. This work presents a grapheme based Statistical Transliteration Model (STM) that learns rules automatically from word-aligned pairs in order to generate transliteration variations. They compared two approaches to MT- (1) The pivot method converts English words into pronunciation symbols by using the STM and then converting these symbols into Korean words by using the Korean standard conversion rule, (2) direct method, without intermediate steps. Finally they proposed a hybrid method for developing more effective transliteration systems. They used automatic Rule Learning method for learning rules of transliteration.

Bilac and Tanaka (2004) [17] proposed Hybrid method that combines the grapheme model and the phoneme model. In the grapheme model, an English word is transliterated to Japanese with some probability and in the phoneme model, a English word is converted to a sequence of phonemes.

Josan and Kaur (2011) [29] presents a hybrid MT that combines strengths of statistical and rule-based translation methodologies. Translations are performed using a rule based engine. The outputs of rule based engine are then corrected based on some statistics.

3   Dataset Preparation

Our data set is bilingual corpus of 1000 unique English-Bengali name pairs. English names have been collected from internet and their Bengali transliterations have done manually. We extracted the TUs from the Bengali names and the corresponding English names, and then Bengali TUs are associated with their English counterparts.

TU is a transliteration units into which a name is decomposed. We decompose each Bengali name and its equivalent English transliteration into a number of TUs. TUs in Bengali word take the pattern A^+B where A represents a vowel or a consonant or a conjunct and B represents the vowel modifier or matra. The English TUs are of the form $A*D*$ where A represents a consonant and D represents a vowel [1]. According to these regular expressions, the Bengali names and English names are segmented into TUs.

<অনিন্দিতা, anindita> →< [অ#নি#ন্দি#তা] , [a#ni#ndi#ta]>

<বৃথিকা, brithika> → <[বৃ#থি#কা], [bri#thi#ka]>

After we retrieved the transliteration units from a Bengali-English name pair, the Bengali TUs are associated with the corresponding English TUs along with the TUs in context.

For example, the following TUs along with their contexts are derived from the name pair, <আশালতা, ashalata>:

Previous Tu	Tu	Next Tu		Previous Tu	Tu
-	আ	শা	<->	-	a
আ	শা	ল	<->	a	sha
শা	ল	তা	<->	sha	la
ল	তা	-	<->	la	ta

According to the above example, for the source TU "শা", the corresponding English TU is "sha" and the context of the source TU is defined by its previous TU "আ" and the next TU "ল" and the context of the target TU "sha" is defined by its previous context "a".

But while decomposing names into TUs using the above stated regular expressions, it is found that the number of TUs derived from a Bengali name and the number of TUs derived from the corresponding English transliteration may differ. This leads to a difficulty in aligning the source TU sequence with the target TU sequence. We resolve this problem using some linguistic rules as stated in [1] that use linguistic knowledge in the form of valid conjuncts and diphthongs in Bengali and their English representation. For example, the [জগমোহন, jogmohan] name pair contains 5 TUs in Bengali name and 4 TUs in English name: [জ#গ#মো#হ#ন<->jo#gmo#ha#n]. In such cases, the system cannot align the TUs automatically so linguistic knowledge is exploited to resolve the confusion. To resolve this, we follow the same method as described in [1]. It is assumed that the problem TU in the English side has always the maximum length. If there are multiple English TUs of same length, the analysis is done from the first one [1]. In the above example, the TU "gmo" has the maximum length and the knowledge base suggests that "gmo" cannot be a valid TU in English because there is no corresponding conjunct representation in Bengali. So "jmo" is split up into 2 TUs "j" and "mo", and the 5 TUs are aligned as [জ#গ#মো#হ#ন<->jo#g#mo#ha#n].

In some cases, the problem of alignment is resolved using the knowledge of Bengali diphthong. In the following example, [সাইমা (সা#ই#মা)<->sai#ma], the number of TUs on one side is different from the other side. In this example, the English TU "sai" have a length which is greater than the other TU "ma". The vowel sequence "ai" is a diphthong in Bengali that has two valid Bengali representations <আই, ঐ> . The TU "ai" is split into "a" and "i" (ai → a#i) and the first one (i.e. a) is attached with the previous TU (i.e. r) and finally the name pair is split as: [[সা#ই#মা)<->sa#i#ma].

There are some exceptional cases where automatic decomposition process may produce some incorrect TU sequence. The cases are as follows.

- The cases where the number of TUs on the both sides do not match and the maximum length English conjunct TU has a valid conjunct representation in Bengali
- The cases where one-to-one correspondence between Bengali TU sequence and English sequence is not possible.

For these cases we followed the same procedure as described in [1], that is, it is manually aligned or the training examples are moved to the direct example base which contains the English names and their in Bengali transliteration.

4 Proposed Methodology

Our proposed method views the MT problem as classification problem where the source TU along with its context is considered as the input to the trained classifier and the classifier assigns one of the possible target TUs (chosen from a set of the distinct TUs in the target language). So, in this classification task, input source TUs along with its context are treated as patterns and the set of distinct TUs in target language are the possible classes. The input name in source language is represented as a sequence of TUs and the task is to predict the target TU for each source TU in the sequence.

For all classifiers, we need to represent a TU as a numerical pattern. Since, for a source TU there may exist more than possible target TU, the context of the source TU would help to disambiguate which target TU should be assigned. To utilize the context of the source TU, we examine a slice of sequence window and assume that the central source TU in that window will be assigned a target TU that is determined by surrounding TUs present in that window. We exploit this idea to represent a TU as a pattern, i.e., a TU is represented as a pattern vector whose entries come from the TU itself and the neighbors of the concerned TU. Thus our proposed MT method has two important steps: feature representation or pattern vector representation and classification which are described in the subsequent subsections.

4.1 Feature Representation

As mentioned earlier in the paper, the source name is represented as a sequence of TUs which are basically represented as pattern vectors. This type of representation is necessary because the most classifiers cannot directly handle TUs in the form of sequence of strings. To make it usable by the classifiers, the input to the classifier should be converted to the numeric values, i.e., the input TU should be represented as vector of values of the features that can discriminate the concerned TU among other TUs in a language. As we mentioned in the earlier sections, the class label (target TU) for a source TU is not only dependent on the source TU itself, but also it is dependent on the other TUs in the context of the source TU.

$$M_{W \times n} = \begin{pmatrix} 1 & 0 & 0 & 0 & 0 & 0 & \dots & 0 \\ 0 & 1 & 0 & 0 & 0 & 0 & \dots & 0 \\ 0 & 0 & 1 & 0 & 0 & 0 & \dots & 0 \\ . & . & . & . & . & . & \dots & . \\ . & . & . & . & . & . & \dots & . \\ 0 & 0 & 0 & 0 & 0 & 0 & \dots & 1 \end{pmatrix}$$

Fig. 2. Pattern representation for TUs in the window

To take care of the effect of these surrounding TUs on the TU under consideration, we consider a window of length W while determining the pattern vector for the central TU. Thus W/2 number of TUs on the left side of the central TU constitutes the left context and W/2 TUs on its right side constitute the right context. Here W is chosen as an odd value. If the total number of distinct TUs in the source language is n and the n-dimensional pattern vector for a source TU corresponds to the sequence $<TU_1, TU_2, TU_3, \dots, TU_i, \dots, TU_n>$ and the pattern vector for any source TU is represented by a binary vector V of length n, where V[i] = 1 if the TU under consideration matches with the TUi and all other vector positions get the value of 0. For example, X is a source TU and X matches with TU_3 then the vector representation of X is $<0, 0, 1,.. 0\dots 0>$. A source TU along with its context in the window is represented by a matrix of order W X n, where W is the number of TUs in the window and n is the length of the binary vector representing a TU. A sample matrix is shown in Fig. 2. Thus the matrix shown in Fig. 2 represents a pattern for the TU at the center of the window and this is also the TU to be transliterated. For an example, if the size of the window is set to 3 and the source TU sequence for the source name রতন is [র#ত#ন], the source TU "র" and the source TU "ত" in the source name রতন [র#ত#ন] are represented by the matrices shown in Figs. 3 and 4 respectively.

TUs	f_1	f_2	f_3	f_4	f_5	...	f_{n-1}	f_n
Null	0	0	0	0	0	...	0	0
র	0	1	0	0	0	...	0	0
ত	0	0	0	0	1	...	0	0

Fig. 3. Pattern representation when the source TU to be transliterated is "র"

TUs	f_1	f_2	f_3	f_4	f_5	...	f_i	...	f_{n-1}	f_n
ব	0	1	0	0	0	...	0	...	0	0
ত	0	0	0	0	1	...	0	...	0	0
ন	0	0	0	0	0	...	1	...	0	0

Fig. 4. Pattern representation when the source TU to be transliterated is "ত"

In Fig. 3, the first row contains n number of 0 s. To obtain the vector of equal size for each TU to transliterated, we need to add n number of 0 s at the beginning when the concerned source TU is the first TU of the source name and window size is 3. Padding of n number of 0 s is also required at the end of the vector when the concerned source TU is the last TU of the source name.

This W x n dimension matrix for a source TU is converted to one dimensional vector by concatenating the rows of the matrix one after another i.e. the feature vector looks like <row_1, row_2 ... row_w> , which has W x n number of features. This one dimensional vector is labeled with the target TU retrieved from the training pair of the source name and the corresponding target name, for example, the concatenated pattern vector for the source TU "ত" in the source name রতন [র#ত#ন] is labeled with the target English TU "ta" which is retrieved from the training pair: <[র#ত#ন], [ra#ta#n]>. Thus, all such labeled pattern vectors representing the source language TUs in the training data are created. This labeled data is then used for training a classifier that learns to classify the pattern vectors representing the source TUs into the possible target TUs.

4.2   Classification

We have used WEKA 3.6 tool kit for classification of the patterns using SVM (SMO) with Polynomial Kernel and K-NN (IBF) (with K = 1). In this section we describe classification details of Bengali-to-English MT and English-to-Bengali back-transliteration using WEKA tool. We have used SVM and KNN as a machine learning algorithm for the classifications of patterns based on variable window sizes. For classification we create the training file which contains feature vectors for TUs of the names in training data. The files are created in WEKA required format which requires each row to contain a m_1-dimension pattern vector (where m_1 = W x n) for a TU in the source name and the last column of the row to contain the label which is the corresponding target TU (English TU) for the source Bengali TU. In a similar way, we have also created the training file for back-transliteration, that is, each row of the training file contains a m_2-dimension pattern vector (where m_2 = W x p, where W is the window size and p is the number of distinct TUs in English language) and the last column of the row is the label which is the corresponding target TU (Bengali TU) for the source English TU. Using these files and WEKA tool kit, the classifier SVM (SMO) and K-NN (IBF) are trained. The test data are also represented in the similar way as the training data. The classification for test data is done using the trained models.

5   Evaluation, Experiments and Results

Since the standard bilingual NE corpus for Bengali-English language pair is not available, the systems have been evaluated using our data set containing 1000 named entities which are person names, place name of Indian origin. The system performance has been measured in terms of Transliteration Unit Agreement Ratio (TUAR) and Word Agreement Ratio (WAR) following the evaluation scheme as described in [1]. WAR measures the correctness of the system generated word, that is, WAR evaluates the system based on word level correctness and TUAR measures the correctness of the system based on Transliteration unit level correctness. Let B be the input Bengali word, E be the English transliteration given by the human and E_s be the system generated transliteration. TUAR is defined as, TUAR = (T-Err)/T, where T is the total number of TUs in test dataset, and Err is the number of wrongly transliterated TUs generated by the system. WAR is defined as, WAR = $(M-Err_s)/M$, where M is the total number of names in the test data and Err_s is the number of erroneous names (i.e. E_s does not match with E) generated by the system.

10-fold cross validation test is performed for each individual MT system. For this purpose, we use the entire labeled data. In this evaluation method, the entire data is divided into equal 10 parts (each part contains the equal number of named entities, i.e. 100 named entities in our case) and one part is held out for testing and the remaining 9 parts (900 named entities) are combined to use for training the system. Thus for each system, 10 test results are collected for the 10 different folds and the final results are averaged over 10 folds.

.5.1   Experiments

We have conducted following three experiments to prove the effectiveness of our proposed SVM based MT model.

Experiment1. In the experiment we implement a probabilistic model presented in [1] which is an existing work in the literature and which is the most similar work to our present work. The details of the joint source noisy channel model can be found [1, 12]. Out of the six different variants of the joint source noisy channel model proposed in [1], authors have experimentally proved that the model F was the best model. We have implemented this model F for comparing to our work.

Experiment2. We have implemented our proposed SVM based MT model for Bengali-to-English transliteration and back-Transliteration.

Experiment3. We apply a K-NN classification model for our MT tasks.

For each experiment, when source language TUs are represented as a pattern vector using the method described in the Sect. 4, the window size is set to 3 since Bengali names contain 3 TUs on an average. For the TUs which occurs at the beginning of the name or at the end of the name, we add n (where n is the number of distinct TUs in the source language) number of 0 s to the beginning or the end to obtain each pattern vector of equal size.

5.2   Results

As mentioned in the earlier sections, system performance has been measured in TUAR and WAR. For system comparisons, 10-fold cross validation has been done. The fold-wise results for each system have been collected. Finally fold-wise results are averaged to obtain a unique system performance score which has been reported in this section.

Comparisons of Bengali-to-English Transliteration Systems. The average TUAR scores obtained by the Bengali-to-English transliteration models are shown in Table 1.

As we can see from Table 1, the performance of SVM model is better than other models. We have also observed that SVM performs better than other two models for almost all folds. Hence, SVM performs significantly better than other two models in terms of TUAR.

Table 1. Average TUAR of each model (Bengali-to-English transliteration)

Models	TUAR (In %)
SVM	80.82
K-NN	75.66
Probabilistic Model [1]	74.379

The overall average performances in terms of WAR obtained by our proposed Bengali-to-English transliteration models and the existing probabilistic model are shown in Table 2. As we can observe from Tables 1 and 2 that transliteration unit agreement ratio (TUAR) obtained by the SVM model is 80.82% and word agreement • ratio is 53.9%, which produces better results than K-NN model and existing probabilistic model [1] for Bengali-to-English transliteration.

Table 2. Average WAR of each model (Bengali-to-English transliteration)

Models	WAR (In%)
SVM	53.9
K-NN	44.4
Probabilistic Model [1]	45

System Performance Comparisons for English-to-Bengali Transliteration. We have also compared the performances of our proposed models along with the existing probabilistic model presented in [1] for English-to-Bengali transliteration. The same performance measures, TUAR and WAR which are used for evaluating Bengali-to-English transliteration systems are also used here.

The overall average performance of English-to-Bengali transliteration systems measured in terms of TUAR is shown in Table 3.

We have shown in Table 4 the comparisons of the performances of the E2B transliteration models in terms of average WAR. We observed from the conducted

Table 3. Average TUAR of each model (English-to-Bengali transliteration)

Models	TUAR (In %)
SVM	75.87
K-NN	70.9
Probabilistic Model [1]	64.73

Table 4. Average WAR of each model (English-to-Bengali transliteration)

Models	WAR (In %)
SVM	45.2
K-NN	36.8
Probabilistic Model [1]	32.4

experiments that SVM model generates the best WAR and TUAR among the proposed models, and existing probabilistic model [1]. It is evident from the above mentioned Tables 3 and 4, that SVM model's transliteration unit agreement ratio is 75.87% and word agreement ratio is 45.2%, which produces better results than K-NN model and existing probabilistic model [1] for English-to-Bengali transliteration. We have also observed that SVM performs better than other two models across the all folds.

5.3 Error Analysis and Discussion

During experimentations with Bengali-to-English transliteration system, we have identified two types of errors committed by the system.

Error type1. When the search TU (TU to be transliterated) is not present in the training data, the system finds an approximate solution for such type of TU, for example, KNN algorithm has the tendency to find the TU whose vector has the maximum similarity to the search TU and to assign the label of the resultant TU vector as label of the search TU. During this approximation process, the system may sometimes commit errors. We are presenting below an example of Bengali name which is wrongly transliterated.

Input: অঙ্কিতা <অ#ক্কি#তা>(ankita)
Output: a#si#ta [system generated string]

When the input source word is অ#ক্কি#তা and the search TU is "ক্কি", we observed that the system transliterates it as "si". Our inspection reveals that "ক্কি" is not present in our training data. We also observe that, for the search TU "ক্কি", the system generates the TU "si". We also observe that there exists two training examples T1 and T2 containing a Bengali TU (say, X) corresponding to the English TU "si" and the previous TU of X in T1 matches with the previous TU ("অ") of the search TU "ক্কি" in our present input and the next TU of X in T2 matches with the next TU ("তা") of the search TU "ক্কি".

Error type2. Another type of error occurred when the sufficient contextual information is not available to accurately identify the English representation for a given search TU.

564   K. Sarkar and S. Chatterjee

We are presenting below an example of Bengali name which is wrongly transliterated due to type 2 errors.

Input: লক্ষী <ল#কথী> (laksmi)
Output: l#tu

Our inspection in the training data for the possible causes of this type of errors reveals the following facts:

- The Bengali TU "ল" have three English representations in the training data like "l", "la" and "lo". The system generates the TU "l". Since the sufficient contextual information is not available, the system choses the transliteration which has the maximum frequency in the training data.
- We also observe that another TU "কথী" in the input source name occurs with the transliteration "ksi" in the training data only once in a context which is different from its current context in our present input. On the hand, the Bengali TU "টু" whose English transliteration is "tu" also occurs only once in the training word with its left context "ল" which is also the left context of the TU "কথী". So, it is equally probable to choose either "ksi" or "tu" as the transliteration of the Bengali TU "কথী". Most likely, that is why the system generates the TU "tu" for the search TU "কথী" as a random choice.

Similar types of errors have also occurred for English-to-Bengali transliteration. Examples are given below. The reasons for such types of errors for English-to-Bengali transliteration are also the same as we discussed earlier in this section.

Error type 1. *Input*. bidya <bi#dya> (বিদ্যা), *Output*. বি#জ

Error type 2. *Input*. soumitra <sou#mi#tra> (সৌমিত্র), *Output*. সৌ#মি#ত্রা

6 Conclusion and Future Work

In this study, we have viewed MT as a pattern classification problem and used the machine learning algorithm SVM and K-NN for the classification of patterns. The experimental results reveal that SVM is more suitable for the Bengali-to-English forward and backward MT tasks. The current system is tested for person names, place names only. It can further be extended for foreign words, organization names and other kinds of named entities. MT can also be useful for normalizing the foreign words to a common form through transliteration and this step when incorporated in the IR system may help in improving the IR system performance. We will investigate such application of MT in future.

Acknowledgments. This research work has received support from the project entitled "Design and Development of a System for Querying, Clustering and Summarization for Bengali" funded by the Department of Science and Technology, Government of India under the SERB scheme.

References

1. Ekbal, A., Naskar, S., Bandyopadhyay, S.: A modified joint source channel model for transliteration. In: Proceedings of the COLING-ACL, Australia, pp. 191–198 (2006)
2. Abdul Jaleel, N., Larkey, L.: Statistical transliteration for English-Arabic cross language information retrieval. In: Proceedings of CIKM, pp. 139–146 (2003)
3. Virga, P., Khudanpur, S.: Transliteration of proper names in cross-language applications. In: 26th Annual International ACM SIGIR Conference on Research and Development in Information Retrieval, pp. 365–366 (2003)
4. Lee, J.S., Choi, K.S.: English to Korean statistical transliteration for information retrieval. J. Comput. Process. Orient. Lang. **12**(1), 17–37 (1998)
5. Jeong, K.S., Myaeng, S.H., Lee, J.S., Choi, K.S.: Automatic identification and back-transliteration of foreign words for information retrieval. J. Inform. Process. Manage. **35**(1), 523–540 (1999)
6. Kim, J.J., Lee, J.S., Choi, K.S.: Pronunciation unit based automatic English-Korean transliteration model using neural network. In: Proceedings of Korea Cognitive Science Association, pp. 247–252 (1999)
7. Lee, J.S.: An English-Korean transliteration and re-transliteration model for Cross lingual information retrieval. Ph.D. thesis, Computer Science Dept. KAIST (1999)
8. Kang, B.J., Choi, K.S.: Automatic transliteration and back-transliteration by decision tree learning. In: 2nd International Conference on Language Resources and Evaluation, pp. 1135–1411 (2000)
9. Kang, I.H., Kim, G.C.: English-to-Korean transliteration using multiple unbounded overlapping phoneme chunks. In: 18th International Conference on Computational Linguistics, pp. 418–424 (2000)
10. Kang, B.J.: A resolution of word mismatch problem caused by foreign word transliterations and English words in Korean information retrieval. Ph.D. thesis, Computer Science Dept., KAIST (2001)
11. Goto, I., Kato, N., Uratani, N., Ehara, T.: Transliteration considering context information based on the maximum entropy method. In: Proceedings of MT-Summit IX, pp. 125–132 (2003)
12. Li, H., Zhang, M., Su, J.: A joint source-channel model for MT. In: Proceedings of ACL, pp. 160–167 (2004)
13. Knight, K., Graehl, J.: MT. In: 35th Annual Meetings of the Association for Computational Linguistics, pp. 128–135 (1997)
14. Jung, S.Y., Hong, S., Paek, E.: An English to Korean transliteration model of extended Markov window. In: 18th Conference on Computational linguistics, pp. 383–389 (2000)
15. Meng, H., Lo, W.-K., Chen, B., Tang, K.: Generating phonetic cognates to handle named entities in English-Chinese cross-language spoken document retrieval. In: Proceedings of Automatic Speech Recognition and Understanding, ASRU 2001, pp. 311–314 (2001)
16. Al-Onaizan, Y., Knight, K.: Translating named entities using monolingual and bilingual resources. In: Proceedings of ACL, pp. 400–408 (2002)
17. Bilac, S., Tanaka, H.: Improving back-transliteration by combining information sources. In: Su, K.-Y., Tsujii, J., Lee, J.-H., Kwong, O.Y. (eds.) IJCNLP 2004. LNCS, vol. 3248, pp. 216–223. Springer, Heidelberg (2005). doi:10.1007/978-3-540-30211-7_23
18. Stalls, B.G., Knight, K.: Translating names and technical terms in Arabic text. In: Proceedings of the Workshop on Computational Approaches to Semitic Languages, pp. 34–41. Association for Computational Linguistics, August 1998

19. Antony, P.J., Ajith, V.P., Soman, K.P.: Kernel method for English to Kannada transliteration. In: International Conference IEEE, Recent Trends in Information, Telecommunication and Computing (ITC), pp. 336–338 (2010)
20. Rathod, H., Dhore, M. L., Dhore, R. M.: Hindi and Marathi to English MT using SVM. Int. J. Natural Lang. Comput. (IJNLC) 2(4), 55–71 (2013)
21. Dhore, M.L., Dixit, S.K., Sonwalkar, T.D.: Hindi to English MT of named entities using conditional random fields. Int. J. Comput. Appl. 48(23), 31–37 (2012)
22. Oh, J.H., Choi, K.S.: An English-Korean transliteration model using pronunciation and contextual rules. In: 19th International Conference on Computational linguistics, Association for Computational Linguistics, vol. 1, pp. 1–7 (2002)
23. Bhalla, D., Joshi, N., Mathur, I.: Rule based transliteration scheme for English to Punjabi. arXiv preprint arXiv:1307.4300 (2013)
24. Deep, K., Goyal, V.: Development of a Punjabi to English transliteration system. Int. J. Comput. Sci. Commun. 2(2), 521–526 (2011)
25. Das, A., Saikh, T., Mondal, T., Ekbal, A., Bandyopadhyay, S.: English to Indian languages MT system at NEWS 2010. In: Proceedings of the 2010 Named Entities Workshop, Association for Computational Linguistics, pp. 71–75 (2010)
26. Haizhou, L., Min, Z., Jian, S.: A joint source-channel model for MT. In: ACL (2004)
27. Rama, T., Gali, K.: Modeling MT as a phrase based statistical machine translation problem. In: Proceedings of the Named Entities Workshop, Shared Task on Transliteration, pp. 124–127. Association for Computational Linguistics (2009)
28. Josan, G., Lehal, G.: A Punjabi to Hindi MT system. Int. J. Comput. Linguist. Chin. Lang. Process. 15(2), 77–102 (2010)
29. Josan, G., Kaur, J.: Punjabi to Hindi statistical MT. system. Int. J. Inform. Technol. Knowl. Manage. 4, 459–463 (2011)

Type-2 Fuzzy Controller with Type-1 Tuning Scheme for Overhead Crane Control

Indrajit Naskar and A.K. Pal⁽✉⁾

Department of AEIE, Heritage Institute of Technology, Kolkata, India
indrajit.naskar@heritaheit.edu,
arabindakumarpal@gmail.com

Abstract. In this paper, a type-1 on-line fuzzy self-tuning scheme is proposed for a type-2 fuzzy PD controller (FPDC). The proposed scheme is applied on an overhead crane to control the cart position as well as the pendulations of the load for smooth material transport. In this study, two separate self-tuning fuzzy logic PD controllers (STFLPDC) are proposed. The STFLPDCs adjust the gain of the controller according to the process requirement by changing the output scaling factors on-line. A comparative study of the crane control is made with respect to other fuzzy controllers.

Keywords: Type-1 fuzzy · Type-2 fuzzy · Overhead crane control · Self-tuning

1 Introduction

The overhead cranes have many uses, but mainly they are employed for the freight transport in ports and also in construction industry for the movement of raw materials [1]. The main problem of transportation through crane system is its pendulation or swing of the load, and this problem of pendulations in the crane is aggravated due to its lightly damped nature that means if any transient motion takes place, it will take a long time to dampen out [2, 3]. In this work, apart from our proposed STFLPDC, type-1 fuzzy logic PD controller (T1FLPDC), type-2 fuzzy logic PD controller (T2FLPDC) and type-1 self-tuning fuzzy logic PD controller (T1STFLPDC) were also investigated on the overhead crane [4, 5]. We have designed the controllers in MATLAB and Simulink environment.

In an industry, an experienced process operator always tracks the output. If any disturbance/error arises in the process an operator through his experience by changing the output of the controller eliminates the error. The output scaling factor (SF) in a fuzzy controller is very important as it directly relates with its gain [4, 6]. Therefore the estimation of the output scaling factor is very crucial for the proper implementation of a fuzzy logic controller (FLC) [7, 8]. Depending on the present process performance, an experienced operator always tries to rectify the controller gain for effective control. Different type-2 fuzzy controllers (T2FLCs) are developed for effective control of uncertainty [9, 10]. Type-1 FLC (T1FLC) and interval T2FLC with different number of if-then rules are designed to control different simulated and real time systems [11, 12]. *Chen et al.* developed the interval T2FLC using different types of membership

© Springer Nature Singapore Pte Ltd. 2017
J.K. Mandal et al. (Eds.): CICBA 2017, Part II, CCIS 776, pp. 567–576, 2017.
DOI: 10.1007/978-981-10-6430-2_44

functions (MFs) [13]. Different T2FLCs were designed to investigate nonlinear and time-varying systems [14–16].

Tuning of T2FLC is very difficult and till now there is no such universal method for tuning of T2FLC [17, 18]. Here, a type-1 self-tuning technique is suggested for T2FLPDC. An improved performance through STFLPDC is expected as it incorporates the dynamics (input error and input change of error) of the process (here, overhead crane). Two FPDCs: one for position controller and another for angle controller are used separately to control the overhead crane. Our dual control scheme approach helps to reduce the computational complexity of the crane control system that is highly nonlinear in behaviour.

2 Proposed Self-tuning Controller Design

The output SF is a very vital parameter for the FLC due its relation to the stability of the whole process. Depending on the input variables *i.e.*, error (e) and change of error (Δe), an operator change the control action by modifying the SF and thereby enhance the process performance [5].

As the MF of T2FLC has a footprint of uncertainty (FOU), which represents the uncertainties in the shape and position of any type-1 fuzzy system [9, 10]. The FOU is restricted by an upper MF (UMF) and a lower MF (LMF), both of which are type-1 type MF. In this work, we design an interval type-2 FPDC with FOU that embedded with 4 T1FLCs. Interval T2FLC is designed by taking the average of T1FLCs. Since FOU of T2FLC offers an additional mathematical feature, so they can be useful in cases where the amount of uncertainty is very high and therefore it is difficult to determine the proper MFs [13] (Fig. 1).

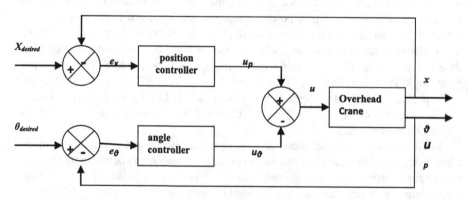

Fig. 1. Dual control structure (position x and angle θ) for overhead crane control

For MFs generation, the left swing of the load is considered as positive swing and the right swing as negative swing. The STFLPDCs use for position and angle control of the crane generate outputs of u_p and u_θ respectively as indicated in Fig. 2. For the overhead crane control using STFLPDC, we incorporate the proposed gain tuning scheme through an on-line gain modifier β, where β is obtained from the output of T1FLCs as shown in Fig. 2. The total control action (u) to drive the cart by STFLPDC is u_p - u_θ. The controller output of STFLPDC is used to operate the DC motor presents in the crane system for position and angle control as shown in Figs. 3 and 4. In the scheme, e_x and e_θ represent errors, Δe_x and Δe_θ represent change of errors, and u_p and u_θ stand for output variable for position and angle controller respectively. Cart position error (e_x) and load sway angle error (e_θ) are obtained from the two encoders mounted for the cart position and swing angle measurement respectively as shown in Fig. 3.

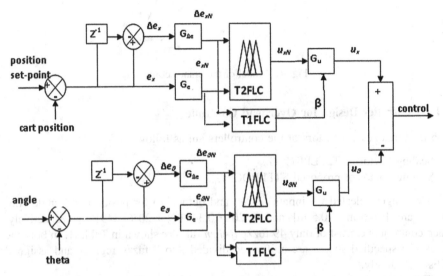

Fig. 2. Dual control and block diagram of STFLPDC for overhead crane control

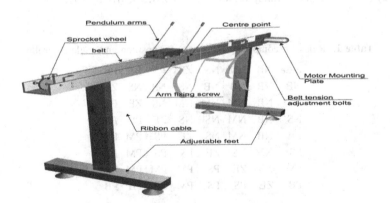

Fig. 3. Laboratory based overhead crane

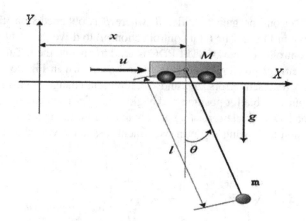

Fig. 4. Model of the crane set-up

2.1   Controller Design for Overhead Controller

The modified scaling factors of the controllers are as follows:

Scaling Factor of T2FLPDC: G_u
Scaling Factor of proposed STFLPDC: $G_u . \beta$

The ranges selected for inputs $(e, \Delta e)$ and output (u) for position and angle controller are $[-0.5 \text{ m}, + 0.5 \text{ m}]$ and $[-20°(-0.3491°), + 20°(0.3491°),]$ respectively. Each controllers consist of only 49 fuzzy *if-then* rules as shown in Table 1. In both the cases, the specified spaces are uniformed divided into 7 fuzzy regions and assigned MFs accordingly.

The term sets (shown in Table 1) $LE = L\Delta E = LU = \{NB, NM, NS, ZE, PS, PM, PB\}$, contain the same linguistic values. Similarly the MFs for β (shown in Table 2) is mapped into 7 fuzzy regions $\{ZE, VS, S, SB, MB, B, VB\}$.

Table 1. Rules for computing output (u) for position and angle controller

e/Δe	NB	NM	NS	ZE	PS	PM	PB
NB	NB	NB	NB	NS	NS	NS	ZE
NM	NB	NM	NM	NM	NS	ZE	PS
NS	NB	NM	NS	NS	ZE	PS	PM
ZE	NB	NM	NS	ZE	PS	PM	PB
PS	NM	NS	ZE	PS	PS	PM	PB
PM	NS	ZE	PS	PM	PM	PM	PB
PB	ZE	PS	PS	PM	PB	PB	PB

Table 2. Fuzzy rules for computing gain factor (β)

$e/\Delta e$	NB	NM	NS	ZE	PS	PM	PB
NB	VB	VB	VB	B	SB	S	ZE
NM	VB	VB	B	B	MB	S	VS
NS	VB	MB	SB	MB	ZE	S	VS
ZE	S	SB	ZE	ZE	S	SB	S
PS	VS	S	ZE	MB	SB	MB	VS
PM	VS	S	MB	B	B	YB	YB
PB	ZE	S	SB	B	VB	VB	VB

2.2 Overhead Crane Model

The proposed controller is demonstrated on a laboratory based Overhead crane (Make: FEEDBACK, UK) as shown in Fig. 3. The working model of the set-up is presented in Fig. 4.

The Overhead crane is an unstable system which, in terms of behavior, means that the plant left without any controller reaches an unwanted, very often destructive state. Thus for such plants it is useful to carry out simulation tests on the models before approaching the real plant. The phenomenological model of the overhead crane is nonlinear, meaning that at least one of the states (x and dx/dt or θ and $d\theta/dt$) is an argument of a nonlinear function.

For modeling Lagrangian approach is considered and thereby derived the load and cart position vectors from Fig. 4, which are given by

$$\overrightarrow{x_l} = \{x + l \sin \theta, -l \cos \theta\}\ \overrightarrow{x_c} = \{x, 0\} \tag{1}$$

The kinetic (K) and potential (P) energy of the gantry crane system are represented by:

$$K = \frac{1}{2} M\ \overrightarrow{\dot{x}_c} . \overrightarrow{\dot{x}_c} + \frac{1}{2} m\ \overrightarrow{\dot{x}_l} . \overrightarrow{\dot{x}_l} \tag{2}$$

and

$$P = -mgl \cos \theta \tag{3}$$

Let corresponding to the generalized displacements $\overrightarrow{q} = \{x, \theta\}$, the generalized force is $\overrightarrow{u} = \{u_x, 0\}$.

Then construct Lagrange's equations for $i = 1, 2$

$$\frac{d}{dt} \left(\frac{\partial L}{\partial \dot{q}_i} \right) - \frac{\partial L}{\partial q_i} = u_i \tag{4}$$

Where, $L = K - P$ and u_i is the external force to the trolley.

Then, the equations of motion of the system with respect to x and θ are obtained through Eqs. (5) and (6) are:

$$(M+m)\frac{d^2x}{dt^2} + K\frac{dx}{dt} = F_v + ml \sin \theta \left(\frac{d\theta}{dt}\right)^2 - ml \cos \theta \frac{d^2\theta}{dt^2} \tag{5}$$

$$\left(I+ml^2\right)\frac{d^2\theta}{dt^2} = mgl \sin \theta - ml \cos \theta \frac{d^2x}{dt^2} \tag{6}$$

The complexity of controlling the overhead crane mainly because of its coupled nature between swing angle and cart psition. The model represented by Eqs. (5) and (6) have four input variables (x and dx/dt or θ and $d\theta/dt$), which are the position variables (x and dx/dt) and angle variables (θ and $d\theta/dt$) are highly nonlinear in nature.

For the purpose of controller design the model has to be linearized and presented in the form of transfer functions. But such a linear equivalent of the nonlinear model is valid only for small deviations of the state values. Thus for the appropriate controller design we develop a nonlinear simulation model from the above equations of motion (Eqs. 5 and 6) as given by Fig. 5.

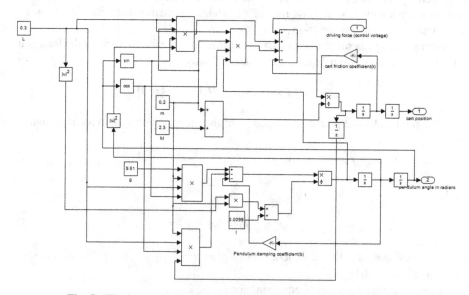

Fig. 5. The inverted pendulum simulink model using Eqs. (5) and (6).

The different constant values of Eqs. (5) and (6) are depicted in Table 3.

Table 3. Overhead crane constants values used for simulation study

m is the mass of the rod in kg	0.2
M is the mass of the moving cart in kg	2.3
g is the acceleration due to gravity in m/s^2	9.81
1 is the distance along the arm to the centre of gravity in m	0.3
I is the moment of inertia of the polem kgm^2	0.0099
K is the cart friction coefficient	0.00005

3 Results

The proposed self-tuning technique is investigated to control an overhead crane with set-points of 0.31 m step for position and π^c (180°) for angle control respectively. The controllers performance also studied with square wave input of amplitude ±0.15 m for position and π^c for angle controller. The control output of T1FLPDC, T1STFLPDC, T2FLPDC and proposed STFLPDC are individually subjected to the overhead crane for effective cart position and swing angle control.

The output of the proposed controllers are investigated under step and square wave inputs as shown in (Figs. 6, 7, 8 and 9). Simulation experiments on the overhead crane illustrated the merits of the proposed tuning scheme over the others. Figures 7 and 9 represent that proposed controller tracks the cart position effectively without much

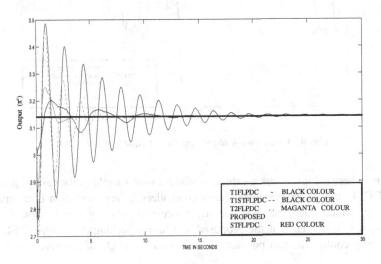

Fig. 6. Crane swing angle control for step input

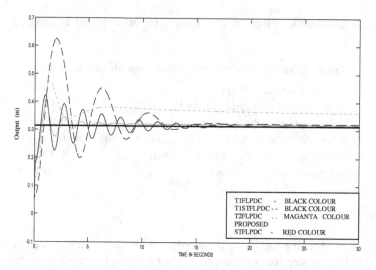

Fig. 7. Crane position control for step input

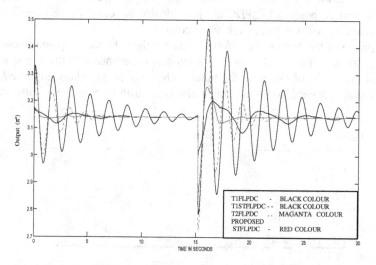

Fig. 8. Crane swing angle control for square wave input

deviation, whereas Figs. 6 and 8 exhibit minimum swing angle in the case of proposed STFLPDC. In case of conventional fuzzy controllers, a large variation is observed in load sway, which could be fatal for any process or loading - unloading systems. Whereas, it is observed that the proposed self-tuning technique for type-2 FLC can satisfactorily control the cart position as well as swing angle of the load attached.

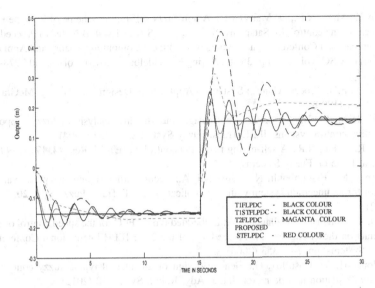

Fig. 9. Crane position control for square wave input

4 Conclusion

The paper presented a type-1 fuzzy based self-tuning technique for a type -2 fuzzy PD controller. Here, output SF in terms of the controller gain is continuously modified on-line through a multiplying factor β, obtained through proposed self-tuning scheme. Study reveals that implementation of our proposed STFLPDC on the overhead crane showed much improved performance compared to T1FLPDC, T2FLPDC and T1STFLPDC with different inputs. A simple dual control scheme is proposed here to ensure rule-reduction as well as model simplification. It is verified from the experimental study that our proposed STFLPDC can fix the cart in its desired location with minimum sway of the load. The suggested controller provides a useful alternative for controlling any such non-linear process, which are difficult to control using conventional methods.

References

1. Hong, K.S., Ngo, Q.H.: Port automation modeling and control of container cranes. In: International Conference on Instrumentation, Control and Automation, pp. 19–26 (2009)
2. Park, M.S., Chwa, D., Hong, S.K.: Antisway tracking control of overhead cranes with system uncertainties and actuator nonlinearity using an adaptive fuzzy sliding mode control. IEEE Trans. Ind. Electron. **55**(11), 3972–3984 (2008)
3. Sorensen, K.L., Singhose, W., Dickerson, S.: A controller enabling precise positioning and sway reduction in bridge and gantry crane. Control Eng. Pract. **15**, 825–837 (2007)
4. Lee, C.C.: Fuzzy logic in control systems: fuzzy logic controller—Parts I, II. IEEE Trans. Syst., Man, Cybern. **20**, 404–435 (1990)

5. Pal, A.K., Mudi, R.K., De Maity, R.R.: A non-fuzzy self-tuning scheme of PD-type FLC for overhead crane control. In: Satapathy, S.C., Udgata, S.K., Biswal, B.N. (eds.) Proceedings of the International Conference on Frontiers of Intelligent Computing: Theory and Applications (FICTA). AISC, vol. 199, pp. 35–42. Springer, Heidelberg (2013). doi:10.1007/978-3-642-35314-7_5

6. Shinskey, F.G.: Process Control Systems—Application, Design, and Tuning. McGraw-Hill, New York (1998)

7. Malki, H.A., Li, H., Chen, G.: New design and stability analysis of fuzzy proportional derivative control systems. IEEE Trans. Fuzzy Syst. **2**, 245–254 (1994)

8. Mudi, R.K., Pal, N.R.: A self-tuning fuzzy PD controller. IETE J. Res. **44**, 177–189 (1998). (Special Issue on Fuzzy Systems)

9. Manceur, M., Essounbouli, N., Hamzaoui, A.: Second-order sliding fuzzy interval type-2 control for an uncertain system with real application. IEEE Trans. Fuzzy Syst. **20**, 262–275 (2012)

10. Lynch, C., Hagras, H., Callaghan, V.: Embedded type-2 FLC for the speed control of marine and traction diesel engines. In: Proceedings of the 2005 IEEE International Conference on Fuzzy Systems, pp. 347–353 (2005)

11. Maldonado1, Y., Castillo1, O.: Genetic design of an interval type-2 fuzzy controller for velocity regulation in a dc motor. Int. J. Adv. Robot. Syst., 1–8 (2012)

12. Blaho, M., Urban, M., Fodrek, P., Foltin, M.: Wireless network effect on PI and type-2 fuzzy logic controller. Int. J. Commun. **6**, 18–25 (2012)

13. Chen, Y., Wang, T.: Interval type-2 fuzzy PID control and simulation. In: 2nd International Conference on Electronic & Mechanical Engineering and Information Technology, pp. 326–330 (2012)

14. Ahmad, M., El-Nagar, M., El-Bardini, A.M.: Practical implementation for the interval type-2 fuzzy PID controller using a low cost microcontroller. Ain Shams Eng. J. **5**, 475–487 (2014)

15. Biglarbegian, M., Melek, W.W., Mendel, J.M.: On the stability of interval type-2 TSK. IEEE Trans. Syst. Man Cybern.—part b: Cybern. **40**(3), 798–818 (2010)

16. Lin, Y.-Y., Chang, J.-Y., Pal, N.R., Lin, C.-T.: A mutually recurrent interval type-2 neural fuzzy system (mrit2nfs) with self-evolving structure and parameter. IEEE Trans. Fuzzy Syst. **21**, 492–509 (2013)

17. Ahmad, M., El-Nagar, M., El-Bardini, A.M.: Parallel realization for self-tuning interval type-2 fuzzy controller. Eng. Appl. Artif. Intell. J. **61**, 8–20 (2017)

18. Xingguo, L., Liu, M.: Optimal design and tuning of PID-type interval type-2 fuzzy logic controllers for delta parallel robots. Int. J. Adv. Rob. Syst. **1**, 1–12 (2016)

A Spatial Domain Image Authentication Technique Using Genetic Algorithm

Amrita Khamrui, Diotima Dutta Gupta$^{(\boxtimes)}$, S. Ghosh, and S. Nandy

Future Institute of Engineering and Management, Kolkata, India
amritakhamrui@rediffmail.com, diotima93@gmail.com,
gsayantani2012@gmail.com, shreyanandy94@gmail.com

Abstract. Since the risk associated with transmission of data over networks is the chance of intrusion and hampering of secrecy, safe transmission of hidden image without hindering the cover image is expected as in image steganography. In this paper, a spatial domain type of image authentication technique by means of Genetic Algorithm has been proposed. Genetic Algorithm is used to improve the quality of stego image. High PSNR values are achieved for various images in comparison with some other existing techniques in this field.

Keywords: Steganography · Genetic Algorithm · Fitness function · PSNR

1 Introduction

Information hiding and sending over digital media is quite common in recent times. But this is always in threat of intrusion. So, when sending encrypted information over digital media, focus must be on its security. When hidden information is associated with an image, steganography is a better option than cryptography. Steganography helps to hide information in an image without letting people know that there is a secret message inside. Steganography finds it use consistently in digital information exchange.

For exchanging information, the first work is embedding of secret messages within an image. After embedding, the stego image is referred to the corresponding receiver where decoding occurs. After decoding, the secret information is available for the intended recipient.

The main problem arises when the secret information can be read by others except the intended recipients before decoding. To avoid this, the secret information is hidden inside an image in such a way that there is not much visible difference between the actual and stego image. This paper aims at minimizing such differences and produces the stego image with better quality.

Steganography is referred as the process of concealing information (in this case, it is an image) within a media file such as image, video, etc. or a file or message (in this case, it is an image too). In this approach, three things are absolutely necessary: the cover image (in which the data or image is to be hidden), the data or image to be hidden (authenticating image) and the resultant stego image (created after the secret data or image is embedded into the original cover image). In this paper image authentication

© Springer Nature Singapore Pte Ltd. 2017
J.K. Mandal et al. (Eds.): CICBA 2017, Part II, CCIS 776, pp. 577–584, 2017.
DOI: 10.1007/978-981-10-6430-2_45

technique using steganographic approach has been proposed in spatial domain where the least significant bits (LSB) are used to embed the secret image.

The comparison between embedded image and optimized stego image is carried on using PSNR which is defined using the mean squared error (MSE). When given a m × n monochrome noise-free image I along with its noisy approximation K, MSE can be defined as:

$$MSE = \frac{1}{mn} \sum_{i=0}^{m-1} \sum_{j=0}^{n=1} [I(i,j) - K(i,j)]^2 \tag{1}$$

The PSNR (in dB) is demarcated as:

$$PSNR = 10 \cdot \log_{10}\left(\frac{MAX_I^2}{MSE}\right)$$

$$or, PSNR = 20 \cdot \log_{10}\left(\frac{MAX_I}{\sqrt{MSE}}\right) \tag{2}$$

$$or, PSNR = 20 \cdot \log_{10}(MAX) - 10 \cdot \log_{10}(MSE)$$

Here, MAX_I is given as the maximum possible value of a pixel of the image. If the pixels are used as 8 bits per image sample, the value of MAX_I must be 255. For colored images where there are three RGB values per image pixel, the PSNR value remains the same except that the MSE gives a different value.

According to the famous Holland's Schemata theorem [12], lower order schematics having more than average value of fitness function grow in consecutive generations exponentially. Therefore, by the execution of the genetic algorithm for a continuous sufficient amount of time it must converge at a global optimum [11]. The upper bound that is obtained after executing the iterations it is observed that it decreases on increasing the population size [13]. In this paper, the genetic algorithm is repeated till all the generations are processed until it delivers the desired result.

The secret image is hidden in the last 4 bit (LSB) of the cover image. In this way the 4 LSB of the pixels of the cover image are fixed in the stego image. So, the remaining 4 bits in the stego image are manipulated to make it as close as possible to the cover image, i.e. we have 16 combinations for optimization. After embedding, the stego image is obtained with 4 LSB fixed values. In this paper, a new fitness function is proposed. The motivation of this fitness function came from the PSNR. Since, more the PSNR value, fitter the individual, a mathematical formula is needed to increase the PSNR value. It means, according to the formula, it is needed to decrease the MSE value in the denominator because the other value is a constant. Now, since MSE value has a square term for eradicating any negative value coming from the difference, modulus can be used instead of it, for the same purpose. Now, the value of PSNR must be greater than one, and the value coming out from the modulus may be less than 1, and so 1 is added to it. This fitness function will take the individuals with the less values. That means, less the fitness value, fitter the individual. It must be kept in mind that crossover rate should be 80%–95% mutation rate should be low i.e. 0.5%–1% assumed as best.

The paper aims at optimization of the stego image as well as minimizing the difference between the stego and the original cover image so that information hidden cannot be easily identified. This research is based on spatial domain image authentication using Genetic Algorithm (GA) in order to increase the visual characteristics along with quality of the stego image. Section 2 deals with reviewing of literature and related papers. Section 3 conveys the proposed technique. Section 4 shows experimental results, comparison with other works and their analysis. Conclusion is drawn at the end.

2 Literature Review

Nowadays, there has been a lot of research in the field of steganography using meta-heuristic algorithms such as PSO and Genetic Algorithm method. Roy R et al. [1] developed a technique of retaining information in image using genetic algorithm by taking PSNR as fitness function. Cheddad A et al. [2] proposed a secure and improved self-embedding algorithm by using 1D hash algorithm along with 2D iFFT. Wang S et al. [3] researched on the RS attack that finds the stego-message by analysing the pixel values statistically. Begum R et al. [4] have used Key-Based Pixel Selection Algorithm in Least Significant Bit embedding to hide data in a cover image because of its low computation complexity as well as high embedding capacity. Li X et al. [5] developed a technique on steganography based on particle swarm optimization method to data on JPEG images. Research has been done by Fard MA et al. [6] on secure steganographic encoding on JPEG images with the help of maximum absolute difference of image quality and fitness function. Chang CC et al. [7], have proposed a secret image sharing algorithm using CRT which improves authentication ability and quality of the stego image. Wang RZ et al. [8] also developed a GA to insert the secret information in moderately significant bit of the cover image and they also projected global substitution step along with local pixel adjustment for increasing the quality of the stego image. Later Wang RZ et al. [9] formulated LSB substitution to hide secret data in the cover images using GA. Jung KH further added Pixel Value Differencing on edge areas when embedding secret data on to cover image by LSB substitution. Nan Jiang [14] proposes two blind LSB steganography algorithms as quantum circuits.

3 The Technique

In this paper a spatial domain image authentication technique using Genetic Algorithm has been proposed. A 3 × 3 mask is used by taking it from the source image in row major order. Four bits taken from each byte of the endorsing image has been extracted and embedded on last four LSB bits of the source image. This process is repeated for the whole source image. The image that is generated from embedding is called stego image. Genetic Algorithm (GA) has been applied on the stego image to generate optimized stego image. The steps of the proposed Genetic Algorithm are discussed in detail.

3.1 Genetic Algorithm

The paper proposes GA as the technique to improve the stego image as close to the cover image. GA is a very popular method for solving optimization problems based on natural selection and random search. The steps of the proposed GA are given as follows:

Initial population: The pixels of the cover image and that of the stego image are separately put into individual arrays. The stego image is produced by hiding the information in the last 4 bits of the cover image. So, out of 8-bits of the cover image, the 4 LSBs are now fixed with the secret information the first 4 MSBs can be changed. In this way, 2^4 combination of individuals are there to start with GA. These 16 individuals are generated randomly by the GA and are treated as the initial population.

Selection: A new fitness function have been proposed to decide the best individuals for cross over. The value of the fitness function is evaluated for each chromosome x in the population and the values are sorted to select the 2 least ones as the most fit individuals.

$$F(x) = 1 + |c[i,j] - s[i,j]| \qquad (3)$$

Here,

F(x) = Fitness Function
c = cover image
S = stego image.

Crossover: Uniform crossover is used in the GA. In uniform crossover, first bit of the pixel of the offspring is of the first parent and the second bit of the child is of the second parent. In this way, the offspring has equal number of chromosomes from both its parents placed alternatively.

Parent 1:	X X X X X X X
Parent 2:	Y Y Y Y Y Y Y
Offspring 1:	X Y X Y X Y X
Offspring 2:	Y X Y X Y X Y

Mutation: Random bit flipping procedure is used in mutation. In this step, a bit between 4–7th bit is selected randomly and flip that bit. This mutated offspring is then again tested according to fitness function and the fittest individual is accepted in the new population.

Accepting: The fittest individuals after mutation are accepted as the new population and the GA is repeated for the new population.

Termination: After execution of all the generations the GA is terminated when the desired results are achieved.

3.2   Insertion Algorithm

Input: source image is of size 512 × 512.
Output: optimized stego image is of size 512 × 512.
Steps:

1. *Consider a mask of size 3 × 3 from the source image.*
2. *Extract bits from the authenticating image. Bits from dimension are extracted first.*
3. *Four bits from the authenticating image is implanted into each byte from the source image.*
4. *Embed dimension of the authenticating image in first thirty two bits of the source image. Width in first sixteen bits and height in next sixteen bits.*
5. *Repeat step 1 to 3 for the whole source image until all bits of the authenticating image is embedded and embedded image or stego image is generated.*
6. *Take 8 × 8 mask from embedded image.*
7. *Generate sixteen random chromosomes for the first byte of the mask. The process is called initialisation.*
8. *Embed secret information in last four bits of each chromosome. The process of embedding is same as the process of forming stego image.*
9. *The fittest two chromosomes are selected through selection process using proposed fitness function. The fittest chromosomes are also called parent chromosome.*
10. *The parent chromosomes are taken for crossover. Crossover generates two offspring.*
11. *Two offspring are processed through mutation.*
12. *The fittest one after mutation is accepted as the next population and the GA is repeated.*
13. *GA is terminated when the desired results are achieved.*
14. *Step 7 to 13 is repeated for the entire mask.*
15. *Step 6 to 14 is repeated for the entire embedded image.*

3.3   Extraction Algorithm

Input: optimized stego image 512 × 512 in size.
Output: hidden authenticating image, cover image 512 × 512 in size.
Steps:

1. *Optimized image mask of size 8 × 8 is taken.*
2. *Reverse Crossover is performed on two consecutive off spring. Uniform cross-over is used. In uniform crossover, first bit of the pixel comes from the first parent and the second bit of the pixel is inherited from the second parent. This process is repeated for the whole optimized image.*

3. *Extract least significant four bits from each byte of the mask.*
4. *Each eight bit extraction form one byte of the authenticating image.*
5. *Extract the width of the authenticating image from the first sixteen bits and height from next sixteen bits.*
6. *Repeat step 3 to 6 until the all pixels of the authenticating image is extracted.*

4   Experimental Results

In research, 512 × 512 grey scale image (8 bit per pixel) Lena, Baboon are used here as cover images as shown in the Fig. 1. The secret image in this case is a 256 × 256 grey scale image in each case.

Fig. 1.   Cover images used here a. Lena b. Baboon

The comparisons of results are done with the PSNR values of the optimized images acquired by the application of the proposed GA relating to the corresponding cover image. The proposed method has been compared with Roy R et al. [1] with same payload that is 4. Table 1 shows the experimental result with two benchmark images Lena and Baboon. It is noticed that after applying GA PSNR has been improved. In Table 2 the proposed technique have compared with existing [1]. It has been seen that the proposed technique shows better result in terms of PSNR than existing [1].

Table 1.   PSNR values obtained from our experiment

Image name	PSNR of the stego image	PSNR of optimized stego image
Lena	35.206337	40.871
Baboon	35.076	40.0134

Table 2. Comparison of PSNR values obtained from our proposed work against existing method (Source: Roy, R et. al [1])

Image name	PSNR calculated by previous method [1]	PSNR calculated by our proposed method
Lena	38.466808	40.87
Baboon	38.4761	40.0134

5 Conclusion

In this work, an effective steganographic method is implemented for embedding secret information in the form of image into images without causing observable distortions. Steganography detection can be used to prevent communication of malicious data. It is hard to detect as message and fundamental image data share same range. The experimental results proves that the proposed method delivers a better technique for embedding data into cover images without producing noticeable alterations in the resultant image.

References

1. Roy, R., et al.: Optimization of stego image retaining information using genetic algorithm with 8-connected PSNR. Procedia Comput. Sci. **60**, 468–477 (2015)
2. Cheddad, A., et al.: A secure and improved self-embedding algorithm to combat digital document forgery. Signal Process. **89**(12), 2324–2332 (2009)
3. Wang, S., et al.: A secure steganography method based on genetic algorithm. J. Inf. Hiding Multimed. Signal Process. **1**(1), 28–35 (2010). ISSN 2073-421
4. Begum, R., et al.: Best approach for LSB based steganography using genetic algorithm and visual cryptography for secured data hiding and transmission over networks. Int. J. Adv. Res. Comput. Sci. Softw. Eng. **4**(6) (2014)
5. Li, X., et al.: A steganographic method based upon JPEG and particle swarm optimization algorithm. Inf. Sci. **177**(15), 3099–3109 (2007)
6. Fard, M.A., et al.: A new genetic algorithm approach for secure JPEG steganography. In: IEEE International Conference Engineering of Intelligent Systems (2006). doi:10.1109/ICEIS.2006.1703168
7. Chang, C.C., et al.: Sharing secrets in stego image with authentication. Sci. Direct Pattern Recogn. **41**(10), 3130–3137 (2008)
8. Wang, R.Z., et al.: Hiding data in images by optimal moderately significant bit-replacement. IEEE Electron. Lett. **36**(25), 2069–2070 (2000)
9. Wang, R.Z., et al.: Image hiding by optimal LSB substitution and genetic algorithm. Pattern Recogn. **34**, 671–683 (2001)
10. Jung, K.H.: High-capacity steganographic method based on pixel value differencing and LSB replacement methods. Imaging Sci. J. **54**(4), 213–221 (2010)
11. Goldberg, D.E.: Genetic Algorithms in Search, Optimization and Machine Learning. Addison Wesley, Boston (1989). ISBN 0-201-15767-5

12. Holland, J.H.: Adaptation in Natural and Artificial Systems: An Introductory Analysis with Applications to Biology, Control and Artificial Intelligence. MIT Press, Cambridge (1998). (NB original printing 1975). ISBN 0-262-58111-6
13. Vo-Van, T., et al.: Modified genetic algorithm-based clustering for probability density functions. J. Stat. Comput. Simul. **87**, 1964–1979 (2017)
14. Jiang, N., Zhao, N., Wang, L.: Int. J. Theor. Phys. **55**: 107 (2016). doi:10.1007/s10773-015-2640-0

Control of Two-Axis Helicopter Model
Using Fuzzy Logic

Abhishek Kar and Nirmal Baran Hui[(✉)]

Department of Mechanical Engineering, National Institute of Technology
Durgapur, Durgapur 713209, West Bengal, India
kar.abhishek946@gmail.com, nirmal.hui@me.nitdgp.ac.in

Abstract. Twin Rotor MIMO System becomes unstable quite easily and control becomes extremely difficult. Present paper is in search of a standard controller to be used for stabilizing such a complex system. Comparison between ZN-tuned PID and fuzzy logic controller has been made in this study. Initially, mathematical model of the system has been developed and simulated in MATLAB. At the end, the developed controllers are tested through a prototype Twin Rotor Multiple Input Multiple Output System (TRMS).

Keywords: Twin Rotor MIMO System · PID controller · Fuzzy logic control · Real experiments

1 Introduction

Modelling of dynamics of Air Vehicles is a challenging task since several nonlinear parameters are associated and states are not easily accessible. It makes the system unstable quite easily and control becomes extremely difficult. TRMS is an experimental set-up to test different control strategies. The TRMS model is highly popular now-a-day among the control engineers since it is difficult to perform direct experiments with air vehicles. Mechanical unit of the TRMS is shown in Fig. 1. It consist of two rotors and a arm. It can well represent a helicopter. The only difference is TRMS is controlled in the absence of aerodynamic effect, which is common for helicopters in reality. Moreover, control of Helicopter is achieved through the altercation of rotor angles. But, in TRMS, it is achieved through the change in speed. A good number of literature is available in this context.

Tastemirov et al. [10] derived the mathematical equations using the Euler-Lagrange. The parameters of the model are estimated and tuned using experimental data. Understanding the non-linearity present in the model, Rahideh et al. [9] modelled the TRMS using neural networks. Later on, Chalupa et al. [11] modelled a TRMS in MATLAB environment and carried out real time experiments to compare with the simulated model. Ahmad et al. [13] derived the analytical model of the TRMS using a system identification method and achieved low settling time and improved stability. Sámano et al. [7] modelled and stabilized an eight rotor helicopter model to achieve hover flight. The main purpose of them was to increase the payload carrying capacity of the rotorcraft without using larger motors and blades. The stabilization of the orientation of the rotorcraft was also tested.

© Springer Nature Singapore Pte Ltd. 2017
J.K. Mandal et al. (Eds.): CICBA 2017, Part II, CCIS 776, pp. 585–598, 2017.
DOI: 10.1007/978-981-10-6430-2_46

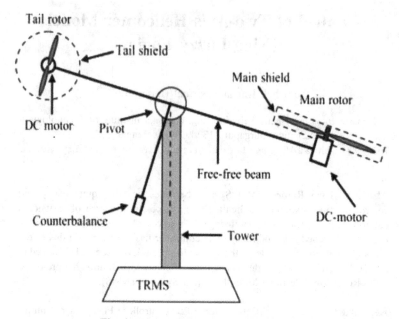

Fig. 1. Twin Rotor MIMO system set up

Since control of TRMS is a difficult task. Different controllers have been tested by various researchers. Chemachema and Zeghlache [8] designed an output feedback linearization based controller for TRMS and tested through computer simulations. Ullah and Lqbal [12] designed a Gaussian controller for a TRMS and its response was observed through computer simulations. Patel et al. [17] and Manoharan and Ramalakshmi [18] applied PID control scheme in TRMS. Later on, Pandey and Laxmi [14] made a comparative study between LQR and PID controller for TRMS control and achieved better performance with LQR.

The performance of PID controller is dependent on its gain parameters. Therefore, quite a few numbers of researchers tried to use soft computing-based controllers either alone or in combination with PID controller. For example, Rahideh and Shaheed [1] presented a fuzzy-PID controller for TRMS. The hybrid controller was found to perform better especially in steady state condition. Toha and Tokhi [2] presented a feed forward and backward control of a TRMS using a GA. This Multi Objective Gentic Algorithm (MOGA)-based controller provided improved tracking performance and significant reduction in vibration was achieved. Deb and Juyal [3] presented an adaptive neuro-fuzzy control applied to SISO and MIMO systems. It has generated good tracking performance, successfully controlled the plant in presence of disturbance input. Saroj and Kar [4] presented a Takagi-Sugeno type fuzzy controller and observer for TRMS. Nasir et al. [5] presented a spiral dynamic algorithm for the similar purpose. Limnaios and Tsourveloudis [6] designed an FLC for a coaxial helicopter and tested for attitude, altitude and position control purposes. Robustness to modelling errors was also assessed in this study. Ahmed and Mohamed [15] used particle swarm optimization for tuning gains of PID controller and tested on a TRMS. According to them, PSO-tuned PID was found to perform better than Ziegler-Nichols-tuned PID controller. In the similar line, Prasad et al. [16] achieved significant improvement in the controller performance when PID gains are tuned using a GA. Hashim and Abido [19] designed a PD fuzzy control scheme tuned by different evolutionary optimization techniques. Gravitational Search Algorithm was found to show the most impressive results in contrast to other algorithms with respect to convergence speed and optimum objective function.

Other than the mentioned above, few more types of controllers have also been applied by the researchers. Kumar and Srivastava [20] made a comparative study between Chebyshev neural network based observer (CNN) and Multi-layer feedforward neural network (MLFFNN) observer to control a TRMS. MLFF neural network resulted better compared to CNN. Rao et al. [21] designed H∞ observer for TRMS. The game theory approach was used to design H∞ filter. It was observed from the simulation results that H∞ observer generates good response in the presence of high level of noise input. Further, Zeghlache et al. [22] presented a type-2 FLC for a TRMS. It has been observed that review report shows that different types of controller (LQR [14], Lead lag controller [12], H∞ [21], PID [17, 18], fuzzy logic-based [22] and NN-based [20]), and different algorithms have been applied to control and stabilize a TRMS. However, the prime objective in developing the controller is to make the system stable in minimum possible time and with less overshoot. Following gaps in the literature have been identified.

- None of the papers reviewed so far has cited simulation or experimental results taking non-linear portion of the coupled dynamic equations.
- Quite a few investigators have shown their interest in experimental validation.
- Report also cites that a concrete algorithms having robust, adaptive, self tuned need to be developed for balancing a highly non-linear system such as TRMS.

In the present paper, an attempt has been made to compare PID and Fuzzy Logic Controller for analyzing the coupled behaviour of the system. Both computer simulations and real experiments will be conducted to see the performance of the controllers.

2 Transfer Function of TRMS

Detailed mathematical equations of the TRMS is available in [23]. These equations in brief are presented below.

$$I_1.\ddot{\varphi} = M_1 - M_{FG} - M_{B\varphi} - M_G \tag{1}$$

$$\text{where, } M_1 = a_1.\tau_1^2 + b_1.\tau_1, \tag{2}$$

$$M_{FG} = M_g.\sin\varphi, - \text{ momentum due to gravity} \tag{3}$$

$$M_{B\varphi} = B_{1\varphi}.\dot{\varphi} + B_{2\varphi}.sign(\dot{\varphi}), - \text{ friction forces momentum} \tag{4}$$

$$M_G = K_{gy}.M_1.\emptyset.\cos\varphi, - \text{gyroscopic momentum} \tag{5}$$

The rotor torwue can be calculated as -

$$\tau_1 = \frac{k_1}{T_{11}s + T_{10}}.u_1 \tag{6}$$

Mathematical equation in horizontal plane could be expressed as -

$$I_2.\ddot{\emptyset} = M_2 - M_{B\emptyset} - M_R \tag{7}$$

$$\text{where, } M_2 = a_2.\tau_2^2 + b_2.\tau_2, \tag{8}$$

$$M_{B\emptyset} = B_{1\emptyset}.\dot{\varphi} + B_{2\emptyset}.sign(\dot{\emptyset}), - \text{friction forces momentum} \tag{9}$$

M_R is the reaction momentum and given by:

$$M_R = \frac{k_c(T_0 s + 1)}{(T_P s + 1)}.\tau_1 \tag{10}$$

Torque expression for tail rotor is given as -

$$\tau_2 = \frac{k_2}{T_{21}s + T_{20}}.u_2 \tag{11}$$

System parameters are determined experimentally and presented in Table 1. From the derived equations, it has been observed that the TRMS consists of two inputs (u_1 and u_2) and two outputs (φ and ψ) and a cross coupling exists among them. Therefore, two linear models u_1 to φ and u_2 to ψ and u_1 to ψ and u_2 to φ are to be identified. As a result, control of such a MIMO system becomes extremely difficult and stability also becomes problematic.

Table 1. TRMS model parameters

Parameter	Value
l_1 - moment of inertia of vertical rotor	$6.8 \cdot 10^{-2}$ kg·m^2
l_2 - moment of inertia of horizontal rotor	$2 \cdot 10^{-2}$ kg·m^2
a_1 - static characteristic parameter	0.0135
b_1 - static characteristic parameter	0.0924
a_2 - static characteristic parameter	0.02
b_2 - static characteristic parameter	0.09
M_g - gravity momentum	0.32 N·m
$B_{1\psi}$ - friction momentum function parameter	$6 \cdot 10^{-3}$ N·m·s/rad
$B_{2\psi}$ - friction momentum function parameter	$1 \cdot 10^{-3}$ N·m·s^2/rad

(continued)

Table 1. (*continued*)

Parameter	Value
$B_{1\varphi}$ - friction momentum function parameter	$1 \cdot 10^{-1}$ N·m·s/rad
$B_{2\varphi}$ - friction momentum function parameter	$1 \cdot 10^{-2}$ N·m·s²/rad
K_{gy} - gyroscopic momentum parameter	0.05 s/rad
k_1 - motor 1 gain	1.1
k_2 - motor 2 gain	0.8
T_{11} - motor 1 denominator parameter	1.1
T_{10} - motor 1 denominator parameter	1
T_{21} - motor 2 denominator parameter	1
T_{20} - motor 2 denominator parameter	1
T_p - cross reaction momentum parameter	2
T_0 - cross reaction momentum parameter	3.5
K_c - cross reaction momentum gain	−0.2

3 TRMS Control

The TRMS control aspect covers two main control areas: Two 1-Degree of freedom (DOF) rotor control and 2-DOF rotor control. Each of these control problems has its own characteristic. Two 1-DOF control systems ignore the dynamical cross-coupling and control the rotors separately, whereas, 2-DOF control system ignores the couplings but controls both the rotors.

The PID control algorithm is one of the most popular control algorithms because of its simplicity. PID controller has been applied separately for 1-DOF pitch and rotor

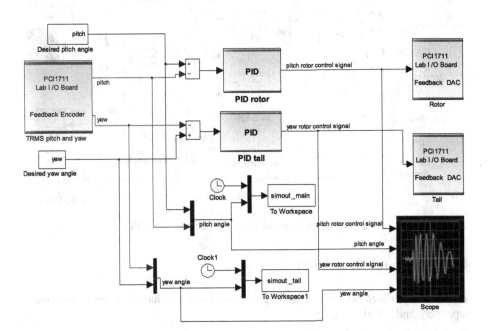

Fig. 2. Real time TRMS 2DOF position control model.

control and 2-DOF rotor control. Figure 2 shows the real-time simulink model of the 2-DOF PID controller for TRMS position control.

3.1 Fuzzy Logic Controller (FLC)

FLC has been applied separately for 1-DOF pitch and rotor control and 2-DOF rotor control. Mamdani-type FLC has been applied with triangular membership function. Linguistic terms used are NL: negative large, NS: negative small, DES: desired, PS: positive small and PL: positive large. Membership function distribution for 1-DOF control of pitch rotor is considered to be linear in nature. Rule base of the FLC for this purpose is presented in Table 2 and simulink model for control of pitch using FLC is shown in Fig. 3.

Table 2. Rule base for FLC for pitch control.

		Pitch error				
		NL	NS	DES	PS	PL
Yaw error	NL	NL	NS	NS	DES	DES
	NS	NS	DES	DES	PS	DES
	DES	NS	DES	DES	DES	PS
	PS	DES	DES	DES	DES	DES
	PL	DES	DES	DES	PS	PS

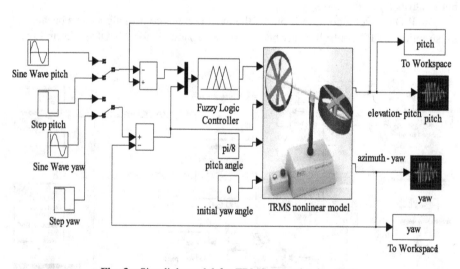

Fig. 3. Simulink model for TRMS control using FLC.

4   Results and Discussion

TRMS is simulated and real experiments have been conducted running two rotors separately and simultaneously.

4.1 Control of Single Rotor

Comparison between real pitch angle and desired pitch angle with Kp = 5, Ki = 8 and Kd = 10 is shown in Fig. 4. Model is simulated for 20 s.

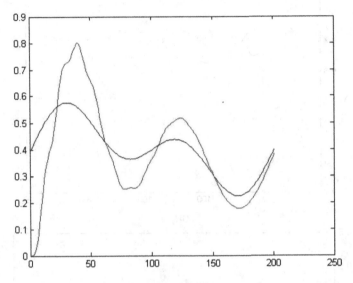

Fig. 4. Pitch rotor movement.

Similarly, Fig. 5 presents comparison between real and desired yaw angles with Kp = 2, Ki = 0.5 and Kd = 5.

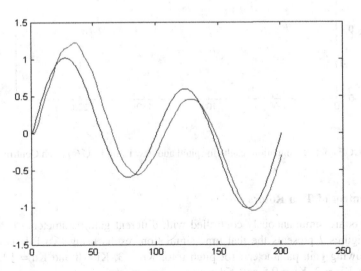

Fig. 5. Yaw rotor movement.

Figure 6 shows the output for pitch rotor and yaw rotor using fuzzy logic controller for pitch rotor.

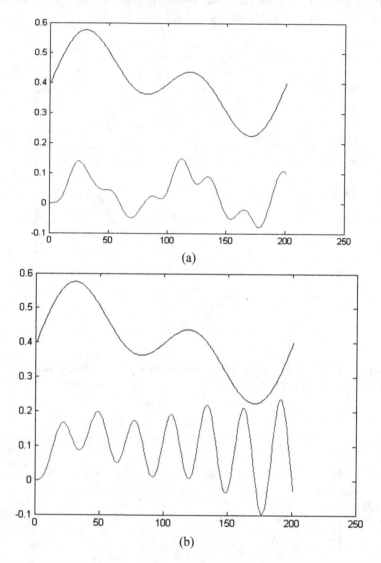

(a)

(b)

Fig. 6. 1DOF control simulation results for pitch and yaw using FLC (a) Pitch Control, (b) Yaw Control.

4.2   Control of Two Rotors

Two rotors are simultaneously controlled with different gain parameters of PID controller. Figures 7 presents the real time simulation results using two PID controllers with following gain parameters: for pitch rotor Kp = 3, Ki = 8 and Kd = 10 and for yaw rotor Kp = 2, Ki = 0.5 and Kd = 5.

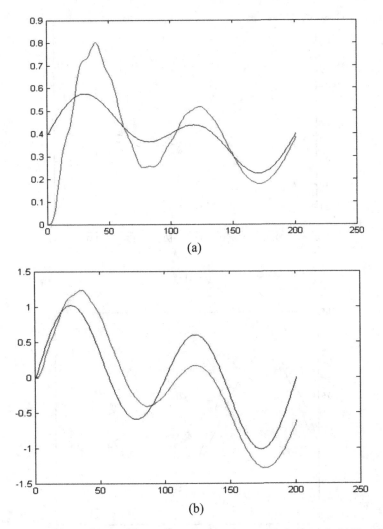

Fig. 7. 2DOF control simulation results for pitch and yaw – (a) Pitch Control, (b) Yaw Control.

Different results have been observed with different values of gain parameters. It is seen that the increase in Ki value slows down the system and cause bigger overshoot. Also we have noticed that the large value of Kd makes the system respond faster. However, very quick response may often break down the control unit. Therefore keeping our focus on the proportional term we designed the Kp value as a function of time. So following are the simulation results where Kp is used as a function of time for pitch rotor. Results with the following gain parameters are shown in Fig. 8: main rotor: $Kp = 5 * 0.1(1 - t + t^2)$, $Ki = 8$ and $Kd = 10$ and PID tail rotor $Kp = 2$, $Ki = 0.5$ and $Kd = 5$. The results obtained after using time varying Kp values for pitch rotor shows a significant variation from the results obtained by using constant Kp.

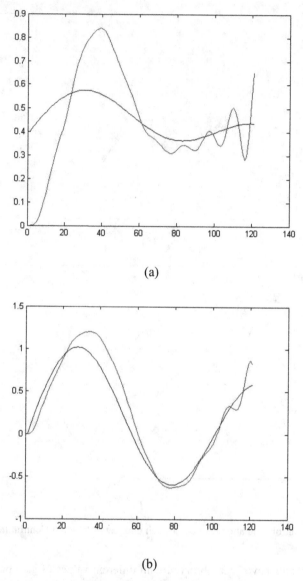

(a)

(b)

Fig. 8. 2DOF control simulation results for pitch and yaw using Kp = 5 * 0.1(1 − t + t²) for pitch rotor (a) Pitch Control, (b) Yaw Control.

Figure 9 shows the output for pitch rotor and yaw rotor using fuzzy logic controller for both pitch rotor and yaw rotor.

The results obtained by using fuzzy logic controller for the pitch rotor and yaw rotor shows that the pitch angle and yaw angle variation shows a similar pattern to the desired angle variation. So by optimizing the rule base and database better control can be achieved and fuzzy logic controller can be used as an alternate to conventional PID controller.

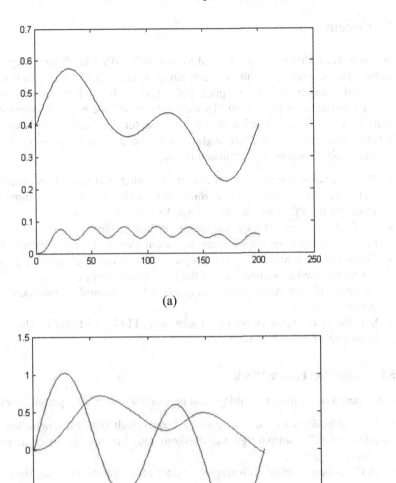

(a)

(b)

Fig. 9. 2DOF control simulation results for pitch and yaw using FLC for both pitch and yaw rotor (a) Pitch Control, (b) Yaw Control.

5 Conclusions

In this work, a PID controller is used to control TRMS with different Kp, Kd and Ki values. The simulation results corresponding to the different cases shows the actual pitch path against the desired pitch path. Then a fuzzy logic control approach is adopted. In the fuzzy logic controller the database and rule base is chosen randomly by trial and error. The simulation results obtained for the fuzzy logic based control of TRMS shows the actual pitch angle against the desired pitch angle. Some of the important observations are mentioned below.

- The simulation results for 1 DOF control of pitch and yaw rotors separately and 2 DOF controls of pitch and yaw rotors in tandem are found to be same for similar values of the PID gain parameters Kp, Ki and Kd.
- For 2 DOF controls of pitch and yaw rotors using different values of PID parameters provided different results and time-dependent gain parameters yielded better results.
- Control of pitch rotor using fuzzy logic controller could not provide good result. It is because the knowledge base of the FLC is not optimized.
- Response of yaw rotor control using fuzzy logic controller was found to be very slow.
- Simultaneous control of both the rotors using FLC gave better results as compared to control of individual rotors.

5.1 Scope for Future Work

In the near future, following things can be made to extend the present work.

- PID controller was found to provide better result than FL Controller. However, tuning of PID controller gain is a tedious job. Attempt can be made to tune PID controller gains.
- FLC has been applied with arbitrary values of Rule Base and Data Base. They may be optimized. Off-line training may be followed initially and trained RB and DB can later be used on-line.

References

1. Rahideh, A., Shaheed, M.H.: Hybrid fuzzy-PID-based control of a Twin Rotor MIMO System. In: IEEE Conference on Industrial Electronics, pp. 48–53 (2006)
2. Toha, S.F., Tokhi, M.O.: Augmented feed forward and feedback control of a twin rotor system using real-coded MOGA. In: 2010 IEEE Congress on Evolutionary Computation (CEC), pp. 1–7 (2010)
3. Deb, A.K., Juyal, A.: Adaptive neuro-fuzzy control of dynamical systems Neural Networks (IJCNN). In: The 2011 International Joint Conference, pp. 2710–2716 (2011)

4. Saroj, D.K., Kar, I.: T-S fuzzy model based controller and observer design for a Twin Rotor MIMO System. In: 2013 IEEE International Conference on Fuzzy Systems (FUZZ), pp. 1–8 (2013). doi:10.1109/FUZZ-IEEE.2013.6622388

5. Nasir, A.N.K., Tokhi, M.O., Omar, M.E., Ghani, N.M.A.: An improved spiral dynamic algorithm and its application to fuzzy modelling of a twin rotor system. In: 2014 World Symposium on Computer Applications & Research (WSCAR), pp. 1–6 (2014)

6. Limnaios, G., Tsourveloudis, N.: Fuzzy logic controller for a mini coaxial indoor helicopter. J. Intell. Rob. Syst. **65**(1), 187–201 (2012)

7. Sámano, A., Castro, R., Lozano, R., Salazar, S.: Modelling and stabilization of a multi-rotor helicopter. J. Intell. Rob. Syst. **69**(1), 161–169 (2013)

8. Chemachema, M., Zeghlache, S.: Output feedback linearization based controller for a helicopter-like Twin Rotor MIMO System. J. Intell. Rob. Syst. **80**(1), 181–190 (2015)

9. Rahideh, A., Shaheed, M.H., Huijberts, H.J.C.: Dynamic modelling of a TRMS using analytical and empirical approaches. Control Eng. Pract. **16**(3), 241–259 (2008)

10. Tastemirov, A., Lecchini-Visintini, A., Morales, R.M.: Complete dynamic model of the Twin Rotor MIMO System (TRMS) with experimental validation. Dept. of Engineering, University of Leicester, University Rd., Leicester, LE1 7RH, UK (2013)

11. Chalupa, P., Přikryl, J., Novák, J.: Modelling of Twin Rotor MIMO System. In: 25th DAAAM International Symposium on Intelligent Manufacturing and Automation (2014)

12. Ullah, K., Lqbal, N.: Modeling and controller design of Twin Rotor System. Helicopter Lab Process Developed at PIEAS, Department of Electrical Engineering. Pakistan Institute of Engineering and Applied Sciences, Nilore, Islamabad. Pakistan

13. Ahmad, S.M., Chipperfield, J., Tokhim, M.O.: Dynamic modelling and control of a 2 DOF Twin Rotor multi-input multi-output system. In: Proceedings of the American Control Conference, Chicago, Illinois, June 2000

14. Pandey, S.K., Laxmi, V.: Optimal control of Twin Rotor MIMO System using LQR technique. In: Jain, L.C., Behera, H.S., Mandal, J.K., Mohapatra, D.P. (eds.) Computational Intelligence in Data Mining - Volume 1. SIST, vol. 31, pp. 11–21. Springer, New Delhi (2015). doi:10.1007/978-81-322-2205-7_2

15. Ahmed, E.-S.M., Mohamed, A.-E.: PID controller tuning scheme for twin rotor multi-input multi-output system based particle swarm optimization approach. J. Eng. Sci. **37**(4), 955–967 (2009)

16. Prasad, G.D., Manoharan, P.S., Ramalakshmi, A.P.S.: PID control scheme for Twin Rotor MIMO System using a real valued genetic algorithm with a predetermined search range. In: 2013 International Conference on Power, Energy and Control (ICPEC), Madurai, India (2013)

17. Patel, A.A., Pithadiya, P.M., Kannad, H.V.: Control of Twin Rotor MIMO System (TRMS) using PID controller. In: National Conference on Emerging Trends in Computer, Electrical & Electronics (ETCEE-2015), International Journal of Advance Engineering and Research Development (IJAERD) (2015)

18. Manoharan, P.S., Ramalakshmi, A.P.S.: Non-linear modeling and PID control of Twin Rotor MIMO System. In: 2012 IEEE Conference on Advanced Communication Control and Computing Technologies (ICACCCT), Madurai, India (2012)

19. Hashim, H.A., Abido, M.A.: Fuzzy controller design using evolutionary techniques for Twin Rotor MIMO System. Comput. Intell. Neurosci. (2015)

20. Kumar, S., Srivastava, S.: On comparison of neural observers for Twin Rotor MIMO System. Int. J. Electron. Electr. Eng. **7**(9), 987–992 (2014)

21. Rao, V.S., Mukerji, M., George, V.I., Kamath, S., Shreesha, C.: System identification and H∞ observer design for TRMS. Int. J. Comput. Electr. Eng. 5(6), 563 (2013)
22. Zeghlache, S., Kara, K., Saigaa, D.: Type-2 fuzzy logic control of a 2-DOF helicopter (TRMS system). Central Eur. J. Eng. 4(3), 303–315 (2014)
23. Feedback Instruments. Twin Rotor Mimo System. Advanced Teaching Manual 1. 33-007-4M5. Feedback Instruments Ltd., Park Road, Crowborough, East Sussex, TN6 2QR, UK, 01 edition, 09 (1998)

Memetic Algorithm Based Feature Selection for Handwritten City Name Recognition

Manosij Ghosh[1(✉)], Samir Malakar[2], Showmik Bhowmik[1],
Ram Sarkar[1], and Mita Nasipuri[1]

[1] Department of Computer Science and Engineering,
Jadavpur University, Kolkata, India
manosij1996@gmail.com, showmik.cse@gmail.com,
raamsarkar@gmail.com, mitanasipuri@gmail.com
[2] Department of Computer Science, Asutosh College, Kolkata, India
malakarsamir@gmail.com

Abstract. Feature selection plays a key role to reduce the high-dimensionality of feature space in machine learning applications by discarding irrelevant and redundant features with the aim of obtaining a subset of features that accurately describe a given problem with a minimum or no degradation of performance. In this paper, a Memetic Algorithm (MA) based Wrapper-filter feature selection framework is proposed for the recognition of handwritten Bangla city names. For evaluating the MA framework, a recently published feature extraction technique, reported in [1], is used for the said pattern recognition problem. Experimentation is conducted on an in-house dataset of 6000 words written in Bangla script. Here, 40 most popular city names of West Bengal, a state in India, have been considered to prepare the dataset. Proposed technique not only reduces the feature dimension, but also enhances the performance of the word recognition technique significantly.

Keywords: Memetic algorithm · Feature selection · Handwritten Bangla word · City name recognition · Filter-wrapper method

1 Introduction

Designing a comprehensive feature vector is a challenging issue in any pattern recognition application. Researchers from all over the world strive to estimate various kinds of features such as shape based, texture based or their combination for developing a near perfect classification system. As a consequence, a trend to design more and more features to enhance the recognition accuracy has been practiced. But this augmentation of feature dimension, at times, does not produce the desired outcome. The key reason for this is that generating more and more features does not ensure non-overlapping and universality properties of feature set i.e., feature values may have redundant information. Moreover, time required for classifying a dataset into the desired classes, an important consideration for supervised learning, increases since this time is directly proportional to the dimension of feature vector used for classification. Therefore, using

© Springer Nature Singapore Pte Ltd. 2017
J.K. Mandal et al. (Eds.): CICBA 2017, Part II, CCIS 776, pp. 599–613, 2017.
DOI: 10.1007/978-981-10-6430-2_47

a large number of features does not always guarantee a better performance at the same time it augments time complexity of the classification system.

This makes features selection (FS) a very important part of any pattern classification problem. Several algorithms are devised to address the problem of reducing irrelevant and redundant features. FS (also called variable elimination) helps in understanding data in a better way, reducing computation need, dipping the effect of curse of dimensionality and improving the performance of the system. Some of the important FS algorithms are branch and bound algorithms [2, 3], genetic algorithm [4], hybrid genetic algorithm [5], sequential search algorithm [6] etc. More such methodologies are found in the surveys reported in [7–10].

1.1 Feature Selection Methods

FS algorithms can broadly be classified as filter method [11, 12], wrapper method [4, 13–16] and embedded method [17, 18]. Filter approach selects best possible feature subset depending on the unique characteristics of the training dataset in predictor independent way. A comprehensive study on different filter methods for FS is described in [12]. Wrapper methods use learning algorithms to evaluate the classification accuracy of train dataset and then the feature combination is selected for which the best recognition accuracy is reached. Some of the wrapper FS approaches are Particle Swarm Optimization (PSO) [13], Genetic Algorithm (GA) [4], Memetic Algorithm (MA) [14–16] etc. It is noteworthy to mention that wrapper methods are computationally costly but provide better feature subset for characterizing the train data than filter approaches since it selects features based on recognition accuracy. Considering only the beneficial part of filter and wrapper methods, the researchers have introduced embedded ways of FS [17, 18]. In these approaches, filter methods are used for selecting feature combination in wrapper methods and consequently enhances recognition outcome with lesser computational cost. Therefore, from the discussion, it is clear that embedded methods for FS is more directed.

1.2 Handwritten Bangla Word Recognition

Handwritten city name recognition, prime pre-requisite for automating postal system [19], is an important as well as difficult job for researchers. The said problem is notionally same as handwritten word recognition (HWR) problem [1, 20–22], but only difference is that the lexicon size is limited and application specific. But this idea can be extended easily to develop systems such as word spotting [23], document clustering [24], document indexing [25] etc. HWR system which considers every word sample as an indivisible pattern unit, while recognizing, is known as holistic approach [1, 20–22]. On contrary, analytical approach segments the word images into characters before doing the recognition [26]. In terms of computational complexity and recognition accuracy, holistic approach weighs better if the lexicon size is limited and predefined [27].

A number of HWR research attempts [1, 19–40] has been found in literature for the scripts like Bangla [1, 19–22, 26, 32–38], Roman [27, 28], Devanagari [29], Arabic [30], Chinese [31] etc. The aim of the present work is find out the optimal feature subset for the recognition of handwritten city names in Bangla. The large number of speakers (250 million [26]) worldwide justifies the consideration of Bangla script in the present work. It is also the second most popular official language (out of 23 official languages) in India and the national language of Bangladesh. More information about Bangla script is reported in [32].

1.3 Brief Survey on Bangla HWR

A number of research attempts [1, 19–22, 26, 33–38] found in literature for Bangla HWR. These works have tried to handle the said problems mainly in two ways. First category of approach [19, 33–38] hypothetically segments the words into sub-parts based on domain knowledge and then using recognition-segmentation combination to recognize the entire words. In case of cursive handwriting, in general, segmentation process proves to be error prone. Therefore, for unconstrained writing, these methods perform some post-processing based on lexicon to generate the final outcome. As a result, these methods are usually computationally expensive. Other category of works [1, 20–22], as already mentioned, consider each word of the lexicon as a pattern class and recognize them as a whole which performs better and takes less time.

But it is to be noted that irrespective of the approaches followed for HWR, only a few works [19, 33–35] have concentrated on reducing the feature dimension to eliminate redundant and misleading features. Interestingly, these works have mainly tried to minimize the feature dimension using down-sampling the localized area i.e., with the cost of some specific feature values. Any sophisticated feature optimization technique for this topic is not reported by the researchers till date.

2 Present Work

Considering the notable facts of FS, said earlier, in the present work, a wrapper-filter based MA is applied to estimate an optimal number of feature values for the recognition of handwritten city names in Bangla script. In [1], different global and/or local feature values are extracted for city name recognition system without knowing the actual importance of the same. Hence, this work is considered here as a case study. To evaluate the proposed approach, an in-house dataset is prepared which comprises 40 most popular city names of West Bengal, an eastern region state of India. Key modules of the present work are described in the subsequent sections.

2.1 Data Collection and Preparation

Data collection is a tiresome but most important task in pattern recognition research. Without appropriate data, research becomes mere theoretical. Here, to exercise the adaptability of devised technique, a collection of 6000 handwritten Bangla word images of 40 different classes (city names) with 150 variations, is prepared. Word samples in the current dataset are written by more than 250 people belonging to different age, sex, professional and educational background. A semi-structured A4 size datasheet is designed to collect the word samples from the individuals. Then all these datasheets are scanned using HP flatbed scanner with 300 dpi resolution and stored as 24 bit BMP file (Fig. 1 shows a sample filled-in datasheet). After that from each such datasheet, word images are cropped programmatically with minimal rectangular bounding box. The selection criterion of the words is described in [1].

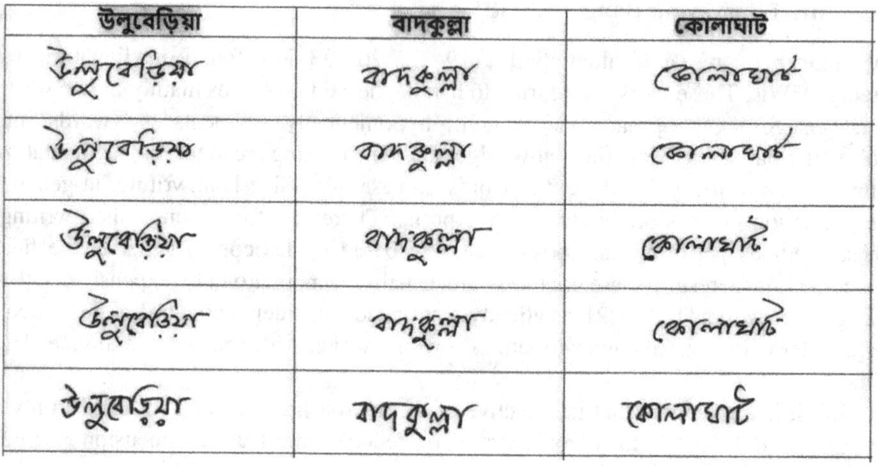

উলুবেড়িয়া	বাদকুল্লা	কোলাঘাট

Fig. 1. Sample scanned datasheet with handwritten word samples written in Bangla

2.2 Feature Extraction

As already mentioned that the prime objective of the current work is to enhance performance of any pattern classification system by reducing feature dimension using MA based embedded FS method. As a case study, feature values are estimated using a recently developed methodology [1] designed for handwritten Bangla city name recognition problem. A brief discussion for same is given below.

Inspired by the concept of the work [22], authors of [1] have designed grid based gradient feature descriptor. Initially, word images are smoothed using Gaussian filter [41]. Next, an $N \times N$ hypothetical grid structure is conceptualized over each input image and then gradient feature calculation is applied on each of the hypothetically segmented sub-images. Figure 2(a–c) represents the input image, gradient representations in terms magnitude and direction inside the hypothetically segmented 6×6 sub-images respectively. In Fig. 3, grid wise gradient variation for some sample images is shown. From close observation, it is clear that said feature values are almost similar for different instances of same city name and vary if the image classes are different. Therefore, it provides the support towards such choice of sub-images generation. However, the work has reported best recognition accuracy for $N = 6$ which means the length of feature vector is 288 ($i.e.6 \times 6 \times 8$).

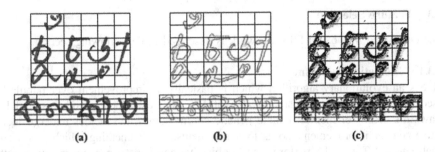

(a)   **(b)**   **(c)**

Fig. 2. Illustration of hypothetically segmented (a) word image; gradient information in terms of (b) magnitude and (c) direction

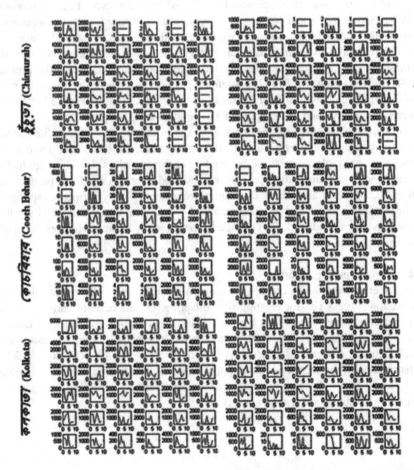

Fig. 3. Illustration of gradient based feature values in different sub-images. Two different instances of a city name are shown in horizontal direction. As each image is segmented into 6 × 6 grids, here, grid wise gradient variation into 8 bins are shown.

2.3   Feature Selection

The developed MA based FS framework is described in the following section.

2.3.1   Memetic Algorithm

MA is an evolutionary algorithm which is basically an improvement over popularly used GA. One of the interesting points of MA is it uses local search inspired by Dawkin's theory of memes. Unlike genetic chromosomes, the memes undergo local refinement or improvements so as to better themselves, something which genes are unable to do. Thus, MA performs multi-objective and constrained optimization with faster convergence rate than that achieved by GA.

As the requirement of any evolutionary algorithm, first, it creates a random population, of chromosomes that represent the selected feature subsets. Each chromosome is a binary string of 0's and 1's where '1' represents a feature is selected whereas '0' represents the complement. Here, this would be randomly selected set of features to be used for city name (written in Bangla) recognition. After that fitness of individual chromosome are checked by setting an objective function. For this problem, Multi-layer Perceptron (MLP) [42] classifier's performance has been chosen, using the set of features each chromosome represents, as the fitness value. Then, the local search (LS) has been performed in the spirit of Lamarckian learning [18].

Chromosomes are kept by the survival of the fittest rule i.e. all the elite chromosomes are preserved and ensue to the next generation. Chromosomes having poor fitness values are replaced by those having higher fitness values. During reproduction, first the genetic operator called crossover is applied. Here, genes from parents (randomly selected) form an entirely different chromosome. Newly formed offspring can then be mutated. This second genetic operator, i.e. mutation, means that the elements of chromosome are a bit altered. This change happens mainly because of errors in copying genes from parents.

2.3.2   Crossover Algorithm

Genetic operator, crossover, creates new combination of genes, plays vital role during reproduction process i.e., for creating new offspring. On the basis of early theoretical and empirical studies, GA [4] has typically used 1 and 2-point crossover operators as the standard mechanisms for implementing reproduction [43]. Here, in the present work, 2-point crossover is used which is described in Algorithm 1. Crossover leads to the distribution of the features of the 2 parents among the children, thereby, creating 2 new feature subsets. It helps in finding an optimal feature subset by testing combinations of available good feature subsets.

Algorithm 1

Randomly selecting 2 parents (p_1 and p_2) from the population using a roulette wheel method [44], and a new random number $prob \in [0,1]$ is generated.
Let a be a positive real number.

if $(prob > a)$
{

    Select 2 points on the chromosome, say, pos_1 and pos_2
    Perform 2 − point crossover, to get $child_1$ and $child_2$
    (Switch the chromosomes between pos_1 and pos_2 between p_1 and p_2)
    Place $child_1$ and $child_2$ in place of worse chromosome

}

2.3.3 Mutation Algorithm

Mutation is a genetic operator which maintains genetic diversity as new generations are created from existing population. It is modeled upon biological concept. Mutation serves to alter one or more gene(s) in the chromosomes (here, selected features). Steps to perform this operation are described in Algorithm 2. Mutation creates a feature subset which is different from the initial.

Algorithm 2

for$(I = 1$ *to length of chromosome)*
    {

        Select a position pos_1 with $pos_1{}^{th}$ bit as '1'
        Select a position pos_2 with $pos_2{}^{th}$ bit as '0'
        Swap the values at pos_1 and pos_2 with probability p.

    }
for ($I = 1$ *to length of chromosome)*
    {

        Randomly flip a bit ('1' to '0' and '0' to '1') with probability p.

    }

2.3.4 Working Principal

The present work mainly focuses on feature dimension reduction without changing their original form, unlike Principal Component Analysis (PCA) [45]. The entire process is depicted in Fig. 4 and a brief description of the same is provided here.

Firstly, feature vector is generated from each input image. Please note that the pre-requisite of MA based FS is a ranked features set. Here, rank of the features is

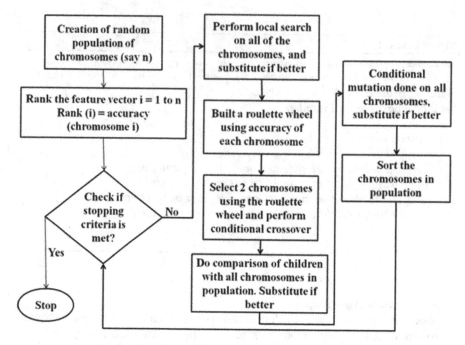

Fig. 4. Flowchart of the present MA based FS framework

carried out using ReliefF [46] function. However, ranking of features is generated only once and is repeatedly used to reduce the computation time.

Next, a random population of chromosomes of size n is created using the random number generator. A chromosome is a string of 0's and 1's where a '0' denotes a feature is not taken and '1' denotes that a feature is taken to build the feature subset. After that, classification accuracy of each feature subset represented by a chromosome is measured. Then the search for new subsets is continued in an iterative manner of the following steps till a satisfactory subset is found out or met the stopping criteria. The stopping criterion, as considered here, is the minimum number of features included and the maximum recognition accuracy achieved. However, an upper limit in the number of iterations is set to stop the searching process when it continues longer without producing significant improvement.

To carry LS by using the said feature ranks each time an ordered pair of random numbers (k, d) is generated to perform k number of additions of the highest ranking features, which have yet not been selected previously and d number of deletions of the lowest ranked features which are already there in the chromosome. However, to prevent the chromosomes from becoming clone due to repeated addition and deletion of same set of features, upper bounds to values of k and d (in our case it is maximum of 5% of total number of features for both k and d) have been set.

Next, conditional crossover is adopted. For this a number is randomly generated between 1 and the maximum allowed number of crossovers. The crossover function for the randomly generated number of times is executed. The chromosomes are selected for crossover using Roulette Wheel [44] selection method so that population keeps the chromosomes producing reasonably good performance among others. Children are compared to all the chromosomes in the population and substituted with the chromosome which founds to have less accuracy with larger number of features. A comparator function which evaluates the goodness of one chromosome against another is also defined here (Algorithm 3). To apply the conditional crossover, here, decision has been taken based on 2 randomly generated real numbers (say, a and b). Crossover is performed if $a > b$.

Finally, conditional mutation on each of the chromosomes is performed and then the performance of the new chromosomes is evaluated. If a better chromosome is observed during mutation, then the mutated chromosome substitutes the parent chromosome. The method of selecting better chromosome is described in Algorithm 3. Better chromosome selection leads to reduction of the number of features used to achieve a particular accuracy without causing the degradation of accuracy below a pre-defined threshold (say, α) [47].

Algorithm 3

```
//a and b are chromosomes.
```
$if\ \left(\left(mod\big(accuracy(a) > accuracy(b)\big)\right) > \alpha\right)$
```
{
    return the chromosome with higher accuracy
}
else
{
```
$val = \left(\big(weight_1 \times accuracy(a)\big) + (weight_2 \times ratio\ of\ unused\ feature\ in\ a)\right)$
$$- \big((weight_1 \times accuracy(b)\big) + (weight_2$$
$$\times ratio\ of\ unused\ feature\ in\ b))$$
```
    if (val > 0)
    {
        return chromosome a as better
    }
    else
    {
        return chromosome b as better
    }
}
```

---

3   Result and Discussion

In this section, initially, the experimental setup is described and then the experimental results are reported in detail along with the graphical representation of the results.

3.1   Experimental Setup

The present experiment is carried out in a PC with Intel Core i3 processor and 8 GB RAM. Windows 7 is used as the Operating System and MATLAB 2013 is used as programming platform. In this experiment, a dataset of 6000 handwritten Bangla word samples with 40 different City names of West Bengal is used. For the recognition purpose, grid based gradient orientation values are extracted from the word images and used as feature vector. As, MA based FS method needs a classifier to verify the fitness of a chromosome, so, MLP is used to meet this objective. An experiment has been conducted to select the best performing number of neurons in hidden layer of MLP. Experimental result is depicted in Fig. 5. It represents the recognition error rate of different number of hidden layer neurons while experimenting on entire dataset with feature vector of length 288. As, least error occurs for 80 number of neurons in hidden layer, hence, this number is fixed for rest of the experiment. For other parameters of MLP, default values are used as set in MTLAB. A detail description regarding the parameter values used in the current experiment is given below,

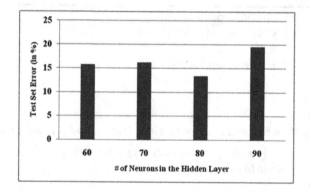

Fig. 5. Shows variation of test set error with varying number of neurons in hidden layer of MLP

- Number of neurons in hidden layer used is selected on a hit and trial basis. Here, this value is set to 80.
- In ReliefF, we have used k (number of nearest neighbors we use per class for classification) as 10.
- Number of features selected *initially* in each chromosome (i.e. number of 1s in each binary string) belongs to $[140, 270]$.
- The weight of accuracy and the weight of ratio of features is selected dynamically with a biased towards accuracy.
- We have taken the size of the population as 10 i.e. population at each iteration will have 10 chromosomes.
- An upper bound on the number of times we perform crossover is set to 5. This boundary has been selected on a hit and trial basis so as to improve the variation of feature subsets in chromosomes of the population.
- The threshold (α) is taken as 5% in Algorithm 3.

During the experimentation, 70%, 15% and 15% of the entire dataset (selected randomly) are used for training, validation and testing purposes respectively. Here, word recognition accuracy (on entire dataset) is calculated using Eq. (1).

$$Accuracy(in\%) = \frac{Number\ of\ correct\ classification}{Total\ number\ of\ word\ samples} \times 100(\%) \qquad (1)$$

3.2 Experimental Result and Analysis

Ample numbers of tests have been conducted to justify the applicability of MA based FS method for handwritten city name recognition. Few results (including maximum and minimum) with varying length of feature vectors are shown in Table 1 and the corresponding graphical presentation is provided in Fig. 6. However, it is to be noted that a given number of features may generate variety of accuracies (even for the exact same feature subset) in each different execution of MA. This is due to the usage of random weights in neural networks to build the model. In addition to this, increase/decrease in recognition accuracies in virtue of feature reduction (Table 1) indicates the usefulness of the designed FS method.

Table 1. Performance of the FS framework. The best 3 results based on optimal recognition accuracy and/or selected feature dimension are highlighted using shaded region

Before Feature Selection		After Feature Selection		Increment in Accuracy (in %)	Reduction in feature size (in %)
Size of feature vector	Recognition Accuracy (%)	Size of feature vector	Recognition Accuracy (%)		
		275	93.33	3.55	4.51
		269	93.75	3.97	6.6
		262	92.13	2.35	9.03
		237	91.08	1.3	17.71
		235	93.91	4.14	18.4
		231	93.92	4.14	19.79
288	89.78	202	91.92	2.14	29.86
		195	92.92	3.14	32.29
		181	85.85	-3.93	37.15
		175	90.80	1.02	39.24
		169	92.42	2.64	41.32
		159	91.77	1.99	44.79
		141	89.73	-0.05	51.04
		112	87.37	-2.41	61.11

It can be said from Fig. 6 that as the number of features is decreased the accuracy in general is seen to decrease. However, for certain specific feature subsets, accuracies are

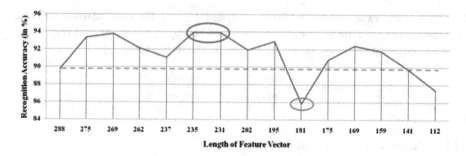

Fig. 6. Variation of accuracy with number of features used for evaluation

Table 2. Comparison of the proposed method with some commonly used FS method

Method	Size of feature vector	Recognition accuracy (in%)	Increment in accuracy (in%)	Reduction in feature size (in%)
No feature selection	288	89.78	–	–
GA*	178	90.1	0.32	38.19
	145	89.33	−0.45	49.65
	154	88.58	−1.2	46.52
Tabu search	220	80.96	−8.82	23.61
Present method*	169	92.42	2.64	41.32
	231	93.92	4.14	19.79
	141	89.73	−0.05	51.04

*The best 3 results are reported based on optimal recognition accuracy and/or selected feature dimension.

far better than the accuracy achieved by applying entire feature set. Hence, on the whole, it can be said it is a trade-off between accuracy and number of features. Compromising on the accuracy to some extent can lead to much smaller feature subsets that in turn help to minimize the execution time of the recognition system. Also, two commonly used meta-heuristic FS mechanisms (GA and Tabu Search [48]) are compared with the proposed method (see Table 2). The results confirm that MA outperforms the other 2 feature selection methods.

Another important conclusion can be drawn from the fact that for certain feature subsets much lower accuracy is found than their neighbors which show that combination of these features have a very low accuracy i.e. some features provide less complementary information to each other.

4 Conclusion

In theory, having a large number of features might seem advantageous, but the curse of dimensionality is not only an inherent problem of high-dimensionality data, but more a mutual problem of the data and the machine learning algorithm being applied. To address this issue, researchers have developed a number of methods to select feature in a pre-processing phase in an attempt to convert the data into a lower-dimensional form. In this paper, MA based Wrapper-filter feature selection framework is applied to reduce the feature dimension while improving the prediction performance of the system. As a case study, we have considered a recently published [1] handwritten city name recognition technique. The proposed work has successfully reduced a good number redundant feature while achieving a significant improvement in recognition accuracy. In future, we plan to apply this feature optimization approach to other handwriting recognition problems. Another aim is to use some meta-heuristic based local guided search to generate more elite chromosome in each evaluation.

References

1. Barua, S., Malakar, S., Bhowmik, S., Sarkar, R., Nasipuri, M.: Bangla handwritten city name recognition using gradient based feature. In: 5th International Conference on Frontiers of Intelligent Computing: Theory and Applications (FICTA) (2016)
2. Narendra, P.M., Fukunaga, K.: A branch and bound algorithm for feature subset selection. IEEE Trans. Comput. **26**(9), 917–922 (1977)
3. Chen, X.W.: An improved branch and bound algorithm for feature selection. Pattern Recogn. Lett. **24**(12), 1925–1933 (2003)
4. Raymer, M.L., Punch, W.F., Goodman, E.D., Kuhn, L.A., Jain, A.K.: Dimensionality reduction using genetic algorithms. IEEE Trans. Evol. Comput. **4**(2), 164–171 (2000)
5. Oh, I.S., Lee, J.S., Moon, B.R.: Hybrid genetic algorithms for feature selection. IEEE Trans. Pattern Anal. Mach. Intell. **26**(11), 1424–1437 (2004)
6. Pudil, P., Novovičová, J., Kittler, J.: Floating search methods in feature selection. Pattern Recogn. Lett. **15**(11), 1119–1125 (1994)
7. Chandrashekar, G., Sahin, F.: A survey on feature selection methods. Comput. Electr. Eng. **40**(1), 16–28 (2014)
8. Valdez, F., Melin, P., Castillo, O.: A survey on nature-inspired optimization algorithms with fuzzy logic for dynamic parameter adaptation. Expert Syst. Appl. **41**(14), 6459–6466 (2014)
9. Guyon, I., Elisseeff, A.: An introduction to variable and feature selection. J. Mach. Learn. Res. **3**((Mar)), 1157–1182 (2003)
10. Kotsiantis, S.: Feature selection for machine learning classification problems: a recent overview. Artif. Intell. Rev., 1–20 (2011)
11. Law, M.H., Figueiredo, M.A., Jain, A.K.: Simultaneous feature selection and clustering using mixture models. IEEE Trans. Pattern Anal. Mach. Intell. **26**(9), 1154–1166 (2004)
12. Sánchez-Maroño, N., Alonso-Betanzos, A., Tombilla-Sanromán, M.: Filter methods for feature selection – a comparative study. In: Yin, H., Tino, P., Corchado, E., Byrne, W., Yao, X. (eds.) IDEAL 2007. LNCS, vol. 4881, pp. 178–187. Springer, Heidelberg (2007). doi:10. 1007/978-3-540-77226-2_19
13. Xue, B., Zhang, M., Browne, W.N.: Particle swarm optimization for feature selection in classification: a multi-objective approach. IEEE Trans. Cybern. **43**(6), 1656–1671 (2013)

14. García-Pedrajas, N., de Haro-García, A., Pérez-Rodríguez, J.: A scalable memetic algorithm for simultaneous instance and feature selection. Evol. Comput. **22**(1), 1–45 (2014)

15. Montazeri, M., Montazeri, M., Naji, H.R., Faraahi, A.: A novel memetic feature selection algorithm. In: 5th Conference on Information and Knowledge Technology (IKT), pp. 295–300. IEEE Press, New York (2013)

16. Yang, C.S., Chuang, L.Y., Chen, Y.J., Yang, C.H.: Feature selection using memetic algorithms. In: Third International Conference on Convergence and Hybrid Information Technology (ICCIT 2008), vol. 1, pp. 416–423. IEEE Press, New York (2008)

17. Cateni, S., Colla, V., Vannucci, M.: A hybrid feature selection method for classification purposes. In: European Modelling Symposium (EMS), pp. 39–44. IEEE Press, New York (2014)

18. Zhu, Z., Ong, Y.S., Dash, M.: Wrapper–filter feature selection algorithm using a memetic framework. IEEE Trans. Syst. Man Cybern. Part B (Cybernetics) **37**(1), 70–76 (2007)

19. Roy, K., Vajda, S., Pal, U., Chaudhuri, B.B.: A system towards Indian postal automation. In: Ninth International Workshop on Frontiers in Handwriting Recognition (IWFHR-9), pp. 580–585. IEEE Press, New York (2004)

20. Bhowmik, S., Polley, S., Roushan, M.G., Malakar, S., Sarkar, R., Nasipuri, M.: A holistic word recognition technique for handwritten Bangla words. Int. J. Appl. Pattern Recogn. **2**(2), 142–159 (2015)

21. Bhowmik, S., Malakar, S., Sarkar, R., Nasipuri, M.: Handwritten bangla word recognition using elliptical features. In: International Conference on Computational Intelligence and Communication Networks (CICN), pp. 257–261. IEEE Press, New York (2014)

22. Bhowmik, S., Roushan, M.G., Sarkar, R., Nasipuri, M., Polley, S., Malakar, S.: Handwritten bangla word recognition using hog descriptor. In: Fourth International Conference of Emerging Applications of Information Technology (EAIT), pp. 193–197. IEEE Press, New York (2014)

23. Frinken, V., Fischer, A., Manmatha, R., Bunke, H.: A novel word spotting method based on recurrent neural networks. IEEE Trans. Pattern Anal. Mach. Intell. **34**(2), 211–224 (2012)

24. Doermann, D.: The indexing and retrieval of document images: a survey. Comput. Vis. Image Underst. **70**(3), 287–298 (1998)

25. Manmatha, R., Han, C., Riseman, E.M.: Word spotting: a new approach to indexing handwriting. In: Proceedings of IEEE Computer Society Conference on Computer Vision and Pattern Recognition (CVPR), pp. 631–637. IEEE Press, New York (1996)

26. Basu, S., Das, N., Sarkar, R., Kundu, M., Nasipuri, M., Basu, D.K.: A hierarchical approach to recognition of handwritten Bangla characters. Pattern Recogn. **42**(7), 1467–1484 (2009)

27. Ishidera, E., Lucas, S.M., Downton, A.C.: Top-down likelihood word image generation model for holistic word recognition. In: Lopresti, D., Hu, J., Kashi, R. (eds.) DAS 2002. LNCS, vol. 2423, pp. 82–94. Springer, Heidelberg (2002). doi:10.1007/3-540-45869-7_11

28. Acharyya, A., Rakshit, S., Sarkar, R., Basu, S., Nasipuri, M.: Handwritten word recognition using MLP based classifier: a holistic approach. Int. J. Comput. Sci. Issues **10**(2), 422–427 (2013)

29. Malakar, S., Sharma, P., Singh, P.K., Das, M., Sarkar, R., Nasipuri, M.: A holistic approach for handwritten hindi word recognition. Int. J. Comput. Vision Image Process. (IJCVIP) **7** (1), 59–78 (2017)

30. AlKhateeb, J.H., Pauplin, O., Ren, J., Jiang, J.: Performance of hidden Markov model and dynamic Bayesian network classifiers on handwritten Arabic word recognition. Knowl.-Based Syst. **24**(5), 680–688 (2011)

31. Gao, J., Li, M., Wu, A., Huang, C.N.: Chinese word segmentation and named entity recognition: a pragmatic approach. Computational Linguistics **31**(4), 531–574 (2005)

32. Sarkar, R., Malakar, S., Das, N., Basu, S., Kundu, M., Nasipuri, M.: Word extraction and character segmentation from text lines of unconstrained handwritten Bangla document images. J. Intell. Syst. **20**(3), 227–260 (2011)

33. Pal, U., Roy, K., Kimura, F.: A lexicon-driven handwritten city-name recognition scheme for Indian postal automation. IEICE Trans. Inf. Syst. **92**(5), 1146–1158 (2009)

34. Pal, U., Roy, R.K., Kimura, F.: Bangla and English city name recognition for Indian postal automation. In: 20th International Conference on Pattern Recognition (ICPR), pp. 1985–1988. IEEE Press, New York (2010)

35. Pal, U., Roy, R.K., Kimura, F.: Handwritten street name recognition for Indian postal automation. In: International Conference on Document Analysis and Recognition (ICDAR), pp. 483–487. IEEE Press, New York (2011)

36. Roy, P.P., Bhunia, A.K., Das, A., Dey, P., Pal, U.: HMM-based Indic handwritten word recognition using zone segmentation. Pattern Recogn. **60**, 1057–1075 (2016)

37. Pal, U., Roy, R.K., Kimura, F.: Multi-lingual city name recognition for Indian postal automation. In: International Conference on Frontiers in Handwriting Recognition (ICFHR), pp. 169–173. IEEE Press, New York (2012)

38. Vajda, S., Roy, K., Pal, U., Chaudhuri, B.B., Belaid, A.: Automation of Indian postal documents written in Bangla and English. Int. J. Pattern Recognit Artif Intell. **23**(08), 1599–1632 (2009)

39. Roy, P.P., Dey, P., Roy, S., Pal, U., Kimura, F.: A novel approach of Bangla handwritten text recognition using HMM. In: 14th International Conference on Frontiers in Handwriting Recognition (ICFHR), pp. 661–666. IEEE Press, New York (2014)

40. Joarder, M.M.A., Mahmud, K., Ahmed, T., Kawser, M., Ahamed, B.: Bangla automatic number plate recognition system using artificial neural network. Asian Trans. Sci. Technol. (ATST) **2**(1), 1–10 (2012)

41. Witkin, A.: Scale-space filtering: a new approach to multi-scale description. In: IEEE International Conference on Acoustics, Speech, and Signal Processing, vol. 9, pp. 150–153. IEEE Press, New York (1984)

42. Gardner, M.W., Dorling, S.R.: Artificial neural networks (the multilayer perceptron)—a review of applications in the atmospheric sciences. Atmos. Environ. **32**(14), 2627–2636 (1998)

43. De Jong, K.A., Spears, W.M.: A formal analysis of the role of multi-point crossover in genetic algorithms. Ann. Math. Artif. Intell. **5**(1), 1–26 (1992)

44. Goldberg, D.E.: Genetic algorithms. Pearson Education India

45. Wold, S., Esbensen, K., Geladi, P.: Principal component analysis. Chemometr. Intell. Lab. Syst. **2**(1–3), 37–52 (1987)

46. Robnik-Šikonja, M., Kononenko, I.: Theoretical and empirical analysis of ReliefF and RReliefF. Mach. Learn. **53**(1–2), 23–69 (2003)

47. Censor, Y.: Pareto optimality in multi objective problems. Appl. Mathe. Optim. **4**(1), 41–59 (1977)

48. Glover, F., Laguna, M.: Tabu Search. Springer, New York (2013)

Improved A-star Algorithm with Least Turn for Robotic Rescue Operations

Ashok M. Chaudhari[1(✉)], Minal R. Apsangi[2], and Akshay B. Kudale[1]

[1] Information Technology, PVG's COET Pune, Pune, Maharashtra, India
ashok78670@gmail.com, akshayak616@gmail.com
[2] Faculty, Information Technology, PVG's COET Pune, Pune, Maharashtra, India
mra_it@pvgcoet.ac.in

Abstract. Nowadays, the robots are widely used in many areas, where Human life cannot be compromised. In the Rescue operation, the robots need to search for the trapped humans. The A-star algorithm and it's variations like Iterative Deepening A-star (IDA-star), Jump Point Search (JPS), etc. are the most popular algorithm in the field of Path-finding in Maze. In those rescue operations, the efficient path between the robot and the trapped person need to be found. But due to their heuristic nature, one cannot predict that whether the output of those algorithms will be cost-efficient or not. Here we are presenting a modified cost function of A-star algorithm in such a way that it will produce a path with less number of rotations.

Keywords: Maze search · Robotic rescue · A-star algorithm

1 Introduction

In the world, the disasters like earthquake, tsunami, etc. could occur at anytime, anywhere. In these situations, the life of human living at that location might be in trouble. In those critical situations, sending more humans like army-officers, commandos, etc. to rescue the trapped one can be very risky. And that's why, for such rescue operation, the use of remote controlled robots are always preferred. In those robotic rescue operations, the humans control the robot remotely, without going to the disaster location. And in those operations, due to disaster, there are some possibilities of broken communication channel. In those situations, the robot should be intelligent enough to find a path in such a way that, the robot will require less amount of time to reach to the trapped person and then take him/her to a safer place. But in doing so it should find the shortest path between him and the human in very less amount of time. Also, the computed path should be efficient enough i.e. it should have as less number of rotations as possible, so that the human will be rescued from those situations in a faster manner.

The Dijkstra's path-finding algorithm is one of the most popular algorithms to find the shortest path in the Maze. As the Dijkstra's uses depth-first search method, it will traverse through all the possible nodes to find the shortest path [6]. Due to which for a sufficient large map, Dijkstra's may discover many unwanted nodes. And hence it will

© Springer Nature Singapore Pte Ltd. 2017
J.K. Mandal et al. (Eds.): CICBA 2017, Part II, CCIS 776, pp. 614–627, 2017.
DOI: 10.1007/978-981-10-6430-2_48

take lots of time in terms of seconds to compute the distance, which is very ineffective [8].

One of the other most popular and efficient path-finding algorithms is A* algorithm. The A* algorithm uses Actual cost and Predicted cost value to find the path between two nodes. The adjustment of Actual cost and Predicted cost trade-off could lead us to either accuracy or to the speed. Like Dijkstra's, the A* algorithm does not search the whole map to find the shortest path, instead, it takes a look to the useful nodes only. Due to this, the A* algorithm can be used in the real-world scenario, where the size of map is quiet large.

2 Background

2.1 Maze

One of the factors that may affect the performance of a path-finding algorithm is the representation of the real-world map into the virtual-world map. The grids are one of the most popular ways of representing the real-world map into the virtual-world map for robotics. A Maze is a 2-Dimensional square grid, in which each node/cell is represented as square [1]. In order to store the real-world map into the virtual-world map, the map is captured as camera image. After capturing the image, a gray-scale filter is applied on the captured image. Then the image is processed and converted into Block maze. The block maze is a type of maze, in which each node is categorized as either walkable or non-walkable block. In block maze, the diagonal movement between nodes is not allowed [4]. In order to create block maze from the gray-scaled image, the image is first divided into many smaller rectangular blocks. And then each block is examined and categorized as a walkable or non-walkable block.

2.2 A* Algorithm

The A* algorithm is best-first search path-finding algorithm. It is based on Actual cost and Heuristic cost of current node/vertex/co-ordinate, due to which it is a flexible algorithm i.e. the performance of A* algorithm can be varied according to the application requirements. It tries to find the path by selecting the nodes having least movement cost. The cost function used by A* algorithm can be represented as follow:

$$f(n) = g(n) + h(n) \tag{1}$$

where,

n is the current node.

$g(n)$ is the Actual cost i.e. the exact cost of moving from source node to current node.

$h(n)$ is the Heuristic cost between the current node and the destination node.

$f(n)$ is the cost of using the current node.

The pseudo-code of A* algorithm is as follow:

```
function find_path( Source, Destination)
{
  OPEN_List = [Source];
  CLOSED_List = [];
  Current_Node = null;
  Neighbours = [];
  Path = [];

  Source.Parent = null;

  while ( OPEN_List is not Empty )
  {
    Current_Node = OPEN_List.remove_least_node();

    if( Current_Node == Destination )
      break;

    CLOSED_List.add(Current_Node);

    Neighbours = Map.search_neighbours( Current_Node
);
    foreach (n in Neighbours)
    {
      examine(n); //The F, G and H cost of n is cal-
culated
      n.Parent = Current_Node;
      OPEN_List.add(n);
    }
  }
  while( Current_Node is not null )
  {
    Path.add( Current_Node );
    Current_Node = Current_Node.Parent;
  }
}
```

The A* algorithm maintains two lists (OPEN List and CLOSED List) to keep track of examined/traversed nodes. The OPEN list contains the nodes, which have been discovered but yet to examine. Whereas, the CLOSED list contains the nodes, which have been discovered as well as examined [7]. In the OPEN list, the nodes are kept in a sorted manner with respect to the Cost value of the Node. While finding the path, the A* algorithm add the Source Node to OPEN list, and then repeatedly remove the node with least cost value from the OPEN list and add their walkable neighbour nodes to OPEN list, until the destination node is removed from the OPEN list. Due to sorted order of nodes in OPEN list, the removal of node with least cost value become very much faster and optimal. The removed node from OPEN list is then examined. If the removed node is the destination node then A* algorithm will be terminated. Otherwise, the walkable neighbour nodes of current node are discovered and then added to OPEN list after calculating cost value of each neighbour node by cost function of A* algorithm. And after adding each walkable neighbour node to OPEN list, the current node is added to CLOSED list [2].

3   Heuristic Cost and Heuristic Function in A*

The Heuristic cost can be calculated by using Heuristic function. This Heuristic function uses the distance metric used to calculate the movement cost. The choice of distance metric is done according to the requirements. The two most popular distance metrics are:

a. Euclidean distance
b. Manhattan distance

The Euclidean distance [3] between two n-dimensional vectors x and y can be defined as:

$$d(x, y) = \sqrt{\sum_{i=1}^{n} (x_i - y_i)^2} \tag{1}$$

And the Manhattan distance [3] between two n-dimensional vectors x and y can be defined as:

$$d(x, y) = \sum_{i=1}^{n} |x_i - y_i| \tag{2}$$

The heuristic cost is estimated by considering that there is no obstacle between the current node and the destination node. The Accuracy and Speed of A* algorithm depend on this heuristic cost.

If the heuristic cost is zero then the A* algorithm will work similar to Dijkstra's algorithm, which will give very accurate output but it will be slow in performance. If the heuristic cost is greater than the cost of moving from current node to destination node, then A* will not guarantee to find the shortest path but it will run faster, i.e. the accuracy will be reduced and the speed will be increased. If the Heuristic cost is equal to the cost of moving from current node to destination node then the A* will only follow the correct path/nodes and avoid exploring irrelevant nodes, making it very fast.

For the accurate (or shortest path) the Euclidean distance can be used. And for faster path-finding, the Manhattan distance can be used.

4 Speed-Accuracy Trade-off in A* Algorithm

Due to this Speed-Accuracy trade-off, the A* have ability to change its behavior according to the requirements. i.e. if path needs to be found in the situations (like video games), where just finding the path in less time is important than optimal path, then the Heuristic cost can be kept greater or equal to the cost of moving from current node to destination node. But, if the path needs to be found in the situations (like rescue operations), where the path should be accurate as well as should be found in less time, then the Heuristic cost should be equal to the cost of moving from current node to destination node [5].

The Speed-Accuracy trade-off of the A* algorithm with respect to Heuristic cost can be given as follow:

Notation: d(n) is the cost of moving from current node to destination.

As shown in Fig. 1, as the value of heuristic function $h(n)$ increases from 0 to infinity, the speed of the algorithm increases i.e. time required by algorithm decreases and the accuracy of algorithm decreases i.e. Path length computed by algorithm increases. Since, at $h(n) = 0$, the A* algorithm will act like Dijkstra's algorithm and will provide accurate result but with less speed. And at $h(n) > d(n)$, the A* algorithm will act like Greedy Best-First-Search algorithm and will provide high speed but with less accurate result.

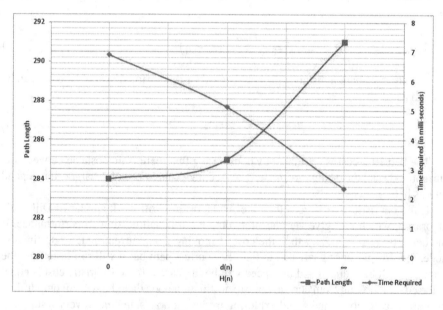

Fig. 1. Speed-Accuracy trade-off

5   Problem

The A* algorithm is heuristic and hence one cannot predict the path computed by it, since there can be multiple paths of same length. Consider the following example:

Figure 2 shows the open maze, in which the path needs to be found. The cost of moving from one node to other node is 1. And the shortest path between them is of length 11. The path from the Source Node and the Destination Node can be given as follow:

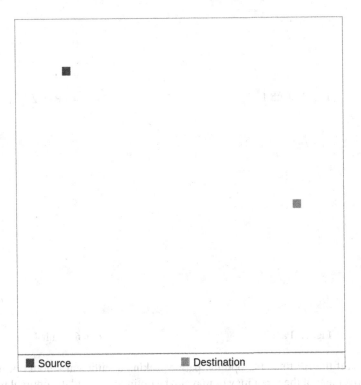

■ Source   ▓ Destination

Fig. 2. Open maze

The Figs. 3, 4, 5 and 6 shows the few possible paths, that can be obtained by traditional A* algorithm. Let's consider that the path is needed to be followed by a robot. And the cost of moving the robot in forward direction is C_m and the cost of rotating the robot in left or right direction is C_R. So the total cost of moving robot from Source to Destination for each path can be given as follow:

$$\text{Cost(Path 1)} = 11C_m + C_R$$
$$\text{Cost(Path 2)} = 11C_m + 2C_R$$
$$\text{Cost(Path 3)} = 11C_m + 4C_R$$
$$\text{Cost(Path 4)} = 11C_m + 8C_R$$

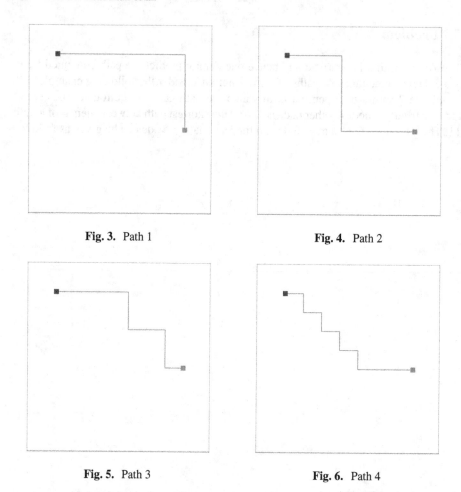

Fig. 3. Path 1

Fig. 4. Path 2

Fig. 5. Path 3

Fig. 6. Path 4

So even if the A* finds the optimal path by taking a sufficient amount of time, the cost of movement of the robot may or may not be optimal. To find the optimal path with optimal movement cost, the cost function f(n) of the A* algorithm need to be modified.

6 Proposed Work

In order to reduce the number of rotations taken by the A* algorithm, the cost function needs to be modified. As the heuristic cost function do not consider any obstacle in between the current node and destination node, it may or may not consider any rotation. But in the case of actual cost function, it takes care of cost of moving from source to current nodes. And by adding a cost to actual cost value for each turn taken by that path, the more accurate result i.e. path with less turn can be achieved. The actual cost function $g(n)$ of the A* algorithm $g(n) = g(parent) + movement\_cost$ can be modified as follow:

$$g(n) = g(parent) + movement\_cost + R \qquad (3)$$

Where, R is the cost of changing the direction i.e. the cost of rotating left or rotating right. The value of R can be defined as follow:

If turn is detected then $R = C_R$
Otherwise $R = 0$

Where, C_R is the cost of rotation. The Cost of Rotation depends on the size of Grid. The larger the grid size, the higher value of rotation cost required. Due to this, after taking each turn the cost value of the node will be increased. And hence, as algorithm chooses the nodes with least cost value from OPEN list, it will also select the nodes with less number of turns, which may result into the path with less number of turns.

7 Experimental Setup

We have used Raspberry Pi 3 – Model B (1.2 GHz 64-bit quad-core ARMv8 CPU) on three 500 × 250 blocks grids. We have used JavaScript programming to achieve the worst case performance, as the JavaScript get less system resources than other programming languages like C, C++ or Java, due to browser restrictions. We have executed the algorithm for 10,000 times to achieve more accurate performance, as the JavaScript's performance may vary according to CPU usage. The Figs. 7, 8 and 9 show the Grids used for testing traditional A* algorithm and Improved A* algorithm.

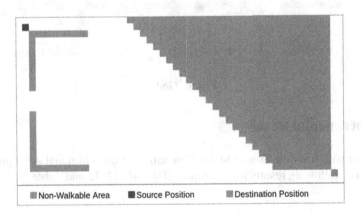

■ Non-Walkable Area   ■ Source Position   ■ Destination Position

Fig. 7. Grid 1

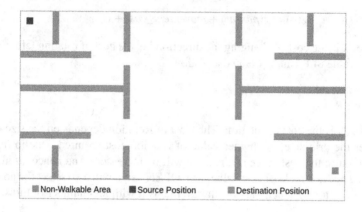

Fig. 8. Grid 2

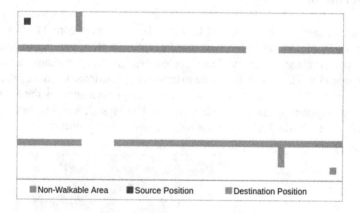

Fig. 9. Grid 3

8   Experimental Result

To find the path from the Source to the Destination, if the traditional A* algorithm is applied. The following results were obtained (Figs. 10, 11, 12 and Table 1).

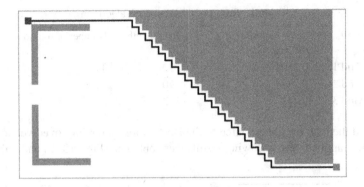

Fig. 10. Grid 1

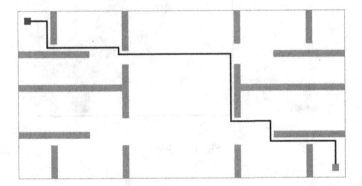

Fig. 11. Grid 2

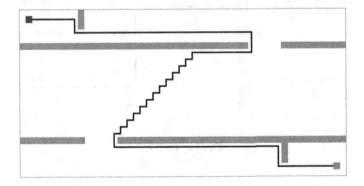

Fig. 12. Grid 3

Table 1. Result of traditional A* algorithm

Grid	Time required (in milliseconds)	Path length	Number of rotations
Grid 1	0.2504	70	44
Grid 2	0.3744	70	9
Grid 3	0.441	112	32

To find the path from the Source to the Destination, if the improved version of A* algorithm is applied. The following results were obtained (Figs. 13, 14 and 15).

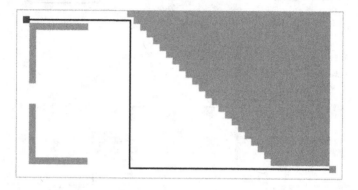

Fig. 13. Grid 1

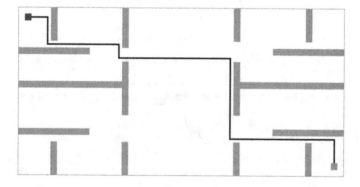

Fig. 14. Grid 2

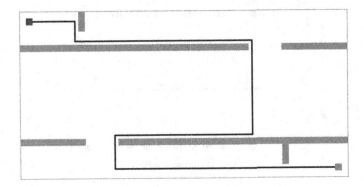

Fig. 15. Grid 3

Rotation Cost: 1
See Table 2.

Table 2. Result of improved A* algorithm

Grid	Time required (in milliseconds)	Path length	Number of rotations
Grid 1	0.3082	70	2
Grid 2	0.4852	70	7
Grid 3	0.5446	112	6

Result Comparison
See Table 3.

Table 3. Result comparison

Grid	Time required (in milliseconds)		Number of rotations	
	A*	Improved A*	A*	Improved A*
Grid 1	0.2504	0.3082	44	2
Grid 2	0.3744	0.4852	9	7
Grid 3	0.4410	0.5446	32	6

The traditional A* algorithm takes less time (in milliseconds) to find the path, but the number of turns in path are more, whereas the improved A* algorithm take few more milliseconds but give less number of turns. As the rotation cost increases gradually, the value of cost function of A* algorithm also increases, as result, the accuracy of algorithm increases, i.e. number of turns taken reduces. While doing so, few extra numbers of node could be also discovered. The Figs. 16 and 17 shows that, as the rotation cost increases gradually, the number of turns decreases, whereas the node space required increases, until the threshold rotation cost is achieved. Whereas the Fig. 18 shows that, as the rotation cost increases gradually, the number of nodes discovered also increases, for those extra discovered nodes, the A* algorithm requires little bit more time, due to this the time required by algorithm also increases gradually.

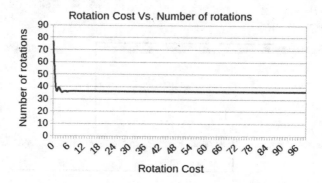

Fig. 16. Effect of rotation cost on number of turns

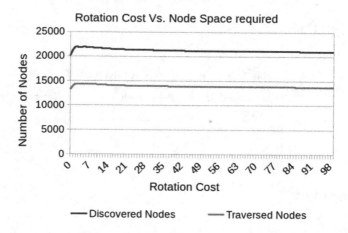

Fig. 17. Effect of rotation cost on number of nodes discovered

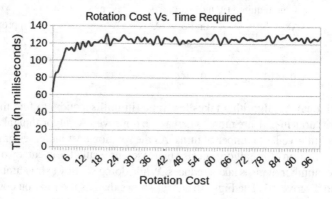

Fig. 18. Effect of rotation cost on time required

9 Conclusion

Keeping in view the threatening situations, the design of Path-finding algorithm become more crucial in rescue operations. We have modified the actual cost function of the traditional A* algorithm. As the rotation cost is added in the cost function, the output of traditional A* algorithm can be improved efficiently. The new cost function will help to find the shortest path with less number of turns, but in doing so, due to Speed-Accuracy trade-off, the time required by the algorithm will be bit more. Due to this, the robot will need more time (in milliseconds) to compute the path, but it will require less time (in seconds/minutes) to reach to the trapped person and bring him/her to a safer place.

References

1. Algfoor, Z., Sunar, M., Kolivand, H.: A comprehensive study on pathfinding techniques for robotics and video games. Int. J. Comput. Games Technol. (2015). doi:10.1155/2015/736138
2. Dong, Z., Li, M.: A routing method of ad hoc networks based on A-star algorithm. In: International Conference on Networks Security, Wireless Communications and Trusted Computing (2009). doi:10.1109/NSWCTC.2009.21
3. Han, J., Kamber, M.: Data Mining: Concepts and Techniques. Morgan Kaufmann Publisher, San Francisco (2001)
4. Joshi, H., Shinde, J.: An image based path planning using A-star algorithm. Int. J. Emerg. Res. Manag. Technol. 3(5), 127–131 (2014)
5. Liu, X., Gong, D.: A comparative study of A-star algorithms for search and rescue in perfect maze. In: Electric Information and Control Engineering (ICEICE) (2011). doi:10.1109/ICEICE.2011.5777723
6. Terzimehic, T., Silajdzic, S., Vajnberger, V., Velagic, J., Osmic, N.: Path finding simulator for mobile robot navigation. In: International Symposium on Information, Communication and Automation Technologies (2011). doi:10.1109/ICAT.2011.6102086
7. Yao, J., Lin, C., Xie, X., Wang, A., Hung, C.: Path planning for virtual human motion using improved A* algorithm. In: Seventh International Conference on Information Technology (2010). doi:10.1109/ITNG.2010.53
8. Zhang, Z., Zhao, Z.: A multiple mobile robots path planning algorithm based on A-star and Dijkstra algorithm. Int. J. Smart Home 8(3), 75–86 (2014)

Author Index

Printed in the United States
By Bookmasters